The American Villain

The American Villain

Encyclopedia of Bad Guys in Comics, Film, and Television

Richard A. Hall

An Imprint of ABC-CLIO, LLC
Santa Barbara, California • Denver, Colorado

Library of Congress Cataloging-in-Publication Data

Names: Hall, Richard A., 1969- author.
Title: The American villain : encyclopedia of bad guys in comics, film, and television / Richard A. Hall.
Description: Santa Barbara, California : Greenwood, [2021] | Includes index.
Identifiers: LCCN 2020005076 (print) | LCCN 2020005077 (ebook) | ISBN 9781440869877 (hardcover ; acid-free paper) | ISBN 9781440869884 (ebook)
Subjects: LCSH: Villains in popular culture—United States—Encyclopedias. | Villains in mass media—United States—Encyclopedias. | Villains in motion pictures—United States—Encyclopedias. | Villains in television—United States—Encyclopedias.
Classification: LCC P96.V48 H35 2021 (print) | LCC P96.V48 (ebook) | DDC 810.9/35269203—dc23
LC record available at https://lccn.loc.gov/2020005076
LC ebook record available at https://lccn.loc.gov/2020005077

ISBN: 978-1-4408-6987-7 (print)
978-1-4408-6988-4 (ebook)

25 24 23 22 21 1 2 3 4 5

This book is also available as an eBook.

Greenwood
An Imprint of ABC-CLIO, LLC

ABC-CLIO, LLC
147 Castilian Drive
Santa Barbara, California 93117
www.abc-clio.com

This book is printed on acid-free paper ∞

Manufactured in the United States of America

Contents

Preface

SPOILER ALERT!

The following work is rife with massive spoilers of some of the most popular fiction of the last half century (with a few examples from far, far earlier). These spoilers are necessary to properly examine the concept of the villain in modern American and some imported fiction. What do modern Americans see as evil or villainous? A growing tendency in television, literature, and film in recent decades has been getting to the heart of *why* villains go bad, presuming that people are inherently good and must have some manner of tragedy to slide them to the dark side. This has not always been the case. Going backward through time from Dracula to Satan, evil was simply evil. Even in the real world, no rational person questions the evil of Adolf Hitler; he is recognized as simply the evilest person to ever live. In the decades since World War II, Western society has become increasingly obsessed with solving the riddle of evil, and that quest has been made manifest throughout popular culture. This work examines some of the most popular—and even comedic—examples ever produced.

Equally fascinating and frightening is that the same culture that creates heroes also creates villains. The same society that inspires individuals to become soldiers, police, or firefighters also inspires some to become mass murderers, domestic abusers, or corrupt politicians and business leaders. Of course this is determined to a large degree by individual experiences and personal background. However, the fact that such fine lines separate good from bad in American society has been an area of concern for most of the country's history. Slavery, perhaps the greatest example of American villainy, was inherently bad. However, there were slave owners who were kinder to their slaves than industrialists in the North were to their free laborers. It is quite possibly this strange gray area that has so fascinated everyone from authors and actors to historians and philosophers who dedicate their careers to examining the human condition.

That quest for understanding lies at the heart of the work that follows. The vast array of villains appearing in this book was specifically chosen for their diversity. Many perusing the following pages will likely notice popular villains who do not appear, and for that, we sincerely apologize. The final list was compiled in the interest of brevity, diversity, and the personal reading and viewing experiences of the authors, and any exclusion should not be interpreted as a lack of the authors' interest or character's importance. In fact, the initial list comprised more than five hundred characters, half of whom were the adversaries of the heroes covered in my previous work, *The American Superhero: Encyclopedia of Caped Crusaders in History* (Greenwood, 2019). Narrowing the list to one hundred was personally excruciating.

My first exposure to villains came in the form of reruns of the 1966–1969 ABC live-action *Batman* series. As a young six-year-old, Penguin, Joker, Riddler, Catwoman, Egghead, King Tut, Mad Hatter, and Mr. Freeze appeared to me to create a constant, nonstop threat to the poor people of Gotham City, with only Batman and Robin—and eventually Batgirl—to protect them. The following year, I was exposed to Darth Vader, who would haunt my young nightmares for years. Then, as I spent my nights in front of the television utilizing my Luke Skywalker action figure to keep the threat of Vader at bay, I could overhear the nightly news as my parents watched television, learning of Americans held hostage in Iran and the constant and growing threat of all-out nuclear war from the Soviet Union, which President Ronald Reagan dubbed an "evil empire." On Sundays in church, I would hear my minister father speak of the never-ending threat of Satan, dedicated to tempting everyone toward an eternity in hell. It was clear that the threat of villains was everywhere—from my own hometown, to a galaxy far, far away. The only comfort to my young mind was that heroes existed to save the day.

As an adult, I noticed that popular culture was beginning to examine why villains turned to the dark side. Good and evil became even more of a gray area. In one interpretation, the Joker was just a failed comedian who experienced one very bad day (Alan Moore and Brian Bolland, *Batman: The Killing Joke*, 1988). Darth Vader was simply a young hero who wanted to save his wife (George Lucas, *Star Wars, Episode III: Revenge of the Sith*, 2005). Quentin Tarantino showed bad guys with good hearts, men and women who did "bad" as their chosen vocation but who, when pressed, were decent people who did the right thing more often than not. As such, when I began my career as a pop culture historian, the concept of villains became a fascinating one, and I began to notice consistent tropes in what writers considered bad or evil.

For most of early American history, "bad guys" were often groups: the British military, "savage" Native tribes, Mexican bandits on the border. That changed with World War II. With the rise of dictators such as Adolf Hitler, Josef Stalin, and Saddam Hussein, Americans began to focus villainy much more on specific individuals with nefarious plans of mass murder and/or global domination. The 1970s saw an epidemic of insane serial killers, often with no rhyme or reason for their blood thirst. Politicians like Richard Nixon and business leaders like Ivan Boesky drove home the frightening prospect that even those entrusted with the foundations of our society possessed their own motives of greed and power. Radical "religious" organizations from Al-Qaeda to the Ku Klux Klan tainted the very idea of religion. These have all become the basis of what Americans consider to be villainous, and their shadow will be seen in each and every one of the examples presented in this volume.

It would be impossible for any single volume to encompass all examples of villains in American pop culture. This volume is not meant as a top one hundred by any stretch, and most readers will doubtless think of countless villains not included. When compiling the list that follows, I attempted to cover the last century of American pop culture and to provide examples that cover a broad swath of types of villainy from every major genre of popular culture. I have also endeavored to create a list that provides some diversity with regard to race, ethnicity, gender, and sexual identity. It was not easy, and roughly half of my original list did not make the final cut. Some extremely impactful franchises, such as *Star Wars* or *Batman*, have multiple entries simply because they provide such a wide array of types of villainy. In the end, no matter how much we study the roots of villainy, it is doubtful that evil will ever be defeated. Villains are a part of who we are as a people, a dark mirror of what we aspire to be. There will always be bad guys. Thankfully, however, there will also always be heroes.

Chronology of Milestone Events

1150
Vita Merlini (*The Life of Merlin*), by Geoffrey of Monmouth, is published.

1485
Le Morte d'Arthur (*The Death of Arthur*), by Sir Thomas Malory, is published.

1667
Paradise Lost, by John Milton, is published, establishing Lucifer/Satan as a sympathetic figure.

1818
Frankenstein; or, The Modern Prometheus, by Mary Shelley, is published; first stage performance in 1823.

1876
Lieutenant Colonel (Brevet Major General) George Armstrong Custer and five companies of his U.S. Cavalry are wiped out by Native Sioux at the Battle of Little Bighorn.

1881
Billy the Kid becomes one of the most famous outlaws in American western history.

1886
Apache War chief Geronimo and 150 of his men surrender to the U.S. Cavalry, representing the last major resistance of the Plains Indian Wars.

1890
Lakota-Sioux chief Sitting Bull is shot and killed by U.S. agents, leading to the massacre at Wounded Knee Creek, ending the Plains Indian Wars.

1892
The Adventures of Sherlock Holmes, by Sir Arthur Conan Doyle, is published; the success of this series of stories spawns countless movies, novels, and television series.

1897
Dracula, by Bram Stoker, is published.

1900

The Wonderful Wizard of Oz, by L. Frank Baum, is published; the success leads to several more *Oz* books.

1916

Mexican revolutionary Pancho Villa gains notoriety in the United States for raiding a small New Mexico town, killing twenty Americans; *The Life of General Villa* becomes one of the first feature-length films released in the United States.

1931

The first *Dracula* movie, starring Bela Lugosi, is produced by Universal Pictures.

The first *Frankenstein* movie, starring Boris Karloff, is produced by Universal Pictures.

1933

Adolf Hitler is elected chancellor of Germany.

1934

DC Comics is established.

1939

Timely Comics is established.

The Hound of the Baskervilles, directed by Sidney Lanfield, is released by Universal Studios/20th Century Fox, the first in the long line of *Sherlock Holmes* films.

The Wizard of Oz, directed by George Cukor, Victor Fleming, Mervyn LeRoy, Norman Taurog, and King Vidor, is released by MGM Pictures.

1959

Goldfinger, the seventh *James Bond* novel, by Ian Fleming, is published; a theatrical version is produced in 1964, directed by Guy Hamilton, and released by United Artists.

Psycho, by Robert Bloch, is published.

The *Sleeping Beauty* animated film is released by Disney Studios.

1960

Psycho, directed by Alfred Hitchcock, is released by Paramount Pictures.

1961

Timely/Atlas Comics becomes Marvel Comics.

Thunderball, the ninth *James Bond* novel, by Ian Fleming, is published.

La Maldicion de La Llorona (*The Curse of the Crying Woman*), directed by Rafael Baledon, is released in Mexico.

1962

One Flew over the Cuckoo's Nest, by Ken Kesey, is published.

1963

Doctor Who debuts on BBC-1; the series runs until 1989, spawning two feature films, one television movie, and a return series that begins in 2005.

X-Men #1, by Marvel Comics, is released, debuting the villain Magneto.

From Russia with Love, the second film in the *James Bond* series, directed by Terence Young, is released by United Artists.

1966

Batman debuts on ABC, starring Adam West; the series runs for three seasons.

Dark Shadows debuts on ABC, running through 1971 and spawning three feature films and a brief return series in 1991.

Star Trek debuts on NBC, running through 1969 and spawning numerous sequel series and films.

1968

The Lord of the Rings, by J. R. R. Tolkien, is first published as a collected trilogy (original novels are published from 1954 to 1955).

1969

The Godfather, by Mario Puzo, is published.

1972

The Godfather, directed by Francis Ford Coppola, is released by Paramount Pictures; two sequels follow in 1974 and 1991.

1973

The Rocky Horror Show, an off-Broadway play by Richard O'Brien, debuts in England; its success leads to the feature film *The Rocky Horror Picture Show*, directed by Jim Sharman, which is released by 20th Century Fox in 1975.

1974

The Texas Chainsaw Massacre, directed by Tobe Hooper, is released by Bryanston Pictures; the success leads to numerous sequels over the years.

1975

One Flew over the Cuckoo's Nest, directed by Milos Forman, is released by United Artists.

1976

Interview with a Vampire, written by Anne Rice, is published, launching what becomes known as *The Vampire Chronicles.*

1977

Star Wars, directed by George Lucas, is released by 20th Century Fox.

1978

Dallas debuts on CBS; the series runs until 1991, and a return series airs on TNT from 2012 to 2014.

Superman: The Movie, directed by Richard Donner, is released by Warner Brothers; the success of the film leads to three sequels throughout the 1980s.

Battlestar Galactica debuts on ABC, starring Lorne Greene.

Halloween, directed by John Carpenter, is released by Compass International Pictures; the success of the film leads to numerous sequels over the decades.

1980

Star Wars: The Empire Strikes Back, directed by Irvin Kirshner, is released by Lucasfilm, distributed by 20th Century Fox.

The "Who Shot J.R.?" season-three cliff-hanger of *Dallas* becomes an international obsession.

Friday the 13th, directed by Sean S. Cunningham, is released by Paramount Pictures; the success of the film leads to numerous sequels and a brief television series.

1981

Dynasty debuts on ABC; a reboot series debuts on the CW in 2017.

Red Dragon, by Thomas Harris, is published.

Excalibur, directed by John Boorman, is released by Orion Pictures.

1982

Star Trek II: The Wrath of Khan, directed by Nicholas Meyer, is released by Paramount Pictures.

1983

Star Wars: Return of the Jedi, directed by Richard Marquand, is released by Lucasfilm, distributed by 20th Century Fox.

G. I. Joe: A Real American Hero, an animated series produced by the toy manufacturer Hasbro, debuts in syndication; numerous animated series and live-action films follow.

1984

Star Trek III: The Search for Spock, directed by Leonard Nimoy, is released by Paramount Pictures.

A Nightmare on Elm Street, directed by Wes Craven, is released by New Line Cinema; the success of the film leads to numerous sequels.

The Transformers, an animated series produced by the toy manufacturer Hasbro, debuts in syndication; numerous animated series and live-action/CGI films follow.

1986

Watchmen graphic novel, by Alan Moore and Dave Gibbons, is published by DC Comics.

1987

Star Trek: The Next Generation debuts on television in syndication.

1988

V for Vendetta miniseries by Alan Moore, David Lloyd, and Tony Weare, is published by Quality Communications in the United Kingdom and Vertigo/DC Comics in the United States.

1989

Batman, directed by Tim Burton, is released by 20th Century Fox.

The Simpsons debuts on FOX.

1991

Silence of the Lambs, directed by Jonathan Demme, is released by Orion Pictures; the success of the Hannibal Lecter character from the Thomas Harris novels spawns several sequels and a television series.

Star Trek VI: The Undiscovered Country, directed by Nicholas Meyer, is released by Paramount Pictures.

1992

Aladdin, directed by Ron Clements and John Musker, is released by Disney Studios.

Batman Returns, directed by Tim Burton, is released by Warner Brothers Studios.

Batman: The Animated Series debuts on FOX. The series runs (under various titles) from 1992 to 1995 and from 1997 to 1999; of all of the films and television series based on *Batman*, this is considered by most to be the most loyal to the source comic book material.

1993

Star Trek: Deep Space Nine debuts on television in syndication.

Superman #75 by DC Comics features the "Death of Superman" at the hands of the villain Doomsday.

The X-Files debuts on FOX. The series runs until 2002, spawning two feature films and a return series in 2016–2017.

1994

Pulp Fiction, directed by Quentin Tarantino, is released by Miramax Films.

Interview with a Vampire, directed by Neil Jordan and starring Tom Cruise as the vampire Lestat, is released by Warner Brothers.

1995

Star Trek: Voyager debuts on UPN.

Batman Forever, directed by Joel Schumacher, is released by Warner Brothers Studios.

Preacher, a comic book by Garth Ennis and Steve Dillon, is published by Vertigo/ DC Comics; the series runs for five years.

1996

Star Trek: First Contact, directed by Jonathan Frakes, is released by Paramount Pictures.

A Game of Thrones, by George R. R. Martin, is published.

Wicked: The Life and Times of the Wicked Witch of the West, by Gregory Maguire, is published.

1997

Buffy the Vampire Slayer debuts on the CW network, starring Sarah Michelle Gellar; it runs for seven seasons and spawns the spin-off series *Angel*.

Harry Potter and the Philosopher's Stone, by J. K. Rowling, is published; released in the United States as *Harry Potter and the Sorcerer's Stone*; the series spawns six sequels.

Batman and Robin, directed by Joel Schumacher, is released by Warner Brothers Studios.

1999

Star Wars, Episode I: The Phantom Menace, directed by George Lucas, is released by Lucasfilm, distributed by 20th Century Fox.

The Matrix, directed by Lana and Lilly Wachowski, is released by Warner Brothers.

The Sopranos debuts on HBO, starring James Gandolfini; the series runs until 2007.

2000

X-Men, directed by Bryan Singer, is released by 20th Century Fox; the success spawns six sequels/prequels.

2001

Smallville debuts on the WB network, starring Tom Welling; the series runs for ten seasons.

Harry Potter and the Sorcerer's Stone, directed by Chris Columbus, is released by Warner Brothers Studios; seven sequels follow over the next ten years.

The Lord of the Rings: The Fellowship of the Ring, directed by Peter Jackson, is released by New Line Cinema; the remaining two chapters are released over the next two years.

2002

Star Wars, Episode II: Attack of the Clones, directed by George Lucas, is released by Lucasfilm, distributed by 20th Century Fox.

Spider-Man, directed by Sam Raimi, is released by Sony Pictures; the success leads to numerous films, sequels, and reboots over the next fifteen years.

2003

The Walking Dead comic book by Robert Kirkman and Tony Moore debuts, published by Image Comics.

Wicked, a musical play by Stephen Schwartz and Winnie Holzman, debuts on Broadway.

The Matrix Reloaded and *The Matrix Revolutions*, both directed by Lana and Lilly Wachowski, are released by Warner Brothers.

Kill Bill, Vol. 1, written and directed by Quentin Tarantino, is produced by Miramax Pictures released; *Kill Bill, Vol. 2* is released one year later.

Pirates of the Caribbean: The Curse of the Black Pearl, directed by Gore Verbinski, is released by Disney Studios; numerous sequels follow.

Battlestar Galactica miniseries debuts on the Sci-Fi Channel, starring Edward James Olmos; the success of the miniseries leads to a full-time series, which runs from 2004 to 2009.

2005

Star Wars, Episode III: Revenge of the Sith, directed by George Lucas, is released by Lucasfilm, distributed by 20th Century Fox.

Batman Begins, directed by Christopher Nolan, is released by Warner Brothers.

Fantastic Four, directed by Tim Story, is released by 20th Century Fox; the moderate success leads to two more films, both considered unsuccessful.

2006

V for Vendetta, directed by James McTeigue, is released by Warner Brothers.

2008

The Dark Knight, directed by Christopher Nolan, is released by Warner Brothers.

Star Wars: The Clone Wars, an animated feature film, is released by Warner Brothers; it is soon followed by an ongoing television series on Cartoon Network.

Breaking Bad debuts on AMC, starring Bryan Cranston; the series runs for five seasons and spawns the spin-off prequel series *Better Call Saul.*

2009

Watchmen, directed by Zack Snyder, is released by Warner Brothers Studios.

2010

Sherlock television series debuts on BBC-1, starring Benedict Cumberbatch.

The Walking Dead television series debuts on AMC, starring Andrew Lincoln; the success of the series spawns a spin-off series, *Fear the Walking Dead.*

2011

Game of Thrones television series debuts on HBO.

Thor, directed by Kenneth Branagh, is released by Marvel Studios; the success of the film leads to two sequels.

Captain America: The First Avenger, directed by Joe Johnston, is released by Marvel Studios; the success of the film leads to two sequels.

American Horror Story debuts on FX; the anthology series runs for ten seasons.

2012

The Avengers, directed by Joss Whedon, is released by Marvel Studios.

The Dark Knight Rises, directed by Christopher Nolan, is released by Warner Brothers.

2013

Man of Steel, directed by Zack Snyder, is released by Warner Brothers.

Star Trek: Into Darkness, directed by J. J. Abrams, is released by Paramount Pictures.

2014

Maleficent, directed by Robert Stromberg, is released by Disney Studios; the success leads to a sequel in 2019.

Gotham debuts on FOX, starring Ben McKenzie.

2015

Avengers: Age of Ultron, directed by Joss Whedon, is released by Marvel/Disney.

Star Wars, Episode VII: The Force Awakens, directed by J. J. Abrams, is released by Lucasfilm/Disney.

2016

Lucifer television series debuts on FOX, starring Tom Ellis; the series runs for three seasons before moving to Netflix.

Batman v. Superman: Dawn of Justice, directed by Zack Snyder, is released by Warner Brothers.

Harry Potter and the Cursed Child, an off-Broadway play by J. K. Rowling, Jack Thorne, John Tiffany, and Imogen Heap, debuts in London.

Fantastic Beasts and Where to Find Them, directed by David Yates, is released by Warner Brothers; the film acts as a prequel series to the *Harry Potter* franchise and spawns numerous sequels.

Suicide Squad, directed by David Ayer, is released by Warner Brothers.

2017

Star Wars, Episode VIII: The Last Jedi, directed by Rian Johnson, is released by Lucasfilm/Disney.

2018

Krypton debuts on the SyFy channel, starring Cameron Cuffe.

Black Panther, directed by Ryan Coogler, is released by Marvel/Disney.

Avengers: Infinity War, directed by Anthony and Joe Russo, is released by Marvel/Disney.

2019

Star Wars, Episode IX: The Rise of Skywalker, directed by J. J. Abrams, is released by Lucasfilm/Disney.

Joker, directed by Todd Phillips, is released by Warner Brothers.

The Curse of La Llorona, directed by Michael Chaves, is released by Warner Brothers.

HBO debuts the live-action series *Watchmen*, a pseudosequel to the popular graphic novel.

Introduction

It is important at the outset to specify the definitions of certain terms. When discussing "villains," what does the term mean? Essentially, a villain is the enemy of the hero in fictional and historical narratives. A villain may also be someone who possesses no personal enemies but conducts themselves in a manner where their behavior is considered evil by the society observing them. In a discussion of villains, one may occasionally refer to the term "nemesis," who can be either a hero or villain. For example, in comic books, the Red Skull is Captain America's nemesis; Captain America is the Red Skull's nemesis. Or it may simply refer to an acrimonious relationship between two individuals, neither of whom is a hero. For example, on the classic television series *Dallas*, Cliff Barnes is J. R. Ewing's nemesis. In the latter example, both characters could be considered villains, but their relationship is one of mutual hatred and constant conflict. The term "villains," in essence, refers to those characters (both fictional and real) that society deems evil or bad, reflecting the opposite of what that society considers good.

The concept of villains is as old as human society. From the evil god Enkidu in The Epic of Gilgamesh (c. 2100 BCE) and the serpent in the book of Genesis in the Bible (written between approximately 1200 BCE and 400 BCE), to the modern-day villains of Thanos in Marvel Studios' *Avengers* films (2012–2019) and the bat-wielding Negan from the comic book and television series *The Walking Dead* (2012 to present), humanity has consistently sought out the source of evil in the world and the hope that good will always prevail in the never-ending battle. As Mike Alsford points out, "What a culture considers heroic and what it considers villainous says a lot about that culture's underlying attitudes. . . . Religions, ideologies, people and activities often serve to provide us with a kind of existential map, an overlay of principles, values and priorities which allow us to make judgments concerning the direction that our lives should take" (Alsford, *Heroes & Villains*, 1, 6).

This book seeks to examine the myriad forms of villainy within American popular culture, not only in the present but also throughout its history. As the United States was initially borne from the empire of Great Britain, much of American culture is still today tied to those British roots. However, as America has become a more diverse society, ideas of villainy from elsewhere have had an impact on what Americans think makes a villain. It is the purpose of this work to provide a side-by-side analysis of a broad variety of examples of villains in American popular culture and to work as a general reference in the future study of villains and villainy in American society.

A BRIEF HISTORY OF VILLAINY

The Judeo-Christian/Islamic world was literally borne from an act of villainy. All three Abrahamic religions recognize the beginning of human existence with God's/Allah's creation of Adam and Eve and their expulsion from paradise when they succumb to the temptations of the mysterious "serpent" in the Garden of Eden. Over the centuries, the story of Adam and Eve has been altered to suggest that the serpent was, in fact, Satan (or the Devil) in disguise. However, depending on the translation, Genesis 3:1 merely describes the serpent as a "subtil" or "crafty" beast. In fact, throughout the Old Testament, the only references to Satan (Hebrew for "adversary") present him as part of God's Heavenly Hosts, although not necessarily a nice one. It is only in the New Testament that Satan is presented as an outright enemy of God, which has been further cemented in the Western world by the later works of Dante and John Milton. Regardless of origin, however, human society since ancient times has been centered on the idea that there exists some supernatural villain out to hurt humankind as part of a millennia-old conflict with the heroic God.

In ancient times, villains in stories tended to be supernatural forces: gods, demigods, demons, or beasts of some kind. That began to change in the last five centuries BCE, with villains in the form of the Persian emperor Xerxes in Herodotus's *Histories* (c. 440 BCE), Brutus's betrayal and assassination of Julius Caesar (44 BCE), and Judas Iscariot's betrayal of Jesus of Nazareth (c. 30 CE). For the last two thousand years, humanity has been keenly aware that evil exists among us and that even those we trust most may turn on us in the end. In the European Middle Ages, the Catholic Church made villains of the neighboring Muslims. During the same period, the earliest Arthurian legends told tales of the evil Sir Mordred and the sorceress Moran le Fey. This was also when the Church and Dante established the Devil as a villain, as later would Milton in the Enlightenment.

The basis of the modern Western villain arose in the 1590s through the collected works of William Shakespeare. Throughout the 1700s, villains were most often built on nationalistic lines: the English seeing the French as villains, and vice versa. In the 1800s, English author Charles Dickens wrote consistently villainous characters based on real-world people who lived among us, often with greed and ambition as the source of their villainy. In the latter half of that century, in the United States, Americans saw the rise of cowboy villains such as Jesse James, Butch Cassidy and the Sundance Kid, and Billy the Kid. However, the twentieth century would see the rise of the evilest villains in human history, establishing the villain for the modern world.

WORLD WAR II AND THE AMERICAN DEFINITION OF VILLAIN

As the United States and the entire Western world were mired in the Great Depression, a radically racist, nationalist organization took over the infant

Weimar Republic in Germany: the Nationalist Socialist German Workers Party (the Nazis). On seizing power in Germany in the mid-1930s, the Nazis and their autocratic leader, Adolf Hitler, sought to eradicate certain "others" in German society—most notably Jews, homosexuals, communists, and any people of color. Once these programs were underway, Hitler next sought global domination, beginning with the conquest of Europe. Although the United States under the leadership of President Franklin Roosevelt worked diligently to provide munitions for the British and, later, the Soviet Union, it would be nearly three years into the conflict before the United States would enter combat operations. Once committed, however, the defeat of the Nazis and the expansionist Japanese Empire in the Pacific would launch the United States to the position of the modern world's leading superpower.

Fascists were mirrored in American pop culture from the beginning of World War II. The Germans, Japanese, and, to a lesser degree, the Italians were all portrayed as villains in movies and comic books throughout the duration of the war. Dictatorship became a haunting possibility as these fascist regimes slowly conquered the world. Heroes, then, were those who would stand up against totalitarianism and stand for freedom, liberty, and democracy. This would, however, lead to any perceived other around the world as a potential replacement for Hitler and the Nazis. Many times, this comparison would be unfair; sometimes, however, it would be spot-on.

Out of the ashes of World War II, emerged the Cold War, a decades-long period of tense relations between the capitalist United States and the communist Soviet Union. This conflict became even more dangerous when both sides possessed atomic/nuclear weapons. Although the political ideologies of fascism and communism were polar opposites, because of their core of totalitarian dictatorship, they appeared to the average American citizen to have much in common. The experiences of these two global conflicts, which defining half of the twentieth century, also narrowed the idea of villainy in American culture. Its impact can easily be seen in American pop culture since World War II. While traditional monster villains, from vampires to the Christian Devil, and, of course, common hoodlums, such as the Mafia, street gangs, drug dealers, and so on, would continue to be popular fictional tropes across all media, many pop culture franchises from comic books to *Star Trek*, *Star Wars*, *G. I. Joe* and beyond would create villains along very similar veins to the real-world villains of the late 1900s.

From World War II and the Cold War, what appears most evident is that what Americans viewed as truly villainous was any attempt to stem personal freedom. Both Nazism and communism denounced religion, a staple of American society from its inception. Both also exemplified totalitarian authoritarianism, something that the United States was specifically created to abhor and resist. From Klingons to the Galactic Empire, and from COBRA Commander to Darth Vader, Americans were united in their distaste for dictatorships. However, other, more capitalist villains, such as television's J.R. and Alexis, were almost seen as antiheroes; their blind ambition for wealth and power, regardless of the cost in a loss of integrity or morals, represented the money-hungry decade of the 1980s and paved the way for the vapid individualism of the century that soon followed.

IMPORTED VILLAINS

As stated earlier, the United States is a country of diversity, populated by peoples from cultures all over the world, perhaps more so than any other modern nation. These immigrants brought with them their own traditions and stories. The overwhelming majority of the first generation of Americans were British. Due in no small part to this history, the United States and United Kingdom have, for two hundred years, maintained what has come to be known as the "special relationship." American schools today teach Shakespeare, Dickens, and Tolkien along with Emerson, Poe, and Hemingway. Everything from Christian Protestantism to Father Christmas (Santa Claus) have roots in our British ancestry. Throughout the nation's history, the United States has imported the fables and fairy tales of central Europe; the Br'er Rabbit tales, brought here by the slaves taken from western Africa; and the haunting tale of La Llorona from Mexico. In the 1990s, pop culture powerhouse Disney even imported the 1,200-to-1,300-year-old legend of Mulan from China.

Of all the imported pop culture in America, however, the British inclusion remains, by far, the greatest. From King Arthur to Shakespeare, Dickens to Tolkien, the Beatles to Led Zeppelin, Monty Python to *Doctor Who*, and culminating with the *Harry Potter* phenomenon of the late 1990s and early 2000s, Americans continue to be obsessed with all things British. Millions of Americans get up in the middle of the night to view British royal weddings and funerals live. Conversely, the British absorb American pop culture in massive numbers. Since the 1980s, popular culture has become America's top export, as the entire world is eager to consume the latest films, music, books, and television programs coming from the United States. Key to the popularity of American pop culture, both at home and abroad, is the vast array of fascinating villains produced by the popular media franchises. While villains have always been key to cultures across the globe, the published world began to share the same idea of villainy at the dawn of the twenty-first century.

THE POST-9/11 VILLAIN

On September 11, 2001, the international terrorist organization Al-Qaeda organized a coordinated attack on the United States that destroyed the World Trade Center in New York City, severely damaged the Pentagon in Washington, DC, and killed 2,977 Americans. This horrendous attack garnered the sympathy of the entire world, minus the relatively few individuals, organizations, and nations who were sympathetic to the terrorists (and terrorism in general). Overnight, the entire world shared a similar definition of "evil" and "villainy." Hatred now defined the villain, and that would be reflected continuously throughout American pop culture for the decades that followed.

Villains have now become those who kill indiscriminately, and a popular counter to that threat has been the antihero. This trope, popularized in the 1970s and 1980s, presents heroes who, more often than not, adopt villainous strategies in order to defeat them (literally fighting fire with fire). Heroes such as Deadpool and the Punisher—both introduced in comic books as villains—were now seen as heroes, willing to slaughter the bad guys in direct response to the threat those villains posed. To a large degree, this provided a cathartic release to audiences who felt helpless against a violent and unpredictable foe. However, this shift to darker, more violent heroes says as much about American society as does those that society deems villains. What moral and ethical lines are Americans willing to cross to stop a "greater" evil? Where did modern ideas of villainy originate? How much have ideas of villains changed since ancient times, and how much have they stayed the same? All of these ideas, and more, will be explored in the thematic essays of this work.

BREAKDOWN OF THE BOOK

While this book at its core is an encyclopedia of villains in American popular culture, it also possesses other aspects that should prove valuable to researchers. Aside from the individual encyclopedic entries, each with its own list of suggested sources on that specific subject, this book also contains a chronology of important dates in the history of villains in popular culture as well as a glossary of terms defining the jargon associated with villain studies. The introduction is followed by five thematic essays, each with its own list of suggested readings. These essays break down as follows.

The first thematic essay is titled "'In the Beginning . . .': The Origins of Villains in the Western World." This essay details the earliest examples of villains in the Middle East and Europe, from the ancient world to the industrial age. The next essay, "'Nazis, Communists, and Terrorists . . . Oh My!': The Rise of the Supervillain and the Evolution of the Modern American Villain," picks up the analysis of villainy from the first essay and brings it to the present day. This essay shows how global events from 1941 to 2001 have impacted American ideas on villainy. Special emphasis in this essay is given to comic book and *Star Trek* villains who have directly reflected real-world events. The third essay is "The Dark Mirror: Evil Twins, *The Twilight Zone*, and the Villain Within," which examines the inner darkness within all people and the potential of anyone to emerge as a villain.

Essay four is "Tarantino and the Antivillain." In 2006, "antivillain" was defined as "an antagonist who isn't purely evil nor entirely unsympathetic—a character who doesn't seem to deserve being cast as the villain" (Laszlo, "Anti-Villain," *Urban Dictionary*). Since the 1990s, Hollywood director Quentin Tarantino had made an art of taking the antihero and turn it on its head, creating villains who, at their heart, are actually sympathetic characters whose actions border on the heroic. Finally, there is the last essay: "The Pathos of Villainy: Getting to the Heart of Why Villains Went Bad." In the late 1980s, American popular culture began spending considerable effort psychoanalyzing popular villains, attempting to understand what makes bad people turn bad (presupposing that all people begin "good"). Villains discussed in this essay span the broad spectrum from serial killer Hannibal Lecter to Darth Vader, and beyond. These essays are designed as a beginning point for further consideration, research, and discussion.

The one hundred entries are listed *A* to *Z*. Each entry opens with a biography listing the character's first appearance, creators, strengths, weaknesses, allies, enemies, and so on. That is followed by an overview of the character: connection to their franchise, origin story, major characteristics and story lines, and the way that they comment on ideas of villainy in America. These portions will contain *massive spoilers*. The next section of each entry is a "see also" section, pointing the reader to other similar examples of villains in pop culture, as well as the thematic essays connected to that character. Last, the reader is provided a list of scholarly/professional works that, to one degree or other, provide even more insight into the character. The entries are followed by the glossary and bibliography.

VILLAINS ARE US

Just as heroes in popular culture reflect a society's highest ideals, hopes, and dreams of what that society and its inhabitants can be, so, too, do villains reflect the societies that produce them. Villains represent the darker sides of ourselves, often providing the warning that with just one bad day—or a succession of really bad days—the greatest among us can quickly become the most dangerous. The villains in the entries that follow represent a wide swath of what Americans view as villainous. Cultlike leaders, murderers, liars, betrayers, and individuals in league with the Devil, as well as the Devil himself, are all evident in the following one hundred entries. Also represented are villains from other cultures whom Americans have imported and made their own because they, too, reflect some aspects of villainy in modern America as much as they did in their own times and in their own countries. Each entry possesses a list of books and articles that relate in one form or fashion to each corresponding villain, as well as a list of other entries in the work that closely relate in some way to that specific villain or villainess. What follows is a vast array of what America sees as bad, from the simply selfish to the devilishly evil and from the horrific to the outright comedic. Throughout, America's darkness is revealed—what we desire to defeat and what we fear to become.

FURTHER READING

Alsford, Mike. 2006. *Heroes & Villains.* Waco, TX: Baylor University Press.

Ashby, LeRoy. 2006. *With Amusement for All: A History of American Popular Culture since 1830.* Lexington: University Press of Kentucky.

Castleman, Harry, and Walter J. Podrazik. 2016. *Watching TV: Eight Decades of American Television.* 3rd ed. Syracuse, NY: Syracuse University Press.

Dolansky, Shawna. 2018. "How the Serpent Became Satan: Adam, Eve, and the Serpent in the Garden of Eden." Biblical Archaeology Society. October 14, 2018. Accessed April 7, 2019. https://www.biblicalarchaeology.org/daily/biblical-topics/bible-interpretation/how-the-serpent-became-satan/.

Dyer, Ben, ed. 2009. *Supervillains and Philosophy: Sometimes, Evil Is Its Own Reward.* Popular Culture and Philosophy Series. Chicago: Open Court.

Faludi, Susan. 2007. *The Terror Dream: Myth and Misogyny in an Insecure America.* New York: Picador.

Fertig, Mark. 2017. *Take That, Adolf!: The Fighting Comic Books of the Second World War.* Seattle, WA: Fantagraphics.

Forasteros, J. R. 2017. *Empathy for the Devil: Finding Ourselves in the Villains of the Bible.* Downers Grove, IL: InterVarsity.

Gavaler, Chris. 2015. *On the Origin of Superheroes: From the Big Bang to "Action Comics No. 1."* Iowa City: University of Iowa Press.

Heit, Jamey. 2011. *Vader, Voldemort and Other Villains: Essays on Evil in Popular Media.* Jefferson, NC: McFarland.

Howe, Sean. 2012. *Marvel Comics: The Untold Story.* New York: Harper-Perennial.

Hutton, Ronald. 2017. *The Witch: A History of Fear, from Ancient Times to the Present.* New Haven, CT: Yale University Press.

Laszlo, Monseignore. 2006. "Anti-Villain." *Urban Dictionary.* July 23, 2006. Accessed July 7, 2019. https://www.urbandictionary.com/define.php?term=anti-villain.

Mahnke, Aaron. 2017. *The World of Lore: Monstrous Creatures.* New York: Del Rey.

Morris, Jon. 2017. *The Legion of Regrettable Supervillains: Oddball Criminals from Comic Book History.* Philadelphia: Quirk Books.

Peaslee, Robert, and Rob Weiner, eds. 2019. *The Supervillain Reader.* Jackson: University of Mississippi Press.

Rosenfeld, Gavriel D. 2014. *Hi Hitler!: How the Nazi Past Is Being Normalized in Contemporary Culture.* Cambridge: Cambridge University Press.

Stark, Steven D. 1997. *Glued to the Set: The 60 Television Shows and Events That Made Us Who We Are Today.* New York: Delta Trade Paperbacks.

Stuller, Jennifer K. 2010. *Ink-Stained Amazons and Cinematic Warriors: Superwomen in Modern Mythology.* London: I. B. Tauris.

Tucker, Reed. 2017. *Slugfest: Inside the Epic 50-Year Battle between Marvel and DC.* New York: Da Capo.

Wright, Bradford W. 2003. *Comic Book Nation: The Transformation of Youth Culture in America.* Baltimore, MD: Johns Hopkins University Press.

Thematic Essays

"In the Beginning . . .": The Origins of Villains in the Western World

"In the beginning," there was a snake . . . or some manner of legged reptile/dragon . . . or the Devil in disguise. Scholars debate this point to this day. Regardless of who the mysterious tempter was in the Garden of Eden, one thing is clear: humans believe that villains have been in the world since the beginning. Centuries after the biblical book of Genesis is believed to have been written, the Greek poet Hesiod wrote the story of Pandora in his book *Works and Days* (c. 700 BCE). Pandora was the wife of Epimetheus, the brother of the mythical figure Prometheus. She was given to her husband by Zeus as revenge on Prometheus for stealing fire from the gods (although, admittedly, a rather roundabout method of revenge and fairly insulting to Pandora). Pandora's curiosity leads her to open a mysterious jar, unleashing all manner of evil and suffering into the world, leading to the term "Pandora's box," an analogy for unintended consequences to the present day.

So, whether a result of a direct creation of God's or the machinations of a fallen angel or the simple curiosity of a young woman, evil is as old as human civilization. Over the millennia, villains with evil intent to one degree or another have been constant staples of all human societies. They have been used both to warn audiences of the dangers of giving in to their darker tendencies and to underscore the heroics of their respective adversaries. Villains have evolved with society, ever broadening the idea of what wrong is. From the beginning, villains in stories have represented who we fear to be but who, deep down, we are each fully aware we possibly could be.

THE ROOT OF ALL EVIL: THE DEVIL

The longest-lasting villain from the ancient world and the one who remains central to western ideas of villainy still today is Satan/the Devil/Lucifer. Although the first book of the Christian Bible, Genesis, is traditionally held to have been

Joseph Campbell

Professor Joseph Campbell (1904–1987) was considered the leading expert in comparative mythologies/religions in the twentieth century. His key works include *Where the Two Came to Their Father* (1943), an evaluation of a Navajo ceremony conducted by two artists; *A Skeleton Key to Finnegans Wake* (1944), an analysis of James Joyce's *Finnegans Wake*; *The Masks of God* (1959–1968), a four-volume work on the history of mythology; and *Historical Atlas of World Mythology* (published posthumously), his final work, an illustrated history of world mythology, completed by his editor, Robert Walker. Campbell's seminal work was *The Hero with a Thousand Faces* (1949).

In this work, Campbell examined and compared stories and mythologies from around the world, establishing the concept of "the hero's journey," a clear structure that all human stories and mythologies exhibit, following the would-be hero from obscurity to heroic status. Writer and director George Lucas has long held that Campbell's hero's journey was an inspiration for his own seminal work, *Star Wars*. After completion of the final film of the original *Star Wars* trilogy, *Return of the Jedi*, Lucas gave a private viewing of all three films for Campbell at his Skywalker Ranch in California, asking the professor for his opinion on the completed work.

In 1988, PBS aired a six-part documentary series titled *Joseph Campbell and the Power of Myth*, with host and interviewer Bill Moyers. In those interviews, Campbell confided to Moyers that George Lucas was the best student he ever had. In 1990, Jean Erdman Campbell, the professor's widow, and Robert Walker (his longtime editor) established the Joseph Campbell Foundation, a nonprofit organization designed to preserve and perpetuate the future of Campbell's work. Campbell died of esophageal cancer at his home in Hawaii in 1987.

Richard A. Hall

written by the Hebrew prophet Moses (c. sixteenth century BCE), many scholars today believe it to have been written much later, closer to the fifth or sixth century BCE (Van Seters, "The Pentateuch," 5). There, in the story of creation and the Garden of Eden, readers are introduced to what the Judeo-Christian world considers the first villain: the serpent. Over the centuries, this "serpent" has become synonymous with the Devil, the ultimate enemy of God and humankind, frequently referred to as Satan, the ancient Hebrew word for "adversary." However, it is important to note that much of what Western society believes today about the Devil does not come from the original scriptures. The Old Testament makes only four references to the supernatural entity "Satan," mostly in the book of Job and, even then, as someone who is in constant direct contact with God. The "serpent" is specified only as an animal: "Now the serpent was more subtil [*sic*] than any beast of the field which the Lord God had made" (Genesis 3:1). Even within the context of Job, Satan is merely a tempter, challenging the faith of the book's protagonist.

The New Testament gives examples that are more in line with modern ideas of the Devil. Satan tempts Christ in the wilderness. Satan "enters" the heart of Judas, the betrayer of Jesus. Satan plays a key role in the "end times" as laid out in the book of Revelation. In all of these stories, Satan is someone who has a direct conflict with God and seeks to extend that conflict to God's greatest creation, humanity. Still, these mentions are few and far between. It would be in the first thousand years of the Catholic Church that Satan would take on the image that is known the world over today: red skinned, horned, spike tailed, and bat winged. It would be centuries after biblical times that what human society recognizes as the Devil would be definitively spelled out. Enoch is mentioned in the early Hebrew scriptures as someone beloved by God who lived a very long time before being taken by God (Genesis 5:24). In the book of Enoch, whose first written text is attributed to the third century BCE, the author describes numerous "fallen angels" who sought to have children with the "daughters of man" and who, if refused, would lead men astray (Enoch 1). This idea would be expanded on in perhaps the most definitive work on Satan, *Paradise Lost*.

In 1667 CE, the English poet John Milton produced his epic poem, *Paradise Lost*. In this narrative, Satan (the angel Lucifer) has just led his unsuccessful rebellion against God in heaven, and he and his followers have been banished to hell. After their defeat, Lucifer convinces his minions to take their vengeance on God's most beloved creation: humankind. It is then that Lucifer disguises himself as a snake and has his historic encounter with Eve. This, however, conflicts with the biblical account, which strongly suggests that the "serpent" had legs, which God removes in punishment for what he has done: "And the Lord God said unto the serpent, Because thou hast done this [tempting the woman], thou art cursed above all cattle, and above every beast of the field; upon thy belly shalt thou go, and dust shalt thou eat all the days of thy life" (Genesis 3:14).

Despite the discrepancy, it is Milton's portrayal of Satan/Lucifer that the Western world has accepted as definitive for the last four hundred years, and the overwhelming majority of fictional portrayals of the Devil throughout that time have been based on this epic poem. Christianity from its inception has presented Satan as humankind's greatest enemy. In the Gospels of the New Testament, written in the decades after the crucifixion of Jesus, Satan takes on a more human form in his attempts to tempt Jesus in the wilderness, and in the book of Revelation, Satan is seen as the mastermind behind the Beast and the Antichrist in an overall war against God and humankind. By the time of Christ, however, human history had already begun to see villainy within itself.

OTHER VILLAINS OF THE ANCIENT WORLD

Ancient civilizations did not possess much in the way of "history" from which to draw cautionary tales regarding examples of good or bad. What they had instead were stories, most of which we regard today as myth, although, at the time, they were considered history or religion (or both). Throughout the ancient world, however, villains were mostly gods or pseudodeities of some form or other. These supernatural supervillains tempted, harassed, and persecuted human beings whom they deemed righteous or in some manner heroic. Occasionally, even heroic gods would do villainous things to humans, either as punishment or tests of character. As human society neared the time of the Jewish prophet Jesus of Nazareth (around whose birth the Western world would define time itself), actual villains began to appear within the scope of actual history, changing from the outlying threat of supernatural phenomenon to the inner darkness of humankind's very soul.

The oldest known written story in human civilization is The Epic of Gilgamesh (c. 2100 BCE). In this story, the hero, Gilgamesh, is a harsh ruler who finds redemption by defeating the evil deity Enkidu. Throughout the Greek myths, produced mostly by such literary giants as Homer and Hesiod in the sixth to eighth centuries BCE, various Olympian deities challenged humans—or, more often, half-human demigods such as Hercules—and taught them the values of honor, duty, and sacrifice to Greek youth. Most of these stories were adopted by the burgeoning Roman civilization for the first half of its domination of the Mediterranean world. In the biblical text of Genesis, one of the earliest human villains was Cain, who brutally murdered his brother, Abel, over his jealousy of God's preference for Abel's animal sacrifices to Cain's plant sacrifices, although they each were offering from the fruits of their respective labors (Genesis 4:1–16). In fact, the entire Old Testament is ripe with examples of human villainy: murder, betrayal, deception, lying, lust, envy, and adultery.

Throughout the ancient Western world, the one key difference between Babylonian, Egyptian, Greek, and Roman stories and those of the ancient Jews is that in the Jewish tales, humans often emerge as villains, whereas the other cultures tend to focus on gods and other supernatural beings as the source of villainy, with humans repeatedly doing what was right in the face of overwhelming paranormal foes. Today, our greatest treasure trove of ancient stories comes from the Greek and Roman myths. In their mythology, the gods exhibit all the weaknesses that, in the centuries since, have been more attributed to humans. The gods exhibit anger and take out revenge. They exhibit lust and often use deceptive tactics to act out on that lustfulness. Whereas in the biblical book of Job, God allows Satan to test Job's devotion by putting him through various hardships and heartaches, the Greek gods tended to put humans through various physical trials to prove their worth. In any event, much of the ancient world saw deities as the progenitors of villainous acts on humanity, while the ancient Hebrews saw the weakness of humans as a source of disappointment to their God.

EARLY HUMAN VILLAINS

Throughout ancient history, villainy was primarily attributed to enemy nations. The Hebrews viewed the Egyptians, Philistines, and Babylonians as villains. The Greeks considered the Persians and Trojans as villains. The Egyptians viewed the Romans as such, and the Romans so viewed the Carthaginians. Occasionally, however, signs of villainy were seen within societies, and the possibility of even the greatest heroes falling into villainous acts was not outside the realm of possibility. Some of the most notable examples of human villainy in the ancient world revolved around the same act: betrayal.

The Roman Republic was founded on a story of villainy. According to the legend of the rape of Lucretia (c. 510 BCE), Sextus Tarquinius, the son of the Etruscan king Tarquinius Superbus ("Tarquin the Proud"), forced Lucretia, the virtuous wife of Sextus's friend, Tarquinius Collatinus, at sword point to have sex with him. At first attempting to seduce her with compliments and, eventually, outright begging, Sextus finally threatens to kill her and place her body next to a dead slave, leading all to believe she has been unfaithful to her husband. This threat forces Lucretia to acquiesce. After confessing to her husband and father (the royal prefect of Rome) what happened, Lucretia commits suicide. In response to this outrage, Collatinus, his father-in-law, and their friends force the king's family from power, vowing that Rome would never again fall under the rule of a king. The Roman Republic would dominate the region for nearly five hundred years before eventually falling once more to monarchy.

In 44 BCE, the Roman senator Marcus Junius Brutus ("Brutus, the Younger") organized a conspiracy of senators to assassinate the Roman dictator Julius Caesar. Although the senators viewed their actions as lawful and justifiable tyrannicide, history has dubbed Brutus a traitor, as Caesar had been his lifelong friend and mentor. There were, in fact, those even at the time who believed the two men may have been more than friends, Caesar having had a decades-long love affair with Brutus's mother, Servilia of the Junii. Regardless of the motivation of or justification for Caesar's assassination, Brutus has been forever branded a villain. Ultimately, their allegedly noble cause was fruitless, as the dictatorship of Caesar would be soon followed by the rise of the Roman emperors for the next five hundred years.

Roughly seventy-five years later, circa 30 CE, the Jewish zealot Judas Iscariot similarly betrayed his teacher and master, Jesus of Nazareth. Although Judas's true motives cannot be known, it has been long-held tradition that Judas, seeing that Jesus was a man of peace rather than the militant messiah he at first believed him to be, turned him over to the Jewish religious authorities for "thirty pieces of silver" (the standard payment for such information at the time). Because Judas's actions led to Jesus's arrest, beating, crucifixion, and death, Christian history has dubbed him a traitor.

To underscore Brutus and Judas as the ultimate in human villainy, the poet Dante Alighieri, in the "Inferno" section of his *Divine Comedy* (1320 CE), presents a horrific image of the large, beastly Satan in the lowest ring of hell, eternally devouring Brutus and Judas as punishment for their sins. However, in his 1952 CE novel, *The Last Temptation of Christ*, author Nikos Kazantzakis suggests that Judas's betrayal was part of Jesus's (and God's) overall plan, drafted by Jesus himself to turn him in to the authorities so that Jesus could complete his assigned mission of sacrifice. In recent decades, revisionist historians and scholars have attempted to defend the actions of Brutus and Judas, but the two have become so embedded in Western culture as villains that a full redemption of either remains unlikely.

HUMAN VILLAINS IN EARLY MODERN FICTION

One of the most popular narratives of medieval Europe was the mythical tales of King Arthur and his Knights of the Round Table. Although no historical records confirm the existence of Britain's most famous monarch, he has become one of the most beloved icons of British history. Alleged to have led the Britons against the invading Saxons in the fifth-to-sixth century CE, the first recorded account of Arthur appeared in the book *Historia Regum Brittanniae* in 1138 CE by Geoffrey of Monmouth. Numerous stories revolving around Arthur and his knights continued over the following centuries, most famously collected in *Le Morte d'Arthur* in 1485 CE, by Sir Thomas Mallory. This would be followed centuries later by *Idylls of the King* (1859–1885 CE) by Alfred, Lord Tennyson, and *The Once and Future King* (1958 CE) by T. H. White. Over the last millennium, the tales of Arthur have been recounted in numerous stories, poems, plays, and films.

In the Arthur legends, the most notorious villain is the king's half sister, the enchantress and witch Morgan le Fay. Early accounts note her only as a witch, but, over time, she is given a backstory that identifies her as Arthur's half sister by their mother, who was seduced by Arthur's father, disguised as Morgan's father (and all of that centuries before modern American soap operas). Morgan later uses the same deception to seduce Arthur into impregnating her. Their child, Sir Mordred, ultimately kills his father in battle. Through Morgan's machinations, audiences saw the villainy of witchcraft, wrath, seduction, and incest, all of which were well established as sinful and villainous through the first millennia of the Catholic Church in Europe.

When it comes to modern ideas of human villainy, however, perhaps the individual most responsible for identifying and dissecting the darker tendencies of humanity is the iconic English playwright William Shakespeare. In just a few decades at the end of the 1500s through the beginning of the 1600s, Shakespeare enthralled the English people with tales of the human condition, some entirely fictional, others based on historical sources. Shakespeare cemented Brutus as a villain in his adaptation of *The Tragedy of Julius Caesar* (1599 CE). In *The Tragedy of Othello, the Moor of Venice* (1603 CE), Shakespeare introduces audiences to the evil Iago, whose racism and ambition lead him to use Othello's trust to play on his insecurities and bring about his downfall.

Writing as he did during the reign of Queen Elizabeth I, the last Tudor monarch of England, Shakespeare's historical plays, by necessity, portrayed the enemies of the Tudors in a villainous light. Shakespeare may be personally responsible for history's judgment of England's King Richard III. In his 1593 play, *Richard III*, the monarch who had been unseated by Elizabeth's grandfather, Henry VII, is portrayed as an ambitious hunchback who killed his nephews and sought to marry his niece in order to secure his throne. Although this story is based on widely held speculations and suspicions of the day, Shakespeare's mastery of storytelling has forever blurred the actual events of the 1480s. Through Shakespeare's works, the Western world received myriad examples of the worst of humanity: betrayal, ambition, lust, envy, and lying. These have become the core base of what the Western world defines as villainous into the present day.

VILLAINY IN THE EARLY INDUSTRIALIZED WORLD

As western Europe and, eventually, the United States began to industrialize, creating the modern world, the authors of popular fiction began to focus on the villainy that evolves with technological advancement. In 1818, twenty-year-old Mary Wollstonecraft Shelley created one of the most popular and important novels of all time: *Frankenstein; or, The Modern Prometheus.* Although many today mistakenly identify "Frankenstein" as the unnatural creature from the novel, the name actually belongs to the character who works as both hero and villain of the piece: the mad scientist Victor Frankenstein. Frankenstein's obsession with uncovering the secret of creating life leads him to bring about the "birth" of an abomination, one that he immediately seeks to destroy, to his own peril. At the time of Shelley's writing, scientists across Europe were experimenting with the use of electricity to revive the dead. Shelly uses her tale to revive subjects that were popular even in ancient times: the dangers of man playing God. Her overarching theme is that with increasing scientific and technological knowledge, there must also come the responsibility of understanding the lines that must never be crossed and the dangers that come with crossing those lines.

With the rise of industrialism and capitalism, greed and man's inhumanity to man became increasingly evident across the Western world in the 1800s. In 1848, Karl Marx and Friedrich Engels published the *Manifesto of the Communist Party* (better known as *The Communist Manifesto*), warning of the eventual uprising of the working class should the greed and inequality of capitalism continue to go unchecked. By that time, English author Charles Dickens was already addressing these issues in his popular fictional works. Most of Dickens's works—*David Copperfield* (1850), *Bleak House* (1853), and *Great Expectations* (1861), to name but a few—underscored the plight of the poor in industrialized England. Most enduring, however, is his 1843 work, *A Christmas Carol in Prose: Being a Ghost-Story of Christmas*, more widely known today simply as *A Christmas Carol.*

Ebenezer Scrooge has become the modern world's icon of the evil capitalist businessman. At the beginning of the story, Scrooge is a money-hungry miser, cruel to his only employee, unwilling to provide any assistance to the poor, and dismissive of his only living relative. It is only through the supernatural machinations of the ghost of his former business partner, Jacob Marley, who was like Scrooge in life, that the villain is shown the error of his ways and allowed to find redemption with what remains of his life. This beloved story has been recounted every Christmas across the Western world in reprinted books and numerous films for the last hundred-plus years. This tale of the redeemed villain remains one of the most beloved stories of all time.

VILLAINS AS ANTIHEROES IN THE AMERICAS

While every country in the world possesses a frontier history—the history of how a country went from smaller to larger—few countries, if any, possess as wild and storied a frontier history as the United States. For the half century following the American Civil War (1861–1865), America's Wild West produced a myriad of characters who, though real, emerged to mythical status, even during their lifetimes. Some of these individuals were heroic in nature: Wyatt Earp, "Buffalo" Bill Cody, and "Wild Bill" Hickock, to name but a few. Others were villains, such as the murderer and train robber Jesse James and the bank/train robbers Butch Cassidy and the Sundance Kid. All of these men existed in the fictional world as well as the real world during their lifetimes. As they had their various adventures out west, eastern publishers produced dime novels for children, with fictionalized accounts of what their parents were reading in the newspapers.

Before the West could be settled, however, the government needed to make the area "safe" from the Native "threat." From 1866 to 1890, the U.S. Army was engaged in what came to be known as the Plains Indian Wars. More than a war, it was actually a massacre of the Plains tribes. The most iconic hero of this war was Lieutenant Colonel (Brevet Major General) George Armstrong Custer. Custer came to an immortalizing end at the Battle of Little Bighorn, when five companies of his men were wiped out by the Cheyenne, Lakota, and Oglala Sioux who had settled in the valley of the Little Bighorn River. For nearly a century, Custer was hailed as a great American hero. In the early 1970s, however, that changed, as Americans began to feel guilt for the Plains Indian Wars and chose its most infamous soldier to serve as the lone scapegoat for the atrocity. Since 1970, in books, film, and television, Custer has served as the ultimate example of the bloodthirsty, racist villain of the American West.

The Lakota-Sioux chief Sitting Bull, present at Little Bighorn but too old to fight, was seen as the primary villain of the period. Word of Sitting Bull in the newspaper could spread fear throughout the region. In the wake of Custer's death (1876), mistakenly hoping that leaving the battlefield would lead the army to call off their crusade, Sitting Bull joined Buffalo Bill in 1884 spent years traveling with its Buffalo Bill's Wild West Show, regaling audiences with the tale of Custer's brave end. Meanwhile, the Apache chief Geronimo, even more feared by the public than Sitting Bull, led the last violent resistance to the United States in the West. His surrender in 1886 and Sitting Bull's death four years later at the hand of government agents led to the end of the Plains Indian Wars. Both men would live on in popular culture up to the present day. In the twenty-first century, during the War on Terror, the U.S. government would ascribe the code name "Geronimo" to Al-Qaeda leader Osama bin Laden.

Once the West was "won," the door was opened to more Americans moving into the region, giving rise to the legends of the Wild West. Of those infamous outlaws and gunslingers, none were more famous—at the time and since—than Billy the Kid. Billy was born Henry McCarty in 1859, but he traveled under the aliases William H. Bonney and William H. Antrum before finally being known as "the Kid." As legend has it, Billy the Kid died at the age of twenty-one, having killed a man for every year he lived. In reality, he likely killed far fewer (although he did kill many). In the New Mexico territory, Billy was seen by the local Mexican populations as a Robin Hood, stealing from the wealthy Irish American landowners and giving to the poorer Mexican Americans. Most of his confirmed kills were revenge killings for the brutal assassination of his benefactor, John Tunstall. Despite this, Billy was, indeed, an often-bloodthirsty murderer. As local law enforcement (hired guns for local businessmen) sought out the Kid, stories from his growing legend were published in popular dime novels in New York and Boston, thrilling legions of young Americans who saw him as more hero than villain.

Billy continued to be the stuff of legend in books and films for over a century following his alleged death in 1881.

Another such villainous antihero was the Mexican revolutionary and outlaw Pancho Villa. Born José Doroteo Arango Arambula in 1878, Francisco "Pancho" Villa became a cattle thief in his youth after killing the son of the landowner for whom his parents were tenant farmers after that son allegedly raped Pancho's sister. During the Mexican Revolution of the 1910s, Villa commanded the armies of northern Mexico against the military government of Victoriano Huerta, briefly becoming the self-appointed governor of the Mexican state of Chihuahua from 1913 to 1914. As he was originally viewed in the United States as a Robin Hood figure, Americans from across the country would flock to the Mexican border with telescopes and binoculars in an attempt to see Villa in action across the border.

Americans' views changed in 1916, however, when Villa and his army crossed the border into New Mexico, killing twenty Americans while stealing supplies. From 1916 to 1917, the American General John "Black Jack" Pershing led the U.S. military's Punitive Expedition, invading Mexico in search of the outlaw. Although he avoided capture by the Americans, Villa was assassinated in an ambush in 1923. In the century since, Pancho Villa has lived on in stories in songs, books, and films, immortalizing the outlaw for all time. Coming into the twentieth century, then, popular ideas of villainy had remained largely unchanged for the last five hundred years. In the 1920s, however, in the ashes of the First World War, new villains were arising in the real world, and their impact on history would redefine evil and villainy for the rest of the twentieth century and beyond.

PREMODERN VILLAINY IN REVIEW

In his seminal analysis, *Heroes & Villains*, Mike Alsford identifies "free will" as a key source of villainy. Just as the serpent chose to tempt Eve, Cain chose to kill Abel, and Sextus chose to rape Lucretia, so, too, do villains—both real and fictional—exhibit the ultimate example of freedom, unrestrained by the limits of morals or ethics of their respective societies. Alsford states,

> The person who operates according to their own rules, who refuses to conform or be limited by convention or taboo has a strength and presence that it is hard to ignore and in some ways is hard not to admire. . . . It seems to me that at the very heart of the notion of the villain is a refusal to submit to the social contract—for whatever reason—and a willful attempt at exploiting the fact that the rest of society chooses to be bound by it. The simple fact of the matter is that, for the most part, villains do not play by the rules. (Alsford, *Heroes & Villains*, 95, 106)

It seems clear from the examples provided that Alsford's take appears to be at the heart of villainy in human society from the very beginning. Whether tempted into nonconformity such as Eve, or given the example to do so by the gods, humanity learned early on that each person is the master of their own destiny and that destiny need not be confined by the accepted rules of society.

By the midtwentieth century, humanity had evolved scientifically and technologically to a degree never imagined just a century before. Access to these advancements allowed humanity to take free will steps beyond anything attempted before—to genocide and/or global conquest. By 1950, the world had seen the rise of Adolf Hitler and Josef Stalin, brutal dictators with the blood of millions on their hands. With these men, the world was introduced to the supervillain, which would define fictional villainy in the Western world for the remainder of the century and beyond. Rising to these threats, the United States and United Kingdom would emerge as superpowers, or superheroes. However, both nations would also have to face the reality prophesied by the British historian, John Dahlberg-Acton, first Baron Acton, in 1887: "All power tends to corrupt and absolute power corrupts absolutely."

FURTHER READING

Adler, Margot. 2014. *Vampires Are Us: Understanding Our Love Affair with the Immortal Dark Side*. Newburyport, MA: Weiser.

Alsford, Mike. 2006. *Heroes & Villains*. Waco, TX: Baylor University Press.

Ashby, LeRoy. 2006. *With Amusement for All: A History of American Popular Culture since 1830*. Lexington: University Press of Kentucky.

Boggs, Johnny D. 2013. *Billy the Kid on Film: 1911–2012*. Jefferson, NC: McFarland.

Castleman, Harry, and Walter J. Podrazik. 2016. *Watching TV: Eight Decades of American Television*. 3rd ed. Syracuse, NY: Syracuse University Press.

Cavendish, Richard. 1968. *The Black Arts: A Concise History of Witchcraft, Demonology, Astrology, and Other Mystical Practices throughout the Ages*. New York: TarcherPerigree.

Cordingly, David. 2006. *Under the Black Flag: The Romance and the Reality of Life among the Pirates*. New York: Random House.

Dolansky, Shawna. 2018. "How the Serpent Became Satan: Adam, Eve, and the Serpent in the Garden of Eden." Biblical Archaeology Society. October 14, 2018. Accessed April 7, 2019. https://www.biblicalarchaeology.org/daily/biblical-topics/bible-interpretation/how-the-serpent-became-satan/.

Donovan, James. 2008. *A Terrible Glory: Custer and the Little Bighorn, the Last Great Battle of the American West*. New York: Little, Brown and Company.

Forasteros, J. R. 2017. *Empathy for the Devil: Finding Ourselves in the Villains of the Bible*. Downers Grove, IL: InterVarsity.

Gavaler, Chris. 2015. *On the Origin of Superheroes: From the Big Bang to "Action Comics No. 1."* Iowa City: University of Iowa Press.

Gloyn, Liz. 2019. *Tracking Classical Monsters in Popular Culture*. London: Bloomsbury Academic.

Hogan, Susan, Albach. 2003. "Was Judas a Good Guy or Bad? Scholars Disagree." Baylor University. April 17, 2003. Accessed April 21, 2019. https://www.baylor.edu/mediacommunications/index.php?id=6435.

Holderness, Graham. 2015. *Re-Writing Jesus: Christ in 20th-Century Fiction and Film*. London: Bloomsbury.

Hutton, Ronald. 2017. *The Witch: A History of Fear, from Ancient Times to the Present*. New Haven, CT: Yale University Press.

Knight, Stephen. 2016. *Toward Sherlock Holmes: A Thematic History of Crime Fiction in the 19th Century World*. Jefferson, NC: McFarland.

Lozano, Gustavo Vasquez, and Charles Rivers, eds. 2016. *Pancho Villa: The Life and Legacy of the Famous Mexican Revolutionary.* Scotts Valley, CA: CreateSpace.

Mahnke, Aaron. 2017. *The World of Lore: Monstrous Creatures.* New York: Del Rey.

Nichols, Catherine. 2018. "The Good Guy/Bad Guy Myth: Pop Culture Today Is Obsessed with the Battle between Good and Evil. Traditional Folk Tales Never Were. What Changed?" Aeon. January 25, 2018. Accessed September 20, 2019. https://getpocket.com/explore/item/the-good-guy-bad-guy-myth.

Pollard, Tom. 2016. *Loving Vampires: Our Undead Obsession.* Jefferson, NC: McFarland.

Russell, Jeffrey B., and Brooks Alexander. 2007. *A History of Witchcraft: Sorcerers, Heretics, & Pagans.* London: Thames & Hudson.

Van Seters, John. 1998. "The Pentateuch." In *The Hebrew Bible Today: An Introduction to Critical Issues*, edited by Steven L. McKenzie and Matt Patrick Graham, 3–49. Westminster, UK: John Knox.

Wallis, Michael. 2007. *Billy the Kid: The Endless Ride.* New York: W. W. Norton & Company.

Woodard, Colin. 2007. *The Republic of Pirates: Being the True and Surprising Story of the Caribbean Pirates and the Man Who Brought Them Down.* Boston: Houghton Mifflin Harcourt.

"Nazis, Communists, and Terrorists . . . Oh My!": The Rise of the Supervillain and the Evolution of the Modern American Villain

Any society, at any point in its history, can be partially defined by who they see as the villain. This provides insight on what that society fears, whether it be an ideology, an economic basis, or a political system. From 1783 to 1940, the United States had not truly had enemies. There had been bad guys: slave holders in the South, outlaws in the West, robber barons in the North, and so on. Other than those examples, America's only conflicts had come primarily from territorial disputes (or outright greed for territorial gain). That changed around 1940. In 1939, Nazi Germany invaded neighboring Poland, going on to conquer most of Europe over the course of the next year. In 1941, Imperial Japan attacked the U.S. Navy port in Pearl Harbor, Hawaii. These provided the first real ideas of American enemies and examples of global villainy. Americans hated—and feared—the idea of totalitarian rule and the oppression of long-held American freedoms and liberties.

Once the threat of international fascism was defeated, the United States was immediately faced with a similar threat: Soviet communism. Fear of Soviet premier Josef Stalin and the perception of the Soviet Union's expansionist goals further reflected this American fear of totalitarianism and a loss of freedom. The Cold War would influence and shape popular culture for most of the next half century. By 1945, the United States had emerged from its long history of isolationism to become the modern world's greatest superpower, bearing the mantle of the world's protector from that date forward. Soon the United States proudly, and often arrogantly, wore the title "Leader of the Free World." However, as comic book legend Stan Lee would later suggest in the pages of *Amazing Fantasy #15* (August 1962), "With great power there must also come—great responsibility."

Until 1940, villains in American popular culture, such as it was, were primarily outlaw gunslingers in dime novels, such as Billy the Kid, and corrupt businessmen such as Ebenezer Scrooge in Charles Dickens's *A Christmas Carol* (both in

"America First"

Although carrying a connotation of American patriotism, the phrase "America First" actually possesses a long-held nationalistic, racist, anti-Semitic history. The America First Committee was first established in 1940 by several college students, most notably R. Douglas Stuart Jr., future U.S. president Gerald Ford, Sargent Shriver (future director of the Peace Corps, brother-in-law to President John Kennedy, and father-in-law to Governor Arnold Schwarzenegger), and Potter Stewart, who would later serve on the U.S. Supreme Court. Originally designed as a noninterventionist organization, strongly protesting American involvement in the burgeoning World War II, it was supported by notable celebrities such as Father Charles Coughlin, Charlie Chaplin, and Henry Ford. Although the group professed to be anti-Nazi, most of its public speakers often utilized blatantly fascist undertones. It openly opposed accepting Jewish refugees from Nazi Europe and quickly took an anti-Semitic turn.

The America First Committee disbanded three days after the Japanese attacks on Pearl Harbor (December 7, 1941), when American noninterventionism all but disappeared overnight. It reemerged in 1943 as the America First Party, and its leader, Gerald L .K. Smith, ran for president under the party's banner in the 1944 election. In the decades since—and particularly in the twenty-first century—it has emerged with a strong anti-immigration platform, strongly supported and promoted by President Donald J. Trump. Throughout the term's history, however, it has represented the thin but vitally important line between patriotism and nationalism, the latter possessing racist, jingoistic, xenophobic, and usually anti-Semitic overtones. It is often sparked by periods of economic uncertainty at home and/or widespread fear of some foreign threat.

Richard A. Hall

the nineteenth century). From 1940 onward, that would forever change. From that point to the present, American villains would be dictators, racists, terrorists, and would-be world conquerors. Americans now feared the rise of murderous sociopaths from within our society, such as the Joker, and would-be world conquerors threatening us from outside, such as the Red Skull. Decades before the rise of Al-Qaeda in the 1990s, pop culture presented Americans with international terrorist organizations such as SPECTRE in the *James Bond* novels and films and COBRA in the *G. I. Joe* cartoons, toy line, and comics. Americans viewed heroes as those who stood against the threats to American freedom and liberty. As such, these villains defined us and shaped our ideas on good and bad.

WORLD WAR II

In the wake of the devastation of World War I (1914–1919), several countries, weakened by the global turmoil, came under fascistic regimes. Fascism as a philosophy has four primary ingredients: nationalism ("My country is better than your country"), imperialism ("My country should rule your country"), racism ("Whatever I am is better than whatever you are"), and atheism ("There is no God; there is only the state"). In 1922, Benito Mussolini and his National Fascist Party took power over the Kingdom of Italy. In 1926, Crown Prince Hirohito became emperor of Japan on the death of his father and was strongly influenced by the powerful imperialistic military elite. In 1936, due to a devastating civil war, fascist general Francisco Franco emerged as caudillo (dictator/strongman) of Spain. By that year, however, the most famous fascist dictator in human history had already risen to the title of führer (leader) of Germany: Adolf Hitler.

Although Austrian by birth, Adolf Hitler had served in the German army during World War I. Devasted by his adopted country's loss and blaming, as many Germans did, the elite Jewish population for complicity in the nation's economic devastation (Germany's delegation to the signing of the Versailles Treaty, which charged Germany with outrageous sums of war reparations to England and France, were all German Jews), Hitler soon joined the fascist National Socialist German Workers Party, better known to history as the Nazi Party. On being chosen chancellor of the German Reichstag (its legislature) in 1933, Hitler oversaw passage of the Enabling Act, essentially giving Hitler the ability to pass laws without consent of the rest of the Reichstag or the president, Paul von Hindenburg. In 1934, von Hindenburg died, and Hitler, again through legislation, merged the offices of chancellor and president, making himself the führer. In direct violation of the Treaty of Versailles, Hitler immediately began to remilitarize Germany, and in 1938, he annexed Austria, followed in 1939 with the invasion of Poland, beginning Nazi Germany's goal of global conquest.

At first, the United States sought to avoid involvement in the growing worldwide conflicts. Japan, Italy, and Germany were all embroiled in imperialistic policies around the globe. In 1941, U.S. president Franklin Delano Roosevelt (FDR), who had been recently elected to an unprecedented third term due in large part to the growing global threats and the continuing Great Depression at home, clearly viewed Hitler as the primary threat to the world, pledging all the support needed by Great Britain and the Soviet Union (the only major powers standing up to Hitler's aggression). Americans en masse continued to be isolationist until December 7, 1941, when, as President Roosevelt said in his December 8, 1941, address to Congress, "The United States of America was suddenly and deliberately attacked [at Pearl Harbor, Hawaii] by naval and air forces of the Empire of Japan." Americans were now united for war, but only against Japan. However, on December 11, 1941, Hitler and Mussolini declared war on the United States, drawing the soon-to-be superpower into the European conflict. This allowed FDR to follow a Hitler First policy, focusing efforts in Europe, which the president deemed a larger threat. In order to rally popular support for the war's European theater, Roosevelt launched a massive propaganda campaign, equating the threats of Japan, Germany, and Italy. From that point on, American popular culture fully backed the president's agenda.

In 1940, Hollywood legend Charlie Chaplin released the film *The Great Dictator*, Chaplin's first talkie, a movie with sound. In it, the actor is clearly portraying Adolf Hitler. His closing speech, however, is a plea to the still-isolationist America to stand against greed and brutality. To that time, Jewish Americans were as despised and mistreated as their relatives were in Europe, and throughout the late 1930s and early 1940s, the United States denied entry to thousands of European Jews (except specific examples such as noted physicist Albert Einstein) attempting to flee Nazi oppression; most of those immigrants went, instead, to Mexico, where they were welcomed. By 1940, however, there was one American industry that was dominated by Jewish Americans: the burgeoning medium of comic books.

Comic books had been a huge hit with American children since their inception in the early 1930s. While they were originally merely reprints of previously released newspaper comic strips, by 1935, the growing number of comic book publishers were looking for original material to print. Since comics were viewed by the rest of the publishing world as a low-brow medium, publishers relied heavily on writers and artists who could not get jobs in mainstream publishing, which proved a boon for Jewish Americans, who were as derided and faced the same levels of prejudice as the infant medium (Wright, *Comic Book Nation*, 2–7). In 1938, two Jewish American boys from Cleveland, Ohio, Jerry Siegel and Joe Shuster, sold an idea to National Allied/DC Comics: Superman.

Superman was unlike any fictional hero since the gods of ancient Greece. An alien and sole survivor of a doomed planet, Superman "possessed powers and abilities far beyond those of mortal men" and was "faster than a speeding bullet . . . more powerful than a locomotive . . . able to leap tall buildings in a single bound" (opening credits, *The Adventures of Superman* radio program, 1940–1951). This introduced the world to the superhero. Ironically, a scant six years later, the United States, to that point a major economic power but little else, emerged as the modern world's first superpower. The massive overnight success of Superman led to a myriad of spandex-clad heroes with super powers to soon follow; including Batman, Captain Marvel ("SHAZAM!"), and Wonder Woman. Originally, superheroes faced off against the standard villains of Depression-era America: corrupt landlords and politicians, street criminals, and organized crime. By 1940, as American newspapers reported accounts of the growing global fascist threat, it became clear that these new superheroes needed to face off against threats that would match and challenge their incredible powers. Enter the supervillain.

The first modern supervillain was the Joker, in the pages of *Batman #1* (Bill Finger and Bob Kane, April 1940). Created by Finger and Kane, Batman had been introduced the year before in *Detective Comics #27* (May 1939). Although identified as a superhero, Batman possessed no super powers. He was highly intelligent, extremely educated, expertly skilled in hand-to-hand combat, and armed with an arsenal of gadgets. Like Superman, Batman originally fought standard urban crime. The Joker changed the game not only for Batman but also for superheroes across the spectrum from 1940 to the present. Created by Finger, Kane, and Jerry Robinson, the Joker represents the ultimate juxtaposition: where the friendly image of a clown is the evil adversary of the frightening image of a bat. Joker was no mere street criminal. He was a psychotic killer, often killing just for the thrill of it. He was a serial killer at a time when that phrase was not as well known as it would become in future decades. As America entered World War II, however, the supervillain was soon to evolve further, reflecting the real-world threat posed by Hitler and his Nazis.

In December 1940, Timely Comics published *Captain America Comics #1.* Created by Jewish Americans Joe Simon and Jack Kirby, Captain America is ninety-eight-pound-weakling Steve Rogers, who desperately wants to serve his country (notably a full year before Pearl Harbor) but is denied because of his inability to pass the basic physical. Rogers is then recruited to take part in a government experiment to create the perfect "super soldier." Injected with what would later be dubbed the "Super Soldier Serum," Rogers' physicality is substantially enhanced, making him the perfect physical specimen. When the scientist who mastered the formula is killed by a Nazi spy, Rogers becomes the only super soldier, serving his country as Captain America, clad in red, white, and blue, and armed only with a similarly colored shield. On the cover of the first issue of *Captain America Comics,* his primary enemy was made quite clear; the hero was punching Adolf Hitler. Captain America's first direct foe is also his most infamous: the Red Skull (Joe Simon and Jack Kirby, *Captain America Comics #1,* December 1940).

Originally, the Red Skull was actually an American industrialist and Nazi sympathizer named George Maxon, who wore a red skull mask. In *Captain America Comics #7* (Joe Simon and Jack Kirby, October 1941), the "real" Red Skull was introduced as Johann Schmidt, a high-ranking member of Hitler's Nazi regime. Throughout World War II, Red Skull would personify the very villainy that Hitler and the Nazis represented: a hatred of the other and a thirst for power, global conquest, and the downfall of America. As the war progressed, however, all the superheroes would express to their audiences the true threat of the real-world menace.

During the war, superhero comic books urged their readers to buy war bonds and recycle their comic books for the war effort against the evil Nazis and Japanese (creating a scarcity that would have a massive impact in future decades on the value of original World War II–era comics). Superman, Batman, and Captain America repeatedly advertised the importance of all Americans, including children, doing their part for the war effort. Midway through the war, Captain America informs his readers of the importance of buying war bonds, explaining to readers how precious every penny is: "485 dimes = 1 M-1903 rifle; 35 dimes = 1 haversack; 25 dimes = 1 hand grenade; 70 dimes = 100 bullets; 55 dimes = feeding 10 soldiers for one day; 350 dimes = 10 bayonettes" (Simon and Kirby, *Captain America Comics #15,* June 1942). By that time, another patriotic-themed superhero had joined the American effort against the Nazis: the Amazonian princess Wonder Woman (William Moulton Marston and H. G. Peter, *All Star Comics #8,* December 1941).

In addition to the six best-selling superheroes of the period—Superman, Batman, Wonder Woman, Captain America, Human Torch, and Sub-Mariner—other comic books focused on the horrors of the Nazis, cementing them in the minds of Americans for generations to come as the ultimate example of evil in the world. The Japanese (the only World War II aggressor to ever actually attack us) were even often referred to as "Japanazis." Roosevelt's conviction that Hitler was the greater threat was quickly embraced by all Americans. Even in the 1950s, long after the war ended, lesser known, nonsuperhero comics such as *Frontline Combat* (E.C., 1951), *Stamps Comics* (Apfelbaum, 1952), *Beware! Terror Tales* (Fawcett, 1953), and *Impact* (E.C., 1955) all presented graphic portrayals of the Holocaust (the mass slaughter of approximately six million European Jews by the

Nazis) and the evil of the Nazis overall (Adams, Medoff, and Yoe, *We Spoke Out*, 21, 33, 42, 49). In 2000, in the feature film *X-Men* (20th Century Fox, director Bryan Singer) and again in the 2011 film *X-Men: First Class* (20th Century Fox, director Matthew Vaughn), the horrors of the Nazis are portrayed through the experiences of the young Jewish mutant Erik Lehnsherr (Magneto).

When the dust of World War II settled, and the Nazi threat was soundly defeated by the new superpower and her allies, good had triumphed over evil. The world's first supervillain had been destroyed. Soon, however, a new threat would emerge, as a former ally became a deadly threat. Just as Nazi Germany and Hitler had threatened the world with the promise of a fascist empire, the Soviet Union and Josef Stalin now posed a similar threat, this time of a communist empire. Although the political ideologies were different—radical conservative fascism versus radical leftist communism—the threat remained the same: totalitarian dictatorship and the loss of personal freedoms and liberties around the world. Once more the new superpower would need to rise to the challenge, and the United States had a new, even more menacing threat to fear. The American people had a new, albeit too familiar, villain.

THE COLD WAR

No sooner had World War II ended than a new struggle confronted the new world superpower. In a speech to Congress in 1947 requesting aide to the troubled countries of Greece and Turkey, President Harry Truman added a section dedicating all of America's efforts to stopping the global spread of communism. This became known as the Truman Doctrine (March 12, 1947), and it officially launched what came to be known as the Cold War (1947–1992). This near-half-century struggle between America's democratic capitalism and the Soviet Union's (and later China's) authoritarian communism became all the more dangerous when the Soviet Union achieved atomic weapons technology in 1949. This led to an arms race, with each side desperately attempting to create more weapons of mass destruction than their opponent. The world sat on edge for forty-five years under a constant threat of total nuclear annihilation. The struggle was called the Cold War because the two major opponents never directly fought militarily. Instead, the conflict was fought through proxy wars in places such as Korea, Cuba, and Vietnam.

For most of the last half of the twentieth century, the Cold War dominated American sociopolitical and popular culture across all media. In the early 1950s, Wisconsin senator Joe McCarthy intensified what was already being called the Second Red Scare (the first Red Scare took place briefly following World War I, thirty years earlier). McCarthy utilized the politics of fear, stoking suspicion within the American populace with the conspiracy theory that communist agents were living among them. With little-to-no evidence to back up his claims, this fearmongering turned neighbor against neighbor, family member against family member, and coworker against coworker. Luckily, McCarthy was exposed by his own hubris when he decided to air his accusatory committee hearings live on television, showing the American people firsthand the depths of his corruption and maliciousness. Once the Red Scare abated, however, the underlying damage done in those few years continued to simmer throughout the rest of the conflict.

Captain America answered the call to America's new threat for a brief period in 1953. After initially cancelling the superhero comic book in 1950, Timely Comics brought back the magazine for three issues as "Captain America: Commie Smasher." In those few stories, Captain America took on the Soviets, China, North Korea, and Vietnam (even though, at the time, the Indochinese country was still occupied by the French). The Red Skull returned, this time in the guise of a proponent of global communism. Although communism is a complete 180-degree difference from fascism, their shared authoritarian core made the villain a natural fit for the new threat. One thing that the communists and fascists had in common was a desire to destroy the freedom and liberty of the United States.

The new Atomic Age kept Americans in a constant state of fear. Children now had to conduct nuclear attack drills along with the standard tornado and fire drills. This fear was made manifest, and given cathartic release to a degree, through the science fiction and monster movies of the 1950s. Films such as *Godzilla* and *Them!* (both in 1954) and *The Fly* (1958) played to the overwhelming fear of science and its possible ramifications, particularly nuclear radiation. In 1947, two unidentified flying object (UFO) sightings gained national attention within just one week, the most notable being the alleged crash at Roswell, New Mexico. The late 1940s and the 1950s would have the largest number of UFO sightings in U.S. history. This, too, was connected to the Cold War. The threat and fear of invasion by the communists could be seen in the equal fear of alien invasion. This was quite visible in films such as *The Day the Earth Stood Still* (1951) and *Invasion of the Body Snatchers* (1956). The villains in these pieces were the threats to individuality and even life itself. Aliens could make Americans their slaves. Science could kill them entirely.

By the 1960s, the respective international spy agencies—America's CIA and the Soviet Union's KGB—had achieved almost-celebrity status in the American zeitgeist. As such, spy novels, films, and television series became wildly popular, with a new form of villain emerging from the genre: the international terrorist organization. Former British intelligence officer Ian Fleming published *Casino Royale* in 1952, introducing the world the superspy James Bond. A decade later, the character made his film debut in *Dr. No.* Avoiding the terrifying reality of the Cold War threat, Fleming pitted his protagonist against the international organization SPECTRE, or the Special Executive for Counterintelligence, Terrorism, Revenge, and Extortion. Decades before religious-based international terrorism became a mainstay around the globe, organizations such as SPECTRE desired one goal: total world domination. Although the group was neither communist nor connected with the Soviet Union, the underlying connection to the communist superpower was clear: the democracies of the West must stand firm against world conquerors.

Other novels and films rode the coattails of *Bond*'s success, some facing other SPECTRE-like international organizations and others against the communist world. Some of the more popular spy films of the period were *The Manchurian Candidate* (1962), *To Trap a Spy* (1964), *Licensed to Kill* (1965, not to be confused with the *Bond* novel and film of the same name), *The Spy Who Came in from the*

Cold (1965), *In Like Flint* (1966), *Funeral in Berlin* (1966), and *The Wrecking Crew* (1969). The villains in these films had one primary factor in common; they all presented a threat to American values and the American way of life. Marvel Comics joined the spy genre in the 1960s. In 1963, the superhero factory introduced the comic book *Sgt. Fury and His Howling Commandos*, set during World War II.

Shortly thereafter, Stan Lee and company brought the World War II soldier to the present, first as a CIA agent and later as head of the international spy agency SHIELD, originally standing for the Strategic Headquarters, International Espionage and Law-Enforcement Division (Stan Lee and Jack Kirby, *Strange Tales #135*, August 1965). Fury and SHIELD soon became the primary overarching connection of all of the Marvel superhero comic books. Fury, his agents, and his army of LMD (life model decoy) robots protected the world from all threats, both terrestrial and extraterrestrial. The overarching theme of the spy genre of the 1960s was that there were powerful threats to the American way of life and that these secret spy agencies were the nation's first line of defense against them.

In 1972, U.S. president Richard Nixon eased tensions with both the Soviet Union and China, as well as ending American military involvement in Vietnam. Throughout the 1970s, it appeared to many as if the Cold War were over, with a whimper rather than a bang. That changed dramatically with the election of Ronald Reagan as president in 1980. President Reagan had been head of the Screen Actors' Guild in the late 1940s, working with the House Un-American Activities Committee in the House of Representatives (under Nixon's leadership) to investigate communist infiltration of Hollywood following World War II. A die-hard anti-communist, Reagan reinflamed the Cold War, spiking U.S. government spending on conventional, nuclear, and experimental weapons, forcing the Soviet Union to follow course, which ultimately played a large role in their eventual economic collapse in the late 1980s and early 1990s. After the socioeconomic doldrums of the 1970s, Reagan came into office proverbially waving the American flag and refocusing American attention on the global threat of international communism.

Hollywood backed the new American militarism with a plethora of patriotic, military-themed films: *Missing in Action* (1984, followed by several sequels); *Commando, Rambo: First Blood, Part II,* and *Invasion USA* (all in 1985); *Delta Force* and *Heartbreak Ridge* (both in 1986); and *Rambo III* (1988), to name but a very, very few. These films made international heroes of actors Chuck Norris, Sylvester Stallone, and Arnold Schwarzenegger. Like the spy films of the 1960s, the primary threats in these films were international threats to the American Dream. On television, children became enthralled by the heroic adventures of *G. I. Joe* (1983–1986), which also ran as a Marvel comic book throughout the decade. The American soldiers of *G. I. Joe*, "the code name for America's daring, highly trained special missions force," fought the forces of COBRA, "a ruthless terrorist organization determined to rule the world" (opening credits, *G. I. Joe: A Real American Hero*). Following the Bond/SPECTRE dynamic of the 1960s, COBRA posed a direct threat to the basic freedoms and liberties of the free nations of the world, just as the Reagan administration presented the Soviet Union.

In December 1991, the Soviet Union collapsed, primarily from the economic devastation of keeping up with Reagan's massive military spending in the 1980s. In February 1992, U.S. president George H. W. Bush and Russian president Boris Yeltsin held a joint press conference in Washington and officially declared an end to the Cold War. After fifty years of fighting Nazis, communists, and fictional international threats, Americans suddenly found themselves without a villain to unite them. This absence of external threats soon led a society used to having an enemy to look inward at themselves and find threats here at home. Beginning in 1964, Americans had grown increasingly suspicious of their own government. Scandals and perceived conspiracies revolving around the assassination of President John F. Kennedy (1963), the Vietnam War (1964–1973), the Pentagon Papers (1971), Watergate (1972–1974), and the Iran-Contra Affair (1984–1987) had shattered American faith in the basic institutions of government.

In December 1991, director Oliver Stone released his award-winning film *JFK*, positing a credible government conspiracy in the assassination of President Kennedy and once more inflaming this decades-long conspiracy theory. The public perception of government secrecy, conspiracy, and villainy was given further voice in the hit television series *The X-Files* (TV: FOX, 1993–2002, 2016, and 2018; movies, 1998 and 2008). In this series, FBI agents Fox Mulder (played by David Duchovny) and Dana Scully (played by Gillian Anderson) investigate cases consisting of the paranormal and/or extraterrestrial. The overarching story line, however, presented a dubious plot—initially thought to be the U.S. government but later exposed as an international cabal of malevolent men—to hide the existence of alien life here on earth. The primary villain of the piece was the mysterious CSM (Cigarette Smoking Man). Throughout the series, CSM represented all that Americans distrusted about their government: secrecy, anonymity, and conspiracy. With no clear international villain to unite the country, divisions within American society grew throughout the 1990s. That changed, quickly, after the events of 9/11.

THE WAR ON TERROR

A decade after the end of the Cold War, America had become complacent, comfortable that external threats to the country were a thing of the past. That changed on the morning of September 11, 2001. On behalf of the international radical jihadist terrorist organization Al-Qaeda, nineteen terrorists hijacked four American passenger planes, flying two into the Twin Towers of the World Trade Center in New York City. The third was flown into the western side of the Pentagon, entering at ground level. Before the fourth plane could reach Washington, the passengers had received word from loved ones by cell phone, still a relatively new technology at the time, of the previous attacks. Several passengers mounted a counteroffensive to take back the plane. Rather than give it up, the terrorists chose to dive-bomb the plane into a field outside Shanksville, Pennsylvania, killing all on board. America's response would come to be known as the War on Terror, beginning with the October 2001 invasion of Afghanistan and its ruling Taliban regime, which had provided safe haven to Al-Qaeda for years.

Al-Qaeda had formed in 1988 under the leadership of the radical Sunni Muslim extremist Osama bin Laden. After the Unites States deployed troops to Saudi Arabia in 1990 in response to Iraqi president Saddam Hussein's invasion and annexation of neighboring Kuwait, bin Laden was outraged over what he viewed as the foreign military occupation of Muslim holy land. Throughout the 1990s, Al-Qaeda had conducted numerous attacks against U.S. interests: a first attempt to destroy the World Trade Center (1993), attacks on U.S. bases in Saudi Arabia (1995–1996), attacks on American embassies in Kenya and Tanzania (1998), and an attack on the U.S. Navy vessel *U.S.S. Cole* (2000). All the while, Americans viewed Al-Qaeda as a just another jihadist organization taking potshots at American interests "over there." The events of 9/11 changed America profoundly, giving Americans a new idea of villainy.

Just weeks after the 9/11 attacks, an issue of the *Captain America* comics laid out the dangers facing the country. Written prior to the surprise attacks, the warning from the longtime Captain America villain Red Skull, lays out a strategy for any of America's would-be enemies to follow: "[America] is a cauldron of hate waiting to erupt . . . a cesspool of violent thoughts looking for release. It's a fuse extending from one coast to the other, waiting for someone to ignite the flame" (Dan Jurgens, *Captain America #46*, October 2001). While Al-Qaeda attacked American interests abroad, Americans at home were attacking each other, conservative versus liberal. Bin Laden had hoped the 9/11 attacks would exacerbate the already-growing divide, but, instead, it unified Americans, albeit briefly, against the new external threat: radical jihadist terrorism.

While many Americans were able to make the distinction between jihadists and mainstream Muslims, many others could not. Fear of, and violence against, Arab and Muslim Americans grew. Terror overall was now the common enemy, and those who practiced or condoned terror were the new American villains. Unlike the Nazis and communists of decades past, terrorists just wanted America—and Americans—gone, completely destroying what they viewed as a "decadent" society. In 2003, the SyFy cable outlet launched a reboot of the 1970s series *Battlestar Galactica* (2003–2010), where a ragtag group of spacefaring humans, their home worlds destroyed, their population decimated, desperately sought escape from the mechanical Cylon race, which the humans had created. Many on the political left were arguing at the time that America had, in essence, created Al-Qaeda through its Middle East policies over the decades. Similarly, in the comic book/television series *The Walking Dead* (comic: 2003–present; television: 2010–present), the threat to humanity (and America) was an overwhelming horde of zombies, the walkers, who cared nothing about "conquering" or "ruling," only consuming and destroying the living and successfully wiping out American society as they did so.

After long wars in Afghanistan and Iraq, Americans began to forget the emotional toil of 9/11. Once it seemed that the threats of Al-Qaeda and its offspring, ISIS/ISIL, were once more only threats "over there," the "Culture Wars" at home resumed, and Americans once more turned on each other, even on the issue of the War on Terror (just as Red Skull had suggested). Americans began defining themselves by which political party they supported, seeing the other party as an enemy to American values. In 2016, Russian president/dictator Vladimir Putin masterminded a coordinated cyberattack on the United States, utilizing social media to further divide the country and manipulate that year's presidential elections in favor of the eventual victor: Donald J. Trump. That same year, FOX relaunched *The X-Files*, as Americans were once more obsessed with their distrust of basic American institutions. An additional season aired in early 2018, a full year into the Trump presidency, and the overall message of the season was that Americans now see everything as a conspiracy and, therefore, nothing really is a conspiracy, allowing true conspiracy to prosper.

CONCLUSION

Prior to World War II, American ideas of villains were the same as most other societies for the last several centuries: murderers, thieves, corrupt officials, and broken systems. The rise of the Nazis, followed by the communists and terrorists, changed the villain dynamic in American society. Villains in any society reflect the fears of that society. Since World War II, what Americans have feared most is the devastation of their freedoms, liberties, values, and society overall. Villains now reflect any threat to our individual reality. The growing problem within America, however, is that threat can be broken down person by person (for example, politically, conservatives may see expanding government power as a threat, whereas liberal might see the lack of it as a threat). The villain can be a foreign dictator or terrorist, or our own government, or even our next-door neighbor. Throughout World War II, the Cold War and the War on Terror, Americans could unify their idea of villains in a common perceived threat. In the absence of those external threats, the villains become ourselves, and the Red Skull stands to be proved frighteningly, devastatingly prescient.

FURTHER READING

Adams, Neal, Rafael Medoff, and Craig Yoe. 2018. *We Spoke Out: Comic Books and the Holocaust.* San Diego, CA: Yoe Books/IDW.

Alsford, Mike. 2006. *Heroes & Villains.* Waco, TX: Baylor University Press.

Ashby, LeRoy. 2006. *With Amusement for All: A History of American Popular Culture since 1830.* Lexington: University Press of Kentucky.

Castleman, Harry, and Walter J. Podrazik. 2016. *Watching TV: Eight Decades of American Television.* 3rd ed. Syracuse, NY: Syracuse University Press.

Costello, Matthew J. 2009. *Secret Identity Crisis: Comic Books & the Unmasking of Cold War America.* New York: Continuum.

Dyer, Ben, ed. 2009. *Supervillains and Philosophy: Sometimes, Evil Is Its Own Reward.* Popular Culture and Philosophy Series. Chicago: Open Court.

Faludi, Susan. 2007. *The Terror Dream: Myth and Misogyny in an Insecure America.* New York: Picador.

Fertig, Mark. 2017. *Take That, Adolf!: The Fighting Comic Books of the Second World War*. Seattle, WA: Fantagraphics.

Gloyn, Liz. 2019. *Tracking Classical Monsters in Popular Culture*. London: Bloomsbury Academic.

Hendershot, Cyndy. 1999. *Paranoia, the Bomb, and 1950s Science Fiction Films*. Bowling Green, KY: Bowling Green State University Popular Press.

Hoberman, J. 2003. *The Dream Life: Movies, Media, and the Mythology of the Sixties*. New York: New Press.

Hoberman, J. 2011. *An Army of Phantoms: American Movies and the Making of the Cold War*. New York: New Press.

Howe, Sean. 2012. *Marvel Comics: The Untold Story*. New York: Harper-Perennial.

Kirshner, Jonathan. 2012. *Hollywood's Last Golden Age: Politics, Society, and the Seventies Film in America*. Ithaca, NY: Cornell University Press.

Peaslee, Robert, and Rob Weiner, eds. 2019. *The Supervillain Reader*. Jackson: University of Mississippi Press.

Rosenfeld, Gavriel D. 2014. *Hi Hitler!: How the Nazi Past Is Being Normalized in Contemporary Culture*. Cambridge: Cambridge University Press.

Rossinow, Doug. 2015. *The Reagan Era: A History of the 1980s*. New York: Columbia University Press.

Starck, Kathleen, ed. 2010. *Between Fear and Freedom: Cultural Representations of the Cold War*. Newcastle Upon Tyne, UK: Cambridge Scholars.

Stark, Steven D. 1997. *Glued to the Set: The 60 Television Shows and Events That Made Us Who We Are Today*. New York: Delta Trade Paperbacks.

Tucker, Reed. 2017. *Slugfest: Inside the Epic 50-Year Battle between Marvel and DC*. New York: Da Capo.

Willis, Susan. 2005. *Portents of the Real: A Primer for Post-9/11 America*. London: Verso.

Wright, Bradford W. 2003. *Comic Book Nation: The Transformation of Youth Culture in America*. Baltimore, MD: Johns Hopkins University Press.

The Dark Mirror: Evil Twins, *The Twilight Zone*, and the Villain Within

While it is true that villains in popular culture reflect the external threats that the society that creates them fears, they also represent the darker natures of that society from within. The most important aspect of popular culture, from an academic perspective, is that more often than not, it holds a mirror to society, reflecting that society in a specific period of time, exposing the good, bad, and downright ugly. Villains in American popular culture reflect the darker aspects of the American Dream. Oftentimes, this is accomplished with a villain who represents the polar opposite of the hero they face (Batman/Joker). Occasionally, however, the villain is a direct antireflection of the specific hero, whether a polar opposite version of that character from an alternate dimension (the Mirror Universe in *Star Trek*) or an evil twin/alternate personality (Angel/Angelus in *Buffy the Vampire Slayer*). In all American pop culture, perhaps the best example of holding a dark mirror to American society was the television program *The Twilight Zone* (CBS, 1959–1964; CBS/Syndication, 1985–1989; UPN, 2002–2003; CBS All Access, 2019–present). While Americans since World War II have had a mostly continuous external threat to fear and oppose, it is the darker nature of America and Americans that terrifies society the most. What we can do to ourselves is as frightening as—if not more than—what others might be able to do to us.

POLAR OPPOSITES

The most popular trope in fictional villains is the idea of the polar opposite: a villain who is the perfect dark mirror of the hero, with all of the same abilities and weaknesses of the hero; in essence, an example of what the hero would look like had they chosen a darker path. Perhaps the earliest example of this in modern storytelling came with the albeit-brief initial appearance of Professor James Moriarty in the Sherlock Holmes adventure "The Adventure of the Final Problem"

Yin and Yang

Yin and yang is an ancient Chinese philosophy underscoring the concept of duality. Its iconic symbol is a circle, made from overlapping teardrop shapes, one black and one white, with a black spot in the white half and a white spot in the black half. The core of the philosophy is that while some forces appear to be opposite in nature, they are, in fact, complementary. In essence, there can be no light without dark, no good without evil. As such, the primary basis of the philosophy has been central to storytelling around the world since the dawn of time. Without the Devil, God could be perceived as an omnipotent dictator, with actually no real purpose other than to be worshipped. Without the Joker, Batman is merely a bully, violating the basic due process rights of alleged criminals. Without the Sith, the Jedi were simply an all-powerful order of super-powered beings acting as overlords to the less powerful. Good, therefore, can only be truly defined by the evil that it confronts.

Without the bad, there can be no appreciation of the good; without the good, there is no hope against the bad. In Chinese cosmology, "yin and yang" define the "*qi*" or "*ch'i*," the basic material out of which the entire universe and all living things were created. Despite its Chinese origins, however, it is a term and symbol that has become embraced by the entire world, with a clear appreciation and acceptance of its core principle: that good and evil are simultaneously opposing and complimentary.

Richard A. Hall

(*Strand Magazine*, December 1893). In this sole appearance, the last of Sir Arthur Conan Doyle's original run of Holmes tales, audiences meet "the World's Greatest Detective's" exact opposite number. Moriarty is equal to Holmes in every way save for the former's darker intentions. Holmes refers to Moriarty as "the Napoleon of Crime."

Nearly a half-century later, comic book readers were introduced to the Red Skull, the first, and ultimately chief, antagonist to the iconic superhero Captain America. Over time, it is revealed that the Skull is also a super soldier, with the same physical abilities as Cap. In 2017, Marvel Comics launched the story line "Secret Empire" (Nick Spencer, April–August 2017). In this story, it is revealed that Captain America is, and has always been, an agent of HYDRA, the international terrorist organization run by Red Skull. In the end, readers discover that Skull had altered Captain America's past, enlisting him into HYDRA as a young child. This story line underscores that with one minor tweak to the past, Steve Rogers could have easily become the Red Skull. Once more, the dark mirror exposes the underlying darkness that lies beneath the surface of the hero, and the villain becomes a manifestation of that altered state.

Comic books presented more polar opposite relationships in the 1960s, with the DC Superman title *Adventure Comics* and the Marvel comic book *The X-Men*. In *Adventure Comics #283* (April 1961), Superman fans were introduced to General Zod, another survivor of Superman's home planet of Krypton. Being from the same world, Zod, like Superman, receives super powers from exposure to Earth's yellow sun. This makes him Superman's physical equal in every way. Zod, however, survived Krypton's demise due to his imprisonment in the Phantom Zone for his attempts to rule Krypton. Zod brings those same world-conquering goals with him to Superman's new home of Earth. Unlike the rest of Superman's rogues' gallery of villains, Zod is a "superman."

In 1963, the newly branded Marvel Comics continued its run of interconnected superhero narratives with *The X-Men #1* (Stan Lee and Jack Kirby, September 1963). This series centered on a group of teenage "mutants," humans born with an evolution-altering "x-gene" granting them special abilities. The first group of X-Men is organized to protect "normal" humans from "evil" mutants. Their leader, Professor Charles Xavier, leads them on their first mission against the evil Magneto. Xavier and Magneto are both Class V mutants, the two most powerful mutants known to exist. Magneto leads the Brotherhood of Evil Mutants in their war against the "normal" humans who hate all mutants. It is soon discovered that Professor X and Magneto were once friends, separated by their different ideas regarding responding to the world's hatred of their kind. Professor X seeks peaceful coexistence with humans, while Magneto prefers a more militant approach, achieving peace through fear.

Many over the years have made the analogy that the Professor X/Magneto relationship was a mirror of real-life civil-rights activists Dr. Martin Luther King Jr. and Reverend Malcolm X. This mirror relationship is expressed most directly in the 1995–1996 story line "Age of Apocalypse," where the insane mutant Legion, Professor X's son, alters history by going into the past and accidentally killing his father. Professor Xavier's death inspires the younger Magneto to respect his fallen colleague's wishes and take up a more humane approach to human-mutant relations. The relationship between the two characters was best explored in the films *X-Men: First Class* (2011), *X-Men: Days of Future Past* (2014), and *X-Men: Apocalypse* (2016).

In 1971, the British sci-fi classic *Doctor Who* launched its eighth season of its original run with a new actor portraying the time-and-space-traveling Time Lord known as the Doctor (the Third Doctor, Jon Pertwee). The first story from that season was "Terror of the Autons," and it introduced perhaps the Doctor's most dangerous foe: the Master. Originally portrayed by Roger Delgado, the Master is one of the Doctor's own species, a Time Lord. As such, he is a perfect match for the Doctor and a clear representation of what the Doctor would be like had he given in to his own darker nature. Whereas the Doctor loves humanity and dedicates his entire existence to keeping the people of Earth safe, the Master sees humanity as nothing more than chattel to be lorded over. For the next forty years, the Master was played by a total of seven actors (Time Lords having the ability to regenerate into a new body on the previous body's death"). In one of the great plot twists of the fifty-plus-year series, from 2014 to 2017, the Master was played by Michelle Gomez, now calling herself "Missy." In the Missy persona, the Doctor was able to get through to—although "coerce" may be a better term—the Master into thinking outside of him/herself, leading her to turn on one of her own previous male incarnations (Steven Moffat, "The Doctor Falls," *Doctor Who*, modern season 10, episode 12, July 1, 2017). Like Holmes long before him, the Doctor sees the Master/Missy as his exact opposite, and through him/her, the Doctor realizes the danger that he, himself, could pose to the universe had he chosen a darker path.

Coming into the 1980s, American television audiences were introduced to the most iconic villain in television history: the Texas oilman J. R. Ewing. *Dallas* (CBS, 1978–1991; TNT, 2012–2014) was a nighttime soap opera centered on the lives, loves, and losses of the powerful Ewing family of Dallas, Texas. J.R. (played by Larry Hagman) immediately emerged as "the Man You Love to Hate," the oldest brother of the Ewing dynasty and heir apparent to his father, Jock's, company, Ewing Oil. J.R. was diabolical and ruthless, using money and power to achieve his nefarious schemes and seduce countless women. The hero of *Dallas* was J.R.'s youngest brother, Bobby (played by Patrick Duffy). Kind, loving, and honest, Bobby was the favorite son of Jock and "Miss Ellie" Ewing. In the series opener, Bobby has just married Pamela Barnes, the daughter of "Digger" Barnes (Jock's sworn enemy) and brother to Cliff Barnes (J.R.'s sworn enemy). Although the series is set on this *Romeo and Juliet* romance, the breakout center of the show soon becomes the villainous J.R. The brothers are equal matches in intelligence, influence, and cunning. When the two begin to lock horns in the series' sixth season, battling each other for control of Ewing Oil as ordained by their father's final wishes, they each begin to see how similar they are to each other, direct opposites in every way. In the series' penultimate season in 2013, J. R. Ewing dies as the Ewing family faces powerful threats from all sides. In order to save the family, Bobby must carry out his brother's final "masterpiece" plan and adopt his villainous brother's methods to ensure the Ewing family's survival. Despite his decades-long opposition to J.R.'s schemes, Bobby discovers how easily he adopts those same methods when pushed.

In the twenty-first century, audiences saw more dark mirrors in the postapocalyptic world of Robert Kirkman's *The Walking Dead* comic book (Image Comics, 2003–2019) and television series (AMC, 2010–present). The hero of *The Walking Dead* is Sheriff Rick Grimes, who suffers a severe gunshot wound that leaves him in a coma for months. When he awakes, the world has changed. Civilization has been wiped out by a plague of flesh-eating zombies. Grimes seeks out his wife and young son, eventually becoming the leader of an ever-growing group of survivors intent on finding a secure place to rebuild a peaceful, kind, and caring society. During their journeys, Grimes and company run across several other groups of survivors, including the Governor, the violent and insane leader of a walled community of survivors called Woodbury. Negan is the self-appointed ruler of a large and well-armed gang of thugs calling themselves "the Saviors," forcing the more peaceful surrounding communities to provide for them out of fear of violent retaliation. Alpha is the leader of a band of nomadic survivors called "the Whisperers," who wear the skins of the undead and wander from place to place mingled in with herds of zombies. All three are dark reflections of Grimes himself. They all represent the insanity brought on by the grief of having lost loved ones and the dangers of absolute power corrupting absolutely, especially in the face of the fall of society. Each represents what could have become of Grimes had he lost his family and not found his group of friends.

Overall, the dark mirror of the polar opposite is as much a message to the hero as to the audience. Every living soul possesses some degree of inner darkness.

Some spend their lives in a constant struggle to keep that darkness at bay (to varying degrees of success). The villains listed above are but a small sample of bad guys who represent the exact opposite number to their corresponding protagonists. They are what the hero could have been, given a succession of really bad days (or just one really, really bad one). Through them, the hero sees what might have been, and the audience sees how close they, themselves, are to falling into the dark mirror.

EVIL TWINS

Occasionally, villains are actually the physical twin, clone, alternate personality, or alternate-universe copy of the hero. The best portrayals of this idea in modern pop culture have come from the film franchise *Star Wars* (Lucasfilm/20th Century Fox, 1977–2005; Lucasfilm/Disney, 2015–present) and the television series *Buffy the Vampire Slayer* (WB, 1997–2001; UPN, 2001–2003). Perhaps the most widely known examples of this phenomenon are the dualistic characters of Jedi hero Anakin Skywalker/Dark Lord of the Sith Darth Vader and the character's grandson, Ben Solo/Kylo Ren.

Writer and director George Lucas introduced Americans to Darth Vader in 1977's *Star Wars* (later referred to as *Episode IV: A New Hope*). The Dark Lord of the Sith soon became one of the most iconic villains in all popular culture. In the film's sequel, *Episode V: The Empire Strikes Back* (1980), it was suggested to viewers that Vader was, in fact, the father of the saga's protagonist, Luke Skywalker. That was confirmed in the final film of the original trilogy, *Episode VI: Return of the Jedi* (1983), and the saga appeared to end with Luke redeeming his father, causing him to turn from Darth Vader to his original identity, the Jedi knight Anakin Skywalker. Sixteen years after *Jedi*, Lucas returned to the "galaxy far, far away" with what became known as the prequel trilogy, telling the story of how a young slave boy named Anakin Skywalker grew up to become a heroic Jedi knight, only to fall to the dark side and become Darth Vader (*Episode I: The Phantom Menace*, 1999; *Episode II: Attack of the Clones*, 2002; *Revenge of the Sith*, 2005). Through the prequels, audiences were able to experience the pain and suffering experienced by the original Skywalker as his obsessive love for his wife drove him to the dark side.

The *Star Wars* saga repeated history with the introduction of Ben Solo/Kylo Ren (*Episode VII: The Force Awakens*, 2015). Anakin's grandson from his daughter, Princess Leia Organa, and her husband, Han Solo, Ben Solo possesses the natural powerful Force abilities of his grandfather, mother, and uncle. When his uncle, Luke Skywalker, senses darkness in his nephew and apprentice due to the machinations of the evil Snoke, Luke briefly considers murdering his nephew, causing the boy to fully commit to the dark side (*Episode VIII: The Last Jedi*, 2017). Although his fall to darkness was different than his grandfather's, the now Kylo Ren possesses the same inner turmoil, frequently feeling the "pull to the light" (*The Force Awakens*). Both dark-side wielders represent the same inner conflict: the constant fight between the light and dark sides of their natures. Both are villains fighting to keep their inner heroes at bay (to equally unsuccessful degrees).

A very similar phenomenon arises in the vampire character Angel in the series *Buffy the Vampire Slayer*. In the very first episode of *Buffy*, Buffy (portrayed by Sarah Michelle Gellar) and the audience are introduced to Angel (played by David Boreanaz), a "vampire with a soul." According to Buffy lore, when a person becomes a vampire, the original human soul dies and leaves the body, and the corpse is reanimated with a demonic soul. Angel's human soul was returned to his body through a curse after his demonic vampire form murdered a young gypsy girl. From then on, Angel survives as an immortal vampire, still dependent on blood to survive but keeping his human conscience, driving him to do good to make up for his past sins. Over time, Angel and Buffy fall in love, and they eventually consummate their relationship. A previously unknown aspect of the curse, however, stated that should Angel ever experience true happiness, his soul would be released, once more giving his demonic spirit control over the body.

After making love to Buffy, Angel feels happiness, and the curse is reversed, bringing forth his demonic personality, Angelus (Joss Whedon, "Innocence," season 2, episode 14, January 20, 1998). Angelus proves to be Buffy's most dangerous foe, fully aware of every aspect of the slayer through Angel's memories. The evil vampire goes on to kill two of the slayer's friends and unleashes a plan to open hell on Earth; his death becomes the only means of stopping the apocalypse. The split second before Buffy is set to kill Angelus, however, the burgeoning witch, Willow (played by Allison Hannigan), successfully casts a spell that returns Angel's soul, causing the slayer to murder her true love to save the world (Whedon, "Becoming, Part 2," season 2, episode 22, May 19, 1998). Angelus would make a few brief returns over the course of the series and its spin-off, *Angel*, but audiences—and Buffy—become keenly aware of the demon that lives within the kindhearted Angel and that the two lovers can never have a happily ever after.

The second *Buffy* example is the character of Dark Willow. By the end of season two, Buffy's sweet, timid friend and classmate, Willow Rosenberg, emerges as an increasingly powerful witch. One of the first examples of a bisexual major character on television, in season four, Willow meets Tara, an equally kind but even more timid witch. Throughout season six, their relationship experiences turbulence as Willow grows increasingly addicted to using her magical powers, even to make her girlfriend forget they were arguing. Shortly after their romantic reunion, Tara is accidentally killed by a stray bullet meant for the slayer.

The pain and agony of losing Tara unleashes Willow's inner darkness, and Dark Willow is borne (Steven S. DeKnight, "Seeing Red," season 6, episode 19, May 7, 2002). Over the final three episodes of the season, Buffy and company strive unsuccessfully to stop Dark Willow's quest for vengeance for Tara's murderer. Willow flays the killer alive before going on to attempt to end the world entirely, too distraught over her loss to care who lives or dies. Ultimately, it is fellow Scooby Gang member Xander (played by Nicholas Brendon), the only member of Buffy's entourage with no supernatural powers, who is able to connect to Willow's inner kindness, allowing her true self to overpower her darker tendencies (David Fury, "Grave," season 6, episode 22, May 21, 2002). Willow is then taken to England under the care of Buffy's watcher, Giles, to learn to deal with her grief, her guilt for the murder she committed, and her powerful abilities. Fear of the reemergence of Dark Willow remains a shroud over the soul over the once-kind witch.

Other evil twins in pop culture history, though not covered in this volume, include *Superman* villain/clone Bizarro and the android "brothers" of Data and Lore in *Star Trek: The Next Generation* (Syndication, 1987–1994). Evil twins take the polar opposite to a much more personal level. In this trope, the evil is not just a representation of what the hero would look like as a villain; more terrifyingly, the hero actually becomes the villain, or very closely related to the villain. Both the polar opposite and the evil twin represent very personal, direct correlations between the hero and the villain. The television series *The Twilight Zone* took a much broader approach, focusing not only on the villain within an individual but also on the villain within society as a whole.

THE TWILIGHT ZONE

In the waning months of the 1950s, writer Rod Serling introduced the world to what would ultimately become widely considered his masterpiece: *The Twilight Zone* (CBS, 1959–1964). Today, the original series is considered not only one of the most popular and artistic series in television history but also one of the most socially important in all of pop culture history. The series was an anthology series, in which each episode was its own separate story with its own distinct cast of characters. As the best of pop culture always does, *The Twilight Zone* held a mirror up to the society of the time, exposing its hopes and aspirations as well as its fears and inner demons. Most episodes examined issues facing America at the time: racism, anxiety over the Cold War, and fear of technological/scientific advancement. Some of the best episodes of the original run focused a magnifying glass onto the inner darkness of American society and the idea that the true enemy of America was America itself.

Perhaps the most memorable and iconic episode of the original series was "The Monsters Are Due on Maple Street" (Rod Serling, *The Twilight Zone*, season 1, episode 22, March 4, 1960). In this story, a seemingly normal suburban street enjoys a weekend afternoon. Some people wash their cars, while others trim their lawns; everyone enjoying a sunny afternoon. A power outage on the block devolves quickly when a young boy mentions that he read a similar story in a comic book, where aliens cut off power to a community just before invading. Although he initially inspires laughter from the block's adults, neighbor soon turns on neighbor when previous suspicious behaviors come to light, causing the growing mob to suspect each other of secretly being an alien agent. As day turns to night, mob violence ensues, with neighbors murdering each other out of fear of the unknown. The episode ends with the camera panning out to expose two actual aliens on an overlooking hill, suggesting that invasion will not be necessary; simply cutting off their electricity for a few hours will lead humans to kill each other. This episode was a frightening reminder of two recent historical events: the

McCarthy Red Scare of 1950–1953, leading Americans to turn on each other to report suspected communists, and the 1956 declaration by Soviet premier Nikita Khrushchev that there was no need for the Soviet Union to invade the United States, as it would be easy to simply wait until Americans turned on each other.

At the heart of the ideological conflict that was the Cold War lay the issue of which economic system was better for a society: capitalism or communism. The primary argument against capitalism was the underlying aspect of greed that drives it. In the episode "The Masks" (Rod Serling, *The Twilight Zone*, season 5, episode 25, March 20, 1964), a dying wealthy man is visited by his greedy daughter, son-in-law, grandson, and granddaughter. Under the guise of Mardi Gras, the man requires that his family each wear horrific masks until midnight or give up any hope of receiving an inheritance. Eager for the old man to die so that they can receive their money, all comply. At midnight, however, as they remove their masks, they discover that the masks are enchanted, altering their faces to match the horrific masks they wore, forever displaying the ugliness of their greed for all to see.

Many episodes of *The Twilight Zone* expose the inner darkness that lies just under the surface of modern America, pointing to how the "land of the free and the home of the brave" has devolved since achieving superpower status into a society consumed with consumption and how Americans have allowed the American Dream to devolve into a society of fear, greed, and selfishness. In Rod Serling's imaginary universe, we are all potential villains. Hidden under our better angels are the demons of avarice and indulgence. Serling, however, does not use *The Twilight Zone* as a means of condemnation but, rather, as cautionary tales to lead the world's guardians of democracy from the darkness and back into the light.

From a psychological standpoint, one of humankind's greatest fears must be the fear of the fall to darkness, of giving in to humanity's baser instincts, and of becoming, in the end, the villain. Through polar opposites, evil twins, and sociopolitical commentary, the fictional narratives of popular culture both warn of the consequences of darkness and influence audiences away from it. Every living soul possesses the potential of falling into the darkness, but all equally possess the ability to rise above it or achieve redemption should they fall. This is the primary role of the villain in popular culture. They hold a mirror to the parts of humanity and society that humanity and society most dread, and they give the hero purpose in leading humanity and society away from that potentially disastrous fate.

FURTHER READING

Alsford, Mike. 2006. *Heroes & Villains*. Waco, TX: Baylor University Press.

Ashby, LeRoy. 2006. *With Amusement for All: A History of American Popular Culture since 1830*. Lexington: University Press of Kentucky.

Brode, Douglas, and Carol Serling. 2009. *Rod Serling and "The Twilight Zone": The 50th Anniversary Tribute*. Fort Lee, NJ: Barricade.

Castleman, Harry, and Walter J. Podrazik. 2016. *Watching TV: Eight Decades of American Television*. 3rd ed. Syracuse, NY: Syracuse University Press.

Costello, Matthew J. 2009. *Secret Identity Crisis: Comic Books & the Unmasking of Cold War America.* New York: Continuum.

Dial-Driver, Emily, Sally Emmons-Featherston, Jim Ford, and Carolyn Anne Taylor. 2008. *The Truth of Buffy: Essays on Fiction Illuminating Reality.* Jefferson, NC: McFarland.

Dolansky, Shawna. 2018. "How the Serpent Became Satan: Adam, Eve, and the Serpent in the Garden of Eden." Biblical Archaeology Society. October 14, 2018. Accessed April 7, 2019. https://www.biblicalarchaeology.org/daily/biblical-topics/bible-interpretation/how-the-serpent-became-satan/.

Dyer, Ben, ed. 2009. *Supervillains and Philosophy: Sometimes, Evil Is Its Own Reward.* Popular Culture and Philosophy Series. Chicago: Open Court.

Eberl, Jason T., and Kevin S. Decker, eds. *The Ultimate Star Wars and Philosophy: You Must Unlearn What You Have Learned.* Hoboken, NJ: Wiley-Blackwell.

Faludi, Susan. 2007. *The Terror Dream: Myth and Misogyny in an Insecure America.* New York: Picador.

Field, Mark. 2017. *Buffy, the Vampire Slayer: Myth, Metaphor & Morality.* N.p.: Amazon Services.

Gavaler, Chris. 2015. *On the Origin of Superheroes: From the Big Bang to Action Comics No. 1.* Iowa City: University of Iowa.

Keetley, Dawn. 2014. *"We're All Infected": Essays on AMC's The Walking Dead and the Fate of the Human.* Contributions to Zombie Studies. Jefferson, NC: McFarland.

Langley, Travis, ed. 2015. *"The Walking Dead" Psychology: Psych of the Living Dead.* Popular Culture Psychology. New York: Sterling.

Leadbeater, Alex. 2019. "*Star Wars* Is Trying to Turn Darth Vader into an Anti-Hero (and That's Very Bad)." Screen Rant. February 4, 2019. Accessed February 4, 2019. https://screenrant.com/star-wars-darth-vader-villain-anti-hero/.

Russell, Jeffrey B., and Brooks Alexander. 2007. *A History of Witchcraft: Sorcerers, Heretics, & Pagans.* London: Thames & Hudson.

South, James B., ed. 2005. *Buffy, the Vampire Slayer and Philosophy: Fear and Trembling in Sunnydale.* Chicago: Open Court.

Stark, Steven D. 1997. *Glued to the Set: The 60 Television Shows and Events That Made Us Who We Are Today.* New York: Delta Trade Paperbacks.

Tye, Larry. 2013. *Superman: The High-Flying History of America's Most Enduring Hero.* New York: Random House.

Van Wormer, Laura. 1985. *Dallas: The Complete Ewing Family Saga, including Southfork Ranch, Ewing Oil, and the Barnes-Ewing Feud—1860–1985.* New York: Doubleday/Dolphin.

Wilcox, Rhonda V., and David Lavery. 2002. *Fighting the Forces: What's at Stake in Buffy, the Vampire Slayer.* Lanham, MD: Rowman & Littlefield.

Wright, Bradford W. 2003. *Comic Book Nation: The Transformation of Youth Culture in America.* Baltimore, MD: Johns Hopkins University Press.

Yuen, Wayne, ed. 2012. *The Walking Dead and Philosophy: Zombie Apocalypse Now.* Popular Culture and Philosophy. Chicago: Open Court.

Yuen, Wayne, ed. 2016. *The Ultimate Walking Dead and Philosophy: Hungry for More.* Popular Culture and Philosophy. Chicago: Open Court.

Tarantino and the Antivillain

Since the 1970s, the antihero has been very popular throughout American culture. Most prominent in the Clint Eastwood *Dirty Harry* movies of the 1970s and 1980s, an antihero is, in essence, a traditionally heroic character who, from time to time, engages in "bad" behavior, such as killing criminals rather than bringing them to justice through the system. Since that time, many popular characters, both from fiction and history, have been dubbed antiheroes, when, in fact, they should more accurately be defined as antivillains. In 2006, Monseignore Lazlo defined antivillain: "The converse of an anti-hero (i.e. a protagonist who isn't purely good or heroic), an anti-villain is an antagonist who isn't purely evil nor entirely unsympathetic—a character who doesn't seem to deserve being cast as the villain, perhaps cast arbitrarily as the villain because they are not the focus of the story but merely present a foil to the central figure, who may be an antihero protagonist. Cf. scapegoat" (Lazlo, "Anti-Villain," *Urban Dictionary*).

Many characters, in both fiction and reality, who have been traditionally defined as either villains or antiheroes may more accurately be defined as antivillains. The person who has mastered the art of the antivillain is legendary Hollywood writer and director Quentin Tarantino. From his masterpiece, *Pulp Fiction* (1994), to his screenplay and collaboration with director Robert Rodriguez, *From Dusk Till Dawn* (1996), to his revenge epic, *Kill Bill, Vols. 1 and 2* (2003–2004), Tarantino has mastered the art of presenting characters whom society, on the surface, would deem villains who, either through immediacy or a desire for redemption, discover the hero that lies within.

ANTIVILLAINS IN THE REAL WORLD

Western culture is replete with complex characters whom history has deemed villains but, on closer inspection, may have some underlying aspects that could be seen as heroic. Much of the Judeo-Christian and Islamic worlds accept the story of the Garden of Eden as legitimate, factual history. In what is viewed as the original

Quentin Tarantino

Born in 1963, Quentin Tarantino is a multi-award-winning Hollywood director and occasional actor. His films have become noteworthy for their complex characters, excessive violence, soundtracks consisting of classic pop and soul tunes, and artistic dialogue laced with pop culture references and profanity. His debut film was the independent movie *My Best Friend's Birthday* (1987), in which he also starred. The script from that film was later transformed into the Warner Brothers film *True Romance* (1993). After selling his script for *Natural Born Killers* (1994) to director Oliver Stone, Tarantino used the money to make his first major feature film, *Reservoir Dogs* (1992). The critical acclaim for *Reservoir Dogs*, gained him the approval and funding for his masterpiece, *Pulp Fiction* (1994), which earned him seven Academy Award nominations. His following films include *Jackie Brown* (1997), *Kill Bill, Vols. 1 and 2* (2003, 2004), *Death Proof* (2007), *Inglorious Basterds* (2009), *Django Unchained* (2012), *The Hateful Eight* (2015), and *Once Upon a Time in Hollywood* (2019).

To date, his films have been nominated for twenty-five Academy Awards, winning five. He is also a frequent collaborator of writer and director Robert Rodriguez, with whom he worked on the film *From Dusk Till Dawn* (1996), in which he also starred. Heavily influenced by the exploitation and blaxploitation films of the early 1970s, Tarantino has taken the antihero concept popularized in that period and essentially turned it on its head, with the antivillain. Whereas antiheroes are heroes who sometimes do villainous acts in their pursuit of justice, antivillains are villains who sometimes do noble or even heroic acts despite themselves. He is often attributed as a major factor in the wildly successful late-in-life acting career of Samuel L. Jackson, who frequently appears in Tarantino films.

Richard A. Hall

act of villainy, the villain of the piece, the serpent (be he Satan or just some crafty creature) tempts humanity out of paradise. However, in the serpent's desire to see humanity suffer, he also introduces humankind to the concept of free will. Similarly, another figure, Judas Iscariot, has traditionally been cast as one of history's ultimate villains, as he betrayed the beloved Christ to his enemies, leading to his death. However, as is examined in Nikos Kazantzakis's 1952 novel, *The Last Temptation of Christ*, Judas may have been personally selected by Christ to perform this "betrayal" in order for the Christ to complete his mission of human redemption.

In American history, one of the most infamous outlaws of the Wild West, Billy the Kid, was, by any definition, a villain. He was a relentless and unapologetic murderer and cattle rustler. He was arrested numerous times, tried and sentenced to death for murder (although he escaped), and finally allegedly killed as a fugitive by Sheriff Pat Garrett in 1881. Despite his clear distinction as a villain, however, most of Billy's murders were revenge killings for the murder of his employer and mentor, John Tunstall, and much of what he stole was given to the local Mexican and Mexican American populations of New Mexico, who conspired to hide the Kid from authorities, viewing him as a Robin Hood stealing from the rich to give to the poor. Given the Wild West's policy of lenience toward justifiable homicide, Billy's willingness to take a life must be weighed against the societal norms of the day, which viewed such killing as a gray area.

A villain contemporary of the Kid was the Apache war chief Geronimo. The mere mention of Geronimo's name was enough to inspire fear in the growing populations of the western frontier. For decades, Geronimo murdered American and Mexican soldiers and civilians without remorse. Like the Kid, Geronimo also stole cattle and other livestock, as well as burned homes, ordered the torture of civilian captives, and allowed the raping of women by his men. During his life, he was the epitome of the American villain. History, however, has forgiven Geronimo's crimes in light of the widespread mistreatment and attempted genocide of his people being conducted by the U.S. government at the time. Geronimo utilized "evil" practices to both exact revenge and seek justice for his people and to attempt to inspire the expanding American society to leave his people alone. He committed villainous acts, but he did so as a form of justice and self-preservation.

Since the 1920s, organized crime, particularly the Italian/Sicilian mob, or Mafia, has been considered villains in the eyes of American society. Over the course of the last century, members of the mob have committed numerous murders; engaged in the manufacture, transportation, and sale of illegal alcohol in the 1920s; overseen the illegal drug trade and prostitution rings; and blackmailed police, government officials, and judges. Despite this widespread criminal activity, some mobsters—such as "Scarface" Al Capone, John Dillinger, and "Pretty Boy" Floyd—have become historical celebrities, exemplifying the epitome of free will as well as profiting from bucking the system and sticking it to the man. Ultimately, their real-world celebrity has altered how Americans view organized crime and the criminals that system creates.

ANTIVILLAINS IN MODERN FICTION

In 1969, author Mario Puzo published *The Godfather* and introduced American society to the fictional Corleone family of New York City. The head of the family, Vito Corleone, is a Sicilian immigrant in the early 1900s, who becomes involved in street-level crime in the 1920s in order to provide for his growing family, earning the title "Godfather" from those in his neighborhood that he protects and cares for. As Don Corleone, he is head of one of the "Five [Crime] Families" of the Sicilian mob in New York, overseeing gambling and prostitution, and protected by the cache of judges, police, and city officials that he has in his pocket. When Don Vito refuses to share his political connections to protect the burgeoning illegal drug trade, the other families have him shot, leading to his retirement and replacement by his youngest son, Michael.

Michael's stories are expanded upon in the sequels to the film of the original novel. Michael Corleone proves a more ruthless and formidable opponent than his aging father, quickly dispatching his enemies by having the heads of the other families assassinated, consolidating all power in New York for himself. As Michael expands the family's influence to Nevada, he is confronted with betrayals within his circle while, simultaneously, facing government investigation into his criminal activities. Once more, Michael protects his interests with unquestioned brutality. When the second-generation Godfather chooses to retire in the late

1970s, his sins come home to haunt him, culminating in the violent death of his daughter and his dying alone.

Puzo's best-selling original novel became even more a part of American popular culture through some of the most iconic gangster films of all time: *The Godfather* (1972), *The Godfather, Part II* (1974), and *The Godfather, Part III* (1990). The Corleones were villains, by any definition of the term; however, they become sympathetic characters due to their dedication to family and the Dons' willingness to proverbially sell their own souls to keep their family safe.

In the wake of the success of *The Godfather* novel and first film, Marvel Comics introduced the character of Frank Castle, "the Punisher" (Gerry Conway, John Romita Sr., and Ross Andru, *The Amazing Spider-Man #129*, February 1974). Viewed today as an antihero, the Punisher was introduced as a villain antagonist for Spider-Man. Castle was a Vietnam veteran who witnessed the murder of his wife and children as innocent bystanders in a gang shootout. Stricken by grief, Castle utilizes his military training to exact vengeance for his family's deaths by "punishing"—murdering—criminals. When he is manipulated into believing that Spider-Man is a villain, the Punisher makes the web-slinger his next target. Unlike previous vigilantes like Spider-Man or Batman, Punisher does not waste time turning wrongdoers in to the proper authorities for the system to dispense justice. He takes the role of judge, jury, and executioner on himself. In the twenty-first century, in films and on Netflix, the Punisher is presented as the greatest of antiheroes, but within the realm of the Marvel Comics Universe, heroes such as Captain America view Castle as a dangerous and unstable criminal. As such, he is much more accurately defined as an antivillain.

From the mid-1970s throughout the 1980s, antiheroes became even more popular in comic books, particularly with one of the most popular comic book heroes of all time, Wolverine. However, the antivillain became just as popular. In 1983, DC Comics introduced the character Lobo. Created by Roger Slifer and Keith Giffen, and introduced in *Omega Men #3* (June 1983), Lobo is an intergalactic bounty hunter who beats and even kills his captives. Originally intended as strictly a villain, the character failed to click with readers and disappeared until he was revamped in the 1990s. Lobo remained primarily a villain. At one point, Lobo attempts to murder Santa Claus, and it is later discovered that Lobo killed everyone on his home world of Czarnia (a peaceful world where he just did not fit in). Once contracted to kill someone, nothing will stop him from fulfilling that contract (Cheeda, "Lobo: 10 Things to Know about SyFy's Main Man"). He is a cold-blooded, bloodthirsty killer who, from time to time, is contracted to kill a bad guy, making him the hero of that particular story. As the character is difficult to fit into the more kid-friendly DC Comics Universe, Lobo has remained largely a background character, disappearing for long stretches of time.

Marvel Comics had much more success with the very similarly themed Deadpool. The "Merc with the Mouth," Deadpool, was created by Rob Liefeld and Fabian Nicieza, and was first introduced in *The New Mutants #98* (February 1991). Originally, Deadpool was a near copy of Lobo, a bounty hunter known for his brutal tactics. Over time in an attempt to turn the villain into an antihero, the *Deadpool* comics began to trend more toward comedy (dark, violent comedy, but comedy nonetheless). In the 2017 film *Deadpool* (20th Century Fox), the titular character (played by Ryan Reynolds) frequently states, "I'm no hero." This is true. In both comics and films, Deadpool is a mercenary and bounty hunter who frequently tortures and/or kills his targets. He is a brutal killer who profits by ridding the world of "worse" villains. By any Western definition of hero or villain, Deadpool is clearly primarily the latter.

On television, the ultimate example of an antivillain, again often mistakenly labeled an antihero, is Tony Soprano. Actor James Gandolfini brought the character of Tony Soprano to life in the hit television series *The Sopranos* (HBO, 1999–2007). Tony is a sort of Godfather for the common man; although similar to the Corleones in many regards, the Sopranos are presented as more upper-middle class than the legendary Corleones. Tony is a mob boss. He kills. He is involved in the drug trade and other nefarious activities. He possesses no qualms about killing relatively innocent people. His love for his family and his obvious regrets for his decisions (made clear to the audience through his psychiatric sessions) make him sympathetic to the audience, and, as the protagonist of the series, he is considered an antihero. Like the previous examples, however, Tony Soprano is clearly a villain, murdering with abandon, consumed by personal gain, and an unapologetic enemy to all that society deems right or good.

The confusion between antihero and antivillain may speak to the sliding values of American society over the last half century, as many Americans are more concerned with greed and getting ahead than with playing by the rules and being a good neighbor. True antiheros are characters with clearly heroic intent who bend the established mores of society because they deem the system damaged and unjust. An antivillain, by contrast, is a character who clearly, willingly, and unapologetically violates the laws and norms of society, usually for personal gain. What differentiates them from an all-out villain is that they possess some core belief or trait that connects them to some degree to the side of right or good. Their villainy has bounds, and they are identifiable for their ability to not cross their own lines of right and wrong. The undisputed master of such characters is the iconic Hollywood writer and director Quentin Tarantino.

ANTIVILLAINS IN TARANTINO FILMS

Quentin Tarantino established himself as a major talent with his screenplay for the 1993 cult hit *True Romance* and his debut writing and directing effort, *Reservoir Dogs* (1992). *Romance*, though written by Tarantino, was directed by Tony Scott. This modern-day *Romeo and Juliet* story centers on awkward comic book store worker Clarence Worley (played by Christian Slater) who meets and very quickly marries the charming call girl Alabama (played by Patricia Arquette). When Clarence hears that his new bride's pimp is violent and dangerous, he takes it upon himself to kill the pimp (egged on to do so by the ghost of Elvis Presley, played by Val Kilmer). After killing the brutal pimp and drug dealer Drexl (played by Gary Oldman), Clarence gathers a suitcase of what he believes to be his wife's clothes, only to discover the next morning that it is a large suitcase of a massive amount of cocaine. Rather than turn the drugs in to authorities, Clarence and Alabama go on the run, leaving Detroit for Los Angeles, where Clarence hopes that his actor friend can help him sell the cocaine to a Hollywood big shot. Pursued by both the Los Angeles Police Department and the crime lord to whom the cocaine belongs, Clarence and Alabama find themselves in a massive gunfight as they sneak away with their money to retire in Mexico. The audience cannot help but cheer on Clarence and Alabama, whose love is at the core of their ultimate goals, but Clarence is a villain. He is a murderer and de facto drug dealer. Although kind and loving, he is a villain.

In 1994, Tarantino released what many consider his masterpiece and one of the most iconic films of the decade: *Pulp Fiction*. Unlike *Reservoir Dogs*, where numerous villains turn on each other, *Pulp Fiction* tells a handful of interweaving stories centered on characters who epitomize the antivillain. Vincent Vega and Jules Winnfield (played by John Travolta and Samuel L. Jackson, respectively) are henchmen for crime boss Marcellus Wallace (played by Ving Rhames). Both men are cold-blooded killers who, throughout the film, gain the sympathy and even admiration of the audience. Vincent is assigned to take his boss's wife out to dinner and show her a good time; meanwhile, rumors abound that Mrs. Wallace (played by Uma Thurman) may be less than loyal to her dangerous husband. Although considerable flirting takes place, Vincent remains ever the gentleman.

In a related story line, aging boxer Butch Coolidge (played by Bruce Willis) makes an arrangement with Marcellus to throw his next fight, allowing Marcellus to bet on the other boxer to make a fortune. Butch, however, double-crosses Marcellus to make more money when he wins the fight. When the two men meet inadvertently on the street, a fight ensues, which is interrupted by a local shop owner, who detains both men and calls his security guard friend so that the two can rape the bloodied combatants. When Butch manages to get loose as Marcellus is being raped, rather than escape and leave Marcellus to his fate, Butch rescues the crime boss, killing their captor in the process. This act of heroism gains Butch a pardon from Marcellus's wrath, and the boxer leaves him to exact revenge on the surviving rapist. In a flashback to the beginning of the film, Jules receives an epiphany when he and Vincent miraculously escape certain death. Jules chooses to change his ways for a more peaceful existence, using the opportunity of an unexpected restaurant robbery to talk the robbers into leaving peacefully without hurting anyone. Throughout the film, most of the main characters are outright villains by any stretch of the word. However, each exhibits noble qualities that show an underlying hero beneath the villainous surface (Tarantino, *Pulp Fiction*, Miramax).

Hot off the successes of Tarantino's *Pulp Fiction* and director Robert Rodriguez's *Desperado* (1995), the two up-and-comers collaborated on the cult classic *From Dusk Till Dawn* (1996). In this screenplay by Tarantino, George Clooney and Tarantino play the Gecko Brothers, notorious bank robbers on the run in Texas. They kidnap widowed minister Jacob Fuller (Harvey Keitel) and his children, Katherine (Juliette Lewis) and Scott (Ernest Liu), to use as hostages to get safely into Mexico. Once across the border, the brothers take their captives to a bar touted as being open "from dusk till dawn" to meet their contact to receive entry into a safe area. Soon after arriving at the bar, the group discovers that the bar is a front operated by vampires who use it to feed off of truckers, bikers, and criminals and to profit from their spoils. Richie Gecko (Tarantino) is quickly killed and turned into a vampire, leaving Seth (Clooney) to turn hero to save not only himself but also his hostages. At the end of the struggle, Seth remains a wanted and unapologetic criminal, but he has spent the evening as the clear hero of the piece (Tarantino, *From Dusk Till Dawn*, Miramax).

Quentin Tarantino's directorial follow-up to *Pulp Fiction* was the 1997 film *Jackie Brown* (Miramax). Unlike all of his other films, *Jackie Brown* was based on someone else's work: the 1992 novel *Rum Punch* by Elmore Leonard. In this film, the title character is played by 1970s blaxploitation queen Pam Grier. Jackie is a flight attendant who runs cash for a dangerous drug dealer and gun runner, Ordell Robbie (played by Samuel L. Jackson). When she is caught, Ordell sets out to kill her before she can turn on him to the police. She makes a deal to do one more big cash run for her boss, giving him enough money to retire and disappear. Instead, Jackie runs a con, setting up Ordell to be taken out by the authorities and taking the bulk of the cash for her own retirement (Tarantino, *Jackie Brown*, Miramax). Although the heroine of the piece, Jackie is, by all rights, a villain. She is a mule for a notorious criminal who only chooses to change her ways once she is caught.

In 2003, Tarantino released the first film of his two-part revenge epic, *Kill Bill*. Like *Pulp*, the film is populated by clear villains. As the story opens, the Bride (played by Uma Thurman) a pregnant woman identified later as Beatrix Kiddo, is shot during her wedding. Although everyone in the chapel is killed, the Bride survives but is in a coma. When she awakens four years later, she embarks on a revenge quest against her would-be killers. The audience soon learns that the Bride was a member of the Deadly Viper Assassination Squad code-named "Black Mamba." The Bride is aware her former team committed the attack—presumably killing her unborn child in the process—and sets out to murder each one on a path of destruction that will culminate in her facing her former boss, Bill. Her first target is her former teammate Vernita Green, code-named "Copperhead" (played by Vivica A. Fox). Although Green has given up her former life and is settled in a nice home raising a child, the Bride dispatches her with abandon, killing her in front of her own daughter.

One by one, the Bride eliminates each member of the team, finally coming face-to-face with the man who ordered her death, Bill (played by David Carradine). Before attacking Bill, however, the Bride discovers that her daughter is alive and living happily with her father, Bill. Through flashbacks, it is discovered that while on an assassination mission, Beatrix discovered she was pregnant with Bill's child; immediately choosing to abandon her mission, her job, and Bill, she made a new life for herself and fell in love with a local record store owner. Initially believing Beatrix to be dead, Bill overreacts when he learns the truth and takes his team to kill Beatrix and her beau at their wedding (Tarantino, *Kill Bill, Vols. 1 and 2*, Miramax). All of the characters are villains, but through the course of the narrative, Beatrix, Vernita, Bill, and Bill's brother, Budd (played by Michael Madsen), are all presented in a sympathetic light to one degree or another.

Tarantino's later films—most notably *Inglourious Basterds* (2009), *Django Unchained* (2012), and *Once Upon a Time in Hollywood* (2019)—tended to focus more on the antihero, but his contributions to the antivillain have defined the genre, firmly distinguishing it from the more popular and often-misused antihero. The appeal of both antiheroes and antivillains is their ability to speak to the darker side of human nature without giving entirely into outright evil. However, whereas the antihero is a good guy who does bad things, the antivillain is the exact opposite. Antivillains are villains as modern Western society defines the term, but narratives of antivillains allow for deeper analysis of the human psyche and argue that even bad guys can have a good heart and even perform heroic deeds without renouncing their villainous ways. They are killers, criminals, and conmen, and they have no compunction to redefine themselves. They epitomize the old adage of "honor among thieves" in a modern world where such honor is seldom seen, even in the mainstream and noncriminal sectors of society. Tarantino's characters, and the others mentioned above, have deepened the narrative of good versus bad. In the post-9/11 world of the twenty-first century, the good guys aren't always good, and the bad guys have the potential to have a heart, stand for what is right, and even save the day.

FURTHER READING

Alsford, Mike. 2006. *Heroes & Villains.* Waco, TX: Baylor University Press.

Ashby, LeRoy. 2006. *With Amusement for All: A History of American Popular Culture since 1830.* Lexington: University Press of Kentucky.

Browne, Nick, ed. 2000. *Francis Ford Coppola's "The Godfather Trilogy."* Cambridge: Cambridge University Press.

Cheeda, Saim. 2019. "Lobo: 10 Things to Know about SyFy's Main Man." *Screen Rant.* July 18, 2019. Accessed July 19, 2019. https://screenrant.com/lobo-facts-trivia-syfy/.

Faludi, Susan. 2007. *The Terror Dream: Myth and Misogyny in an Insecure America.* New York: Picador.

Forasteros, J. R. 2017. *Empathy for the Devil: Finding Ourselves in the Villains of the Bible.* Downers Grove, IL: InterVarsity.

Geronimo, and S. M. Barrett. (1906) 2005. *Geronimo: My Life.* Chicago: Dover.

Greene, Richard, and K. Silem Mohammad, eds. 2007. *Quentin Tarantino and Philosophy: How to Philosophize with a Pair of Pliers and a Blowtorch.* Chicago: Open Court.

Grevas, Andrew. 2019. "'You Understand the Human Condition': *The Sopranos*, Mental Health, & Me." 25YL. May 2019. Accessed June 1, 2019. https://25yearslatersite.com.

Hines, Ree. 2013. "Tony Soprano Character Altered Face of TV, Paving Way for Antiheroes." Today. June 2013. Accessed June 1, 2019. https://www.today.com/popculture/tony-soprano-character-altered-face-tv-paving-way-antiheroes-6C10387810.

Hogan, Susan, Albach. 2003. "Was Judas a Good Guy or Bad? Scholars Disagree." Baylor University. April 17, 2003. Accessed April 21, 2019. https://www.baylor.edu/mediacommunications/index.php?id=6435.

Howe, Sean. 2012. *Marvel Comics: The Untold Story.* New York: Harper-Perennial.

Laszlo, Monseignore. 2006. "Anti-Villain." *Urban Dictionary.* July 23, 2006. Accessed July 7, 2019. https://www.urbandictionary.com/define.php?term=anti-villain.

Lebo, Harlan. 2005. *The Godfather Legacy*. Rev. ed. New York: Fireside.

Leibovitz, Annie, and Sam Kashner. 2012. "The Family Hour: An Oral History of *The Sopranos*." *Vanity Fair*. April 2012. Accessed June 1, 2019. https://www.vanityfair.com/hollywood/2012/04/sopranos-oral-history.

Peary, Gerald, ed. 2013. *Quentin Tarantino: Interviews, Revised and Updated*. Jackson: University of Mississippi Press.

Pruner, Aaron. 2019. "How the Godfather of TV Antiheroes Tony Soprano Changed Television Forever." Rotten Tomatoes. January 2019. Accessed June 1, 2019. https://editorial.rottentomatoes.com/article/tony-soprano-introduced-the-tv-antihero/.

Roche, David. 2018. *Quentin Tarantino: Poetics and Politics of Cinematic Metafiction*. Jackson: University of Mississippi Press.

Shone, Tom. 2017. *Tarantino: A Retrospective*. San Rafael, CA: Insight Editions.

Wallis, Michael. 2007. *Billy the Kid: The Endless Ride*. New York: W. W. Norton.

The Pathos of Villainy: Getting to the Heart of Why Villains Went Bad

It has been said that villains see themselves as the hero in their own story; they do not view their deeds as evil but actually as good. While this has been the case in many narratives, there remain just as many narratives where villains are fully aware that they are bad and that their actions are villainous. It may be more accurate and all-encompassing to state that villains usually sees themselves as the victim of their own story, and it is their response to this victimization that has led them down a darker path. There is a large degree of pathos in many of the most popular villains in American pop culture. When audiences are first introduced to a villain, they may see the villain's actions as horrendous, or even ghastly, secure in the knowledge that they—the audience—could never commit such atrocities.

As the villain is explored, the story often goes back to a very innocent time in the character's past, most often childhood, and audiences discover that some horrible trauma turned a once-kind, normal person into a monster. This pathos can also make the villain all the more frightening when the audience is forced to admit, even if only to themselves, that given the same circumstances, anyone might follow the path of darkness in the wake of such an experience. Readers and viewers of pop culture are fascinated by villains because of the realization that every single person possesses the potential to become the villain. Prior to the 1980s, villains had essentially simply been accepted as evil, with no real exploration as to how or why. That changed with the late 1980s' exploration into the mind of comic book villain, the Joker; throughout the 1990s and into the twenty-first century, more villains would be placed on the proverbial couch to get to the heart of why they went bad.

THE JOKER

Since 1940, the Joker, who is widely considered the first supervillain in American comic books, had been simply a maniacal serial killer and trickster foe to the

Paradise Lost

Paradise Lost is a narrative, blank verse poem first published in 1667 by the poet John Milton (1608–1674). It is divided into twelve (originally ten) books. The overall story has two arcs: the fall of man, the story of Adam and Eve in the Garden of Eden, and a de facto biograph of Lucifer/Satan. The story begins in the aftermath of the legendary battle between the angels of heaven and Satan's legion of fallen angels. Now banished to hell—or Tartarus, the ancient Greek for hell—Satan vows to traverse the Abyss between hell and Earth and tempt the new creation, humans, into disobeying God.

The story follows the basic events as described in Genesis, with a few notable exceptions: the Bible does not identify the "serpent" as Satan, but in Milton's epic, Satan takes on the form of a serpent, cementing popular dogma; Adam and Eve enjoyed a sexual relationship before the fall (though without the sin of lust); and Adam willingly disobeys God, fully aware of what Eve has done (a part of the story left more ambiguous in the Scriptures). Satan returns to hell triumphant, but soon he and all his followers are transformed into snakes (as the "serpent" was in Scriptures for his part in events). Although still the villain, Satan is portrayed more sympathetically in *Paradise Lost*, providing some context for his rebellion. Satan is in no way repentant for any of his actions, stating in the text that "It is better to rule in Hell than to serve in Heaven." Much of what Western society considers as fact regarding the character of Lucifer/Satan actually comes more from *Paradise Lost* than from anything in Scripture.

Richard A. Hall

"Dark Knight Detective," Batman. In 1988, legendary comic book writer Alan Moore and artist Brian Bolland produced the noncanonical one-shot graphic novel *Batman: The Killing Joke* (DC Comics, March 1988). The primary plot of the story revolves around the Joker shooting Batgirl/Barbara Gordon in the stomach and severing her spine in front of her father, Gotham police commissioner James Gordon. The Joker then kidnaps Commissioner Gordon, strips him naked, runs him through an abandoned fun park's tunnel of love, and forces him to look at photographs of his suffering daughter. The intent is to prove to Gordon and to Batman that it only takes one bad day to drive even the most noble of men insane. In flashbacks, however, the reader sees the backstory for the one bad day that made the Joker.

In this story, the pre-Joker is an unnamed engineer who walks away from his job to take a chance at being a stand-up comedian. His attempts, however, fail miserably, and his supportive, pregnant wife and he are forced to live in abject poverty. In an attempt to support his family while continuing to follow his dream, the young man agrees to help some common criminals by leading them through his former employer's factory so that they can rob the neighboring factory unnoticed. Before the job, however, police inform the young man that there has been a fire at his tenement apartment and that his pregnant wife and unborn child have died.

Forced to go through with assisting the criminals, he is also forced to don the identity of the Red Hood—a reference to the first Joker origin story in *Detective Comics #168* (Bill Finger, Lew Sayre Schwartz, and Win Mortimer, February

1951)—an identity the two criminals use to set up as a patsy in case they are caught. Ultimately, the two criminals are killed by security guards, and the Red Hood jumps into a vat of chemicals to escape Batman via the underground sewer system. When the young man washes ashore downriver, he discovers that the chemicals have left his skin permanently bleached white and his hair permanently dyed green, giving him the appearance of a traditional playing-card joker. This trauma, along with the loss of his wife and unborn child, warps his mind to a degree that he becomes the Joker. Although the Joker's attempt to similarly traumatize the commissioner fails, his backstory underscores the potential results of one bad day (Alan Moore, *The Killing Joke*, 1988).

A quasi-backstory was given in the television series *Gotham* (FOX, 2014–2019). Although the television series sought to examine the formative years of young Bruce Wayne between the murders of his parents and his rise as Batman, Warner Brothers, the owners of DC Comics and the DC TV/movie franchises, gave explicit orders that the series could not use the character of the Joker in any way. Instead, writers introduced the character of Jerome Valeska (played by Cameron Monaghan), a young, physically and emotionally abused son of a circus snake charmer. When he is exposed as having murdered his mother, Jerome—a seemingly innocent young boy to that point—erupts in maniacal laughter, with a psychotic grin (causing audiences to believe that this boy would be the Joker).

Over seasons two to four, hints continued to pop up in the narrative to suggest that this character would eventually become the "Clown Prince of Crime." Primrose Hill, the producers of the series, insisted he was not, and they possibly faced lawsuit if he was. In season four, Jerome dies. By that time, viewers have been introduced to Jerome's twin brother, Jeremiah (also played by Monaghan), a sweet, quiet, brilliant engineer. Jerome claims that it is, in fact, Jeremiah who was always the "bad" son, who convinced their mother that Jerome was crazy when it was actually Jeremiah who was guilty for much of what Jerome was accused. In a posthumous "gift," Jerome exposes Jeremiah to an overdose of his mysterious gas (Joker gas?), which drives Jeremiah insane, bleaches his skin, and eventually turns his hair green. In a fight with Bruce near the end of season five, Jeremiah falls into a vat of chemicals, severely scarring his face and making most of his hair fall out. Jeremiah remains in a catatonic state for ten years, until Bruce returns to Gotham. In the character's final scene, having been rescued from the asylum by his harlequin-dressed henchwoman, he tries to come up with his name and is seemingly stuck on "J." While the studio stuck to the letter of their agreement with Warner Brothers, it was quite clear to all Batman fans that Jeremiah Valeska was clearly the Joker. If so, *Gotham* created a fascinating backstory to comic books' most iconic villain.

In 2019, Warner Brothers released the controversial film *Joker*, directed by Todd Phillips and starring Joaquin Phoenix as the titular iconic villain. In this noncanonical origin story, Joker begins life as Arthur Fleck, an economically downtrodden and deeply disturbed young man with a neurological disorder that causes him to laugh sporadically, often at inappropriate times, who works a dead-end job as a clown for hire. Throughout the course of the story, Fleck experiences a rapid succession of bad days, culminating in his finding true freedom by releasing his frustrations against society in a more violent manner. Although many fans were unhappy with the Joker having such a detailed story and identity, the psychological analysis of who the Joker could have originated as provides considerable depth to the character.

J. R. EWING

Throughout the 1980s, J. R. Ewing (played by Larry Hagman), the antagonist of the hit nighttime soap opera *Dallas* (CBS, 1978–1991; TNT, 2012–2014), was known worldwide as "the Man You Love to Hate." For the first half of the original series' run, there appeared to be no limit to J.R.'s villainy, even when it came to members of his own family. He manipulated the destruction of his brother, Bobby's, marriage to first wife, Pamela Barnes (played by Patrick Duffy and Victoria Principal, respectively). He manipulated his own wife's alcoholism to work toward his goal of gaining custody of their young son. He mortgaged the family home, Southfork, to finance a highly risky business venture. When it appeared that his parents, Jock and Ellie Ewing (played by Jim Davis and Barbara Bel Geddes, respectively), were going to divorce, he attempted to split the family company, Ewing Oil, off from the rest of the family assets so that he would not lose it in the divorce. More than twenty years after the original series was cancelled, he attempted to steal Southfork from his brother in a scheme with a Venezuelan crime boss, which ultimately endangered the lives of his entire family. He was the epitome of evil.

Over the last few seasons of the original series and the final episodes of the return series' second season, audiences received a different perspective on J.R. His evil manipulations, regardless of how they appeared or whom they appeared to hurt, were for the overall good of the family, and his evil machinations could be relied upon to save the family when faced with overwhelming outside threats. At the end of the original series' eighth season, audiences were surprised with the sudden death of Bobby Ewing (Leonard Katzman, "Swan Song," season 8, episode 30, May 17, 1985). In the ensuing ninth season, J.R. began to emerge as the series' hero, renewing his relationship with wife Sue Ellen (played by Linda Gray) when she hit rock bottom with her alcoholism.

When a dip in ratings led to the decision to bring Bobby back from the dead, the tenth season established that season nine had, in fact, been a dream, thus returning J.R. to the role as villain. Despite this, however, viewers began to see a heart in the villain. For example, despite his utter contempt and hatred of rival Cliff Barnes (played by Ken Kercheval), J.R. never expressed, or even alluded to, this hatred when in the company of nephew Christopher (who was also Cliff's nephew). When Hagman passed away in November 2012, writers of the return series' second season had to work in the death of J.R. In the wake of J.R.'s death, viewers were informed of the many lengths that he had gone to in order to protect his family from outside threats while simultaneously battling cancer.

Throughout the series' original run, numerous hints at the source of J.R.'s villainy were dropped to provide audiences more insight and sympathy for the character. Despite his never-ending goal to gain his father's pride and affection, both of his parents openly and blatantly preferred younger brother Bobby to him. Further, although J.R. had numerous extramarital affairs while married to Sue Ellen, he never personally cared for the women he was using; meanwhile, Sue Ellen's own affairs were romantic in nature. She would fall deeply in love with the men she cheated with and thus wounded J.R., who psychologically separated love from sex. Finally, at the end of the original series, having lost his father, wives, and sons, J.R. contemplates suicide, leaving audiences to wonder whether or not he does (Leonard Katzman, "Conundrum," season 14, episodes 22–23, May 3, 1991).

At his core, J.R. was a forgotten son who sought his parents' approval by being the total opposite of his brother and a husband who, viewing nonromantic sexual encounters as innocent, hurt, scarred, and even threatened the life of the only woman he ever loved. He was a pessimist concerning the world at large, willing to do what he believed necessary to keep his family safe and to spare them from falling from the heights he viewed them as holding.

THE CIGARETTE SMOKING MAN

On the hit television series *The X-Files* (FOX, 1993–2002; 2016; 2018), audiences were introduced to the mysterious Cigarette Smoking Man ("CSM," "Smokey," or "Cancer Man"), the shadowy overall antagonist of the series. The character (played by William B. Davis), personified the nameless, seemingly anonymous government agents at the heart of most American conspiracy theories. In the episode "Musings of a Cigarette Smoking Man" (Glen Morgan, season 4, episode 7, November 17, 1996), audiences were finally given a backstory to this figure, or, at the very least, the backstory compiled by the Lone Gunman conspiracy investigators who frequently assist FBI agents Mulder and Scully. According to this story, CSM begins his top-secret career as a U.S. Army captain stationed at Fort Bragg, North Carolina.

The captain—a dedicated nonsmoker—is drafted in 1962 by nameless intelligence personnel to assassinate an American citizen on American soil. The citizen in question is later identified as President John F. Kennedy. Under the pseudonym "Mr. Hunt" (an allusion to longtime CIA agent E. Howard Hunt, a central figure to many Kennedy assassination conspiracy theories), the captain conducts the mission, simultaneously setting up local former marine Lee Harvey Oswald as the patsy. It is during this mission that the captain begins his smoking habit. Over the next five years, CSM unsuccessfully attempts to publish a spy novel under the pseudonym "Raul Bloodworth." He is then involved in planning the assassinations of both Dr. Martin Luther King Jr. and Senator Bobby Kennedy (King assassin James Earl Ray claimed that a co-conspirator named Raul was involved in that killing). In the 1990s, after revealing his involvement in everything from the U.S. victory over the Soviet hockey team in the 1980 Olympics to the Anita Hill controversy during the 1991 confirmation hearings for Supreme Court nominee

Clarence Thomas, CSM finally gets a story published, only to discover that the publisher changed his ending; this final failure leads him to dedicate his full attention to his more nefarious intelligence operations (Glen Morgan, "Musings of a Cigarette Smoking Man," 1996).

Although this backstory fails to address the allegations that CSM was involved in the Roswell incident in 1947 or the fact that he is the biological father of Agent Mulder, whose infant picture Bill Mulder shows him in 1962, the audience is left with the possibility that this backstory cannot be verified and may be a construction of CSM meant to be discovered. Regardless, it shows the possibility, or probability, that CSM was never a man with evil intent but, rather, a man whose patriotism and sense of duty was used by nefarious sources to coerce him into a life of villainy (exacerbated by his own failures at his desired profession). For the remainder of the series as well as its two later return seasons, CSM continued to be a malicious figure with dreams of global domination through subterfuge. The backstory does, however, attempt to put a more human face to a character previously shown to be evil incarnate.

VOLDEMORT

In 1997, author J. K. Rowling published what would become the most successful series of children's novels—and novels overall—in publishing history: the *Harry Potter* series. In the first book, *Harry Potter and the Sorcerer's Stone* (titled *Harry Potter and the Philosopher's Stone* outside the United States), readers are introduced to the evil Lord Voldemort, the dark wizard responsible for the deaths of Harry Potter's parents and the source of the lightning-shaped scar on the young boy's forehead. Believed dead, Voldemort spends the first four books of the series attempting to regain his full power and revived body. In the second book, *Harry Potter and the Chamber of Secrets* (1998, United Kingdom; 1999, United States), Harry, now in his second year at Hogwarts School of Witchcraft and Wizardry, discovers an enchanted journal belonging to a former student, Tom Marvolo Riddle, whose spirit resides in the book. At the climax of the story, Riddle's spirit reveals to Harry that he is, in fact, the younger version of Lord Voldemort.

Although Voldemort despises all Muggles (nonmagical people) and Mudbloods (witches and wizards with one or more nonmagical parents), Tom Riddle, himself, is the son of a witch and a Muggle. Tom's muggle father abandons his wife shortly before Tom is born, and his mother dies while Tom is still young. Confined to an orphanage, Tom is visited by Professor Albus Dumbledore, headmaster of Hogwarts, and is informed that the reason he can do so many wondrous things with his mind is that he is, in fact, a wizard. At Hogwarts, Tom poses as a model student but already holds his dark agenda against all nonmagical and half-magical people. It is this darkness that causes Dumbledore to later deny Tom the position of Defense Against the Dark Arts professor. Riddle then changes his name and raises an army of like-minded wizards and witches eventually known as "Death Eaters" (Riddle's full name is, in fact, an anagram for "I Am Lord Voldemort"). Before graduating, Riddle learns from Professor Horace Slughorn how to create horcruxes, objects in which pieces of a witch or wizard's soul can be hidden to be later reincorporated. The downside to the spell is that it can only be done through murder (J. K. Rowling, *Harry Potter and the Half-Blood Prince*, 2005). Lord Voldemort, then, becomes the epitome of someone with severe abandonment and self-loathing issues, aiming his hurt and hatred toward the half of his heritage responsible for his abandonment.

DARTH VADER

In the late 1970s, audiences around the world were introduced to one of the most iconic villains in pop culture history: Darth Vader, Dark Lord of the Sith (George Lucas, *Star Wars*, 1977). In the last chapter of the original *Star Wars* trilogy, it is revealed that Vader had once been the Jedi knight hero Anakin Skywalker. It then becomes the mission of Luke Skywalker, Vader's son, to redeem his fallen father, which he does prior to the Dark Lord's death (Lucas, *Star Wars, Episode VI: Return of the Jedi*, 1983). In 1999, Lucas returned to the *Star Wars* saga with a prequel trilogy, beginning with *Star Wars, Episode I: The Phantom Menace*. This film introduced audiences to the ten-year-old slave boy Anakin Skywalker (played by Jake Lloyd). When Jedi master Qui-Gon Jinn (played by Liam Neeson) believes Anakin to be the "Chosen One" of Jedi legend, prophesied to bring balance to the Force, the elder Jedi decides to take on the boy as an apprentice. When Qui-Gon dies at the hands of the Sith Lord Darth Maul, Anakin's training falls to newly appointed Jedi knight Obi-Wan Kenobi (played by Ewan McGregor).

Over the course of the next two films, *Star Wars, Episode II: Attack of the Clones* (2002) and *Star Wars, Episode III: Revenge of the Sith* (2005), Lucas unfolds the tale of how the young hero falls to darkness. Throughout the years of Anakin's training, he comes under the side tutelage of Republic chancellor Palpatine (who is secretly the Sith Lord Darth Sidious). Over the course of the Clone Wars, Anakin slowly becomes disenchanted by the Jedi Order, seeing them as arrogant and prideful, the antithesis of what they claimed to believe. Added to this, Anakin breaks official Jedi policy by falling in love with and marrying Senator Padme Amidala.

When the young Jedi, established as being able to foresee the future, has dreams of his wife's death, he becomes obsessed with saving her life. After Anakin discovers Palpatine's true identity, the evil Sith tells him that his own master had discovered how to prevent death. When the Jedi seek to kill Palpatine, Anakin saves the Sith Lord's life, committing himself to his teachings if Palpatine will, as compensation, teach Anakin how to save Padme. Anakin is then named Darth Vader and, on Palpatine's orders, slaughters all of the Jedi at the Jedi Temple, including dozens of younglings, children in their early years of training. Anakin then kills all of the members of the Confederacy of Independent Star Systems, ending the Clone Wars. These murders fully cement the dark control of Anakin's soul. Ultimately, Padme dies because of Anakin's fall. With the loss of the only thing in the universe that he loves, Darth Vader fully embraces the dark side of the Force and becomes one of the evilest villains in pop culture.

LEX LUTHOR

Lex Luthor first appeared in comic books simply as Luthor, a mad scientist foe for Superman (Jerry Siegel and Joe Shuster, *Action Comics #23*, April 1940). The first origin story for the character appeared in 1960. In that story, a young Lex Luthor resides in Superman's hometown of Smallville, where he rescues the young Superboy from an encounter with Kryptonite. Superboy then builds a lab for the aspiring young scientist, where Lex attempts to create a permanent antidote for Kryptonite. When a fire breaks out, Superboy extinguishes it with his "freeze breath," inadvertently spilling chemicals on Lex and causing the boy to go bald. The trauma is used to explain Luthor's eventual turn to evil and hatred of Superman (Siegel and Al Plastino, *Adventure Comics #271*, April 1960). A more detailed, deeper, and defining origin story emerges through the television series *Smallville* (WB, 2001–2006; CW, 2006–2011).

In the series, the young adult Lex Luthor (played by Michael Rosenbaum) befriends the teenage Clark Kent (played by Tom Welling) when Clark rescues Lex after his car hits Clark and then runs off a bridge into a river. The son of the prominent billionaire and head of LuthorCorp Lionel Luthor (played by John Glover), Lex becomes obsessed with young Clark, believing that the boy is hiding details of the rescue, which Lex's team of scientists deem physically impossible (Alfred Gough and Miles Millar, "Pilot," season 1, episode 1, October 16, 2001). Over the ensuing seasons, the relationship between Lex and Clark becomes increasingly strained as Lex is repeatedly there for whatever Clark needs, while Clark is clearly lying to Lex and hiding secrets about his abilities. This continued perceived betrayal is exacerbated by Lionel's own designs to turn his son and heir into a proper Luthor: manipulative, deceitful, and treacherous. Eventually, the original Lex is killed by the Green Arrow, but a fully grown clone later emerges, with all of the original Lex's memories intact, including the memory before his death of Clark's secret origin. In the end, just as Clark emerges as Superman, Lex's secret sister, Tess Mercer (played by Cassidy Freeman), exposes Lex to a concoction that deletes his memories, yet with his hatred of Clark inexplicably intact. This sets up the world of Superman as previously established in the comics (Al Septien, Kelly Souders, and Brian Peterson, "Finale, Part 2," season 10, episode 22, May 13, 2011).

The Lex Luthor of *Smallville* is a truly sympathetic character. Already scarred by his father's dysfunctional parenting, the overwhelming sense of betrayal by the person Lex considered to be his best friend only proved to enhance what his father had always warned him about trusting anyone. A key component of the overall story, however, is Clark's parents' distrust of Lionel Luthor and their firm belief that Lex's apple does not fall far from the family tree. There are numerous times when Clark considers confiding in his friend and just as many situations suggesting that Lex might use Clark's abilities to his own advantage, thus proving the Kents correct. Rosenbaum's nuanced performance leaves audiences to debate to this day whether Clark's trust could have swayed Lex from his evil fate. What remains certain, however, is that *Smallville* succeeds in making Lex Luthor a more sympathetic character than the comics, films, and other television incarnations ever attempted to build.

THE PATHOS OF THE VILLAIN

Many of the villains in the entries that follow—Angelique Bouchard-Collins, the Governor, Hannibal Lecter, Maleficent, Norman Bates, O-Ren Ishii, and Two-Face, to name but a very few—also possess similarly sympathetic origin stories. Since the 1980s, it has been a growing trend in American popular culture to examine the origins of villainy and to get to the heart of why villains went bad. Many are victims of the one bad day examined in Alan Moore's *The Killing Joke*. Others, like J.R., Darth Vader, and Lex Luthor, are the victims of a lifetime of childhood trauma that leaves them permanently scarred and with a twisted view of right and wrong. Many Americans fear their darker nature, constantly fearing that they, too, might turn to the dark side. This has led to this obsession with the heart of villainy and the promise of redemption. As science learns more about the human condition, the inner workings of the human brain, and the psychology of those society deems villains, popular culture will continue to pursue answers to these questions through analyses of the many villains of popular culture. The first step in solving any problem is identifying that there is one. How many villains could have been "saved" had the seeds of their villainy been identified early on?

FURTHER READING

Alsford, Mike. 2006. *Heroes & Villains*. Waco, TX: Baylor University Press.

Arp, Robert, ed. 2017. *"The X-Files" and Philosophy: The Truth Is in Here*. Chicago: Open Court.

Ashby, LeRoy. 2006. *With Amusement for All: A History of American Popular Culture since 1830*. Lexington: University Press of Kentucky.

Baggett, David, Shawn E. Klein, and William Irwin, eds. 2004. *Harry Potter and Philosophy: If Aristotle Ran Hogwarts*. Chicago: Open Court.

Barker, Cory, Chris Ryan, and Myc Wiatrowski, eds. 2014. *Mapping Smallville: Critical Essays on the Series and Its Characters*. Jefferson, NC: McFarland.

Campbell, Joseph. (1949) 2004. *The Hero with a Thousand Faces: Commemorative Edition*. Princeton, NJ: Princeton University Press.

Castleman, Harry, and Walter J. Podrazik. 2016. *Watching TV: Eight Decades of American Television*. 3rd ed. Syracuse, NY: Syracuse University Press.

Dyer, Ben, ed. 2009. *Supervillains and Philosophy: Sometimes, Evil Is Its Own Reward*. Popular Culture and Philosophy Series. Chicago: Open Court.

Eberl, Jason T., and Kevin S. Decker, eds. *The Ultimate Star Wars and Philosophy: You Must Unlearn What You Have Learned*. Hoboken, NJ: Wiley-Blackwell.

Faludi, Susan. 2007. *The Terror Dream: Myth and Misogyny in an Insecure America*. New York: Picador.

Friedman, Lester D., and Allison B. Kavey. 2016. *Monstrous Progeny: A History of the Frankenstein Narratives*. New Brunswick, NJ: Rutgers University Press.

Gavaler, Chris. 2015. *On the Origin of Superheroes: From the Big Bang to Action Comics No. 1*. Iowa City: University of Iowa.

Grau, Christopher, ed. 2005. *Philosophers Explore The Matrix*. Oxford: Oxford University Press.

Greene, Richard, and K. Silem Mohammad, eds. 2007. *Quentin Tarantino and Philosophy: How to Philosophize with a Pair of Pliers and a Blowtorch.* Chicago: Open Court.

Irwin, William, ed. 2002. *The Matrix and Philosophy: Welcome to the Desert of the Real.* Chicago: Open Court.

Irwin, William, and Gregory Bassham, eds. 2010. *The Ultimate Harry Potter and Philosophy: Hogwarts for Muggles.* Hoboken, NJ: John Wiley & Sons.

Kreeft, Peter. 2005. *The Philosophy of Tolkien: The Worldview behind The Lord of the Rings.* San Francisco, CA: Ignatius.

Langley, Travis. 2012. *Batman and Psychology: A Dark and Stormy Knight.* New York: John Wiley & Sons.

Langley, Travis, ed. 2015. "*The Walking Dead*" *Psychology: Psych of the Living Dead.* Popular Culture Psychology. New York: Sterling.

Leadbeater, Alex. 2019. "*Star Wars* Is Trying to Turn Darth Vader into an Anti-Hero (and That's Very Bad)." Screen Rant. February 4, 2019. Accessed February 4, 2019. https://screenrant.com/star-wars-darth-vader-villain-anti-hero/.

Lewis, Courtland, and Paula Smithka, eds. 2010. *Doctor Who and Philosophy: Bigger on the Inside.* Chicago: Open Court.

Lewis, Courtland, and Paula Smith, eds. 2015. *More Doctor Who and Philosophy: Regeneration Time.* Chicago: Open Court.

Nichols, Catherine. 2018. "The Good Guy/Bad Guy Myth: Pop Culture Today Is Obsessed with the Battle between Good and Evil. Traditional Folk Tales Never Were. What Changed?" Aeon. January 25, 2018. Accessed September 20, 2019. https://getpocket.com/explore/item/the-good-guy-bad-guy-myth.

Peaslee, Robert, and Rob Weiner, eds. 2020. *The Supervillain Reader.* Jackson: University of Mississippi Press.

Pierson, David P., ed. 2014. *Breaking Bad: Critical Essays on the Contexts, Politics, Style, and Reception of the Television Series.* Lanham, MD: Lexington Books.

Porter, Lynnette. 2012. *Sherlock Holmes for the 21st Century: Essays on New Adaptations.* Jefferson, NC: McFarland.

Sweet, Derek R. 2015. *Star Wars in the Public Square: The Clone Wars as Political Dialogue.* Critical Explorations in Science Fiction and Fantasy Series, edited by Donald E. Palumbo and Michael Sullivan. Jefferson, NC: McFarland.

Tye, Larry. 2013. *Superman: The High-Flying History of America's Most Enduring Hero.* New York: Random House.

White, Mark D., ed. 2009. *Watchmen and Philosophy: A Rorschach Test.* The Blackwell Philosophy and Pop Culture Series, edited by William Irwin. Hoboken, NJ: Wiley.

Wright, Bradford W. 2003. *Comic Book Nation: The Transformation of Youth Culture in America.* Baltimore, MD: Johns Hopkins University Press.

Yeffeth, Glenn, ed. 2003. *Taking the Red Pill: Science, Philosophy and the Religion of The Matrix.* Dallas, TX: BenBella.

Yuen, Wayne, ed. 2012. *The Walking Dead and Philosophy: Zombie Apocalypse Now.* Popular Culture and Philosophy. Chicago: Open Court.

Yuen, Wayne, ed. 2016. *The Ultimate Walking Dead and Philosophy: Hungry for More.* Popular Culture and Philosophy. Chicago: Open Court.

A–Z Entries

Agent Smith

First Appearance:	*The Matrix* (release date: March 31, 1999)
Creators:	Lana and Lilly Wachowski
Other Media:	Comics, video games, *The Lego Batman Movie*
Primary Strength:	Computer interaction, computer virus abilities
Major Weakness:	Disruption of the Matrix
Weapons:	Simulated guns, manipulation of the Matrix
Base of Operations:	The Matrix (simulated reality)
Key Allies:	Oracle, fellow Matrix agents
Key Enemies:	Morpheus, Neo, human members of the resistance
Actual Identity:	N/A
Nicknames/Aliases:	N/A

The Matrix film trilogy was written and directed by sisters Lana and Lilly Wachowski and was produced and distributed by Warner Brothers from 1999 to 2003. The general plot of the franchise is that sometime in the twenty-first century, artificial intelligence (AI) waged war on humanity on Earth; when humanity cut off the robots' supply of solar energy, the machines fought back by discovering how to feed off of human bioelectric energy. To maintain their power supply, the AI forces created a simulated reality—the Matrix—keeping all of humanity in a hibernated state, allowing them to live out their lives within this simulated reality, unaware of their actual state. Some humans, such as Morpheus and Neo, are aware of this false reality and choose to resist. The overarching AI of the program (Oracle) dispatches simulated agents to prevent the resistance from achieving their goals and maintaining the peace and continuance of the Matrix.

Chief among these agents is Agent Smith. Portrayed in the films by Hugo Weaving and voiced in the video games by Christopher Corey Smith, Agent Smith wears the simulated appearance similar to the legendary men in black: black suit and tie, dark sunglasses. At the beginning of the first film, Smith appears to be a government agent out to capture Thomas Anderson, a computer hacker who is actually "the One" to lead the resistance, known by his hacker ID of "Neo." Agent Smith is the most formidable of the many Matrix agents, avoiding deletion by "linking" to Neo's connection to the Matrix. Over time, Smith gains the ability to create copies of himself by merging with any entity within the Matrix. He eventually gains the ability to "overwrite" the human consciousness of his victims, absorbing their memories and abilities and even allowing him to exist in the "real" world. Smith ultimately absorbs the Oracle in a last-ditch attempt to defeat Neo.

The Matrix trilogy, like the *Terminator* films before them, is a warning about humanity's reach extending its grasp. Agent Smith, as well as Oracle and the Matrix itself, speaks to a continuing fear that Americans have had since the 1950s: that artificial intelligence will one day take over human society, eventually eliminating biological life in favor of the mechanical. Like the Daleks, Cybermen, Terminators, and Borg before him, as well as the Cylons (before and after), Agent Smith and the Matrix represent the pinnacle of human achievement and the dangers that those achievements represent. The final lesson of the story is to always choose the red pill (a life of hard reality) over the blue pill (the illusion that "ignorance is bliss"). The more humanity seeks out an existence of ease, the more they threaten the continuation of that very existence. Through *The Matrix*, the Wachowski sisters send a message to all of humanity: face the challenges of who you actually are rather than take the easy road of who society deems you to be.

Richard A. Hall

See also: Borg Queen/Borg, Brainiac, Cybermen, Davros/Daleks, Frankenstein's Monster, Number Six/Cylons, Ultron; *Thematic Essays*: "Nazis, Communists, and Terrorists . . . Oh My!": The Rise of the Supervillain and the Evolution of the Modern American Villain.

Further Reading

Alsford, Mike. 2006. *Heroes & Villains.* Waco, TX: Baylor University Press.

Ashby, LeRoy. 2006. *With Amusement for All: A History of American Popular Culture since 1830.* Lexington: University Press of Kentucky.

Grau, Christopher, ed. 2005. *Philosophers Explore The Matrix.* Oxford: Oxford University Press.

Irwin, William, ed. 2002. *The Matrix and Philosophy: Welcome to the Desert of the Real.* Chicago: Open Court.

Yeffeth, Glenn, ed. 2003. *Taking the Red Pill: Science, Philosophy and the Religion of The Matrix.* Smart Pop Series. Dallas, TX: BenBella.

Alexis Carrington-Colby-Dexter

First Appearance:	*Dynasty*, season 1, episode 15 (air date: April 20, 1981)
Creators:	Richard and Esther Shapiro
Other Media:	N/A
Primary Strength:	Seduction
Major Weakness:	Greed
Weapons:	Money
Base of Operations:	Denver, Colorado (original); Atlanta, Georgia (reboot)
Key Allies:	Cecil Colby, "Dex" Dexter, Fallon Colby, Adam Carrington

Key Enemies:	Blake Carrington, Krystle Carrington, Sable Colby
Actual Identity:	N/A
Nicknames/Aliases:	"The Bitch"

Dynasty was one of the most popular nighttime soap operas of the 1980s. Airing on ABC from 1980 to 1989, the series, created by Richard and Esther Shapiro, was a direct response to the worldwide success of CBS's *Dallas*. The show centered on the oil-rich Carrington family of Denver, Colorado, headed by family patriarch Blake Carrington (John Forsyth). In the show's premier season, Blake marries his former secretary, Krystle Jennings (Linda Evans), much to the chagrin of daughter Fallon (originally played by Pamela Sue Martin, later by Emma Samms). The show's greatest controversy—and therefore a contributing factor to its taboo popularity—was the openly gay character of son Steven Carrington (originally played by Al Corley, later by James MacKay). The one key ingredient missing from the first season was a clear villain, one that more closely resembled *Dallas*'s iconic J. R. Ewing. When Blake accidentally kills Steven's lover in a fit of rage and is placed on trial for murder, a surprise witness to Blake's history of violence appears in the final scene of the season's final episode: Blake's long-absent first wife, Alexis (Edward De Blasio, "The Testimony," *Dynasty*, April 20, 1981).

Alexis was portrayed with villainous glee by Joan Collins. At first, she becomes the nemesis of the new Mrs. Carrington, Krystle. In the third season, however, Alexis marries Blake's longtime rival, Cecil Colby, and, on Cecil's death, she inherits his multimillion dollar company, ColbyCo. This places Alexis as an equal to the heroic Blake and makes her as powerful as her CBS Texan male counterpart. In the fourth season, Alexis becomes romantically involved with "Dex" Dexter, the son of one of Blake's oldest business partners. Despite the relationship's ups and downs—usually due to Alexis having to make a choice between love and power—the bond between the two remains one of the constants of the show. Throughout the remaining seasons, Dex clearly respects Alexis as she is and admires her all the more. At no point does any male character on the show suggest that Alexis is in over her head or that she has no place in a "man's" world. Whenever the character enters the room, it is clear that she is the dominant force and worthy of respect, no matter how one feels about her personally.

The key difference between *Dynasty* and *Dallas* was the former's emphasis on high fashion and over-the-top soap-operatic tropes. Many of the most extravagant fashions were worn by Alexis. Throughout the series, Alexis gains power as she gains husbands, carrying the names of each as she goes along. By the end of the series, Alexis Carrington-Colby-Dexter-Rowan is an unstoppable force of nature, utilizing guile and seduction comparable to any businessman of the 1980s. Due to rapidly declining ratings in 1989, the series was cancelled, with a true-to-its-form cliff-hanger ending leaving the fate of Alexis, Blake, and Krystle in question. A two-part reunion miniseries aired in 1991 to tie up loose ends, but the result was panned by fans and critics alike.

Dynasty was rebooted in 2017 on the CW, changing the location of the series from Colorado to Atlanta, Georgia. The new Alexis was portrayed by nighttime

Joan Collins as Alexis Carrington-Colby-Dexter on the ABC nighttime soap opera *Dynasty*. She was queen of the 1980s soap opera villainesses. (Nik Wheeler/Alamy Stock Photo)

soap favorite Nicollette Sheridan. However, it is Joan Collins's original portrayal that is forever stamped on the American zeitgeist. In every scene, Collins's Alexis is clearly in command of all she surveys. From her gaze, to her 1980s-shoulder-pad-enhanced stance, to her powerful British accent, Alexis does not have to prove that she is a force to be reckoned with. It is evident. She invokes respect and fear to equal degrees. In 2013, *TV Guide* named Alexis the number seven "nastiest" villain in TV history ("TV Guide Picks TV's 60 Nastiest Villains," *TV Guide*).

Alexis represented the ultimate embodiment of a 1980s post–women's lib woman: independent, powerful, and in complete control of her life, her choices, and her destiny. She proved herself capable of playing in a previously "man's" world, and she did so by playing by the rules they had established. Her increasingly hyphenated last name was a double-edged sword. On the one hand, it was a testament—a proverbial trophy case—to the chain of powerful men she had used to achieve her ends. On the other hand, it suggested that it was only through those men that she had gained such success. What is without argument is the fact that Alexis inspired as much fear, loathing, and thirst for revenge as any comparable male character on television. As her primary enemy was also the father of her children, Alexis would frequently use her children's love as a weapon against her ex-husband, but, to the same degree, she would not hesitate to use her power to help or protect her children. Her popular "cat fights" with her nemesis, Krystle, tended to emphasize long-standing stereotypes of women, even as her boardroom machinations broke down those same stereotypes. This makes Alexis a complex and complicated character, and one of the more interesting villains of the Decade of Greed.

Richard A. Hall

See also: Angelique Bouchard-Collins, Cersei Lannister, Ebenezer Scrooge, Ernst Stavro Blofeld/SPECTRE, Fiona Goode/The Supreme, Fish Mooney, Heisenberg/Walter White,

J. R. Ewing, Maleficent, The Master/Missy, Morgan le Fay, Nurse Ratched, Sherry Palmer, Sue Sylvester, Wicked Witch of the West; *Thematic Essays*: The Pathos of Villainy: Getting to the Heart of Why Villains Went Bad.

Further Reading

Alsford, Mike. 2006. *Heroes & Villains.* Waco, TX: Baylor University Press.

Ashby, LeRoy. 2006. *With Amusement for All: A History of American Popular Culture since 1830.* Lexington: University Press of Kentucky.

Bates, Billie Rae. 2004. *Dynasty High: A Guide to TV's Dynasty and Dynasty II: The Colbys.* Charleston, SC: BookSurge.

Castleman, Harry, and Walter J. Podrazik. 2016. *Watching TV: Eight Decades of American Television.* 3rd ed. Syracuse, NY: Syracuse University Press.

Rossinow, Doug. 2015. *The Reagan Era: A History of the 1980s.* New York: Columbia University Press.

Shapiro, Esther. 1984. *Dynasty: The Authorized Biography of the Carringtons.* New York: Doubleday.

Stark, Steven D. 1997. *Glued to the Set: The 60 Television Shows and Events That Made Us Who We Are Today.* New York: Delta Trade Paperbacks.

"TV Guide Picks TV's 60 Nastiest Villains." 2013. *TV Guide.* April 22, 2013. Accessed January 1, 2019. http://wordsmithonia.blogspot.com/2013/04/tv-guide-picks-tvs-60-nastiest-villains.html.

Alpha/The Whisperers

First Appearance:	**Alpha:** *The Walking Dead #132* (cover date: October 2014) **The Whisperers:** *The Walking Dead #130* (cover date: August 2014)
Creators:	Robert Kirkman (with artists Charlie Adlard, Stefano Gaudiano, and Cliff Rathburn)
Other Media:	Television series
Primary Strength:	**Alpha:** Brutality, inspiring loyalty **The Whisperers:** Numbers
Major Weakness:	Blinded by ideology
Weapons:	Knives/bladed objects
Base of Operations:	Eastern United States
Key Allies:	Lydia, Beta
Key Enemies:	Lydia, Rick Grimes (comics only), Carl Grimes (comics only), Daryl Dixon (television only), Michonne, King Ezekiel, Negan
Actual Identity:	Unknown
Nicknames/Aliases:	N/A

The Walking Dead is a comic book created by Robert Kirkman and Tony Moore in 2003, published through Image Comics. The story centers on the survivors of a zombie apocalypse, led by a Kentucky sheriff's deputy, Rick Grimes. Through the struggles of the survivors, Rick and his group also encounter other human survivors who are, more often than not, greater threats than the undead. In 2010, the cable television network AMC launched a series based on the comic, shifting Grimes's origins to Georgia and adding a new character, the redneck tracker Daryl Dixon. Of the many human threats encountered both in the comics and television series, one of the most horrifying was Alpha and her band of "Whisperers."

In both the comic and the television series, the Whisperers are a group of the living who have learned to survive not by avoiding the undead "walkers" but by becoming them. They make masks and disguises from the flesh of the dead, nomadically moving among them. Their name comes from the fact that as they walk with the dead, they are forced to speak to each other only in brief, elongated, whispered words or phrases (so as to not be discovered by their undead companions). Over time, the Whisperers learn to herd the walkers.

As Rick (in the comics; Daryl on television) and the communities he has helped to create and preserve begin to encroach on Whisperer land, Alpha, the female leader of the Whisperers, comes into conflict with Rick (in the comics; Daryl on TV), especially when Alpha's daughter, Lydia, meets and becomes involved with Carl Grimes, Rick's son. In the television series, Lydia meets Henry, the adopted son of King Ezekiel. Alpha claims that certain territory belongs to the Whisperers and that if the community members wander into that territory, there will be deaths. To prove her point, Alpha orders the decapitation of numerous members of the communities, using their zombified heads to demarcate the line between Whisperer land and the communities. In the comics, Rick ultimately relies on Negan, his former enemy, to deal with the Alpha "problem," which he does with typical Negian glee.

As the television series allows for a more cinematic overview of land and large herds of walkers, the scope of the issue of territory becomes clearer than is possible on the printed page. On the series, the Whisperer story line did not begin until February, 2019; with Alpha portrayed with menacing aplomb by Samantha Morton. By that time, Rick Grimes actor Andrew Lincoln had left the show, making Norman Reedus's Daryl the de facto Rick. Although the Whisperers are viewed as villains in both series, the television incarnation presents undertones of the way Native Americans used to be portrayed in 1940s and 1950s western films: as savages attempting to stop the "progress" of civilization. Like that old stereotype, the "civilized" communities do not recognize Whisperer land, as the Whisperers are not "utilizing" it; instead, they are simply roaming nomadically from place to place with no settlement or "society" to speak of. Alpha and the Whisperers, on the other hand, see theirs as the only proper way to live in the new apocalyptic world, and they want no part of Rick's or Daryl's so-called progress.

The coming of Alpha is forewarned by her daughter, Lydia, who is captured by Rick in the comics and Daryl on TV. As Lydia shares her own origin story, readers and viewers soon discover that Alpha is a brutally abusive mother. When the zombie outbreak begins, Alpha's natural aggressiveness is a benefit to herself, her daughter, and those who choose to follow her. Living as the Whisperers do in a proverbial human wolf pack, identifying the leader as the "alpha" makes all the more sense. As the comic book and television series diverged in very different directions just prior to the appearance of Alpha on TV, it is unclear if the TV Alpha will meet the same fate as her comic book counterpart, but regardless, Alpha proves a cunning and deadly foe for the heroes of *The Walking Dead.* Through Alpha and the Whisperers, audiences are confronted with a frightening but logical alternative to attempting to reclaim "civilization" in the wake of a zombie apocalypse. Alpha knows no rules of gender or traditional gender roles. Those ideas have passed with the undead. In the new world, there is only the Alpha. She does not fear or avoid the undead; she understands that the living and the dead must now share the world together.

Richard A. Hall

See also: Alexis Carrington-Colby-Dexter, Angelique Bouchard-Collins, Asajj Ventress, Bellatrix Lestrange, Borg Queen/Borg, Captain Phasma/Stormtroopers, Catwoman, Cersei Lannister, Dark Willow, Elle Driver/California Mountain Snake, Faith the Vampire Slayer, Fiona Goode/The Supreme, Fish Mooney, The Governor, Harley Quinn, Kahless/Klingons, La Llorona, Maleficent, Morgan le Fay, Negan/The Saviors, Number Six/Cylons, Nurse Ratched, O-Ren Ishii/Cottonmouth, Poison Ivy, Reverend Stryker/The Purifiers, Sue Sylvester, Tia Dalma/Calypso, Wicked Witch of the West; *Thematic Essays*: The Pathos of Villainy: Getting to the Heart of Why Villains Went Bad.

Further Reading

Alsford, Mike. 2006. *Heroes & Villains.* Waco, TX: Baylor University Press.

Keetley, Dawn. 2014. *We're All Infected: Essays on AMC's The Walking Dead and the Fate of the Human.* Contributions to Zombie Studies. Jefferson, NC: McFarland.

Langley, Travis, ed. 2015. *The Walking Dead Psychology: Psych of the Living Dead.* Popular Culture Psychology. New York: Sterling.

Yuen, Wayne, ed. 2012. *The Walking Dead and Philosophy: Zombie Apocalypse Now.* Popular Culture and Philosophy. Chicago: Open Court.

Yuen, Wayne, ed. 2016. *The Ultimate Walking Dead and Philosophy: Hungry for More.* Popular Culture and Philosophy. Chicago: Open Court.

Angelique Bouchard-Collins

First Appearance:	*Dark Shadows*, episode 368 (air date: November 22, 1967)
Creators:	Dan Curtis and Art Wallace
Other Media:	Comics, novels, audioplays, movies
Primary Strength:	Witchcraft/magic
Major Weakness:	Obsessive love for Barnabas Collins; as vampire: crosses, silver
Weapons:	Poppets (essentially, voodoo dolls)
Base of Operations:	Collinsport, Maine

Key Allies:	Nicholas Blair, Quentin Collins, Barnabas Collins, Diabolos
Key Enemies:	Barnabas Collins, Josette Collins
Actual Identity:	N/A
Nicknames/Aliases:	Miranda Du Val, Cassandra Blair, Valerie Collins

Dark Shadows (ABC, 1966–1971) was one of the most popular daytime soap operas of the late 1960s. Originally established as a Gothic romance centered on Victoria Winters, a young governess for the wealthy Collins family of Collinsport, Maine, the show's poor ratings led creator Dan Curtis to take a more supernatural approach. In 1967, the show introduced Barnabas Collins, played by Jonathan Frid, as a vampire villain. The popularity of the character led the writers to change Barnabas into a heroic reluctant vampire (the first of what would become a popular trope in vampire fiction). Beginning in November 1967, the series began its first of many time-travel story lines. Running for over a year, the 1795 story line showed the origins of Barnabas's vampire curse and introduced viewers to Barnabas's most fearsome foe: his wife, Angelique.

Angelique Bouchard, played with devious glee by actress Lara Parker, was introduced as the maidservant to the Countess DuPres, the aunt of Josette DuPres, fiancée to Barnabas Collins, the son and heir to the wealthy Joshua Collins (Sam Hall, *Dark Shadows #368*, November 22, 1967). Viewers soon discovered that while visiting the island of Martinique, Barnabas had an affair with Angelique, and the young servant girl hopes to continue the romance while at Collinwood.

Dan Curtis

Dan Curtis (1927–2006) was an American writer, director, and producer most famous for his creation of the daytime soap opera *Dark Shadows* (ABC, 1966–1971). Originally designed as a *Wuthering Heights*–style gothic narrative, the show slowly began to incorporate supernatural elements, which gained the show massive viewership and national popularity, particularly among younger viewers. By 1968, the peak of the series' popularity, *Dark Shadows* was the highest-rated program on daytime television, a title that would only be surpassed a decade later with *General Hospital.* Aside from villain-turned-hero vampire Barnabas Collins, the series also featured werewolves, a witch, a gypsy, zombies, ghosts, time travel, and the concept of alternate realities (a popular trope in the 1960s). Despite its low budget, the show was renowned at the time for its state-of-the-art special effects.

The enduring popularity of the program inspired three feature films and a short-lived remake of the series twenty years after the original series was cancelled. Curtis also produced and directed two of the most popular television miniseries of all time: *The Winds of War* (1983) and *War and Remembrance* (1988–1989), World War II epics that both aired on ABC and were based on novels from Herman Wouk. Curtis did not live to see the 2012 theatrical comedic homage by director Tim Burton and starring Johnny Depp as Curtis's vampire antihero, Barnabas Collins, but four original cast members made cameos in the film. Although Curtis received massive acclaim for his numerous television projects over the decades, it is *Dark Shadows* for which he will be most remembered.

Richard A. Hall

When Barnabas rejects her, Angelique shows herself to be a witch, casting a spell on Josette that makes her fall in love with Barnabas's uncle, Jeremiah. Heartbroken, Barnabas turns once more to Angelique, agreeing to marry her. By this time, it is clear that a witch exists. When Barnabas discovers that Angelique is the witch, he attempts to kill her. Angelique then casts a spell on Barnabas, and he is soon bitten by a bat, leading to his death and resurrection as a vampire (Gordon Russell, *Dark Shadows #411*, January 22, 1968).

Once Barnabas's origin has been revealed, the story soon shifts back to the present, 1968. Soon, the long-believed-dead witch returns in the form of the now-brunette Cassandra Blair Collins, new wife to Barnabas's present-day "cousin," Edward. Angelique's true identity is soon revealed, and she allies with the demonic Nicholas Blair, who possesses devious machinations against the Collins family. For a brief time, Angelique becomes a vampire. Over the remaining years of the series, Angelique frequently returns as an adversary and, more often, a powerful ally to Barnabas and, eventually, his immortal cousin, Quentin. Throughout the character's run on the original series, Angelique is consistently portrayed as the most powerful of all the supernatural creatures in the *Dark Shadows* universe.

Although Angelique appears in all of the various time-traveling story lines, the original character comes to her end in the final 1840 story line. Having traveled back to the year 1840 by way of a mysterious "stairway through time," Barnabas and his constant companion, Dr. Julia Hoffman, encounter Angelique at a younger point in her time line, unaware of their future adventures as allies. This past Angelique, still her villainous self from the 1795 story line, once more becomes an ally to Barnabas, losing her powers in the process. As she lies dying from a gunshot wound, Barnabas confesses that he does love her; after this, Barnabas and Julia return to the present, and the standard time line of *Dark Shadows* comes to an end (Hall, *Dark Shadows #1179*, January 27, 1971). The series was abruptly cancelled, its final episode airing on April 2, 1971. Throughout the series, Parker's portrayal exhibits the combination of forlorn longing and indignant outrage of the proverbial woman scorned, while, at the same time, it underscores her increasing independence as she grows in power and prestige in her ex-lover's eyes.

The popularity of the series led to two noncanonical theatrical releases. The original, *House of Dark Shadows* (MGM, 1970, director Dan Curtis), centered on a dark retelling of the original Barnabas story line from the series. The sequel, *Night of Dark Shadows* (MGM, 1971, dictor Dan Curtis), told another noncanonical story, centering on Quentin Collins and his wife, Tracy. The young couple moves into the estate of Collinwood, and Quentin soon begins having flashbacks of his ancestor, Charles (also played by Quentin actor David Selby), who had an affair with the witch Angelique over a century before. Although it returned the character of Angelique to her darker, more villainous origins, the film was widely panned by critics and fans alike, and Lara Parker's four-year stint as Angelique came to an end.

Curtis and MGM attempted to revive the series in 1991 on NBC, retelling the original stories in a more rapid, weekly, nighttime format. The midseason series was cancelled after twelve episodes, as it failed to garner an audience in its Friday nighttime slot against the final season of the popular nighttime soap *Dallas*. In this brief series, Angelique was portrayed by Lysette Anthony. A pilot for another reboot was filmed in 2004, casting Ivana Milicevic as Angelique; but the WB decided against airing it. In 2012, a theatrical release was produced by director Tim Burton, starring Johnny Depp as Barnabas and Eva Green as Angelique. Green's Angelique, unfortunately, falls into old stereotypes, focusing on the anger more than the heartbreak or the agency that comes with her power. The film was panned by critics and fans alike, and its release against Marvel's *The Avengers* all but guaranteed its box office failure.

Over the decades, *Dark Shadows* had a few short runs in comic book form, and Angelique appeared in all of those series. In 1998, original Angelique actress Lara Parker wrote her first of many *Dark Shadows* novels, *Angelique's Descent*. This novel told the story of how the young Angelique became a witch in the late 1700s. The popularity of the book led to an audio drama version by Big Finish Productions in the early 2010s. Parker continues to write *Dark Shadows* novels and to portray Angelique on various Big Finish productions. In the genre of horror storytelling, Angelique stands out as one of the most powerful witches in fiction, alternating between villain and heroine. She is also significant as one of the earliest portrayals of a powerful woman in American popular culture. Above all, she stands as the ultimate representation of the old saying "hell hath no fury like a woman scorned."

Richard A. Hall

See also: Angelus, Bellatrix Lestrange, Dark Willow, Dracula, Fiona Goode/The Supreme, Fish Mooney, Grindelwald, Maleficent, Morgan le Fay, Nurse Ratched, Tia Dalma/Calypso, Ursula, Wicked Witch of the West; *Thematic Essays*: Tarantino and the Antivillain, The Pathos of Villainy: Getting to the Heart of Why Villains Went Bad.

Further Reading

Alsford, Mike. 2006. *Heroes & Villains*. Waco, TX: Baylor University Press.

Ashby, LeRoy. 2006. *With Amusement for All: A History of American Popular Culture since 1830*. Lexington: University Press of Kentucky.

Castleman, Harry, and Walter J. Podrazik. 2016. *Watching TV: Eight Decades of American Television*. 3rd ed. Syracuse, NY: Syracuse University Press.

Cavendish, Richard. 1968. *The Black Arts: A Concise History of Witchcraft, Demonology, Astrology, and Other Mystical Practices throughout the Ages*. New York: TarcherPerigree.

Cutrara, Daniel S. 2014. *Wicked Cinema: Sex & Religion on Screen*. Austin: University of Texas Press.

Hamrick, Craig, and R. J. Jamison. 2012. *Barnabas & Company: The Cast of the TV Classic Dark Shadows*. Bloomington, IN: iUniverse.

Hutton, Ronald. 2017. *The Witch: A History of Fear, from Ancient Times to the Present*. New Haven, CT: Yale University Press.

Russell, Jeffrey B., and Brooks Alexander. 2007. *A History of Witchcraft: Sorcerers, Heretics, & Pagans*. London: Thames & Hudson.

Ryan, Hannah. 2020. "Vilifications: Conjuring Witches Then and Now." In *The Supervillain Reader*, edited by Rob Weiner and Rob Peaslee, 156–171. Jackson: University of Mississippi Press.

Scott, Kathryn Leigh, and Jim Pierson. 2012. *Dark Shadows: Return to Collinwood*. New York: Pomegranate.

Angelus

First Appearance:	*Buffy the Vampire Slayer*, season 1, episode 1 (air date: March 10, 1997)
Creators:	Joss Whedon and David Greenwalt
Other Media:	Comics, novels
Primary Strength:	Strength, regenerative powers
Major Weakness:	Sunlight, wooden stakes (or enchanted objects) through heart, crosses
Weapons:	N/A
Base of Operations:	Sunnydale, California; Los Angeles, California
Key Allies:	Spike, Drusilla, Faith, the Master
Key Enemies:	Buffy Summers, Rupert Giles, Willow Rosenberg
Actual Identity:	Angel (as vampire), Liam (as a human)
Nicknames/Aliases:	N/A

Buffy the Vampire Slayer (WB, 1997–2001; UPN, 2001–2003) is a cult-classic television series that has gained an international following. Creator Joss Whedon wanted to take the tired concept of the girl being attacked by the monster and flip the idea so that the girl attacks the monster (Billson, *Buffy the Vampire Slayer*, 24–25). The show centers on Buffy Summers, a run-of-the-mill high school teenager who also happens to be the latest in a centuries-long line of "Chosen Ones," teenage girls who serve, one at a time, as "the slayer," the one girl in all the world who can save us from demons, vampires, and all threats of the supernatural. Every slayer is trained by a watcher, chosen by the Watchers' Council to oversee the slayer's training and guide her on her overall mission. When the series begins, Buffy and her recently divorced mother move to the small California town of Sunnydale, which happens to sit directly on a Hellmouth, a portal/magnet of concentrated evil, mostly in the form of vampires. In the very first episode, Buffy meets Angel, a mysterious figure with clear knowledge of the supernatural and a desire to be of assistance to the new slayer (Joss Whedon, "Welcome to the Hellmouth," *Buffy the Vampire Slayer*, season 1, episode 1, March 10, 1997). Viewers soon discover that the heroic young man—and Buffy's burgeoning love interest—is, in fact, a vampire.

Angelus/Angel is born as Liam in 1700s Ireland. After becoming a vampire, he becomes Angelus, one of the most sadistic killers in vampire history. According to Buffy lore, when a human becomes a vampire, the human soul leaves the body, and a demonic vampire essence takes over the body. It is later established that Angelus was present during the 1898 Boxer Rebellion in China. Sometime in the early 1900s, Angelus murders a young gypsy girl, and the gypsy's family retaliates by returning Liam's human soul to his now-vampire body, making Angel, as he would now call himself, the ultimate dichotomy: a vampire with a soul, tortured with an immortal bloodlust while possessing the conscience of a human

David Boreanaz played the "Jekyll and Hyde" character of Angel/Angelus in *Buffy the Vampire Slayer.* (UPN/Twentieth Century Fox/RGR Collection/Alamy Stock Photo)

(David Greenwalt, "Angel," *Buffy the Vampire Slayer*, season 1, episode 7, April 14, 1997).

In season two, Angel and Buffy finally consummate their love, and the experience of true happiness causes Angel to once more lose his soul, as his curse was to live in pain and guilt over his crimes (Marti Noxon, "Surprise," *Buffy the Vampire Slayer*, season 2, episode 13, January 9, 1998). Now Angelus once more, the vampire returns to his villainous ways, emotionally torturing Buffy until their final confrontation leads to the slayer slaying him, sending him to hell. Unknown to Buffy, however, her friends were working on a plan to return Angel's soul, and they succeed just as Buffy is about to penetrate his heart. Unfortunately, by that time, Angelus's/Angel's death is necessary to stop an impending apocalypse, thus necessitating sending the "good" vampire to a hellish fate.

However, as is the fate with fictional heroes and villains, death is not permanent. Angel returns and continues to be the love interest and partner to the slayer until he finally decides to leave town, aware that he and Buffy can never truly be happy or his evil self will return. Angel then moves to Los Angeles and begins working as a private detective. In season four of the spin-off series, *Angel* (WB, 1999–2004), Angelus is once more brought forth to confront an enemy known only as "the Beast," which he, of course, does. With his soul once more restored by the witch Willow, Angel begins to ponder the concept of good and evil and the necessity to occasionally utilize the dark for the greater good. By this time, the formerly villainous vampire Spike has emerged in Los Angeles and is now another vampire with a soul. In 2013, *TV Guide* declared Angelus the number eleven "nastiest" villain in TV history ("TV Guide Picks TV's 60 Nastiest Villains," *TV Guide*).

Angelus was the latest incarnation of the idea of the reluctant vampire. This idea began in the 1960s with the soap opera *Dark Shadows* (ABC, 1966–1971) and its vampire villain-turned-hero, Barnabas Collins, and it continued with the vampire Louis in Anne Rice's *Vampire Chronicles* novels (1976–present). The primary difference is the dual personality. Angelus and Angel are, in fact, two different individuals, struggling for control of the same body. Angel possesses a human soul, with all of the potential for redemption that the condition implies. Angelus is a pure demonic force, with no ties to humanity, possessing unbridled cruelty and a lust not only for murder but also for the most cruel and violent murder he can imagine.

Since the publication of *Dracula* in 1897, vampire lore has been wildly popular in American culture. From the first Hollywood incarnation of *Dracula* in 1931 to the *Twilight* novels (2005–2008) and corresponding films, Americans have been obsessed with tales of the undead. However, whereas Americans prefer their vampires to be good, Angelus brought the genre back to its evil-incarnate roots. He represents the darkness that dwells beneath the good, the dark mirror to what humanity aspires to be.

Richard A. Hall

See also: Angelique Bouchard-Collins, Dark Willow, Dracula, Faith the Vampire Slayer, Spike and Drusilla; *Thematic Essays*: The Dark Mirror: Evil Twins, *The Twilight Zone*, and the Villain Within, The Pathos of Villainy: Getting to the Heart of Why Villains Went Bad.

Further Reading

Adler, Margot. 2014. *Vampires Are Us: Understanding Our Love Affair with the Immortal Dark Side*. Newburyport, MA: Weiser.

Alsford, Mike. 2006. *Heroes & Villains*. Waco, TX: Baylor University Press.

Ashby, LeRoy. 2006. *With Amusement for All: A History of American Popular Culture since 1830*. Lexington: University Press of Kentucky.

Billson, Anne. 2005. *Buffy the Vampire Slayer*. London: British Film Institute.

Castleman, Harry, and Walter J. Podrazik. 2016. *Watching TV: Eight Decades of American Television*. 3rd ed. Syracuse, NY: Syracuse University Press.

Dial-Driver, Emily, Sally Emmons-Featherston, Jim Ford, and Carolyn Anne Taylor. 2008. *The Truth of Buffy: Essays on Fiction Illuminating Reality*. Jefferson, NC: McFarland.

Field, Mark. 2017. *Buffy, the Vampire Slayer: Myth, Metaphor & Morality*. N.p.: Amazon Services.

Gross, Edward, and Mark A. Altman. 2017. *Slayers & Vampires: The Complete, Uncensored, Unauthorized Oral History of Buffy & Angel*. New York: Tor.

Jowett, Lorna. 2005. *Sex and the Slayer: A Gender Studies Primer for the Buffy Fan*. Middletown, CT: Wesleyan University Press.

Lavery, David. 2013. *Joss Whedon, a Creative Portrait: From Buffy, the Vampire Slayer to Marvel's "The Avengers."* London: I. B. Tauris.

Lavery, David, and Cynthia Burkhead, eds. 2011. *Joss Whedon: Conversations*. Jackson: University of Mississippi Press.

Pender, Patricia J. 2016. *I'm Buffy and You're History*. London: I. B. Tauris.

Pollard, Tom. 2016. *Loving Vampires: Our Undead Obsession*. Jefferson, NC: McFarland.

Short, Sue. 2011. "*Buffy the Vampire Slayer*: Beauty and the 'Big Bad.'" In *Cult Telefantasy Series: A Critical Analysis of The Prisoner, Twin Peaks, The X-Files, Buffy the Vampire Slayer, Lost, Heroes, Doctor Who, and Star Trek*, 84–107. Jefferson, NC: McFarland.

South, James B., ed. 2005. *Buffy, the Vampire Slayer and Philosophy: Fear and Trembling in Sunnydale*. Chicago: Open Court.

"TV Guide Picks TV's 60 Nastiest Villains." 2013. *TV Guide*. April 22, 2013. Accessed January 1, 2019. http://wordsmithonia.blogspot.com/2013/04/tv-guide-picks-tvs-60-nastiest-villains.html.

Wilcox, Rhonda V., Tanya Cochran, Cynthea Masson, and David Lavery, eds. 2014. *Reading Joss Whedon*. Syracuse, NY: Syracuse University Press.

Wilcox, Rhonda V., and David Lavery. 2002. *Fighting the Forces: What's at Stake in Buffy, the Vampire Slayer*. Lanham, MD: Rowman & Littlefield.

Yeffeth, Glenn, ed. 2003. *Seven Seasons of Buffy: Science Fiction and Fantasy Writers Discuss Their Favorite Television Show*. Dallas, TX: BenBella.

Yeffeth, Glenn, ed. 2004. *Five Seasons of Angel: Science Fiction and Fantasy Writers Discuss Their Favorite Vampire*. Smart Pop Series. Dallas, TX: BenBella.

Archie Bunker

First Appearance:	*All in the Family*, season 1, episode 1 (air date: January 12, 1971)
Creators:	Norman Lear
Other Media:	N/A
Primary Strength:	Argument
Major Weakness:	Bigotry, hypocrisy
Weapons:	N/A
Base of Operations:	New York City
Key Allies:	Edith Bunker, Michael "Meathead" Stivic, Gloria Stivic
Key Enemies:	Michael "Meathead" Stivic, Gloria Stivic, George Jefferson, Maude Findlay
Actual Identity:	Archibald Bunker
Nicknames/Aliases:	N/A

All in the Family (CBS, 1971–1979) is a sitcom created by television legend Norman Lear. It starred Carroll O'Connor as lower-middle-class New Yorker Archie Bunker. Every episode of this landmark television program centered on a central argument over the issues facing America at the time: race, women's rights, the LGBT+ community, politics, and income inequality, to name a few. These arguments took place primarily in the Bunker living room, between Archie and his unemployed college-student son-in-law, Michael Stivic (played by Rob Reiner). Michael's wife/Archie's daughter, Gloria (played by Sally Struthers), most often sided with her husband, while Archie's wife, Edith (played by Jean Stapleton), desperately sought to keep the peace. It is considered not only one of the most successful programs in television history but one of the most socially important as well.

Archie came across as an almost "lovable" villain, as it was clear to the audience that his vile opinions and clear lack of understanding of basic reality came from a place of utter ignorance all too present in pre–baby boomer white America. The series—and Archie in particular—frequently used strong, offensive language as a means of driving home to the audience the importance of the subject matter and the depths of the entrenchment of bigoted ideas in what was considered mainstream America. Archie frequently spoke to black and/or LGBT+ people in direct, offensive language, confident that his bigoted ideas were not only reality but also acknowledged as such by those minority groups.

The character was so expertly written and performed as not only to expose the ignorance of radical conservative beliefs concerning race and gender but also to do in such a way that the source of the ignorance did not necessarily define the ignorant individual as evil. Perhaps Archie's most formidable opponent was his wife's cousin, Maude Findlay. Masterfully portrayed by Bea Arthur—to such a degree that Maude would receive her own spin-off program—Maude was the ultimate example of the empowered feminist of the 1970s. Going far beyond calling out Archie's ignorance, Maude could disarm any opponent with such a degree of wit and sarcasm to make the target of her tirades agree with her simply to make the insults cease.

All in the Family—and its fellow 1970s Norman Lear spin-offs, *Maude*, *Good Times*, and *The Jeffersons*—played a vital role in broadening the discussion of the major sociopolitical issues of the day. It educated as well as informed, and it helped audiences to learn from the inequalities of the past in order to work toward a better tomorrow. As the character of Archie Bunker so brilliantly portrays, much of the ignorance behind American bigotry can be overcome simply by exposing the bigot to reality, putting a human face on the victims of hatred, and speaking to the humanity within most Americans.

Richard A. Hall

See also: Bellatrix Lestrange, Davros/Daleks, Frank Burns, General Custer, Grindelwald, Magneto, Red Skull, Sue Sylvester, Voldemort, Zod; *Thematic Essays*: The Pathos of Villainy: Getting to the Heart of Why Villains Went Bad.

Further Reading

Alsford, Mike. 2006. *Heroes & Villains.* Waco, TX: Baylor University Press.

Ashby, LeRoy. 2006. *With Amusement for All: A History of American Popular Culture since 1830.* Lexington: University Press of Kentucky.

Behnken, Brian D., and Gregory D. Smithers. 2015. *Racism in American Popular Media: From Aunt Jemima to the Frito Bandito.* Westport, CT: Praeger.

Castleman, Harry, and Walter J. Podrazik. 2016. *Watching TV: Eight Decades of American Television.* 3rd ed. Syracuse, NY: Syracuse University Press.

McCrohan, Donna. 1988. *Archie & Edith, Mike & Gloria: The Tumultuous History of All in the Family.* New York: Workman.

Asajj Ventress

First Appearance:	*Star Wars: Clone Wars*, season 1, chapter 6 (air date: November 14, 2003)
Creators:	George Lucas, Genndy Tartakovsky, and Dermot Power
Other Media:	CGI feature film, novels, and comic books
Primary Strength:	The Force
Major Weakness:	Abandonment issues
Weapons:	Lightsabers
Base of Operations:	Dathomir
Key Allies:	Count Dooku/Darth Tyrannus (originally), Ahsoka Tano (temporarily), QuinlanVos (finally), the Nightsisters
Key Enemies:	Obi-Wan Kenobi, Count Dooku/Darth Tyrannus
Actual Identity:	N/A
Nicknames/Aliases:	N/A

In 1977, writer and director George Lucas introduced the world to his iconic film *Star Wars*. The massive worldwide success of the original film has spawned numerous sequels, prequels, animated television series, made-for-TV movies, novels, and comic books. Set a "long time ago . . . in a galaxy far, far away," *Star Wars* tells a generational saga of a galaxy at war between the forces of good and evil. The movie *Star Wars, Episode II: Attack of the Clones* (Lucasfilm, 2002, director George Lucas) introduced a period of galactic history long-referred to as the Clone Wars. As the following film was set to end this conflict, Lucas green-lit two animated television series to cover the events of the war itself: *Clone Wars* (Cartoon Network, 2003, 2005) and *The Clone Wars* (Cartoon Network, 2008–2013; Netflix, 2014; Disney+ streaming service, 2019). Of the new and interesting characters introduced in the two series, one of the most complex and popular was the villain Asajj Ventress.

Ventress was introduced in the sixth episode of the animated series *Clone Wars* as a potential apprentice to the Sith Lord, Count Dooku, secretly known as Darth Tyrannus. As Dooku is testing potential assassins, a mysterious woman appears wielding two lightsabers and quickly dispatches all contenders. Claiming a desire to become a Sith, Ventress apprentices to Dooku as part of the Sith Lord's private plan to usurp his own master, Darth Sidious (Genndy Tartakovsky, *Clone Wars*, "Chapter 6," 2003). Ventress serves Dooku on numerous missions against the Jedi knights, specifically against Obi-Wan Kenobi, Anakin Skywalker (the future Darth Vader), and Ahsoka Tano. Most notably, she assists Dooku in a plan to frame the Jedi for the kidnapping of the young Huttling, Rotta the Hutt, son and heir of the crime lord Jabba the Hutt (George Lucas, *The Clone Wars* feature film, Lucasfilm/Warner Brothers, 2008). Eventually, Sidious discovers Dooku's plan and orders his apprentice to kill Ventress as a test of his loyalty. Dooku's attempt

Sith apprentice Asajj Ventress preparing for battle on the animated series *Star Wars: The Clone Wars*. (RGR Collection/Alamy Stock Photo)

fails, sending Ventress on a mission to find her own way, primarily as a bounty hunter.

In the third season of the CGI-animated series, viewers discover that Ventress was from the planet Dathomir, where she was sold as a child by the Nightsister clan. Young Ventress was discovered by an abandoned Jedi knight, who sensed her connection to the Force, the intangible essence known to provide powers to both Jedi and Sith. When her master is killed by pirates, Ventress eventually escapes, now dedicated to destroying the Jedi, whom she sees as having abandoned both herself and her master. After some time on her own, Ventress returns to Dathomir to become an official Nightsister, but the entire clan is destroyed by Dooku's forces, once more leaving Ventress alone. In the 2016 novel *Dark Disciple* by Christie Golden, Ventress begins a romance with the fallen Jedi knight Quinlan Voss. Dooku finally succeeds in killing his former apprentice, and Voss returns her body to her home planet so that her spirit can join those of her sisters.

Although often falling into the stereotype of the woman scorned, Asajj Ventress is also the first prominent Force-wielder in the *Star Wars* canon, as well as one of the most sympathetic characters in the franchise. Abandoned or betrayed by everyone she trusted, Ventress becomes the very symbol of self-sufficiency and frequently proves herself capable against any foe, good or evil. While she is often presented as lithe and sexual, at no time does her sexuality become a defining aspect of her character. Her power and cleverness match all men she confronts. Although her death may preclude her inclusion in future *Star Wars* projects, her enduring popularity and importance to the Clone Wars era cement her place in the hearts and minds of *Star Wars* fans across the globe.

Richard A. Hall

See also: Angelique Bouchard-Collins, Bellatrix Lestrange, Billy the Kid, Boba Fett, Dark Willow, Fiona Goode/The Supreme, Fish Mooney, Grindelwald, Imperial Officers, Jabba the Hutt, Maleficent, The Master/Missy, Morgan le Fay, Nurse Ratched, Sherry Palmer, Sith Lords, Tia Dalma/Calypso, Voldemort, Wicked Witch of the West; *Thematic Essays*: The Pathos of Villainy: Getting to the Heart of Why Villains Went Bad.

Further Reading

Alsford, Mike. 2006. *Heroes & Villains*. Waco, TX: Baylor University Press.

Eberl, Jason T., and Kevin S. Decker, eds. *The Ultimate Star Wars and Philosophy: You Must Unlearn What You Have Learned*. Hoboken, NJ: Wiley-Blackwell.

Faludi, Susan. 2007. *The Terror Dream: Myth and Misogyny in an Insecure America*. New York: Picador.

Jones, Brian Jay. 2016. *George Lucas: A Life*. New York: Little Brown and Company.

Kaminski, Michael. 2008. *The Secret History of Star Wars: The Art of Storytelling and the Making of a Modern Epic*. Kingston, ON, Canada: Legacy Books.

Reagin, Nancy R., and Janice Liedl, eds. *Star Wars and History*. New York: John Wiley & Sons.

Sunstein, Cass R. 2016. *The World According to Star Wars*. New York: Dey Street Books.

Sweet, Derek R. 2015. *Star Wars in the Public Square: The Clone Wars as Political Dialogue*. Critical Explorations in Science Fiction and Fantasy Series, edited by Donald E. Palumbo and Michael Sullivan. Jefferson, NC: McFarland.

Taylor, Chris. 2015. *How Star Wars Conquered the Universe: The Past, Present, and Future of a Multibillion Dollar Franchise*. New York: Basic Books.

B

Bellatrix Lestrange

First Appearance:	*Harry Potter and the Goblet of Fire* (novel) (release date: July 8, 2000)
Creators:	J. K. Rowling
Other Media:	Movies, Pottermore website
Primary Strength:	Witchcraft/magic
Major Weakness:	Blind loyalty to Voldemort
Weapons:	Wand
Base of Operations:	Britain
Key Allies:	Lord Voldemort, Narcissa Malfoy (sister), Lucius Malfoy (brother-in-law), Death Eaters
Key Enemies:	Dumbledore, Harry Potter, Sirius Black (cousin)
Actual Identity:	N/A
Nicknames/Aliases:	N/A

In 1997, author J. K. Rowling introduced readers to the magical world of Harry Potter with *Harry Potter and the Philosopher's Stone* (released in the United States as *Harry Potter and the Sorcerer's Stone*). The series follows young wizard Harry Potter from the ages of eleven to seventeen, through his years at Hogwarts School of Witchcraft and Wizardry in Great Britain. During his time at Hogwarts, Harry must also face numerous threats to his friends and school, most often centering on the evil wizard, Lord Voldemort ("He Who Must Not Be Named"), who murdered Harry's parents when he was a young child and who threatens the very existence of Harry's wizarding world as he knows it. While Harry is assisted by his friends and professors, Voldemort relies on the assistance of his dedicated followers, known as "Death Eaters."

Of the army of Death Eaters, perhaps the most blindly dedicated is Bellatrix Lestrange. In the book series, Bellatrix made her debut in the fourth installment, *Harry Potter and the Goblet of Fire* (2000), but in the film series, she first appeared in the fifth movie, *Harry Potter and the Order of the Phoenix* (2007), where she was portrayed by Helena Bonham Carter. She is the aunt of Harry's archnemesis at school, Draco Malfoy, and the cousin of Harry's godfather, Sirius Black. After Lord Voldemort's initial defeat when he attempted to kill young Harry, most of his followers went underground, claiming that they either never supported the Dark Lord or that they only supported him under duress. Bellatrix, however, never

Death Eaters

The Death Eaters are the legions of wizards and witches devoted to the Dark Lord Voldemort in the *Harry Potter* novels and films. Prior to the Dark Lord's fall, the Death Eaters were notorious for their murders and torturing of Muggles (nonmagical people), as well as their same treatment of wizards and witches who refused to serve Voldemort. They were recognizable for their wrist tattoos: a skull with a snake emerging from it. Voldemort could summon his minions by pressing his wand to his own tattoo. Notable members mentioned in the books include Lucius Malfoy, Narcissa Malfoy, Bellatrix Lestrange, Peter Pettigrew, Barty Crouch Jr., Fenrir Greyback, and Antonin Dolohov. Professor Igor Karkaroff, headmaster of Durmstrang Academy, was once a Death Eater, as was Professor Severus Snape, potions master at Hogwarts School for Witchcraft and Wizardry, who turned sides to join Professor Albus Dumbledore after Voldemort's murder of Lilly Potter, mother of Harry and Snape's lifelong love. Keeping his new allegiance secret, Snape proved a valuable asset in defeating Voldemort for good.

The Death Eaters briefly took control of the Ministry of Magic after the death of Dumbledore. Voldemort's legions played a vital role in the Battle for Hogwarts in the seventh book, and eighth film, of the series. Of the above-mentioned Death Eaters, only the Malfoys and Dolohov survived the final battle; their ultimate fates remain unknown. In the popular zeitgeist, the Death Eaters represent the legions of devoted racist, bigoted, fanatical devotees often associated with maniacal demagogues such as Voldemort.

Richard A. Hall

wavered in her dedication, eventually being sentenced to Azkaban Prison for the torture of Frank and Alice Longbottom, parents of Harry's friend and classmate Neville. Once Voldemort returns to full health near the end of *Goblet of Fire*, Bellatrix escapes from prison to return to his side.

Bellatrix is part of a team of Death Eaters who fight Harry and his friends, calling themselves "Dumbledore's Army," at the Ministry of Magic. It is during this battle that she murders her cousin Sirius (*Harry Potter and the Order of the Phoenix* (book), 2003). After the Death Eaters have taken control of the ministry, Bellatrix's minions capture Harry, whose identity is hidden, and his friends, and she begins to torture young Hermione Granger for information. Harry, Hermione, and their friends are rescued by Lucius Malfoy's former slave, Dobby the House Elf (*Harry Potter and the Deathly Hallows* (book), 2007). The evil witch is killed during the Battle of Hogwarts, when Molly Weasley kills her for attempting to murder Molly's daughter and Harry's girlfriend, Ginny (*Harry Potter and the Deathly Hallows*, 2007).

Unlike many witches in popular culture, Bellatrix Lestrange is in complete thrall to a male master, Lord Voldemort. All of her evil deeds are in direct service to him. Although this may be seen as weakness or even playing into traditional stereotypes of women, it is also important to note that Bellatrix is one of the very few Death Eaters to maintain her loyalty and dedication, even in the face of certain imprisonment in Azkaban (while readers and viewers are never shown the extent of the horrors of Azkaban, they are alluded to numerous times in both the books and films). Her stalwart commitment to her master and his cause belies a strength that none of the primary male Death Eaters possess, as they choose instead a path of safety and cowardice. Bellatrix Lestrange represents a woman of considerable power, unwavering loyalty, and absolute evil.

Richard A. Hall

See also: Angelique Bouchard-Collins, Archie Bunker, Dark Willow, Fiona Goode/The Supreme, Fish Mooney, Grindelwald, Maleficent, Morgan le Fay, Nurse Ratched, Tia Dalma/Calypso, Ursula, Voldemort, Wicked Witch of the West; *Thematic Essays*: "In the Beginning . . .": The Origins of Villains in the Western World, "Nazis, Communists, and Terrorists . . . Oh My!": The Rise of the Supervillain and the Evolution of the Modern American Villain, The Pathos of Villainy: Getting to the Heart of Why Villains Went Bad.

Further Reading

Alsford, Mike. 2006. *Heroes & Villains*. Waco, TX: Baylor University Press.

Baggett, David, Shawn E. Klein, and William Irwin, eds. 2004. *"Harry Potter" and Philosophy: If Aristotle Ran Hogwarts*. Chicago: Open Court.

Barratt, Bethany. 2012. *The Politics of "Harry Potter."* London: Palgrave Macmillan.

Cavendish, Richard. 1968. *The Black Arts: A Concise History of Witchcraft, Demonology, Astrology, and Other Mystical Practices throughout the Ages*. New York: TarcherPerigree.

Hutton, Ronald. 2017. *The Witch: A History of Fear, from Ancient Times to the Present*. New Haven, CT: Yale University Press.

Irwin, William, and Gregory Bassham, eds. 2010. *The Ultimate "Harry Potter" and Philosophy: Hogwarts for Muggles*. Hoboken, NJ: John Wiley & Sons.

Reagin, Nancy R. 2011. *"Harry Potter" and History*. Hoboken, NJ: John Wiley & Sons.

Rothman, Ken. 2011. "Hearts of Darkness: Voldemort and Iago, with a Little Help from Their Friends." In *Vader, Voldemort and Other Villains: Essays on Evil in Popular Media*, edited by Jamey Heit, 202–217. Jefferson, NC: McFarland.

Russell, Jeffrey B., and Brooks Alexander. 2007. *A History of Witchcraft: Sorcerers, Heretics, & Pagans*. London: Thames & Hudson.

Ryan, Hannah. 2020. "Vilifications: Conjuring Witches Then and Now." In *The Supervillain Reader*, edited by Rob Weiner and Rob Peaslee, 156–171. Jackson: University of Mississippi Press.

Bill/Snake Charmer

First Appearance:	*Kill Bill, Vol. 1* (release date: October 10, 2003)
Creators:	Quentin Tarantino
Other Media:	N/A
Primary Strength:	Martial arts, expert marksman, expert swordsman
Major Weakness:	Obsession
Weapons:	Samurai swords, guns
Base of Operations:	Various
Key Allies:	Deadly Viper Assassination Squad: Budd/Sidewinder, Elle Driver/California Mountain Snake, O-Ren Ishii/Cottonmouth, Vernita Green/Copperhead

Key Enemies:	Beatrix Kiddo/Black Mamba/The Bride
Actual Identity:	Unknown
Nicknames/Aliases:	"Snake Charmer"

Kill Bill (volumes one and two) is the ultimate cinematic revenge epic by writer and director Quentin Tarantino. Released in two parts in 2003 and 2004, the film stars Uma Thurman as the enigmatic Bride, bent on revenge against the gang that placed her in a coma after trying to kill her on her wedding day and presumably killing her unborn child in the process. As she moves one by one through the colorful and dangerous members of the Deadly Viper Assassination Squad, audiences learn numerous things about the mysterious Bride: she was once a member of the Deadly Vipers, known as "Black Mamba"; she was once romantically involved with the Viper leader, Bill ("Snake Charmer"); and her child was saved and currently lives with her father, Bill (Quentin Tarantino, *Kill Bill, Vols. 1 & 2*, 2003–2004). Throughout the piece, Bill is shown to have a softer, though dangerously obsessed, side that actually makes him all the deadlier.

In the films, Bill (no last name ever given) is portrayed by 1970s icon David Carradine, most famous for his role as the wandering monk Caine on the television series *Kung Fu* (ABC, 1972–1975). Fatherless from a young age, Bill spent his early life collecting father figures, most notably the Mexican criminal Esteban Vihaio (played by Michael Parks) and the Chinese kung fu master Pai Mei (played by Gordon Liu). When his young love interest, Beatrix, goes missing after failing to complete an assassination mission, Bill obsessively searches for her, eventually finding her in a small Texas town about to marry a local record store owner. Enraged, Bill and his team of assassins kill everyone in the small chapel (or so they believe). While Beatrix kills his team one by one, Bill hides in his Mexican villa with his and Beatrix's now-four-year-old daughter, B.B. After a touching and sporadically violent reunion, Beatrix kills Bill with the ancient Five Point Palm Exploding Heart Technique, which she learned from her and Bill's former mentor, Pai Mei (Quentin Tarantino, *Kill Bill, Vol. 2*, 2004).

An avid fan of 1970s exploitation and martial arts films, Tarantino created Bill along the lines of traditional gangster with a kung fu twist. From the opening shot of the first film, Bill is shown to be a cold-blooded killer, making Beatrix all-the-more the hero for seeking revenge against him and his team. Over time, however, a softer side becomes visible. Bill attempts to warn his brother, Budd, of Beatrix's impending visit. He has been lovingly raising young B.B., proving to be an apparently loving and attentive father, something Bill himself never had. In the end, however, Bill proves to be equally loving and deadly, similar in many ways to other fictional crime icons Vito and Michael Corleone and Walter White. The mixture of evil with a heart has become a popular trope in modern fiction, and Bill represents this in traditionally genius Tarantino form.

Richard A. Hall

See also: Billy the Kid, Boba Fett, The Corleone Family, Elle Driver/California Mountain Snake, Ernst Stavro Blofeld/SPECTRE, Fish Mooney, Gus Fring, Heisenberg/Walter

White, Jabba the Hutt, Marsellus Wallace, Negan/The Saviors, O-Ren Ishii/Cottonmouth, Pancho Villa, Ra's al Ghul, Tony Montana, Tony Soprano; *Thematic Essays*: Tarantino and the Antivillain.

Further Reading

Alsford, Mike. 2006. *Heroes & Villains*. Waco, TX: Baylor University Press.

Greene, Richard, and K. Silem Mohammad, eds. 2007. *Quentin Tarantino and Philosophy: How to Philosophize with a Pair of Pliers and a Blowtorch*. Chicago: Open Court.

Kirshner, Jonathan. 2012. *Hollywood's Last Golden Age: Politics, Society, and the Seventies Film in America*. Ithaca, NY: Cornell University Press.

Peary, Gerald, ed. 2013. *Quentin Tarantino: Interviews, Revised and Updated*. Jackson: University of Mississippi Press.

Roche, David. 2018. *Quentin Tarantino: Poetics and Politics of Cinematic Metafiction*. Jackson: University of Mississippi Press.

Shone, Tom. 2017. *Tarantino: A Retrospective*. San Rafael, CA: Insight Editions.

Billy the Kid

First Appearance:	Born: New York City, late 1859; first national newspaper accounts/dime novels: early 1881
Creators:	Parents: Patrick McCarty and Catherine Devine
Other Media:	Novels, movies, radio, television, stage plays, comics, songs, video games
Primary Strength:	Sharpshooter
Major Weakness:	Ego
Weapons:	Six-shooters, rifles
Base of Operations:	New Mexico Territory
Key Allies:	John Henry Tunstall, Alexander McSween, Dick Brewer, Lincoln County Regulators
Key Enemies:	Murphy/Dolan Cartel, Sheriff Pat Garrett
Actual Identity:	Henry McCarty
Nicknames/Aliases:	William H. Bonney, William H. Antrim, "Kid" Antrim, "El Chivato"

In the history of fictional villains in American history, some were actually borne from the real world. This was particularly true of the period of U.S. history known as the Wild West. From 1870 to 1920, several legends of American westward expansion became legends of fiction as well, often during their own lifetimes, such as Jesse James, "Doc" Holiday, and Butch Cassidy and the Sundance Kid. By far the greatest legend to emerge from the Wild West—and the one that has had the longest continual impact on American popular culture—was the young outlaw known as Billy the Kid (1859–1881). When the Kid was allegedly killed by Sheriff Pat Garrett in 1881, the twenty-one-year-old Kid is said to have killed a man for every year he lived. Although he is frequently portrayed as a Robin Hood figure and an antihero in American popular culture, many in New Mexico at the time, particularly his victims, viewed the Kid as a murderous, bloodthirsty outlaw. The truth, whether outlaw or hero, has been forever blurred by the passage of time and his constant presence in American pop culture.

When Henry McCarty was fifteen years old, his mother died in New Mexico. He left his younger brother and stepfather to go the Arizona territory, where he committed his first robbery. At sixteen, McCarty committed his first murder, allegedly in self-defense, against a man with whom he was arguing. McCarty then returned to New Mexico. In 1877, he began working as a cattle rustler, calling himself William H. Bonney. In 1878, Bonney began working for English immigrant and rancher John Tunstall, who was in competition with the local faction of powerful Irish ranchers, the Murphy/Dolan Cartel. When the Irish businessmen sent local sheriff Bill Brady to confiscate Tunstall's property, the English rancher was killed by the posse. Bonney and fellow ranch hand Dick Brewer swore affidavits against Sheriff Brady and his men and rallied Tunstall's other young ranch hands to form the Lincoln County Regulators, tasked by the local U.S. marshall to bring in the Murphy/Dolan boys. The Regulators, however, soon took justice into their own hands, murdering the men they were tasked with arresting, making Bonney and his cohorts outlaws. This began the Lincoln County Wars.

One of only two known photographs of the infamous outlaw, Billy the Kid. (Library of Congress)

Escaping capture numerous times, the Kid, as he was now widely known, endeared himself to the local Mexican populations by stealing from the Irish ranchers and giving most of his spoils to the local Mexican villages. The Irish magnates soon turned to recently elected Sheriff Pat Garrett, a former compatriot of the Kid, to hunt down the outlaw. Garrett captured the Kid, but he once more escaped, killing two deputies in the process. On July 14, 1881, Garrett went to the home of Pete Maxwell, a friend of Billy's, to question him about the Kid's whereabouts. Unbeknown to Garrett (and possibly Maxwell), the Kid was there visiting one of his paramours, Pete's sister, Paulita. As legend has it, in the middle of the night, the Kid went to the kitchen unarmed. Hearing Pete talking to someone, the Kid opened the door and asked, "*Quien es*?" ("Who's there?"). Garrett fired, killing the Kid. Garrett buried his old friend the next day, taking no photographs or proof of what happened, and went on to publish his book, *The Authentic Life of Billy, the Kid*, in 1882. According to all accounts, numerous people witnessed the corpse and verified that it was Billy.

The country accepted Garrett's account of the outlaw's demise, and Billy remained a legend in popular culture for decades. Nearly seven decades later, in 1948, a Texas resident named Ollie "Brushy Bill" Roberts claimed to be the Kid and went to a local magistrate to seek a pardon from the New Mexico governor for the murders of Billy the Kid (as had once been promised to the Kid in a ruse to capture him). The local judge dismissed Roberts's claim, and Roberts died shortly after, leaving open the mystery of whether or not he was Billy the Kid. According to birth records, Brushy Bill was born in 1868, in Buffalo Gap, Texas, making him nine years younger than the Kid, but it is unclear whether the Kid may have stolen this identity. To date, numerous tests have been conducted and facial recognition software has been used to determine the actual grave of Billy the Kid, thus far to no definitive conclusion.

Billy the Kid has been a constant mainstay in American popular culture for 140 years. He has been the subject of twenty-two feature films to date, beginning in 1911 and most recently in the 2019 film *The Kid*. Perhaps his most memorable and popular portrayal was by the actor Emilio Estevez in the films *Young Guns* (1988) and *Young Guns II* (1990). While the debate over whether Billy the Kid was an outlaw or antihero will continue for time immemorable, during his life, by the strictest definition of the law, Billy the Kid was a villain: a thief, a murderer, and a fugitive from justice. He was, without question, a gunslinger, often for hire. Rather than as outlaw or antihero, perhaps the best way to define Billy the Kid would be to call him an antivillain: a bad guy who, from time to time, would do beneficent deeds.

Richard A. Hall

See also: Asajj Ventress, Bill/Snake Charmer, Boba Fett, Captain Hector Barbossa, Catwoman, Elle Driver/California Mountain Snake, Fish Mooney, General Custer, Geronimo, Joker, Loki, Negan/The Saviors, O-Ren Ishii/Cottonmouth, Pancho Villa, Tony Montana, Tony Soprano, Two-Face; *Thematic Essays*: "In the Beginning . . .": The Origins of Villains in the Western World, Tarantino and the Antivillain, The Pathos of Villainy: Getting to the Heart of Why Villains Went Bad.

Further Reading

Alsford, Mike. 2006. *Heroes & Villains*. Waco, TX: Baylor University Press.

Ashby, LeRoy. 2006. *With Amusement for All: A History of American Popular Culture since 1830*. Lexington: University Press of Kentucky.

Boggs, Johnny D. 2013. *Billy the Kid on Film: 1911–2012*. Jefferson, NC: McFarland.

Serena, Katie. 2018. "Brushy Bill Roberts: The Man Who Claimed to Be Billy the Kid." All That's Interesting. December 25, 2018. Updated January 17, 2019. Accessed June 29, 2019. https://allthatsinteresting.com/brushy-bill-roberts.

Wallis, Michael. 2007. *Billy the Kid: The Endless Ride*. New York: W. W. Norton.

Boba Fett

First Appearance:	*The Star Wars Holiday Special*, CBS (air date: November 17, 1978)
Creators:	George Lucas, Ralph McQuarrie, and Joe Johnston
Other Media:	Live-action feature films, CGI animated series, novels, and comic books
Primary Strength:	Hunting
Major Weakness:	Blind devotion to contracts
Weapons:	Blasters, wrist cables, flamethrower
Base of Operations:	Kamino (originally)
Key Allies:	Jango Fett (father), Aura Sing, Bossk, Dengar, Jabba the Hutt, Darth Vader
Key Enemies:	Mace Windu, Han Solo
Actual Identity:	N/A
Nicknames/Aliases:	"The Best Bounty Hunter in the Galaxy"

In 1977, writer and director George Lucas introduced the world to his iconic film *Star Wars*. The massive worldwide success of the original film has spawned numerous sequels, prequels, animated television series, made-for-TV movies, novels, and comic books. Set a "long time ago . . . in a galaxy far, far away," *Star Wars* tells a generational saga of a galaxy at war between the forces of good and evil. One of the most popular characters from this epic saga is the bounty hunter Boba Fett, first introduced in live-action form in the 1980 sequel, *Star Wars: The Empire Strikes Back* (episode five of the overall saga). Creator George Lucas gave a small taste of the character in an animated short that aired during the televised 1978 holiday special. In the decades since his inception, Boba Fett has come to define the ultimate antivillain in the *Star Wars* universe.

After Fett's debut in the holiday special (voiced by Don Francks) introduced him as a bounty hunter working for the evil Darth Vader, young fans were excited for his film debut. However, in his first feature film, *Star Wars: The Empire Strikes Back*, the mysterious bounty hunter speaks only five sentences (four to Vader and one instructing workers to place the frozen Han Solo in his ship). His only line in the following film, *Star Wars: Return of the Jedi* (1983), was a "Wilhelm Scream" (it is a scream of German man used decades ago in a film and frequently inserted in modern films when a scream is needed) as he fell to his apparent death in the Sarlacc pit on Tatooine (in both films, Fett was portrayed by Jeremy Bulloch).

Despite this, Boba Fett merchandise was among the best-selling of all *Star Wars* merch. In the expanded universe novels of the 1990s and 2000s, Fett is shown to have survived his fall and has numerous adventures until the 2012 purchase of Lucasfilm by Disney erased all expanded universe canon, placing the bounty hunter's fate once more in doubt.

Much of the character's popularity revolved around the mystery surrounding him. Similar to Clint Eastwood's "Man with No Name" from his spaghetti westerns of the 1960s and 1970s, or the comic book superhero Wolverine at Marvel Comics, Boba Fett's past was shrouded in mystery. Although he wears the armor of the Mandalorian race, it was never established in the films if Fett, himself, is Mandalorian or if Boba Fett is even his real name. The Marvel *Star Wars* comics had suggested he is a product of the mythical Clone Wars, which had been mentioned briefly in the original film but were never expanded on in the original trilogy (David Michelinie and Gene Day, *Star Wars, Vol. 1 #68*, February 1983).

In response to continued fan adoration, Lucas provided some backstory in his prequel trilogy. In *Star Wars, Episode II: Attack of the Clones* (2002), fans discovered that Boba is actually an unaltered clone of the bounty hunter Jango Fett; as a child, he witnesses the killing of his father by the Jedi knight Mace Windu. Fans would receive more of young Fett in the animated series *Star Wars: The Clone Wars* (2008–2014), where his connections to bounty hunters is shown to have continued beyond his father's death (Fett was portrayed by Daniel Logan in *Episode II*, and he voiced the character in *Clone Wars*). Although rumors continued of a possible Boba Fett movie, Lucasfilm head Kathleen Kennedy confirmed in 2018 that plans for a Boba Fett were, in fact, "dead" (White, "Star Wars: Kathleen Kennedy Confirms the Boba Fett Movie Is Dead).

Although Boba Fett is portrayed as a villain in the *Star Wars* films, it is only due to his employment by the villains Jabba the Hutt and Darth Vader. From the perspective of the character, if those he is hired to retrieve had done nothing wrong themselves, then he would not have been hired to retrieve them. He is a traditional bounty hunter, a gun for hire. He is seen as villainous because his bounty is the hero Han Solo. In the decanonized *Legacy of the Force* novels (2006–2008), an elderly Fett trains Jaina Solo, daughter of Han Solo and Princess Leia, to take down her brother-turned-villain, Jacen Solo/Darth Caedus. By that time, the villain had achieved antihero status.

Bounty hunters have gained a certain notoriety in American history due in large part to their pre–Civil War role in tracking down runaway slaves. They are seen as individuals who place more value on money than people. In the case of Han Solo, though a hero by the time of *Empire Strikes Back*, he had skipped out on a debt owed to the crime lord Jabba the Hutt. While the future of Boba Fett in *Star Wars* remains uncertain, it is believed that he will be, at the very least, mentioned in the streaming series *The Mandalorian* (2019–Present). Whether or not fans have seen the last of Boba Fett, his place in the history of *Star Wars* and among villains in American popular culture overall has already been cemented.

Richard A. Hall

See also: Asajj Ventress, Bill/Snake Charmer, Billy the Kid, The Comedian, Elle Driver/California Mountain Snake, Geronimo, Jabba the Hutt, Imperial Officers, Killmonger, O-Ren Ishii/Cottonmouth, Sith Lords, Tony Soprano; *Thematic Essays*: Tarantino and the Antivillain.

Further Reading

Alsford, Mike. 2006. *Heroes & Villains.* Waco, TX: Baylor University Press.

Ashby, LeRoy. 2006. *With Amusement for All: A History of American Popular Culture since 1830.* Lexington: University Press of Kentucky.

Eberl, Jason T., and Kevin S. Decker, eds. *The Ultimate Star Wars and Philosophy: You Must Unlearn What You Have Learned.* Hoboken, NJ: Wiley-Blackwell.

Jones, Brian Jay. 2016. *George Lucas: A Life.* New York: Little Brown & Company.

Kaminski, Michael. 2008. *The Secret History of Star Wars: The Art of Storytelling and the Making of a Modern Epic.* Kingston, ON, Canada: Legacy.

Reagin, Nancy R., and Janice Liedl, eds. *Star Wars and History.* New York: John Wiley & Sons.

Sunstein, Cass R. 2016. *The World According to Star Wars.* New York: Dey Street.

Taylor, Chris. 2015. *How Star Wars Conquered the Universe: The Past, Present, and Future of a Multibillion Dollar Franchise.* New York: Basic.

White, James. 2018. "*Star Wars*: Kathleen Kennedy Confirms the Boba Fett Movie Is Dead." Empire. October 28, 2018. Accessed January 23, 2019. https://www.empireonline.com/movies/news/star-wars-kathleen-kennedy-confirms-boba-fett-movie-dead/.

Borg Queen/Borg

First Appearance:	**Borg:** *Star Trek: The Next Generation*, season 2, episode 16 (air date: May 8, 1989) **Borg Queen:** *Star Trek: First Contact* (release date: November 22, 1996)
Creators:	Rick Sternbach (Designer of the Borg)
Other Media:	Novels, comics
Primary Strength:	Assimilation, hive mind
Major Weakness:	Disruption of the hive mind
Weapons:	Nanoprobes, laser/phaser (energy-based beam weaponry)
Base of Operations:	Delta Quadrant
Key Allies:	N/A
Key Enemies:	Captain Jean-Luc Picard, Lieutenant Commander Data, Captain Kathryn Janeway, United Federation of Planets, Species 8472
Actual Identity:	N/A
Nicknames/Aliases:	N/A

Star Trek is a popular science fiction franchise developed for television by Gene Roddenberry in 1966. It was originally set in the twenty-third century, when humanity has long been exploring deep space and Earth is a member of the United Federation of Planets. The original series has spawned an animated series, five sequel and prequel live-action series, and thirteen feature films to date. The first live-action spin-off series was *Star Trek: The Next Generation*, which debuted in syndication on September 28, 1987. The series, dubbed *TNG* by fans, focuses on the adventures of Captain Jean-Luc Picard and the crew of the *USS Enterprise-D* (making it the fifth Federation starship to bear the name).

In the second season of the series, the omnipotent being Q uses his powers to cast the *Enterprise* to the far reaches of space, introducing them to the species Borg, a hive-minded cybernetic race who relentlessly seek to assimilate other races into their collective (Maurice Hurley, "Q Who," *Star Trek: The Next Generation*, season 2, episode 16, May 8, 1989). Awareness of humanity leads the Borg to make their way to Federation space and become a seemingly unstoppable enemy and a constant threat freedom and individuality across the stars. At the end of the third season, the Borg arrived in Federation space, encounter the *Enterprise*, capture and assimilate Captain Picard, and give him a new identity: Locutus of Borg, the Borg's representative to the people of the Federation (Michael Piller, "The Best of Both Worlds, Parts 1 and 2," *Star Trek: The Next Generation*, season 3, episode 26 to season 4, episode 1, June 18, 1990, and September 24, 1990).

In 1996, the first feature film to present the *TNG* cast in their own movie, *Star Trek: First Contact*, was released. In this film, the Borg travel back to the late twenty-first century in an attempt to assimilate humanity before they reach the stars. Captain Picard, long since recovered from his attempted assimilation, leads the crew of the *Enterprise-E* back in time to stop them. During this adventure, Picard and his crew discover that the Borg have a leader, the Borg Queen (played by Alice Krige), a centralized, individual Borg controlling the entire hive (Brannon Braga and Ronald Moore, *Star Trek: First Contact*, November 22, 1996). The threat of the Borg and their queen would next be prominent on the series *Star Trek: Voyager* (UPN, 1995–2001), which featured the adventures of Captain Kathryn Janeway and the crew of the Federation starship *USS Voyager* trapped in the Delta Quadrant, tens of thousands of light-years from home.

In an attempt to gain free passage through Borg space on their way home, Captain Janeway agrees to assist the Borg in their fight against their enemy, Species 8472. This arrangement also gained *Voyager* a new crew member, Seven-of-Nine, a Borg female detached from the collective (Braga and Joe Menosky, "Scorpion, Parts 1 and 2," *Star Trek: Voyager*, season 3, episode 26 to season 4, episode 1, May 21, 1997, and September 3, 1997). In the series finale, Admiral Janeway, having long since made it home to Earth with most of her crew intact after twenty-three years in the Delta Quadrant, travels back through time and across the stars to engage in a battle of wits with the Borg Queen (once more portrayed by Krige) in order for *Voyager* to change history and come home more than fifteen years earlier with more of the crew intact (Rick Berman, Brannon Braga, and Kenneth Biller, "Endgame," *Star Trek: Voyager*, season 7, episodes 25–26, May 23, 2001).

On a list of TV's "nastiest" villains compiled in 2013 by *TV Guide*, the Borg were listed at number four ("TV Guide Picks TV's 60 Nastiest Villains," *TV Guide*). In the realm of science fiction, the Borg are similar in almost every way to the Cybermen of *Doctor Who*. Like the Cybermen, the Borg seek to assimilate other races and cultures into their own, strengthening themselves through numbers. This makes them similar to the communists in history, seeking to expand their influence through assimilation, making them different from the Nazis or the Daleks from *Doctor Who*, who seek racial purity through extermination of the other. The primary difference between Borg and Cybermen is the unifying leadership of the Borg Queen. Aside from her power as the centralizing authority of the hive, the Borg Queen also possesses the power of seduction, tempting any who would resist to join her in the collective. The blind single-minded ambition of the Leninist/Stalinist Borg Queen makes the Borg even more like the villainous Soviet communists so vilified in American culture.

Richard A. Hall

See also: Agent Smith, Alpha/The Whisperers, Brainiac, Captain Phasma/Stormtroopers, COBRA, The Court of Owls, Cybermen, Davros/Daleks, Doomsday, Ernst Stavro Blofeld/SPECTRE, Fish Mooney, Grand Nagus/Ferengi, Kahless/Klingons, Negan/The Saviors, Number Six/Cylons, Nurse Ratched, Q, Reverend Stryker/The Purifiers, Ultron; *Thematic Essays*: "Nazis, Communists, and Terrorists . . . Oh My!": The Rise of the Supervillain and the Evolution of the Modern American Villain, The Dark Mirror: Evil Twins, *The Twilight Zone*, and the Villain Within, The Pathos of Villainy: Getting to the Heart of Why Villains Went Bad.

Further Reading

Alsford, Mike. 2006. *Heroes & Villains*. Waco, TX: Baylor University Press.

Ashby, LeRoy. 2006. *With Amusement for All: A History of American Popular Culture since 1830*. Lexington: University Press of Kentucky.

Castleman, Harry, and Walter J. Podrazik. 2016. *Watching TV: Eight Decades of American Television*. 3rd ed. Syracuse, NY: Syracuse University Press.

Crome, Andrew, and James McGrath, eds. 2013. *Time and Relative Dimensions in Faith: Religion and Doctor Who*. London: Darton, Longman, and Todd.

Gross, Edward, and Mark A. Altman. 2016. *The Fifty-Year Mission, the First 25 Years: The Complete, Uncensored, Unauthorized Oral History of Star Trek*. New York: St. Martin's.

Gross, Edward, and Mark A. Altman. 2016. *The Fifty-Year Mission, the Next 25 Years: The Complete, Uncensored, Unauthorized Oral History of Star Trek*. New York: St. Martin's.

Kistler, Alan. 2013. *Doctor Who: Celebrating Fifty Years, a History*. Guilford, CT: Lyons.

Lewis, Courtland, and Paula Smithka, eds. 2010. *Doctor Who and Philosophy: Bigger on the Inside*. Chicago: Open Court.

Lewis, Courtland, and Paula Smithka, eds. 2015. *More Doctor Who and Philosophy: Regeneration Time*. Chicago: Open Court.

Reagin, Nancy R. 2013. *Star Trek and History*. Hoboken, NJ: John Wiley & Sons.

Rosenfeld, Gavriel D. 2014. *Hi Hitler!: How the Nazi Past Is Being Normalized in Contemporary Culture*. Cambridge: Cambridge University Press.

Rossinow, Doug. 2015. *The Reagan Era: A History of the 1980s*. New York: Columbia University Press.

"TV Guide Picks TV's 60 Nastiest Villains." 2013. *TV Guide*. April 22, 2013. Accessed January 1, 2019. http://wordsmithonia.blogspot.com/2013/04/tv-guide-picks-tvs-60-nastiest-villains.html.

Brainiac

First Appearance:	*Action Comics #242* (cover date: July, 1958)
Creators:	Otto Binder and Al Plastino
Other Media:	Animated and live-action television series, animated home video
Primary Strength:	Computer interaction
Major Weakness:	Computer interaction
Weapons:	Near-godlike intelligence, tendrils, shrinking ray, robot legions
Base of Operations:	Interstellar space
Key Allies:	N/A
Key Enemies:	Superman, Supergirl, Seg-El, Lyta-Zod, Adam Strange
Actual Identity:	Doctor/Professor Milton Fine (when in human form)
Nicknames/Aliases:	"The Terror of Kandor," "The Collector of Worlds"

The *Superman* franchise is one of the most successful in pop culture history. Created by the Jewish American team of writer Jerry Siegel and artist Joe Shuster, Superman is an alien named Kal-El, whose home world of Krypton was destroyed shortly after his birth. Aware of the impending doom, his parents placed him in a space capsule and sent him into space to save him. He landed in Smallville, Kansas, and was raised by Jonathan and Martha Kent under his adopted name, Clark Kent. On reaching adulthood, Clark discovered that he had "powers and abilities far beyond those of mortal men" and dedicated himself to protecting the world as Superman, the world's first superhero. Because of his near-godlike powers, his only weakness being Kryptonite (meteor fragments of his home world), Superman requires antagonists of particularly daunting abilities. One of the most formidable of these is Brainiac.

In 1958, readers were introduced to Brainiac. Over the years, Brainiac has had numerous interpretations, although he is usually presented as a humanoid with green skin, a bald head, and violet-colored nodules on his head. Essentially, at his core, Brainiac appears to be a cyborg, with both organic and inorganic components. Originally, he is described as being from the planet Bryak (sometimes,

Lobo

Lobo is a popular bounty hunter antihero/antivillain in DC Comics. Created by Roger Slifer and Keith Giffen, Lobo first appeared in *Omega Men #3* (June 1983). Lobo is an alien from the planet Czarnia who possesses enhanced strength and stamina (and, eventually, regenerative abilities). His name means "he who devours your entrails and thoroughly enjoys it." Arriving shortly after the rise of similar dark heroes and villains such as the Punisher and Wolverine at Marvel Comics, DC readers did not warm to the character as quickly.

He would return in his own series in the 1990s in response to the booming popularity of more violent heroes, an issue DC Comics touched upon in their landmark publication *Kingdom Come* by Mark Waid and Alex Ross in 1996. In DC Comics' "New 52" reboot, Lobo emerged as a slave trader who murdered his entire race (Rob Liefeld, *Deathstroke #9–12*, July–October 2012). In the "Rebirth" reboot, Lobo was returned to his original backstory, becoming a member of the Suicide Squad (Joshua Williamson and Jason Fabok, *Justice League vs. Suicide Squad #1–6*, February–March 2017). In 2019, the character was introduced into the second season of the SyFy cable television series *Krypton*, where he was portrayed by Emmett J. Scanlan. In all incarnations, Lobo strictly adheres to the contracts he makes with his clients. Gleefully enjoying gore-filled violence and murder, he is an unstoppable force of nature while on a hunt. He also enjoys hard drinking, vulgar language, and womanizing. His personality is reflected in his Earth-style motorcycle-gang-member clothing and accoutrements; he even rides a motorcycle-themed space cycle on his adventures. He is not a hero who occasionally crosses the line; he is a villain who, for the right price, will do good.

Richard A. Hall

however, referred to as "Colu," "Yod," or "Yod-Colu"), although, in some incarnations, he is Kryptonian. He travels the universe, miniaturizing cities from planets on the verge of destruction, placing them in bottles, and preserving them, with the side effect that he also now rules them. A key story line explains that he bottled the Kryptonian city of Kandor before the planet's destruction, essentially making Superman no longer the lone survivor of the doomed planet (Otto Binder and Al Plastino, *Action Comics #242*, July 1958). Numerous variations and alterations to the original concept developed over the decades. In 2011, as part of DC Comics' "New 52" reboot, Brainiac returned to his collecting modus operandi, with an intergalactic spacecraft larger than any planet and legions of drone spacecraft as well as his armies of robots.

On the television series *Smallville* (WB, 2001–2011), Brainiac is, in fact, the AI creation of Superman's father, Jor-El; "Brainiac" is an acronym for Brain InterActive Construct. Like Clark, he escaped Krypton, arriving on Earth in another spaceship, which was discovered roughly fifteen years after Clark's. Played on *Smallville* by James Marsters, Brainiac proves a near-indomitable foe for the up-and-coming Superman. In later seasons, he appears to Clark as Brainiac 5, a future, reprogrammed incarnation, working alongside the Legion of Superheroes in the thirty-first century. In 2018, yet another version of the character appeared on the SyFy cable network series *Krypton*. Once more the intergalactic collector of comic book origins, this version of Brainiac is portrayed by Blake Ritson and is pitted against Superman's grandfather, Seg-El.

Whether cyborg or robot, however, the artificial intelligence entity known as Brainiac has consistently proven to be one of Superman's most dangerous foes. Like the Borg of *Star Trek*, Brainiac sees his collection of species as beneficial to them, preserving cultures that would otherwise go completely extinct. Like Ultron of Marvel Comics, he is a computer that sees all organic life as faulty and in need of cyberenhanced evolution. As villains go, he represents modern man's ultimate fear: that our creations will one day destroy us, even if it is out of a benevolent intention of preserving us. The character has been further examined in the documentary, *Necessary Evil: Super-Villains of DC Comics*, directed by Scott Devine and J. M. Kenny (Warner Home Video, 2013).

Richard A. Hall

See also: Borg Queen/Borg, Cybermen, Davros/Daleks, Doctor Doom, Doomsday, Lex Luthor, Number Six/Cylons, Thanos, Ultron, Zod; *Thematic Essays*: "Nazis, Communists, and Terrorists . . . Oh My!": The Rise of the Supervillain and the Evolution of the Modern American Villain, The Pathos of Villainy: Getting to the Heart of Why Villains Went Bad.

Further Reading

Alsford, Mike. 2006. *Heroes & Villains*. Waco, TX: Baylor University Press.

Ashby, LeRoy. 2006. *With Amusement for All: A History of American Popular Culture since 1830*. Lexington: University Press of Kentucky.

Barker, Cory, Chris Ryan, and Myc Wiatrowski, eds. 2014. *Mapping Smallville: Critical Essays on the Series and Its Characters*. Jefferson, NC: McFarland.

Daniels, Les. 2004. *Superman: The Complete History—the Life and Times of the Man of Steel*. New York: DC Comics.

Loader, Paul. 2009. "Brainiac's Brain, Brainiac's Body." In *Supervillains and Philosophy: Sometimes, Evil Is Its Own Reward*, edited by Ben Dyer, 189–198. Chicago: Open Court.

Wright, Bradford W. 2003. *Comic Book Nation: The Transformation of Youth Culture in America*. Baltimore, MD: Johns Hopkins University Press.

Captain Hector Barbossa

First Appearance:	*Pirates of the Caribbean: The Curse of the Black Pearl* (release date: June 28, 2003)
Creators:	Ted Elliot, Terry Rossio, Stuart Beattie, and Jay Wolpert
Other Media:	Novels
Primary Strength:	Immortality (briefly)
Major Weakness:	Greed
Weapons:	Sword
Base of Operations:	*The Black Pearl*
Key Allies:	Jack (his monkey), crew of *The Black Pearl*
Key Enemies:	Captain Jack Sparrow, "Bootstrap" Bill Turner, Will Turner, Elizabeth Swan, Davy Jones, Calypso, British East India Company
Actual Identity:	N/A
Nicknames/Aliases:	N/A

In 2003, Disney launched its *Pirates of the Caribbean* film franchise, based loosely on the popular ride at their theme parks and set in the early 1700s. The first film, subtitled *The Curse of the Black Pearl,* introduced viewers to the antihero pirate Captain Jack Sparrow (played with overly exuberant glee by Johnny Depp) and his archnemesis, the pirate Captain Hector Barbossa (played with slithering charisma by Geoffrey Rush). The unexpected worldwide success of the first film led to four sequels: *Dead Man's Chest* (2006), *At World's End* (2007), *On Stranger Tides* (2011), and *Dead Men Tell No Tales* (2017). In 2018, Disney announced that it would be rebooting the franchise rather than commit to future films from the current saga.

As *The Curse of the Black Pearl* opens, Barbossa has been captain of the *Pearl* for ten years, having led a mutiny against her original captain, Jack Sparrow. In the interim, Barbossa and his crew stole some cursed Aztec gold. By the time they realize they have been cursed with being "living dead"—creatures that cannot die but also cannot experience the simple joys of real life—they have spent much of the treasure. Barbossa then leads his men on a quest to retrieve all of the gold to return it and lift their curse. The last piece is in the possession of Elizabeth Swan, the daughter of the British governor of the Caribbean colony of Port Royal. Swan had taken the coin as a child from the young Will Turner, son of "Bootstrap" Bill Turner, part of Sparrow's original crew. After succeeding in saving his crew, Barbossa is killed by Sparrow, who resumes command of the *Pearl* (Ted Elliot and Terry Rossio, *Pirates of the Caribbean: The Curse of the Black Pearl*, 2003).

Barbossa, however, is revived by the witch Tia Dalma, who, unknown to all, is really the sea goddess Calypso, and she then recruits him to assist in retrieving Sparrow from Davy Jones' Locker (Ted Elliot and Terry Rossio, *Pirates of the Caribbean: Dead Man's Chest*, 2006). Once they are successful, Barbossa calls together the Brethren Court, made up of the nine Pirate Lords, to unite against the power of the British East India Company (BEIC). After destruction of the BEIC fleet, Barbossa once more steals the *Pearl* from Sparrow intending to find the Fountain of Youth (Ted Elliot and Terry Rossio, *Pirates of the Caribbean: At World's End*, 2007).

Ten years later, Barbossa has lost the *Pearl*, and his right leg, to the dread pirate Blackbeard. Working off his crimes for the British Royal Navy, Barbossa teams with Sparrow to hunt down Blackbeard and find the Fountain of Youth. Barbossa kills Blackbeard, confiscates his ship as repayment for his leg, and once more hits the seas as a pirate (Ted Elliot and Terry Rossio, *Pirates of the Caribbean: On Stranger Tides*, 2011). Five years later, Barbossa is a commodore, commanding a fleet of pirate ships. He once more teams with Sparrow to defeat the undead pirate hunter Captain Armando Salazar, sacrificing his life in the process in order to save his daughter, Carina (Jeff Nathanson, *Pirates of the Caribbean: Dead Men Tell No Tales*, 2017). With Disney's previously discussed announcement concerning the franchise, this can be considered the end of Captain Barbossa's story.

Captain Hector Barbossa represents the stereotypical 1700s pirate, though with a supernatural twist. He travels the Seven Seas, commanding a crew of men with the sole mission of raping, pillaging, and stealing from whomever they encounter. Even after suffering a fate worse than death—existing as the undead—and later

Geoffrey Rush played Captain Hector Barbossa in the first five *Pirates of the Caribbean* movies. (Walt Disney Pictures/AF Archive/Alamy Stock Photo)

given the opportunity to make amends for his crimes as a legitimate sailor, Barbossa reverts to his criminal ways time and time again. His only moral compass is the pirate code, to which Barbossa adheres strictly when it suits him to do so. He possesses a clear addiction to the thrill of flouting authority and living by his own rules.

He also, however, represents the concept of honor among thieves, often placing his own self-interest aside for his crew; Will Turner; Elizabeth Swan; his daughter, Carina; and even—to the surprise of all—his archnemesis, Jack Sparrow. He is a villain with a streak of nobility, again consistent with the stereotype of early modern pirates. When compared to modern-day pirates—both literal and figurative—Barbossa may seem to lean more to the heroic, or antiheroic. However, that aspect of the character speaks more to the degrading of the concept of honor among thieves that, in the early 1700s, would not have been considered a positive characteristic. Captain Barbossa is a pirate as the twenty-first-century zeitgeist remembers them from three hundred years past.

Richard A. Hall

See also: Alexis Carrington-Colby-Dexter, Billy the Kid, Cersei Lannister, Fish Mooney, Geronimo, Goldfinger, Gus Fring, Heisenberg/Walter White, J. R. Ewing, Lex Luthor, Marsellus Wallace, Ozymandias, Pancho Villa, Tia Dalma/Calypso, Tony Montana, Tony Soprano; *Thematic Essays*: Tarantino and the Antivillain, The Pathos of Villainy: Getting to the Heart of Why Villains Went Bad.

Further Reading

Alsford, Mike. 2006. *Heroes & Villains.* Waco, TX: Baylor University Press.

Ashby, LeRoy. 2006. *With Amusement for All: A History of American Popular Culture since 1830.* Lexington: University Press of Kentucky.

Cavendish, Richard. 1968. *The Black Arts: A Concise History of Witchcraft, Demonology, Astrology, and Other Mystical Practices throughout the Ages.* New York: TarcherPerigree.

Cordingly, David. 2006. *Under the Black Flag: The Romance and the Reality of Life among the Pirates.* New York: Random House.

Woodard, Colin. 2007. *The Republic of Pirates: Being the True and Surprising Story of the Caribbean Pirates and the Man Who Brought Them Down.* Boston: Houghton Mifflin Harcourt.

Captain Phasma/Stormtroopers

First Appearance:	**Captain Phasma:** *Star Wars, Episode VII: The Force Awakens* (release date: December 18, 2015) **Stormtroopers:** *Star Wars: From the Adventures of Luke Skywalker* (publication date: November 12, 1976)
Creators:	**Captain Phasma:** J. J. Abrams and Lawrence Kasdan **Stormtroopers:** George Lucas

Other Media:	Novels, animated series, and comic books
Primary Strength:	Intimidation
Major Weakness:	Inability to accurately hit moving or stationary targets
Weapons:	Blasters
Base of Operations:	Death Star (Stormtroopers only), Starkiller Base, Imperial Fleet (Stormtroopers only), First Order Fleet, Imperial Outposts (Stormtroopers only)
Key Allies:	Darth Vader, Emperor Palpatine, Grand Moff Tarkin (Stormtroopers only), Kylo Ren, Supreme Leader Snoke, General Hux
Key Enemies:	Rebel Alliance (Stormtroopers only); Resistance
Actual Identity:	N/A
Nicknames/Aliases:	N/A

In 1977, writer and director George Lucas introduced the world to his iconic film *Star Wars*. The massive worldwide success of the original film has spawned numerous sequels, prequels, animated television series, made-for-TV movies, novels, and comic books. Set a "long time ago . . . in a galaxy far, far away," *Star Wars* tells a generational saga of a galaxy at war between the forces of good and evil. From the very opening shots of the original film, Stormtroopers were the frightening, faceless, nameless shock troops of the Galactic Empire, doing the bidding of the evil Emperor Palpatine and his chief henchman, Darth Vader. Their name invokes mental images of the shock troops of Adolf Hitler in Nazi Germany. In the sequel trilogy that began with *Episode VII: The Force Awakens*, Stormtroopers were finally given a singular, overall commander: Captain Phasma.

Emperor Palpatine came to power first as Chancellor Palpatine of the Galactic Republic, similar, again, in many ways to how Adolf Hitler advanced to rule Germany. At the time of Palpatine's transition from elected leader to absolute ruler, the republic was protected by a Clone Army. These nameless legions were clones of the bounty hunter, Jango Fett (George Lucas, *Star Wars, Episode II: Attack of the Clones*, 2002). At some point during the devolution from republic to empire, these clones were slowly replaced with volunteers and draftees—Clone Troopers became Stormtroopers. With their white armor and black eye lenses, their ghostly appearance stands as a staunch juxtaposition of Darth Vader's all-black armor. Although the crux of the original trilogy focuses on Vader, logistically in order for Princess Leia and her rebellion to truly defeat the empire, they must battle legions upon legions of Stormtroopers.

After the events of 1983's *Return of the Jedi*, it was assumed that the threat of the empire—and, therefore, Stormtroopers—was over. However, by *Episode VII*, set thirty years after the events of *Return of the Jedi*, a new threat has arisen to strike fear in that galaxy far, far away: the First Order. Led by the mysterious Supreme Leader Snoke, this new empire requires a new, and different, generation of Stormtroopers. Rather than clones or volunteers, the First Order Stormtroopers are taken at birth and programmed to be obedient foot soldiers for the First Order. Like previous generations of troopers, the new Stormtroopers are given alphanumeric designations rather than names. One such trooper, FN-2187, resists his programming on his first combat mission, escaping the First Order and joining the new resistance as Finn. This new generation of Stormtroopers has a clearly designated head trooper in Captain Phasma (J. J. Abrams and Lawrence Kasdan, *Star Wars, Episode VII: The Force Awakens*, 2015).

Phasma is a woman warrior from the planet Parnassos. According to the 2017 novel, *Star Wars: Phasma* by Delilah S. Dawson, after assisting First Order general Hux, who crashed on the planet, she is offered a position with the First Order. Phasma stands out from her legions not only by her towering height but also by her chrome-colored armor, as opposed to the standard Stormtrooper white, and flowing cape. She is captured by Finn, Han Solo, and Chewbacca during their secret raid to disable the shields of Starkiller Base and is allegedly thrown into a trash compactor before the planet base is destroyed (J. J. Abrams and Lawrence Kasdan, *The Force Awakens*, 2015). Although she is believed dead, Finn encounters her again aboard the Star Destroyer *Supremacy*, after his failed mission to disable its tracking device. Phasma falls to her death, presumably, during her battle with Finn (Rian Johnson, *Star Wars, Episode VIII: The Last Jedi*, 2017).

The purpose of both Imperial and First Order Stormtroopers, and Captain Phasma as well, is to act as simple shock troops, automaton pawns utilized to enforce and defend the actions of their respective imperious masters. Like the Nazi Stormtroopers of German history, they are villainous due to their blind loyalty and seemingly endless numbers. Some, however, like Finn, show that they need not be blindly loyal. Some can break their programming and find redemption. The vast number, however, are forever trapped, both by their programming and their fear of reprisal for insubordination. They represent the unstoppable force, and they underscore the sacrifice necessary to protect freedom and liberty in any galaxy.

Richard A. Hall

See also: Alpha/The Whisperers, Boba Fett, Borg Queen/Borg, Cybermen, Davros/Daleks, Fish Mooney, Imperial Officers, Jabba the Hutt, Number Six/Cylons, Nurse Ratched, Sith Lords; *Thematic Essays*: "Nazis, Communists, and Terrorists . . . Oh My!": The Rise of the Supervillain and the Evolution of the Modern American Villain, The Pathos of Villainy: Getting to the Heart of Why Villains Went Bad.

Further Reading

Alsford, Mike. 2006. *Heroes & Villains*. Waco, TX: Baylor University Press.

Eberl, Jason T., and Kevin S. Decker, eds. *The Ultimate Star Wars and Philosophy: You Must Unlearn What You Have Learned.* Hoboken, NJ: Wiley-Blackwell.

Jones, Brian Jay. 2016. *George Lucas: A Life*. New York: Little Brown & Company.

Kaminski, Michael. 2008. *The Secret History of Star Wars: The Art of Storytelling and the Making of a Modern Epic.* Kingston, ON, Canada: Legacy.

Reagin, Nancy R., and Janice Liedl, eds. *Star Wars and History.* New York: John Wiley & Sons.

Sunstein, Cass R. 2016. *The World According to Star Wars.* New York: Dey Street.
Taylor, Chris. 2015. *How Star Wars Conquered the Universe: The Past, Present, and Future of a Multibillion Dollar Franchise.* New York: Basic.

Catwoman

First Appearance:	*Batman #1* (cover date: June 1940)
Creators:	Bill Finger and Bob Kane
Other Media:	Animated and live-action television series, movies
Primary Strength:	Stealth, hand-to-hand combat, acrobatics
Major Weakness:	Affection for Batman
Weapons:	Whip
Base of Operations:	Gotham City
Key Allies:	Batman, Gotham City Sirens, Birds of Prey, Female Furies
Key Enemies:	Batman
Actual Identity:	Selina Kyle
Nicknames/Aliases:	"The Cat," Irena Dubrovna

The *Batman* franchise is, perhaps, second only to *Superman* in regard to its impact on popular culture. Created by writer Bill Finger and artist Bob Kane, Batman is billionaire playboy Bruce Wayne, who, after witnessing a mugger murder his parents when he was a young boy, vowed to dedicate his life battling crime in his hometown of Gotham City. In order to strike fear in criminals, Wayne chose to disguise himself as a bat, and "the Batman" (originally "Bat-Man") was born (Bill Finger and Bob Kane, *Detective Comics #33*, November 1939). Unlike his counterpart Superman, Batman is a mere mortal, with no "super" powers of any kind. Instead, Batman is armed only with his keen intellect and a myriad of gadgets and vehicles that he uses in his fight against crime. Over the decades, in comics as well as on television and film, Batman has gained arguably the most impressive rogues' gallery of villains in all of popular culture. One of the earliest—and, therefore, longest lasting—is Catwoman.

Catwoman is Selina Kyle, a particularly skilled cat burglar. When she debuted in 1940, she was referred to only as "the Cat," clad originally in a full-length purple dress and cat mask. Her iconic skintight black costume emerged in the campy 1960s *Batman* television series, which starred Adam West as Batman and Burt Ward as Robin, the Boy Wonder. In the series and corresponding theatrical release, Catwoman was portrayed by three actresses: Julie Newmar in the first two seasons of the series, Lee Meriwether in the theatrical release, and African American singer/actress Eartha Kitt in the third and final season of the show. For these first live-action appearances, all three actresses chose to include a recurring purring in their speech and sexually suggestive movements meant to tempt the

Caped Crusader. From time to time over the decades, Catwoman has stepped away from her criminal behavior to become a temporary ally to the Dark Knight Detective.

In 1987, as part of the "Batman: Year One" story line, Selina's backstory was reimagined, making her a sex worker who is inspired by the new bat vigilante to take on her own secret identity and start a new career as a cat burglar (Frank Miller and David Mazzucchelli, *Batman #404*, February 1987). Her next live-action appearance was in the 1992 film *Batman Returns*, where she was portrayed by Michelle Pfeiffer. In this incarnation, Selina is a meek secretary to an evil businessman who discovers that she has overheard his conversation of his criminal activities and seemingly kills her. When she is revived by an army of stray cats, she emerges a more aggressive and confident woman, donning the role of Catwoman to take vengeance on the world that had mistreated her. She falls in love with Bruce Wayne but ultimately falls victim to her growing insanity and seemingly dies again, although the final shot of the film shows her silhouette against the Gotham skyline (Daniel Waters and Sam Hamm, *Batman Returns*, Warner Brothers, director Tim Burton, 1992). Both in comics and the historic *Batman: The Animated Series* (FOX, 1992–1997) and later Saturday-morning cartoon *The Batman* (FOX-Kids, 2004–2008), Catwoman remained both enemy and occasional ally to Batman, with their relationship constantly revolving from sexual tension to outright romance.

In the much-derided 2004 film *Catwoman*, Halle Berry played a different incarnation of the character altogether. Berry's Catwoman was professional artist Patience Phillips. Like Selina in *Batman Returns*, Patience is meek, accidentally overhears criminal activity, is murdered, and is revived by a stray cat. The revived Patience, again like the previous film version, is more assertive and in possession of catlike reflexes. This Catwoman is a standard vigilante, with no connection to cat burglary or crime in any way. Unconnected to the *Batman* franchise or the Selina identity, the film was panned by critics and fans alike.

The next film version of the character was in the 2012 movie *The Dark Knight Rises*, directed by Christopher Nolan. Oozing with sexual charisma, this Selina, never referred to as "Catwoman" although she dons the familiar catlike leotard and ears, is played by Anne Hathaway, and once more she is a cat burglar-turned-ally to Christian Bale's Batman. The most recent live-action Catwoman has appeared on the television series *Gotham* (FOX, 2014–2019). Played by newcomer Camren Bicondova, this preteen Selina Kyle is a street criminal who witnesses the murder of Bruce Wayne's parents; she becomes a close friend and an on-again, off-again love interest to the young Bruce Wayne. By the end of the series, she emerges as the Catwoman, choosing a life of crime over a life with Bruce. Recently, in the comics, the decades-long on-and-off romance between Batman and Catwoman appeared to come to a happy ending with the impending nuptials of the couple. However, Catwoman chooses in the end to leave Batman at the altar, having been convinced that a happy Batman would be a useless Batman and that Gotham needed the Dark Knight more than she did (Tom King, *Batman #50*, July 2018).

Throughout her long and storied history, Catwoman has remained a burglar, unlike the myriad male murderers who usually require Batman's attention. Her

Anne Hathaway played Selina Kyle (aka Catwoman) in the 2012 film *The Dark Knight Rises*. (Warner Bros. Pictures/TCD/Prod.DB/Alamy Stock Photo)

villainy, then, never rises beyond that of basic larceny. However, her thirst for the adventure and excitement of getting away with complex crimes keeps her forever tied to the wrong side of the law and, therefore, Batman. Although she has frequently, especially in modern times, played the role of reluctant hero, her heart will always be on the side of the villain. In a society that still, to a large degree, expects women to take a lesser role, Catwoman remains a symbol of complete independence: from men, from the norms of society, and from the confines of the law. The character has been further examined in the documentary *Necessary Evil: Super-Villains of DC Comics*, directed by Scott Devine and J. M. Kenny (Warner Home Video, 2013).

Richard A. Hall

See also: Alexis Carrington-Colby-Dexter, Borg Queen/Borg, Dr. Frank-N-Furter, Elle Driver/California Mountain Snake, Faith the Vampire Slayer, Fiona Goode/The Supreme, Fish Mooney, Harley Quinn, Joker, The Master/Missy, Morgan le Fay, Number Six/Cylons, Nurse Ratched, O-Ren Ishii/Cottonmouth, Pancho Villa, Poison Ivy, Scarecrow, Tia Dalma/Calypso, Two-Face; *Thematic Essays*: The Dark Mirror: Evil Twins, *The Twilight Zone*, and the Villain Within, The Pathos of Villainy: Getting to the Heart of Why Villains Went Bad.

Further Reading

Alsford, Mike. 2006. *Heroes & Villains*. Waco, TX: Baylor University Press.

Ashby, LeRoy. 2006. *With Amusement for All: A History of American Popular Culture since 1830*. Lexington: University Press of Kentucky.

Beard, Jim, ed. 2010. *Gotham City 14 Miles: 14 Essays on Why the 1960s Batman TV Series Matters*. Edwardsville, IL: Sequart Research & Literacy Organization.

Douglas, Susan J. 1995. *Where the Girls Are: Growing Up Female with the Mass Media.* New York: Three Rivers.

Faludi, Susan. 2007. *The Terror Dream: Myth and Misogyny in an Insecure America.* New York: Picador.

Heldenfels, Richard. 2020. "The Bat, the Cat . . . and the Eagle?: Irene Adler as Inspiration for Catwoman." In *The Supervillain Reader*, edited by Rob Weiner and Rob Peaslee, 146–155. Jackson: University of Mississippi Press.

Langley, Travis. 2012. *Batman and Psychology: A Dark and Stormy Knight.* New York: John Wiley & Sons.

O'Neil, Dennis, ed. 2008. *Batman Unauthorized: Vigilantes, Jokers, and Heroes in Gotham City.* Smart Pop Series. Dallas, TX: BenBella.

Stuller, Jennifer K. 2010. *Ink-Stained Amazons and Cinematic Warriors: Superwomen in Modern Mythology.* London: I. B. Tauris.

Weldon, Glen. 2016. *The Caped Crusade: Batman and the Rise of Nerd Culture.* New York: Simon & Schuster.

Wright, Bradford W. 2003. *Comic Book Nation: The Transformation of Youth Culture in America.* Baltimore, MD: Johns Hopkins University Press.

Cersei Lannister

First Appearance:	*A Game of Thrones* (publication date: August 1, 1996)
Creators:	George R. R. Martin
Other Media:	Song, poems, movies, games, and TV shows
Primary Strength:	Cunning
Major Weakness:	Blind Ambition
Weapons:	N/A
Base of Operations:	Westeros
Key Allies:	Jaime Lannister, Qyburn, Euron Greyjoy, House of Lannister, and House of Baratheon of King's Landing, Houses: Payne, Swyft, Mrbrand, Lyndden, Lefford, Crakehall, Serrett, Broom, Clegane, Prester, and Westerling
Key Enemies:	House of Tyrells
Actual Identity:	N/A
Nicknames/Aliases:	"Protector of the Realm," "Protector of the Seven Kingdoms," "Lady Paramount of the Westerlands," "Lady of Casterly Rock," "Light of the West," "Queen Dowager," "Queen Reagent," "Queen of the Seven Kingdoms," "Queen of the Andals," "The First Man"

George R. R. Martin introduced the world to his fantasy epic, *A Song of Ice and Fire*, with the series' first novel, *A Game of Thrones*, in 1996. Similar in many ways to Tolkien's Middle-earth, the world of *Ice and Fire* is very much like our world and yet very different as well. There are kings, queens, nobles, and dragons. The drama begins with the unexpected death of the king of the Seven Kingdoms, Robert Baratheon. The throne then falls to his heir, his (presumed) son, Joffrey. The succeeding narratives follow the political intrigue into who should sit on the Iron Throne as the true ruler of the realms. The massive success of the series led to a television adaptation, the acclaimed series *Game of Thrones* (HBO, 2011–2019). One of the key antagonists of the book and television series is King Joffrey's mother, Cersei.

Cersei, from the House of Lannister, is described as a beautiful woman, of fair skin, emerald eyes, and golden hair. She becomes queen to King Robert Baratheon (the seventeenth ruler of the Seven Kingdoms). The oldest child and only daughter to Tywin and Joanne Lannister, she is also the twin sister to Jaime Lannister, called "the King Slayer" for his assassination of the Mad King. Their father noted in *Clash of Kings* (1998, the second novel of the series) that they look so much alike that he could not tell them apart when they were children. Their mother died when they were four years old, after giving birth to their youngest brother, Tyrion Lannister, whom Cersei always blamed for her mother's death and described as a monster and a beast. Her father secured her position of power through his personal fortune by restoring the profitability of gold mining and making the house of Lannister one of the wealthiest in Westeros. When King Baratheon needed economic support to secure the throne, he agreed to married Cersei Lannister. She had three children, fathered by her twin brother, Jaime Lannister: Joffrey Baratheon, Myrcella Baratheon, and Tommen Baratheon. In the TV series, she is played by Lena Headey and Nell Williams (as child).

Cersei Lannister has been described by others in *Game of Thrones*, *Dance with Dragons* (2011, the fifth novel of the series), and *Clash of Kings* as a female version of her father: ambitious, cunning, power hungry, astute, and greedy. In combination with the HBO series, she can be said to represent two of the archetypes of the fantasy genre: shadow queen and mother (Patel, "Expelling a Monstrous Matriarchy"; Jones, "A Game of Genders"). She has become perhaps the most powerful and feared villain in the story, but only after the HBO adaptation by David Benioff and D. B. Weiss made some changes to her character. In the beginning of the novels, all the audience knows about Cersei is from the point of view of other characters. In many ways, the audience only observes the shadow part, the villain, through the eyes of the victims of her actions. Insight into her own point of view does not truly appear until *A Feast for Crows*, the fourth book in the series, which offers several chapters from different character's perspectives.

It has been argued that the TV show made Cersei more empathetic, stronger, and less temperamental (Jones, "A Game of Genders"). Because of this, Cersei in the book can be perceived as more of a typical female villain. By giving her a voice of her own, the TV series allowed audiences to empathize with her and provided rationalization for her evil. These scenes are either not present in the books or modified for the TV audience. In season one, episode three, Cersei is nurturing her son Joffrey's wounds from a bite from the wolf Nymeria, belonging to Arya Stark, which shows her motherly side. As part of the scene, she shows her shadow

Lena Headey played Cersei Lannister in the HBO series *Game of Thrones*. (PictureLux/ The Hollywood Archive/Alamy Stock Photo)

or dark side when she encourages her son to lie and ensures him that soon the world will be as "he deems it to be." This can be viewed as a twisted form of motherhood, whereas it may be an attempt grow closer to her child or to allow her son to view her as an advisor, a kind of ally, and therefore retain some level of power. In season one, episode five, there is an honest conversation between Cersei and King Baratheon about strategy and hate and the way that hate unites them and allows the kingdom to stay together. These do not happen in the novel. They present Cersei at the same level of men in a world historically dominated by men.

Some of the show's changes give Cersei a more impactful presence. Cersei loses a baby fathered by King Baratheon. In the season one, episode two of the show, she says that the baby died after battling a fever; to Lady Catelyn, Ned Stark's wife, she presents the loss as a traumatic event and attempts empathy towards Bran Starks's tragic fall and expected death, even after it was Cersei and Jaime who are responsible for the fall, which Lady Catelyn does not know. In the novel, the baby is purposely aborted with Moon Tea as to safeguard the bloodline (George R. R. Martin, *Game of Thrones*, chapter 45). In one scene, Ned Stark confronts Cersei about the parentage of the children, and they have a conversation in which they discuss King Baratheon hitting her. In season one, episode two of the TV show, Cersei insinuates that it only happened once, but in the book, she notes that it has happened before but never in the face (George R. R. Martin, *Game of Thrones*, chapter 45).

The changes in the show make her empathetic and emphasize her motherly dimension, but they also show her shadow side. She becomes the face of evil through complicated schemes, sadism, temperamental violent reactions, pretenses of family protection, consolidation of power, and payback. Some of the very evil scenes in both the book and the TV series include slaying Sansa's wolf, Lady, because Nymeria could not be found; drowning Melara (her childhood friend) because she dares to dream of marrying Jamie; killing all of King Baratheon's illegitimate children; buying the testimony of Shae, Tyrion's love, to frame him for King Joffrey's assassination; massacring the Baelor; beheading Missandei—a slave interpreter freed by Daeneryes—in front of Daenerys; and forcing Ellaria from the house Martell to watch her daughter perish in front of her in pain while both are tied up and she is unable to do anything about it.

A fortune teller from Lannisport, Maggy the Frog, shows important elements of Cersei's character. She allows Cersei three questions, which result in three prophecies. First, Cersei asks about being queen, and Maggy tells her, "Queen you shall be (for a time) . . . until there comes another, younger and more beautiful, to cast you down and take all you hold dear." Second, she asks about having children with the king, to which the response is, "Six-and-Ten for him, and three for you. Gold shall be their crowns and gold their shrouds." Finally, Cersei asks about her death and is told, "When your tears have drowned you, the valonqar shall wrap his hands about your pale white throat and choke the life from you" (George R. R. Martin, *A Feast of Crows*, chapter 36; *Game of Thrones*, season 5, episode 1, April 12, 2015). It is said that these are the prophecies that influence the character the most; she seems keep them in mind as elements to consider in the Game of Thrones, and in attempting to prevent them, she brings her fate to pass.

An analysis of her villainy raises many questions about Cersei. Did her gender, her position within the realm, and her relationships reveal perceived limits to the parameters of her actions? In other words, is Cersei a villain? The intentions of Cersei's actions around power, greed, and pride make her a villain to remember because of the way she uses fear, violent retaliation, manipulation for the sake of self-gain or survival, and murder and massacre. These actions leave a memory of horror and tangibly represent her shadow, her dark side, her villainy. However, these are also necessary to set the stage for the heroic. As such, she is a villain in that she expresses those characteristics that modern society has deemed to be villainous, such as greed, lust, and envy. These traits are not gender exclusive, but Western society has deemed such behavior from a woman to be eviler than when done by men, who might simply be described as "ambitious." Through Cersei, then, audiences see a woman playing a "man's" game in a "man's" world and doing it just as successfully . . . if not more so.

Maria Antonieta Reyes

See also: Alexis Carrington-Colby-Dexter, Angelique Bouchard-Collins, Borg Queen/Borg, The Corleone Family, The Court of Owls, Fiona Goode/The Supreme, Fish Mooney, Loki, Sherry Palmer, Sue Sylvester, Ursula; *Thematic Essays*: The Pathos of Villainy: Getting to the Heart of Why Villains Went Bad.

Further Reading

Clapton, William, and Laura J. Shepherd. 2017. "Lessons from Westeros: Gender and Power in *Game of Thrones*." *Politics* 37, no. 1: 5–18.

Craven, Bruce. 2019. *Win or Die: Leadership Secrets from Game of Thrones*. New York: Thomas Dunne.

Jones, Rebecca. 2012. "A Game of Genders: Comparing Depictions of Empowered Women between A Game of Thrones Novel and Television Series." *Journal of Student Research* 1, no. 3: 14–21.

Patel, C. 2014. "Expelling a Monstrous Matriarchy: Casting Cersei Lannister as Abject in *A Song of Ice and Fire*." *Journal of European Popular Culture* 5, no. 2: 135–147.

Silverman, Eric J., and Robert Arp, eds. 2017. *The Ultimate Game of Thrones and Philosophy: You Think or Die*. Chicago: Open Court.

COBRA

First Appearance:	*G. I. Joe: A Real American Hero* Toy Line (release date: summer 1982)
Creators:	Larry Hama
Other Media:	Animated TV series, comic books, live-action films
Primary Strength:	Seemingly endless financial resources
Major Weakness:	Ineptitude
Weapons:	Military-grade weapons and vehicles
Base of Operations:	Various
Key Allies:	Destro, Zartan, Drednoks
Key Enemies:	G. I. Joe
Actual Identity:	N/A
Nicknames/Aliases:	Cobra Command

G. I. Joe is a popular toy, comic book, and animated television series line from the Hasbro toy company. The original 12-inch dolls were the brainchild of Stan Weston in 1963, who sold the idea to Hasbro. In 1964, the initial line of Joes was launched, with one representing each branch of U.S. military service. In the 1970s, a black Joe and a nurse were introduced, as well as the legendary kung-fu grip. By the end of the 1970s, boys' preferences shifted to the smaller 3.75-inch action figures made famous by the *Star Wars* line. In 1982, Hasbro relaunched the line with the assistance of Marvel Comics; this time it had a series of 3.75-inch figures and rebranded *G. I. Joe* as an elite team of U.S. servicemen and -women organized to fight the international terrorist organization COBRA. Designed by Marvel Comics writer Larry Hama, COBRA was initially led by the mysterious masked Cobra Commander; his weapons manufacturer, Destro; and the field commander of COBRA forces, Major Bludd.

Cobra Commander was an egomaniacal dictator with delusions of grandeur, his plans to thwart G. I. Joe are consistently examples of reach exceeding one's grasp.

Over time, Destro organized a coup to create a new commander with his love interest/COBRA spy the Baroness; COBRA chief scientist, Dr. Mindbender; COBRA corporate executives; twin brothers Tomax and Xamot; and the mercenary Zartan. The new commander was born from combining the DNA of some of history's most famous warriors—Alexander the Great, Attila the Hun, Vlad Dracula, Genghis Khan, Hannibal, Julius Caesar, and Napoleon—to create the new COBRA emperor, Serpentor. This relegated Cobra Commander to second-in-command status (Buzz Dixon and Larry Hama, *Arise, Serpentor, Arise!*, 1986). Unfortunately for COBRA and the members of the coup, Serpentor proved even more egomaniacal and unstable than Cobra Commander. COBRA's constant lack of proper and loyal leadership proved its primary weakness against the more disciplined and dedicated G. I. Joe.

The COBRA organization consisted of numerous branches. Destro controlled the weapons manufacturing branch, while Doctor Mindbender oversaw the organization's scientific research. In response to the growing real-world stigma of criminality on the part of corporate America, Marvel and Hama created a corrupt corporate branch of COBRA, Extensive Enterprises, under the direction of twin brothers Tomax and Xamot and their private army of elite Crimson Guard soldiers. Mindbender and Destro eventually created an army of android warriors called Battle Android Troopers (or BATs). As the toy line demanded more and more new figures, Hama and his team developed more COBRA personalities, including Storm Shadow (a ninja), Zartan (a mercenary and leader of the Drednoks), and Firefly (a saboteur/demolitions expert).

In 1987, it was shown that Cobra Commander was actually a fugitive of the mystical land of Cobra-La, a civilization of mutated life-forms combining human and animal traits. The leader of Cobra-La had sent his greatest scientist, Cobra Commander, to go into the world and conquer it, reclaim the planet for Cobra-La, and eliminate the human species. Cobra Commander, however, became greedy, seeking out his own personal quest to rule (Buzz Dixon and Ron Friedman, *G. I. Joe: The Movie*, Nelson Entertainment, 1987). Far less successful than the animated *Transformers* theatrical release the same year, *G. I. Joe: The Movie* signaled the beginning of the end of the animated series and a severe downturn in comic book sales. In the decades since, numerous attempts have been made to revitalize the franchise, including two live-action feature films from Paramount Pictures: *G. I. Joe: The Rise of Cobra* (2009) and *G. I. Joe: Retaliation* (2013), the latter starring Bruce Willis and Dwayne "the Rock" Johnson. To date, however, nothing has returned the franchise to the popularity it enjoyed in the 1980s.

In the opening credits to the 1980s animated series, COBRA is described as "a ruthless terrorist organization determined to rule the world." Then, international terrorism was only beginning to be an issue that concerned Americans. From 1979 to 1981, fifty-two Americans were held hostage by the nation of Iran. Throughout the 1980s, numerous small terrorist organizations hijacked international passenger flights. The idea of an organized international hierarchical terrorist group was still years away in the real world. As such, COBRA represented a precursor to later groups like Al-Qaeda or ISIS. The key difference, other than the fantastical personalities associated with COBRA, was motivation. Whereas

Al-Qaeda and ISIS represent terrorist organizations based on a fundamentalist interpretation of religion, COBRA conducted its activities on the basis of power and wealth alone. In the panorama of popular culture, COBRA represents the organized army that poses a threat not only to a specified protagonist but also to society as a whole.

Richard A. Hall

See also: Alpha/The Whisperers, Billy the Kid, Borg Queen/Borg, Captain Phasma/Stormtroopers, The Corleone Family, The Court of Owls, Cybermen, Davros/Daleks, Ernst Stavro Blofeld/SPECTRE, Geronimo, Grand Nagus/Ferengi, Negan/The Saviors, Number Six/Cylons, Pancho Villa, Red Skull; *Thematic Essays*: "Nazis, Communists, and Terrorists . . . Oh My!": The Rise of the Supervillain and the Evolution of the Modern American Villain, The Dark Mirror: Evil Twins, *The Twilight Zone*, and the Villain Within.

Further Reading

Alsford, Mike. 2006. *Heroes & Villains.* Waco, TX: Baylor University Press.

Ashby, LeRoy. 2006. *With Amusement for All: A History of American Popular Culture since 1830.* Lexington: University Press of Kentucky.

Beard, Jim. 2018. *The Joy of Joe: Memories of America's Movable Fighting Man from Today's Grown-Up Kids.* N.p.: CreateSpace.

Bellomo, Mark. 2018. *The Ultimate Guide to G. I. Joe: 1982–1994.* 3rd ed. Iola, WI: Krause.

Castleman, Harry, and Walter J. Podrazik. 2016. *Watching TV: Eight Decades of American Television.* 3rd ed. Syracuse, NY: Syracuse University Press.

Howe, Sean. 2012. *Marvel Comics: The Untold Story.* New York: Harper-Perennial.

Rosenfeld, Gavriel D. 2014. *Hi Hitler!: How the Nazi Past Is Being Normalized in Contemporary Culture.* Cambridge: Cambridge University Press.

Rossinow, Doug. 2015. *The Reagan Era: A History of the 1980s.* New York: Columbia University Press.

Stevens, J. Richard. 2020. "Making America Great Again, You Foolsssss: Neoliberal Snake Charmers in Marvel's *G. I. Joe: A Real American Hero*." In *The Supervillain Reader*, edited by Rob Weiner and Rob Peaslee, 288–299. Jackson: University of Mississippi Press.

The Comedian

First Appearance:	*Watchmen #1* (cover date: September, 1986)
Creators:	Alan Moore and Dave Gibbons
Other Media:	Motion comics, live-action film
Primary Strength:	Advanced marksmanship, advanced hand-to-hand combat
Major Weakness:	Greed, lust
Weapons:	Military-grade weapons
Base of Operations:	Various
Key Allies:	The Watchmen

Key Enemies:	Moloch, Viet-Cong
Actual Identity:	Eddie Blake
Nicknames/Aliases:	N/A

In 1986, writer Alan Moore and artist Dave Gibbons produced the groundbreaking comic book miniseries/graphic novel *Watchmen.* In this twelve-issue series, Moore examines how if superheroes existed in the real world, they would prove to be extremely flawed and possibly psychologically disturbed individuals. In the premier issue, the story begins with the murder of retired hero and government agent Eddie Blake, "the Comedian" (Alan Moore and Dave Gibbons, *Watchmen #1,* September 1986). The mystery is soon taken up by fellow former hero Rorschach, himself a deeply disturbed individual. As the story unfolds, readers become aware that the Comedian was more villainous than most of his enemies; a heartless murderer and rapist, in flashback scenes from the 2009 film, he is shown to be responsible for the assassination of President John F. Kennedy. His part in the assassination is suggested in the original comic, along with the suggestions that he also killed Watergate investigating reporters Woodward and Bernstein and rescued the American hostages held in Iran in 1979 (Alan Moore and Dave Gibbons, *Watchmen #1–12,* September 1986–October 1987).

Although the series is set in 1985, Moore's narrative reveals the history of superheroes in his fictional America since World War II. In these flashbacks, the

Alan Moore

Alan Moore (b. 1953) is a legendary comic book writer. Born in Northampton, England, Moore grew up poor and had low-paying jobs before discovering his gift for writing, an outlet for his own anarchist political leanings. His first major success was with the serial *V for Vendetta* (1980), which appeared in the British periodical *Warrior* magazine. In 1983, DC Comics editor Len Wein tagged Moore to begin writing the comic book *Swamp Thing.* Moore's new take on the character, *The Saga of the Swamp Thing* gained both critical acclaim and commercial success. His first original piece in the United States was *Watchmen* (DC Comics, September 1986–October 1987), a twelve-issue miniseries that, along with Frank Miller's *Batman: The Dark Knight Returns* (DC Comics, February–June 1986), revolutionized the comic book industry, garnering attention and acclaim from the literary world.

Working later for the company America's Best Comics, Moore published *The League of Extraordinary Gentlemen* (volume one: March 1999–September 2000; volume two: September 2002–November 2003), a narrative bringing together iconic figures from British literature—most notably, Alan Quartermain, Dr. Jekyll/Mr. Hyde, Captain Nemo, and Mina (Harker) Murray—as the latest members of the League, assigned with keeping the British Empire safe. A third volume was published in the United States by Top Shelf Productions from May 2009 to June 2012. While *V for Vendetta, Watchmen,* and *League* were all developed into major motion pictures in the 2000s, Moore refused to allow his name to be attached to the film projects, feeling that the commercialization of his works diluted their original intent as political theses. He remains one of the most respected comic book writers in the medium's history.

Richard A. Hall

Comedian is shown to have been part of the original superhero team, the Minutemen, in 1939. During one flashback, Comedian attempts to rape his teammate Silk Spectre (Sally Jupiter). Later, in the early 1970s, Comedian is serving the U.S. government in Vietnam alongside fellow hero Doctor Manhattan. Before leaving Vietnam, he murders a young Vietnamese girl who claims she is pregnant with his child. Still later in the 1970s, Comedian is shown dispersing an angry crowd alongside the second Nite Owl (Daniel Dreiberg), leaping into the crowd, and shooting people at random (Alan Moore and Dave Gibbons, *Watchmen #1–12*, September 1986–October 1987). In that last scene, as portrayed in the live-action film, Nite Owl asks, "Whatever happened to the American dream?" The Comedian responds, "Whatever happened to the American dream? It came true!" (David Hayter and Alex Tse, *Watchmen*, Warner Brothers, director Zach Snyder, 2009). In the film version, Comedian is played with villainous glee by Jeffrey Dean Morgan.

The Comedian's original story line was altered by the 2014 DC Comics series *Before Watchmen* and the 2017–2019 DC series *Doomsday Clock*. As a hero, Comedian is best described as an antihero, a hero who crosses the lines of acceptable or legal behavior. Comedian, however, is a villain by any sense of the word. As Mike Alsford says, "What a culture considers heroic and what it considers villainous says a lot about that culture's underlying attitudes" (Alsford, *Heroes & Villains*, 2). This idea is central to Moore's primary thesis. In the world of *Watchmen*, Comedian is recognized by the government as a hero, as he successfully disposes of enemies to the American people. However, his brutality and utter lack of moral compass are anathema to what Americans claim to be their ethical core. The character is a solid and frightening glance into what Americans viewed as acceptable heroic behavior in the Reagan Era of the 1980s. His continued popularity in the 2009 film expresses how little American values have changed during the time in between.

Richard A. Hall

See also: Asajj Ventress, Bill/Snake Charmer, Billy the Kid, Boba Fett, CSM/The Cigarette Smoking Man, Frank Burns, Geronimo, Heisenberg/Walter White, Negan/The Saviors, Ozymandias, Pancho Villa, Tony Soprano; *Thematic Essays*: "Nazis, Communists, and Terrorists . . . Oh My!": The Rise of the Supervillain and the Evolution of the Modern American Villain, The Dark Mirror: Evil Twins, *The Twilight Zone*, and the Villain Within, The Pathos of Villainy: Getting to the Heart of Why Villains Went Bad.

Further Reading

Alsford, Mike. 2006. *Heroes & Villains*. Waco, TX: Baylor University Press.

Ashby, LeRoy. 2006. *With Amusement for All: A History of American Popular Culture since 1830*. Lexington: University Press of Kentucky.

Faludi, Susan. 2007. *The Terror Dream: Myth and Misogyny in an Insecure America*. New York: Picador.

Hillerbrand, Rafaela, and Anders Sandburg. 2009. "Who Trusts the Watchmen." In *Supervillains and Philosophy: Sometimes, Evil Is Its Own Reward*, edited by Ben Dyer, 103–112. Chicago: Open Court.

Rossinow, Doug. 2015. *The Reagan Era: A History of the 1980s*. New York: Columbia University Press.

Tucker, Reed. 2017. *Slugfest: Inside the Epic 50-Year Battle Between Marvel and DC.* New York: Da Capo.

White, Mark D., ed. 2009. *Watchmen and Philosophy: A Rorschach Test.* The Blackwell Philosophy and Pop Culture Series, edited by William Irwin. Hoboken, NJ: Wiley.

Wright, Bradford W. 2003. *Comic Book Nation: The Transformation of Youth Culture in America.* Baltimore, MD: Johns Hopkins University Press.

The Corleone Family

First Appearance:	*The Godfather* (publication date: March 10, 1969)
Creators:	Mario Puzo
Other Media:	Movies, novels
Primary Strength:	Wealth, political connections
Major Weakness:	Honor
Weapons:	Standard hand guns, machine guns, bombs
Bases of Operations:	New York City/Lake Tahoe, Nevada
Key Allies:	The Corleone Family: Carmela, Santino (Sonny), Frederico (Fredo), Constanzia (Connie), Tom Hagen, Apollonia, Katherine (Kay), Mary and Anthony; Genco Abbandando, Peter Clemenza, Salvatore Tessio, Don Tommasino, Albert "Al" Neri
Key Enemies:	Don Ciccio, Don Fanucci, Don Barzini, Don Tattaglia, Virgil Solozzo, Hyman Roth, Don Altobello, Joey Zasa, Don Lucchesi
Actual Identities:	Vito and Michael Corleone
Nicknames/Aliases:	"The Don," "The Godfather" (the head of the family)

When *The Godfather* was first published, it remained on the best-seller lists for more than a year and sold over nine million copies. Prior to going to print, the publisher released sample chapters, which caught the eye of Paramount Pictures, and the film rights were locked down before the novel even hit the shelves. The movie went on to be considered one of the greatest movies of all time and spawned two sequels (*The Godfather, Part II*, 1974; and *The Godfather, Part III*, 1991). *The Godfather, Part II* is the only sequel in Academy Award history to win more Oscars than the original movie.

The plot of the novel is detailed, using flashbacks and many side stories that were dropped completely from the movies. It was decided that the format of the novel might be a barrier to audiences, so the decision was made to focus the first movie on the 1945–1955 story. When the second movie was greenlit, the story of Vito's early life (1901–1923) from the novel was woven into the story of Michael's struggles of 1958–1960. The third movie, not taken from the original novel, is set from 1976 to 1980 and jumps to 1997 in the final scene. The popularity of the novel and the movies spawned two additional books written by Mark Winegardner, *The Godfather Returns*, 2004; and *The Godfather's Revenge*, 2006 which are set in the two time periods between the movies of the trilogy. The following comes from a combination of the novel and film versions.

Vito Andolini is born in 1891. In 1901, the local Mafia chieftain, Don Ciccio, orders the death of Vito's father, Antonio. Vito's older brother, Paolo, takes to the hills to seek vengeance, but he is gunned down during their father's funeral. Vito's mother takes him to see Don Ciccio in an effort to plead for his life. Don Ciccio refuses, and she is gunned down at point-blank range. The young Vito (played in the film by Oreste Baldini) escapes and is hunted by Don Ciccio's men, but friends of the family smuggle him out of the village and he sails for America. While being processed at Ellis Island, Vito refuses to give the customs agent his last name, so the agent dubs him "Vito Corleone." After his release from Ellis Island, Vito is taken in by the Abbandando family, and he grows up with their son, Genco (Puzo 1969, 194). Vito (now played by Robert De Niro) works in the family grocery store. By 1917, he has married Carmela, and Santino is over a year old. This is also the time frame (1917–1920) when Vito runs afoul of Don Fanucci, a member of the Black Hand. First, Fanucci forces Signor Abbandando to employ his nephew, putting Vito out of a job.

Soon after, Vito meets Peter Clemenza and Salvatore Tessio, joining their gang. They make their living by hijacking trucks carrying women's dresses. After Vito's first night on this new job, he is approached by Don Fanucci demanding a piece of the action. Clemenza and Tessio are cowed by Fanucci and want to cave to his demands. Vito convinces them to give him a quarter of the amount Fanucci demanded and promises he will handle it. When pressed as to how, Vito utters his famous phrase for the first time: "I make an offer he don't refuse." After a terse meeting, Vito follows Fanucci home and guns him down. By dealing with the Fanucci situation on his own initiative, Vito's stature is immediately raised, and he goes from being equal partners with Clemenza and Tessio to their leader. From there, Vito's power and influence continue to grow (Puzo 1969, 198–208).

Michael Corleone (played by Al Pacino) is born a little before the execution of Fanucci in 1920. After Pearl Harbor, Michael enlists in the U.S. Marine Corps against the express wishes of his father. Michael serves with distinction in the Pacific theater, winning numerous medals. He is discharged in early 1945 after being wounded. The discharge was engineered by Vito without Michael's knowledge. After a few weeks' rest, Michael enrolls at Dartmouth, which is where he meets Kay Adams (Puzo 1969, 17). Michael originally has no interest in joining the family business, and Vito (now played by Marlon Brando) wants Michael to surpass him in the legitimate world. Michael is set upon a different path when Vito is shot in a failed assassination attempt after refusing to lend his influence and protection to the narcotics operation proposed by Virgil "the Turk" Sollozzo.

While Vito rests in his sickbed, a war rages throughout the underworld, with Sonny leading the Corleone family. Only the death of Sonny finally goads Vito out of his sickbed to resume command of his family. After Santino's funeral, he calls a meeting of the Five Families and invites families from across the country to a summit to hammer out a peace. According to the novel, it is during Vito's final speech for this summit that he coins the term "cosa nostra" or "this thing of ours" (Puzo 1969, 292–294). After returning from self-imposed exile in Sicily, Michael learns the family business, has Vito's political contacts and other aspects of the business transferred to him, and marries Kay. At the end of that three-year period, Michael begins the process of moving the family to Nevada. The move is supposed to be complete after another year, but that is cut short when Vito dies of a massive heart attack in 1955. Following Vito's funeral, Michael stands as godfather to Connie's baby, settles the family business, and cements his position as Don and Godfather.

Michael continues working with crime boss Hyman Roth, meeting with him in Havana to discuss partnering with the Batista government in Cuba. While on this trip, Fredo inadvertently reveals himself to be the source of Roth's information. Back in New York, a Roth-sanctioned hit on Frank Pentangeli, the Corleone family leader on the East Coast, fails and is set up to make Frank think that it was sanctioned by Michael. This leads to Frank cooperating with the FBI and a Senate committee investigation against Michael. When it is Frank's turn at the microphone during the public hearings, Michael sits in the audience next to Frank's brother from Sicily. For some reason, the sight of his brother causes Frank to completely recant everything he has said before, and the entire investigation falls apart (Francis Ford Coppola, *The Godfather, Part II*, Paramount, 1974).

In 1979, Michael begins in earnest to finally make the Corleone family legitimate. His way forward is to gain controlling interest in Immobiliare, a global real-estate holding company controlled by many players, including the Catholic Church. Pope Paul VI grants Michael the Order of St. Sebastian. Soon thereafter, Michael deposits $600 million in the Vatican Bank to help cover its debt in return for the Vatican vote for the Immobiliare deal. At this time, Sonny's illegitimate son, Vincent, is brought into the family business working for Michael. This pulls Michael back into the underworld, where he is forced to deal with threats from Joey Zasa. While all of this is going on, Michael is beginning to really feel the guilt of his past sins. After Vincent proves himself a worthy successor, Michael hands the reins of power over to him because, as he tells Connie, "I just can't do it anymore." Michael reiterates to Kay that everything he has done in his life was to protect his family. This is proven to be ineffective, as a bullet meant to kill him passes through his shoulder and kills his daughter and closest child, Mary. Michael is racked with guilt and grief over this and retires to Sicily, where he dies alone, presumably of a heart attack like his father, in 1997 at approximately seventy-seven years old (Francis Ford Coppola, *The Godfather, Part III*, Paramount, 1991).

Mario Puzo has been criticized for glamorizing the Mafia. In the novel, Vito Corleone comes off as an amalgamation of George Patton, George Washington, and Thomas Jefferson. He is the far-seeing, all-wise statesman and general who is merely trying to take care of his family in a cruel dog-eat-dog world. This attitude toward some criminals is reminiscent of the American attitude toward some of the famous bank robbers of the early twentieth century, such as John Dillinger. This idealization of criminals who are just doing what they must in the face of an unfair larger society can be traced back to Robin Hood or even further. The popularity of the books and the movies and the endurance of their characters and ideals show that Americans can be tolerant of crime when they are seen as punching up. If Don Corleone was randomly murdering people in his old neighborhood, he would be seen as a craven killer. Killing Don Fanucci was seen as an act of heroism because Fanucci represented all the institutions of society that are overbearing and unfair to "the little people." By assuming Fanucci's station without Fanucci's cruelty, Vito Corleone and, later on, Michael Corleone are the "little guy's" protector, even their Godfather.

Keith R. Claridy

See also: Alexis Carrington-Colby-Dexter, Bill/Snake Charmer, Borg Queen/Borg, Cersei Lannister, COBRA, The Court of Owls, Davros/Daleks, Doctor Doom, Ernst Stavro Blofeld/SPECTRE, Fiona Goode/The Supreme, Fish Mooney, Goldfinger, Grand Nagus/Ferengi, Gus Fring, Heisenberg/Walter White, J. R. Ewing, Lex Luthor, Marsellus Wallace, Negan/The Saviors, Ozymandias, Sherry Palmer, Tony Montana, Tony Soprano, Zod; *Thematic Essays*: The Pathos of Villainy: Getting to the Heart of Why Villains Went Bad.

Further Reading

Browne, Nick, ed. 2000. *Francis Ford Coppola's "The Godfather Trilogy."* Cambridge: Cambridge University Press.

Cowie, Peter. 1997. *The Godfather Book.* London: Faber.

Lebo, Harlan. 2005. *The Godfather Legacy.* Rev. ed. New York: Fireside.

Lewis, Jon. 2010. *The Godfather.* London: Palgrave MacMillan.

McCarty, John. 2004. *Bullets over Hollywood: The American Gangster Picture from the Silents to "The Sopranos."* Cambridge, MA: Da Capo.

Puzo, Mario. 1969. *The Godfather.* New York: G.P. Putnam's Sons.

Renga, Dana, ed. 2011. *Mafia Movies: A Reader.* Toronto, ON, Canada: University of Toronto Press.

The Court of Owls

First Appearance:	*Batman* # 3, volume 2 (publication date: October 2011)
Creators:	Scott Snyder and Greg Capullo
Other Media:	Television, home video movies
Primary Strength:	Control over assassins known as the Talons
Major Weakness:	Blinded by ideology
Weapons:	Massive collected wealth
Base of Operations:	Gotham City
Key Allies:	Bane, Cluemaster
Key Enemies:	Batman, Nightwing, Robin, Batgirl, Calvin Rose
Actual Identities:	Several wealthy and powerful citizens of Gotham City

In taking on the flagship book of the *Batman* line, creators Scott Snyder and Greg Capullo decided that rather than reuse a preexisting member of the Dark Knight's formidable rogue's gallery, they would introduce a new threat. Over his long crime-fighting career, one constant was that Batman was confident in his familiarity with every aspect of Gotham City. Snyder wanted to take this strength the superhero believed he possessed and transform it into a weakness. He did this by giving the city itself a secret: the Court of Owls, an evil cabal that has been dwelling in Gotham since its foundation.

For centuries, the Court of Owls was believed to be a myth intertwined throughout the history of Gotham. The subject of a macabre nursery rhyme, they conduct their plans under a shroud of secrecy. If people stand in their way, they will "send a Talon for your head." The Talons referred to are the reanimated corpses of circus performers who act as their assassins. The membership of the Court of Owls boasts a number of wealthy prominent families who manipulate the social and political order of the city. Although they are mainly based in an underground labyrinth, Gotham contains a number of secretive hideaways they use as sanctuaries; Bruce Wayne's own ancestor even designed a series of buildings with hidden thirteenth floors for them to use. Like most Gothamites, Batman is skeptical of their existence, until the body of one of their victims surfaces, which puts the Dark Knight on their trail.

In *Batman* #5 (December 2011), an issue praised for its artistically disorienting style, the Court of Owls drug the Caped Crusader and force him to navigate a labyrinth with the intention of driving him mad. Inevitably Batman escapes, forcing their hand into launching a full assault during the Night of the Owls across all *Batman*-related comics. Every ally of the Caped Crusader is called upon to defend the city from the Court of Owls and the Talons on multiple fronts. Of all Batman's compatriots, it is arguably his closest, Dick Grayson (Nightwing), who has the greatest personal challenge during this arc. As a former circus acrobat, he is at one point intended to be a Talon until circumstances put him under Batman's care. While protecting the mayor from a Talon who was one of his ancestors, Nightwing learns that he was destined to be the court's Gray Son (Kyle Higgins and Eddie Barrows, *Nightwing* #8, June 2012). The attack on the city is thwarted, and in its aftermath, Batman gains the information need to deal a disastrous blow to the court. In doing so, he discovers that one of his frequent acquaintances, mayoral candidate Lincoln March, has been pulling the strings as a leader of the Owls.

During the event Forever Evil, the defeat of the Justice League inspires supervillains across the DC Universe to fearlessly operate in the open. In Gotham City, Batman's famed rogues' gallery becomes embroiled in a civil war for control. For their part, the court plan to lie low during the chaos and then strike when the moment is advantageous. When an army of frozen Talons is discovered beneath Blackgate Penitentiary, the supervillains involved in the conflict vie for the court's alliance. Although they initially side with Bane to allow him to empower the Talons with the strength-enhancing chemical Venom, the Owls do eventually turn on him.

The Owls achieve one of their greatest victories during the events of "Robin War." After a battle with the Joker leaves Batman dealing with amnesia, the superhero community of Gotham is thrust into turmoil. Lincoln March sees this as his opportunity to finally bring Dick Grayson into his fold. Manipulating a member of the city council, the Owls orchestrate a complex plan utilizing the police as their personal army. Grayson and his fellow Robin alumni form an alliance with a group of teenage vigilantes fighting under the Robin banner in an attempt to save the city from falling apart. Despite a valiant effort from the young heroes, Dick Grayson is given a difficult ultimatum and reluctantly joins the Owls.

With momentum from this victory, the Court of Owls expands globally and declares themselves the Parliament of Owls. They embark on a project to build a new secretive community for their most elite members, called Parliament Grove. While they work to build this, the Owls find themselves in conflict with the fanatical Kobra Cult. Unfortunately for them, the dream of Parliament Grove never becomes a reality, as Nightwing betrays the Parliament of Owls, bringing a halt to their operations.

Considering that Batman is one of the most adapted characters in popular culture, it was only a matter of time before the Court of Owls appeared outside of the comic book pages. Given their ties to Gotham City's history, they were utilized by the writers of the series *Gotham* in the show's third season. In the direct-to-video movie *Batman vs. Robin* (2015), the Owls serve as the primary antagonists. Despite the plethora of iconic villains in Batman's rogues' gallery, the Court of Owls have managed to stake their claim as one of the biggest threats in Gotham in a relatively short amount of time.

Joshua Plock

See also: Alexis Carrington-Colby-Dexter, Catwoman, Cersei Lannister, COBRA, The Corleone Family, CSM/The Cigarette Smoking Man, Doctor Doom, Ernst Stavro Blofeld/SPECTRE, Fish Mooney, Grand Nagus/Ferengi, Gus Fring, Harley Quinn, Heisenberg/Walter White, Joker, J. R. Ewing, Lex Luthor, Marsellus Wallace, Ozymandias, Penguin, Poison Ivy, Ra's al Ghul, Red Skull, Scarecrow, Sherry Palmer, Sith Lords, Tony Montana, Tony Soprano, Two-Face; *Thematic Essays*: "Nazis, Communists, and Terrorists . . . Oh My!": The Rise of the Supervillain and the Evolution of the Modern American Villain, The Pathos of Villainy: Getting to the Heart of Why Villains Went Bad.

Further Reading

Geaman, Kristen L., ed. 2015. *Dick Grayson, Boy Wonder: Scholars and Creators on 75 Years of Robin, Nightwing, and Batman.* Jefferson, NC: McFarland.

Manning, Scott. 2017. "Classical Reception: Batman and the Court of Owls." Historian on the Warpath. Accessed December 18, 2018. https://scottmanning.com/content/ancient-roots-batman-and-the-court-of-owls/.

Pearson, Roberta, William Uricchio, and Will Brooker, eds. 2015. *Many More Lives of the Batman.* London: BFI Palgrave.

Wallace, Daniel. 2012. *Batman: The World of the Dark Knight.* London: Dorling Kindersley.

Weldon, Glen. 2015. *The Caped Crusade: Batman and the Rise of Nerd Culture.* New York: Simon & Schuster.

CSM/The Cigarette Smoking Man

First Appearance:	*The X-Files*, season 1, episode 1 (air date: September 10, 1993)
Creators:	Chris Carter
Other Media:	Films, novels, comics
Primary Strength:	Seemingly endless resources, political and financial connections, cunning
Major Weakness:	Obsession with Agents Mulder and Scully
Weapons:	Extreme cleverness
Base of Operations:	Various
Key Allies:	FBI, CIA, NSA, Syndicate, FBI Deputy Director Skinner, Jeffrey Spender
Key Enemies:	FBI Agents Fox Mulder and Dana Scully
Actual Identity:	Unknown
Nicknames/Aliases:	"Cancer Man," "Smokey," C. G. B. Spender, Carl Gerhard Busch

In 1993, creator Chris Carter debuted his historic television series, *The X-Files* (FOX, 1993–2002; 2016; 2018). Running originally for nine seasons, followed by two feature films and two brief return seasons, the series starred David Duchovny and Gillian Anderson as FBI agents Fox Mulder and Dana Scully, respectively. Mulder and Scully worked on the FBI's X-Files, unsolved mysteries, largely centered on supernatural or paranormal phenomenon. At the center of *The X-Files* was the conspiracy: a secret cabal of individuals—many within the U.S. government—connected in some way to several alien species currently hiding around the planet, with unknown but suspected dubious motives. Every few episodes returned to the overall conspiracy story line. At the center of this conspiracy was a mysterious figure, always shrouded in his own cigarette smoke, whom the other characters and the fans referred to only as "CSM" or the "Cigarette Smoking Man," portrayed with frightening menace by William B. Davis.

Throughout its twenty-five-year run, only a few tidbits of actual information concerning CSM ever emerged to satiate viewers' curiosity. In the premier episode, when Dr. Dana Scully receives her new assignment to use science to debunk Agent Mulder's investigations into the paranormal, CSM is standing in the corner as FBI deputy director Walter Skinner (played by Mitch Pileggi) gives Scully her orders. From that point forward, any time Mulder and Scully investigate a case that takes them closer to the aforementioned conspiracy, CSM appears in the shadows, an obvious obstacle to the agents' goal. Viewers soon learn that Mulder's secret informant within the conspiracy—known only as Deep Throat, the former moniker of the secret source for reporter Bob Woodward during his investigation into the Watergate conspiracy of the 1970s—has worked alongside CSM and Mulder's father, Bill Mulder, for decades.

Men in Black

Although most today associate the term "men in black" with the popular comic book and movie franchise, those fictional heroes are actually based on real-world villains. In the realm of ufology (the study of unidentified flying object [UFO] phenomenon), there are numerous accounts over the decades from individuals who claim to have had UFO encounters and whose experiences were soon followed by visitations from mysterious "men in black": nameless men notable for their black suits, ties, hats, and sunglasses. These men are regularly associated with the key government organizations tasked with investigating UFO phenomenon: Operation Blue Book and its predecessor, the Majestic-12. The men in black exist in the shadows, frequently threatening those who have encountered UFO events into remaining silent on the matter.

Several individuals who claim to have witnessed events surrounding the iconic Roswell incident, where a crashed alien spacecraft and alien bodies were discovered outside Roswell, New Mexico, in 1947, have reported being visited by men in black, who warned them of the consequences of telling anyone about what they experienced. To date, no such men in black have been identified or even confirmed by the U.S. government. The pop culture franchise of the same name was created by Lowell Cunningham as a comic book (Aircel Comics, 1990; Malibu Comics, 1991). The first film, starring Will Smith and Tommy Lee Jones, was released by Sony pictures in 1997. It was followed by two sequels starring Smith and Jones before a fourth film, *Men in Black: International*, starring Chris Hemsworth and Tessa Thompson, was released in 2019.

Richard A. Hall

The closest that fans came to an origin story for CSM was in the episode "Musings of a Cigarette Smoking Man." In this episode, the conspiracy investigators known as the Lone Gunmen report to Mulder and Scully what they have uncovered about their mysterious opponent. What they have learned, and even they admit that they cannot confirm that this story is more than smoke and mirrors, is that CSM was an army officer stationed at Fort Bragg, North Carolina, in 1962, where he was recruited to assassinate President John F. Kennedy. Unknown to Mulder and his friends, CSM is eavesdropping on their conversation, occasionally smiling; this makes it even more unclear to viewers how much of what is being said is fact and how much is CSM's own fiction. Afterward, CSM becomes more and more embroiled in numerous conspiracies for the U.S. government over the decades that follow. Meanwhile, in the present, viewers see that CSM is also a failed science fiction author, who would rather be a writer than what he has become (Glen Morgan, "Musings of a Cigarette Smoking Man," *The X-Files*, season 4, episode 7, November 17, 1996).

From time to time, when Agent Scully is out of action, Mulder is teamed with other agents. In season two, Mulder is briefly teamed with Agent Alex Krycek (played by Nicholas Lea) and, in season five, with Agent Jeffrey Spender (played by Chris Owens). Both are eventually revealed to be working for CSM; Agent Spender is actually CSM's own son. Later in the series, it is revealed that when CSM and Bill Mulder worked together, CSM had an affair with Bill's wife and is, in fact, Fox Mulder's father. Throughout the series, CSM appears to have died several times, once allegedly from lung cancer (shortly after that, he reappeared, now smoking through an implant in his throat). In the final episode of the original run of the series, CSM is literally blown up by helicopters in his secret cave lair (Chris Carter, "The Truth," *The X-Files*, season 9, episode 20, May 19, 2002). By that time, the first *X-Files* feature film had been released, and CSM did not appear in the second; as such, viewers were left to believe that the mysterious villain had, indeed, died in the series finale.

William B. Davis played the mysterious "Cigarette Smoking Man" in the long-running FOX series *The X-Files*. (Fox Broadcasting/Photofest)

When the series returned for a miniseason in 2016, it was revealed that CSM was still alive, with a mysterious master plan to eradicate millions of people across the globe, this time with the assistance of Mulder and Scully's former ally, FBI agent Monica Reyes (played by Annabeth Gish). Part of his plan is to find Mulder and Scully's son, William, whom the two had hidden away at his birth to protect him from CSM and the mysterious Syndicate. In the second miniseason in 2018, viewers discovered that young William possesses special abilities due to alien DNA that he inherited from his mother, Scully, and that, in fact, CSM is William's father, making him, then, Fox Mulder's half brother. In that season, currently billed as the series' last, viewers were left hanging about William's fate and if CSM was finally and definitively defeated.

In 2013, CSM was named listed as twenty-first on *TV Guide*'s list of "60 Nastiest Villains" in television history ("TV Guide Picks TV's 60 Nastiest Villains," *TV Guide*). In the realm of villains in popular culture, CSM speaks to a real-world fear. Beginning in 1964, with the government's official report on the assassination of President Kennedy, through the nightmare of Vietnam, the assassinations of Dr. Marin Luther King Jr. and Senator Bobby Kennedy, the release of the Pentagon Papers, and the Watergate scandal that brought down President Richard Nixon, Americans were haunted by the idea that their government was dishonest, involved in a revolving door of conspiracies that went against American ideals and even safety. CSM speaks to this lingering fear. He is the nameless, smoke-shrouded darkness at the heart of the federal government, secretly working against the best interests of the American people and selling us out to unknown alien threats. Also, unlike many villains in other pop culture franchises, he is more powerful than the heroes, and he cannot be definitively stopped.

Richard A. Hall

See also: Asajj Ventress, Bill/Snake Charmer, Frank Burns, General Custer, Heisenberg/Walter White, Imperial Officers, Martin Brenner, Sherry Palmer; *Thematic Essays*: "Nazis, Communists, and Terrorists . . . Oh My!": The Rise of the Supervillain and the Evolution of the Modern American Villain, The Dark Mirror: Evil Twins, *The Twilight Zone*, and the Villain Within, The Pathos of Villainy: Getting to the Heart of Why Villains Went Bad.

Further Reading

Alsford, Mike. 2006. *Heroes & Villains*. Waco, TX: Baylor University Press.

Arp, Robert, ed. 2017. *The X-Files and Philosophy: The Truth Is in Here*. Chicago: Open Court.

Ashby, LeRoy. 2006. *With Amusement for All: A History of American Popular Culture since 1830*. Lexington: University Press of Kentucky.

Faludi, Susan. 2007. *The Terror Dream: Myth and Misogyny in an Insecure America*. New York: Picador.

Handlen, Zack, and Todd VanDerWerff. 2018. *Monsters of the Week: The Complete Critical Companion to The X-Files*. New York: Harry N. Abrams.

Mooney, Darren. 2017. *Opening The X-Files: A Critical History of the Original Series*. Jefferson, NC: McFarland.

Short, Sue. 2011. "*The X-Files*: Trust, Belief, and Broken Promises." In *Cult Telefantasy Series: A Critical Analysis of The Prisoner, Twin Peaks, The X-Files, Buffy the Vampire Slayer, Lost, Heroes, Doctor Who, and Star Trek*, 55–83. Jefferson, NC: McFarland.

Terry, Paul. 2019. *The X-Files: The Official Archives: Cryptids, Biological Anomalies, and Parapsychic Phenomenon*. New York: Abrams.

"TV Guide Picks TV's 60 Nastiest Villains." 2013. *TV Guide*. April 22, 2013. Accessed January 1, 2019. http://wordsmithonia.blogspot.com/2013/04/tv-guide-picks-tvs-60-nastiest-villains.html.

Cybermen

First Appearance:	*Doctor Who*, original season 4, episode 5 (air date: October 8, 1966)
Creators:	Gerry Davis and Kit Pedler
Other Media:	Comics, audioplays, novels, movies
Primary Strength:	Biomechanical assimilation, flight (in modern era), strength of numbers
Major Weakness:	Gold
Weapons:	Wrist lasers, assimilating nanotechnology

Base of Operations:	Mondas/Parallel Earth
Key Allies:	N/A
Key Enemies:	The Doctor
Actual Identity:	N/A
Nicknames/Aliases:	N/A

Doctor Who has had two runs on BBC: from 1966 to 1989 and from 2005 to the present (the second run airing as well on the cable TV outlet BBC-America). The series was created by Sydney Newman and Verity Lambert. The hero is an unnamed Time Lord who, centuries ago, ran away from his home world in a stolen TARDIS (an acronym for his time-and-space ship, Time And Relative Dimension In Space), to live a life exploring all of time and space. He calls himself "the Doctor," with no other name ever given. The Time Lords possess the ability to regenerate when they die, giving them a new living body; they can officially regenerate a total of twelve times before they die for good. Over a span of, to date, more than 1,500 years, the Doctor has saved people, planets, galaxies, and, occasionally, the entire universe. During these travels, the Doctor's many incarnations have had frequent engagements with a race of cybernetic life-forms known as Cybermen.

The Cybermen were introduced during the adventures of the first Doctor (played by William Hartnell). In the 1966 episode "The Tenth Planet," it was explained that, originally, Earth had a twin planet in our solar system called Mondas. Like Earth, Mondas had a human population. When Mondas shifted its orbit, the result was catastrophic environmental chaos. The human population survived through the implementation of cybernetic devices. Over centuries of improvements and upgrades, the Cybermen evolved. Now they exist as mindless automatons, a collective hive mind, who travel time and space seeking to enhance their numbers by "upgrading" whatever life forms they encounter (Gerry Davis and Kit Pedler, "The Tenth Planet," *Doctor Who,* original season 4, episode 5–8, October 8–29, 1966). In the more recent run of the series, their story has been slightly changed so that the Cybermen actually originated on Earth in a parallel universe. The Cybermen have an anthropomorphic appearance: a head, body, two arms, two legs, all mechanical. The options given to their victims are to be either "upgraded" or "deleted," which share very obvious parallels with the cybervillains the Borg from the American television series *Star Trek: The Next Generation.*

What makes the Cybermen even more frightening is that they were once like us. They represent the nightmare scenario of science gone insane, humans playing God in their endless pursuit of immortality. To accomplish this goal, however, the Cybermen have sacrificed everything that had made them human to being with. They are now something different, something, in their eyes at least, more evolved, something pure. According to the story line "The Tomb of the Cybermen," with the second Doctor (played by Patrick Troughton), the original idea of upgrading humanity came from the enigmatic Brotherhood of Logicians (Gerry Pedler and Kit Davis, "Tomb of the Cybermen," *Doctor Who,* original season 5, episodes 1–4, September 2–23, 1967).

On the one hand, Cybermen are, by now, completely robotic in nature, incapable of feeling either desire or hatred. However, it was their initial desire to survive, and that desire is still evident in their primary programming. Their all-encompassing goal is the survival of their kind. They would, then, define their actions of assimilation as good. Likewise, they see anyone who opposes their mission of assimilation as a threat to their continued existence. Since they originally viewed the end of their existence with fear and presumably hatred, their base programming would cause them to hate anyone or anything they viewed as a threat to that existence and, therefore, evil. From the Cyberman perspective, then, they are the good guys, and the Doctor is the bad guy; their idea of racial purity is seen as beneficial to both the collective and the upgraded.

In a more recent Cybermen story, they were used as pawns by another of the Doctor's nemeses, Missy (previously known as "the Master"). Missy is the most recent regeneration of an "evil" Time Lord (or Lady, in this guise) who was once a childhood companion of the Doctor. In the two-part story, Missy has uploaded untold numbers of human souls at the time of death to a Time Lord–inspired hard drive, leaving their lifeless corpses to be upgraded by a new breed of Cybermen, presumably to have their human souls reintroduced, although the purpose for this reintroduction is unclear, as it would insert individuality into the collective (Steven Moffat, "Dark Water"/"Death in Heaven," *Doctor Who*, modern season 8, episodes 11–12, November 1–8, 2014). In this story line, the general mission of the Cybermen is unchanged. They still seek to assimilate new life into the cybercollective. They still view a mortal, biological life as inferior.

Unlike the Ku Klux Klan or the Nazis—or even fellow *Doctor Who* villains the Daleks—the Cybermen do not seek to eliminate the other (unless, of course, that other rejects assimilation). Cybermen are more like the communists during the Cold War, seeking to increase the strength of their society by adding to the collective. So the question then becomes, were the communists villains? The answer, of course, is that, by Western standards, yes. What makes them villainous by Western ethics is that they choose the collective over the individual and accomplish their goal by force. British and American history, in particular, are grounded in a strong resistance to authoritarianism, be it king, dictator, or universal collective. The Doctor, on the other hand, although he has no compulsion about eradicating all Cybermen from existence in a universal mass slaughter given the opportunity, is the hero. The Doctor represents the ultimate individual, saving humanity from itself, preserving individuality throughout time.

Richard A. Hall

See also: Agent Smith, Alpha/The Whisperers, Borg Queen/Borg, Brainiac, Captain Phasma/Stormtroopers, Davros/Daleks, Doomsday, Grand Nagus/Ferengi, Kahless/Klingons, The Master/Missy, Number Six/Cylons, Red Skull, Ultron; *Thematic Essays*: "In the Beginning . . .": The Origins of Villains in the Western World, "Nazis, Communists, and Terrorists . . . Oh My!": The Rise of the Supervillain and the Evolution of the Modern American Villain, The Pathos of Villainy: Getting to the Heart of Why Villains Went Bad.

Further Reading

Alsford, Mike. 2006. *Heroes & Villains.* Waco, TX: Baylor University Press.

Crome, Andrew, and James McGrath, eds. 2013. *Time and Relative Dimensions in Faith: Religion and Doctor Who.* London: Darton, Longman, and Todd.

Kistler, Alan. 2013. *Doctor Who: Celebrating Fifty Years, a History.* Guilford, CT: Lyons Press.

Lewis, Courtland, and Paula Smithka, eds. 2010. *Doctor Who and Philosophy: Bigger on the Inside.* Chicago: Open Court Press.

Lewis, Courtland, and Paula Smithka, eds. 2015: *More Doctor Who and Philosophy: Regeneration Time.* Chicago: Open Court Press.

Muir, John Kenneth. 2007. *A Critical History of Doctor Who on Television.* Jefferson, NC: McFarland.

Short, Sue. 2011. "*Doctor Who* and *Star Trek*: Twenty-First Century Reboots." In *Cult Telefantasy Series: A Critical Analysis of The Prisoner, Twin Peaks, The X-Files, Buffy the Vampire Slayer, Lost, Heroes, Doctor Who, and Star Trek,* 166–194. Jefferson, NC: McFarland.

Dark Willow

First Appearance:	*Buffy the Vampire Slayer*, season 6, episode 19 (air date: May 7, 2002)
Creators:	Joss Whedon
Other Media:	Comics, novels
Primary Strength:	Witchcraft/magic
Major Weakness:	Dedication to friends
Weapons:	Potions, poppets, amulets
Base of Operations:	Sunnydale, California
Key Allies:	N/A
Key Enemies:	Buffy Summers, Rupert Giles, The Trio
Actual Identity:	Willow Rosenberg
Nicknames/Aliases:	N/A

Buffy the Vampire Slayer (WB, 1997–2001; UPN, 2001–2003) is a cult-classic television series that has gained an international following. Creator Joss Whedon wanted to take the tired concept of the girl being attacked by the monster and flip it so that the girl attacks the monster (Billson, *Buffy the Vampire Slayer*, 24–25). The show centers on Buffy Summers, a run-of-the-mill high school teenager who also happens to be the latest in a centuries-long line of "Chosen Ones," teenage girls who serve, one at a time, as the slayer, the one girl in all the world who can save us from demons, vampires, and all threats of the supernatural. Every slayer is trained by a watcher, chosen by the Watchers' Council to oversee the slayer's training and guide her on her overall mission. When the series begins, Buffy and her recently divorced mother move to the small California town of Sunnydale, which happens to sit directly on a Hellmouth, a portal/magnet of concentrated evil, mostly in the form of vampires.

In the very first episode, Buffy meets Willow Rosenberg, a standard, run-of-the-mill high school nerd, considered unpopular by the "it" crowd. Buffy immediately befriends the young lady, and she becomes a valuable member of Buffy's Scooby Gang: her circle of friends who assist her in her slayer duties, saving the world and Buffy time and time again (Whedon, "Welcome to the Hellmouth," *Buffy the Vampire Slayer*, season 1, episode 1, March 10, 1997). Although originally the tech-savvy member of the group, Willow soon begins to dabble in the dark arts, becoming a powerful witch. On the television series, Willow was played by Allison Hannigan. At the end of the series' sixth season, her involvement in witchcraft overcomes her naturally benign demeanor, and she devolves into Dark Willow.

Although Willow had spent most of her high school years in a romantic relationship with the werewolf Daniel "Oz" Osbourne (played by Seth Green), after their breakup, once Willow begins college in season four, she soon begins a lesbian relationship with fellow witch Tara Maclay (played by Amber Benson). The two witches are deeply in love, but their relationship is tested throughout season six, when it becomes clear that Willow has become addicted to witchcraft, often using it to make her life easier, even if that means using it on her friends and Tara without their knowledge. No sooner does the couple reconcile than Tara is accidentally shot and killed from a stray bullet when Trio member Warren shoots Buffy outside the women's house. Tara's death unleashes Willow's burgeoning darker side, and as she screams over Tara's dead body, her skin goes white(r), her eyes go pitch black, and her red hair turns a darker red, shaded with black. Dark Willow has emerged (Steven S. DeKnight, "Seeing Red," *Buffy the Vampire Slayer*, season 6, episode 19, May 7, 2002).

Dark Willow now embarks on a mission to kill all three members of the villainous/comedic Trio. When she learns that Buffy, too, is fighting for her life, she uses her powers to save the slayer. The revived Buffy fails to reach Willow before the witch slaughters Warren, flaying him alive (Marti Noxon, "Villains," *Buffy the Vampire Slayer*, season 6, episode 20, May 14, 2002). However, when Buffy and the rest of the Scooby Gang attempt to block her mission of murder, Willow turns on Buffy, and the two titans fight. Willow is briefly subdued by the surprise appearance of Rupert Giles, Buffy's former watcher, who arrives endowed with his own considerable level of magic (Doug Petrie, "Two to Go," *Buffy the Vampire Slayer*, season 6, episode 21, May 21, 2002). When Willow manages to overpower Giles and Buffy, she sets out to complete her mission by destroying the entire world. In the end, the only one who can stop her is Scooby member Xander, not through any kind of supernatural power but through his professed love for his deeply hurt friend and his willingness to die with her (David Fury, "Graves," *Buffy the Vampire Slayer*, season 6, episode 22, May 21, 2002). Her friend's love not only stops Dark Willow's plan but also redeems her to her former self. She then agrees to go with Giles back to England to undergo treatment for her addiction and learn to control her powers.

On the surface, Dark Willow represents the standard wicked witch. On a deeper level, however, the emergence of Dark Willow speaks to the darkness that exists deep within even the kindest of people; just one event of unspeakable heartbreak may be enough for anyone to tap into their darker selves and unleash their own level of destruction on the lives of those around them. Hers is a story of addiction and untapped potential, and it is the ultimate example of the old adage, most commonly attributed to comic book writer Stan Lee, that "with great power, there must also come great responsibility."

Richard A. Hall

See also: Alexis Carrington-Colby-Dexter, Alpha/The Whisperers, Angelique Bouchard-Collins, Angelus, Asajj Ventress, Bellatrix Lestrange, Borg Queen/Borg, Cersei Lannister, Elle Driver/California Mountain Snake, Faith the Vampire Slayer, Fiona Goode/The Supreme, Grindelwald, Harley Quinn, Jafar, La Llorona, Loki, Lucifer/Satan, Maleficent, Morgan le Fay, Nurse Ratched, O-Ren Ishii/Cottonmouth, Poison Ivy, Sauron/Saruman, Sherry Palmer, Sith Lords, Spike and Drusilla, Tia Dalma/Calypso, Ursula, Voldemort, Wicked Witch of the West; *Thematic Essays*: The Dark Mirror: Evil Twins, *The Twilight Zone*, and the Villain Within, The Pathos of Villainy: Getting to the Heart of Why Villains Went Bad.

Further Reading

Alsford, Mike. 2006. *Heroes & Villains.* Waco, TX: Baylor University Press.

Ashby, LeRoy. 2006. *With Amusement for All: A History of American Popular Culture since 1830.* Lexington: University Press of Kentucky.

Billson, Anne. 2005. *Buffy the Vampire Slayer.* London: British Film Institute.

Castleman, Harry, and Walter J. Podrazik. 2016. *Watching TV: Eight Decades of American Television.* 3rd ed. Syracuse, NY: Syracuse University Press.

Cavendish, Richard. 1968. *The Black Arts: A Concise History of Witchcraft, Demonology, Astrology, and Other Mystical Practices throughout the Ages.* New York: TarcherPerigree.

Dial-Driver, Emily, Sally Emmons-Featherston, Jim Ford, and Carolyn Anne Taylor. 2008. *The Truth of Buffy: Essays on Fiction Illuminating Reality.* Jefferson, NC: McFarland.

Faludi, Susan. 2007. *The Terror Dream: Myth and Misogyny in an Insecure America.* New York: Picador.

Field, Mark. 2017. *Buffy, the Vampire Slayer: Myth, Metaphor & Morality.* N.p.: Amazon Services.

Forasteros, J. R. 2017. *Empathy for the Devil: Finding Ourselves in the Villains of the Bible.* Downers Grove, IL: InterVarsity.

Gross, Edward, and Mark A. Altman. 2017. *Slayers & Vampires: The Complete, Uncensored, Unauthorized Oral History of Buffy & Angel.* New York: Tor.

Hutton, Ronald. 2017. *The Witch: A History of Fear, from Ancient Times to the Present.* New Haven, CT: Yale University Press.

Jowett, Lorna. 2005. *Sex and the Slayer: A Gender Studies Primer for the Buffy Fan.* Middletown, CT: Wesleyan University Press.

Lavery, David. 2013. *Joss Whedon, A Creative Portrait: From Buffy, the Vampire Slayer to Marvel's The Avengers.* London: I. B. Tauris.

Lavery, David, and Cynthia Burkhead, eds. 2011. *Joss Whedon: Conversations.* Jackson: University of Mississippi Press.

Pender, Patricia J. 2016. *I'm Buffy and You're History.* London: I. B. Tauris.

Russell, Jeffrey B., and Brooks Alexander. 2007. *A History of Witchcraft: Sorcerers, Heretics, & Pagans.* London: Thames & Hudson.

Ryan, Hannah. 2020. "Vilifications: Conjuring Witches Then and Now." In *The Supervillain Reader*, edited by Rob Weiner and Rob Peaslee, 156–171. Jackson: University of Mississippi Press.

Short, Sue. 2011. "*Buffy the Vampire Slayer*: Beauty and the 'Big Bad.'" In *Cult Telefantasy Series: A Critical Analysis of The Prisoner, Twin Peaks, The X-Files, Buffy the Vampire Slayer, Lost, Heroes, Doctor Who, and Star Trek*, 84–107. Jefferson, NC: McFarland.

South, James B., ed. 2005. *Buffy, the Vampire Slayer and Philosophy: Fear and Trembling in Sunnydale.* Chicago: Open Court.

Wilcox, Rhonda V., Tanya Cochran, Cynthea Masson, and David Lavery. 2014. *Reading Joss Whedon.* Syracuse, NY: Syracuse University Press.

Wilcox, Rhonda V., and David Lavery. 2002. *Fighting the Forces: What's at Stake in Buffy, the Vampire Slayer.* Lanham, MD: Rowman & Littlefield.

Yeffeth, Glenn, ed. 2003. *Seven Seasons of Buffy: Science Fiction and Fantasy Writers Discuss Their Favorite Television Show.* Dallas, TX: BenBella.

Davros/Daleks

First Appearance:	**Davros:** *Doctor Who*, original series, season 12, episode 11 (air date: March 8, 1975) **Daleks:** *Doctor Who*, original series, season 1, episode 5 (air date: December 21, 1963)
Creators:	Terry Nation
Other Media:	Comics, audioplays, novels, movies
Primary Strength:	Strength of numbers
Major Weakness:	All-consuming hatred
Weapons:	**Davros:** Control panel for Daleks **Daleks:** Laser gun, sucker manipulation claw
Base of Operations:	Skaro
Key Allies:	N/A
Key Enemies:	The Doctor, Time Lords
Actual Identity:	N/A
Nicknames/Aliases:	"Pepper Pots" (Daleks)

Doctor Who has had two runs on BBC: from 1966 to 198 and from 2005 to the present (the second run airing as well on the cable TV outlet BBC-America). The series was created by Sydney Newman and Verity Lambert. The hero is an unnamed Time Lord who, centuries ago, ran away from his home world in a stolen TARDIS (an acronym for his time-and-space ship, Time And Relative Dimension In Space), to live a life exploring all of time and space. He calls himself "the Doctor," with no other name ever given. The Time Lords possess the ability to regenerate when they die, giving them a new living body; they can officially regenerate a total of twelve times before they die for good. Over a span of, to date, more than 1,500 years, the Doctor has saved people, planets, galaxies, and, occasionally, the entire universe. During these travels, the Doctor's many incarnations have had frequent engagements with a race of cybernetic life-forms known as Daleks and their megalomaniacal creator, Davros.

The Daleks were first introduced during the adventures of the first Doctor (played by William Hartnell). They were the first aliens other than the Doctor and

Terry Nation

Terry Nation (1930–1997) was a British television writer born in Cardiff, Wales. In 1963, he was assigned by the British Broadcasting Corporation (BBC) to write for the new science fiction program, *Doctor Who*. The series centers on the adventures of the alien time and space traveler known only as the Doctor. In the series' first season, Nation developed a villainous alien species that became not only the most popular *Doctor Who* villain but also one of the most iconic villains in sci-fi history: the Daleks. Odd for contract writers at the time, Nation possessed the forethought to secure the copyright for the Daleks, and once they became an overnight success, Nation began work on a script titled *The Dalek's Master Plan* with cowriter Dennis Spooner. Nation attempted to sell his script to the United States for a potential Dalek-themed television series in America. Unfortunately, the United States had not yet experienced *Doctor Who*, so the concept was not well received. In 1975, Nation wrote "Genesis of the Daleks," one of the most popular Dalek stories in *Doctor Who* history. He then went on to create two more sci-fi series for the BBC: *Survivors* (1975–1977) and *Blake's 7* (1978–1981). At the time of his death in 1997, Nation was working on a reboot of *Blake's 7*. His wise move to copyright the Daleks made him a considerable fortune in merchandising rights.

Richard A. Hall

his granddaughter, Susan, to be introduced in the series. In the 1963 story line "The Daleks," viewers were introduced to the planet Skaro. Two intelligent species lived on Skaro: the humanlike Thals, who lived on the surface, and the mechanical Daleks, who looked like squat, salt-and-pepper shakers, with three noticeable appendages of a single eyestalk (symbolizing their singular, narrow worldview), a laser gun, and a plunger-like sucker, used to manipulate devices as needed. According to the story, centuries ago Skaro ended a thousand-year war with a neutron bomb, which kills without disturbing the architectural and electronic surroundings. The Dals retreated underground, mutating over time into gelatinous, squid-like creatures who enclosed themselves in their tanklike devices to protect themselves and became the Daleks. It is not quite clear how the Thals survived unchanged (Terry Nation, "The Daleks," *Doctor Who*, original series, season 1, episodes 5–11, December 21, 1963–February 1, 1964).

Over time, the history of the Daleks was rewritten. In the 1975 story line "Genesis of the Daleks," the fourth Doctor (played by Tom Baker), is sent by the Time Lords to earlier in Skaro's history in order to prevent the Daleks from ever developing. At this point in the planet's history, the thousand-year war is nearing its end. The Thals are at war with the equally humanlike Kaleds. The Kaled's chief scientist, a deformed and mutated half-cybernetic scientist named Davros, has developed the Daleks, shown to be squid-like mutations of the Kaleds, to become the most effective killing machines in the universe and the final solution to the Thal problem.

With the opportunity to destroy the Daleks before they can be incorporated into their mechanical shells, the Doctor pauses, asking, "Have I the right?" After contemplating the millions of lives that may be spared by the Daleks never existing, the Doctor also weighs the countless planets that found peace and cooperation in the face of the Dalek threat. He poses a question to his companion Sarah Jane: if you were to go back in time and find a child that you knew would grow up to be a brutal dictator, could you, then, kill that child? He ultimately decides that he cannot commit genocide in the name of good (Terry Nation, "Genesis of the Daleks," *Doctor Who*, original series, season 12, episodes 11–16, March 8–April 12, 1975). With this retcon, viewers, and the Doctor, discover that the Daleks did not simply evolve, as had the Cybermen; they were specifically designed from the beginning to be killing machines.

In more recent years, in the episodes "Asylum of the Daleks" and "Time of the Doctor," the eleventh Doctor (played by Matt Smith) encounters Dalek drones, individuals that have been allowed to maintain their outward humanoid appearance but have been transformed into Daleks on the inside (their eyestalks and laser guns protrude when needed). The primary purpose of these slave-like creations is subterfuge in order to allow the Daleks to get as close as possible to the Doctor without him noticing (Steven Moffat, "Asylum of the Daleks," *Doctor Who*, modern series, season 7, episode 1, September 1, 2012; Steven Moffat "Time of the Doctor," Christmas special, December 25, 2013). What is unclear is the ultimate fate of these drones. Are they eliminated once their usefulness has been completed, as their form is anathema to the Dalek idea of purity? Do they continue in their drone existence as beings that would always be seen, and presumably treated, as inferior by "real" Daleks? Or are they eventually given a full transformation into actual Daleks? Regardless of their ultimate fate, it is clear that the Daleks have no problem with creating a slave subrace of Dalek-esque creatures when the situation requires it.

It is also in "Asylum of the Daleks" and the later episode "Into the Dalek" that the viewer discovers that Daleks view hatred as "divine" and "beautiful." In both instances, the Doctor responds with natural disgust. The Daleks suggest that this may be why they have never been able to kill the Doctor, because they view his hatred of them as divine. In "Into the Dalek," a damaged Dalek goes so far as to suggest that the Doctor himself would make a good Dalek, due to his deep hatred of them (Steven Moffat and Phil Ford, "Into the Dalek," *Doctor Who*, modern series, season 8, episode 2, August 30, 2014). This adds a moral element to the Daleks. To them, hatred is a highly regarded value. Since that moral is in direct opposition to the accepted norms of our society, the Daleks are villains. By human standards of morality, they are evil.

It is this very issue that defines the Daleks as villains. They do not pose questions about tolerating diversity. They do not invite others to become a part of their society or seek to explain or defend their philosophies. They exterminate all others, except those they can use as slaves. To what degree, then, does a society that encourages diversity and ethical relativism pass judgment on a society that holds such different moral ideas of right and wrong? If what a Dalek does is hate and exterminate, is it not being true to itself when it does so? Further, would attempting to change its nature—by educating it to make it less evil in our eyes—in fact be forcing it to be what it is not? Daleks hate, and they exterminate. That is their reason for existence. They see beauty in it because that is all that they know, and they see no reason to alter that worldview.

Daleks see only Dalek life as legitimate. Once exposed to the Doctor and the idea that life exists outside their world, their mission of racial purity reaches to the stars and all of time. It can be said, then, that the Doctor is responsible for unleashing this monster on the universe. Their mission results in the Time War against the Time Lords, which is so intense that it threatens the entire universe, causing the Doctor to commit double genocide in order to save the lives of the countless billions affected by the two warring races (Steven Moffat, "Day of the Doctor," fiftieth anniversary special, November 23, 2013). This is a recurring theme of the series: weighing the importance of the individual over the collective. In 2013, *TV Guide* listed the Daleks as the number twenty-three "nastiest" TV villains of all time ("TV Guide Picks TV's 60 Nastiest Villains," *TV Guide*).

In the most recent appearance of Davros, the Doctor finds himself on a war-torn planet and finds a young child in the middle of a minefield. As the Doctor attempts to save the child, he asks the child's name. The child responds, "Davros." The Doctor is now confronted with the very question he had posed centuries before, and he chooses to leave the child in the minefield. In the future, Davros, near death, summons the Doctor, and the hero, out of guilt about his earlier sin, acquiesces. The seemingly innocent request proves, naturally, to be a trick; Davros seeks to utilize the Doctor's regeneration energy to lengthen his own life. In his attempt to escape, the Doctor discovers that the Daleks have somehow developed the concept of mercy. Realizing the only answer to this conundrum, the Doctor then returns to the stranded child and rescues him (Steven Moffat, "The Magician's Apprentice"/"The Witch's Familiar," *Doctor Who*, modern series, season 9, episodes 1–2, September 19–26, 2015). Davros and the Daleks, then, speak to one of the most fearsome forms of villainy: a seemingly unstoppable enemy with a singular goal to exterminate the other.

Richard A. Hall

See also: Agent Smith, Alpha/The Whisperers, Borg Queen/Borg, Brainiac, Captain Phasma/Stormtroopers, Cybermen, Doomsday, Grand Nagus/Ferengi, Kahless/Klingons, Martin Brenner, The Master/Missy, Number Six/Cylons, Ultron; *Thematic Essays*: "In the Beginning . . .": The Origins of Villains in the Western World, "Nazis, Communists, and Terrorists . . . Oh My!": The Rise of the Supervillain and the Evolution of the Modern American Villain, The Pathos of Villainy: Getting to the Heart of Why Villains Went Bad.

Further Reading

Alsford, Mike. 2006. *Heroes & Villains*. Waco, TX: Baylor University Press.

Crome, Andrew, and James McGrath, eds. 2013. *Time and Relative Dimensions in Faith: Religion and Doctor Who*. London: Darton, Longman, and Todd.

Kistler, Alan. 2013. *Doctor Who: Celebrating Fifty Years, a History*. Guilford, CT: Lyons.

Larsen, Kristine. 2011. "Frankenstein's Legacy: The Mad Scientist Remade." In *Vader, Voldemort and Other Villains: Essays on Evil in Popular Media*, edited by Jamey Heit, 46–63. Jefferson, NC: McFarland.

Lewis, Courtland, and Paula Smithka, eds. 2010. *Doctor Who and Philosophy: Bigger on the Inside*. Chicago: Open Court.

Lewis, Courtland, and Paula Smithka, eds. 2015. *More Doctor Who and Philosophy: Regeneration Time*. Chicago: Open Court.

Muir, John Kenneth. 2007. *A Critical History of Doctor Who on Television*. Jefferson, NC: McFarland.

Rosenfeld, Gavriel D. 2014. *Hi Hitler!: How the Nazi Past Is Being Normalized in Contemporary Culture*. Cambridge: Cambridge University Press.

Short, Sue. 2011. "*Doctor Who* and *Star Trek*: Twenty-First Century Reboots." In *Cult Telefantasy Series: A Critical Analysis of The Prisoner, Twin Peaks, The X-Files, Buffy the Vampire Slayer, Lost, Heroes, Doctor Who, and Star Trek*, 166–194. Jefferson, NC: McFarland.

"TV Guide Picks TV's 60 Nastiest Villains." 2013. *TV Guide*. April 22, 2013. Accessed January 1, 2019. http://wordsmithonia.blogspot.com/2013/04/tv-guide-picks-tvs-60-nastiest-villains.html.

Doctor Doom

First Appearance:	*Fantastic Four* #5 (cover date: July, 1962)
Creators:	Stan Lee and Jack Kirby
Other Media:	Movies, television
Primary Strength:	Genius intellect
Primary Weakness:	Obsession with Reed Richards
Weapons:	Doombots, various laser weapons, sorcery
Base of Operations:	Latveria
Key Allies:	Red Skull, Green Goblin
Key Enemies:	Fantastic Four, Avengers
Actual Identity:	Victor Von Doom
Nicknames/Aliases:	N/A

With the creation of the Fantastic Four, comic legends Stan Lee and Jack Kirby introduced the world to the Marvel Universe. The duo knew that this universe of heroes needed a face of evil, and the face they created wore a metal mask. Born in the fictional nation of Latveria, Victor Von Doom hailed from a persecuted clan of gypsies. When the tyrannical government left Doom orphaned, the young man became practiced in the occult and science and used this knowledge to avenge his family. Von Doom's revolutionary actions earned him a global attention, and Empire State University offered him a chance to study at their institution (Stan Lee and Jack Kirby, *Fantastic Four Annual #2*, September 1964).

Although his ego did not make him popular in general, Victor ended up striking a particular rivalry with fellow scientist, Reed Richards. Working in secret, Doom utilized the resources of the university to build a machine that would allow him to communicate with his mother in the afterlife. As Reed Richards warned, his invention malfunctioned, leaving his face disfigured. Expelled from Empire

State, Doom donned his now-iconic mask and cloak and returned to Latveria to liberate and rule it.

When Doctor Doom finally made his comic debut, it was to take revenge on Reed Richards, now known as Mr. Fantastic, the patriarch of the Fantastic Four. He trapped the team in their headquarters and forced the team into conducting a time-traveling heist. Although his plan failed, Doom ultimately escaped by outwitting the heroes. Given his personal connection to Richards, he quickly established himself as their greatest enemy. The Latverian ruler's sinister plots were often of a grandiose nature, even going so far as to steal the Silver Surfer's power cosmic (Stan Lee and Jack Kirby, *Fantastic Four* #57, December 1966).

Doctor Doom became such a popular character that he began to be featured in comics like *Astonishing Tales* and *Super-Villain Team Up.* This established him as an influential character in the Marvel Universe, outside of the Fantastic Four's sphere of influence. In particular, *Astonishing Tales* #8 (October, 1971) gave readers one of the defining tales of this villain. Creators Gerry Conway and Gene Colan revealed that as an annual tradition, Doom battles the devil himself in an attempt to save his mother's soul. Not only did this story add a layer of humanity to the evil ruler, but it also established his mother as an important figure in his life. This plot point was continually built on and culminated in 1989's *Doctor Doom and Doctor Strange: Triumph and Torment.*

Julian McMahon was the first actor to play a live-action version of Victor Von Doom/Doctor Doom in an officially released film in 2005's *Fantastic Four,* and its 2007 sequel, *Fantastic Four: Rise of the Silver Surfer.* (Twentieth Century Fox/Marvel Enterprises/Photofest)

In the pages of *Iron Man,* Doom would have a memorable battle with the Armored Avenger in the story arc "Doomquest." A failed business deal between Latveria and Stark Industries naturally thrusts Doom into confrontation with Iron Man. In the heat of battle, the two are transported to the Middle Ages, where Victor Von Doom agrees to an alliance with the legendary witch Morgan le Fay. In exchange for le Fay using her magic to rescue his mother from hell, Doom agrees to lead her army against King Arthur. As one would expect, Iron Man forges an alliance with the legendary king, bringing the hero and villain into battle.

During John Byrne's *Fantastic Four* run, readers were treated to a moment that once had seemed impossible. The son of the Latveria's former king, Prince Zorba deposed Doctor Doom and began his own reign of terror. For the sake of his people, he reluctantly appealed to the Fantastic Four for help (Byrne, *Fantastic Four* #246–247, September–October 1982). During the ensuing years, the Four and Doom would forge temporary truces during dire circumstances. This even included Doom's assistance in the complicated birth of Reed and Sue Richard's daughter, Valeria. In 1984, Marvel Comics published one of the first universe-wide crossovers with the series *Secret Wars*. A being known as the Beyonder transported the heroes and villains of Earth to Battleworld in order to engage in an epic showdown. Despite the sprawling cast of characters, Doctor Doom found a way to stand out in this saga by taking a leadership role among the villains and even stealing the Beyonder's power. The cover to *Secret Wars #10* (1984), which portrays a battle-worn yet defiant Doom, has proven one of the defining images of the classic event.

When Victor Von Doom made a pact with the demonic Hazareth Three to gain greater occult powers, he showed that his penchant for manipulating would-be allies knew no bounds. This would lead to a short-lived victory as Doom was ultimately sent to hell and the Fantastic Four took on the role of leading Latveria, dismantling as much of his work as possible. When he returned, he found the stability of the Marvel Universe increasingly thrown into turmoil thanks to the first civil war and an invasion from the Skrulls. In this chaotic atmosphere, he joined other key villains in forming the Cabal. Naturally, as he never wishes to share power, Doom turned against them when the moment was right.

Three decades after the original *Secret Wars*, a sequel was published. This time the event was kicked off when Doctor Doom accomplished what so many other villains have tried and failed to do: conquer the universe. Doom destroyed the multiple time lines of the Marvel Universe and remade them to his own desires. He even went so far as to make the Invisible Woman and her children his own family. While he was defeated in a grand battle with Reed Richards and normalcy was restored, Doom realized that absolute power surprisingly left him unfulfilled. Inspired by begrudging respect for Tony Stark, Victor went through a period of using his resources and knowledge to be a hero. As expected, this was only a temporary realignment, as once Mister Fantastic returned from a hiatus, Doctor Doom reverted to his evil ways.

The Marvel Universe is filled with a plethora of supervillains, yet Doctor Doom is arguably their most famous. He is a character driven solely by ego and spite, but he also has the intellect and power to support his inflated sense of self-worth. Beyond the iconic look of the character Jack Kirby crafted, he has a depth that few villains in comics are given. The character is consistently ranked among the greatest villains of all time, as the ruler of Latveria has established himself as arguably the standard bearer of evil for Marvel Comics.

Joshua Plock

See also: Angelique Bouchard-Collins, Bellatrix Lestrange, Brainiac, Cersei Lannister, Dark Willow, Ernst Stavro Blofeld/SPECTRE, Fiona Goode/The Supreme, Green Goblin, Grindelwald, Killmonger, Lex Luthor, Loki, Magneto, Ozymandias, Red Skull, Sauron/

Saruman, Sith Lords, Thanos, Ultron, Zod; *Thematic Essays*: "Nazis, Communists, and Terrorists . . . Oh My!": The Rise of the Supervillain and the Evolution of the Modern American Villain, The Pathos of Villainy: Getting to the Heart of Why Villains Went Bad.

Further Reading

Dyer, Ben, ed. 2009. *Supervillains and Philosophy.* Chicago: Open Court.

Gresh, Lois H., and Robert Weinberg. 2005. *The Science of Supervillains.* Hoboken, NJ: John Wiley & Sons.

Howe, Sean. 2013. *Marvel Comics: The Untold Story.* New York: Harper/Perennial.

Lee, Stan. 1976. *Bring on the Bad Guys: Origins of Marvel Villains.* New York: Marvel Comics.

Doomsday

First Appearance:	*Superman: The Man of Steel #18* (cover date: December 1992)
Creators:	Brett Breeding, Dan Jurgens, Jerry Ordway, Louise Simonson, and Roger Stern
Other Media:	Movies, television (animated and live action), animated home video
Primary Strength:	Indestructible
Major Weakness:	N/A
Weapons:	N/A
Base of Operations:	N/A
Key Allies:	N/A
Key Enemies:	Superman, Supergirl, Superboy
Actual Identity:	N/A
Nicknames/Aliases:	"The Creature"

The *Superman* franchise is one of the most successful in pop culture history. Created by the Jewish American team of writer Jerry Siegel and artist Joe Shuster, Superman is an alien named Kal-El, whose home world of Krypton was destroyed shortly after his birth. Aware of the impending doom, his parents placed him in a space capsule and sent him into space to save him. He landed in Smallville, Kansas, and was raised by Jonathan and Martha Kent under his adopted name, Clark Kent. On reaching adulthood, Clark discovered that he had "powers and abilities far beyond those of mortal men" and dedicated himself to protecting the world as Superman, the world's first superhero. Because of his near-godlike powers, his only weakness being Kryptonite (meteor fragments of his home world), Superman requires antagonists of particularly daunting abilities. Of Superman's rogues' gallery of villains, the most physically daunting—and the sole *Superman* villain to definitively defeat the Man of Steel—is Doomsday.

Heading toward the mid-1990s, the comic book industry was facing the beginning of the end of the so-called Collectors' Bubble. The explosion of comic book sales from roughly 1988 to 1995, spurred on by would-be collectors who viewed comic books as sound financial investments more than simple consumer products or entertainment medium, required the various comic book publishers to come up with ever-escalating events that would boost sales. In 1993, *Superman* comic sales were quickly diminishing, leading the team of writers of the four *Superman* titles to work together on a big event. Their initial idea was to finally marry Superman to his longtime girlfriend, Lois Lane. That plan was put on hold by the publisher due to the upcoming television series *Lois and Clark: The New Adventures of Superman* (ABC, 1993–1997), which would begin the iconic relationship from its beginning.

Left to come up with a new gimmick, writer Jerry Ordway suggested killing the Man of Steel. While it was not uncommon for comic book superheroes to "die" (only to come back the next issue), the creative team decided that this death would be more pronounced, essentially showing the world what it would be like without the world's first superhero. To kill the most powerful hero of all time, however, would require the most powerful villain of all time (Interview with Louise Simonson, "A Hero Can Be Anyone (1978–Present)," *Superheroes: A Never-Ending Battle*, PBS-DVD, 2013).

Doomsday is a genetically engineered creature from the planet Krypton. Originally meant to be the perfect living being, the creature's lack of emotion or empathy made him instead the perfect killing machine. Originally called the Ultimate, Doomsday escaped Krypton, burning a path of murder and destruction across the universe before finally being "killed" and buried in an impenetrable prison cocoon, which eventually made its way to Earth. Naturally, the only being on Earth who could fight him was Superman. Their ultimate confrontation was portrayed in *Superman (Vol. 2) #75*, the best-selling single comic book issue in DC Comics history, and one of the best-selling in the industry as a whole. Ultimately, although Superman lands a killing blow to the creature, he receives one as well, and both titans fall in death (Dan Jurgens and Brett Breeding, *Superman #75*, January 1993). As with all popular comic book characters, however, Doomsday would return to threaten the world again and again.

Outside of comics, Doomsday first appeared in season eight of the television series *Smallville* (WB, 2001–2006; CW, 2006–2011). In the series, Doomsday is portrayed as a seemingly normal human who slowly transforms into the unstoppable beast and who is actually stopped fairly easily in the final episode of the season. An even different form of the villain appears in the film *Batman v. Superman: Dawn of Justice* (Warner Brothers, 2016), created by Lex Luthor from the DNA of the deceased General Zod. A more comic-accurate version was portrayed on the cable television series *Krypton* (SyFy, 2018–2019). In season two, it is established that over a thousand years prior to the age of Superman, Doomsday was originally a Kryptonian citizen named Dax, who volunteered to be the subject of an experiment by the houses of El (Superman's ancestors) and Zod (General Zod's ancestors) and to be mutated into the ultimate weapon to save Krypton from its warring ways (Joel Anderson Thompson, "Zods and Monsters," *Krypton*, season 2, episode 7, July 24, 2019). The original overall "Death of Superman" story line has been released in two animated home video releases from DC/Warner Brothers.

What Doomsday most represents in the realm of American pop culture villainy is the idea of the unstoppable force. Although a biological entity, Doomsday is a killing machine, no different from the Borg, Cybermen, Cylons, Daleks, or Terminators. He is the ultimate representation of the unstoppable force meeting the immovable object (Superman). He cannot be permanently stopped or irrevocably killed. Doomsday, as his name suggests, is America's fear of that obstacle that will ultimately destroy everything in its path. He is the dark mirror of Superman, as well as the representation of science gone horribly wrong. In this way, Doomsday speaks to American fears on every level. The character has been further examined in the documentary *Necessary Evil: Super-Villains of DC Comics*, directed by Scott Devine and J. M. Kenny (Warner Home Video, 2013).

Richard A. Hall

See also: Agent Smith, Borg Queen/Borg, Brainiac, Cybermen, Davros/Daleks, Dracula, Frankenstein's Monster, Freddy Krueger, Jason Voorhees, La Llorona, Lex Luthor, Lucifer/Satan, Martin Brenner, Michael Myers, Number Six/Cylons, Ultron, Zod; *Thematic Essays*: The Dark Mirror: Evil Twins, *The Twilight Zone*, and the Villain Within.

Further Reading

Alsford, Mike. 2006. *Heroes & Villains*. Waco, TX: Baylor University Press.

Ashby, LeRoy. 2006. *With Amusement for All: A History of American Popular Culture since 1830*. Lexington: University Press of Kentucky.

Barker, Cory, Chris Ryan, and Myc Wiatrowski, eds. 2014. *Mapping Smallville: Critical Essays on the Series and Its Characters*. Jefferson, NC: McFarland.

Daniels, Les. 2004. *Superman: The Complete History—the Life and Times of the Man of Steel*. New York: DC Comics.

Tucker, Reed. 2017. *Slugfest: Inside the Epic 50-Year Battle between Marvel and DC*. New York: Da Capo.

Tye, Larry. 2013. *Superman: The High-Flying History of America's Most Enduring Hero*. New York: Random House.

Wright, Bradford W. 2003. *Comic Book Nation: The Transformation of Youth Culture in America*. Baltimore, MD: Johns Hopkins University Press.

Dracula

First Appearance:	*Dracula* (publication date: May 26, 1897)
Creators:	Bram Stoker
Other Media:	All media
Primary Strength:	Immortality, shape-shifting, hypnotism
Major Weakness:	Sunlight, wooden stakes, crucifixes
Weapons:	Sharp fangs
Base of Operations:	Transylvania

Key Allies:	Renfield, Brides
Key Enemies:	Abraham Van Helsing, Lorrimer Van Helsing, Blade (in comics)
Actual Identity:	N/A
Nicknames/Aliases:	Count Alucard (*Son of Dracula*), D. D. Denham (*Satanic Rites of Dracula*), Kah (*Legend of the Seven Golden Vampires*)

In 1897, author Bram Stoker introduced readers to a new fictional evil: Dracula. Named for a brutal East European ruler from the 1400s, this was an undead creature who survived by drinking the blood of the living. Leaving his castle in the mountains of Transylvania, Dracula ventures across the sea to England to terrorize a new nation of victims. The novel *Dracula* was a success and has since inspired creators in every other form of media to bring their own vision to this vampire. Stoker's story was first adapted to film in 1922 with the silent German film *Nosferatu: A Symphony of Horror*. This unauthorized adaptation of the novel gave audiences the antagonist Count Orlock, Dracula in all but name. Ultimately the Stoker estate took legal action against the film, and it was locked away.

Dracula had his proper cinematic debut in 1931 with the Universal film *Dracula*. Hungarian actor Bela Lugosi took the leap from stage to screen and created arguably the definitive take on the character. His interpretation was divorced from the decrepit creature of the source material. Dracula now donned a tuxedo and cape, with a foreign mystique to compliment his charming demeanor. After destroying the mind of real estate agent Renfield, Dracula makes his way to the shores of England. There he ingratiates himself with Dr. Seward; his daughter, Mina; and her fiancé, Jonathan. Slowly he begins turning Mina into a creature of the night like himself, and he would have succeeded were it not for Professor Van Helsing. The film ends with Van Helsing driving a stake through the vampire's heart. However, a good monster never remains dead, and after sitting out the sequel, *Dracula's Daughter*, he returned in 1943's *Son of Dracula*, which moved the action out of Europe and onto a plantation in the American South. From there, Dracula would appear with his fellow members of the Universal Monsters stable in monster mash films, like *House of Frankenstein* (1944), *House of Dracula* (1945), and *Abbott & Costello Meet Frankenstein* (1948).

After the era of the Universal Monsters, Dracula appeared in further movies, from the underrated *Return of Dracula* (1958) to *Billy the Kid Versus Dracula* (1966). But it was British studio Hammer Film Productions that took over and made prominent additions to the character's legacy. Beginning with *Horror of Dracula* in 1958, actor Christopher Lee donned the cape for the studio and remained in the role for eight films. By the end of each franchise installment, the count was slain, but his followers would utilize various macabre rituals to resurrect him each time. This version of Dracula was darker and more sadistic, largely to compete with the increasingly edgier American horror films of the era. Hammer ultimately moved their monster into a contemporary era with *Dracula AD*

Bela Lugosi immortalized himself as the ultimate "Dracula" in the 1931 film. (Allstar Picture Library/Alamy Stock Photo)

1972. Resurrected in 1970s London, Dracula began a campaign of preying on counterculture youths and battling the descendants of Van Helsing. With the studio's final *Dracula* picture, they collaborated with famed Chinese company Shaw Brothers Studios for the cult classic *Legend of the Seven Golden Vampires* (1979). This film combined the gothic horror of the Dracula movies with fast-paced martial arts as Dracula traveled to feudal China to confront Van Helsing and a family terrorized by the supernatural.

The silver screen was not the only place terrorized by Dracula, as Marvel Comics brought the undead creature into the pages of their publications. In 1972, acclaimed creators Gene Colan and Gerry Conway created the horror series *Tomb of Dracula*, featuring the legendary vampire. While he occasionally crossed paths with the publisher's iconic heroes, it was the supernaturally based characters created in this series with whom he frequently clashed. Largely assembled by Quincy Harker was a network including vampire-human hybrid Blade, detective Hannibal King, generational vampire hunter Dr. Rachel Van Helsing, and Dracula's own descendant, Frank Drake. Although he was a villain, *Tomb of Dracula* also gave the bloodsucker a chance to be an occasional antihero. In 2004, Dracula's battles with Blade and Hannibal King even made the leap to the silver screen in *Blade Trinity*.

By the time the 1980s rolled around, hipper, younger bloodsuckers dominated movie theaters. However, Dracula did serve as the primary antagonist, uniting his fellow monsters in the 1987 cult classic *The Monster Squad.* Actor Duncan Regehr won praise from fans and critics for his truly sinister performance in the role. Dracula returned to the big screen in full-force in 1991 under the helm of legendary filmmaker Francis Ford Coppola, with a grandiose take on the mythos in *Bram Stoker's Dracula.* Adhering closer to the source material than many of the previous adaptations, this film saw acclaimed character actor Gary Oldman in the lead role. This time Dracula is portrayed as a romantic warrior who was cursed when he turned his back on God after losing the love of his life. Reusing a plot point from a 1973 TV movie from Dan Curtis, Dracula recognizes that his former lover is reincarnated as Mina Murray, and this drives him to turn her into an undead creature like himself.

Dracula may have begun merely as a monster in a Victorian novel, but he has grown to a cultural icon. He is arguably the most filmed fictional character in history and has largely shaped the way our culture views vampire mythology as a whole. Today Dracula conjures images of a charismatic monster in a cape rather than a fifteenth-century warlord. Across the decades, a number of legendary actors have portrayed the infamous bloodsucker, and each have left their mark on the character. There is little doubt that Dracula will continue to evolve in new ways to continue to entertain and terrify society.

Joshua Plock

See also: Angelique Bouchard-Collins, Angelus, Frankenstein's Monster, Freddy Krueger, Jason Voorhees, Leatherface, Lucifer/Satan, Michael Myers, Spike and Drusilla; *Thematic Essays*: "In the Beginning . . .": The Origins of Villains in the Western World, The Pathos of Villainy: Getting to the Heart of Why Villains Went Bad.

Further Reading

Hunter, Jack, ed. 1996. *House of Horror: The Complete Hammer Films Story.* London: Creation.

Hutchings, Peter. 2003. *Dracula: A British Film Guide.* London: I. B. Tauris.

Joslin, Lyndon W. 2017. *Count Dracula Goes to the Movies.* Jefferson, NC: McFarland.

Mallory, Michael. 2009. *Universal Monsters: A Legacy of Horror.* New York: Universe.

Schoell, William. 2014. *The Horror Comics: Fiends, Freaks, and Fantastic Creatures.* Jefferson, NC: McFarland.

Silver, Alain and James Ursini. 1993. *The Vampire Film.* New York: Limelight.

Unger, Steven P. 2010. *In the Footsteps of Dracula.* New York: Audience Artist Group.

Dr. Frank-N-Furter

First Appearance:	*The Rocky Horror Show* (stage play) (first performance: June 19, 1973)
Creators:	Richard O'Brien
Other Media:	Movies
Primary Strength:	Brilliant scientist
Major Weakness:	Passion/lust

Weapons:	Medusa transducer
Base of Operations:	Denton, Texas; the planet Transsexual in the galaxy of Transylvania
Key Allies:	Riff Raff, Magenta, Colombia, Rocky
Key Enemies:	Dr. Everett Scott, Brad Majors, Janet Weiss, Eddie, Riff Raff
Actual Identity:	N/A
Nicknames/Aliases:	"Sweet Transvestite from Transsexual, Transylvania"

The Rocky Horror Show is a rock opera from the 1970s, the brainchild of writer and composer Richard O'Brien. The immediate success of the stage play led to a major motion picture directed by Jim Sharman and distributed by 20th Century Fox in 1975. Though a box office failure, the film gained a cult following and continued massive success with midnight showings throughout the 1970s and beyond. Die-hard fans of the film have created interactive traditions for audiences to take part in the fun. The main character, Dr. Frank-N-Furter (immortalized by the stage and screen performance of Tim Curry), is an alien mad scientist bent on releasing everyone from their sexual rigidity. He is the first major open LGBTQ+ character in American popular culture and became a symbol of the Gay Liberation Front/Lavender Menace movements of the 1970s. Although the character has been portrayed by numerous actors and actresses over the years, Curry's portrayal remains dominant in American pop culture.

Set in Denton, Texas, in 1974, newly engaged conservative couple Brad and Janet (played by Barry Bostwick and Susan Sarandon) head to the home of their former professor, Dr. Everett Scott, to tell him of their pending nuptials. A flat tire on a rainy night lead them to seek a phone at the nearby castle of Dr. Frank-N-Furter, where the two and the audience are introduced to two of the greatest musical numbers of the 1970s: "The Time Warp," performed by servants Riff Raff, Magenta, and Colombia, and "Sweet Transvestite," introducing all to the mysterious Frank-N-Furter. Frank shows the couple his latest creation: the perfect man, Rocky. The sexual norms of the day are put into a tailspin, with the gender-bending Frank opening Brad and Janet to "absolute pleasure." When his previous experiment, Colombia's boyfriend Eddie, is released from "the vaults," the young couple become aware that Frank is a murdering psychopath. Dr. Everett Scott arrives at the castle, looking for his nephew, Eddie. As Brad, Janet, and even Dr. Scott become more open to giving in to pleasure, Riff Raff and his sister, Magenta, turn on Frank, killing him so that they can return to their home planet of Transsexual.

On the surface, Dr. Frank-N-Furter is the standard mad scientist, along the model of Dr. Victor Frankenstein from Mary Shelley's immortal 1818 novel, *Frankenstein; or, The Modern Prometheus*, with Rocky representing a more successful version of the classic monster. Frank is also, as stated earlier, a cold-blooded murderer. He falls into the realm of antivillain, however, through his overall message

Tim Curry brought his iconic performance of Dr. Frank-N-Furter to the big screen in 1975's *The Rocky Horror Picture Show.* (Twentieth Century Fox/AF Archive/Alamy Stock Photo)

of "don't dream it; be it," opening the minds of Brad, Janet, and the audience to overturning the social norm in favor of a more freeing lifestyle of acceptance of one's desires and pleasures (a very 1970s concept). He is also groundbreaking for his place in LGBTQ+ history.

Richard A. Hall

See also: Doctor Doom, Dracula, Frankenstein's Monster, Heisenberg/Walter White, Lex Luthor, Martin Brenner, The Master/Missy, Number Six/Cylons; *Thematic Essays*: Tarantino and the Antivillain.

Further Reading

Alsford, Mike. 2006. *Heroes & Villains.* Waco, TX: Baylor University Press.

Ashby, LeRoy. 2006. *With Amusement for All: A History of American Popular Culture since 1830.* Lexington: University Press of Kentucky.

Larsen, Kristine. 2011. "Frankenstein's Legacy: The Mad Scientist Remade." In *Vader, Voldemort and Other Villains: Essays on Evil in Popular Media*, edited by Jamey Heit, 46–63. Jefferson, NC: McFarland.

Thompson, Dave. 2016. *The Rocky Horror Picture Show FAQ: Everything Left to Know about the Campy Cult Classic.* Logan Village, QLD, Australia: Applause.

Weinstock, Jefferey Andrew. 2008. *Reading Rocky Horror: The Rocky Horror Picture Show and Popular Culture.* Basingstoke, UK: Palgrave Macmillan.

Ebenezer Scrooge

First Appearance:	*A Christmas Carol. In Prose. Being a Ghost Story of Christmas* (original publication date: December 19, 1843)
Creators:	Charles Dickens
Other Media:	Radio, television, film, comics
Primary Strength:	Wealth
Major Weakness:	Fear of the future
Weapons:	N/A
Base of Operations:	London, England
Key Allies:	Fred (his nephew and sole living relative), Bob Cratchit, "Tiny" Tim Cratchit, Jacob Marley, Ghosts of Christmas Past, Present, and Yet-to-Come ("Future")
Key Enemies:	Himself (proverbially)
Actual Identity:	N/A
Nicknames/Aliases:	"A Squeezing, Wrenching, Grasping, Scraping, Clutching, Covetous Old Sinner"

Originally published in 1843, *A Christmas Carol* has become the most commercially successful Christmas tradition in the history of the holiday. Unlike most stories, which center on a hero, Dickens's classic tale centers on the primary villain, Ebenezer Scrooge. Scrooge is a product of industrial-era Victorian England. He is a money-lender, a representation of the very sinners beaten by Jesus of Nazareth in the New Testament (John 2:13–16). As the story opens, it is Christmas Eve in London, and Scrooge professes his distaste for the holiday, berating his nephew, Fred; two gentlemen requesting donations for the poor; and his sole employee, Bob Cratchit. When Scrooge returns home for the evening, he is confronted by the ghost of his longtime business partner, Jacob Marley. Marley tells Scrooge of his horrible afterlife due to his greed and avarice in his lifetime and warns Scrooge that he also will meet this same fate if he does not change his evil ways. In order to move his friend, Marley sends three spirits to visit Scrooge over the course of the next three nights.

Scrooge is then visited by the Ghost of Christmas Past, who shows him how much he has changed since his kinder days as a young man. That spirit is followed

The Grinch

The Grinch has become a Christmas mainstay in American popular culture. Best described as an American Ebenezer Scrooge, the Grinch was first introduced in 1957 in the children's book *How the Grinch Stole Christmas* by Dr. Seuss (Theodor Seuss Geisel, 1904–1991). While his species is never identified, he is a cold-hearted, furry green humanoid who lives on a mountain overlooking the top of Whoville, home to the kindhearted, light-skinned (and nonfurry) Whos.

In his original and most iconic story, the Grinch is particularly angry because of the upcoming celebration of Christmas, when the Whos will be partying, enjoying themselves, and making considerable joyful noise. He ultimately plans to disrupt this frivolity by sneaking into Whoville on Christmas Eve and stealing all of the gifts from all of the homes, in anticipation of enjoying the resulting sadness that the town will experience. When he discovers that the Whos are still joyful and happy despite the lack of presents, the Grinch's heart—already established as "two sizes too small"—grows "three sizes that day." He abruptly returns to Whoville with all of the gifts intact and is warmly welcomed into the Whos' celebrations. Like the British classic *A Christmas Carol, How the Grinch Stole Christmas* is a tale of redemption, showing that the spirit of Christmas can warm even the coldest of hearts. The book was translated into an animated television special narrated by Boris Karloff (1887–1969), a live-action film (2000) starring Jim Carrey (b. 1962) as the Grinch, and a CGI-animated feature film with the character voiced by Benedict Cumberbatch (b. 1976).

Richard A. Hall

by the Ghost of Christmas Present, who presents to Scrooge how others celebrate the holiday with love, with no care for money or worldly possessions. It is while he is with Christmas Present that Scrooge discovers that his employee, Bob, has a lame son, Tiny Tim, who is kindhearted child despite his lot in life. Present is followed by the Ghost of Christmas Yet-to-Come (the Ghost of Christmas Future). Taking the form of the Grim Reaper, this last spirit shows a not-too-distant future where Tiny Tim has died from his ailments and Scrooge also is dead, to the delight of all who knew him. Scrooge awakens to discover that all three spirits have visited him in just one night and that it is now Christmas Day. Having learned his lesson, Scrooge commits himself to being a kinder and more generous man and to seeing to it that Tiny Tim receives the medical attention he needs to survive, which, the narrator informs the reader, he does. The villain emerges as a hero, showing that no one is beyond redemption.

The cable television network FX aired the latest rendition of this classic tale in 2019. The new incarnation, directed by Nick Murphy and starring Guy Pierce as Ebenezer Scrooge, presents perhaps the coldest and cruelest Scrooge in the story's long history. For the first time ever, audiences see deceased partner Jacob Marley in the afterlife as he is handed his mission to announce Scrooge's chance for redemption. Also, the Ghost of Christmas Past presents audiences with the unimaginable horror that led Scrooge to lose his faith and concern for humanity, and in another first, the final shot of the miniseries provides audiences insight into why, of all the cold, cruel humans on Earth, Scrooge was chosen for this shot at redemption. After a century of Scrooge being presented, more or less, as a grumpy old man, FX's *A Christmas Carol* elevates Scrooge to true, unapologetic villainy, making his predetermined redemption an even greater message of hope for a twenty-first century world.

In the nearly two hundred years since its original publication, *A Christmas Carol* has been reprinted countless times and adapted, revised, and reimagined in every media of popular culture. Scrooge has inspired characters from Disney's Uncle Scrooge McDuck to Dr. Seuss's the Grinch. The timeless tale of redemption has become a holiday classic that still holds resonance in the twenty-first century. Ebenezer Scrooge is the ultimate greedy, self-absorbed businessman. He is J. R. Ewing. He is Lex Luthor. He is Donald Trump. Forever representing the evils of capitalism, Ebenezer Scrooge is the ultimate example of the darker side of humanity, one who, fortunately for him, has a friend on the other side of existence willing to break the barrier between life and death to give his friend fair warning of what is to come after death. Despite this lesson—repeated every Christmas season across the Western world—its lessons go disregarded as early as December 26 every year, and greed and avarice continue to thrive.

Richard A. Hall

See also: Alexis Carrington-Colby-Dexter, Archie Bunker, Cersei Lannister, Frank Burns, Grand Nagus/Ferengi, J. R. Ewing, Lex Luthor, Marsellus Wallace; *Thematic Essays*: "In the Beginning . . .": The Origins of Villains in the Western World, The Pathos of Villainy: Getting to the Heart of Why Villains Went Bad.

Further Reading

Alsford, Mike. 2006. *Heroes & Villains.* Waco, TX: Baylor University Press.

Ashby, LeRoy. 2006. *With Amusement for All: A History of American Popular Culture since 1830.* Lexington: University Press of Kentucky.

Dickens, Charles. 2015. *A Christmas Carol (Annotated): An Annotated Version of A Christmas Carol with Full Novel and In-Depth Analysis.* N.p.: Amazon Services.

Gavaler, Chris. 2015. *On the Origin of Superheroes: From the Big Bang to Action Comics No. 1.* Iowa City: University of Iowa.

Marx, Karl, and Friedrich Engels. 2019. *The Communist Manifesto.* Scotts Valley, CA: CreateSpace.

Standiford, Les. 2011. *The Man Who Invented Christmas: How Charles Dickens's A Christmas Carol Rescued His Career and Revived Our Holiday Spirits.* New York: Broadway.

Elle Driver/California Mountain Snake

First Appearance:	*Kill Bill, Vol. 1* (release date: October 10, 2003)
Creators:	Quentin Tarantino
Other Media:	N/A
Primary Strength:	Martial arts, expert swordsman
Major Weakness:	Blind hatred of Beatrix Kiddo
Weapons:	Samurai swords, guns

Base of Operations:	Various
Key Allies:	Deadly Viper Assassination Squad: Bill/Snake Charmer, Budd/Sidewinder, O-Ren Ishii/Cottonmouth, Vernita Green/Copperhead
Key Enemies:	Beatrix Kiddo/Black Mamba/The Bride
Actual Identity:	Elle Driver
Nicknames/Aliases:	California Mountain Snake

Kill Bill (volumes one and two) is the ultimate cinematic revenge epic by writer and director Quentin Tarantino. Released in two parts in 2003 and 2004, the film stars Uma Thurman as the enigmatic Bride, bent on revenge against the gang that placed her in a coma after trying to kill her on her wedding day and presumably killing her unborn child in the process. As she moves one by one through the colorful and dangerous members of the Deadly Viper Assassination Squad, audiences learn numerous things about the mysterious Bride: she was once a member of the Deadly Vipers, known as "Black Mamba"; she was once romantically involved with the Viper leader, Bill ("Snake Charmer"); and her child was saved and currently lives with her father, Bill (Quentin Tarantino, *Kill Bill, Vols. 1 & 2*, 2003–2004). Of the members of the Deadly Vipers, the one who appears to despise Beatrix the most is Elle Driver ("California Mountain Snake"), played by Daryl Hannah.

In *Kill Bill, Vol. 1* (2003), audiences first see Elle Driver disguised as a nurse and wearing an eye patch to cover a lost eye; she is sent to the hospital where Beatrix lays in a coma to finish the job initiated by the gang. At the last moment, Bill contacts her to abort her mission (much to her disgust). Elle is seen next in *Kill Bill, Vol. 2* (2004), where it is discovered that Elle has replaced Beatrix as Bill's romantic interest. When Bill's brother, Budd ("Sidewinder") informs Elle that he has captured Beatrix and buried her alive and asks for a reward for his service, Elle arrives the following day with a case of cash. After giving Elle the location of Beatrix's "grave," he discovers that his case of cash also contains a live black mamba snake. The snake strikes Budd several times, and within a minute, he is dead. Elle telephones Bill to report that she has found Budd dead, presumably killed by Beatrix ("Black Mamba"), but that Budd succeeded in burying her alive first. Leaving Budd's trailer, Elle is confronted by the very-much-alive Beatrix, and the two embark on a bloody swordfight, which Beatrix ultimately wins by plucking out Elle's remaining eye, leaving the assassin to an uncertain fate, blind and in a trailer with the still-alive deadly snake.

In the realm of fiction, Elle is an example of the dark mirror, the polar opposite of the heroine, Beatrix. Elle and Beatrix are both blond, blue-eyed, deadly assassins and romantically linked to Bill. However, unlike Beatrix, Elle embraces her murderous occupation. Elle also exemplifies the gun for hire, an assassin comfortable with taking any life for the right amount of money. In the universe of Tarantino characters, literally filled with colorful eccentric characters, Elle Driver is one of the darkest. She is an unstoppable killing machine, and as the audience does not specifically witness her death, it can be assumed that this killer remains on the loose and a dangerous threat (albeit a blind one).

Richard A. Hall

See also: Bill/Snake Charmer, Billy the Kid, Boba Fett, The Corleone Family, Ernst Stavro Blofeld/SPECTRE, Fish Mooney, Gus Fring, Heisenberg/Walter White, Jabba the Hutt, Marsellus Wallace, Negan/The Saviors, Nurse Ratched, O-Ren Ishii/Cottonmouth, Pancho Villa, Ra's al Ghul, Tony Montana, Tony Soprano; *Thematic Essays*: The Dark Mirror: Evil Twins, *The Twilight Zone*, and the Villain Within, Tarantino and the Antivillain.

Further Reading

Alsford, Mike. 2006. *Heroes & Villains.* Waco, TX: Baylor University Press.

Greene, Richard, and K. Silem Mohammad, eds. 2007. *Quentin Tarantino and Philosophy: How to Philosophize with a Pair of Pliers and a Blowtorch.* Chicago: Open Court.

Kirshner, Jonathan. 2012. *Hollywood's Last Golden Age: Politics, Society, and the Seventies Film in America.* Ithaca, NY: Cornell University Press.

Peary, Gerald, ed. 2013. *Quentin Tarantino: Interviews, Revised and Updated.* Jackson: University of Mississippi Press.

Roche, David. 2018. *Quentin Tarantino: Poetics and Politics of Cinematic Metafiction.* Jackson: University of Mississippi Press.

Shone, Tom. 2017. *Tarantino: A Retrospective.* San Rafael, CA: Insight Editions.

Ernst Stavro Blofeld/SPECTRE

First Appearance:	*Thunderball* (publication date: March 27, 1961)
Creators:	Ian Fleming
Other Media:	Movies
Primary Strength:	Strategy, seemingly endless resources
Major Weakness:	Mad for power
Weapons:	Handguns, henchmen
Base of Operations:	Various
Key Allies:	Dr. No, Auric Goldfinger
Key Enemies:	James Bond/Agent 007, British Secret Service/MI-6, CIA
Actual Identity:	Franz Oberhauser (Blofeld)
Nicknames/Aliases:	"SPECTRE Agent #1" (Blofeld)

In 1953, former British military intelligence officer Ian Fleming introduced the world to the most famous superspy in fiction: James Bond, commander in the British Royal Navy and British Secret Service Agent, code-named "007." Bond first appeared in the novel *Casino Royale*, and the successful novel and film franchises that succeeded it followed 007 on various adventures to save the world, visiting

Dr. Evil

Dr. Evil was the brainchild of comedian Mike Myers (b. 1963), who portrayed the character, along with the role of Austin Powers, in the film *Austin Powers: International Man of Mystery* (1997), as well as its sequels: *Austin Powers: The Spy Who Shagged Me* (1999) and *Austin Powers in Goldmember* (2002, all from New Line Cinema). The character's appearance was directly copied from the iconic *James Bond* villain Ernst Stavro Blofeld, specifically, the version played by Donald Pleasence in the 1967 film *You Only Live Twice*, and his voice was an impersonation of Myers's former *Saturday Night Live* boss, Lorne Michaels (b. 1944). Ironically, Pleasence (1919–1995) starred in the horror film franchise *Halloween*, whose murdering antagonist was named Michael Myers.

In the *Austin Powers* series, Dr. Evil is the standard evil mastermind behind an international criminal organization, frequently devising numerous ridiculous plans to conquer the world, only to be defeated every time by the titular British superspy. In the third film, it was discovered that Dr. Evil is, in fact, Dougie Powers, Austin's long-lost brother. Dr. Evil has a son, Scott (played by Seth Green, b. 1974), by his henchwoman, Frau Farbissina (played by Mindy Sterling, b. 1953), who is an amalgamation of several female SPECTRE agents from the *Bond* films. Dr. Evil also possesses a clone of himself (one-eighth of his size), "Mini Me" (played by Verne Troyer, 1969–2018). The character and films are excellent parodies of the ludicrous nature of 1960s spy movie plots.

Richard A. Hall

exotic locales, drinking vodka martinis ("shaken, not stirred"), and seducing beautiful women. He utilizes his "license to kill" to save the world from various threats: communists, terrorists, and the international organization known as SPECTRE, the Special Executive for Counterintelligence, Terrorism, Revenge, and Extortion. When the successful novels led to a massively successful film franchise, the first half-dozen *Bond* films centered on SPECTRE and its mysterious leader: Agent #1/Ernst Stavro Blofeld.

From an early age, Blofeld proved brilliant, receiving degrees in history, economics, and engineering. After World War II, Blofeld formed SPECTRE, an international organization comprised of multinational companies and banks. The hierarchy consists of top-level members of criminal and intelligence organizations from around the world. In the *Bond* films, Blofeld has been portrayed by Donald Pleasance (*You Only Live Twice*, 1967), Telly Savalas (*On Her Majesty's Secret Service*, 1969), Charles Gray (*Diamonds Are Forever*, 1971), and Christoph Waltz (*Spectre*, 2015). In the 2015 film, it is revealed that Blofeld was born Franz Oberhauser; that when he and Bond were children, Oberhauser's father had adopted the orphaned Bond; and that Bond soon became their father's favorite, leading Franz to murder his father, stage his death, change his name to Ernst Stavro Blofeld, and form SPECTRE.

In the 1960s, at the height of the Cold War, American and Western European fears of communist aggression, invasion, and/or nuclear attack drew audiences to spy films by the millions; the successes of the spy heroes acted as a cathartic release for Cold War anxieties. Of these spy films and novels, *James Bond* was, by far, the most successful. The specter of global conquest by authoritarianism made the need for a James Bond even greater. Blofeld, then, represents the greatest fear of the Cold War era: an overpowering threat to basic freedoms and liberties around the world. He would be copied elsewhere in popular culture in comic book villains such as Marvel's updated version of Red Skull and animated and toy franchises such as *G. I. Joe*'s COBRA. In 2017, *Esquire* magazine listed Blofeld as the number seven *Bond* villain of all time (Hall, "All 104 Bond Villains Ranked"). In the twenty-first century, with fears of similar international organizations such as Al-Qaeda and ISIS/ISIL, Blofeld and SPECTRE remain relevant villains in the United States. Blofeld is the threat to life as Americans know it and a malevolent specter of what may lie around the corner for the Western democracies.

Richard A. Hall

See also: Borg Queen/Borg, Cersei Lannister, COBRA, The Corleone Family, The Court of Owls, Cybermen, Davros/Daleks, Fish Mooney, Goldfinger, The Governor, Grand Nagus/Ferengi, Heisenberg/Walter White, Jabba the Hutt, J. R. Ewing, Kahless/Klingons, Lex Luthor, Marsellus Wallace, Negan/The Saviors, Ra's al Ghul, Red Skull, Sherry Palmer, Zod; *Thematic Essays*: "Nazis, Communists, and Terrorists . . . Oh My!": The Rise of the Supervillain and the Evolution of the Modern American Villain, The Dark Mirror: Evil Twins, *The Twilight Zone*, and the Villain Within.

Further Reading

Alsford, Mike. 2006. *Heroes & Villains.* Waco, TX: Baylor University Press.

Ashby, LeRoy. 2006. *With Amusement for All: A History of American Popular Culture since 1830.* Lexington: University Press of Kentucky.

Brittany, Michele, ed. 2014. *James Bond and Popular Culture: Essays on the Influence of the Fictional Superspy.* Jefferson, NC: McFarland.

Hall, Jacob. 2017. "All 104 James Bond Villains Ranked: From Masterminds to Henchmen, the Final Word on 007's Furious Foes." *Esquire.* May 24, 2017. Accessed July 4, 2019. https://www.esquire.com/entertainment/movies/g2496/best-james-bond-villains-ranked/.

Hoberman, J. 2003. *The Dream Life: Movies, Media, and the Mythology of the Sixties.* New York: New Press.

Starck, Kathleen, ed. 2010. *Between Fear and Freedom: Cultural Representations of the Cold War.* Newcastle upon Tyne, UK: Cambridge Scholars.

F

Faith the Vampire Slayer

First Appearance:	*Buffy the Vampire Slayer*, season 3, episode 3 (air date: October 13, 1998)
Creators:	Joss Whedon and David Greenwalt
Other Media:	Comics, novels
Primary Strength:	Enhanced strength, speed, and agility
Major Weakness:	Need for acceptance
Weapons:	Wooden stakes, crossbows
Base of Operations:	Sunnydale, California; Los Angeles, California
Key Allies:	Buffy Summers, Angel, Mayor Wilkins, Wolfram and Hart
Key Enemies:	Buffy Summers, Scooby Gang
Actual Identity:	Unknown
Nicknames/Aliases:	"The Chosen One" (in theory)

Buffy the Vampire Slayer (WB, 1997–2001; UPN, 2001–2003) is a cult-classic television series that has gained an international following. Creator Joss Whedon wanted to take the tired concept of the girl being attacked by the monster and flip it so that the girl attacks the monster (Billson, *Buffy the Vampire Slayer*, 24–25). The show centers on Buffy Summers, a run-of-the-mill high school teenager who also happens to be the latest in a centuries-long line of "Chosen Ones," teenage girls who serve, one at a time, as the slayer, the one girl in all the world who can save us from demons, vampires, and all threats of the supernatural. Every slayer is trained by a watcher, chosen by the Watchers' Council to oversee the slayer's training and guide her on her overall mission. When the series begins, Buffy and her recently divorced mother move to the small California town of Sunnydale, which happens to sit directly on a Hellmouth, a portal/magnet of concentrated evil, mostly in the form of vampires. In the very first episode, Buffy meets Willow Rosenberg, a standard, run-of-the-mill high school nerd, considered unpopular by the "it" crowd. Buffy immediately befriends the young lady, and she becomes a valuable member of Buffy's Scooby Gang: her circle of friends who assist her in her slayer duties, saving the world and Buffy time and time again (Joss Whedon, "Welcome to the Hellmouth," season 1, episode 1, March 10, 1997).

At the end of season one, Buffy briefly dies (Joss Whedon, "Prophecy Girl," season 1, episode 12, June 2, 1997). Although she is revived, her death sets off an automatic calling of the next slayer, turning on the powers of Buffy's would-be

Eliza Dushku played the villainess/antihero Faith in the television series *Buffy the Vampire Slayer.* (UPN/Photofest)

successor, Kendra. As a result, a strange anomaly exists: two slayers at once. While she is a more disciplined slayer, Kendra soon dies (Joss Whedon, "Becoming, Part 1," season 2, episode 22, May 19, 1998). Though an active slayer remains, the death of one automatically calls another: Faith. Portrayed by Eliza Dushku, Faith proves to be an even more rebellious slayer than Buffy, soon becoming a bad influence on the true Chosen One. When rebuffed by Buffy and her friends, the jilted Faith turns to Sunnydale's mayor, Richard Wilkins. The mayor is, in fact, an evil demonic entity bent on killing everyone in Sunnydale and ruling the Hellmouth. After attempting to murder the heroic vampire Angel, Buffy's boyfriend, Faith teams with Buffy for one final battle, which leaves Faith in a coma.

Faith briefly returns the following season as a means of transitioning the character to the spin-off series, *Angel* (WB, 1999–2004), where the ersatz slayer finds some manner of redemption, bonding with the vampire, who understands dealing with one's inner demons. Faith returns to *Buffy* in the final, seventh season to assist the heroes in their final defense of the Hellmouth. In general, Faith represents the dark mirror, the polar opposite of the good slayer, Buffy. Faith is what Buffy could have become had it not been for the love and support of her friends and family. Through Faith, audiences can see the darker parts of themselves made manifest and the dangers and hardships into which such darkness can lead.

Richard A. Hall

See also: Alexis Carrington-Colby-Dexter, Alpha/The Whisperers, Angelique Bouchard-Collins, Angelus, Asajj Ventress, Bellatrix Lestrange, Borg Queen/Borg, Cersei Lannister, Dark Willow, Dracula, Elle Driver/California Mountain Snake, Fiona Goode/The Supreme, Harley Quinn, La Llorona, Maleficent, Morgan le Fay, Nurse Ratched, O-Ren Ishii/Cottonmouth, Poison Ivy, Sherry Palmer, Spike and Drusilla, Tia Dalma/Calypso, Wicked Witch of the West; *Thematic Essays*: The Dark Mirror: Evil Twins, *The Twilight Zone*, and the Villain Within, The Pathos of Villainy: Getting to the Heart of Why Villains Went Bad.

Further Reading

Alsford, Mike. 2006. *Heroes & Villains.* Waco, TX: Baylor University Press.

Billson, Anne. 2005. *Buffy the Vampire Slayer.* London: British Film Institute.

Castleman, Harry, and Walter J. Podrazik. 2016. *Watching TV: Eight Decades of American Television.* 3rd ed. Syracuse, NY: Syracuse University Press.

Cavendish, Richard. 1968. *The Black Arts: A Concise History of Witchcraft, Demonology, Astrology, and Other Mystical Practices throughout the Ages.* New York: TarcherPerigree.

Dial-Driver, Emily, Sally Emmons-Featherston, Jim Ford, and Carolyn Anne Taylor. 2008. *The Truth of Buffy: Essays on Fiction Illuminating Reality.* Jefferson, NC: McFarland.

Field, Mark. 2017. *Buffy, the Vampire Slayer: Myth, Metaphor & Morality.* N.p.: Amazon Services.

Gross, Edward, and Mark A. Altman. 2017. *Slayers & Vampires: The Complete, Uncensored, Unauthorized Oral History of Buffy & Angel.* New York: Tor.

Hutton, Ronald. 2017. *The Witch: A History of Fear, from Ancient Times to the Present.* New Haven, CT: Yale University Press.

Jowett, Lorna. 2005. *Sex and the Slayer: A Gender Studies Primer for the Buffy Fan.* Middletown, CT: Wesleyan University Press.

Lavery, David. 2013. *Joss Whedon, A Creative Portrait: From Buffy, the Vampire Slayer to Marvel's The Avengers.* London: I. B. Tauris.

Lavery, David, and Cynthia Burkhead, eds. 2011. *Joss Whedon: Conversations.* Jackson: University of Mississippi Press.

Pender, Patricia J. 2016. *I'm Buffy and You're History.* London: I. B. Tauris.

Russell, Jeffrey B., and Brooks Alexander. 2007. *A History of Witchcraft: Sorcerers, Heretics, & Pagans.* London: Thames & Hudson.

Short, Sue. 2011. "*Buffy the Vampire Slayer*: Beauty and the 'Big Bad.'" In *Cult Telefantasy Series: A Critical Analysis of The Prisoner, Twin Peaks, The X-Files, Buffy the Vampire Slayer, Lost, Heroes, Doctor Who, and Star Trek,* 84–107. Jefferson, NC: McFarland.

South, James B., ed. 2005. *Buffy, the Vampire Slayer and Philosophy: Fear and Trembling in Sunnydale.* Chicago: Open Court.

Wilcox, Rhonda V., Tanya Cochran, Cynthea Masson, and David Lavery. 2014. *Reading Joss Whedon.* Syracuse, NY: Syracuse University Press.

Wilcox, Rhonda V., and David Lavery. 2002. *Fighting the Forces: What's at Stake in Buffy, the Vampire Slayer.* Lanham, MD: Rowman & Littlefield.

Yeffeth, Glenn, ed. 2003. *Seven Seasons of Buffy: Science Fiction and Fantasy Writers Discuss Their Favorite Television Show.* Dallas, TX: BenBella.

Fiona Goode/The Supreme

First Appearance: *American Horror Story*, season 3, episode 1 (air date: October 9, 2013)
Creators: Ryan Murphy and Brad Falchuk
Other Media: N/A

Primary Strength:	Witchcraft/magic
Major Weakness:	Vanity, ego
Weapons:	Potions, poppets, amulets
Base of Operations:	New Orleans, Louisiana
Key Allies:	Cordelia Foxx (daughter), Coven, Spalding
Key Enemies:	Marie Laveau
Actual Identity:	N/A
Nicknames/Aliases:	"The Supreme"

American Horror Story is an anthology television series created by Ryan Murphy and Brad Falchuk that began airing in the fall of 2011 on the FX cable network. Each season presents a different overall thematic story line, though it often utilizes many cast members from previous seasons in different roles. The third season was subtitled "Coven," focusing on two competing covens of witches in modern-day New Orleans: the Caucasian witches, descended from the survivors of the Salem witchcraft trials of 1692, and the black voodoo witches, whose ancestors have been in New Orleans from the beginning. The white witches live at Miss Robichaux's Academy, led by Headmistress Cordelia Foxx (played by Sarah Paulson). Cordelia's mother, Fiona Goode (played by Jessica Lange), is globally recognized by the magical world, minus the voodoo witches of New Orleans, as "the Supreme," the most powerful witch in the world and official leader of the magic community.

As the season begins, Fiona is in desperate search for a scientific remedy to restore her youth. She is aware that her life is nearing an end after decades of drug and alcohol abuse. She returns to Miss Robichaux's and receives a cold reception from her daughter, the kindhearted Cordelia. Several threats face the academy

Marie Laveau

Marie Laveau (1801–1881) is a legendary voodoo priestess who lived in nineteenth century New Orleans. She was born free to a woman of mixed Native American, African, and French descent and a local white French politician. She opened a beauty parlor in New Orleans and was widely known as a practitioner of magic. Although records indicate that she died peacefully in 1881 at the age of seventy-nine, rumors circulated of individuals seeing her around the city long after her death, giving rise to rumors that through her voodoo practice, she had achieved mortality. A more likely scenario, however, is that one of her daughters, also named Marie Laveau, continued her mother's two occupations.

Regardless of the actual course of events, people to this day visit her grave, leaving written requests for the local legend. In the third season of the FX cable television series *American Horror Story* (2011–present) subtitled *Coven* (2013–2014), the character of the original, immortal Marie Laveau was portrayed by Angela Bassett (b. 1958). Staying true to the real-world legend, Bassett's Laveau is still alive and youthful in the twenty-first century, still the proprietor of a New Orleans beauty salon, and still the voodoo queen. The legend of Marie Laveau is a fascinating addition to American popular culture and a key component to the rich history, mystery, and nuance that has always surrounded the city of New Orleans.

Richard A. Hall

throughout the season, often requiring Fiona's intervention. Ultimately, Fiona must ally herself with her longtime adversary, the seemingly immortal voodoo priestess Marie Laveau (portrayed by Angela Bassett and based on the real-life nineteenth-century New Orleans voodoo priestess of the same name). As the season and story line end, Fiona dies, damned to an eternity of bland existence, and Cordelia emerges as the new Supreme. The witches of Coven (without Fiona) later returned in season eight, subtitled "Apocalypse," where Cordelia leads the charge against the Antichrist.

Fiona represents all of the female empowerment often associated with witchcraft stories. She is the ultimate power in a world thought to be ruled by men. She also represents the fear that comes with facing one's mortality. As someone who has hedonistically enjoyed all that life has to offer, the idea of death is particularly devastating for someone like Fiona (female or male). Additionally, Fiona represents the idea of absolute power corrupting absolutely. She has been the most powerful being on Earth for decades, and as her powers fade with her dwindling health, even those who dislike her vanity and ego cannot help but feel for her slow decline from her former greatness. She is both a warning against wasting one's live on frivolity and a call for people to live to their ultimate potential. As she is called to utilize her powers to repeatedly save the coven, she transitions from banal queen to antivillain.

Richard A. Hall

See also: Alexis Carrington-Colby-Dexter, Alpha/The Whisperers, Angelique Bouchard-Collins, Angelus, Asajj Ventress, Bellatrix Lestrange, Borg Queen/Borg, Cersei Lannister, Dark Willow, Elle Driver/California Mountain Snake, Faith the Vampire Slayer, Harley Quinn, Jafar, La Llorona, Loki, Lucifer/Satan, Maleficent, Morgan le Fay, Nurse Ratched, O-Ren Ishii/Cottonmouth, Poison Ivy, Sauron/Saruman, Sherry Palmer, Sith Lords, Spike and Drusilla, Tia Dalma/Calypso, Ursula, Voldemort, Wicked Witch of the West; *Thematic Essays*: Tarantino and the Antivillain, The Pathos of Villainy: Getting to the Heart of Why Villains Went Bad.

Further Reading

Alsford, Mike. 2006. *Heroes & Villains*. Waco, TX: Baylor University Press.

Castleman, Harry, and Walter J. Podrazik. 2016. *Watching TV: Eight Decades of American Television*. 3rd ed. Syracuse, NY: Syracuse University Press.

Cavendish, Richard. 1968. *The Black Arts: A Concise History of Witchcraft, Demonology, Astrology, and Other Mystical Practices throughout the Ages*. New York: TarcherPerigree.

Faludi, Susan. 2007. *The Terror Dream: Myth and Misogyny in an Insecure America*. New York: Picador.

Forasteros, J. R. 2017. *Empathy for the Devil: Finding Ourselves in the Villains of the Bible*. Downers Grove, IL: InterVarsity.

Hutton, Ronald. 2017. *The Witch: A History of Fear, from Ancient Times to the Present*. New Haven, CT: Yale University Press.

Russell, Jeffrey B., and Brooks Alexander. 2007. *A History of Witchcraft: Sorcerers, Heretics, & Pagans*. London: Thames & Hudson.

Ryan, Hannah. 2020. "Vilifications: Conjuring Witches Then and Now." In *The Supervillain Reader*, edited by Rob Weiner and Rob Peaslee, 156–171. Jackson: University of Mississippi Press.

Fish Mooney

First Appearance:	*Gotham*, season 1, episode 1 (air date: September 22, 2014)
Creators:	Bruno Heller
Other Media:	Comics
Primary Strength:	Cunning, tenacity
Major Weakness:	Blinded by vengeance
Weapons:	Various (eventually psychic control of whomever she touches)
Base of Operations:	Gotham City
Key Allies:	Butch Gilzean
Key Enemies:	Oswald Cobblepot, Carmine Falcone, Sal Moroni, Francis Dulmacher, Hugo Strange
Actual Identity:	N/A
Nicknames/Aliases:	N/A

The *Batman* franchise is, perhaps, second only to *Superman* in regard to its impact on popular culture. Created by writer Bill Finger and artist Bob Kane, Batman is billionaire playboy Bruce Wayne, who, after witnessing a mugger murder his parents when he was a young boy, vowed to dedicate his life battling crime in his hometown of Gotham City. In order to strike fear in criminals, Wayne chose to disguise himself as a bat, and "the Batman" (originally "Bat-Man") was born (Bill Finger and Bob Kane, *Detective Comics #33*, November 1939). In 2014, Bruno Heller produced the live-action television series *Gotham* (FOX, 2014–2019) to examine Bruce Wayne's formative years, from his parents' death to his rise as Gotham's Dark Knight Detective. Most of the characters on the series, both major and minor, were drawn directly from the source comic book material. One character, however, was unique to the series: minor crime boss Fish Mooney (played by Jada Pinkett Smith).

Fish is introduced as a key source of information for Gotham City Police detective Harvey Bullock (played by Donal Logue) and a chief lieutenant for Gotham's primary crime boss, Don Carmine Falcone. All of season one revolves around a gang war initiated by the deceptions of Fish's "umbrella boy," Oswald Cobblepot, "the Penguin" (played by Robin Lord Taylor). Forced to flee Falcone's wrath, Fish escapes Gotham by ship, only to be taken by the henchmen of Dr. Francis Dulmacher, "the Doll Maker" (played by Colm Feore), who takes needed body parts from captured individuals for his patients. Fish utilizes her cunning and charm to fool Dulmacher into trusting her, only to assist in the escape of several other captives and make her way back to Gotham and vengeance on Falcone and Cobblepot. When Cobblepot's machinations come to full fruition, he faces off against his one-time employer, throwing Fish from a high building into the Gotham River, presumably to her death.

In the second season, audiences learn that Fish's body has been recovered by Dr. Hugo Strange (played by B. D. Wong), who experiments on recently deceased villains, toying with their DNA. His experiments bring Fish back to life, but with the mutated ability to take control of any person she touches. When the inmates of Indian Hill escape, Fish leads an army of the mutants to take Gotham. When she is eventually accidentally killed by Detective James Gordon (played by Ben McKenzie) in season three, her dying words are words of advice to Penguin to take Gotham or destroy it. Pinkett Smith had an opportunity unique among her castmates: to create a character entirely from scratch, without the weight of decades of established canon to live up to.

Fish Mooney takes the traditional gangster character and adds a sense of feminism and woman power. She utilizes stereotypical womanly wiles and manages to add a sense of female empowerment, making her a character that her male nemeses are unable to ever fully understand or outsmart. Although she is eventually defeated by the Penguin, he credits all that he knows about deception and subterfuge to her tutelage. She is the embodiment of the twenty-first-century woman, taking what has traditionally been a "man's" world and making it a world of her own design. Her popularity will doubtless lead to her addition to the overall rogues' gallery in the *Batman* comics and other media in the years to come.

Richard A. Hall

See also: Alexis Carrington-Colby-Dexter, Bill/Snake Charmer, Borg Queen/Borg, Catwoman, Cersei Lannister, COBRA, The Corleone Family, The Court of Owls, Elle Driver/California Mountain Snake, Ernst Stavro Blofeld/SPECTRE, Goldfinger, Green Goblin, Gus Fring, Harley Quinn, Joker, Lex Luthor, O-Ren Ishii/Cottonmouth, Poison Ivy, Ra's al Ghul, Scarecrow, Tony Montana, Tony Soprano, Two-Face; *Thematic Essays*: "Nazis, Communists, and Terrorists . . . Oh My!": The Rise of the Supervillain and the Evolution of the Modern American Villain.

Further Reading

Alsford, Mike. 2006. *Heroes & Villains*. Waco, TX: Baylor University Press.

Faludi, Susan. 2007. *The Terror Dream: Myth and Misogyny in an Insecure America*. New York: Picador.

Weldon, Glen. 2016. *The Caped Crusade: Batman and the Rise of Nerd Culture*. New York: Simon & Schuster.

Frank Burns

First Appearance:	*MASH: A Novel about Three Army Doctors* (publication date: 1968)
Creators:	Richard Hooker
Other Media:	Film, television
Primary Strength:	Tenacity
Major Weakness:	Hypocrisy, limited intellect
Weapons:	N/A

Base of Operations:	4077th Mobile Army Surgical Hospital, thirty-eighth parallel, South Korea
Key Allies:	Major Margaret Houlihan
Key Enemies:	Captain Benjamin Pierce, Captain John McIntyre, Captain B. J. Hunnicutt, Lieutenant Colonel Henry Blake, Colonel Sherman Potter, Corporal Walter O'Reilly, Corporal Maxwell Klinger
Actual Identity:	Major Franklin Delano Marion Burns
Nicknames/Aliases:	"Frank," "Needle Nose," "Ferret Face"

*M*A*S*H,* the military acronym for Mobile Army Surgical Hospital, was a pop culture phenomenon in the 1970s. Following the popularity of the 1968 novel, which centered on the antics and experiences of draftee army surgeons during the Korean conflict (1950–1953), 20th Century Fox released a theatrical version in 1970. The popularity of that film led to the television series, which ran on CBS from 1972 to 1983. The final feature-length episode of the series remains one of the most watched original network-television episodes in television history. The primary protagonist of all three incarnations was Captain Benjamin Franklin "Hawkeye" Pierce (played by Donald Sutherland in the film and Alan Alda in the series), a nonconformist draftee and brilliant surgeon. The primary antagonist of the novel, film, and the first four seasons of the series was Major Frank Burns, a radically conservative—and, in the novel and film, ultrareligious—draftee, substandard surgeon, and second in command of the 4077th MASH.

In the novel and film (where he was portrayed by Robert Duvall), Frank stood in stark contrast to the leftist antics of Hawkeye and his partner in crime, Captain "Trapper John" McIntyre (played by Elliot Gould in the film and Wayne Rogers in the series). In all three incarnations, the married Burns carried on an extramarital affair with the MASH unit's head nurse, Major Margaret "Hot Lips" Houlihan (played by Sally Kellerman in the film and Loretta Swit in the series). The "regular army" Houlihan was attracted to Burns's strict adherence to military protocols and discipline (other than, of course, the regulations against fraternization and extramarital relations). In the series, perhaps the most iconic representation in the American zeitgeist, Burns was portrayed by Larry Linville. Linville's Burns was far less intelligent than the novel and film versions, making him an easy target for Hawkeye and Trapper's considerably sharp wit. Burns frequently attempted to charge Hawkeye and Trapper with violations of army regulations, of which they were consistently admittedly guilty. On every occasion, however, the army's need for Hawkeye and Trapper's considerable surgical skills outweighed the necessity for strict adherence to regulations by civilian draftees in a war zone.

Frank Burns epitomized the worst examples of real-world military leadership. Veterans of all branches have experienced a Frank Burns in their careers, and the constant ridicule of Burns on the program served as a cathartic release for servicemen and -women who had suffered such incompetence. In all three incarnations, Burns was ultimately returned stateside due to a mental breakdown. In the novel and film, the breakdown was brought on by Hawkeye and Trapper's relentless antics. In the series, Burns was promoted and transferred stateside after a mental breakdown when Houlihan broke off their relationship to marry someone else. Also in the series, the irritation caused by Burns's idiocy was exacerbated by his incompetence as a surgeon, risking the lives of soldiers that the hero doctors so diligently attempted to save.

Burns also frequently exhibited staunch prejudices and bigotry. In one episode, he considers reporting a gay soldier brought into the unit for medical attention, and his attempt is thwarted when Hawkeye and Trapper blackmail Burns and threaten to inform his wife of his relationship with Houlihan. He also relentlessly despised North Koreans and Chinese, to the point of even refusing to treat them when enemy soldiers were brought into the unit. Even outside of "the enemy," Burns's comments frequently exhibited a complete and utter ignorance of Asian people and cultures (viewing no difference between Chinese, Japanese, and Koreans). Although he never expressed racism toward the few black characters on the show and was admittedly far less sexist than the womanizing Hawkeye and Trapper, Burns did repeatedly show contempt for any and all who were lower ranked than he was, which, as a major, meant the overwhelming majority of the other characters, primary, secondary, and guest stars.

In the realm of American villainy, Frank Burns is one of the more comedic examples. Hilarity aside, he represents the dangers of authority figures blinded by strict adherence to regulations, even if doing so threatens the safety or lives of those under his command or placed in his care. In the 1970s, he was yet another example, along with *All in the Family*'s Archie Bunker, of television's underscoring the frequently ludicrous nature of the more radical elements of political conservatism at the time. No serviceman or -woman would ever want to serve under a Burns, nor would any patient ever want to be placed in his care. He is an example of the dangers of incompetence at the higher levels of any organization.

Richard A. Hall

See also: Archie Bunker, General Custer, Imperial Officers, Martin Brenner, Sue Sylvester; *Thematic Essays*: The Pathos of Villainy: Getting to the Heart of Why Villains Went Bad.

Further Reading

Alsford, Mike. 2006. *Heroes & Villains*. Waco, TX: Baylor University Press.

Ashby, LeRoy. 2006. *With Amusement for All: A History of American Popular Culture since 1830*. Lexington: University Press of Kentucky.

Castleman, Harry, and Walter J. Podrazik. 2016. *Watching TV: Eight Decades of American Television*. 3rd ed. Syracuse, NY: Syracuse University Press.

Kalter, Suzy. 1988. *The Complete Book of M*A*S*H*. New York: Harry N. Abrams.

Reiss, David S. 1983. *M*A*S*H: The Exclusive, Inside Story of TV's Most Popular Show*. London: Macmillan.

Frankenstein's Monster

First Appearance:	*Frankenstein; or, The Modern Prometheus* (publication date: January 1, 1818)
Creators:	Mary Wollstonecraft Shelley
Other Media:	Stage, radio, movies, television, comic books, songs
Primary Strength:	Enhanced strength
Major Weakness:	Slow movement and intelligence (in films)
Weapons:	N/A
Base of Operations:	Central Europe (in the novel and films)
Key Allies:	Igor (in the films)
Key Enemies:	Victor Frankenstein
Actual Identity:	N/A
Nicknames/Aliases:	"The Creature"

For over more than two hundred years, *Frankenstein* has been one of the most powerful and popular novels ever written. Since its initial publication in 1818, when author Mary Shelley was only twenty years old, it has been retold, reimagined, and rebooted in every medium of popular culture. The initial story revolved around scientist Victor Frankenstein, in early nineteenth-century central Europe, and his desire to play God by creating a man. In the original novel and most retellings, the creature is stitched together from cadavers. In the twentieth century, electricity became the source for giving the creature life. After Frankenstein turns his back on the abomination he has created, the monster demands a mate, murdering members of his creator's family until Frankenstein consents, changing his mind (in the novel) before the female can be finished. Frankenstein then embarks on a quest around the globe to find and stop his monster, happening upon the stranded crew of Captain Robert Walton at the North Pole. Frankenstein passes his tale to the captain before dying; his creature then takes his corpse and disappears into the dark.

Frankenstein's Monster is a villain only through his murderous tendencies. He is a victim of fear and hatred—even from his own creator—that push him to violence. This aspect of the narrative remains throughout its numerous retellings. Unlike the original novel, the Universal Pictures *Frankenstein* films of the 1930s and 1940s kept the Creature mute and of slow intelligence, a lumbering, horrifying threat to the people of the countryside. In 1948, DC Comics introduced its version; over the decades, they made him part of the military organization Super Human Advanced Defense Executive (SHADE). The DC version is more loyal to the original source, with the monster exhibiting significant intelligence as well as enhanced physical strength.

A central theme of the original novel that most of the story's retellings and reimaginings use is that of the dangers of playing God. In the twentieth century, this central theme has been manifested in numerous science fiction franchises: the

Mary Shelley

Mary Wollstonecraft Shelley (1797–1851) was the author of one of the most important novels in the history of the Western world: *Frankenstein; or, The Modern Prometheus* (1818). She was the daughter of Mary Wollstonecraft (1759–1797), one of the key founders of feminism and the author of *A Vindication of the Rights of Woman* (1792). As her mother died shortly after her birth, the younger Mary was raised by her father, William Godwin (1756–1836), one of the early founders of modern anarchism and author of *An Enquiry Concerning Political Justice* (1793). At the age of seventeen, Mary began a romance with the married poet Percy Bysshe Shelley (1792–1822), which ultimately led to Shelley abandoning his wife, who died soon thereafter, and marrying the young Wollstonecraft.

It was during the summer of 1816, while she was staying with the famous poet George Gordon Byron, sixth Baron Byron (Lord Byron, 1788–1824), at a villa on Lake Geneva that Mary first conceived of her story, *Frankenstein*. During a particularly rainy period, the group passed the time retelling ghost stories, allegedly leading Byron to suggest the challenge that members of the party write their own horror stories. An immediate critical and commercial success, *Frankenstein* has, over the last two centuries, become one of the most popular stories in Western pop culture. It has been revived, rebooted, copied, and satirized in every medium of popular culture. The name "Frankenstein" has become synonymous with the dangers of playing God and the horrors associated with humankind's technological advances exceeding the evolution of its wisdom. The story has become analogous of real-world incidents such as Dr. J. Robert Oppenheimer's part in development of the atomic bomb in 1945.

Richard A. Hall

Godzilla films of the 1950s, 1960s, and twenty-first century; the Cybermen of *Doctor Who*; the Borg of *Star Trek*; the dinosaurs of the *Jurassic Park* novels and films; and the Cylons of *Battlestar Galactica*. The zombie genre, from the 1968 film *Night of the Living Dead* to the twenty-first-century comic book/television series *The Walking Dead*, owes most of its credit to Shelley's creation. In most zombie narratives, the living dead are the result of some scientific accident due to humankind's hubris, and the creatures themselves are, like the Creature, walking, murdering reanimated corpses. Frankenstein's Monster has also been an analogy for scientific and technological advances in the real world such as atomic/nuclear weapons technology, cloning, and artificial intelligence. Despite the dangers presented in so many facets of popular culture, however, humanity as a whole continues to fail to learn Mary Shelley's lesson, and the fate of Dr. Frankenstein remains a distinct possibility for the entirety of the real world.

Throughout popular culture, the overall zeitgeist memory of Frankenstein's Monster is the 1931 Universal Pictures version, brought to life by director James Whale, makeup artist Jack Pierce, and the immortal performance of Boris Karloff. Society has, for a century, mistakenly referred to the monster as "Frankenstein," and in the popular image of him, he has green skin, a flattened head, and electrical nodes on either side of his neck and lumbers in large, platform shoes, his arms extended like a mindless zombie. The idea of an unstoppable, undead murderer has also emerged in the *Friday the 13th*, *Nightmare on Elm Street*, and *Child's*

Boris Karloff created the iconic version of Frankenstein's Monster in the 1931 film *Frankenstein* and its first two sequels. (United Archives GmbH/Alamy Stock Photo)

Play horror film franchises. Modern retellings of the original tale tend to focus more on the sin of Frankenstein and his search for redemption.

Audiences of all media see the Creature as a villain primarily because of his frightening appearance and the abomination of his birth. However, it is not the monster that is the true villain of the piece but, rather, the creator by whose name he is best known. Dr. Frankenstein's quest to play God is the ultimate villainy in Western culture. In the end, Frankenstein's Monster is a cautionary tale against people allowing their proverbial reach to extend their grasp. Through her monster, Shelley warns us of the consequences of hubris; with an underlying message of not judging a book by its cover, she urges her audiences to look beneath the surface before judging good or evil. Frankenstein's Monster is a villain of our own making, posing the question of whether the true evil lies within the villain or within those who drove villains to their evil ways.

Richard A. Hall

See also: Agent Smith, Asajj Ventress, Borg Queen/Borg, Brainiac, Cybermen, Davros/ Daleks, Doomsday, Dracula, Dr. Frank-N-Furter, Ebenezer Scrooge, Faith the Vampire Slayer, Freddy Krueger, Jason Voorhees, Martin Brenner, Michael Myers, Number Six/ Cylons; *Thematic Essays*: "In the Beginning . . .": The Origins of Villains in the Western World, The Pathos of Villainy: Getting to the Heart of Why Villains Went Bad.

Further Reading

Alsford, Mike. 2006. *Heroes & Villains.* Waco, TX: Baylor University Press.

Ashby, LeRoy. 2006. *With Amusement for All: A History of American Popular Culture since 1830.* Lexington: University Press of Kentucky.

Friedman, Lester D., and Allison B. Kavey. 2016. *Monstrous Progeny: A History of the Frankenstein Narratives.* New Brunswick, NJ: Rutgers University Press.

Gavaler, Chris. 2015. *On the Origin of Superheroes: From the Big Bang to Action Comics No. 1.* Iowa City: University of Iowa.

Gloyn, Liz. 2019. *Tracking Classical Monsters in Popular Culture.* London: Bloomsbury Academic.

Hitchcock, Susan Tyler. 2007. *Frankenstein: A Cultural History*. New York: W.W. Norton.

Larsen, Kristine. 2011. "Frankenstein's Legacy: The Mad Scientist Remade." In *Vader, Voldemort and Other Villains: Essays on Evil in Popular Media*, edited by Jamey Heit, 46–63. Jefferson, NC: McFarland.

Maddrey, Joseph. 2004. *Nightmares in Red, White, and Blue: The Evolution of the American Horror Film*. Jefferson, NC: McFarland.

Mahnke, Aaron. 2017. *The World of Lore: Monstrous Creatures*. New York: Del Rey.

Murphy, Bernice M. 2013. *The Rural Gothic in American Popular Culture: Backwoods Horror and Terror in the Wilderness*. London: Palgrave Macmillan.

Skal, David J. 2001. *The Monster Show: A Cultural History of Horror*. Rev. ed. New York: Farrar, Straus and Giroux.

Freddy Krueger

First Appearance:	*A Nightmare on Elm Street* (release date: November 9, 1984)
Creators:	Wes Craven
Other Media:	Television, comic books, music videos
Primary Strength:	Dream manipulation
Major Weakness:	Overconfidence
Weapons:	Razor glove
Base of Operations:	Boiler room, dream world
Key Allies:	Jason Voorhees
Key Enemies:	Nancy Thompson, Kristen Parker, Alice Johnson
Actual Identity:	N/A
Nicknames/Aliases:	"Bastard Son of One Hundred Maniacs"

The 1980s introduced moviegoers to a host of boogeymen to terrorize the silver screen. Among all the blade-wielding maniacs, one in particular solidified himself as an icon of the decade: Freddy Krueger. Created by writer and director Wes Craven, Krueger made his debut in the 1984 horror classic *A Nightmare on Elm Street*. The peace of suburban Elm Street was shattered when a murderer named Freddy Krueger began preying on the children of the neighborhood. When the legal system failed to stop him, the parents of the community banded together and burned Freddy to death in a boiler room. However, this proved to be only the beginning of their nightmares.

Many years later, the teenagers of Elm Street begin to have nightmares wherein they are stalked by a man covered in burns armed with a razor-clawed glove. As the body count rises, Nancy Thompson, the impromptu leader of the youth, digs into what is going on and discovers the truth of who Freddy is and what their parents have done. Utilizing her scrappy ingenuity, Nancy is able to bring Freddy out of the dream world he controls and into the real world, where she seemingly is able to defeat him.

Like any good movie monster, Freddy Krueger was far from done with his bloody ways. The sequel, *A Nightmare on Elm Street 2: Freddy's Revenge*, was released shortly thereafter in 1985. Retooled from an unrelated screenplay, the film followed Jessie, who moved into Nancy's old house and finds himself possessed by a returning Freddy. The film divided audiences at the time but has gained a modern cult following. For the third film in the franchise, Wes Craven was back to develop a story that would serve as a follow-up to the original film. *A Nightmare on Elm Street 3: Dream Warriors* (1987) focuses on a group of teenagers committed to the mental hospital Westin Hills as a result of Freddy invading their dreams. Despite the doctors' that this is a delusion, their fears are all too real, and the teens are systematically killed through violently ironic means in their sleep. Nancy Thompson is now a psychiatric professional who trains the kids to defeat Kruger utilizing their dream powers. While Freddy is once again temporarily defeated, he is successful in finally slaying his old enemy Nancy. *Dream Warriors* is a particular favorite in the franchise, as it perfectly showcases the killer's morbid humor, which became a staple gimmick and set him apart from many of his fellow movie slashers. It also gave moviegoers their first glimpse at the character's backstory as a child conceived by a nun who suffered a horrific crime at the hands the criminally insane.

The survivors of Westin Hill then try to move on from the events they experienced, but they are still haunted by Freddy. A strange sequence featuring a dog leads to the return of the slasher, who picks up where he left off. As he slices through the surviving Dream Warriors, they pass their powers to their friend Alice, who will be the latest young woman to oppose Freddy. Their rivalry takes a personal turn when Krueger uses her unborn child as a means to transition from the dream world into the real world. In the elaborate climax of *A Nightmare on Elm Street V: The Dream Child* (1989), the slasher has his final confrontation with Alice and is killed by her child, Jacob, and the ghost of his own mother.

As the *Nightmare* franchise needed a new direction, Craven once again returned to continue Krueger's saga with a twist to the character. In *Wes Craven's New Nightmare* (1994), the filmmaker explores the idea of Freddy Krueger being the modern incarnation of a demonic entity who haunts dreams. With a foot firmly planted in the real world, Freddy does not terrorize the character of Nancy, but rather the actress behind her, Heather Langenkamp. Thanks to the masses being terrorized by the *Nightmare on Elm Street* film series, Freddy has been empowered to attack our reality.

In 2003, fans of horror saw a long-held dream fulfilled as New Line Cinema finally had the legal rights necessary to pit Freddy against fellow slasher Jason Voorhees. Appropriately titled *Freddy vs. Jason*, this movie saw Freddy utilize Jason to terrorize a new generation of Elm Street teens, inspiring the fear necessary to restore him to prominence. Inevitably a rivalry is sparked between the bloodthirsty boogeymen with a collective of teenagers caught in the middle. In the film's climax, the two icons battle it out on Jason's familiar stomping ground of Camp Crystal Lake. While the hockey-masked killer seemingly beheads Freddy,

Robert Englund forever immortalized himself with his portrayal of nightmare monster Freddy Krueger in the original *Nightmare on Elm Street* films of the 1980s. (New Line Cinema/Allstar Picture Library/Alamy Stock Photo)

it is hinted in the end that Krueger survives so that he and Jason can continue to battle.

The production company Platinum Dunes sought to bring Krueger back to the big screen after a lengthy absence with a remake of *A Nightmare on Elm Street* (2010). For the first time in the character's history, he was played by someone besides Robert Englund, as Oscar nominee Jack Earle Haley donned the claws. While 2010's *A Nightmare on Elm Street* had a strong initial box office success, audiences dwindled, and critical reception was poor. Despite this, Freddy Krueger remains one of the key figures of 1980s popular culture and one of moviedom's most popular monsters. His burn-scarred face has graced any piece of merchandise conceivable. On the small screen, he served as the host for *Freddy's Nightmares* (Syndication, 1988–1990), a short-lived anthology. *A Nightmare on Elm Street* was even referenced by President Ronald Reagan in a 1988 speech. In 2003, the American Film Institute honored Freddy Krueger by recognizing him as one of the greatest movie villains ever.

Joshua Plock

See also: Doomsday, Dracula, Frankenstein's Monster, Jason Voorhees, Leatherface, Michael Myers; *Thematic Essays*: The Pathos of Villainy: Getting to the Heart of Why Villains Went Bad.

Further Reading

Clover, Carol. 1993. *Men, Women, and Chainsaws: Gender in Modern Horror Film.* Princeton, NJ: Princeton University Press.

Hutson, Thommy. 2016. *Never Sleep Again: The Elm Street Legacy.* Brentwood, TN: Permuted.

McNeill, Dustin. 2017. *Slash of the Titans: The Road to Freddy vs. Jason.* San Jose, CA: Harker.

Muir, John Kenneth. 2012. *Horror Films of the 1980s.* Jefferson, NC: McFarland.

Skal, David J. 2001. *The Monster Show.* New York: Farrar, Straus and Giroux.

Wooley, John. 2011. *Wes Craven: The Man and His Nightmares.* Hoboken, NJ: Wiley & Sons.

G

General Custer

First Appearance:	Born: New Rumley, Ohio, December 5, 1839; first national newspaper accounts: mid-1863
Creators:	Parents: Emanuel Henry Custer and Marie Ward Kirkpatrick
Other Media:	Novels, movies, radio, television, stage plays, comics, songs
Primary Strength:	Tactics
Major Weakness:	Ego/narcissism, thirst for glory
Weapons:	Pistols, sword, rifles
Base of Operations:	The Great Plains
Key Allies:	Elizabeth "Libby" Custer (spouse), General Philip Sheridan, Seventh U.S. Cavalry
Key Enemies:	Confederate Army, Sitting Bull, Crazy Horse, Black Kettle, Plains Sioux, Major Marcus Reno, Captain Frederick Benteen, President Ulysses S. Grant
Actual Identity:	Lieutenant Colonel [Brevet Major General] George Armstrong Custer
Nicknames/Aliases:	"Autie," "The Boy General," "Long Hair," "Yellow Hair," "Son of the Morning Star Who Attacks at Dawn"

Prior to World War II, American ideas of heroes and villains came primarily from the real world. From the heroic Davey Crockett to the villainous Pancho Villa and the antivillain Billy the Kid, Americans drew their heroes and villains from the pages of newspapers, immortalizing them in the popular culture of the day, leading them to be celebrated in popular culture for the centuries to come. One historical figure who has served as both hero and villain since his death in 1876 has been General George A. Custer. After becoming a national hero during the American Civil War (1861–1865), the youngest man to ever reach the rank of brigadier and, later, major general, the demoted Lieutenant Colonel Custer was sent to the Great Plains in command of the newly formed Seventh Cavalry to defeat the "renegade," "hostile" Native Americans in order to pave the way for American expansion. The celebrity he attained from his heroic exploits during the

Sitting Bull

The legendary Hunkpapa Lakota chief Sitting Bull (1831–1890) was one of the most feared individuals in America during the Plains Indian Wars (1866–1890). According to an interview with his great-grandson in 2007, Sitting Bull's birth name was Jumping Badger, disputing the long-held story that Sitting Bull was one of the very few Plains Indians to keep the same name from birth to adulthood. Sitting Bull famously refused to sign the Treaty of 1868, stating that the Lakota did not "wish to eat from the hand of the grandfather [U.S. President Andrew Johnson]." In 1876, he assisted in getting women and children to safety during the Battle of Little Bighorn, the greatest Native victory against the white man in all Native American history.

In 1881, he and his family surrendered to the U.S. government, and in 1885, he joined Buffalo Bill's Wild West Show, entertaining audiences with his accounts of Custer's Last Stand. In 1890, he returned to the Black Hills of South Dakota, calling all who wished to come to him so that they could conduct the Ghost Dance, a ceremony requesting advice from the spirits of their ancestors. When U.S. government agents learned of this, they feared another Little Bighorn and went to the Black Hills to take him into custody. When one of Sitting Bull's men attempted to prevent his leader's capture, a shot was fired, killing Sitting Bull on the spot. His followers fled and were eventually taken out by the U.S. Army at what came to be known as the Massacre at Wounded Knee (Creek). During his adult life, the name "Sitting Bull" struck terror in the hearts of U.S. citizens seeking to populate the Great Plains. He was a hero to his people and a villain in the eyes of the U.S. military.

Richard A. Hall

Civil War was exacerbated by his flamboyant personality and endless quest for personal glory.

On the Plains, Custer achieved even more glory with numerous victories against the Plains tribes. In 1876, when President Grant ordered that all Natives report to their respective reservations or be considered "hostile," Custer and the Seventh were sent to the Montana Territory to take out the Sioux Chief Sitting Bull and his "renegade" followers. There, Custer met a brutal defeat, outnumbered nearly ten to one. When he and five companies of men were killed at the Battle of Little Bighorn on June 25, 1876, news of the event shattered the celebratory atmosphere of the centennial celebrations in the East. For nearly a century after his death, Custer was immortalized in popular culture through books, stage plays, radio programs, comic books, films, and television programs as the martyred hero of American expansionism.

Shortly after Custer's death, popular entertainer Buffalo Bill Cody opened his stage play, *Buffalo Bill: First Scout for Custer*, and throughout the 1880s, Cody employed Sitting Bull to regale audiences with his firsthand account of Custer's heroism. Decades later, in 1941, Hollywood legend Erol Flynn starred as Custer in the movie *They Died with Their Boots On*, a heroic tale cementing further Custer's status as fallen icon of the West. A short-lived live-action television series titled simply *Custer* (ABC, 1967) was the last heroic portrayal of Custer before history dubbed him the scapegoat for America's Native policy and the Plains Indian Wars.

Custer's celebrity took a dramatic turn in the opposite direction in 1970. By that time, the American Indian Movement had begun their crusade for Native civil rights. American guilt over the centuries of atrocities against Native Americans required a scapegoat. In the 1970 film *Little Big Man*, directed by Arthur Penn, actor Richard Mulligan portrayed Custer at Little Bighorn as an insane, bloodthirsty psychopath. From that moment, General Custer has become the face of the white man's atrocities against the Natives. Since then, Custer has been portrayed in books, film, and made-for-TV movies as a vainglorious egoist, more concerned with his personal glory than the lives of innocent Natives (or even his own men). Since the 1990s, scholars have attempted to repair Custer's reputation, but popular culture remains the standing account of what Americans view as the truth. While, in the end, Custer was likely neither as heroic nor as villainous as he has been portrayed, his image in the American zeitgeist has cemented him as an historical example of white racism against the indigenous Americans alongside Christopher Columbus and Andrew Jackson.

George Armstrong Custer has become a symbol for the atrocities committed against Native Americans by the U.S. government. (Library of Congress)

A more even account of Custer was presented in the book and TV miniseries *Son of the Morning Star*. The book, *Son of the Morning Star: Custer and the Little Big Horn*, was written by Evan S. Connell in 1984. The two-part miniseries aired on ABC in 1991, starring Gary Cole as the infamous cavalry commander. Both reflect Custer's indominable ego as well as his utter disregard for the massive body counts on both sides of his battles. They also show the general's respect and sympathy for the Sioux and his disgust with the U.S. government's mistreatment of the Native peoples. In the end, the U.S. government is the true villain of the piece, and Custer becomes the avatar for their villainy. History requires a scapegoat for atrocities, and history has chosen the most flamboyant and publicly noted figure of the period to play that role.

Today, despite decades of historians attempting to correct the record and place him in a more proper context, General Custer stands in the zeitgeist as an example of villainy with regard to America's greatest sin: racism. Even if, as many scholars have noted, Custer was merely a cog in the government machine, a soldier following orders against a group the American government and people deemed a dangerous enemy, following orders has not, in modern times, been an acceptable excuse for atrocities in war. In the years following Little Bighorn, surviving Native warriors defended the actions of Custer and his men when the government, at first, attempted to blame the Boy General for the catastrophic defeat in Montana. Whether hero or villain, Custer was the most famous face of U.S. Native policy in the last half of the 1800s and works in his role in American popular culture as an example of the villainy of America's past as it strives to not repeat that villainy in the future.

Richard A. Hall

See also: Billy the Kid, CSM/The Cigarette Smoking Man, Frank Burns, Geronimo, Grindelwald, Imperial Officers, Martin Brenner, Pancho Villa, Voldemort; *Thematic Essays*: "In the Beginning . . .": The Origins of Villains in the Western World.

Further Reading

Alsford, Mike. 2006. *Heroes & Villains.* Waco, TX: Baylor University Press.

Ashby, LeRoy. 2006. *With Amusement for All: A History of American Popular Culture since 1830.* Lexington: University Press of Kentucky.

Connell, Evan S. (1984) 2001. *Son of the Morning Star: Custer and the Little Bighorn.* New York: History Book Club.

Donovan, James. 2008. *A Terrible Glory: Custer and the Little Bighorn, the Last Great Battle of the American West.* New York: Little, Brown and Company.

Hutton, Paul Andrew, ed. 1992. *The Custer Reader.* Lincoln: University of Nebraska Press.

Wert, Jeffry D. 1996. *Custer: The Controversial Life of George Armstrong Custer.* New York: Simon & Schuster.

Geronimo

First Appearance:	Born: New Mexico, June, 1829; first national newspaper accounts: early 1880s
Creators:	Grandfather: Mahko
Other Media:	Novels, movies, radio, television, stage plays, comics, songs
Primary Strength:	Tactics, fearlessness
Major Weakness:	Hatred
Weapons:	Pistols, rifles
Base of Operations:	New Mexico
Key Allies:	Apache Sioux
Key Enemies:	U.S. Army
Actual Identity:	Goyakle/"The One Who Yawns" (in Mescalero-Chiricahua/Athabaskan)
Nicknames/Aliases:	N/A

In the early decades of the United States, villains were primarily national enemies: Britain, France, and Mexico. After the Civil War (1861–1865), villains in America still came from the real world, and for the last half of the 1800s, the primary villain in America and popular culture were the "hostile," "renegade" Native Americans of the West: Sitting Bull, Crazy Horse, and Quanah Parker. Of the Native "enemies" of the United States, however, one struck such terror in the hearts of the American citizenry that, in the twenty-first century, the U.S. Army would give the code name "Geronimo" to the infamous international terrorist Osama bin Laden. Geronimo and his band of Apache warriors represented the last armed resistance in what has come to be known as the Plains Indian Wars. More than a century after his death, Geronimo lives on in American popular culture across all media.

Legend has it that at a young age, Geronimo received a vision from the "Great Force" that no bullet would ever touch him. This is said to be the basis of his endless fearlessness on the battlefield, fighting both the American and Mexican militaries throughout his long life. In 1886, down to just around 150 men, Geronimo surrendered to the U.S. government with the assurance that he and his men would serve only a couple years in prison. Ultimately, they would spend decades in prison, moved from Florida to Oklahoma. In his final years, Geronimo was allowed to leave prison during the day to go into town and sign autographs. In February 1909, on his way back to the prison, Geronimo was thrown from his horse and spent the night in the cold. He died shortly after of pneumonia, never having been struck by a bullet.

During the Plains Indian Wars (1866–1890), the Apache chief Geronimo was one of the most feared warriors in the American West. (Library of Congress)

By the time of his death, Geronimo was already a staple of American popular culture. During his imprisonment, Americans would come from all over the country to see Geronimo shoot buffalo and to get his autograph. Over the last hundred years, he has been the topic of songs and books. He has been portrayed in numerous television programs set in the West, and there have been four feature films telling the story of his life, the two most recent in 1993. Since his capture in 1886, Geronimo has been viewed less as a villain and is more noted for his undaunted bravery. American military paratroopers and civilian skydivers call upon the dead warrior's bravery and shout, "Geronimo!" before jumping. In the fifth through the seventh seasons of the modern incarnation of the British television science-fiction series *Doctor Who*, the eleventh Doctor would shout, "Geronimo!" before embarking on adventure.

During his life in the West, however, Geronimo was viewed as one of the most feared villains in American history. In the realm of pop culture villains, Geronimo represents the unstoppable force, an enemy whose mere name strikes terror in all who face him. The legend of his immunity to being shot added a supernatural element to his already fearsome reputation. Civilians taken hostage by Natives in the West faced the most gruesome of fates if caught by the Apache, who were universally viewed as the baddest of the bad, and of these most terrifying of Natives, Geronimo was far and above the most terrifying. The fact that his name was invoked as a code name for Osama bin Laden shows how deeply the terror Geronimo once struck in American society has not been forgotten, even if it has been long since forgiven. In the end, Geronimo represents a Frankenstein's Monster of America's own creation. The United States viewed him as a monster, despite the fact that it was American policy and determined westward expansion that put him in that role.

Richard A. Hall

See also: Asajj Ventress, Billy the Kid, Frankenstein's Monster, General Custer, Kahless/Klingons, Pancho Villa; *Thematic Essays*: "In the Beginning . . .": The Origins of Villains in the Western World.

Further Reading

Alsford, Mike. 2006. *Heroes & Villains.* Waco, TX: Baylor University Press.

Ashby, LeRoy. 2006. *With Amusement for All: A History of American Popular Culture since 1830.* Lexington: University Press of Kentucky.

Behnken, Brian D., and Gregory D. Smithers. 2015. *Racism in American Popular Media: From Aunt Jemima to the Frito Bandito.* Westport, CT: Praeger.

Gavaler, Chris. 2015. *On the Origin of Superheroes: From the Big Bang to Action Comics No. 1.* Iowa City: University of Iowa.

Geronimo, and S. M. Barrett. (1906) 2005. *Geronimo: My Life.* Chicago: Dover.

Leach, Mike, and Buddy Levy. 2015. *Geronimo: Leadership Strategies of an American Warrior.* New York: Gallery.

Sweeney, Edwin R. 2012. *From Cochise to Geronimo: The Chiricahua Apaches, 1874–1886.* Norman: University of Oklahoma Press.

Goldfinger

First Appearance:	*Goldfinger* (publication date: March 23, 1959)
Creators:	Ian Fleming
Other Media:	Movie, song
Primary Strength:	Strategy, seemingly endless resources
Major Weakness:	Greed
Weapons:	Handguns, henchmen, GB poison (sarin), gold paint

Base of Operations:	Various
Key Allies:	Oddjob, SMERSH (Directorate of Special Departments within NKVD USSR), Mr. Ling, American Mafia
Key Enemies:	James Bond/Agent 007, British Secret Service/MI-6, CIA
Actual Identity:	Auric Goldfinger
Nicknames/Aliases:	"The Man with the Midas Touch"

In 1953, former British military intelligence officer Ian Fleming introduced the world to the most famous superspy in fiction: James Bond, commander in the British Royal Navy and British Secret Service Agent, code-named "007." Bond first appeared in the novel *Casino Royale*, and the successful novel and film franchises that succeeded it followed 007 on various adventures to save the world, visiting exotic locales, drinking vodka martinis ("shaken, not stirred"), and seducing beautiful women. He utilizes his "license to kill" to save the world from various threats: communists, terrorists, and the international criminal organizations. When the successful novels lead to a massively successful film franchise, the third, and one of the most iconic and successful, of the franchise was *Goldfinger* (1964).

In the film, Auric Goldfinger is played by German actor Gert Frobe. The story finds James Bond, played for the third time by Sean Connery, ordered to investigate the international gold magnate and uncover his gold smuggling operation. Bond eventually discovers that aside from his smuggling operations, Goldfinger

Pinky and the Brain

"Pinky and the Brain" was a recurring minicartoon on the animated television series *Animaniacs* (FOX-Kids, 1993–1995; Kids' WB, 1995–1998) and later their own spin-off series, *Pinky, Elmyra & the Brain* (Kids' WB, 1998–1999), produced by Warner Brothers Animation and Stephen Spielberg's Amblin Entertainment. Pinky and Brain are genetically altered laboratory mice. The tall, slender Pinky (voiced by Rob Paulson, b. 1956) is the less intelligent of the two, extremely hyperactive and easily distracted. By contrast, the short, squat, large-headed Brain (voiced by Maurice LeMarche, b. 1958) is massively intelligent with delusions of grandeur and repeated plans for world conquest.

Every episode would begin with Pinky asking, "What are we doing tonight, Brain?" Brain would respond maliciously, "The same thing we do every night, Pinky . . . try to take over the world!" As often as not, Brain's plans would be as thwarted by his own failure to think the plan through as by Pinky's incompetence. Ultimately, they are a brilliant parody of the would-be world-conquering villains of the *James Bond* franchise. They are also a hilarious, rather hyperbolic commentary on the risks of genetically altering animals. "Pinky and the Brain," along with the rest of the cast of *Animaniacs*, were an attempt by Spielberg to revive the wacky yet intelligent comedy of the Warner Brothers cartoons of the 1930s and 1940s featuring such animation classics as Bugs Bunny, Daffy Duck, and Porky Pig. While perhaps not as successful in longevity, Pinky and the Brain were popular and beloved animated characters in the 1990s.

Richard A. Hall

plans to contaminate the U.S. gold supply at Fort Knox, rendering the metal useless for decades and destroying the American economy while, at the same time, dramatically increasing international gold prices. Agent 007, of course, saves the day, taking Goldfinger to prison in Washington, DC. During the flight, Goldfinger manages to get loose, and in a struggle with Bond, a gun is fired, decompressing the aircraft and pulling Goldfinger out of the plane and to his death.

In 2017, *Esquire* magazine listed Goldfinger as the number five *Bond* villain of all time (Hall, "All 104 James Bond Villains Ranked"). In the realm of American villainy, Goldfinger represents a type of villain that has become even more popular in the decades since the book and film that introduced him to American audiences: the wealthy and unscrupulous businessperson. Goldfinger cares nothing for the consequences of his actions on others but only for how his actions further enrich his already considerable wealth. As the wealth gap in America becomes more and more a major sociopolitical issue, the threat of a Goldfinger becomes all the more frightening to American audiences. He represents the embodiment of egoism, with an utter lack of altruism, which stands as one of the ultimate acts of villainy in American popular culture.

Richard A. Hall

See also: The Corleone Family, The Court of Owls, Ernst Stavro Blofeld/SPECTRE, Fish Mooney, Grand Nagus/Ferengi, Heisenberg/Walter White, Jabba the Hutt, Lex Luthor, Marsellus Wallace, Negan/The Saviors, Sherry Palmer; *Thematic Essays*: "Nazis, Communists, and Terrorists . . . Oh My!": The Rise of the Supervillain and the Evolution of the Modern American Villain.

Further Reading

Alsford, Mike. 2006. *Heroes & Villains.* Waco, TX: Baylor University Press.

Ashby, LeRoy. 2006. *With Amusement for All: A History of American Popular Culture since 1830.* Lexington: University Press of Kentucky.

Brittany, Michele, ed. 2014. *James Bond and Popular Culture: Essays on the Influence of the Fictional Superspy.* Jefferson, NC: McFarland.

Hall, Jacob. 2017. "All 104 James Bond Villains Ranked: From Masterminds to Henchmen, the Final Word on 007's Furious Foes." *Esquire.* May 24, 2017. Accessed July 4, 2019. https://www.esquire.com/entertainment/movies/g2496/best-james-bond-villains-ranked/.

Hoberman, J. 2003. *The Dream Life: Movies, Media, and the Mythology of the Sixties.* New York: New Press.

Starck, Kathleen, ed. 2010. *Between Fear and Freedom: Cultural Representations of the Cold War.* Newcastle upon Tyne, UK: Cambridge Scholars.

Gollum

First Appearance:	*The Hobbit* (publication date: September 21, 1937)
Creators:	J. R. R. Tolkien
Other Media:	Movies, cartoons

Primary Strength:	Stealth
Major Weakness:	Obsession
Weapons:	N/A
Base of Operations:	Middle-earth
Key Allies:	N/A
Key Enemies:	Bilbo Baggins, Frodo Baggins, Sauron
Actual Identity:	Smeagol, Trahald
Nicknames/Aliases:	N/A

In 1937, British author J. R. R. Tolkien introduced the world and generations of readers to the world of Middle-earth in his novel *The Hobbit.* He continued his tale of hobbits and the wizard Gandalf in *The Lord of the Rings* trilogy from 1954 to1955. The stories were translated to stage, radio, and television before director Peter Jackson brought *The Lord of the Rings* to theaters from 2001 to 2003, followed by breaking *The Hobbit* into a trilogy of films from 2012 to 2014. The overall story revolves around the One Ring, a ring of invisibility forged by the evil Sauron in the fires of Mount Doom on Middle-earth. The wizard Gandalf the Grey guides two generations of hobbits as part of the overall crusade to stop the Dark Lord from taking over the world. In *The Hobbit*, Bilbo Baggins steals the ring from the mysterious Gollum to assist in his approach of the dragon Smaug. A generation later, Gollum attempts to steal the ring back from its new owner, Frodo Baggins, who seeks to return the ring to Mount Doom to destroy it.

Gollum is a severely deformed centuries-old hobbit whose obsession with the One Ring, which he creepily refers to as "My Precious," slowly ate away at his body and soul, transforming him into the grotesque Gollum. In *The Hobbit*, Bilbo Baggins crosses paths with Gollum while attempting to escape from the Misty Mountains and agrees to a test of riddles from Gollum in exchange for guidance out of the dark. Baggins discovers the One Ring and takes it with him, and it proves a valuable find when finally facing Smaug. In the novel *The Fellowship of the Ring* (and the movie *The Return of the King*), it is discovered that Gollum was originally the hobbit Smeagol. One year, on his birthday, Smeagol went fishing with his friend Deagol, who discovered the ring in the river. Smeagol's immediate obsession with the ring led him to murder his friend to retrieve it. He then ran away to the Misty Mountains to hide from his crime, eventually misplacing the ring over time. In *The Lord of the Rings* trilogy, Gollum pursues and briefly teams up with Frodo Baggins in an attempt to retrieve his stolen property. When Frodo successfully drops the ring into the lava rivers of Mount Doom, Gollum leaps to grab it, falling into the fires and his death.

The world of the hobbits is one of peace and tranquility. Smeagol's murder of Deagol is reminiscent of Cain's murder of Abel, and like Cain, Smeagol leaves his home for the wilderness to escape his sin. Gollum's story continues, however, with his crazed obsession with the One Ring. Gollum's desire cannot be satiated, to the point that he is willing to take any life—including, ultimately his own—to possess the ring. He represents the darker nature of humanity and the inherent dangers of obsession and greed. Though a murderer, he is also a sympathetic villain, as his actions and loneliness come from his blind obsession with an inanimate object that can never return his affections.

Richard A. Hall

See also: Asajj Ventress, Doomsday, Faith the Vampire Slayer, Frankenstein's Monster, Sauron/Saruman; *Thematic Essays*: The Pathos of Villainy: Getting to the Heart of Why Villains Went Bad.

Further Reading

Alsford, Mike. 2006. *Heroes & Villains.* Waco, TX: Baylor University Press.

Ashby, LeRoy. 2006. *With Amusement for All: A History of American Popular Culture since 1830.* Lexington: University Press of Kentucky.

Hammond, Wayne G., and Christina Scull. 2005. *The Lord of the Rings: A Reader's Companion.* San Diego, CA: Houghton Mifflin Harcourt.

Kreeft, Peter. 2005. *The Philosophy of Tolkien: The Worldview behind The Lord of the Rings.* San Francisco, CA: Ignatius.

The Governor

First Appearance:	*The Walking Dead* #27 (cover date: April, 2006)
Creators:	Robert Kirkman (with artists Charlie Adlard and Cliff Rathburn)
Other Media:	Television series, novels
Primary Strength:	Inspiring loyalty
Major Weakness:	Blinded by power and grief
Weapons:	Guns
Base of Operations:	Woodbury, Georgia
Key Allies:	Bob Stookey, Andrea, Lilly Chambler
Key Enemies:	Rick Grimes, Michonne, Daryl Dixon (television series only)
Actual Identity:	Brian Blake (comics and novels), Philip Blake (television series)
Nicknames/Aliases:	N/A

The Walking Dead is a comic book created by Robert Kirkman and Tony Moore in 2003, published through Image Comics. The story centers on the survivors of a zombie apocalypse, led by a Kentucky sheriff's deputy, Rick Grimes. Through the struggles of the survivors, Rick and his group also encounter other human survivors who are, more often than not, greater threats than the undead. In 2010, the cable television network AMC launched a series based on the comic, shifting Grimes's origins to Georgia and adding a new character, the redneck tracker Daryl Dixon. Once Rick and his group of survivors get used to the idea that the dead walk the Earth and are a constant threat to their own lives, they soon discover that the living can be as fearsome as the dead. The first human threat they face is the Governor, the leader of the walled community of Woodbury.

In the comics, Brian Blake and his brother, Philip, discover the community of Woodbury under the command of a National Guard unit that rules with an iron fist. After leading a revolt to overtake the Guard, Brian is chosen as governor. When Rick Grimes, along with Glenn and Michonne, discover the community, the Governor cuts off Rick's hand, severely beats Glenn, and rapes and tortures Michonne. When Rick and Glenn escape, Michonne exacts her revenge, removing the Governor's eye, arm, fingernails, and genitalia. She also murders the Governor's undead niece, Penny, whom the Governor was keeping alive by feeding her the remains of his victims. The crazed Governor then leads his people against Rick's prison refuge, destroying its walls and killing one of Rick's people before his own people turn on him and his girlfriend Lilly shoots him and throws him to the walkers. In both the comics and the television series, the Governor punishes "guilty" people by means of a Roman-style arena fight to the death surrounded by walkers.

The television version of the Governor's story is actually only slightly different. Played by David Morrissey, his name on the series is Philip, presumably with no brother, and Penny is his daughter. Additionally, Michonne does not get raped, although it first appears that Glenn's girlfriend, Maggie, may be, and Michonne only takes the Governor's eye (and kills Penny). Also, after his initial assault on the prison, his people turn on him, and he wanders away, coming across Lilly and her family and joining another group that he leads into the same fate as the comics in a final assault on the prison. After a brutal fight with Rick, Michonne puts her katana sword through his chest, and Lilly shoots him in the face. One final departure from the comics is that the Governor causes Andrea to be bitten by a walker, leading her to commit suicide, whereas in the comics, Andrea continued for some time as Rick's love interest. In 2013, *TV Guide* listed the Governor as the number twenty-eight "nastiest" TV villain of all time ("TV Guide Picks TV's 60 Nastiest Villains," *TV Guide*).

David Morrissey brought the comic book villain the Governor to life on the AMC television series *The Walking Dead*. (PictureLux/The Hollywood Archive/Alamy Stock Photo)

In both incarnations, the Governor represents one of the most reviled aspects of modern villain in fiction: the would-be ruler. Although the Governor comes to power through heroic deeds, he soon succumbs to the age-old adage that "power corrupts and absolute power corrupts absolutely." In the comics, his goal of attacking the prison is merely to capture supplies for Woodbury; on the television program, he wants to take the prison itself, seeing it as more secure than Woodbury. Regardless of medium, however, he is the ultimate example of a man driven mad by power. His violence only grows as his power increases. He is a murderer, rapist, and torturer; his only true affection is for the animated corpse of a little girl. He represents that which Americans most fear: a would-be dictator whose kind face hides a dark soul.

Richard A. Hall

See also: Alpha/The Whisperers, Asajj Ventress, Doctor Doom, Ernst Stavro Blofeld/SPECTRE, Killmonger, Lex Luthor, Martin Brenner, Negan/The Saviors, Sherry Palmer, Voldemort, Zod; *Thematic Essays*: "Nazis, Communists, and Terrorists . . . Oh My!": The Rise of the Supervillain and the Evolution of the Modern American Villain, The Pathos of Villainy: Getting to the Heart of Why Villains Went Bad.

Further Reading

Alsford, Mike. 2006. *Heroes & Villains.* Waco, TX: Baylor University Press.

Keetley, Dawn. 2014. *We're All Infected: Essays on AMC's The Walking Dead and the Fate of the Human.* Contributions to Zombie Studies. Jefferson, NC: McFarland.

Kirkman, Robert. 2018. *The Quotable Negan: Warped Witticisms and Obscene Observations from The Walking Dead's Most Iconic Villain.* New York: Skybound.

Langley, Travis, ed. 2015. *The Walking Dead Psychology: Psych of the Living Dead.* Popular Culture Psychology. New York: Sterling.

"TV Guide Picks TV's 60 Nastiest Villains." 2013. *TV Guide.* April 22, 2013. Accessed January 1, 2019. http://wordsmithonia.blogspot.com/2013/04/tv-guide-picks-tvs-60-nastiest-villains.html.

Yuen, Wayne, ed. 2012. *The Walking Dead and Philosophy: Zombie Apocalypse Now.* Popular Culture and Philosophy. Chicago: Open Court.

Yuen, Wayne, ed. 2016. *The Ultimate Walking Dead and Philosophy: Hungry for More.* Popular Culture and Philosophy. Chicago: Open Court.

Grand Nagus/Ferengi

First Appearance:	**Ferengi:** *Star Trek: The Next Generation*, season 1, episode 5 (air date: October 19, 1987) **Grand Nagus:** *Star Trek: Deep Space Nine*, season 1, episode 11 (air date: March 21, 1993)
Creators:	Gene Roddenberry and Herb Wright (designer of Ferengi) David Livingston (designer of Grand Nagus)
Other Media:	Novels, comics

Primary Strength:	Cunning
Major Weakness:	Greed
Weapons:	N/A
Base of Operations:	Ferenginar, Alpha Quadrant
Key Allies:	N/A
Key Enemies:	United Federation of Planets
Actual Identity:	Zek (Grand Nagus)
Nicknames/Aliases:	N/A

Star Trek is a popular science fiction franchise originally developed for television by Gene Roddenberry in 1966. It was originally set in the twenty-third century, when humanity has long been exploring deep space and Earth is a member of the United Federation of Planets. The original series has spawned an animated series, five sequel and prequel live-action series, and thirteen feature films to date. The first live-action spin-off series was *Star Trek: The Next Generation*, which debuted in syndication on September 28, 1987. The series, dubbed *TNG* by fans, focuses on the adventures of Captain Jean-Luc Picard and the crew of the *USS Enterprise-D* (making it the fifth Federation starship to bear the name). The success of *TNG* led to a third live-action series: *Star Trek: Deep Space Nine* (*DS9*), which first aired in syndication on January 3, 1993. This series moved from the usual backdrop of a traveling starship to the fixed location of a space station under the command of Commander, and later Captain, Benjamin Sisko, the first African American lead in a *Star Trek* series. A fascinating alien species first introduced on *TNG* and then more fully explored on *DS9* were the Ferengi.

Early in the first season of *TNG*, audiences were introduced to the Ferengi in the episode "The Last Outpost," one of the last contributions to the series by creator Gene Roddenberry, which aired on October 19, 1987. The first thing that viewers discover about this new race, and really the only aspect to their culture explored on *TNG*, is that their entire culture is centered on the acquisition of wealth, preferably in the form of Gold Pressed Latinum. This made the Ferengi a timely addition to the *Star Trek* universe, arriving as they do at the height of the greed-obsessed 1980s. Their greed-based villainy, at first, appears to be the only aspect of Ferengi culture, with no redeeming qualities to the species evident in their *TNG* appearances. However, just as *TNG* would add depth to the Klingon villains from the original series and the later series *Star Trek: Voyager* would do for the *TNG* villains, the Borg, the Ferengi would be explored in far more depth in the *TNG* follow-up, *DS9*.

One of the main characters on *DS9* was Quark (played by Armin Shimerman), the Ferengi owner of a bar-casino on the promenade of the space station. Quark had come to the station when it was called Terok Nor and was a base for the evil Cardassian Empire during their occupation and enslavement of the planet Bajor. When the United Federation of Planets liberated Bajor, they took control of the station, renaming it Deep Space Nine. The new Starfleet commander, Benjamin Sisko, convinces (i.e., blackmails) Quark into remaining on the station to promote business and becoming a community leader, much to the chagrin of Sisko's Bajoran first officer and the station's security chief, Odo. Quark continues to underscore the core Ferengi belief in acquiring wealth, often quoting the Ferengi Rules of Acquisition, including the following: rule one, "Once you have their money, you never give it back"; rule six, "Never allow family to stand in the way of opportunity"; rule nine, "Opportunity plus instinct equals profit"; and rule 10, "Greed is eternal" (Wrobel, *The Complete Ferengi Rules of Acquisition*). The Ferengi are also an extremely sexist culture by the standards of literally all other *Star Trek* species. Women are not allowed to own property, hold office, or even wear clothes. As the fourth rule states, "A woman wearing clothes is like a man in the kitchen."

Ferengi culture was expanded upon in the *DS9* episode "The Nagus" (David Livingston, season 1, episode 10, March 21, 1993). In this episode, fans were finally introduced to the leader of the Ferengi society, Grand Nagus Zek (played by Wallace Shawn). In this episode, the Grand Nagus arrives at DS9 to appoint Quark his successor just before dying. When Zek's son conspires with Quark's brother, Rom, to kill Quark, Zek returns, confessing that his "death" was a ploy to test what his son would do. Over time, Zek falls in love with Quark's mother, whose strong will and free spirit inspires him to grant equality to Ferengi women (and allow them to start wearing clothes). Over the course of the series, Quark, Rom, and Rom's son, Nog, are inspired by their Starfleet neighbors to become more thoughtful, caring individuals, and Nog becomes the first Ferengi to join Starfleet, where he become a war hero and disabled veteran.

Although almost always played for comedic fodder, the Ferengi as they appeared on *TNG* were a venomous species, whose greed often overrode their own considerable cunning. In the realm of American villainy, the Ferengi represent the greed, lust, and avarice that has come to consume American society in the decades since World War II. They are a cautionary tale of who humanity could become, while simultaneously expressing the overall ridiculousness of allowing greed to overpower the better angels of sentient nature. They are an exaggerated form of us, with the underlying note that even if one is consumed by the acquisition of wealth, one can still limit that desire when confronted with a choice of right or wrong.

Richard A. Hall

See also: Alpha/The Whisperers, Borg Queen/Borg, Captain Hector Barbossa, Catwoman, COBRA, The Court of Owls, Ernst Stavro Blofeld/SPECTRE, Fish Mooney, Goldfinger, Kahless/Klingons, Negan/The Saviors, Q, Sherry Palmer; *Thematic Essays*: "Nazis, Communists, and Terrorists . . . Oh My!": The Rise of the Supervillain and the Evolution of the Modern American Villain, The Dark Mirror: Evil Twins, *The Twilight Zone*, and the Villain Within, The Pathos of Villainy: Getting to the Heart of Why Villains Went Bad.

Further Reading

Alsford, Mike. 2006. *Heroes & Villains*. Waco, TX: Baylor University Press.

Ashby, LeRoy. 2006. *With Amusement for All: A History of American Popular Culture since 1830*. Lexington: University Press of Kentucky.

Castleman, Harry, and Walter J. Podrazik. 2016. *Watching TV: Eight Decades of American Television*. 3rd ed. Syracuse, NY: Syracuse University Press.

Gross, Edward, and Mark A. Altman. 2016. *The Fifty-Year Mission, the First 25 Years: The Complete, Uncensored, Unauthorized Oral History of Star Trek.* New York: St. Martin's.

Gross, Edward, and Mark A. Altman. 2016. *The Fifty-Year Mission, the Next 25 Years: The Complete, Uncensored, Unauthorized Oral History of Star Trek.* New York: St. Martin's.

Reagin, Nancy R. 2013. *Star Trek and History.* Hoboken, NJ: John Wiley & Sons.

Rossinow, Doug. 2015. *The Reagan Era: A History of the 1980s.* New York: Columbia University Press.

Wrobel, Ron, III. 2016. *The Complete Ferengi Rules of Acquisition: Aphorisms, Guidelines, and Principles to Life in Ferengi Culture.* Scotts Valley, CA: CreateSpace.

Green Goblin

First Appearance:	*The Amazing Spider-Man #14* (cover date: July 1964)
Creators:	Stan Lee and Steve Ditko
Other Media:	Movie, animated television series
Primary Strength:	Cunning, genius
Major Weakness:	Drug-induced insanity, obsession
Weapons:	Pumpkin bombs
Base of Operations:	New York City
Key Allies:	Doctor Octopus
Key Enemies:	Spider-Man
Actual Identity:	Norman Osborn (later Harry Osborn and others)
Nicknames/Aliases:	N/A

When Marvel Comics editor-in-chief Stan Lee launched what came to be known as the Marvel Age of Comics in the early 1960s, one of the earliest superheroes introduced, who went on to become one of the most popular and commercially successful superheroes of all time, was his collaboration with artist Steve Ditko: Spider-Man. Spider-Man is really awkward high-schooler Peter Parker who is bitten by a radioactive spider, granting him the proportional speed, strength, agility, and senses of a spider. After losing his uncle to a street criminal that Peter, as Spider-Man, could have stopped, the young hero dedicates himself to the concept that "[w]ith great power there must also come—great responsibility" (Stan Lee and Steve Ditko, *Amazing Fantasy #15*, August 1962). Over the decades, *Spider-Man* has accumulated one of the most extensive and fascinating rogues' galleries in all of comics. Of all of Spider-Man's foes, however, arguably the most terrifying is one of his earliest: the Green Goblin.

The original Green Goblin was actually the genius millionaire scientist and industrialist Norman Osborn, father to Peter Parker's high school friend Harry. The mystery of the Goblin's identity went on for two years before his secret identity and origin story were revealed to readers. During an experiment, Osborn had been exposed to unstable chemicals, which increased his physical strength while simultaneously slowly decaying his sanity (Stan Lee and Steve Ditko, *The Amazing Spider-Man #40*, September 1966). The most iconic Green Goblin story, "The Night Gwen Stacy Died," brings a deadly showdown between Goblin and the web-slinger when Goblin throws Peter Parker's girlfriend, Gwen Stacy, from New York City's George Washington Bridge. Spider-Man allows Goblin to get away in order to attempt to save Stacy with a web line to catch her before she hits the water. However, when the web line goes taut, the sudden break to her fall causes her head to snap backward, killing the young woman. Goblin later appears to die in combat with Spider-Man, leading his son Harry, who is dealing with his own drug issues, to take up the mantle of Green Goblin (Gerry Conway and Gil Kane, *The Amazing Spider-Man #121–122*, June–July 1973).

Over the decades, others have donned the mantle of Green Goblin, ultimately to relinquish it on Norman Osborn's numerous returns. Numerous Goblin spin-offs have developed in the comics over the years, including Hobgoblin, Proto-Goblin, Goblin King, and others. To date, the only live-action version of the character has been in the feature film *Spider-Man* (Sony Pictures, director Sam Raimi, 2002). In that film, Norman Osborn/Green Goblin was portrayed by Willem DaFoe; the original Goblin story line, without Stacy's death, is sped up, culminating with the character's death when he accidentally impales himself with his own glider, as he does in the comics. Also like the comics, Norman's death inspires Harry (played by James Franco) to turn evil and take up the Goblin mantle.

Unlike most comic book supervillains, Green Goblin possesses no overall evil plan. He does not seek world conquest, and his petty crimes tend to be more about accumulating resources for further developing his arsenal of weapons. His ultimate goal is the personal destruction of death of Peter Parker/Spider-Man, whose secret identity is known to Osborn. His one, obsessive desire is death and destruction. The Harry Osborn Goblin likewise seeks Spider-Man's destruction, but more for revenge for the hero's perceived involvement in his father's death. Overall, he represents the antithesis to Peter's "great power" mantra, representing, instead, the idea that with great power, there comes the ability to do whatever one desires regardless of consequences.

Richard A. Hall

See also: Asajj Ventress, Brainiac, Catwoman, The Comedian, The Court of Owls, Doctor Doom, Doomsday, Dr. Frank-N-Furter, Faith the Vampire Slayer, Frankenstein's Monster, Harley Quinn, Joker, Killmonger, Lex Luthor, Loki, Magneto, Martin Brenner, Ozymandias, Penguin, Poison Ivy, Ra's al Ghul, Red Skull, Scarecrow, Sherry Palmer, Thanos, Two-Face, Ultron, Zod; *Thematic Essays*: "Nazis, Communists, and Terrorists . . . Oh My!": The Rise of the Supervillain and the Evolution of the Modern American Villain, The Dark Mirror: Evil Twins, *The Twilight Zone*, and the Villain Within, The Pathos of Villainy: Getting to the Heart of Why Villains Went Bad.

Further Reading

Alsford, Mike. 2006. *Heroes & Villains*. Waco, TX: Baylor University Press.

Ashby, LeRoy. 2006. *With Amusement for All: A History of American Popular Culture since 1830*. Lexington: University Press of Kentucky.

Costello, Matthew J. 2009. *Secret Identity Crisis: Comic Books & the Unmasking of Cold War America.* New York: Continuum.

DeFalco, Tom. 2004. *Comics Creators on Spider-Man.* London: Titan.

Howe, Sean. 2012. *Marvel Comics: The Untold Story.* New York: Harper-Perennial.

Starck, Kathleen, ed. 2010. *Between Fear and Freedom: Cultural Representations of the Cold War.* Newcastle upon Tyne, UK: Cambridge Scholars.

Tucker, Reed. 2017. *Slugfest: Inside the Epic 50-Year Battle between Marvel and DC.* New York: Da Capo Press.

Wright, Bradford W. 2003. *Comic Book Nation: The Transformation of Youth Culture in America.* Baltimore, MD: Johns Hopkins University Press.

Grindelwald

First Appearance:	*Harry Potter and the Philosopher's [Sorcerer's] Stone* (novel) (release date: June 26, 1997)
Creators:	J. K. Rowling
Other Media:	Movies, Pottermore website
Primary Strength:	Witchcraft/magic
Major Weakness:	Racism, megalomania
Weapons:	The Elder Wand (one of the three Deathly Hallows)
Base of Operations:	Europe
Key Allies:	Albus Dumbledore (originally), Credence Barebone (Aurelius Dumbledore), Queenie Goldstein
Key Enemies:	Albus Dumbledore, Aberforth Dumbledore, Newt Scamander, Theseus Scamander, Tina Goldstein
Actual Identity:	Gellert Grindelwald
Nicknames/Aliases:	N/A

In 1997, author J. K. Rowling introduced readers to the magical world of Harry Potter with *Harry Potter and the Philosopher's Stone* (released in the United States as *Harry Potter and the Sorcerer's Stone*). The series follows young wizard Harry Potter from the ages of eleven to seventeen, through his years at Hogwarts School of Witchcraft and Wizardry in Great Britain. Through the course of these novels and the later films, audiences discover that before Lord Voldemort, the greatest dark wizard of all time had been Gellert Grindelwald, a childhood friend of wizarding legend Albus Dumbledore. After the final book, *Harry Potter and the Deathly Hallows*, was released as a film, author J. K. Rowling revealed that Dumbledore actually possessed romantic feelings for Grindelwald, setting up her forthcoming Potterverse prequel film series, beginning with *Fantastic Beasts and Where to Find Them* (Warner Brothers, 2016). This *Fantastic Beasts* series would examine the rise and fall of Grindelwald, culminating in the legendary duel between Dumbledore and Grindelwald, hailed in the novels as the greatest wizarding duel in history. In the new film series, Grindelwald was played by Hollywood legend Johnny Depp.

At a young age, Gellert Grindelwald became obsessed with the legend of the Deathly Hallows, three magical objects of immense power: the Resurrection Stone; the Cloak of Invisibility; and the Elder Wand. Grindelwald was still a child when he moved to the small community of Godric's Hollow, the location of the graves of the brothers who originally owned the Hallows. It was there that he met a young Albus Dumbledore, and the two became fast friends. Grindelwald had a vision of the wizarding world taking over the Muggle (nonmagical) world and ruling over them for their own good. Dumbledore, at first, agreed with his friend, until he finally discovered Grindelwald's true, eviler intent. A duel between Dumbledore's brother Aberforth and Grindelwald led Albus to side with his brother, delivering simultaneous killing curses with Grindelwald, one of which struck and killed Dumbledore's young sister, Ariana.

Years later, when Dumbledore was serving as Defense against the Dark Arts professor at Hogwarts, Grindelwald, now in possession of the Elder Wand, launched his final mission to conquer the world for wizardkind. Bound by a blood oath to never cross his old friend again, Dumbledore sends his former student Newt Scamander to stop Grindelwald. During a rally where Grindelwald conjures images of the forthcoming World War II as a reason for the wizarding world to stop and control the Muggles, a group of aurors led by Theseus Scamander stops the rally but fails to capture Grindelwald. Grindelwald then reveals that young Credence Barebone, a deeply disturbed young wizard in possession of the phoenix Fawks, is secretly Dumbledore's younger brother, Aurelius (J. K. Rowling, *Fantastic Beasts: The Crimes of Grindelwald*, Warner Brothers, 2018).

In the realm of Western villainy, Gellert Grindelwald can most closely be associated with real-world villain Adolf Hitler. Aside from his fanatical goal of global conquest, Grindelwald also possesses an intense hatred of Muggles and Mudbloods (witches and wizards with one or more Muggle parent). With the combined power of the Elder Wand (the most powerful wand in wizarding history) and his own considerable Hitleresque talent for swaying large crowds to believe and follow him, Grindelwald is, to date, the most frightening and powerful villain to appear in Rowling's magical world. He also, unfortunately, directly reflects the growing xenophobia currently acting as a cancer across the Western world. As Hitler's deeds fall farther into the past, and fewer and fewer people remain who remember the nightmare of the Nazis, characters such as Grindelwald play a vital role in society as a cautionary tale of where current trends in Western society could lead.

Richard A. Hall

See also: Angelique Bouchard-Collins, Archie Bunker, Bellatrix Lestrange, Dark Willow, Fiona Goode/The Supreme, Maleficent, Morgan le Fay, Sauron/Saruman, Sith Lords, Voldemort, Wicked Witch of the West; *Thematic Essays*: "In the Beginning . . .": The Origins of Villains in the Western World, "Nazis, Communists, and Terrorists . . . Oh My!": The Rise of the Supervillain and the Evolution of the Modern American Villain, The Pathos of Villainy: Getting to the Heart of Why Villains Went Bad.

Further Reading

Adams, Neal, Rafael Medoff, and Craig Yoe. 2018. *We Spoke Out: Comic Books and the Holocaust*. San Diego, CA: Yoe Books/IDW.

Alsford, Mike. 2006. *Heroes & Villains*. Waco, TX: Baylor University Press.

Baggett, David, Shawn E. Klein, and William Irwin, eds. 2004. *Harry Potter and Philosophy: If Aristotle Ran Hogwarts*. Chicago: Open Court.

Barratt, Bethany. 2012. *The Politics of Harry Potter*. London: Palgrave MacMillan.

Cavendish, Richard. 1968. *The Black Arts: A Concise History of Witchcraft, Demonology, Astrology, and Other Mystical Practices throughout the Ages*. New York: TarcherPerigree.

Hutton, Ronald. 2017. *The Witch: A History of Fear, from Ancient Times to the Present*. New Haven, CT: Yale University Press.

Irwin, William, and Gregory Bassham, ed. 2010. *The Ultimate Harry Potter and Philosophy: Hogwarts for Muggles*. Hoboken, NJ: John Wiley & Sons.

Reagin, Nancy R. 2011. *Harry Potter and History*. Hoboken, NJ: John Wiley & Sons.

Russell, Jeffrey B., and Brooks Alexander. 2007. *A History of Witchcraft: Sorcerers, Heretics, & Pagans*. London: Thames & Hudson.

Gus Fring

First Appearance:	*Breaking Bad*, season 2, episode 11 (air date: May 17, 2009)
Creators:	Vince Gilligan
Other Media:	N/A
Primary Strength:	Cunning, persistence
Major Weakness:	Obsessive hatred of Don Salamanca
Weapons:	Box cutter, guns, explosives
Base of Operations:	Albuquerque, New Mexico
Key Allies:	Mike Ehrmantraut, Walter White/Heisenberg, Gale Boetticher, Don Eladio
Key Enemies:	Drug Enforcement Agency (DEA), Don Hector Salamanca, Walter White (Heisenberg)
Actual Identity:	Gustavo Fring
Nicknames/Aliases:	"The Chicken Man," "The Chilean"

Breaking Bad debuted in 2009 to favorable reviews, and it was generally accepted that the writing was some of the best on television in recent history. Maintaining that level of greatness can be difficult if the only bad guys Walter White (played by Bryan Cranston) takes on are low-level thugs who may be tougher than Walt but nowhere near his league in terms of cunning and intelligence. The debut of Gustavo "Gus" Fring (played by Giancarlo Esposito) at the end of season two marked the beginning of a whole new type of foe for Walt; because Gus was Walt's intellectual equal, maybe even a little smarter, it would take much more cunning and guile from Walt to succeed in the struggle against this new opponent.

The character of Gus Fring is one of contradictions or maybe even dualities. To the general public, Gus Fring is a mild-mannered, sometimes painfully boring, owner of the chicken restaurant franchise Los Pollos Hermanos. He is active in the community and even sponsors events for the Drug Enforcement Agency. What a much smaller group of people know is that Gus sits atop a vast drug manufacturing and distribution network at the behest of some of the worst cartels in Mexico. He uses his company's trucks to move product, his company's laundromat to camouflage a meth superlaboratory and to provide a cover for all the chemicals required in the manufacture of methamphetamine, and his goodwill curried throughout the community to keep himself beyond suspicion.

Gus initially does not want to work with Walt because of some undefined "reservations" about him (Vince Gilligan, "Box Cutter," *Breaking Bad*, season 4, episode 1, July 17, 2011), but the purity of Walt's product eventually convinces Gus to seriously consider a partnership. Thus he brings Walt into his orbit and convinces Walt to come work for him in his superlab under the laundromat. The only catch is that Gus wants nothing to do with Jesse Pinkman (played by Aaron Paul), whom he sees as nothing more than a meth addict. In Walt's first meeting with him, Gus warns him to never trust an addict, referring to Jesse (George Mastras, "Mandala," *Breaking Bad*, season 2, episode 11, May 17, 2009).

The men's partnership is fraught with disagreements and distrust from the beginning. Walt suspects that Gus merely intends to learn his recipe and then have him and Jesse killed. Gus finds Walt to be careless and a man of poor judgment. They are both right. What is new for Walt is that while Gus may not be a step ahead of him, he is hardly ever lagging far behind. This means that when Walt finally decides that the struggle with Gus has gotten a little too existential, he must draw upon all of his intelligence and ingenuity to get rid of him. The final showdown happens at the Casa Tranquila, a nursing home where Don Hector Salamanca, Gus's long-time archnemesis, lives.

Don Hector has no love for Walt, but his hatred for Gus goes back decades. This makes it easy for Walt to enlist Don Hector in his plan. Gus visits Don Hector to taunt him and ultimately kill him. During their exchange, Gus notices just a heartbeat too late that something is not right and begins to stand just as the bomb Walt planted under Don Hector's wheelchair detonates. The very next scene shows Gus standing in the door of the room seemingly unharmed, but the camera then reveals the right side of his head, which is devoid of flesh and shows the exposed skull underneath. Gus straightens his tie and falls over dead (Vince Gilligan, "Face Off," *Breaking Bad*, season 4, episode 13, October 09, 2011).

The character of Gus Fring was fairly well received at the time, and compared to every other rival of color Walt faced, Gus was definitely the strongest (Prioleau, "Walter White and Bleeding Brown"). He was different from Walter in many respects, but they were both extremely intelligent men who claimed to want what was best for their families. This was a welcome change to a show that is accused of utilizing the "Mighty Whitey" trope, where a white person enters a world usually inhabited by people of color and winds up being better than everyone else

(Harris, "Walter White Supremacy"). Ultimately, though, the trope wins out, when Walt uses Gus and Don Hector's hatred of each other to his advantage. The passing of Gus Fring signaled the end of the single person who could equal Walter White. The final season of the show required entire groups the DEA and Neo-Nazis to achieve the same effect of the single figure of Gustavo Fring. That final image of Gus, half his face stripped away, provides a canvas upon which many interpretations of dualistic symbolism can be painted, or it can just be enjoyed as a suitably incredible end to an unmatched incredible character.

Keith R. Claridy

See also: Bill/Snake Charmer, Captain Hector Barbossa, The Corleone Family, The Court of Owls, Ernst Stavro Blofeld/SPECTRE, Fish Mooney, Goldfinger, Grand Nagus/Ferengi, Heisenberg/Walter White, Jabba the Hutt, Marsellus Wallace, Negan/The Saviors, Tony Montana, Tony Soprano; *Thematic Essays*: The Dark Mirror: Evil Twins, *The Twilight Zone*, and the Villain Within.

Further Reading

Harris, Malcolm. 2013. "Walter White Supremacy." *New Inquiry*. September 2013. Accessed August 10, 2019. https://thenewinquiry.com/walter-white-supremacy/.

Peters, Andy. 2015. "Beyond Good and *Bad*: The Linguistic Construction of Walter White's Masculinity in *Breaking Bad*." University of Michigan. Accessed June 8, 2019. https://lsa.umich.edu/content/dam/english-assets/migrated/honors_files/PETERS%20A.%20Beyond%20Good%20&%20Bad.pdf.

Prioleau, Chris. 2013. "Walter White and Bleeding Brown: On *Breaking Bad*'s Race Problem." *Apogee Journal*. October 2013. Accessed August 10, 2019. https://apogeejournal.org/2013/10/03/walter-white-bleeding-brown-on-breaking-bads-race-problem/.

Sandel, Adam Adatto. 2018. "Breaking Bad: Walter White as Nietzschean Hero." *American Affairs Journal*. Fall 2018. Accessed August 10, 2019. https://americanaffairsjournal.org/2018/08/breaking-bad-walter-white-as-nietzschean-hero/.

Tannenbaum, Rob. 2013. "Gus from *Breaking Bad* Wants Walt's Head on a Pike." *Rolling Stone*. September 2013. Accessed August 10, 2019. https://www.rollingstone.com/tv/tv-news/gus-from-breaking-bad-wants-walts-head-on-a-pike-205633/.

VanDerWerff, Emily Todd. 2013. "*Breaking Bad* Ended the Anti-Hero Genre by Introducing Good and Evil." *AV Club*. September 2013. Accessed June 24, 2019. https://tv.avclub.com/breaking-bad-ended-the-anti-hero-genre-by-introducing-g-1798240891.

Hannibal Lecter

First Appearance:	*Red Dragon* (novel) (release date: October 1981)
Creators:	Thomas Harris
Other Media:	Movies, television
Primary Strength:	Cunning
Major Weakness:	Overconfidence
Weapons:	Various
Base of Operations:	N/A
Key Allies:	N/A
Key Enemies:	Will Graham, Clarice Starling
Actual Identity:	Dr. Hannibal Lecter
Nicknames/Aliases:	"Hannibal the Cannibal," Count Hannibal Lecter VIII

In his 1981 novel, *Red Dragon*, author Thomas Harris introduced the world to the serial killer Dr. Hannibal Lecter. Though an ancillary character in his first literary appearance, he overwhelmingly captured the imaginations of audiences, leading to a greater role in the novel's follow-up, *The Silence of the Lambs* (1988). He, finally, emerges as the protagonist in the final two books, *Hannibal* (1999) and *Hannibal Rising* (2006). It was on film, however, that the character gained a dominant foothold in American pop culture. Although Brian Cox originally played Lecter in the 1986 film *Manhunter* (based on *Red Dragon*), it was with Sir Anthony Hopkins' seething portrayal of the suave killer in the 1991 version of *The Silence of the Lambs*. Hopkins returned for the film versions of *Hannibal* (2001) and *Red Dragon* (2002). While Hannibal has been embraced by modern audiences as an antihero, he is much more accurately an antivillain. He is not a hero who occasionally kills wrongdoers; he is a brutal serial killer who occasionally kills wrongdoers.

Lecter was born in Lithuania, where, as a young child, he witnessed the murder—and eating—of his sister by local Nazi sympathizers, who claimed that Lecter also partook of his dead sister. Like many textbook sociopaths, Lecter possesses no remorse for his murders, and he tortured and killed small animals as a child. In *Red Dragon*, however, FBI agent Will Graham claims that Lecter is more than a sociopath, defining him instead as "a monster." Lecter grew up to become a man of high society, attributed in part to his royal Lithuanian heritage, and an acclaimed surgeon and psychiatrist. Lecter views his murders as social services,

Anthony Hopkins shot to super-stardom with his Oscar-winning portrayal of Dr. Hannibal Lecter in the 1991 film *The Silence of the Lambs*. (Universal Pictures/AF Archive/Alamy Stock Photo)

separating the wheat from the chaff, cutting away the "lesser" in human society in order to purify it.

In *The Silence of the Lambs*, even confinement does not stop him; he causes fellow prisoner Multiple Miggs to swallow his own tongue just by whispering to him in retaliation for Miggs's crude behavior toward FBI agent Clarice Starling. At the end of both the film and novel of *The Silence of the Lambs*, an escaped Lecter hunts his former warden, Dr. Frederick Chilton, whom Lecter believes to be a subpar psychiatrist. In the novel and film for *Hannibal Rising* and the television series *Hannibal* (NBC, 2013–2015), the narratives attempt to provide some meaning and explanation for Hannibal's fall into madness, making him a more sympathetic character, which, in the minds of the audience, excuses his atrocities.

In the end, however, Dr. Hannibal Lecter is a cold-blooded murderer and one who, in spite of Western society's disgust of the mere concept, devours his victims. He combines the unquenchable bloodthirst of slasher-film icons such as Jason Voorhees or Leatherface with the purifying agenda of a Grindelwald or Magneto. His charm and sophistication both disarm and terrify his victims and audiences alike. He is Hitler gone solo and ravenous. In the realm of villainy, he represents the unstoppable killing machine that threatens anyone he deems unworthy of being in society, regardless of race, ethnicity, gender, sexual orientation, or socioeconomic status. Anyone who has ever made a mistake can be a future target, and future meal, for Hannibal the Cannibal.

Richard A. Hall

See also: Angelus, Bellatrix Lestrange, Billy the Kid, The Comedian, Doomsday, Dracula, Elle Driver/California Mountain Snake, Freddy Krueger, Grindelwald, Jason Voorhees, Joker, Leatherface, Magneto, Martin Brenner, The Master/Missy, Michael Myers, Negan/The Saviors, Norman Bates, Nurse Ratched, Pancho Villa, Ra's al Ghul, Red Skull, Reverend Stryker/The Purifiers, Sith Lords, Spike and Drusilla, Thanos, Ultron, Voldemort, Zod; *Thematic Essays*: "In the Beginning . . .": The Origins of Villains in the Western World, "Nazis, Communists, and Terrorists . . . Oh My!": The Rise of the Supervillain and the Evolution of the Modern American Villain, Tarantino and the Antivillain, The Pathos of Villainy: Getting to the Heart of Why Villains Went Bad.

Further Reading

Alsford, Mike. 2006. *Heroes & Villains.* Waco, TX: Baylor University Press.

Ashby, LeRoy. 2006. *With Amusement for All: A History of American Popular Culture since 1830.* Lexington: University Press of Kentucky.

Dyer, Ben, ed. 2009. *Supervillains and Philosophy: Sometimes, Evil Is Its Own Reward.* Popular Culture and Philosophy Series. Chicago: Open Court.

Forasteros, J. R. 2017. *Empathy for the Devil: Finding Ourselves in the Villains of the Bible.* Downers Grove, IL: InterVarsity.

Lafferty, Sarah. 2011. "Exploring the Relay Gaze in Hollywood Cinema: Serial Killers and the Women Who Hunt Them." In *Vader, Voldemort and Other Villains: Essays on Evil in Popular Media*, edited by Jamey Heit, 97–112. Jefferson, NC: McFarland.

Szumskyj, Benjamin, ed. 2008. *Dissecting Hannibal Lecter: Essays on the Novels of Thomas Harris.* Jefferson, NC: McFarland.

Westfall, Joseph, ed. 2016. *Hannibal Lecter and Philosophy: The Heart of the Matter.* Chicago: Open Court.

Harley Quinn

First Appearance:	*Batman: The Animated Series*, season 1, episode 7 (air date: September 11, 1992)
Creators:	Paul Dini and Bruce Timm
Other Media:	Animated home video, comics, film
Primary Strength:	Hand-to-hand combat, acrobatics
Major Weakness:	Obsession with Joker
Weapons:	Large mallet, guns
Base of Operations:	Gotham City
Key Allies:	Joker, Poison Ivy, Suicide Squad
Key Enemies:	Batman
Actual Identity:	Harleen Quinzel
Nicknames/Aliases:	N/A

The *Batman* franchise is, perhaps, second only to *Superman* in regard to its impact on popular culture. Created by writer Bill Finger and artist Bob Kane,

Batman is billionaire playboy Bruce Wayne, who, after witnessing a mugger murder his parents when he was a young boy, vowed to dedicate his life battling crime in his hometown of Gotham City. In order to strike fear in criminals, Wayne chose to disguise himself as a bat, and "the Batman" (originally "Bat-Man") was born (Bill Finger and Bob Kane, *Detective Comics #33*, November 1939). Unlike his counterpart, Superman, Batman is a mere mortal, with no "super" powers of any kind. Instead, Batman is armed only with his keen intellect and a myriad of gadgets and vehicles that he uses in his fight against crime. Over the decades, in comics as well as on television and film, Batman has gained arguably the most impressive rogues' gallery of villains in all of popular culture. One of the most recent and most popular is Harley Quinn.

Unlike the vast majority of comic book supervillains, Harley Quinn did not originate in the pages of comic books. She was first introduced in the groundbreaking television series *Batman: The Animated Series* (Fox Kids, 1992–1995). Originally meant merely as a background henchwoman for the Joker, her bubbly personality and overall air of innocence—as well as her stylish harlequin/jester costume—set her up immediately to be much more than a henchwoman. She had all the makings of the perfect girlfriend for the Clown Prince of Crime. Her origin story was revealed in the one-shot comic book *The Batman Adventures: Mad Love* (1994). In that story, Harley Quinn originated as psychiatrist Dr. Harleen Quinzel, newly assigned to Arkham Asylum and to treating the Joker. Through their sessions, Quinzel falls in love with the murderous psychopath, speaking directly to real-world scenarios where various "normal" women fell passionately in love with incarcerated serial killers. She eventually becomes Joker's accomplice, assisting in his escape and becoming his henchwoman and faithful girlfriend. Although Joker is a physically and emotionally abusive boyfriend, the newly minted Harley Quinn is endlessly devoted, even going so far as to refer to the mad murderer as "Puddin'" (Paul Dini and Bruce Timm, *Mad Love*, February 1994).

Harley quickly made the transition from television to comics, becoming one of the most popular DC Comics characters of the last quarter century. During her many breakups with Joker, Harley teams up with other female villains to commit various crimes, most notably, Poison Ivy. In 2011, as part of DC Comics' "New 52" relaunch, Harley began the transition from villain to antihero (or, more accurately, antivillain). After being captured and incarcerated once again, Harley is forcibly enlisted into the ranks of the U.S. government's latest Suicide Squad: a group of imprisoned supervillains, under the guidance of government agent Amanda Waller, who are sent on suicide missions against various threats to society; should members of the squad attempt to escape, an implanted explosive device would kill them immediately (Adam Glass and Federico Dallocchio, *Suicide Squad, Vol. 4, #1*, November 2011). By this time, Harley's appearance had been dramatically altered from her more innocent *Batman: The Animated Series* days, and she had a much more sexualized costume and appearance. It was this more sexualized version that made her first live-action appearance in the film *Suicide Squad* (Warner Brothers, 2016), where the character was portrayed by actress

Margot Robbie. In recent years, Harley Quinn has been a continuingly popular character for DC Comics, whether as villain, antivillain, or some grayer area in between.

In the realm of American villainy, Harley Quinn represents the dangers of passionate obsession. She is deeply mentally disturbed, both through contact with and abuse at the hands of the Joker. Despite the inherent sadness of the character, Harley never fails to entertain with her wit, her antics, and her off-center brand of heroics. She is tied to villainy, not through malicious intent but, rather, through blind devotion to a dedicated maniacal villain. Once she removes herself from her villainous influence, the Joker, and strikes out on her own, her tendency continues to bend toward villainy, because this is the path she has chosen, and the criminal world, whether financially lucrative or not, provides a sense of freedom that living by the rules never can. The character has been further examined in the documentary *Necessary Evil: Super-Villains of DC Comics*, directed by Scott Devine and J. M. Kenny (Warner Home Video, 2013).

Richard A. Hall

See also: Alexis Carrington-Colby-Dexter, Borg Queen/Borg, Catwoman, Elle Driver/California Mountain Snake, Faith the Vampire Slayer, Fiona Goode/The Supreme, Joker, The Master/Missy, Morgan le Fay, Number Six/Cylons, Nurse Ratched, O-Ren Ishii/Cottonmouth, Poison Ivy, Scarecrow, Tia Dalma/Calypso, Two-Face; *Thematic Essays*: The Pathos of Villainy: Getting to the Heart of Why Villains Went Bad.

Further Reading

Alsford, Mike. 2006. *Heroes & Villains.* Waco, TX: Baylor University Press.

Barba, Shelley E., and Joy M. Perrin, eds. 2017. *The Ascendance of Harley Quinn: Essays on DC's Enigmatic Villain.* Jefferson, NC: McFarland.

Beard, Jim, ed. 2010. *Gotham City 14 Miles: 14 Essays on Why the 1960s Batman TV Series Matters.* Edwardsville, IL: Sequart Research & Literacy Organization.

Cruz, Joe, and Lars Stoltzfus-Brown. 2020. "Harley Quinn, Villain, Vixen, Victim: Exploring Her Origins in *Batman: The Animated Series.*" In *The Supervillain Reader*, edited by Rob Weiner and Rob Peaslee, 203–213. Jackson: University of Mississippi Press.

Douglas, Susan J. 1995. *Where the Girls Are: Growing Up Female with the Mass Media.* New York: Three Rivers.

Faludi, Susan. 2007. *The Terror Dream: Myth and Misogyny in an Insecure America.* New York: Picador.

Langley, Travis. 2012. *Batman and Psychology: A Dark and Stormy Knight.* New York: John Wiley & Sons.

O'Neil, Dennis, ed. 2008. *Batman Unauthorized: Vigilantes, Jokers, and Heroes in Gotham City.* Smart Pop Series. Dallas, TX: BenBella.

Stuller, Jennifer K. 2010. *Ink-Stained Amazons and Cinematic Warriors: Superwomen in Modern Mythology.* London: I. B. Tauris.

Weldon, Glen. 2016. *The Caped Crusade: Batman and the Rise of Nerd Culture.* New York: Simon & Schuster.

Wright, Bradford W. 2003. *Comic Book Nation: The Transformation of Youth Culture in America.* Baltimore, MD: Johns Hopkins University Press.

Heisenberg/Walter White

First Appearance:	*Breaking Bad*, season 1, episode 1 (air date: January 20, 2008)
Creators:	Vince Gilligan
Other Media:	N/A
Primary Strength:	Knowledge of chemistry, cunning
Major Weakness:	Concern for family, greed
Weapons:	Handguns
Base of Operations:	Albuquerque, New Mexico
Key Allies:	Skyler White, Walter White Jr., Holly White, Hank Schrader, Marie Schrader, Jesse Pinkman, Saul Goodman, Gustavo "Gus" Fring, Mike Ehrmantraut, Todd Alquist
Key Enemies:	Drug Enforcement Agency, Gus Fring, Don Hector Salamanca, Tuco Salamanca
Actual Identity:	Walter White
Nicknames/Aliases:	Heisenberg

Vince Gilligan, creator of *Breaking Bad* (A&E, 2008–2013) and its prequel series, *Better Call Saul* (AMC, 2015–2021), cut his teeth on another iconic show, *The X-Files* (FOX, 1993–2002, 2016–2018), where he served as writer, coexecutive producer, executive producer, coproducer, and supervising producer. After the spinoff of that show, *The Lone Gunmen* (FOX, 2001; which Gilligan cocreated and executive produced), failed to catch on, Gilligan did some varied spec writing. Then in 2004, Gilligan and a friend of his, Thomas Schnauz, were having a conversation about a recent news story of a man cooking meth in his apartment, and as the conversation progressed, the subject of Saddam Hussein's supposed mobile chemical weapons labs also came up. Thomas Schnauz remembers, "Neither of us were working and we were like two 70-year-old men who like to complain about the world. And somehow we spun off into the idea of driving around in a mobile lab, cooking meth. It was a joke . . . but a couple days later Vince called back and said: 'Remember we were talking about that mobile lab and meth? Do you mind if I run with that?'" (Wagner, "The Capitalist Nightmare at the Heart of *Breaking Bad*"). Gilligan ran with the idea and went on to create one of the most iconic shows of the early twenty-first century.

Walter White (played by Bryan Cranston) lives a life that is basically the embodiment of the color beige. A shot of a plaque on the wall of the den shows that he was a "Contributor to Research Awarded the Nobel Prize" as the "Crystallography Project Leader for Proton Radiography" over twenty years earlier (Vince Gilligan, "Pilot," *Breaking Bad*, season 1, episode 1, January 20, 2008). His life has taken a decidedly sharp downturn since then. He is married with one son and a daughter on the way. The research he took part in that the plaque commemorates landed him the dream job of a high school chemistry teacher. The sadness of his regular life does not end there; when school is out, Walt has a second job at a car wash with a terrible boss and gets harassed by students just so that he can make ends meet. At his birthday party, Walt learns just how lucrative the drug trade can be from his brother-in-law, the DEA agent Hank.

The next day, Walt collapses and is rushed to the hospital, where he is given the bad news that he has inoperable lung cancer. The first episode spends a good deal of time showing the viewer that the White family is not doing well financially. This is all so that it will make sense when Walt resorts to drastic measures to ensure that his family will be financially secure after he is gone. At his birthday party, Hank (played by Dean Norris) offers to take Walt on a ride along to see a bust in person. After his diagnosis, Walt takes him up on it. During the bust, Walt sees his old student Jesse Pinkman (played by Aaron Paul) make his escape. He also asks Hank to let him take a look at the lab's setup. All of this has given Walt the idea that he could use his superior chemistry knowledge to make meth, have Jesse sell it, and stockpile enough cash to take care of his family after he's gone. Why worry about prison when you only have a couple years to live at best?

Thus begins Walter White's descent into the seedy underworld of drug cartels. Using his superior knowledge of chemistry, Walt is able to create very pure meth, and it becomes highly desirable. Eventually assuming the identity of Heisenberg, Walt takes on low-level street dealers and the Mexican drug cartels, avoids the DEA, and works for and then kills Gustavo "Gus" Fring (played by Giancarlo

Bryan Cranston in his "Heisenberg" persona on the AMC television series *Breaking Bad*. (WENN US/Alamy Stock Photo)

Esposito). Walt kills many people during the run of the show, but most of them can be excused by the viewer as necessary because it was either kill or be killed for Walter. The first "inexcusable" death that shows Walt has crossed the Rubicon comes in the second season. Jesse has been in a relationship with Jane (played by Krysten Ritter), and the two of them have been enjoying heroin together. Walt disapproves of Jesse's drug use and is not a big fan of Jane. One evening, Walt goes to Jesse's house and finds Jesse passed out. He also sees that Jane has overdosed and is choking on her own vomit. Walt begins to move as though he is going to roll her over to save her life, but he stops himself and watches her die (John Shiban, "Phoenix," *Breaking Bad*, season 2, episode 12, May 24, 2009). This is the first death connected to Walt that is more a matter of from convenience for Walt and his business rather than survival.

As he descends into his Heisenberg life, Walter's personal life suffers. His wife, Skyler (played by Anna Gunn), figures out what he is up to and wants a divorce. Walt eventually convinces her to help him launder the money by buying the car wash, but their relationship is beyond repair. As events begin to unravel around Walt, he becomes more frantic to hold everything together. Hank figures out that Walt is Heisenberg and relaunches an investigation into his own brother-in-law, which leads to Hank's murder by Neo-Nazis (Moira Walley-Beckett, "Gliding Over All," *Breaking Bad*, season 5, episode 8, September 2, 2012; Moira Walley-Beckett, "Ozymandias," *Breaking Bad*, season 5, episode 14, September 15, 2013). Walt meets his end during a police raid of the Neo-Nazi compound where he has gone to free Jesse (Vince Gilligan, "Felina," *Breaking Bad*, season 5, episode 16, September 29, 2013).

This story of turning "Mr. Chips into Scarface," in the words of creator Vince Gilligan (Segal, "The Dark Art of *Breaking Bad*"), is considered one of the greatest shows in television history. While it can be argued that *Breaking Bad* explores the same antihero territory first blazed by *The Sopranos*, it can also be argued that Walter White is an extreme version of all of us (VanDerWerff, "*Breaking Bad* Ended the Anti-Hero"). Tony Soprano the mob boss isn't likely to parallel most of the viewers' lives, but Walter White the chemistry teacher who is barely making ends meet and now has a devastating medical diagnosis could be anyone. The character of Walter White puts a mirror in front of the audience and shows them what they could be if pushed to the limit. Walt shows them what lengths they might go to if facing certain death and financial ruin for their family. The audience is also shown that there is definitely a price to be paid for these actions. The final episode perfectly portrays creator Vince Gilligan's personal belief that "karma kicks in at some point, even if it takes years . . . to happen" (Segal, "The Dark Art of *Breaking Bad*").

Keith R. Claridy

See also: Alexis Carrington-Colby-Dexter, Bill/Snake Charmer, Billy the Kid, Captain Hector Barbossa, The Corleone Family, The Court of Owls, Ebenezer Scrooge, Ernst Stavro Blofeld/SPECTRE, Fish Mooney, Grand Nagus/Ferengi, Gus Fring, J. R. Ewing, Lex Luthor, Marsellus Wallace, Negan/The Saviors, Ozymandias, Sherry Palmer, Tony Montana, Tony Soprano; *Thematic Essays*: Tarantino and the Antivillain, The Pathos of Villainy: Getting to the Heart of Why Villains Went Bad.

Further Reading

McKeown, B., D. B. Thomas, J. C. Rhoads, and D. Sundblad. 2015. "Falling Hard for *Breaking Bad*: An Investigation of Audience Response to a Popular Television Series." *Participations: Journal of Audience & Receptions Studies*. November 2015. Accessed June 15, 2019. https://www.participations.org/Volume%2012/Issue%202/8.pdf.

Peters, Andy. 2015. "Beyond Good and *Bad*: The Linguistic Construction of Walter White's Masculinity in *Breaking Bad*." University of Michigan. Accessed June 8, 2019. https://lsa.umich.edu/content/dam/english-assets/migrated/honors_files/PETERS%20A.%20Beyond%20Good%20&%20Bad.pdf.

Pierson, David P., ed. 2014. *Breaking Bad: Critical Essays on the Contexts, Politics, Style, and Reception of the Television Series*. Lanham, MD: Lexington Books.

Segal, David. 2011. "The Dark Art of *Breaking Bad*." *New York Times*. July 2011. Accessed June 24, 2019. https://www.nytimes.com/2011/07/10/magazine/the-dark-art-of-breaking-bad.html.

VanDerWerff, Emily Todd. 2013. "*Breaking Bad* Ended the Anti-Hero Genre by Introducing Good and Evil." *AV Club*. September 2013. Accessed June 24, 2019. https://tv.avclub.com/breaking-bad-ended-the-anti-hero-genre-by-introducing-g-1798240891.

Wagner, Erica. 2014. "The Capitalist Nightmare at the Heart of *Breaking Bad*." *New Statesman America*. December 2014. Accessed June 15, 2019. https://www.newstatesman.com/culture/2014/12/capitalist-nightmare-heart-breaking-bad.

I

Imperial Officers

First Appearance:	*Star Wars: From the Adventures of Luke Skywalker* (publication date: November 12, 1976)
Creators:	George Lucas
Other Media:	Television (animated and live-action), comics, novels
Primary Strength:	Strategy, politics
Major Weakness:	Blind devotion to the Galactic Empire
Weapons:	Death Star (space station), Star Destroyers (battlecruiser starships)
Base of Operations:	The Galactic Empire ("a galaxy far, far away")
Key Allies:	Emperor Palpatine, Darth Vader, Stormtroopers, AT-AT Drivers, TIE pilots
Key Enemies:	The Rebel Alliance (and, to a degree, each other)
Actual Identity:	Grand Moff/Governor Wilhuff Tarkin, Grand Admiral Mitth'raw'nuruodo ("Thrawn"), Director Orson Krennic (to name but a very few)
Nicknames/Aliases:	N/A

In 1977, writer and director George Lucas introduced the world to his iconic film *Star Wars* (Lucasfilm/20th Century Fox). The massive worldwide success of the original film has spawned numerous sequels, prequels, animated television series, made-for-TV movies, novels, and comic books. Set a "long time ago . . . in a galaxy far, far away," *Star Wars* tells a generational saga of a galaxy at war between the forces of good and evil. Six months prior to the original film's release, ghostwriter Alan Dean Foster brought Lucas's story to the printed page in the novelization of the film. The original *Star Wars* set up the basics of what would become the *Star Wars* universe and one of the most successful franchises in pop culture history. The novel and film introduced audiences to the ranks of imperial officers, the upper echelon of the imperial military machine and blind loyalists to the empire and its ruler, Emperor Sheev Palpatine (secretly, the Sith Lord Darth Sidious).

Perhaps the most famous imperial officer in *Star Wars* lore was one of the first introduced to audiences in the 1970s: Grand Moff Wilhuff Tarkin. The highest-ranked officer in the imperial military, Tarkin was granted the title of governor of the empire's moon-sized battle station, the Death Star, a spherical station built around a powerful superlaser possessing the ability to destroy an entire planet. In the original film, Tarkin (played by veteran actor Peter Cushing) first appears during a meeting of the highest-ranked officers on board the Death Star as they debate among themselves the power of the station versus the dangers of its discovery by the Imperial Senate. Tarkin informs his officers that the emperor has just permanently dissolved the Senate, wiping away forever the last vestiges of the democratic Old Republic. When questioned as to how the empire will maintain control of the galaxy without the bureaucracy, Tarkin further informs them that "regional governors" will now have absolute control over their respective star systems, backed by the might of the Death Star.

His role in the overall *Star Wars* saga was initially brief, as he is killed when the Rebel Alliance successfully destroys the Death Star at the end of the first film. The enduring popularity of the character, however, brought him back, originally in novels published between 1991 and 2012 and also in the two animated prequel television series: *The Clone Wars* (Cartoon Network, 2008–2013; Netflix, 2014; Disney+, 2019–present) and *Rebels* (Disney-XD, 2014–2018), voiced by Stephen Stanton in both series. The character was resurrected once more in the live-action prequel film *Rogue One: A Star Wars Story* (Lucasfilm/Disney, 2016), as a CGI re-creation of Cushing. Tarkin's backstory has been established in James Luceno's 2014 novel, *Star Wars: Tarkin*.

One of the most popular imperial officers in the *Star Wars* canon since the original film trilogy ended has been Grand Admiral Thrawn. Originally presented in the 1991 novel *Star Wars: Heir to the Empire* by Timothy Zahn, Thrawn—unlike *all* other imperial officers—was not human, but Chiss, a blue-skinned, red-eyed humanoid species known for their cunning. Set five years after the events of the "last" film, *Return of the Jedi* (Lucasfilm, 1983), Grand Admiral Thrawn had rallied the scattered remnants of the defeated empire to threaten the burgeoning New Republic and to reclaim the empire's former glory. A strategic genius, Thrawn defeated his enemies by closely studying their culture—art, religion, music, and so on—seeing this as the key to understanding any species.

Although the *Heir* trilogy was some of the most critically and commercially successful novels in the franchise, they, and every *Star Wars* novel published from 1991 to 2012, were ret-conned after Lucasfilm was acquired by the Walt Disney Corporation, as they desired to reboot the entire franchise other than the released films and television series. The decision was met with considerable resistance from fans, leading Lucasfilm to begin reincorporating some of the more popular aspects of the novels, now dubbed "*Star Wars* Legends," into the new canon. Thrawn's enduring popularity led to his return in the animated series *Rebels*, and the original author, Zahn, was brought back to tell the character's "new" backstory in a trilogy of canonical novels.

Another noteworthy addition to the imperial officer corps is that of Director Orson Krennic. Director Krennic was first introduced in 2019 in the canonical novel *Catalyst: A Rogue One Novel* by James Luceno and then, a month later, in the live-action anthology prequel film *Rogue One: A Star Wars Story* (Lucasfilm/Disney, 2016), where the character was played by Ben Mendelsohn. Krennic, a young imperial engineer, politically maneuvers himself to command the construction of the original Death Star, drafting the hesitant scientist Galen Erso into assisting with creating the station's superweapon. Ultimately, Krennic's ambitions lead to his own demise, as the brilliant Erso builds a weakness into the station, which he secretly leaks to the growing Rebel Alliance. Krennic dies during the alliance's mission to steal the plans to the Death Star, which sets up the events of the original film.

Other, less notable officers also met unfortunate fates due to their involvement with the empire. In the original film, Darth Vader (Sith Lord and right hand to the emperor) uses his control of the mystical Force to choke Death Star commander Admiral Motti after the officer mocks Vader's religion (although Tarkin's intervention ultimately saves Motti from Vader's wrath). In the following film, *The Empire Strikes Back* (Lucasfilm, 1980), Vader utilizes the same Force power to kill both imperial fleet commander Admiral Ozzel and star destroyer commander Captain Needa when the two men fail in their respective assignments. In the third original film, *Return of the Jedi* (Lucasfilm, 1983), Moff Jerjerrod, commander of the second Death Star, dies alongside countless other officers and enlisted personnel when the Rebel Alliance destroys the new station.

Other than Thrawn, all other imperial officers to date have been human (speaking to the empire's fascistic racism), and all but two have been men. The two exceptions so far have been Admiral Daala, protégée and love interest of Tarkin, originally appearing in the Jedi Academy trilogy of novels by Keven J. Anderson in 1994, and Commander Iden Versio of Inferno Squad, originally appearing in the 2017 tie-in novel *Star Wars Battlefront II: Inferno Squad* by Christie Golden, setting up the video game of the same name. Although Daala has, to date, been rendered "Legend," in both of these cases, the women officers ultimately switch sides and become good guys, suggesting that women are not as blind in their devotions as are the men. Other than Versio (and, of course, Thrawn), all other imperial officers are not only human but white as well.

In the realm of American villainy, imperial officers are intentionally reminiscent of the Nazi officer corps from World War II. Their uniforms, cruelty, and racism depict the very essence of the fascist German regime from the midtwentieth century. They represent the tendency, dangers, and ultimate inadvisability of blindly following a dictatorial regime. All of the (male) officers listed above exhibit traits of sadism, ambition, and the corruptions of power. Their respective downfalls represent the predictable fate of blindly following the wrong side. Their personality traits reflect the worst of human nature, and although science fiction/fantasy characters, they are all too eerily reminiscent of that which many real-world human beings are capable of becoming.

Richard A. Hall

See also: Archie Bunker, Asajj Ventress, Boba Fett, Captain Phasma/Stormtroopers, COBRA, Frank Burns, General Custer, Jabba the Hutt, Martin Brenner, Negan/The Saviors, Nurse Ratched, Red Skull, Sith Lords; *Thematic Essays*: "Nazis, Communists, and Terrorists . . . Oh My!": The Rise of the Supervillain and the Evolution of the Modern American Villain.

Further Reading

Alsford, Mike. 2006. *Heroes & Villains*. Waco, TX: Baylor University Press.

Ashby, LeRoy. 2006. *With Amusement for All: A History of American Popular Culture since 1830*. Lexington: University Press of Kentucky.

Eberl, Jason T., and Kevin S. Decker, eds. *The Ultimate Star Wars and Philosophy: You Must Unlearn What You Have Learned*. Hoboken, NJ: Wiley-Blackwell.

Jones, Brian Jay. 2016. *George Lucas: A Life*. New York: Little Brown & Company.

Kaminski, Michael. 2008. *The Secret History of Star Wars: The Art of Storytelling and the Making of a Modern Epic*. Kingston, ON, Canada: Legacy.

Reagin, Nancy R., and Janice Liedl, eds. *Star Wars and History*. New York: John Wiley & Sons.

Sunstein, Cass R. 2016. *The World According to Star Wars*. New York: Dey Street.

Sweet, Derek R. 2015. *Star Wars in the Public Square: The Clone Wars as Political Dialogue*. Critical Explorations in Science Fiction and Fantasy Series, edited by Donald E. Palumbo and Michael Sullivan. Jefferson, NC: McFarland.

Taylor, Chris. 2015. *How Star Wars Conquered the Universe: The Past, Present, and Future of a Multibillion Dollar Franchise*. New York: Basic.

J

Jabba the Hutt

First Appearance:	*Star Wars: From the Adventures of Luke Skywalker* (publication date: November 12, 1976)
Creators:	George Lucas
Other Media:	Television, comics, novels
Primary Strength:	Cunning, wealth
Major Weakness:	Greed
Weapons:	N/A
Base of Operations:	Tatooine ("a galaxy far, far away")
Key Allies:	Boba Fett, Rotta the Hutt (son), Prince Xixor (in "Legends" stories)
Key Enemies:	Ziro the Hutt (uncle), Luke Skywalker
Actual Identity:	Jabba Desilijic Tiure
Nicknames/Aliases:	N/A

In 1977, writer and director George Lucas introduced the world to his iconic film *Star Wars*. The massive worldwide success of the original film has spawned numerous sequels, prequels, animated television series, made-for-TV movies, novels, and comic books. Set a "long time ago . . . in a galaxy far, far away," *Star Wars* tells a generational saga of a galaxy at war between the forces of good and evil. Six months prior to the original film's release, ghostwriter Alan Dean Foster brought Lucas's story to the printed page in the novelization of the film. The original *Star Wars* set up the basics of what would become the *Star Wars* universe and one of the most successful franchises in pop culture history. The novel and film introduced audiences to the interplanetary crime lord Jabba the Hutt. The brief mention of the character in the original novel, however, would be ret-conned with the character's first onscreen appearance in the film *Star Wars, Episode VI: Return of the Jedi* (Lucasfilm, 1983).

Other than the brief scenes in the novelization and comic book adaptation of the original *Star Wars* (immediately ret-conned out of official canon due to George Lucas's uncertainty about how he wanted the character depicted), the audience's only understanding of Jabba the Hutt from the films was the mentions of him in *Star Wars* and the first sequel, *The Empire Strikes Back* (1980), where it was established that Jabba was a powerful crime boss to whom hero Han Solo owed money. At the end of the film, Solo was captured by the empire, frozen, and given to the bounty hunter Boba Fett for delivery to Jabba. At the opening of *Return of the Jedi*

(1983), Luke Skywalker and the other saga heroes embark on a rescue operation, taking them deep into the lair of the mysterious crime lord.

When audiences in 1983 finally received their first glimpse of the character, they were met with a giant slug-like creature with large eyes and mouth and small arms and hands. He proudly displayed the frozen Solo as an ornament and warning to all of the ultimate fate for those who failed the gangster. Ultimately, Jabba was killed during the rescue attempt by Rebel Alliance leader—and Han Solo's love interest—Princess Leia Organa, whom the crime lord had chained to his throne as yet another treasure. The enduring popularity of the character, however, led to his return in several comic books published by Dark Horse in the 1990s. In 1997, as part of the special edition rereleases of the original trilogy, a poorly received CGI version appeared in a previously cut scene from the original film, and in 1999, Jabba returned once more in a cameo in *Star Wars, Episode I: The Phantom Menace* (Lucasfilm). Fans received even more Jabba in several episodes of the animated television series *The Clone Wars* (Cartoon Network, 2008–2013; Netflix, 2014; Disney+, 2019–present).

In the realm of American villainy, Jabba the Hutt represents the typical mob boss, with a massive crime empire spanning the galaxy. His physicality reflects his ultimate sins: lust, gluttony, and greed. Though imposing, he is equally physically weak due to the limited mobility brought on by his massive girth and slug-like body. His strength comes solely from his personal cunning and his considerable wealth. However, as his henchmen are primarily guns for hire, their respective loyalties go only as far as Jabba's ability to pay. As such, there is no one on upon

The vile crime lord Jabba the Hutt with a captured Princess Leia in the 1983 film *Star Wars: Return of the Jedi*. (PictureLux/The Hollywood Archive/Alamy Stock Photo)

whom the crime boss can consistently rely. This vulnerability proves his greatest weakness and is a key factor in his ultimate downfall.

Richard A. Hall

See also: Alexis Carrington-Colby-Dexter, Asajj Ventress, Bill/Snake Charmer, Boba Fett, Captain Phasma/Stormtroopers, COBRA, The Corleone Family, Ernst Stavro Blofeld/SPECTRE, Fish Mooney, Goldfinger, Grand Nagus/Ferengi, Gus Fring, Heisenberg/Walter White, Imperial Officers, J. R. Ewing, Lex Luthor, Marsellus Wallace, Negan/The Saviors, O-Ren Ishii/Cottonmouth, Ozymandias, Penguin, Ra's al Ghul, Red Skull, Sith Lords, Tony Montana, Tony Soprano, Two-Face; *Thematic Essays*: "Nazis, Communists, and Terrorists . . . Oh My!": The Rise of the Supervillain and the Evolution of the Modern American Villain.

Further Reading

Alsford, Mike. 2006. *Heroes & Villains.* Waco, TX: Baylor University Press.

Ashby, LeRoy. 2006. *With Amusement for All: A History of American Popular Culture since 1830.* Lexington: University Press of Kentucky.

Eberl, Jason T., and Kevin S. Decker, eds. *The Ultimate Star Wars and Philosophy: You Must Unlearn What You Have Learned.* Hoboken, NJ: Wiley-Blackwell.

Jones, Brian Jay. 2016. *George Lucas: A Life.* New York: Little Brown & Company.

Kaminski, Michael. 2008. *The Secret History of Star Wars: The Art of Storytelling and the Making of a Modern Epic.* Kingston, ON, Canada: Legacy.

Reagin, Nancy R., and Janice Liedl, eds. *Star Wars and History.* New York: John Wiley & Sons.

Sunstein, Cass R. 2016. *The World According to Star Wars.* New York: Dey Street.

Sweet, Derek R. 2015. *Star Wars in the Public Square: The Clone Wars as Political Dialogue.* Critical Explorations in Science Fiction and Fantasy Series, edited by Donald E. Palumbo and Michael Sullivan. Jefferson, NC: McFarland.

Taylor, Chris. 2015. *How Star Wars Conquered the Universe: The Past, Present, and Future of a Multibillion Dollar Franchise.* New York: Basic.

Jafar

First Appearance:	*Aladdin* (release date: November 25, 1992)
Creators:	Ron Clements and John Musker
Other Media:	Live-action film, animated television series, animated home-video, Broadway play
Primary Strength:	Cunning, limited magic, "phenomenal cosmic power" (temporarily as a genie)
Major Weakness:	Greed, ambition
Weapons:	N/A
Base of Operations:	Agrabah (near the Jordan River in the Middle East)
Key Allies:	Iago
Key Enemies:	Aladdin, Princess Jasmine, Genie
Actual Identity:	N/A
Nicknames/Aliases:	N/A

By the 1990s, Walt Disney Studios was firmly cemented as *the* name in American animated feature films. Frequently centered on established Western fairy tales, Disney began a second Golden Age of animation with the release of *The Little Mermaid* in 1989, followed by *Beauty and the Beast* in 1991. In 1992, Disney's thirty-first animated feature release was *Aladdin*, a Disney-fied retelling of one of the Arabian Nights tales from *One Thousand and One Nights*, a collection of Arab folktales collected in the eighteenth century. Disney's *Aladdin* focuses on a common "street rat" boy named Aladdin who is used as a guinea pig to enter the dangerous Cave of Wonders to retrieve a mysterious golden lamp for the evil would-be wizard Jafar. Left to presumably die in the cave, Aladdin discovers the lamp and releases the magical Genie within, who then grants the boy three wishes, which Aladdin uses to escape from the cave and win the heart of the Princess Jasmine. Once Jafar discovers that the handsome new prince in court is, in reality, the boy Aladdin, he embarks on a quest to attain the lamp and take over the sultanate of Agrabah.

The character of Jafar, along with several other elements in *Aladdin*, was borrowed from the classic 1940 film *The Thief of Baghdad* (United Artists). In the Disney incarnation, Jafar holds the position of grand vizier to the sultan of Agrabah, Princess Jasmine's kind but scatterbrained father. Jafar is also, secretly, an evil wizard in search of the mystical Genie of the Lamp to grant him unlimited power. He also seeks Princess Jasmine's hand in marriage in order to cement his claim to the throne. The character acts as a modern-day Iago from William Shakespeare's *Othello*, slyly whispering insecurities into Aladdin's ear in order to manipulate the hero. This similarity is underscored by the fact that Jafar's pet parrot is named Iago. These machinations included casting a spell on the sultan causing him to give Jasmine's hand in marriage to Jafar. Eventually, Jafar does attain the lamp, making the benevolent Genie his slave. Aladdin, then, utilizes his own cunning to convince Jafar to wish to become an "all powerful Genie," knowing that with that power come the limits of being tied to a lamp and forever a slave to others who find him.

The massive popularity of the animated feature led to a Broadway version in 2011, and in 2019, Disney released a live-action/CGI version of the original film, starring Will Smith as the Genie. In the original animated film, Jafar was voiced by Jonathan Freeman, who would reprise the role on Broadway. In the 2019 film, Jafar was played by Marwan Kenzari. In the realm of Western and American villainy, Jafar is the modern incarnation of the classic Shakespearean villain, representing the darker natures of the human spirit, most notably greed, ambition, and a lust for power. In the more modern lexicon of villains, Jafar represents the dark wizard. He is the Voldemort to Aladdin's Harry Potter and the Grindelwald to Aladdin's Dumbledore. He is the dark mirror that often appears in wizard and witchcraft fables. He is Iago with dark magic. In the narrower realm of Disney villains, he is derivative of all other villains in Disney animated features. Jafar is a cautionary tale of absolute power corrupting absolutely.

Richard A. Hall

See also: Angelique Bouchard-Collins, Bellatrix Lestrange, CSM/The Cigarette Smoking Man, Dark Willow, Doctor Doom, Fiona Goode/The Supreme, Grand

Nagus/Ferengi, Grindelwald, Loki, Lucifer/Satan, Maleficent, The Master/Missy, Morgan le Fay, Red Skull, Sauron/Saruman, Sith Lords, Sue Sylvester, Ursula, Voldemort, Wicked Witch of the West; *Thematic Essays*: "In the Beginning . . .": The Origins of Villains in the Western World, The Dark Mirror: Evil Twins, *The Twilight Zone*, and the Villain Within.

Further Reading

Alsford, Mike. 2006. *Heroes & Villains*. Waco, TX: Baylor University Press.

Ashby, LeRoy. 2006. *With Amusement for All: A History of American Popular Culture since 1830*. Lexington: University Press of Kentucky.

Cavendish, Richard. 1968. *The Black Arts: A Concise History of Witchcraft, Demonology, Astrology, and Other Mystical Practices throughout the Ages*. New York: TarcherPerigree.

Darcy, Jen. 2016. *Disney Villains: Delightfully Evil: The Creation, the Inspiration, the Fascination*. New York: Disney Editions.

Gavaler, Chris. 2015. *On the Origin of Superheroes: From the Big Bang to Action Comics No. 1*. Iowa City: University of Iowa.

Hutton, Ronald. 2017. *The Witch: A History of Fear, from Ancient Times to the Present*. New Haven, CT: Yale University Press.

Jason Voorhees

First Appearance:	*Friday the 13th* (release date: November 25, 1992)
Creators:	Sean S. Cunningham, Victor Miller, Rob Kurz, and Tom Savini
Other Media:	Comic books, novels
Primary Strength:	Immortality
Major Weakness:	Limited intellect
Weapons:	Machete (other sharp implements)
Base of Operations:	Camp Crystal Lake (later New York City and space)
Key Allies:	Mrs. Voorhees (mother)
Key Enemies:	Various teenagers
Actual Identity:	N/A
Nicknames/Aliases:	N/A

In 1978, John Carpenter's *Halloween* ushered in the modern era of slasher horror films. Two years later, writer Victor Miller and director Sean S. Cunningham began one of the most successful slasher franchises in the genre, *Friday the 13th* (Paramount, 1980). The film takes its title from the centuries-old myth that any Friday that lands on the thirteen of any month is an unlucky day; this tradition dates to Friday, October 13, 1307, when the legendary Knights Templar were arrested en masse by King Philip IV of France. The film is set at the fictional Camp Crystal Lake, where legend has it that the spirit of a young boy who drowned during summer camp in 1957, due to the camp counselors having sex and not paying attention to their charges, haunts the camp, waiting to kill more counselors out of vengeance. That child's name was Jason Voorhees.

Jason would terrify teenage victims and audiences throughout the 1980s and on into the twenty-first century, appearing in twelve feature films to date. Recognizable for his iconic hockey goalie mask hiding his physical disfigurement and his machete, Jason is an unstoppable force of nature. Despite being "killed" at the end of each film, the killer returns in the next installment, ending each story with a considerable body count. His primary targets are teenagers, particularly those who engage in drugs or sexual activity. At the end of *Friday the 13th, Part IV: The Final Chapter* (1984), Jason is dismembered by the young survivor, Tommy Jarvis (played by Corey Feldman). In the next chapter, *Friday the 13th, Part V: A New Beginning* (1985), "Jason" proves to be a distraught father whose son died similarly to Jason. In *Friday the 13th, Part VI: Jason Lives* (1986), the now-grown Tommy (played by Thom Matthews) is obsessed with Jason's possible return and exhumes Jason's body, stabbing it repeatedly with a steel spike during a lightning storm. The spike ultimately becoming a lightning rod that revives the monster. Jason would return in four more sequels before teaming up and battling with fellow slasher icon Freddy Krueger in *Freddy vs. Jason* (New Line, 2003). In 2009, a reboot of the franchise was attempted with a loose remake of the original.

The image of Jason in the popular zeitgeist often fails to remember that in the original 1980 film, Jason was not the murderer. In that film, it was Jason's mother, Mrs. Voorhees, who committed the murders in her son's name. In the sequel, *Friday the 13th, Part II* (1981), Jason wears a simple burlap sack as a cowl, rather than his iconic hockey mask. In the realm of American villainy, Jason represents the unstoppable killing machine, along the lines of Frankenstein's Monster in literature or Doomsday in comic books. He cannot be stopped, killed, or reasoned with. He is a mindless monster, not unlike the great white shark in *Jaws* (Paramount, 1975). Jason is a constant reminder that, like him, death cannot be escaped and that "the wages of sin is death" (Romans 6:23). Unlike serial killers such as Hannibal Lecter or even Freddy Krueger, Jason does not understand why he kills, only that he must.

Richard A. Hall

See also: Alpha/The Whisperers, Doomsday, Dracula, Frankenstein's Monster, Freddy Krueger, Hannibal Lecter, Joker, Leatherface, Michael Myers, Norman Bates; *Thematic Essays*: "Nazis, Communists, and Terrorists . . . Oh My!": The Rise of the Supervillain and the Evolution of the Modern American Villain.

Further Reading

Alsford, Mike. 2006. *Heroes & Villains*. Waco, TX: Baylor University Press.

Ashby, LeRoy. 2006. *With Amusement for All: A History of American Popular Culture since 1830*. Lexington: University Press of Kentucky.

Hitchcock, Susan Tyler. 2007. *Frankenstein: A Cultural History*. New York: W. W. Norton.

Maddrey, Joseph. 2004. *Nightmares in Red, White, and Blue: The Evolution of the American Horror Film*. Jefferson, NC: McFarland.

Mahnke, Aaron. 2017. *The World of Lore: Monstrous Creatures*. New York: Del Rey.

Murphy, Bernice M. 2013. *The Rural Gothic in American Popular Culture: Backwoods Horror and Terror in the Wilderness.* London: Palgrave Macmillan.
Skal, David J. 2001. *The Monster Show: A Cultural History of Horror.* Rev. ed. New York: Farrar, Straus and Giroux.

Joker

First Appearance:	*Batman #1* (cover date: June, 1940)
Creators:	Jerry Robinson, Bill Finger, and Bob Kane
Other Media:	Animated and live-action television series, movies
Primary Strength:	Cunning, tenacity
Major Weakness:	Insanity
Weapons:	Joker gas
Base of Operations:	Gotham City
Key Allies:	Harley Quinn
Key Enemies:	Batman, Robin, Batgirl, Police Commissioner James Gordon
Actual Identity:	Unknown (in some incarnations, Jack Napier; on television series *Gotham*, Jeremiah Valeska, though not technically the Joker)
Nicknames/Aliases:	"The Clown Prince of Crime," "The Harlequin of Hate," "Mr. J."

The *Batman* franchise is, perhaps, second only to Superman in regard to its impact on popular culture. Created by writer Bill Finger and artist Bob Kane, Batman is billionaire playboy Bruce Wayne, who, after witnessing a mugger murder his parents when he was a young boy, vowed to dedicate his life battling crime in his hometown of Gotham City. In order to strike fear in criminals, Wayne chose to disguise himself as a bat, and "the Batman" (originally "Bat-Man") was born (Bill Finger and Bob Kane, *Detective Comics #33*, November 1939). Unlike his counterpart, Superman, Batman is a mere mortal, with no "super" powers of any kind. Instead, Batman is armed only with his keen intellect and a myriad of gadgets and vehicles that he uses in his fight against crime. Over the decades, in comics as well as on television and film, Batman has gained arguably the most impressive rogues' gallery of villains in all of popular culture. His most iconic villain, and the world's first supervillain, is the Joker. In more than eight decades, throughout all popular media, the Joker is one of the most famous villains in the Western world.

When the Joker was introduced in 1940, he was simply a maniacal serial killer dressed as a circus clown. When DC Comics began to make the Batman books more kid friendly, Joker took on the mantle of the Clown Prince of Crime, with various outlandish schemes to become Gotham City's chief crime boss. This incarnation continued in the popular 1960s television series *Batman* (ABC,

1966–1969), where Cesar Romero gave the first live-action performance of the character. The Romero version of Joker was listed in 2013 by *TV Guide* as the number thirty-three "nastiest" villain in television history ("TV Guide Picks TV's 60 Nastiest Villains," *TV Guide*). In the 1970s, under the pen name of Dennis O'Neil, Joker returned to his darker roots, often with outlandish puzzle-ridden plans to outsmart the Dark Knight Detective, usually with high body counts. His most frequent weapon of choice is his ominous Joker gas, a concoction that causes its victims to literally laugh themselves to death with frozen Joker smiles on their corpses.

The first origin story for the Joker appeared in 1951. This story presented Joker as originally a simple criminal working under the name "the Red Hood," for the red-domed helmet and cape that he wore. During what was meant to be his final caper at a chemical plant, the Red Hood leaped into a vat of chemicals in an attempt to escape from Batman. Exposure to the chemicals left the unidentified white man with bleached-white skin, green hair, and a permanent "smile." It also left him deeply and permanently insane (Bill Finger, "The Man behind the Red Hood," *Detective Comics #168*, February 1951). In 1988, this origin story would be given more depth in the one-shot graphic novel *Batman: The Killing Joke*, where the unidentified "criminal" was shown to actually be a failed stand-up comic who was drafted by a criminal gang to portray the Red Hood for this one caper. The young man agrees in order to provide for his pregnant wife and move her out of their cheap, rat-infested apartment. After experiencing the aforementioned fall into the vat and physical disfigurement, he discovers that his apartment building has burned down, his wife and unborn child inside. The ensuing trauma leads him to become the Joker (Alan Moore, *Batman: The Killing Joke*, 1988).

Of the many popular Joker stories over the decades, perhaps the one that best encapsulates the totality of the character's mania is also the last Joker story as presented by writer and artist Frank Miller in his landmark 1986 work, *Batman: The Dark Knight Returns*. In this story, set in the not-too-distant future, it has been ten years since the last appearance of Batman in Gotham City. Since that time, Joker has been in a vegetative state in Arkham Asylum. When a television in the hospital's common area reports that Batman has returned, Joker smiles and awakens from his catatonia, stuttering to say, "Batman!" Joker soon manipulates his psychiatrist, Dr. Wolper, to convince the authorities to release him; the psychiatrist is convinced that Joker and other Gotham supervillains were victims of Batman's own psychosis.

Wolper views Joker as his ticket to fame, getting the killer an interview on a late-night talk show. During the taping, however, Joker kills the show's host, the audience, and Wolper before escaping into the night. Joker next plans a massive assault at a carnival, where he confronts Batman for the last time. During their fight, Batman hits Joker in the eye with one of his batarangs (small, bladed projectiles), before paralyzing the Clown Prince in the carnival's Tunnel of Love. As the police close in, Joker uses what mobility he has to break his own neck, setting Batman up for murder. When a flamethrower catches the tunnel interior on fire, Batman watches from the sidelines as the corpse of his longtime nemesis burns (Alan Miller, *Batman: The Dark Knight Returns #1–4*, February–June 1986).

Perhaps the most iconic version of the Joker in the overall American zeitgeist is the animated version from the legendary television series *Batman: The Animated Series* (FOX-Kids, 1992–1995). The visual image of Joker in this series was highly adopted from the 1950s comic book version. However, the performance of voice actor Mark Hamill added an air of evil rarely touched upon in previous television and film incarnations. This series was also distinctive for introducing the Joker's love interest, Harley Quinn. Hamill's haunting maniacal laugh added further menace to the murderous clown, and the series overall further underscored the depths of Joker's insanity and obsession with Batman.

A more recent incarnation of the Joker appeared in the live-action film *The Dark Knight* (Warner Brothers, director Chris Nolan, 2008,). In this story, the Joker (played by Heath Ledger, who would win a posthumous Academy Award for his performance) is an anonymous anarchist who wears clown makeup. He is hired by Gotham City mobsters to rid them of the new vigilante, Batman. Instead, Joker leaves a trail of bodies in an alleged attempt to force Batman to reveal his true identity. In actuality, however, his overall scheme is to show Batman that no one is a good person worthy of the Dark Knight's protection. He manipulates a situation in which a boatload of innocent civilians must choose between murdering a boatload of convicted felons before those felons have the opportunity to murder them, with the added caveat that if neither boat chooses to kill the other, both boats will explode. In his mania, Joker admits that he has no overall plan; rather, he just likes to "do things."

Joaquin Phoenix gained considerable critical acclaim and professional accolades for his introspective portrayal of the iconic comic book villain in the 2019 film *Joker*. (Warner Bros. Pictures/TCD/Prod.DB/Alamy Stock Photo)

What can be considered a de facto prequel to Ledger's Joker came in the 2019 film *Joker* (Warner Brothers, director Todd Phillips). In this film, Arthur Fleck (played by Joaquin Phoenix) is a down-on-his-luck clown for hire who aspires to be a stand-up comedian. He lives with his ailing mother (played by Frances Conroy), who suffers from the delusion that her son is the product of an imaginary romance between her and billionaire Thomas Wayne (played by Brett Cullen). Arthur suffers a neurological condition that causes him to spontaneously laugh, even when he is sad or angry. A series of bad luck pushes Arthur to the brink of insanity, culminating with learning that he is adopted and that his mother exposed him to continuous physical abuse from her various boyfriends in his youth. After killing three bullies on a train, Arthur's seemingly endless travails lead him down a path of violence and a dedication to chaos. By the end of the film, neither Arthur nor the audience knows who he truly is, and shades of *The Dark Knight* Joker are evident (Todd Phillips and Scott Silver, *Joker*, Warner Brothers, 2019).

In the character's long and storied history, Joker has remained Batman's most noteworthy opponent. He is the Professor Moriarty to Batman's Sherlock Holmes, the two characters destined to perform their respective roles against each other over and over again for all of eternity. In the realm of American villainy, Joker is the threat to stability that most terrorizes American society. He is an unstable element in a world that demands stability. He does not kill for thrill, money, or vengeance. He kills for only one purpose: to challenge and provide purpose for his only true "love," Batman. As an element of social commentary, Joker represents the broken nature of both the criminal justice and psychiatric care systems. He is what all Americans fear they could become with just one bad day.

Richard A. Hall

See also: Angelus, Catwoman, The Court of Owls, Fish Mooney, Freddy Krueger, Green Goblin, Hannibal Lecter, Harley Quinn, Jason Voorhees, Leatherface, Lex Luthor, Michael Myers, Norman Bates, Penguin, Poison Ivy, Ra's al Ghul, Red Skull, Scarecrow, Two-Face; *Thematic Essays*: "Nazis, Communists, and Terrorists . . . Oh My!": The Rise of the Supervillain and the Evolution of the Modern American Villain, The Dark Mirror: Evil Twins, *The Twilight Zone*, and the Villain Within, The Pathos of Villainy: Getting to the Heart of Why Villains Went Bad.

Further Reading

Alsford, Mike. 2006. *Heroes & Villains*. Waco, TX: Baylor University Press.

Ashby, LeRoy. 2006. *With Amusement for All: A History of American Popular Culture since 1830*. Lexington: University Press of Kentucky.

Barba, Shelley E., and Joy M. Perrin, eds. 2017. *The Ascendance of Harley Quinn: Essays on DC's Enigmatic Villain*. Jefferson, NC: McFarland.

Beard, Jim, ed. 2010. *Gotham City 14 Miles: 14 Essays on Why the 1960s Batman TV Series Matters*. Edwardsville, IL: Sequart Research & Literacy Organization.

Faludi, Susan. 2007. *The Terror Dream: Myth and Misogyny in an Insecure America*. New York: Picador.

Heit, Jamey. 2011. "No Laughing Matter: The Joker as a Nietzschean Critique of Morality." In *Vader, Voldemort and Other Villains: Essays on Evil in Popular Culture*, edited by Jamey Heit, 175–188. Jefferson, NC: McFarland.

Langley, Travis. 2012. *Batman and Psychology: A Dark and Stormy Knight*. New York: John Wiley & Sons.

Moseley, Daniel. 2009. "The Joker's Comedy of Existence." In *Supervillains and Philosophy: Sometimes, Evil Is Its Own Reward*, edited by Ben Dyer, 127–136. Chicago: Open Court.

O'Neil, Dennis, ed. 2008. *Batman Unauthorized: Vigilantes, Jokers, and Heroes in Gotham City*. Smart Pop Series. Dallas, TX: BenBella.

Sanborn, K. 2015. "Who Killed Jason Todd: The Joker, Himself, His Writer, or the Fans?" The Graphic Novel. October 18, 2015. Accessed February 20, 2019. http://graphicnovel.umwblogs.org/2015/10/18/who-killed-jason-todd-the-joker-himself-his-writer-or-the-fans/.

Smith, Michael. 2011. "'And Doesn't All the World Love a Clown?': Finding the Joker and the Representation of His Evil." In *Riddle Me This, Batman!: Essays on the Universe of the Dark Knight*, edited by Kevin K. Durand and Mary K. Leigh, 187–200. Jefferson, NC: McFarland.

"TV Guide Picks TV's 60 Nastiest Villains." 2013. *TV Guide*. April 22, 2013 Accessed January 1, 2019. http://wordsmithonia.blogspot.com/2013/04/tv-guide-picks-tvs-60-nastiest-villains.html.

Weldon, Glen. 2016. *The Caped Crusade: Batman and the Rise of Nerd Culture*. New York: Simon & Schuster.

White, Mark D., and Robert Arp, eds. 2008. *Batman and Philosophy: The Dark Knight of the Soul*. The Blackwell Philosophy and Pop Culture Series. Hoboken, NJ: Wiley.

Wright, Bradford W. 2003. *Comic Book Nation: The Transformation of Youth Culture in America*. Baltimore, MD: Johns Hopkins University Press.

J. R. Ewing

First Appearance:	*Dallas*, season 1, episode 1 (air date: April 2, 1978)
Creators:	David Jacobs
Other Media:	Novels, songs
Primary Strength:	Wealth, blackmail, cunning
Major Weakness:	Greedy, untrustworthy
Weapons:	Money, information
Base of Operations:	Dallas, Texas
Key Allies:	Jock Ewing (father), Ellie Ewing (mother), Bobby Ewing (brother), Sue Ellen Ewing (first wife), Callie Ewing (second wife), James Beaumont (son), John Ross Ewing III (son), Kristin Shepard (sister-in-law/lover), Detective Harry McSween (henchman), Sly Lovegren (secretary), Marilee Stone, Police Detective Ratigan, April Ewing, Vaughn Leland (originally)
Key Enemies:	Cliff Barnes, Pamela Barnes-Ewing, Stephen "Dusty" Farlow, Jeremy Wendell, Carter McKay, Katherine Wentworth, Kristin Shepard, Bobby Ewing (occasionally), Allan Beam, Sue Ellen Ewing (occasionally), James Beaumont (eventually), Michelle Stevens, Jeb Ames, Willie Joe Garr, Jamie Ewing-Barnes, Vaughn Leland (ultimately), Marilee Stone (occasionally)
Actual Identity:	John Ross Ewing Jr.
Nicknames/Aliases:	"The Man You Love to Hate," "The Human Oil Slick"

"Who Shot J.R.?"

By the third season of the television nighttime soap opera *Dallas*, the series was one of the most popular on American television, even gaining massive audiences in Europe and the Middle East. Once the third season (1979–1980) was under way, CBS requested an additional two episodes (bringing the season to twenty-five episodes total). The submitted scripts had already ended the season with episode twenty-three; writers and the show's creator, David Jacobs, decided to build up to a cliff-hanger, creating a list of potential suspects eager to kill the show's antagonist, J. R. Ewing. In the season's final episode, "A House Divided" (March 21, 1980), the final scene shows the villainous J.R. in his office late at night. Then a first-person-perspective camera shot emerges from the office elevator, leading J.R. to go to his office door, where shots come from the camera perspective. A wounded J.R. is left on the floor in agony as the credits roll.

The summer of 1980 saw the entire Western world consumed with the question "Who Shot J.R.?" J.R. actor Larry Hagman left the country, opening the possibility that he would not return to the show. This led CBS to grant Hagman a new contract of $100,000 per episode plus royalties on J.R.-related merchandise, making him the highest-paid actor in television history to that point. A strike by the Writers' Guild of America in the summer of 1980 postponed both the production of the series and the opening of the fall season, pushing back further the reveal and raising momentum for the series even more. Approximately 83 million Americans and 350 million people worldwide tuned in to see the episode "Who Done It" (season 4, episode 4) on November 21, 1980, and *Dallas* became the defining American television program of the 1980s.

Richard A. Hall

J. R. Ewing holds the distinction of being chosen the number one "nastiest" villain in television history ("TV Guide Picks TV's 60 Nastiest Villains," *TV Guide*). Although the title was granted just five months after Larry Hagman (who immortalized the character with his portrayal) had passed away during filming of the second season of the renewed 1980s soap opera *Dallas* (CBS, 1978–1991, 1996, 1998; TNT, 2012–2014), by that time, J.R. was known worldwide and was mysteriously equally reviled and beloved. *Dallas* debuted in 1978, at a time when overall American morale was at its lowest point since the Great Depression. Unlike anything else on television at the time, the series centered on the fictional oil and cattle baron Ewing family of Dallas, Texas. The program was originally designed as a modern-day *Romeo and Juliet*, with Ewing heir Bobby having recently married Pamela Barnes, the daughter of Willard "Digger" Barnes, decades-long enemy of Jock Ewing, Bobby's father (and sister to Cliff Barnes, J. R. Ewing's constant nemesis). The focus of the show soon shifted to the series' antagonist, Bobby's older brother, J.R. The global popularity of *Dallas* quickly spawned a train of copycat nighttime soap operas focused on the lives of the rich and powerful, and the series and J.R. would come to epitomize the greed and corruption of America in the 1980s.

J. R. Ewing was the oldest of the three sons of Jock and Ellie Ewing. Jock Ewing (played by Jim Davis) was the founder of Ewing Oil Company, and "Miss Ellie" (played by Barbara Bel Geddes) was the heiress to the sprawling cattle ranch known as Southfork. Miss Ellie's favorite son was the absent and alcoholic middle child, Gary, and princely Bobby (played by Patrick Duffy) was a favorite of both of his parents. J.R., then, was on a constant quest to be his father's favorite. To do this, J.R. sought to become the most powerful and ruthless independent oilman in Texas, aspiring to inherit majority control of Ewing Oil. Over time, a fourth son, Ray Krebs (played by Steve Kanaly), emerged when it was discovered that the longtime Southfork ranch foreman was, in fact, Jock Ewing's love child from a World War II romance. Since, by that time, Jock had dedicated his golden years to ranching, the bond between the new father and son grew stronger, much to J.R.'s chagrin. Most of the first two seasons of *Dallas* centered on J.R.'s schemes to break up his brother Bobby's marriage to Pamela Barnes (played by Victoria Principal). Meanwhile, social crusader Cliff Barnes (played by Ken Kercheval) declared war on the Ewings, seeking to destroy the wealthy clan and gain revenge for his own father, Digger Barnes, who claimed that Jock had stolen his half of what became Ewing Oil, as well as the heart of his true love, Ellie Southworth.

After the disappearance and presumed death of patriarch Jock in season five (due to the actor's untimely death), season six centered on the battle for Ewing Oil. In his revised will, Jock had established a challenge for J.R. and Bobby: split Ewing Oil in half for one year, and whoever makes the most profit in that year gains majority control of the company. While Bobby's business practices were always honest, honorable, and above board, J.R. sought victory through conniving, lying, and double-crossing. Some of J.R.'s more dubious deeds include having a sustained affair with his wife, Sue Ellen's (played by Linda Gray), sister; manipulating Sue Ellen's established alcoholism to create the illusion that she was an unfit mother in order to win custody of their son, John Ross; mortgaging all Ewing Oil assets (including the family home, Southfork) to fund oil leases in Southeast Asia; financing a counterrevolution in the southeast Asian country that had stripped him of those same oil wells and selling those same oil leases to his closest business associates when he learned that they were about to become

Larry Hagman portrayed "The Man You Love to Hate," J. R. Ewing, one of the most iconic villains of the 1980s in the CBS television series *Dallas*. (Pictorial Press Ltd/Alamy Stock Photo)

worthless; and manipulating his weak/alcoholic brother Gary to run away, abandoning his new wife and child, and then having henchmen forcibly remove the new bride to her home in Tennessee, leaving the newborn daughter in the custody of Jock and Ellie.

They also include creating numerous schemes to set up rival Cliff Barnes for failure (even driving Barnes to attempt suicide at one point); convincing his now-ex-sister-in-law, Pamela, that her recently deceased new beau was actually alive and thus sending her on a wild goose chase around the globe; setting up a former henchman on false rape charges; manipulating Bobby—the eventual owner of Southfork—to unknowingly sell the ranch to J.R.; and posthumously setting up Cliff Barnes for J.R.'s murder, when he had, in fact, died from cancer. These are but a few highlights from the seventeen-season run of the original series and its return twenty years later.

In the second season of the series' return (2013), the Ewing family found itself under siege from numerous threats, all tied to longtime family nemesis Barnes. Although Bobby and the rest of the family had, for decades, denounced J.R.'s methods and tactics, it was to him that they turned in their hour of need. The response to this threat was met with J.R.'s promise that this would be his "masterpiece." Unknown to the family, J.R. was already dying from cancer. He spent his final weeks setting up a far-reaching scheme to take down all of the Ewings' enemies after his death (even going so far, as mentioned above, as to use his own death as part of the scheme). In this regard, J.R. becomes, in the end, an antivillain, utilizing vile and villainous deeds to perpetuate an overall good: the protection of his family. J.R. has had many memorable quotes over the decades, but the one that best describes him is the following: "The best way to get to know a man is to talk to his friends . . . and his enemies. My friends are in the statehouse . . . my enemies are a lot harder to find" (Cynthia Cidre, "Hedging Your Bets," *Dallas* series 2, season 1, episode 2).

Dallas became a global phenomenon after the season three cliff-hanger, "Who Shot J.R." When the culprit was ultimately exposed as being his sister-in-law/former secretary and mistress, Kristin Shepard (played primarily by Mary Crosby), the desperate scorned woman claimed to be pregnant with J.R.'s child. Rather than allow his family to go through the scandal that would ensue, J.R. exiled Kristin in California, sending her monthly checks to provide for her and his child. After giving birth, Kristin returned to Dallas, where audiences learn that she was actually blackmailing several local oilmen by claiming that her child was, in fact, theirs. When she finds J.R. alone at Southfork, an argument ensues as she attempts to squeeze him for more money. After a cutaway to other scenes, Cliff Barnes, then the assistant to now–state senator Bobby, arrives at Southfork and discovers a woman's body facedown in the family swimming pool. After jumping into the pool to save the woman, Cliff discovers her dead and looks up to find J.R. standing on an overlooking balcony in front of a broken railing, drink in hand. Audiences never discover whether Kristin fell or was pushed.

When the series returned in 2012 on the cable network TNT, twenty-one years had passed since the original series finale (the two made-for-TV movies that aired in the 1990s were dismissed as noncanonical). J.R. has been in a depressed state in an upper-class seniors' facility for nearly all of that time, having lost his personal fortune to his brother and ex-wife, Sue Ellen. He is brought out of his catatonic state when his grown son, John Ross (played by Josh Henderson), comes to his father with a scheme to take Southfork from Bobby. The legendary villain then spends his final year of life pushing and training his son to be his worthy successor. When it becomes clear by the end of the return's first season that J.R. has succeeded in this endeavor, he toasts his son, claiming, "Now that's my son . . . from tip to tail" (Cynthia Cidre and Robert Rovner, "Revelations," *Dallas* series 2, season 1, episode 10, August 8, 2012).

The series in general—and J.R. specifically—epitomized 1980s America. The rise of Donald Trump as a celebrity businessman in the 1980s undoubtedly owes much to the popularity of J.R., and the inspiration the character provided to a generation of burgeoning businessmen. In the realm of fictional villains, J.R. stands as the ultimate example of power corrupting and the appeal of greed, lust, and a driving ambition to rule. While staunchly protective of his family, J.R. has no qualms about personally destroying members of that same family if it suits his own personal quests. He is a liar, cheater, backstabber, and womanizer. When the character was reawakened in the tech-heavy, politically correct 2010s, he succeeded in showing how the "old ways" of doing dirty business still applied in modern times. His was a sympathetic tale of a neglected son, and he was the epitome of how evil one human being with money can be.

Richard A. Hall

See also: Alexis Carrington-Colby-Dexter, The Corleone Family, CSM/The Cigarette Smoking Man, Ebenezer Scrooge, Ernst Stavro Blofeld/SPECTRE, Fish Mooney, Goldfinger, Heisenberg/Walter White, Lex Luthor, Ozymandias, Sherry Palmer, Sue Sylvester, Tony Montana, Tony Soprano; *Thematic Essays*: "Nazis, Communists, and Terrorists . . . Oh My!": The Rise of the Supervillain and the Evolution of the Modern American Villain, The Dark Mirror: Evil Twins, *The Twilight Zone*, and the Villain Within, Tarantino and the Antivillain, The Pathos of Villainy: Getting to the Heart of Why Villains Went Bad.

Further Reading

Alsford, Mike. 2006. *Heroes & Villains.* Waco, TX: Baylor University Press.

Ashby, LeRoy. 2006. *With Amusement for All: A History of American Popular Culture since 1830.* Lexington: University Press of Kentucky.

Bates, Billie Rae. 2007. *Destination: Dallas—A Guide to TV's Dallas.* Charleston, SC: BookSurge.

Castleman, Harry, and Walter J. Podrazik. 2016. *Watching TV: Eight Decades of American Television.* 3rd ed. Syracuse, NY: Syracuse University Press.

Curran, Barbara A. 2005. *Dallas: The Complete Story of the World's Favorite Prime-Time Soap.* Nashville, TN: Cumberland House.

Gillespie, Nick, and Matt Welch. 2008. "How 'Dallas' Won the Cold War." *Washington Post.* April 27, 2008. Accessed September 26, 2019. http://www.washingtonpost.com/wp-dyn/content/article/2008/04/25/AR2008042503103.html.

Kalter, Suzy. 1984. *The Complete Book of Dallas: Behind the Scenes at the World's Favorite Television Program.* New York: Harry N. Abrams.

Rossinow, Doug. 2015. *The Reagan Era: A History of the 1980s.* New York: Columbia University Press.

Stark, Steven D. 1997. *Glued to the Set: The 60 Television Shows and Events That Made Us Who We Are Today.* New York: Delta Trade Paperbacks.

"TV Guide Picks TV's 60 Nastiest Villains." 2013. *TV Guide.* April 22, 2013. Accessed January 1, 2019. http://wordsmithonia.blogspot.com/2013/04/tv-guide-picks-tvs-60-nastiest-villains.html.

Van Wormer, Laura. 1985. *Dallas: The Complete Ewing Family Saga, Including Southfork Ranch, Ewing Oil, and the Barnes-Ewing Feud—1860–1985.* New York: Doubleday/Dolphin.

Kahless/Klingons

First Appearance:	**Kahless:** *Star Trek*, season 3, episode 22 (air date: March 7, 1969) **Klingons:** *Star Trek*, season 1, episode 26 (air date: March 23, 1967)
Creators:	Gene Roddenberry (Kahless and Klingons), Gene L. Coon (Klingons)
Other Media:	Film, novels, comics
Primary Strength:	Strategy, cunning, tenacity
Major Weakness:	Intolerance
Weapons:	Energy-based weaponry, bat'leth/mek'leth (bladed weapons), starships with cloaking technology
Base of Operations:	Qo'nos (pronounced "Kronos"), Alpha Quadrant
Key Allies:	Romulans (occasionally), United Federation of Planets (eventually)
Key Enemies:	Captain James T. Kirk, United Federation of Planets (until twenty-fourth century)
Actual Identity:	N/A
Nicknames/Aliases:	"The Unforgettable" (Kahless)

Star Trek is a popular science fiction franchise originally developed for television by Gene Roddenberry in 1966. It was originally set in the twenty-third century, when humanity has long been exploring deep space and Earth is a member of the United Federation of Planets. The original series has spawned an animated series, five sequel and prequel live-action series, and thirteen feature films to date. The original series debuted on NBC on September 8, 1966, and focused on the adventures of Captain James T. Kirk and the crew of the *USS Enterprise*. The first live-action spin-off series, set a century after the original, was *Star Trek: The Next Generation*, which debuted in syndication on September 28, 1987. The series, dubbed *TNG* by fans, focuses on the adventures of Captain Jean-Luc Picard and the crew of the *USS Enterprise-D* (making it the fifth Federation starship to bear the name). Of the many alien species introduced by the several incarnations of *Star Trek*, one of the most enduring has been the original antagonists of the series: the Klingons.

Marc Okrand

Marc Okrand (b. 1948) is a gifted linguist. He is most noted for his contributions to the alien languages of the *Star Trek* franchise. Originally tasked with creating Vulcan dialogue for the film *Star Trek II: The Wrath of Khan* (Paramount, 1982), he is perhaps most famous for creating the complete Klingon language throughout his work on the films *Star Trek III: The Search for Spock* (Paramount, 1984), *Star Trek V: The Final Frontier* (Paramount, 1989), and *Star Trek VI: The Undiscovered Country* (Paramount, 1991).

Rather than simply utilizing strange guttural sounds as a pseudolanguage, Okrand's Klingonese is a complete language, with grammar, word tenses, slang, and dialects. His books on the language include *The Klingon Dictionary* (1985, revised 1992), *The Klingon Way* (1996), and *Klingon for the Galactic Traveler* (1997). He has also produced two *Rosetta Stone*–style audiocourses: *Conversational Klingon* (1992) and *Power Klingon* (1993). He cowrote the world's first Klingon opera, *'u,'* performed in the Netherlands in 2010. Perhaps his most popular work on the language has been *The Klingon Hamlet* (1996), a complete translation of Shakespeare's seminal play. This was a reference to piece of dialogue from *Star Trek VI*, where the Klingon general Chang tells his human hosts that Shakespeare could only be truly appreciated in "the original Klingon." In 2018, Okrand was called back into service for *Star Trek*, continuing to develop alien languages for the enduring franchise.

Richard A. Hall

The Klingons were developed for the original series by Gene L. Coon. Their first appearance established the Organian Peace Treaty between the United Federation of Planets and the Klingon Empire. Coming as the series did during the height of the Cold War, the Klingons were directly representative of the communist Soviet Union: they were conquerors, allowed no freedom to the people under their rule, and were brutal killers (as the West viewed the Soviets to be). Their physical appearance, however, was originally derivative of Asian stereotypes of the 1930s and 1940s movie serials. They had dark skin, pronounced slanted eyebrows, and long Fu Manchu moustaches and goatees, in a not-so-subtle nod to the fact that a growing part of East Asia was becoming communist. While they only appeared in a handful of episodes of the original series, they were repeatedly mentioned as the greatest threat to the Federation, with only the agreed-upon Neutral Zone acting as a barrier between the two superpowers.

A decade after the original series was cancelled, Paramount pictures released *Star Trek: The Motion Picture* (1979). Beginning with the feature films, the Klingons' appearance dramatically changed with the incorporation of ridged foreheads (Fu Manchu facial hair remaining intact). Though only appearing in a cameo in the original feature film—and not appearing at all in the first sequel—the Klingons played a much more important role in three of the six films featuring the original *Star Trek* cast: *Star Trek III: The Search for Spock* (1985); *Star Trek V: The Final Frontier* (1989); and *Star Trek VI: The Undiscovered Country* (1991). In the films, not only did the appearance of the Klingons change but also their overall culture was examined a bit more closely. The Klingons were now portrayed as a seminoble warrior race, placing honor in battle among all other values in their society.

Beginning with the first spin-off series, *Star Trek: The Next Generation* (Syndication, 1987–1994), set a century after the original, peace had been established between the empire and the UFP, and the first Klingon to join Starfleet (Lieutenant Worf, played by Michael Dorn) served aboard the new *USS Enterprise*. Shortly after the series debuted, the Cold War began its slow decline, ultimately ending before the series' initial run concluded. As such, the pseudo-Russians were portrayed more as reluctant and often-misunderstood allies. The series began to explore Klingon culture more closely, underscoring the importance of accepting other cultures that would come to define post–Cold War U.S. foreign policy. The strained alliance would be further explored in the third live-action *Trek* series, *Star Trek: Deep Space Nine* (Syndication, 1993–1999; often referred to as *DS9*). When writer and director J. J. Abrams relaunched the *Trek* franchise with his feature film *Star Trek* (Paramount, 2009), the Klingons' appearance was altered even more, with further-deepened dark skin (now a dark blackish hue), but the failure of the new franchise after its third installment made any further exploration of differences impossible. The latest prequel television series, *Star Trek: Discovery* (CBS-All Access, 2017–present) promises to alter the Klingons even more.

In the original series episode "The Savage Curtain" (Gene Roddenberry, season 3, episode 22, March 7, 1969), a picture is seen of Kahless, an important historical figure in Klingon history. Twenty-four years later, in the *TNG* episode "Rightful Heir" (James Brooks and Ronald D. Moore, season 6, episode 23, May 17, 1993), this character is explored more deeply. In that episode, viewers learn that Kahless the Unforgettable was the Klingon warlord who united the Klingon people some 1,500 years earlier, establishing the system of honor that all Klingon warriors were pressed to follow. As the Klingon Empire by this time in the *TNG* story line was growing divisive, with warring families forming alliances against each other, devoted followers of Kahless's teachings cloned the original warrior from blood left on one of his swords. This cloned copy then became the new Klingon emperor (sold to the Klingon people as the resurrected original). Under his "leadership" (his "emperor" status would be as more of a figurehead since the Klingon High Council knew that he was just a clone), the empire would begin to long for its conquering past, making it more aggressive in the forthcoming Dominion War, a key story line for the last four seasons of *DS9*.

Throughout their history on television and film, the Klingons have been direct representations of the Soviet Union/Russia. During the Cold War, they represented the greatest threat to the freedom of the many peoples of the United Federation of Planets. Once the Cold War ended, they continued to represent uneasy allies, with both sides wary of the other's motives and actions (just like the real-world relationship between the United States and Russia). Their warlike nature and thirst for glory in battle make them an unstable element to the peace promoted by the Federation. With real-world tensions between the United States and Russia continuing to worsen in the twenty-first century, it will be important to examine how the Klingons will be represented in future *Trek* adventures.

Richard A. Hall

See also: Alpha/The Whisperers, Borg Queen/Borg, Captain Phasma/Stormtroopers, COBRA, The Court of Owls, Cybermen, Davros/Daleks, Ernst Stavro Blofeld/SPECTRE, General Custer, Geronimo, Grand Nagus/Ferengi, Negan/The Saviors, Number Six/Cylons, Q; *Thematic Essays*: "Nazis, Communists, and Terrorists . . . Oh My!": The Rise of the Supervillain and the Evolution of the Modern American Villain, The Dark Mirror: Evil Twins, *The Twilight Zone*, and the Villain Within.

Further Reading

Alsford, Mike. 2006. *Heroes & Villains.* Waco, TX: Baylor University Press.

Ashby, LeRoy. 2006. *With Amusement for All: A History of American Popular Culture since 1830.* Lexington: University Press of Kentucky.

Castleman, Harry, and Walter J. Podrazik. 2016. *Watching TV: Eight Decades of American Television.* 3rd ed. Syracuse, NY: Syracuse University Press.

Gross, Edward, and Mark A. Altman. 2016. *The Fifty-Year Mission, the First 25 Years: The Complete, Uncensored, Unauthorized Oral History of Star Trek.* New York: St. Martin's.

Gross, Edward, and Mark A. Altman. 2016. *The Fifty-Year Mission, the Next 25 Years: The Complete, Uncensored, Unauthorized Oral History of Star Trek.* New York: St. Martin's.

Reagin, Nancy R. 2013. *Star Trek and History.* Hoboken, NJ: John Wiley & Sons.

Rossinow, Doug. 2015. *The Reagan Era: A History of the 1980s.* New York: Columbia University Press.

Killmonger

First Appearance:	*Jungle Action #6* (cover date: September 1973)
Creators:	Don McGregor and Rich Buckler
Other Media:	Film, television
Primary Strength:	Strategy, cunning
Major Weakness:	Obsessive vengeance
Weapons:	Bladed weapons, guns
Base of Operations:	Wakanda; Harlem, New York (in comics); Oakland, California (in film)
Key Allies:	N'Jobu (father), Baran Macabre (in comics), Ulysses Klaue (in film)
Key Enemies:	Ulysses Klaue, Black Panther
Actual Identity:	N'Jadaka/Erik Killmonger (in comics), Prince N'Jadaka/Erik Stevens (in film)
Nicknames/Aliases:	"Killmonger" (in film)

In 1961, Marvel Comics editor-in-chief Stan Lee launched what has come to be known as the Marvel Age of superhero comics with publication of *Fantastic Four #1* (Stan Lee and Jack Kirby, November 1961). Five years later, in the pages of that same comic, Lee and Kirby introduced the world's first black superhero, the Black

Panther (*Fantastic Four #52*, July 1966). Black Panther was actually King T'Challa of the African kingdom of Wakanda, a nation untouched by European colonization or slave trading and rich in deposits of vibranium, the most powerful substance in the Marvel Universe. The enduring popularity of that character led to his being featured in his own comic in the 1970s, *Jungle Action*. One of the first antagonists presented in *Jungle Action* is also one of the more sympathetic and heartbreaking villains in superhero comic books: Killmonger. In 2018, a revised—but equally sympathetic—version of Killmonger would appear in the groundbreaking, record-smashing feature film *Black Panther*, cementing the villain in the overall zeitgeist of American pop culture.

In the comics, when the international pirate, mercenary, and weapons dealer Ulysses Klaue invades Wakanda to steal vibranium, he forcefully enlists a local Wakandan, N'Jobu. When Black Panther successfully repels Klaue's attempted theft, N'Jobu dies, and his family, including his young son, N'Jadaka, is exiled to the United States. Growing up as Erik Killmonger in Harem, New York, N'Jadaka attends college, studying engineering. King T'Challa allows Killmonger to return to Wakanda, where the disillusioned young man becomes a political subversive, criticizing T'Challa for the king repeatedly allowing "outsiders" (the Fantastic Four and Avengers) into the country, as well as for frequently leaving Wakanda to assist the Avengers. Ultimately, however, Killmonger is killed in his attempted coup (Don McGregor and Billy Graham, *Jungle Action #17*, September 1975). Killmonger—and the entire *Black Panther* run of the 1970s—was a response to the popular blaxploitation films of the era.

In the feature film *Black Panther* (Marvel Studios/Disney, 2018), a modern twist is given to the original 1970s villain. In this film, Erik Stevens (played by Michael B. Jordan) is a former U.S. Marine (who gained the nickname "Killmonger" for his impressive kill ratio), raised in the poor black community of Oakland, California. Stevens, however, was actually Prince N'Jadaka, the son of Crown Prince N'Jobu, brother to T'Chaka, king of Wakanda. N'Jobu takes it upon himself to steal vibranium from Wakanda in order to give it to African-descended people around the world displaced by the centuries of the slave trade, many of whom live in abject poverty—especially in the United States—due to systemic racism. By N'Jobu's reckoning, the vibranium is their right, and it will give them advantages too long denied them.

When T'Chaka orders N'Jobu's arrest, N'Jobu is killed in the process, and T'Chaka orders his men to hide the truth of his brother's actions. Decades later, after T'Chaka's death, T'Challa is crowned king and given the mantle of the Black Panther. When Stevens arrives in Wakanda, he announces his true identity, challenges his cousin's claim to the throne, and defeats him in combat to become king. Killmonger then decides to complete his father's original mission to help African descendants around the world. Although T'Challa defeats him and reclaims his throne and the mantle of Black Panther, he is sympathetic to his cousin's (and uncle's) beliefs and commits to doing what he can to help those communities however he can peacefully (Ryan Coogler and Joe Robert Cole, *Black Panther*, 2018).

The original Killmonger from comics was not dissimilar to Bruce Wayne, traumatized by a parent's death and seeking some semblance of justice or vengeance.

The Killmonger of the film adds to this. While also traumatized by the loss of his father and seeking justice and vengeance against those he deems responsible, his overall mission to help black people around the world displaced by slavery and subjugated by institutional racism to the present day. In the realm of American villainy, Killmonger definitely qualifies as an antivillain. Although his overall global mission is derived from a place of devotion and duty toward millions around the world who suffer needlessly, his tactics are villainous, scarred by the trauma of his childhood. This is evident in the hero's commitment to addressing the issues raised by his nemesis. T'Challa sees some of his own nobility in Killmonger and how easy it is to go from hero to villain.

Richard A. Hall

See also: Boba Fett, Doctor Doom, Grindelwald, Gus Fring, Kahless/Klingons, Magneto, Marsellus Wallace, O-Ren Ishii/Cottonmouth, Pancho Villa, Sherry Palmer, Tia Dalma/Calypso, Tony Montana, Zod; *Thematic Essays*: The Dark Mirror: Evil Twins, *The Twilight Zone*, and the Villain Within, The Pathos of Villainy: Getting to the Heart of Why Villains Went Bad.

Further Reading

Alsford, Mike. 2006. *Heroes & Villains.* Waco, TX: Baylor University Press.

Ashby, LeRoy. 2006. *With Amusement for All: A History of American Popular Culture since 1830.* Lexington: University Press of Kentucky.

Behnken, Brian D., and Gregory D. Smithers. 2015. *Racism in American Popular Media: From Aunt Jemima to the Frito Bandito.* Westport, CT: Praeger.

Boyd, Todd. 1997. *Am I Black Enough for You?: Popular Culture from the 'Hood and Beyond.* Bloomington: Indiana University Press.

Faludi, Susan. 2007. *The Terror Dream: Myth and Misogyny in an Insecure America.* New York: Picador.

Howe, Sean. 2012. *Marvel Comics: The Untold Story.* New York: Harper-Perennial.

Langley, Travis, and Alex Simmons, eds. 2019. *Black Panther Psychology: Hidden Kingdoms.* New York: Sterling.

Nama, Adilifu. 2011. *Super Black: American Pop Culture and Black Superheroes.* Austin: University of Texas Press.

Wright, Bradford W. 2003. *Comic Book Nation: The Transformation of Youth Culture in America.* Baltimore, MD: Johns Hopkins University Press.

L

La Llorona

First Appearance:	Aztec pantheon
Creators:	Unk
Other Media:	Song, poems, movies, games, and TV shows
Primary Strength:	Clairvoyance
Major Weakness:	N/A
Weapons:	N/A
Base of Operations:	Near bodies of water (natural or artificial), caves, and the borderlands
Key Allies:	N/A
Key Enemies:	N/A
Actual Identity:	N/A
Nicknames/Aliases:	*La dama en blanco, La Malinche, La Catrina,* "The Lady in White," "The Lady of the River"

La Llorona is an Ibero American family of folkloric tales (the term "Ibero America" refers to the Iberian Peninsula and describes American countries that were colonized by Spain, and/or Portugal). As a result, this tale has had different and numerous interpretations, as they have been passed down orally through different cultures. Some historic reviews have established its origin to be older than the period of colonization, *prehispano,* and rooted in Mexican ancient Mayan legends. This can be found in the Florentine Codex, a work by Franciscan friar Bernardino de Sahagun during the conquest of America, and later work by Dominican friar Diego Duran. In these recording of the Nahua people, La Llorona is linked to Cihuacoatl and Coatlicue: goddesses of fertility, mother earth, and of war. Both goddesses appear as warnings or omens prior to the conquest and both perform lamentations of futility, such as "Oh, my children." Because of this, La Llorona has been accepted as a Mexican folk tale that has now been recovered and transformed through Chicana literary and oral traditions.

Although different in minor ways among the different cultures, the tale has common elements. La Llorona is the story of a ghost, specter, or ethereal woman who cries out for her dead children at night. This cry or lament is said to be a warning, an omen of imminent danger, and to come from her guilt of having drowned her own children. In many cases, she is said to roam as penance in despair around bodies of water looking for her children. She often wears a white tunic and has black hair. She emerges in a town and walks toward a river, lake, or creek, where she often disappears. There are cultures where she may disappear into caves, but a body of water is always present. In recent years, the borderlands have become part of the background of the legend.

The parable is said to be a cautionary tale, a warning to children to avoid bodies of water or La Llorona might take them, confusing them for her own children. In many of these stories, the drowning is done out of spite or anger, an infanticide. From the beginning, the tale has been understood to be historically and culturally significant in its relation to classism, patriarchy, displacement, eradication of culture, as well as historical conflicts based on class and/or ethnicity. In other words, La Llorona also carries cultural teachings about consequences of behaving outside the social norm. In many cases the drowned children become the expression of disempowerment—citizens betrayed by their town, authority, or nature. This further results in dishonor, desecrated land, and shame. The tale then becomes a representation of different issues of priority that a community may be experiencing, like the suppressed indigenous voice and the often ignored role of women in society.

The tale's main action is a mother killing her children; therefore, the most common archetype of La Llorona is the scary murderous, crazy, unfit mother. However, as a tale, it has many more elements that make it and La Llorona more complex. Depending on the culture, the tale may focus on La Llorona being abandoned by her lover, who tends to be of different social class or belong to a different group of people. The drowning of the children is then done out of spite or protection of the children, who will now not belong to either group. Other stories may focus on her sexual promiscuity or actions that may be considered unacceptable, like nontraditional motherhood or drinking. Other stories compare her to La Malinche, who is seen to have betrayed her people by facilitating translation for Hernan Cortez when he was conquering Mexico and therefore aiding the conquest.

In most tales, it is unclear whether La Llorona is victim or the victimizer, mother or murderer, enchantress or monster, goddess or witch. Aitana and Alberto Martos Garcia note that La Llorona cannot be viewed in dualistic terms but must be seen more like the Triple Goddess, or the Dark goddess. This is because as specter, her hollering and lamenting also make La Llorona an oracle, and therefore ambiguous. La Llorona brings warnings against rising water, negligence, imbalance, abuse, and war. They note that, as with any oracle, she requires a tribute, a sacrifice. In this case, the sacrifice or tribute is the children (the members of a society, or children of Mother Earth). As a goddess, she is more like the archetype of the sacred feminine, where she represents life and death, day and night, calm water, and storm. She then also becomes the voice of the unheard, empowerment, and nature. This has become more evident in recent writings emerging from Chicana literature and culture, where the myth is perceived as a general patriarchal warning of bad mothers or women, mad or crazy mother figures, often as a recovery of the story's initial intent from Aztec oral history (Martos Garcia and Martos Garcia, "Nuevas Lecturas de la Llorona: Imaginarios, identidad y Discurso Parabolico").

In popular culture, La Llorona can be found in movies and popular TV shows. When elements of sociopolitical, economic, or ethnic struggles are not present, part of the folktale is lost, which is often perceived as cultural appropriation; it is argued that the tale stops representing its intended message and turns La Llorona into a ghost of phantasmagoric nature, a boogey man, horror. Some of these have been the 2005 pilot for the TV-show *Supernatural* (Eric Kripke, "Pilot," season 1, episode 1, September 13, 2005; Series Run: The WB, 2005–2006; The CW, 2006–2020), *J-ok'el* (2007); *Grimm* (Akela Cooper, "La Llarona," season 2, episode 9, October 26, 2012; Series Run: NBC, 2011–2017), in many ways even the feature film *The Curse of La Llorona* (2019). Attempts at reinterpretations outside patriarchy in myth can be seen in the films *Chasing Papi* (2003) and *Y tu Mama Tambien* (2001), and primarily in Chican@ literature: *Summer of Mariposas* by Guadalupe Garcia McCall (2012), *The Legend of La Llorona* by Rodolfo Anaya (2011), *Woman Hollering Creek* by Sandra Cisneros (1991), *Ceremony* by Leslie M. Silko (1977), *La Llorona on the Longfellow Bridge* by Alicia Gaspar de Alba (2003), and *Boderlands/La Frontera: The New Mestiza* by Gloria Anzaldua (1987). She is a villain in that she represents what we fear: the supernatural, a woman capable of killing her own children, and a danger to those we hold most dear.

Maria Antonieta Reyes

See also: Alexis Carrington-Colby-Dexter, Angelique Bouchard-Collins, Cersei Lannister, Dark Willow, Fiona Goode/The Supreme, Maleficent, Poison Ivy, Tia Dalma/Calypso, Ursula, Wicked Witch of the West; *Thematic Essays*: "In the Beginning . . .": The Origins of Villains in the Western World, The Pathos of Villainy: Getting to the Heart of Why Villains Went Bad.

Further Reading

Herrera, Cristina. 2016. "Cinco Hermanitas: Myth and Sisterhood in Guadalupe Garcia McCalls Summer of the Mariposas." *Children's Literature* 44: 96–114.

Martos Garcia, Alberto, and Aitana Martos Garcia. 2015. "Nuevas Lecturas de la Llorona: Imaginarios, identidad y Discurso Parabolico." *Universum* 30, no. 2: 179–195.

Montelongo Flores, Monica. 2013. "Placing La Llorona as Curandera: Leslie Marmon Silko's *Ceremony* and Chicano Culture Theory." *Southwestern American Literature* 31, no. 1: 42–54.

Perez, Domino R. 2008. *There Was a Woman: Llorona from Folklore to Popular Culture.* Austin: University of Texas Press.

Spinoso Arcocha, Rosa Maria. 2003. *La Llorona: Mito, Género, y Control Social en México.* Mexico: Servicios de Publicaciones y Divulgación Científica e la Universidad de Malaga.

Leatherface

First Appearance:	*The Texas Chainsaw Massacre* (release date: October 1, 1974)
Creators:	Kim Henkel and Tobe Hooper

Other Media:	Comic books, novels
Primary Strength:	Near indestructible, unstoppable
Major Weakness:	Limited intellect
Weapons:	Chainsaw, butcher implements
Base of Operations:	Texas
Key Allies:	Sawyer Family: Drayton/The Cook, Nubbins, Chop Top/Plate Head, Eddie/Tex, Tech/Tinker, Alfredo/Fred, Vilmer, and W.E.
Key Enemies:	Various teenagers
Actual Identity:	Thomas Brown Hewitt (2003 remake continuity)
Nicknames/Aliases:	N/A

John Carpenter's 1978 film, *Halloween*, is considered by most to have ushered in the modern era of slasher horror films. However, four years earlier, the cult classic *The Texas Chainsaw Massacre* horrified audiences to the same degree as later slasher films. Directed by Tobe Hooper and cowritten by Hooper and Kim Henkel, the independent film (distributed by Bryanston Distributing Company) was set in present-day (1974) rural Texas, where a group of five friends are on a trip to visit the grave of the grandfather of two members of the group. Along the way, they pick up a strange—and ultimately violent—hitchhiker, who wounds one of the group before being thrown from the van. When the group reaches their destination, they are low on fuel. Stumbling upon an old house, they go in search of gas. At this point, the group first encounters Leatherface (played by Gunnar Hansen).

In the original film, audiences never see the true visage of Leatherface, so named because of the mask he wears, made from the actual face of one of his previous victims. It is established that Leatherface works (or once worked) as a butcher alongside his brother, "the Cook" (referred to in later films as Drayton Sawyer). As it turns out, the family's once-popular barbeque was actually made from human victims. The series continued with six sequels before its 2003 reboot, The carnage and violence of this slasher film predates that of the *Halloween, Friday the 13th, A Nightmare on Elm Street,* or *Child's Play* franchises (to name only the most commercially successful of the genre). In 2003, director Marcus Nispel relaunched the franchise with a modern remake, the success of which inspired a prequel film, *The Texas Chainsaw Massacre: The Beginning* (New Line Cinema, 2006).

In the 2006 film, an abandoned baby is found in a dumpster in 1939. The woman who finds him names him Thomas and raises him with her other sons. In 1969, the adult Thomas murders his boss at the recently closed slaughterhouse where the boy was found thirty years earlier. When the local sheriff attempts to arrest Thomas, his adopted brother Charlie murders the sheriff, assuming the policeman's identity. The story then follows the same tropes as the earlier films; lost teens stumble across the family, and slaughter ensues. This film, then, follows the popular trend of the late 1990s and early 2000s of providing a backstory to explain the evil actions of pop culture villains. In this case, Leatherface is influenced by the violence and insanity of the family who raised him.

At his core, Leatherface is just another of the popular *Frankenstein*-esque unstoppable monsters of the slasher movie genre. Like Michael Myers and Jason Voorhees, Leatherface is a masked, murderous, unstoppable force, whose thirst for blood cannot be quenched. He represents the fear of the hidden identity, as well as the fear of impending and unavoidable death. Placed within the context of the period in which these films were most popular, the mid-1970s through the mid-1990s, the source of this fear is difficult to ascertain; as such, one can only conclude that the carnage has been the source of attraction.

Richard A. Hall

See also: Alpha/The Whisperers, Doomsday, Dracula, Frankenstein's Monster, Freddy Krueger, Hannibal Lecter, Jason Voorhees, Joker, Michael Myers, Norman Bates; *Thematic Essays*: "Nazis, Communists, and Terrorists . . . Oh My!": The Rise of the Supervillain and the Evolution of the Modern American Villain, The Pathos of Villainy: Getting to the Heart of Why Villains Went Bad.

Further Reading

Alsford, Mike. 2006. *Heroes & Villains*. Waco, TX: Baylor University Press.

Ashby, LeRoy. 2006. *With Amusement for All: A History of American Popular Culture since 1830*. Lexington: University Press of Kentucky.

Hitchcock, Susan Tyler. 2007. *Frankenstein: A Cultural History*. New York: W. W. Norton.

Maddrey, Joseph. 2004. *Nightmares in Red, White, and Blue: The Evolution of the American Horror Film*. Jefferson, NC: McFarland.

Mahnke, Aaron. 2017. *The World of Lore: Monstrous Creatures*. New York: Del Rey.

Murphy, Bernice M. 2013. *The Rural Gothic in American Popular Culture: Backwoods Horror and Terror in the Wilderness*. London: Palgrave Macmillan.

Skal, David J. 2001. *The Monster Show: A Cultural History of Horror*. Rev. ed. New York: Farrar, Straus and Giroux.

Lex Luthor

First Appearance:	*Action Comics #23* (cover date: April, 1940)
Creators:	Jerry Siegel and Joe Shuster
Other Media:	Movies, television (animated and live action), animated home video
Primary Strength:	Cunning
Major Weakness:	Obsession with Superman
Weapons:	N/A
Base of Operations:	Metropolis
Key Allies:	Mercy Graves, Lionel Luthor (on television), LexCorp, Intergang, Legion of Doom, Injustice League/Gang

Key Enemies:	Superman, Supergirl, Superboy, Lois Lane, Lionel Luthor (on television)
Actual Identity:	Alexander Joseph Luthor
Nicknames/Aliases:	"The Greatest Criminal Mind of Our Time" (self-proclaimed, in movies)

The *Superman* franchise is one of the most successful in pop culture history. Created by the Jewish American team of writer Jerry Siegel and artist Joe Shuster, Superman is an alien named Kal-El whose home world of Krypton was destroyed shortly after his birth. Aware of the impending doom, his parents placed him in a space capsule and sent him into space to save him. He landed in Smallville, Kansas, and was raised by Jonathan and Martha Kent under his adopted name, Clark Kent. On reaching adulthood, Clark discovered that he had "powers and abilities far beyond those of mortal men" and dedicated himself to protecting the world as Superman, the world's first superhero. Because of his near-godlike powers, his only weakness being Kryptonite (meteor fragments of his home world), Superman requires antagonists of particularly daunting abilities. Of Superman's rogues' gallery of villains, one of the earliest, long established as Superman's archnemesis, is Lex Luthor.

When the character of Lex Luthor was first introduced, simply called Luthor, he was a basic criminal mastermind bent on world destruction. Over time, he is established as a mad scientist, which is how he continues throughout the late 1940s and into the mid-1980s. He finally received the first name Lex with a ret-conned

Montgomery Burns

Charles Montgomery Burns, "Mr. Burns," first appeared in *The Simpsons* episode "Simpsons Roasting on an Open Fire" (season 1, episode 1, December 17, 1989). The creation of *Simpsons* creator Matt Groening (b. 1954), Mr. Burns was originally voiced by Christopher Collins (1949–1994) in the first season of the show and has been voiced by Harry Shearer (b. 1943) ever since. On *The Simpsons* (FOX, 1989–present), Mr. Burns is the evil owner of the Springfield Nuclear Power Plant and the employer to the series' hapless hero, Homer Simpson (voiced by Dan Castellaneta). He is the source of all evil in Springfield and the epitome of the corrupt 1980s businessman. Known for his dated jokes—his age, although unknown, is clearly quite advanced—and menacingly exclaiming, "Excellent!" as he drums his fingers together in stereotypically villainous fashion, he has only one friend and ally: his loyal assistant, Waylon Smithers (also voiced by Shearer), who is also secretly in love with the dastardly villain.

On April 22, 2013, *TV Guide* listed Mr. Burns as the second "nastiest" villain in television history, although some lists position him at number one ("TV Guide Picks TV's 60 Nastiest Villains," *TV Guide*). Mr. Burns is also a parody of some of pop culture history's more notorious businessman villains, such as J. R. Ewing and Lex Luthor. Despite the occasional attempts of *Simpsons* writers to add some depth and sympathy to the character, Mr. Burns is most popular—and effective—when he oozes complete and utter villainy.

Richard A. Hall

backstory published in 1960. In that story, it is revealed that Lex actually grew up with a young Clark Kent in Smallville. In that story, teenage up-and-coming scientist Lex Luthor saves Superboy from an encounter with Kryptonite, the only substance known to kill him. Superboy then builds Lex an impressive laboratory as a thank-you. When a fire breaks out at the lab, Superboy uses his "freeze breath" to put out the flames, inadvertently blowing chemicals onto Lex, causing the red-haired boy to go bald. This incident turns Lex against Superboy/Superman forever (Jerry Siegel and Al Plastino, "How Luthor Met Superboy," *Adventure Comics #271*, April 1960). Luthor continued to be a mad scientist—garbed in a specially engineered war suit to better battle the Man of Steel—until the universe-altering *Crisis on Infinite Earths* (Marv Wolfman and George Perez, DC Comics, April 1985–March 1986).

By that time, Superman had made the transition from comic books and television to the big screen. In *Superman: The Movie* (Warner Brothers, 1978), an updated version of Superman's origin story is told, and the new hero faces his first big threat in the form of criminal mastermind Lex Luthor (played by Gene Hackman). This live-action version of Luthor was more comedic and zanier, as it focused more on the insanity of the villain. Hackman continued this version of the character in two of the three following sequels: *Superman II* (1981) and *Superman IV: The Quest for Peace* (1987). This interpretation of Luthor returned in a pseudosequel to *Superman II* that retconned the critical disasters of *Superman III* and *IV*: *Superman Returns* (2006). In that film, Kevin Spacey continued Hackman's take on the character. The most recent feature film incarnation was presented in *Batman v. Superman: Dawn of Justice* (2016). In that film, actor Jesse Eisenberg merges the Hackman/Spacey incarnations with the now-long-established comics incarnation of the wealthy businessman.

Gene Hackman brought a comedic spin to the comic book villain Lex Luthor in the original *Superman* film in 1978. (Warner Bros. Pictures/AF Archive/Alamy Stock Photo)

In the post-*Crisis* comics, the modern take and most popular version in the overall American zeitgeist on Lex Luthor began. In 1986, legendary comics writer John Byrne and artist Dick Giordano relaunched the *Superman* franchise with their six-part miniseries, *The Man of Steel* (October–December 1986). In that series, Lex Luthor is reintroduced as a wealthy 1980s businessman, originally once more with red hair (John Byrne and Dick Giordano, "Enemy Mine . . . ," *The Man of Steel #4*, November 1986). From that point forward, this is how Lex Luthor would be portrayed across all media, from the live-action television series *Lois & Clark: The New Adventures of Superman* (ABC, 1993–1997), where Luthor was portrayed by John Shea, to *Superman: The Animated Series* (Kids' WB/WB, 1996–2000), where Luthor was voiced by Clancy Brown. In the immediate aftermath of 9/11, however, the most nuanced and popular version of the character would be introduced on the live-action television series *Smallville* (WB, 2001–2006; CW, 2006–2011).

On *Smallville*, Lex Luthor (played by Michael Rosenbaum) is introduced as the early twenties son of billionaire Lionel Luthor (played by John Glover), banished to oversee LuthorCorp's facility in Smallville as punishment for continued bad behavior in Metropolis. There Lex meets high schooler Clark Kent when Lex's car inadvertently hits Clark on a bridge, sending car, driver, and pedestrian into the river below. Clark rescues the unconscious Lex from the sinking car. Lex and Clark then become the best of friends, and Lex secretly begins to investigate his mysterious savior when his salvage team insists that Clark's rescue was impossible. As the years pass and it becomes increasingly clear that Clark is not being completely honest with Lex, their relationship becomes strained. As a side story, Lionel Luthor strives to turn his son into the devious cutthroat businessman that Lionel believes he needs to be. This combination of a brutal father and a lying best friend ultimately leads Lex down his inevitable path of villainy. In 2013, Rosenbaum's Lex was named the thirty-eighth nastiest TV villain of all time ("TV Guide Picks TV's 60 Nastiest Villains," *TV Guide*). This version of Lex was very similar to the comic book miniseries *Superman: Birthright* (Mark Waid and Leinil Francis Yu, September 2003–September 2004).

Jeph Loeb and Tony Harris published the story "Lex Luthor: Triumph over Tragedy" (*Superman: Lex 2000*, January 2001), which set up Luthor to become president of the United States. Primarily a social commentary on the corresponding inauguration of wealthy businessman George W. Bush as U.S. president, the story and the ensuing overarching story line are eerily prescient of the emergence of Donald Trump as president in 2016. Throughout all of the various incarnations of Lex Luthor since 1940, however, one key aspect has remained constant: Luthor's obsession with destroying Superman and his belief that this alien "god" poses more threat to humanity than savior. In the overall realm of American villainy, Lex Luthor is the ultimate criminal mastermind intent on achieving power and on the belief that his leadership is the world's only true hope. Megalomaniacal, narcissistic, and unstoppable, Lex Luthor is the very epitome of an American villain.

Richard A. Hall

See also: Alexis Carrington-Colby-Dexter, Archie Bunker, Brainiac, Cersei Lannister, The Court of Owls, Doctor Doom, Doomsday, Dr. Frank-N-Furter, Ernst Stavro Blofeld/SPECTRE, Fish Mooney, Goldfinger, Green Goblin, Joker, J. R. Ewing, Martin Brenner, Ozymandias, Professor Moriarty, Thanos, Zod; *Thematic Essays*: The Dark Mirror: Evil Twins, *The Twilight Zone*, and the Villain Within, The Pathos of Villainy: Getting to the Heart of Why Villains Went Bad.

Further Reading

Alsford, Mike. 2006. *Heroes & Villains*. Waco, TX: Baylor University Press.

Ashby, LeRoy. 2006. *With Amusement for All: A History of American Popular Culture since 1830*. Lexington: University Press of Kentucky.

Barker, Cory, Chris Ryan, and Myc Wiatrowski, eds. 2014. *Mapping Smallville: Critical Essays on the Series and Its Characters*. Jefferson, NC: McFarland.

Daniels, Les. 2004. *Superman: The Complete History—The Life and Times of the Man of Steel*. New York: DC Comics.

Robichaud, Christopher. 2009. "Bright Colors, Dark Times." In *Supervillains and Philosophy: Sometimes, Evil Is Its Own Reward*, edited by Ben Dyer, 61–70. Chicago: Open Court.

Tucker, Reed. 2017. *Slugfest: Inside the Epic 50-Year Battle between Marvel and DC*. New York: Da Capo Press.

"TV Guide Picks TV's 60 Nastiest Villains." 2013. *TV Guide*. April 22, 2013. Accessed January 1, 2019. http://wordsmithonia.blogspot.com/2013/04/tv-guide-picks-tvs-60-nastiest-villains.html.

Tye, Larry. 2013. *Superman: The High-Flying History of America's Most Enduring Hero*. New York: Random House.

Wright, Bradford W. 2003. *Comic Book Nation: The Transformation of Youth Culture in America*. Baltimore, MD: Johns Hopkins University Press.

Loki

First Appearance:	Unknown/Scandinavian folk tales; earliest written appearances: *Poetic Edda*, *Prose Edda*, and *Heimskringla*, compiled in the thirteenth century; most popular rendition: *Journey Into Mystery #85* (cover date: October 1962)
Creators:	**Folklore:** Unknown **Marvel Comics:** Stan Lee, Larry Lieber, and Jack Kirby
Other Media:	Movies, television (animated and live-action), animated home video
Primary Strength:	Cunning, deception, shape-shifting, magic
Major Weakness:	Obsession with Thor Odinson (in comics)
Weapons:	Various mystical implements
Base of Operations:	Asgard
Key Allies:	**Folklore:** Hel (son), Fenrir (wolf/son), Jormungandr (world serpent/son), Sigyn (wife), Sleipnir (eight-legged horse/son when in horse form) **Marvel Comics:** Hela (daughter/goddess of Hel), Enchantress, Doctor Doom, Mephisto
Key Enemies:	Odin Allfather, Thor Odinson, Baldr the Brave, The Warriors Three (in comics), Lady Sif (in comics), Jane Foster/"Lady Thor" (in comics), The Avengers (in comics)

Actual Identity:	Loki Laufeyson (also Loki Odinson), Svaoilfari (in mare form)
Nicknames/Aliases:	"God of Mischief," "God of Lies," "God of Evil"

All ancient human societies had their own collections of myths, consisting of gods and supernatural creatures. These myths held to primary purposes: to explain the world and to teach right and wrong. The Norse mythology of Scandinavia revolved around the prime god Odin (or Woden). Unlike Ancient Greek/Roman mythology or the Judeo-Christian/Islamic religious traditions, where there was one primary evil being, the Norse had secondary villains in the forms of the god Hel and the wolf Fenrir, both of whom were the offspring of the primary Norse villain Loki. Loki is the antagonist to the Allfather, Odin, and Odin's son, Thor, god of thunder and lightning. For centuries, Loki and the Norse gods were the realm of ancient mythological studies. However, in 1962, Marvel Comics editor-in-chief Stan Lee, writer Larry Lieber, and artist Jack Kirby reintroduced Loki to modern audiences in their new superhero comic book *Journey into Mystery*, which centered in a modern incarnation of the ancient god Thor and turned the ancient myth into modern superhero. It is primarily through the Marvel Comics and Cinematic Universes that Americans have become aware of Loki. Through the Marvel feature films since their 2011 movie *Thor*, Loki (as portrayed by Tom Hiddleston) has become one of the most popular villains in American popular culture.

Like many of the ancient mythologies, the Norse stories are littered with inconsistencies. This is due to the fact that by the time the myths were collected and written down, the stories were already well traveled, passed down generation to generation for centuries. What can be derived concerning Loki is that he was the father of Hel, the godling overseer of the realm of Hel, home to lost souls (very similar to the Christian hell). In most renditions, he is also the son of the gods Farbauti and Laufey. In the myths, Laufey is Loki's mother; in his later incarnation in Marvel Comics, Laufey is Loki's biological father, a frost giant. In the myths, as in the later comics and movies, Loki is defeated by Thor, with the assistance of his enchanted hammer, Mjolnir. This is recorded in the collections of the *Poetic Edda*. In the twentieth century, when Stan Lee sought to make a Superman-type hero for his burgeoning Marvel Comics Universe, Lee looked to the past, bringing the myths of Thor to the present and putting a sci-fi twist to the ancient tales.

In the comics and feature films, Loki is the adopted son of Odin Allfather, taken in by the chief god after Loki's biological father, Laufey, is defeated by Odin in battle. Loki, then, grows up with his adoptive brother, Thor, constantly in the shadow of his powerful, handsome sibling. Through this choice, Lee and the Marvel writers have been able to add the age-old subject of sibling rivalry (in essence, making Loki and Thor a modern-day Cain and Abel, albeit with a happier ending). In the comics, Loki is considered the god of mischief, evil, and lies. When he discovers his true parentage, it makes Odin's perceived favoritism of Thor all the more evident. Loki, then, turns his powers against his brother and father, seeking to dethrone Odin and rule Asgard and all of the Nine Realms, including Midgard (Earth).

In the 2012 film *The Avengers*, Loki makes a deal with the Mad Titan Thanos to open a portal through which the alien Chitauri can invade Earth, with the understanding that once Thanos has conquered the universe, Loki will rule Earth, the place his brother, Thor, holds most dear. When that plan fails, Loki fakes his own death and uses his shape-shifting abilities to unseat his father, Odin, taking on his identity while hiding the aging god in a human retirement home on Earth (*Thor: The Dark World*, 2013; *Thor: Ragnarok*, 2017).

As a god, Loki sees himself above other life-forms in the universe. Like his Judeo-Christian counterpart, the Devil, he has a particular dislike for Earth's humans. This is best expressed in his speech as he attempts to take over and rule the Earth: "Is not this simpler? Is this not your natural state? It's the unspoken truth of humanity, that you crave subjugation. The bright lure of freedom diminishes your life's joy in a mad scramble for power, for identity. You were made to be ruled. In the end, you will always kneel" (Loki, *The Avengers*, Marvel Studios, writer/director Joss Whedon, 2012). Here, Loke places himself alongside the Devil not only as the enemy of humanity but also as a critic of their devotion to their God, who requires a degree of servitude in addition to their free will. In this way, he does not consider himself the villain but, rather, the hero, allowing humanity to see themselves for what they truly are: subservient creatures from the beginning.

In the comics, Loki has appeared as a woman and a young male child (both when his previous, adult male form had been "killed"). He has frequently allied himself with the demon Mephisto and the human dictator Doctor Doom, as well as the Asgardian Enchantress. When Lee sought to create a team of superheroes, Loki became the threat that first united the Avengers: Thor, Iron Man, Ant-Man, the Wasp, and the Hulk (Stan Lee and Jack Kirby, *The Avengers #1*, July 1963). In the two-part animated home-video release *Hulk vs.* (Marvel Studios/Lionsgate, 2009), Loki uses the Enchantress to split the Hulk into his human and monster halves and then use the monster as a de facto puppet to destroy Asgard and kill Odin. In 2019, it was announced that Tom Hiddleston would reprise his film role in a television series on the new Disney+ streaming service. The god of ancient Scandinavia has gone global and remains a mainstay in popular culture.

In the realm of Western villainy, Loki is a representation of Lucifer/Satan. He is powerful tempter and liar, urging—often through spells—humans to do his bidding and going against the better angels of their nature. In modern times, he is driven by jealousy and a sense of not belonging. This connects him to the Lucifer of John Milton's *Paradise Lost* (1667). Hiddleston's portrayal has often added layers of sympathy for the character and an underlying affection for his adopted father and brother, while simultaneously playing his villainy with malicious glee. In the twenty-first century, Loki speaks to anyone who has ever felt isolated or less than or who has had a sense of not belonging. Overall, however, he is a menacing threat and a sign of how those negative feelings can lead to self-destructive behavior.

Richard A. Hall

See also: Alexis Carrington-Colby-Dexter, Angelique Bouchard-Collins, Bellatrix Lestrange, Dark Willow, Doctor Doom, Green Goblin, Grindelwald, Jafar, J. R. Ewing, Lucifer/Satan, Magneto, Maleficent, The Master/Missy, Morgan le Fay, Poison Ivy, Professor Moriarty, Q, Red Skull, Sauron/Saruman, Sith Lords, Sue Sylvester, Thanos, Tia Dalma/Calypso, Ultron, Ursula, Voldemort, Wicked Witch of the West; *Thematic Essays*: "In the Beginning . . .": The Origins of Villains in the Western World, The Dark Mirror: Evil Twins, *The Twilight Zone*, and the Villain Within, The Pathos of Villainy: Getting to the Heart of Why Villains Went Bad.

Further Reading

Alsford, Mike. 2006. *Heroes & Villains.* Waco, TX: Baylor University Press.

Campbell, Joseph. (1949) 2004. *The Hero with a Thousand Faces: Commemorative Edition.* Princeton, NJ: Princeton University Press.

Costello, Matthew J. 2009. *Secret Identity Crisis: Comic Books & the Unmasking of Cold War America.* New York: Continuum.

Dyer, Ben, ed. 2009. *Supervillains and Philosophy: Sometimes, Evil Is Its Own Reward.* Popular Culture and Philosophy Series. Chicago: Open Court.

Gaiman, Neil. 2018. *Norse Mythology.* New York: W. W. Norton.

Gavaler, Chris. 2015. *On the Origin of Superheroes: From the Big Bang to Action Comics No. 1.* Iowa City: University of Iowa.

Gloyn, Liz. 2019. *Tracking Classical Monsters in Popular Culture.* London: Bloomsbury Academic.

Howe, Sean. 2012. *Marvel Comics: The Untold Story.* New York: Harper Perennial.

Kelly, Henry Ansgar. 2006. *Satan: A Biography.* Cambridge: Cambridge University Press.

Mahnke, Aaron. 2017. *The World of Lore: Monstrous Creatures.* New York: Del Rey.

McCoy, Daniel. 2016. *The Viking Spirit: An Introduction to Norse Mythology and Religion.* Scotts Valley, CA: CreateSpace.

Milton, John. (1667) 2005. *Paradise Lost.* Mineola, NY: Dover.

Russell, Jeffrey B., and Brooks Alexander. 2007. *A History of Witchcraft: Sorcerers, Heretics, & Pagans.* London: Thames & Hudson.

Wright, Bradford W. 2003. *Comic Book Nation: The Transformation of Youth Culture in America.* Baltimore, MD: Johns Hopkins University Press.

Lucifer/Satan

First Appearance:	Tanakh (seventh to eighth century BCE); the book of Job (original publication unknown)
Creators:	Unknown
Other Media:	Movies, television (animated and live action), novels, short stories, comic books, songs, poems, art
Primary Strength:	Cunning, deception, shape-shifting, black magic, seduction
Major Weakness:	Obsession with destroying God's creation, humans (in most incarnations)

Weapons:	N/A
Base of Operations:	Hell, Earth
Key Allies:	Legions of demons/fallen angels, the Beast, the Antichrist
Key Enemies:	God/YHWH/Allah
Actual Identity:	Lucifer/Lucifer Morningstar
Nicknames/Aliases:	"The Devil," "Prince of Hell," "Lord of Lies," "The Tempter," "The Adversary"

Lucifer, or Satan, may well be the oldest villain in world history. Although it is impossible to definitively identify his first appearance in written lore, religion, and mythology, the earliest known written accounts are in the Hebrew Tanakh, where "the Satan" is referred to as a prosecutor and part of God's legions of angels, and the book of Job, where, again, Satan appears to live in heaven with God, working to tempt and test the human Job's faith in and devotion to God. In the Gospels of the New Testament, Satan appears only once, tempting Jesus three times during the Christ's forty-day fast in the wilderness. Satan is referred to over a dozen times in the Judeo-Christian religious texts and is traditionally associated with being the true identity of the "serpent" in the Garden of Eden that leads humanity to its original sin of disobedience to God. The modern image of the Devil—red skinned, horned, leather winged, and wielding a pitchfork—came centuries later, promoted by the Catholic Church and continuing throughout the

Hela and Mephisto

In order to provide villains of equal stature to superheroes, comic book creators often find themselves pressed for ideas with particularly powerful heroes such as the Norse god Thor or the Sorcerer Supreme, Doctor Strange. In the 1960s, however, limited by the strict Comics Code Authority (CCA), comic books were unable to use Satan, the original supervillain, as a potential foe. Marvel Comics circumvented this rule by making Satan-like characters such as Hela and Mephisto.

Hela was introduced in *Journey Into Mystery #102* (March 1964) by Stan Lee and Jack Kirby. She is the goddess ruler of the Norse realm of Hel (a twist on the originally male Norse god Hel). She is the daughter of Loki, god of mischief, and a key foe to Thor, god of thunder. Like Satan, she rules over the realm of damned souls. In the feature film *Thor Ragnarok* (2017), Hela, played by Cate Blanchett (b. 1969), was reconceived as the secret sister of Thor and Loki, freed from Hel on the death of her father, Odin.

Mephisto was an even-closer match for Satan, introduced in *The Silver Surfer #3* (December 1968), by Lee and artist John Buscema. Mephisto was Satan in all but name; with red skin, red clothing, pointed ears, he lorded over a hellish dimension. In 1972, after the CCA was amended to allow the use of Satan as a character, Mephisto was presented as a lesser demon, jealous of fellow demon Zarathos. Mephisto then merges Zarathos with the human Johnny Blaze, creating the avenging superhero Ghost Rider (Roy Thomas, Gary Friedrich, and Mike Ploog, *Marvel Spotlight #5*, August 1972). Over the years, Mephisto has also been a frequent adversary to Doctor Strange, master of the mystic arts.

Richard A. Hall

history of Christianity to the present day. This image was further embedded in the popular zeitgeist by the epic poem "Inferno," the first of the three-part work *Divine Comedy* by Dante Alighieri published from 1308 to 1320 CE.

Ironically, most of what the world knows about Lucifer/Satan today comes neither from biblical texts or Christian sources. In 1667 CE, the poet John Milton published his epic masterpiece, *Paradise Lost*. Milton's story begins in the immediate aftermath of Lucifer's attempted war on heaven, where he and his legions of fallen angels have been banished to hell. Lucifer concocts a master plan to crawl up to Earth, disguise himself as a serpent, and tempt the humans Adam and Eve into disobeying God, presumably dooming humanity to his own fate. This is the source of modern ideas of Satan being the source of original sin. The book of Genesis merely describes the "serpent" as an intelligent beast, originally with arms and legs; this can be deduced from the fact that the serpent's punishment for tempting Eve is that he would slither on the ground for the rest of his days, leading to the explanation as to why snakes are the only reptiles without legs. Milton's Lucifer has become the definitive biography of Satan in the modern world.

The final book of the Christian Bible, the book of Revelation (also known as Apocalypse), provides a vague and often difficult-to-understand account of humanity's final days, when Satan will work through the Beast and the Antichrist to claim as many human souls as possible before the final confrontation with God and the heavenly armies led by Jesus Christ. The vagueness of the text has caused many over the centuries to mistake Satan as *being* the Beast, Antichrist, or both. Regardless of interpretation, however, Lucifer/Satan has, for two thousand years, been considered the ultimate villain in human history and the primary enemy of all humankind. His fate, as described in Revelation, is that he will ultimately be condemned to hell to suffer for all eternity. However, Milton and numerous other modern traditions claim that Satan will rule over hell, being responsible for punishing the lost souls condemned there.

Lucifer/Satan—portrayed here in an engraving by Gustave Doré for an 1866 reprint of John Milton's *Paradise Lost*—is the oldest villain in western literature. (*Milton's Paradise Lost—Illustrated by Gustave Doré*, 1866)

Over the centuries, Lucifer/Satan has been a mainstay in Western popular culture. In 1936, Stephen Vincent Benet published the short story "The Devil and Daniel Webster." In this tale, Jabez Stone, an American farmer, makes a deal with a

Mister Scratch to sell his soul for seven years of prosperity and good luck (later extended to ten years). When the day comes to pay up, Stone wants out of the deal, hiring the legendary nineteenth-century lawyer and congressman Daniel Webster to defend his case. A judge and jury of Mister Scratch's choosing, a collection of damned souls from American history, are ultimately swayed by Webster's oratory, freeing Stone from his contract (*The Saturday Evening Post*, October 24, 1936). A similar story appeared in song decades later. In 1979, the Charlie Daniels Band released the song "The Devil Went Down to Georgia." In this song, the Devil approaches a "fiddle player" named Johnny and challenges him to a fiddling duel. If Johnny wins, he will receive a golden fiddle, but if the Devil wins, Johnny loses his soul. The song is designed to showcase the considerable violin talents of Charlie Daniels, but the ultimate moral of the story is that the Devil can be defeated by his own hubris. In 1993, legendary singer Johnny Cash released "The Devil Comes Back to Georgia," where the Devil is once more defeated by the talented Johnny.

The 1968 film *Rosemary's Baby* and the film franchise of *The Omen*—*The Omen* (1976), *Damien: Omen II* (1978), *Omen III: The Final Conflict* (1981), and *Omen IV: The Awakening* (1991)—all centered on the idea of a human son of Satan. *The Omen* goes so far as to make this son of Satan eventually rise as the Antichrist. Demonic possession is central to *The Exorcist* film franchise: *The Exorcist* (1973), *Exorcist II: The Heretic* (1977), *The Exorcist III* (1990), *Exorcist: The Beginning* (2004), and *Dominion: Prequel to The Exorcist* (2005). All of these films and countless others cash in on society's overwhelming fear of the Devil and his hellish legions. The poems, stories, songs, novels, comic books, television series, and films featuring the Devil/Satan/Lucifer number in the hundreds, if not thousands.

A more comedic Satan is portrayed in the animated series *South Park* (Comedy Central, 1997–present). On this series, the stereotypical Satan—red skinned, horned, and demonic—is an emotionally needy figure. Over the course of the series and its one theatrical feature film, Satan develops a romantic relationship with real-world Iraqi dictator Saddam Hussein. Satan is clearly homosexual, providing a subtext that homosexuality is in some way sinful or wrong. However, it is also an abusive relationship, with Satan the victim of the more sadistic Hussein. Overall, *South Park*'s Satan desires to be loved and adored and responds violently when that adoration does not meet his expectations.

On the television series *Supernatural* (WB, 2005–2006; CW, 2006–2020), Lucifer is introduced in the fifth season. In that incarnation, Lucifer is a fallen archangel, cast from heaven for refusing God's decree that angels should love humans more than him, as clearly God loved humans more than his angels. Lucifer's hatred for humans goes far beyond that; he despises them for their treatment of Earth and for using him as a scapegoat for their own evil actions. The character is portrayed by several actors, as the series established that he could only interact with humans by inhabiting one. In 2013, *TV Guide* listed the *Supernatural* version of Lucifer as the thirty-seventh "nastiest" villain in television history ("TV Guide Picks TV's 60 Nastiest Villains," *TV Guide*).

The most recent incarnation of the character, directly derived from the Milton version, has been the television series *Lucifer* (FOX, 2016–2018; Netflix,

2019–2020). Loosely based on the late 1980s and early 1990s DC Comics books *The Sandman* and *Lucifer*, the series stars Tom Ellis as Lucifer Morningstar, the Devil. Bored by centuries of torturing damned souls, Lucifer has escaped hell, leaving it rudderless, to make a life for himself in modern-day Los Angeles, California. The owner of the popular bar and dance club Lux, Lucifer lives a life of utter debauchery, aided by his demon bodyguard, Mazikeen/Maze (played by Lesley-Ann Brandt). Lucifer's "brother," the angel Amenadiel (played by D. B. Woodside) is sent to Earth by God to force the errant son to return to his appointed duties. The series underscores Lucifer's hatred of his "father" as described in Milton's poem, but it ultimately makes him a sympathetic character and antivillain, as he often uses his powers for good to assist the Los Angeles Police Department and Detective Chloe Decker (played by Lauren German), to whom Lucifer is inexplicably emotionally drawn. An overarching theme of the series is that the Devil does nothing more than open humans up to follow their deepest desires, freeing them from the de facto "slavery" expected by their creator.

In recent decades, Lucifer has been granted a more sympathetic viewpoint than in millennia past. If it is, truly, "better to rule in Hell than to serve in Heaven," what does this former angel know that humanity does not? The traditional phrase "the Devil made me do it" no longer holds validity, as the Devil, clearly, does not "make" humans do anything other than consider their options and give in to their desires. As such, it could be argued that the Devil is more a proponent of free will than is God. Despite this, the Devil/Satan/Lucifer remains the ultimate representation of evil in the Western world. He has become a symbol to be feared, as well as a scapegoat used to defend against humanity's basest instincts and actions. Many films and television series have portrayed individuals faced with choosing right or wrong with images of themselves as an angel on one shoulder and the Devil on the other. Modern Satanists tend to focus on the freedom promised by following the Devil's example of disobedience to God. In the twenty-first century, humanity has come to use Satan as an excuse for sin while simultaneously possessing a fear of seeing him in the afterlife.

Richard A. Hall

See also: Angelique Bouchard-Collins, Bellatrix Lestrange, Dark Willow, Fiona Goode/The Supreme, Freddy Krueger, J. R. Ewing, La Llorona, Loki, Maleficent, Morgan le Fay, Q, Reverend Stryker/The Purifiers, Sauron/Saruman, Sith Lords, Ursula, Voldemort; *Thematic Essays*: "In the Beginning . . .": The Origins of Villains in the Western World, The Pathos of Villainy: Getting to the Heart of Why Villains Went Bad.

Further Reading

Alsford, Mike. 2006. *Heroes & Villains*. Waco, TX: Baylor University Press.

Ashby, LeRoy. 2006. *With Amusement for All: A History of American Popular Culture since 1830*. Lexington: University Press of Kentucky.

Campbell, Joseph. (1949) 2004. *The Hero with a Thousand Faces: Commemorative Edition*. Princeton, NJ: Princeton University Press.

Carey, John. (1999) 2020. "Milton's Satan." In *The Supervillain Reader*, edited by Rob Weiner and Rob Peaslee, 125–139. Jackson: University of Mississippi Press.

Cavendish, Richard. 1968. *The Black Arts: A Concise History of Witchcraft, Demonology, Astrology, and Other Mystical Practices throughout the Ages*. New York: TarcherPerigree.

Dolansky, Shawna. 2018. "How the Serpent Became Satan: Adam, Eve, and the Serpent in the Garden of Eden." Biblical Archaeology Society. October 14. Accessed April 7, 2019. https://www.biblicalarchaeology.org/daily/biblical-topics/bible-interpretation/how-the-serpent-became-satan/.

Forasteros, J. R. 2017. *Empathy for the Devil: Finding Ourselves in the Villains of the Bible*. Downers Grove, IL: InterVarsity.

Forbes, Daniel A. 2011. "The Aesthetic of Evil." In *Vader, Voldemort and Other Villains: Essays on Evil in Popular Media*, edited by Jamey Heit, 13–27. Jefferson, NC: McFarland.

Gavaler, Chris. 2015. *On the Origin of Superheroes: From the Big Bang to Action Comics No. 1*. Iowa City: University of Iowa.

Gloyn, Liz. 2019. *Tracking Classical Monsters in Popular Culture*. London: Bloomsbury Academic.

Hogan, Susan, Albach. 2003. "Was Judas a Good Guy or Bad? Scholars Disagree." Baylor University. April 17, 2013. Accessed April 21, 2019. https://www.baylor.edu/mediacommunications/index.php?id=6435.

Holderness, Graham. 2015. *Re-Writing Jesus: Christ in 20th-Century Fiction and Film*. London: Bloomsbury.

Kelly, Henry Ansgar. 2006. *Satan: A Biography*. Cambridge: Cambridge University Press.

Mahnke, Aaron. 2017. *The World of Lore: Monstrous Creatures*. New York: Del Rey.

Milton, John. (1667) 2005. *Paradise Lost*. Mineola, NY: Dover.

Russell, Jeffrey B., and Brooks Alexander. 2007. *A History of Witchcraft: Sorcerers, Heretics, & Pagans*. London: Thames & Hudson.

"TV Guide Picks TV's 60 Nastiest Villains." 2013. *TV Guide*. April 22, 2013. Accessed January 1, 2019. http://wordsmithonia.blogspot.com/2013/04/tv-guide-picks-tvs-60-nastiest-villains.html.

Van Seters, John. 1998. "The Pentateuch." In *The Hebrew Bible Today: An Introduction to Critical Issues*, edited by Steven L. McKenzie and Matt Patrick Graham, 3–49. Westminster, UK: John Knox.

Winstead, Antoinette F. 2011. "The Devil Made Me Do It!: The Devil in 1960s–1970s Horror Film." In *Vader, Voldemort and Other Villains: Essays on Evil in Popular Media*, edited by Jamey Heit, 28–45. Jefferson, NC: McFarland.

Magneto

First Appearance:	*The X-Men #1* (cover date: September, 1963)
Creators:	Stan Lee and Jack Kirby
Other Media:	Movies, television (animated)
Primary Strength:	Control of magnetic fields and metals
Major Weakness:	Racism
Weapons:	N/A
Base of Operations:	Genosha, Asteroid M/Avalon
Key Allies:	Brotherhood of (Evil) Mutants, Mystique, Toad, X-Men (occasionally), Professor Charles Xavier (occasionally), Quicksilver (son), Scarlett Witch (daughter), Polaris (daughter), Hellfire Club (temporarily), Acolytes
Key Enemies:	The X-Men (often), X-Factor, X-Force, Professor Charles Xavier, Wolverine
Actual Identity:	Erik Lehnsherr (in movies and originally in comics), Max Eisenhardt (more recently in comics)
Nicknames/Aliases:	"Magnus," "Master of Magnetism"

In 1963, Marvel Comics editor-in-chief Stan Lee and artist Jack Kirby introduced the last of their new Marvel Age of heroes: the X-Men. Although commercially the least successful of these new heroes, the X-Men were the most socially relevant to the period. Professor Charles Xavier ran a school for "gifted youngsters," or "mutants," teenagers born with a mutated gene that provided them with exceptional super powers. Unlike the previous Marvel heroes who received their powers from some manner of scientific accident, the X-Men were born with enhanced abilities that manifested during puberty. Due to their strange natural powers, mutants were hated by "normal" humans. Professor X sought peaceful coexistence between mutants and humans.

In the premier issue, the X-Men fought the villain Magneto. Over time, readers discovered that Magneto and Professor X were once close friends, but they became enemies due to Magneto's strong belief that humans would never accept mutants and that mutants, therefore, must use their powers to enforce acceptance. Over the decades, numerous comic book professionals, academics, and fans have made a connection between the Professor X and Magneto dynamic and that of real-world

Stan Lee

Comic book legend Stan "the Man" Lee (1922–2018) was born Stanley Martin Lieber in New York City. At the age of seventeen, Lee went to work for Timely Comics as an office boy. Timely was owned by Martin Goodman (1908–1992), who was married to Lee's cousin. In 1941, when Timely editor Joe Simon (1913–2011) left the company, the eighteen-year-old Lee was promoted to editor. He left Timely briefly from 1942 to 1945 to serve in World War II, first for the U.S. Army Signal Corps and then for the Training Film Division, when his experience in publishing came to the army's attention. In 1947, Lee married Joan Boocock (1922–2017). The two were married for seventy years, having only two daughters (one who died in infancy). Lee continued to write and edit for Timely through the 1950s.

In 1961, with the assistance of artists Jack Kirby (1917–1994) and Steve Ditko (1927–2018), Lee initiated the Marvel Age of Comics, changing the company's name to Marvel Comics. Over the course of two years, Lee and his team created some of the most iconic superheroes in comic book history: the Fantastic Four, the Hulk, Spider-Man, Iron Man, Ant-Man and the Wasp, Thor, the Avengers, Daredevil, Doctor Strange, and the X-Men. Lee was also instrumental in the creation of the heroes Black Panther (the first black superhero) and the Falcon (the first African American superhero) in the late 1960s. With such a vast array of heroes, Lee was also required to concoct some equally powerful supervillains: Doctor Doom, Green Goblin, Loki, Magneto, Hela, and Mephisto, to name but a very few. Lee spent over a half century promoting Marvel Comics. With the worldwide popularity of the Marvel feature films since 2008, Stan Lee's legacy as a pop culture icon has been secured.

Richard A. Hall

civil-rights activists Dr. Martin Luther King Jr. and the Reverend Malcolm X, whose takes on civil rights for blacks ranged from the former's policy of nonviolence and the latter's more militant stance. Over the decades, the X-Men have consistently presented an analogy for all people in society who feel that they are other: racial/ethnic minorities, the LGBT+ community, nerds, the socially awkward, or any individual or group that society deems different.

While Magneto's origin has been ret-conned and tweaked over the decades, the origin that is most well known in the overall zeitgeist is the one presented in the film *X-Men* (20th Century Fox, 2000) and later expanded upon in the film *X-Men: First Class* (20th Century Fox, 2011). In those films, young Erik Lehnsherr is a European Jew during World War II. He and his parents are captured by the Nazis and sent to a concentration camp. When the guards attempt to separate him from his parents, his mutant powers over magnetism manifest, bringing him to the attention of Nazi scientist Klaus Schmidt, who murders Erik's mother in front of him to call forth the boy's powers. This backstory perfectly establishes the otherness of mutants in the X-Men universe, connecting them to the persecution of Jews during the war, and it cements the future Magneto's dislike for "normal" humans (*homo sapien* versus the mutant designation *homo superior*). By the end of 20th Century Fox's *X-Men* franchise, Magneto and Professor X have resolved their differences and work together for the protection of mutants worldwide.

When Professor X leaves Earth to join his alien-queen wife among the stars, he asks Magneto to take charge of his school and teach and train the next generation of X-Men, dubbed "the New Mutants." Although the original X-Men strongly oppose the idea, refusing to take the field of battle of their former foe, Magneto does respect his old friend's wishes and attempts to redeem himself by following Xavier's example (Christ Claremont and Mary Wilshire, *New Mutants #35*, January 1986). His redemption, however, is short lived, and he soon returns to his more militant approach to humanity. Years later, after the X-Men succeed in stopping Magneto from using his satellite base Asteroid M/Avalon to amplify his powers and destroy the tectonic plates of the Earth, the United Nations—in an attempt to appease his antihuman stance—offer him the recently decimated island nation of Genosha, whose mutant slave population has recently received emancipation, where he could rule a new mutant society (Fabian Nicieza and Alan Davis, *X-Men #86–87*, March–April 1999).

In the realm of Western villainy, Magneto is one of the more sympathetic villains. His hatred and racism are born from hatred and racism against him and his kind. He utilizes his super powers to militantly protect and avenge his brothers and sisters from a society that hates and fears them. He fights fire with fire, injustice with injustice, and violence with violence. His villainy is derived not from evil but from pain. He is the tortured animal that learns to fight back. He fervently wishes that the world was as his friend Xavier sees it, but he is confronted daily by the realities of the hatred and bigotry that continues to plague the species. Above all, he is a cautionary tale of the eventual outcome of continued persecution and prejudice: a violent revolutionary fervor for equality and acceptance.

Richard A. Hall

See also: Borg Queen/Borg, Brainiac, Catwoman, The Comedian, The Court of Owls, Doctor Doom, Doomsday, Dracula, Green Goblin, Grindelwald, Harley Quinn, Joker, Killmonger, Lex Luthor, Loki, Morgan le Fay, Ozymandias, Penguin, Poison Ivy, Ra's al Ghul, Red Skull, Reverend Stryker/The Purifiers, Scarecrow, Thanos, Two-Face, Ultron, Voldemort, Zod; *Thematic Essays*: The Dark Mirror: Evil Twins, *The Twilight Zone*, and the Villain Within, The Pathos of Villainy: Getting to the Heart of Why Villains Went Bad.

Further Reading

Alsford, Mike. 2006. *Heroes & Villains.* Waco, TX: Baylor University Press.

Costello, Matthew J. 2009. *Secret Identity Crisis: Comic Books & the Unmasking of Cold War America.* New York: Continuum.

De Falco, Tom. 2006. *Comics Creators on X-Men.* London: Titan.

Howe, Sean. 2012. *Marvel Comics: The Untold Story.* New York: Harper-Perennial.

Levin, Noah. 2009. "Mutation and Moral Community." In *Supervillains and Philosophy: Sometimes, Evil Is Its Own Reward*, edited by Ben Dyer, 137–146. Chicago: Open Court.

Poon, Jared. 2009. "What Magneto Cannot Choose." In *Supervillains and Philosophy: Sometimes, Evil Is Its Own Reward*, edited by Ben Dyer, 53–60. Chicago: Open Court.

Powell, Jason. 2016. *The Best There Is at What He Does: Examining Chris Claremont's X-Men.* Edwardsville, IL: Sequart.

Wright, Bradford W. 2003. *Comic Book Nation: The Transformation of Youth Culture in America*. Baltimore, MD: Johns Hopkins University Press.

Maleficent

First Appearance:	*Sleeping Beauty* (release date: January 29, 1959)
Creators:	Marc Davis and Eric Cleworth
Other Media:	Novels, fairy tales, books, live-action and CGI movies, TV shows
Primary Strength:	Magic
Major Weakness:	Insecurity
Weapons:	Staff
Base of Operations:	Moors
Key Allies:	Tree Ogres, Vine Dragon, and Diaval (a raven-turned-man)
Key Enemies:	Prince Phillip, King Henry, Stefan, humans
Actual Identity:	Dark Fae, Maleficent
Nicknames/Aliases:	"Evil Godmother," "Mistress of All Evil," "Guardian of the Moors," "Queen Maleficent of the Moors"

Maleficent originated in the Walt Disney animated feature film *Sleeping Beauty* (1959). She was created by Disney animator Marc Davis, made a dragon by Eric Cleworth , and revised in 2014 by Linda Woolverton. She was voiced in the film by Eleanor Audley and portrayed in the revised live-action version by Angelina Jolie. Her appearance tends to emphasize her dark heart. She is portrayed as a tall, slender, horned femme fatale, dressed in black. In the animated film, the black is combined with purple and resembles a combination of a witch and vampire attire and allure. She is an evil fairy or dark fairy who cast a curse of death on Princess Aurora, the protagonist of the 1959 film, for mistakenly presuming that she did not get invited to the princess's christening. The curse stated that the princess would prick herself on the spindle of a spinning wheel at the age of sixteen and die. As part of the story, there are three more fairy godmothers: Flora, Fauna, and Merryweather. Merryweather, having the opportunity to bestow upon the princess a gift at her christening after the curse was cast, protects the princess by making her fall into a deep sleep until "true love's kiss" awakens her.

This tale, and therefore the character on which Maleficent is based, are older than the 1959 animated film. The film is part of a series of Walt Disney's animation of very old fairy tales. *Sleeping Beauty* was the sixteenth of these retelling of tales. This tale is based on Charles Perrault's *Sleeping Beauty* (a French fairy tale from the seventeenth century) and the Brothers Grimm's *Little Briar Rose* (a German fairy tale from the nineteenth century). In both tales, the Maleficent character is an evil fairy godmother, and the retelling of the tale left the overall elements of the story intact. However, there is an even older tale related to *Sleeping Beauty. Sun, Moon and Talia,* by Giambattista Basile from England, was published in 1634 in the book *The Tale of Tales*. Feminists in the modern age have been attempting to recover some of the fairy tales because they tend to be "overly simplistic, naïve, sexist, or even culturally offensive" (Bowman, "The Dichotomy of the Great Mother Archetype in Disney Heroines and Villainesses," *Vader, Voldemort and Other Villains*, 2011, 80; Sivan, "The Secret History of Maleficent," 2014). Recovering Basile's older tale allowed for the "intertextual transformation" of *Sleeping Beauty* and, most interestingly, of Maleficent (Üner, "Intertextual Transformation of a Fairy Tale from Sleeping Beauty to Maleficent," 374). Intertextualization allows for the tale to remain the same while retelling the story from a different character's perspective as the protagonist (in this case, Maleficent). It allows for recovery and inclusion of other aspects of the story that still revolve around good and evil from outside a binary understanding. This can be seen in the 2014 film by Walt Disney *Maleficent* and its sequel, *Maleficent: Mistress of Evil*, in 2019.

In this tale, the story revolves around Maleficent. She is a powerful fairy now presented as queen and guardian of the Moors, an enchanted forest inhabited by numerous magical creatures, from invasion by humans. King Henry attempts to invade, and Maleficent fights the humans with the help of the inhabitants of Moors. The king then offers succession to the throne to the one who can avenge him. In this story, Maleficent befriends a human when she is a child, Stefan, with whom

Maleficent was first added to the *Sleeping Beauty* story in the 1959 film from Walt Disney Studios. (Walt Disney Productions/Entertainment Pictures/Alamy Stock Photo)

she falls in love. He decides to be the one to avenge King Henry and, putting Maleficent to sleep, cuts her wings, presenting them as proof of defeat. Stefan becomes the king and has a child, Princess Aurora, who is then cursed by Maleficent at the royal christening to prick herself in a spindle into an eternal slumber. While observing her growth in order to ensure the fulfillment of her curse, Maleficent develops a motherly love for Aurora, true love, and it is her kiss that ends up awakening Aurora from her sleep (Linda Woolverton, *Maleficent*, 2014).

Maleficent is known as the Mistress of All Evil, and her name means "doing evil or harm." Whether in the 1959 movie or the most recent movies by Walt Disney Studios, the evil elements remain. Maleficent is prideful and exercises wickedness, unforgiveness, and vanity, and she uses menacing curses of magic to destroy (even if as a response to being wronged). Her evil doing is still present, even if presented as part tragedy. This continues to emphasize the descriptors of a "bad woman" or "bad mother." The modern live-action films present a more sympathetic view of this traditional witch, making her emotionally vulnerable and explaining her wickedness. While Maleficent has received a moment of overcoming her evil tendencies, granting her some redemption, when tested, her wickedness survives, which makes her a villain to remember, understand, and love.

Maria Antonieta Reyes

See also: Alexis Carrington-Colby-Dexter, Angelique Bouchard-Collins, Asajj Ventress, Bellatrix Lestrange, Cersei Lannister, Dark Willow, Fiona Goode/The Supreme, Grindelwald, Jafar, La Llorona, Loki, Lucifer/Satan, Morgan le Fay, Poison Ivy, Sauron/Saruman, Tia Dalma/Calypso, Ursula, Wicked Witch of the West; *Thematic Essays*: "In the Beginning . . .": The Origins of Villains in the Western World, Tarantino and the Antivillain, The Pathos of Villainy: Getting to the Heart of Why Villains Went Bad.

Further Reading

Alsford, Mike. 2006. *Heroes & Villains*. Waco, TX: Baylor University Press.

Ashby, LeRoy. 2006. *With Amusement for All: A History of American Popular Culture since 1830*. Lexington: University Press of Kentucky.

Ashlin, D. L. 1998. "Sleeping Beauty. Folklore and Mythology: Pittsburg University." Accessed December 27, 2019. http://www.pitt.edu/~dash/type0410.html#basile.

Bowman, Sarah Lynne. 2011. "The Dichotomy of the Great Mother Archetype in Disney Heroines and Villainesses." In *Vader, Voldemort and Other Villains: Essays on Evil in Popular Media*, edited by Jamey Heit, 80–96. Jefferson, NC: McFarland.

Cavendish, Richard. 1968. *The Black Arts: A Concise History of Witchcraft, Demonology, Astrology, and Other Mystical Practices throughout the Ages*. New York: TarcherPerigree.

Darcy, Jen. 2016. *Disney Villains: Delightfully Evil: The Creation, the Inspiration, the Fascination*. New York: Disney Editions.

Davis, Amy M. 2007. *Good Girls and Wicked Witches: Women in Disney's Feature Animation*. East Barnet, UK: John Libbey.

Faludi, Susan. 2007. *The Terror Dream: Myth and Misogyny in an Insecure America*. New York: Picador.

Hutton, Ronald. 2017. *The Witch: A History of Fear, from Ancient Times to the Present*. New Haven, CT: Yale University Press.

Mahnke, Aaron. 2017. *The World of Lore: Monstrous Creatures*. New York: Del Rey.

Russell, Jeffrey B., and Brooks Alexander. 2007. *A History of Witchcraft: Sorcerers, Heretics, & Pagans*. London: Thames & Hudson.

Sivan. 2014. "The Secret History of Maleficent: Murder, Rape, and Woman-Hating in *Sleeping Beauty*." Reviving Herstory. Accessed December 27, 2019. http://www.revivingherstory.com/rhblog/2014/11/3/the-secret-history-of-maleficent-murder-rape-and-woman-hating-in-sleeping-beauty.

Üner, Ayse Melda. 2017. "Intertextual Transformation of a Fairy Tale from Sleeping Beauty to Maleficent." *Journal of Social Sciences Institute* 20, no. 38: 371–382.

Marsellus Wallace

First Appearance:	*Pulp Fiction* (release date: October 14, 1994)
Creators:	Quentin Tarantino
Other Media:	N/A
Primary Strength:	Wealth
Major Weakness:	Obsessive vengeance
Weapons:	Guns
Base of Operations:	Los Angeles, California
Key Allies:	Mia Wallace (wife), Jules Winnfield, Vincent Vega, Winston Wolfe
Key Enemies:	Butch Coolidge (temporarily)
Actual Identity:	N/A
Nicknames/Aliases:	N/A

Pulp Fiction, the second film by Quentin Tarantino, is considered by many to be his ultimate masterpiece. It was nominated for seven Academy Awards, winning only one, for Best Original Screenplay. The story of the film, told out of sequence, centers on two primary arcs: the retrieval of an unnamed but presumably supernatural artifact and the hunt for a professional boxer who refused to win a fight he'd originally agreed to throw. The character connecting both arcs is Marsellus Wallace (played by Ving Rhames), a local crime boss. Shortly after sending henchmen Jules Winnfield (played by Samuel L. Jackson) and Vincent Vega (played by John Travolta) to retrieve the strange artifact, he orders all of his forces to pursue and capture the renegade boxer, Butch Coolidge (played by Bruce Willis). The fact that Wallace is black is a throwback to the blaxploitation films of the 1970s that strongly influenced Tarantino.

As mentioned, the story is told out of sequence. As such, the first audiences see of Wallace is when he is recruiting the aging boxer, Butch, to throw his upcoming fight so that Wallace can benefit from betting on a sure thing. Later, when Butch is on the run from Wallace's men, the two inadvertently meet on the street, resulting in a chase that leads them to a pawnshop, where both are subdued by the shop's owner. The two rivals soon discover that they are about to be raped by the shop owner and his friend, Zed. As Wallace is being brutalized by Zed, Butch breaks free; rather than escape, which he momentarily considers, he rescues Wallace. After forgiving the boxer, Wallace allows Butch to leave while he waits for some of his men to arrive and "go medieval" on his captors (this is the end of Wallace's overall story, though told out of order). Wallace's final appearance is during the film's final sequences, a flashback to before his first appearance, when the crime lord sends a fixer, Winston Wolfe (played by Harvey Keitel), to assist Winnfield and Vega with an unexpected situation concerning a dead body and bloodied vehicle.

Overall, Marsellus Wallace is a standard organized-crime boss. He has an army of henchmen, a trophy wife (played by Uma Thurman), and a fixer all at his command. Outside of fixing boxing matches, the nature of his criminal activity is never made clear. Is he involved in drugs? Gambling? Prostitution? The audience never discovers. The only sign, in fact, that he is a criminal is the violent nature of his associates, combined with his obvious wealth. In the end, however, he is presented as an Al Capone figure of power and danger. His villainy is implied and supported by the tropes surrounding him and the accepted stereotypical beliefs of the audience.

Richard A. Hall

See also: Bill/Snake Charmer, Billy the Kid, Boba Fett, The Corleone Family, Elle Driver/California Mountain Snake, Ernst Stavro Blofeld/SPECTRE, Fish Mooney, Gus Fring, Heisenberg/Walter White, Jabba the Hutt, Negan/The Saviors, O-Ren Ishii/Cottonmouth, Pancho Villa, Ra's al Ghul, Tony Montana, Tony Soprano; *Thematic Essays*: Tarantino and the Antivillain.

Further Reading

Alsford, Mike. 2006. *Heroes & Villains*. Waco, TX: Baylor University Press.

Greene, Richard, and K. Silem Mohammad, eds. 2007. *Quentin Tarantino and Philosophy: How to Philosophize with a Pair of Pliers and a Blowtorch*. Chicago: Open Court.

Kirshner, Jonathan. 2012. *Hollywood's Last Golden Age: Politics, Society, and the Seventies Film in America*. Ithaca, NY: Cornell University Press.

Peary, Gerald, ed. 2013. *Quentin Tarantino: Interviews, Revised and Updated*. Jackson: University of Mississippi Press.

Roche, David. 2018. *Quentin Tarantino: Poetics and Politics of Cinematic Metafiction*. Jackson: University of Mississippi Press.

Shone, Tom. 2017. *Tarantino: A Retrospective*. San Rafael, CA: Insight Editions.

Martin Brenner

First Appearance:	*Stranger Things*, season 1, episode 1 (release date: July 15, 2016)
Creators:	Matt and Ross Duffer
Other Media:	Novels, comics
Primary Strength:	Government resources
Major Weakness:	Cruelty

Weapons:	Various
Base of Operations:	Hawkins, Indiana
Key Allies:	Hawkins National Laboratory, U.S. Department of Energy
Key Enemies:	Jane Hopper/Eleven, Kali Prasad/Eight, the Soviet Union
Actual Identity:	N/A
Nicknames/Aliases:	"Papa"

In 2016, the Duffer brothers launched their nostalgic series, *Stranger Things* (Netflix, 2016–present). The series, set in the mid-1980s, centers on four teenage boys from Indiana: Mike (played by Finn Wolfhard), Dustin (played by Gaten Matarazzo), Lucas (played by Caleb McLaughlin), and Will (played by Noah Schnapp). In the first season, the boys meet a mysterious girl known only as Eleven (played by Millie Bobby Brown), who possesses supernatural telekinetic powers. The girl has escaped from nearby Hawkins Laboratory, where she underwent government experiments conducted by her "Papa," Dr. Martin Brenner (played by Matthew Modine). Aside from his experiments on Eleven and others, Brenner is also researching a strange phenomenon, a portal to another dimension that comes to be known as the Upside Down, which is populated by a malevolent creature intent on breaking through to our world. Set during the waning years of the Cold War, it is soon discovered that the communist superpower, the Soviet Union, is also researching the other dimension.

Kali Prasad/Eight

Kali Prasad, also known as "Eight" or "008," was introduced in the second season of the Netflix series *Stranger Things*. Like the show's protagonist, Eleven, Kali was taken by Hawkins Laboratory and subjected to numerous painful experiments to test the limits of her supernatural powers, which, in her case, cause anyone she chooses to experience hallucinations. When Eleven uses her psychokinetic powers to locate Eight, the teenage girl is living with a group of other homeless teenagers who steal to survive and spend their time seeking out people who have hurt them in the past and killing them.

Kali represents the dark mirror of Eleven. Both girls experienced the same cruelties and violence, but whereas Eleven escaped to find kindness and love through her new group of friends and adults, Kali found only other downtrodden victims. Through Kali, Eleven sees what her life might have been like had she not encountered her friends. Both seek justice for the crimes done to them, but Kali opts to utilize her powers to achieve that justice on her own: sentencing those who hurt her to death, thus showing the difference between justice and vengeance. At present, the rest of Kali's story remains untold. Will she continue down the dark path of vengeance until she becomes the very weapon that she was intended to be? Or will she, through Eleven or others, find a path to redemption and find happiness as her "sister" has done?

Richard A. Hall

Through flashback sequences, audiences discover that Dr. Brenner has been conducting cruel experiments testing the limits of Eleven's powers, with no regard to the young girl herself. In the first season, the boys and their tangential allies seek to protect Eleven from Brenner, while simultaneously attempting to save their friend, Will, from the clutches of the Upside Down and the monstrous Demogorgon. Over the succeeding seasons, the depth of U.S.-Soviet involvement in Hawkins Lab's activities becomes clear. In the episode "The Lost Sister," audiences are introduced to Eight, another young girl tested by Brenner alongside Eleven, who now uses her powers to hunt down and punish lab employees she sees as responsible for her suffering (Justin Doble, "The Lost Sister," *Stranger Things*, season 2, episode 7, October 27, 2017). Although Brenner is believed dead by the end of season one, hints suggest his possible return in future seasons.

Brenner is, at his heart, a typical mad scientist, more concerned with discovery than his subjects (or even his staff and coworkers). With very little screen time, his villainy is seen through the nightmares and flashbacks of the victimized Eleven. He is that malevolent secret government agent who commits his evil in what he views as the overall national interest. Brenner's replacement at Hawkins Lab, Sam Owens (played by Paul Reiser), proves a much more human and humane government agent, showing that Brenner may be the exception rather than the rule within the government. Ultimately, Brenner is a modern-day Frankenstein, intent on creating a monster that he can never truly control.

Richard A. Hall

See also: COBRA, CSM/The Cigarette Smoking Man, Dr. Frank-N-Furter, Ernst Stavro Blofeld/SPECTRE, Frankenstein's Monster, Green Goblin, Hannibal Lecter, Imperial Officers, Lex Luthor, Nurse Ratched; *Thematic Essays*: "Nazis, Communists, and Terrorists . . . Oh My!": The Rise of the Supervillain and the Evolution of the Modern American Villain.

Further Reading

Alsford, Mike. 2006. *Heroes & Villains*. Waco, TX: Baylor University Press.

Costello, Matthew J. 2009. *Secret Identity Crisis: Comic Books & the Unmasking of Cold War America*. New York: Continuum.

Faludi, Susan. 2007. *The Terror Dream: Myth and Misogyny in an Insecure America*. New York: Picador.

Rossinow, Doug. 2015. *The Reagan Era: A History of the 1980s*. New York: Columbia University Press.

Starck, Kathleen, ed. 2010. *Between Fear and Freedom: Cultural Representations of the Cold War*. Newcastle upon Tyne, UK: Cambridge Scholars.

Vogel, Joseph. 2018. *Stranger Things and the '80s: The Complete Retro Guide*. St. London, ON, Canada: Cardinal.

Wetmore, Kevin J., Jr. 2019. *Uncovering Stranger Things: Essays on Eighties Nostalgia, Cynicism and Innocence in the Series*. Jefferson, NC: McFarland.

Willis, Susan. 2005. *Portents of the Real: A Primer for Post-9/11 America*. London: Verso.

The Master/Missy

First Appearance:	*Doctor Who*, original series, season 8, episode 1 (air date: January 2, 1971)
Creators:	Robert Holmes
Other Media:	Novels, comic strips, TV movie, audiodramas
Primary Strength:	Time travel, regeneration, hypnotic abilities, possessions
Major Weakness:	Limited regenerations (in theory)
Weapons:	Tissue compressor eliminator
Base of Operations:	All of time and space
Key Allies:	Cybermen (temporarily)
Key Enemies:	The Doctor
Actual Identity:	Unknown
Nicknames/Aliases:	Professor Yana, Prime Minster Harry Saxon

The Master is a recurring character created for the British science fiction television series *Doctor Who,* a series about a Time Lord known only as the Doctor from the planet Gallifrey, a race that has discovered the secrets of time travel. Gallifreyans had come to an understanding that time travel should be limited and only done in cases of "neutral . . . peaceful observation of developing cultures" (Muir, *A Critical History of "Doctor Who" on Television*, 3). The Doctor does not completely agree with this approach, and taking a time-and-space machine called a TARDIS, he travels through time and space, eventually becoming a guardian of Earth and many other planets in many different universes and defending them against the incursion of threats and monsters. In the telling of the Doctor's stories, different villains were created, some in overarching story lines that have allowed the Doctor to establish longevity and significance in British popular culture. Some of these were the Autons, the Cybermen, the Daleks, the Zygons, the Silence, the Weeping Angels, and the Doctor's archnemesis, the Master.

The Master was created around 1971 by Robert Holmes, as a serious challenge to the Doctor, a twisted reflection, a Moriarty type of villain with "a brilliant, calculating mind . . . but who chose the darker path" (Kistler, *"Doctor Who": Celebrating Fifty Years, a History*, 89). At some point, it was even considered to make the master a woman, as a symbol of opposite reflection, which came to fruition through regenerations in 2014 with the introduction of Missy (Kistler, 88). The Master, who, just like the Doctor, is a Time Lord with no name, became a physical manifestation of the "hero's dark side" (Kistler, 90, 130). This starts with an intimate connection between the hero and the villain from a long time past. The Master and the Doctor are not only from the same planet but also from the same clan, Prydonian, known for cunning and manipulation (Kistler, 90, 131). This means that they grew up in the same place and attended school (the Academy) together, where they became friends (Kistler, 131). It has even been insinuated that they may have even been half brothers (Kistler, 193–194). This intertwined story serves to emphasize their special bond; one could not be without the other.

This can be further understood in their opposing philosophical approaches to their own challenge to the Gallifreyan law against intrusive time travel. The Doctor travels in time and space and gets involved, but always with the intention of helping. The Master seeks to conquer. His catch phrase has been "I am the Master, you will obey me" (Kistler, 90). As a Gallifreyan, the Master has the power to regenerate and the understanding, and in many cases the ability, to time travel; therefore, he has the ability to do evil deeds across space and time. The character was first introduced in the first episode of the "Terror of Autons" story line (Robert Holmes, *Doctor Who*, original series, season 8, episode 1, January 2, 1971), during what should have been his last natural regeneration (Time Lords are only supposed to be able to regenerate a total of twelve times, giving them thirteen lives). However, the origin story of the Master can be found in the episode "Utopia" (Russell T. Davies, *Doctor Who*, modern series, season 3, episode 11, June 16, 2007), where we learn that when the Master looked into the Untempered Schism (a natural tear in the time-and-space continuum) as a child as part of a cultural practice, it caused him to go mad. This establishes the Master as a villain who expresses his madness through any means necessary, and his madness can be recurring because of his regenerative abilities.

The Master has been personified by eight different actors in the TV series. Roger Delgado (from 1971 to 1973) was the first, in many cases referred to as the original. His personification of the Master is his last natural regeneration. Roger Delgado passed away before he could do a final episode. The Master is then brought back in "Deadly Assassin" (Robert Holmes, *Doctor Who,* original series, season 14, episode 9, October 30, 1976), as a decaying body, where the face of the Master is unrecognizable (out of respect for Delgado and Delgado's fans). This Master is personified by Peter Pratt, which establishes that the Master is still alive, and in the episode "The Keeper of Traken" (Johnny Byrne, *Doctor Who*, original series, season 18, episode 21, January 31, 1981), the Master is personified by Geoffrey Beevers. In this story, The Master makes an attempt to regain life through a power in the planet of Traken called the Source. The Doctor stops him, but not before he could transfer himself into the body of Tremas, the Counsel of Traken, personified by Anthony Ainley. This gives the Master an opportunity to prolongate his life, and Ainley personified the Master until the original series was canceled in 1989.

In 1996, an attempt was made to bring back the series with an American TV movie, *Doctor Who* (FOX, May 14, 1996), and the Master was part of the story line. This is the only time that an American was cast as the Master. The story involves a peace treaty between the Time Lords and the Daleks, and the Master is captured and killed by the Daleks. However, once again, before dying, he transfers himself into a snakelike creature, a Deathworm Morphant, which allows him to transfer into Bruce (played by Eric Roberts), who becomes the Master in human form. He then falls into the Eye of Harmony of the eighth Doctor's TARDIS and is imprisoned until he is rescued by the Time Lords in an effort to recruit allies during the Time Wars. It is then that he is given a new set of regenerations.

Running away and using a Chameleon Arch, he disguises himself as a human, Professor Yana. Professor Yana is a character played by legendary British actor Dereck Jacobi in the episode "Utopia" (Russell T. Davies, *Doctor Who*, modern series, season 3, episode 11, June 16, 2007), in which the Master gets reintroduced again, eventually dying and regenerating into actor John Simms, who played the Master from 2007 to 2010 in the return series. This was the very first natural regeneration on TV for the Master. He then conquers Earth by becoming the prime minister of Great Britain, Harold Saxon. The Doctor (in his tenth incarnation) defeats him once more, and as audiences learn later, the Master ends up on a Mondasyan Colony Ship, where he encounters Missy (his own future regeneration).

Missy (played by Michelle Gomez) is, to date, the most recent regeneration of the Master and the first time the character was played by a woman. Audiences first meet her in the episode "Deep Breath" (Steven Moffat, *Doctor Who*, modern series, season 8, episode 1, August 23, 2014), but she is not revealed to be the Master until the season's penultimate episode, "Dark Water" (Moffat, *Doctor Who*, modern series, season 8, episode 11, November 1, 2014). After several interactions with the twelfth Doctor (played by Peter Capaldi) that appear to start the character down a nobler path, Missy meets her end by her own hand, stabbed by Simms's incarnation in the episode "The Doctor Falls" (Moffat, *Doctor Who*, modern series, season 10, episode 12, July 1, 2017), which takes place on the aforementioned Mondasyan Colony Ship, when Missy is on the ship helping the Doctor. This is a common thread that unites the classic *Doctor Who* representation of the Master and the modern impersonations: throughout the characters' history, the Doctor and the Master have to work together in several episodes in order to save the day, or, in the case of the Master, survive to war another day.

With the Doctor and the Master, each is an opposite reflection of the other,. The renegade hero, the Doctor, is the healer, the interventionist for the better outcome with kindness and compassion. He travels in time for exploration and engagement. On the other hand, the renegade villain, the Master, travels in time to conquer, to dominate, and to create chaos, and he does so cruelly and mercilessly, or simply with total disregard for others. The Doctor seems to strive to prove that goodness exists, not acknowledging that through his example, he brings into existence that goodness. The Master acts out of a void of hope, constantly bringing into existence the dark side, his accepted understanding of the meaninglessness of it all. The Master, then, is the formidable and most true reflection of the hero, a true close companion, the villain.

Maria Antonieta Reyes

See also: Alexis Carrington-Colby-Dexter, Angelique Bouchard-Collins, Angelus, Cybermen, Davros/Daleks, Doctor Doom, Ernst Stavro Blofeld/SPECTRE, Green Goblin, Grindelwald, Joker, J. R. Ewing, Lex Luthor, Loki, Lucifer/Satan, Magneto, Professor Moriarty, Red Skull, Zod; *Thematic Essays*: The Dark Mirror: Evil Twins, *The Twilight Zone*, and the Villain Within, The Pathos of Villainy: Getting to the Heart of Why Villains Went Bad.

Further Reading

Alsford, Mike. 2006. *Heroes & Villains*. Waco, TX: Baylor University Press.

Crome, Andrew, and James McGrath, eds. 2013. *Time and Relative Dimensions in Faith: Religion and Doctor Who*. London: Darton, Longman, and Todd.

Kistler, Alan. 2013. *Doctor Who: Celebrating Fifty Years, a History*. Guilford, CT: Lyons.

Lewis, Courtland, and Paula Smithka, eds. 2010. *Doctor Who and Philosophy: Bigger on the Inside*. Chicago: Open Court.

Lewis, Courtland, and Paula Smithka, eds. 2015. *More Doctor Who and Philosophy: Regeneration Time*. Chicago: Open Court.

Muir, John K. 1999. *A Critical History of Doctor Who on Television*. Jefferson, NC: McFarland.

Short, Sue. 2011. *Cult Telefantasy Series: A Critical Analysis of The Prisoner, Twin Peaks, The X-Files, Buffy the Vampire Slayer, Lost, Heroes, Doctor Who, and Star Trek*. Jefferson, NC: McFarland.

Michael Myers

First Appearance:	*Halloween* (release date: October 25, 1978)
Creators:	John Carpenter and Debra Hill
Other Media:	Comic books and novels
Primary Strength:	Apparent immortality
Major Weakness:	Limited intellect
Weapons:	Large kitchen knife (other sharp implements)
Base of Operations:	Haddonfield, Illinois
Key Allies:	N/A
Key Enemies:	Dr. Samuel Loomis, Laurie Strode
Actual Identity:	N/A
Nicknames/Aliases:	N/A

In 1978, John Carpenter's *Halloween* ushered in the modern era of slasher horror films. Although *The Texas Chainsaw Massacre* had hit theaters four years earlier, it is *Halloween* that is most often associated with launching the genre. In the original film, the story begins in 1963, when Michael Myers (then six years old) dressed in a clown costume murders his sister on Halloween night. The story then moves forward fifteen years, and Myers has escaped from the nearby mental institution and is heading back to his hometown. Wearing a featureless white mask with a shock of unkept brown hair, he stalks local teenager Laurie Strode (played by Jamie Lee Curtis), making her, her friends, and the children in her charge his latest targets for carnage. Michael's psychiatrist, Dr. Sam Loomis (played by Donald Pleasence), comes to Haddonfield in pursuit of his patient. As Michael moves to take the killing blow against Laurie, Loomis shoots him, sending the murderer falling from the second-floor window, presumably to his death (or, at the very least, paralysis). As paramedics take Laurie to the hospital, Loomis discovers that Michael's body is missing from the yard, seemingly having stalked off into the night (John Carpenter and Debra Hill, *Halloween*, Compass International, 1978).

The massive popularity of the independent film demanded a sequel, *Halloween II* (1981), which picks up where the original ended. Michael follows Laurie to the hospital, continuing his attempts to kill her. Meanwhile, Loomis discovers that Laurie is actually Michael's younger sister, only a toddler when he committed his original murder. In the sequel, Michael appears to have been killed in an explosion. The third film in the series, *Halloween III: Season of the Witch* (1982) was unrelated to the rest, with no connection to the Michael Myers story. In *Halloween 4: The Return of Michael Myers* (1988), it has been ten years since the original, and the silent, faceless, lumbering murderer continues his path of carnage, this time pursuing the young daughter of Laurie, who, audiences learn, has died since the second film. This story continues in the fifth film, *Halloween 5: The Revenge of Michael Myers* (1989). In the sixth film of the original series, *Halloween: The Curse of Michael Myers* (1995), Dr. Loomis discovers that a cult called the Cult of Thorn has kidnapped and impregnated the young Jamie Strode and is the source of Michael's obsession with killing his family.

In the 1998 film *Halloween H20: 20 Years Later*, the events of parts four through six are ret-conned, and Curtis returns as Laurie, who once more faces Michael after he awakens from a twenty-year coma. In 2007 and 2009, director Rob Zombie reimagined the original two films with remakes of *Halloween* and *Halloween II*, focusing more on the young Michael and the source of his madness. In 2018, David Gordon Green directed the film *Halloween*, a direct sequel to the original film, ret-conning *Halloween II, 4, 5,* and *H20* and the Rob Zombie films, and erasing the story line that Laurie was Michael's sister. In this film, presumably the official bookend to the original, Curtis returns as Laurie, and Myers is once more seemingly killed in the end.

Like other slasher film icons, such as Leatherface, Jason Voorhees, and Freddy Krueger, Michael Myers is the unstoppable killing machine. His continued resurrections, due entirely to the ongoing popularity of the franchise, add to his fearsomeness. He cannot be reasoned with or contained for long. "Killing" him, though only temporary, is the only respite his potential victims can hope for. He is the walking embodiment of death, from which no one can escape for long. Additionally, he speaks to everyone's fear of impending death. As long as audiences fear the inevitable, Michael Myers will doubtlessly continue to live on.

Richard A. Hall

See also: Alpha/The Whisperers, Doomsday, Dracula, Frankenstein's Monster, Freddy Krueger, Hannibal Lecter, Jason Voorhees, Joker, Leatherface, Norman Bates; *Thematic Essays*: "Nazis, Communists, and Terrorists . . . Oh My!": The Rise of the Supervillain and the Evolution of the Modern American Villain.

Further Reading

Alsford, Mike. 2006. *Heroes & Villains.* Waco, TX: Baylor University Press.

Ashby, LeRoy. 2006. *With Amusement for All: A History of American Popular Culture since 1830.* Lexington: University Press of Kentucky.

Hitchcock, Susan Tyler. 2007. *Frankenstein: A Cultural History*. New York: W. W. Norton.

Maddrey, Joseph. 2004. *Nightmares in Red, White, and Blue: The Evolution of the American Horror Film*. Jefferson, NC: McFarland.

Mahnke, Aaron. 2017. *The World of Lore: Monstrous Creatures*. New York: Del Rey.

Murphy, Bernice M. 2013. *The Rural Gothic in American Popular Culture: Backwoods Horror and Terror in the Wilderness*. London: Palgrave Macmillan.

Skal, David J. 2001. *The Monster Show: A Cultural History of Horror*. Rev. ed. New York: Farrar, Straus and Giroux.

Morgan le Fay

First Appearance:	*Vita Merlini* (first published: approximately 1150)
Creators:	Unknown
Other Media:	Comics, novels, movies, stage plays
Primary Strength:	Witchcraft/magic, immortality
Major Weakness:	Obsessive vengeance
Weapons:	Spells, potions
Base of Operations:	Britain
Key Allies:	Sir Mordred (son or nephew in Arthurian legends), Merlin the Magician (briefly)
Key Enemies:	Merlin the Magician, King Arthur, Spider-Woman (in comics), Doctor Strange (in comics)
Actual Identity:	Also spelled "Morgana," "Morganna," "Morgen," "Moryen," and "Morien"
Nicknames/Aliases:	N/A

Morgan le Fay is, perhaps, the oldest witch in Western fiction. She is most commonly known for her appearance in the Arthurian legends of the British Middle Ages. Of these tales, the one that is most established in the overall zeitgeist is Sir Thomas Malory's *Le Morte d'Arthur* in 1485. In 1978, writer Marv Wolfman and artist Carmine Infantino introduced her into the Marvel Comics Universe as a recurring supervillain (*Spider-Woman #2*, May 1978). Her most noteworthy appearance on film was in the 1981 movie *Excalibur*, directed by John Boorman, where the ancient witch was portrayed by Helen Mirren. Over the centuries, her character has remained relatively unchanged, often playing into the stereotype of the woman as seductress, with malevolent intent toward men.

Unlike earlier versions that portray both Morgan and Merlin as equally good and evil, in Malory's text, Morgan is utterly evil and Merlin utterly good. Whereas other texts identify Merlin as Morgan's teacher in the magical arts, in Malory, she learns the black arts while living in a nunnery. In numerous incarnations, Morgan is the half sister of King Arthur, whose father, King Uther Pendragon, utilizes

Merlin's magic to disguise himself as the husband of Queen Igraine (Morgan's mother). In many of those texts, Morgan seduces her brother using the same spell, giving birth to the evil Sir Mordred, although Malory writes Mordred as Morgan's nephew, the son of Morgause, Morgan's sister and Arthur's half sister. In all of these tales, Morgan's hatred of her half brother appears to stem from the toll Uther's subterfuge placed on her parents' otherwise-happy marriage. In the film *Excalibur*, based primarily on Malory's text, Merlin escapes Morgan's slumber spell to trick the witch into releasing the magic that has kept her young and beautiful, and her "son," Morgan, kills her out of fright.

For most of the last thousand years, Morgan le Fay has been the base source for the Western idea of a witch. All modern incarnations of witches, from *Dark Shadows*' Angelique to Bellatrix Lestrange from the *Harry Potter* series, are derived from this medieval sketch. From the fictional prose of Malory to the real-world accusations of Salem, Morgan has remained the embodiment of the term "witch." She speaks to both the stereotypes of the seductive power of women and the more empowering image of a strong and independent woman. As long as witches remain a popular trope in Western fiction, the image of Morgan le Fay will live on, underscoring the character's immortality.

Richard A. Hall

See also: Angelique Bouchard-Collins, Bellatrix Lestrange, Dark Willow, Fiona Goode/The Supreme, Fish Mooney, Grindelwald, Maleficent, Nurse Ratched, Sith Lords, Tia Dalma/Calypso, Ursula, Voldemort, Wicked Witch of the West; *Thematic Essays*: Tarantino and the Antivillain, The Pathos of Villainy: Getting to the Heart of Why Villains Went Bad.

Further Reading

Alsford, Mike. 2006. *Heroes & Villains.* Waco, TX: Baylor University Press.

Cavendish, Richard. 1968. *The Black Arts: A Concise History of Witchcraft, Demonology, Astrology, and Other Mystical Practices throughout the Ages.* New York: TarcherPerigree.

Cutrara, Daniel S. 2014. *Wicked Cinema: Sex & Religion on Screen.* Austin: University of Texas Press.

Gloyn, Liz. 2019. *Tracking Classical Monsters in Popular Culture.* London: Bloomsbury Academic.

Hutton, Ronald. 2017. *The Witch: A History of Fear, from Ancient Times to the Present.* New Haven, CT: Yale University Press.

Russell, Jeffrey B., and Brooks Alexander. 2007. *A History of Witchcraft: Sorcerers, Heretics, & Pagans.* London: Thames & Hudson.

Ryan, Hannah. 2020. "Vilifications: Conjuring Witches Then and Now." In *The Supervillain Reader*, edited by Rob Weiner and Rob Peaslee, 156–171. Jackson: University of Mississippi Press.

N

Negan/The Saviors

First Appearance:	**Negan:** *The Walking Dead #100* (cover date: July 2012) **The Saviors:** *The Walking Dead* #97 (cover date: May 2012)
Creators:	Robert Kirkman and Charlie Adlard
Other Media:	Television series, novels
Primary Strength:	**Negan:** Cunning, brutality, inspiring loyalty **The Saviors:** Numbers
Major Weakness:	Blinded by Ideology
Weapons:	**Negan:** Lucille (a barbed-wire-covered baseball bat) **The Saviors:** Guns
Base of Operations:	The Sanctuary, rural Virginia
Key Allies:	**Negan:** Eventually: Carl Grimes, The Communities of Alexandria, The Kingdom, and The Hilltop, Judith Grimes (television only)
Key Enemies:	Rick Grimes, Carl Grimes, Daryl Dixon (television only), Michonne, King Ezekiel, Maggie Rhee, Jesus, Father Gabriel, Rosita, Eugene (all members of the above-mentioned communities)
Actual Identity:	N/A
Nicknames/Aliases:	N/A

The Walking Dead is a comic book created by Robert Kirkman and Tony Moore in 2003, published through Image Comics. The story centers on the survivors of a zombie apocalypse, led by a Kentucky sheriff's deputy, Rick Grimes. Through the struggles of the survivors, Rick and his group also encounter other human survivors who are, more often than not, greater threats than the undead. In 2010, the cable television network AMC launched a series based on the comic, shifting Grimes's origins to Georgia and adding a new character, the redneck tracker Daryl Dixon. Of the many human threats encountered both in the comics and television series, one of the most formidable foes to overcome was the band of thugs known as "the Saviors" and their sadistic leader, Negan.

In both the comics and television series, Rick Grimes and the Alexandria community are introduced to an enigmatic character who goes by "Jesus," due to his physical similarity to Jesus of Nazareth. Jesus introduces Rick and his survivors to a fellow community, the Hilltop, who provide de facto slave labor for a gang known as the Saviors. The Saviors offer protection from the undead in exchange for goods and services (not unlike 1920s Chicago gangs). Rick and his crew agree to rid the Hilltop of these bullies, declaring, in essence, a war against the gang. As it turns out, the Saviors are far larger in numbers than Rick was led to believe, and he and his some of his group are captured and taken to the gang's sadistic leader, Negan. Before the zombie apocalypse, Negan was a high school coach, married to a kind, loving woman. The nightmare of this new world leads Negan to follow a philosophy that only the strong survive and that the weak must be "saved." His good intentions, as he sees them, are soon twisted into a megalomaniacal pseudo-dictatorship, controlled by the brutality of his beloved barbed-wire-covered baseball bat named Lucille, after his dead wife.

In his first appearance, Negan is forced to show Rick who is in fact in charge in this new world. As punishment for killing some of his men, Negan brutally beats Rick's close friend Glenn Rhee to death with Lucille (on the television series, he kills Abraham for the murders and soon after kills Glenn for Daryl's failure to obey Negan's established rule of silence during this first meeting). At first, Rick is shocked into submission, but the hero soon finds himself, declaring all-out war on Negan and the Saviors. Once defeated, Negan is spared death; instead, Rick imprisons him for years so that the mad leader can see how Rick's more peaceful methods work better than Negan's harsh rule. Over his years of imprisonment, Negan befriends Rick's son, Carl, and eventually evolves to a more antiheroic figure. Later, when Rick and the communities are faced with the even-deadlier threat of the Whisperers and their brutal leader, Alpha, Negan is released, as Rick is forced to accept that Alpha's brutality can only be met with someone of equally relentless violence. In the comic book, Negan disappears after the Whisperer War story arc, returning only in cameo in the comics' final issue.

On the television series, Negan is portrayed with slithery glee by Jefferey Dean Morgan. The overall story of the show changes dramatically from the comic after the events of "All Out War," as Carl dies from a zombie bite during the war and Rick disappears for years shortly after defeating Negan. It falls, therefore, to Rick's adopted daughter, Judith, to achieve an emotional connection to Negan and to bring out the villain's deeper heart. At the time of this writing, the Whisperer War story line is only beginning on the television series, and it remains unknown how the Negan character will be utilized on the series moving beyond that, especially as the comics' main heroes of Rick and Carl are no longer part of the television series. Although more of an antihero following "All Out War" in both incarnations of the franchise, because of Negan's own tendencies toward—and even enjoyment of—brutal violence, the character can never be truly heroic in the traditional sense of the word.

At their core, Negan and the Saviors are the ultimate representation of street gang ideology. They use their strength and numbers to frighten the weak into doing their bidding and providing them the essentials of survival. This relationship is underscored by promises of the most brutal of physical violence. Negan kills to teach a lesson. That, alone, is villainous. The fact that he simultaneously enjoys the violence and thrives on the fear he evokes. During the Whisperer War, only Negan's brutality can match the threat of the Whisperers' leader, Alpha, suggesting that fire can only be defeated by fire, violence for violence. Negan is a classic representation of power corrupting and the ease with which the kindest of people can be driven to be the darkest of monsters.

Richard A. Hall

See also: Alpha/The Whisperers, Bill/Snake Charmer, Borg Queen/Borg, Fish Mooney, The Governor, Kahless/Klingons, Number Six/Cylons, Reverend Stryker/The Purifiers; *Thematic Essays*: The Pathos of Villainy: Getting to the Heart of Why Villains Went Bad.

Further Reading

Alsford, Mike. 2006. *Heroes & Villains.* Waco, TX: Baylor University Press.

Keetley, Dawn. 2014. *We're All Infected: Essays on AMC's The Walking Dead and the Fate of the Human.* Contributions to Zombie Studies. Jefferson, NC: McFarland.

Kirkman, Robert. 2018. *The Quotable Negan: Warped Witticisms and Obscene Observations from The Walking Dead's Most Iconic Villain.* New York: Skybound.

Langley, Travis, ed. 2015. *The Walking Dead Psychology: Psych of the Living Dead.* Popular Culture Psychology. New York: Sterling.

Yuen, Wayne, ed. 2012. *The Walking Dead and Philosophy: Zombie Apocalypse Now.* Popular Culture and Philosophy. Chicago: Open Court.

Yuen, Wayne, ed. 2016. *The Ultimate Walking Dead and Philosophy: Hungry for More.* Popular Culture and Philosophy. Chicago: Open Court.

Norman Bates

First Appearance:	*Psycho* (publication date: April 10, 1959)
Creators:	Robert Bloch
Other Media:	Films
Primary Strength:	Deception
Major Weakness:	Obsessive compulsion
Weapons:	Large kitchen knife
Base of Operations:	Bates Motel
Key Allies:	"Mother" (an alternate personality of Bates's dead mother)
Key Enemies:	"Mother" (the same alternate personality)
Actual Identity:	N/A
Nicknames/Aliases:	N/A

In 1960, Alfred Hitchcock, perhaps the greatest thriller director in Hollywood history, released his masterpiece, *Psycho,* based on the 1959 novel of the same name. The center of the story is the young, humble motel clerk, Norman Bates, who lives alone with his mother in their home overseeing the family business. Bates's mother is a harsh, verbally abusive woman who relentlessly belittles her meek son, a taxidermist by hobby. In recent years, the Bates Motel has fallen on hard times, as the new interstate highway system has diverted traffic from the once-busy back-road highway, a fate of numerous such businesses due to the real-world interstate system. One evening, a beautiful young woman named Mary Crane arrives at the out-of-the-way motel, seeking a night's rest, as she is on the run, having just stolen a large sum of money from her employer.

After overhearing an argument between Bates and his mother, Mary suggests to the kind young man that he should have his mother committed to an institution. She later hears "Mother" vowing to kill her and retires to her room. Later that evening, a shadowy old woman appears in Mary's bathroom and kills the young woman in the shower. Horrified at what his mother has done, Norman hides the body and the young woman's car in a lake behind the motel. Meanwhile, Mary's sister, Lila, hires a private detective to find her, who, after interrogating Norman, also meets an untimely demise from the old woman. Lila and Mary's boyfriend, Sam, then go to investigate themselves. The two discover that Mrs. Bates was long dead and that young Norman had suffered a breakdown as a result of his mother dying by suicide after murdering her boyfriend. Lila and Sam soon discover that Norman is, in fact, the murderer; that he suffers from a personality disorder, speaking to his mother's stuffed corpse and responding to himself in her voice; and that Norman dresses as his mother to commit his crimes. Norman is placed in an institution, where his "Mother" persona completely takes over his mind.

Robert Bloch continued Norman Bates's story in succeeding novels. In *Psycho II* (1982), Bates escapes treatment and ultimately dies, his identity stolen by a copycat killer. In *Psycho House* (1990), the Bates Motel has been turned into a sideshow attraction, with "Norman" merely a robotic attraction. Finally, in the prequel novel, *Psycho: Sanitarium* (2016), Norman's long-lost—and even more insane—twin brother is revealed. The novels, however, did not catch on in the overall American zeitgeist to the degree that the film franchise did. Today, *Psycho* is much more synonymous with Hitchcock and actor Anthony Perkins, who brought Norman Bates to chilling life in the original film and its successive sequels.

In the film *Psycho II* (1983), a cured Norman Bates returns to the Bates Motel, where he soon meets his real mother, who gave him up at birth. After killing and mummifying this new mother, Bates returns to his murderous ways. In *Psycho III* (1986), set soon after events of the previous film, Norman falls in love, only to have "Mother" kill the woman. A reporter uncovers the fact that Mrs. Spool (Norman's new mother), was, in fact, his aunt, who was in love with Norman's father and killed him when he chose her sister over her. Believing him to be hers, she kidnapped infant Norman, only to be caught and institutionalized; therefore, this story reestablishes Norman's original mother as his true one. Norman destroys the new mother's corpse and is reinstitutionalized. In the final film of the series, *Psycho IV: The Beginning* (1990), the previous two films are ret-conned, erasing their stories from canon. Now released after thirty years, Bates is married with a child on the way. Convinced that his insanity is hereditary, he considers killing the unborn child but, instead, burns down the Bates Motel, presumably living happily ever after.

The television series *Bates Motel* (A&E, 2013–2017) acts as a prequel to the original novel and film, examining the brutal upbringing of Norman Bates (now played by Freddie Highmore) by his abusive mother (played by Vera Farmiga) and setting the stage for his murderous adult life. In the overall realm of villainy in American pop culture, Norman Bates is a more sympathetic character. Driven insane by an abusive mother, Bates is a deeply deranged serial killer. His pain and trauma are manifested through violence, but as Norman is, by nature, a kind soul, he can only manifest this violence through the alternate personality of "Mother." This aspect of the character differentiates him from other fictional serial killers such as Michael Myers, Leatherface, or Jason Voorhees, and it places him in a more realistic light, making him more similar to real-world psychotic serial killers such as Jeffrey Dahmer and Son of Sam. Bates does, however, speak to that inner fear that many have as they question their own sanity and the depths they may fall to were they to give in to their darker natures.

Richard A. Hall

See also: Doomsday, Dracula, Freddy Krueger, Hannibal Lecter, Jason Voorhees, Joker, Leatherface, Michael Myers; *Thematic Essays*: The Pathos of Villainy: Getting to the Heart of Why Villains Went Bad.

Further Reading

Alsford, Mike. 2006. *Heroes & Villains*. Waco, TX: Baylor University Press.

Ashby, LeRoy. 2006. *With Amusement for All: A History of American Popular Culture since 1830*. Lexington: University Press of Kentucky.

Deutelbaum, Marshall, and Leland Poague. 2009. *A Hitchcock Reader*. 2nd ed. Hoboken, NJ: Wiley-Blackwell.

Maddrey, Joseph. 2004. *Nightmares in Red, White, and Blue: The Evolution of the American Horror Film*. Jefferson, NC: McFarland.

Murphy, Bernice M. 2013. *The Rural Gothic in American Popular Culture: Backwoods Horror and Terror in the Wilderness*. London: Palgrave Macmillan.

Skal, David J. 2001. *The Monster Show: A Cultural History of Horror*. Rev. ed. New York: Farrar, Straus and Giroux.

Spoto, Donald. 1991. *The Art of Alfred Hitchcock: Fifty Years of His Motion Pictures*. Norwell, MA: Anchor.

Number Six/Cylons

First Appearance:	**Number Six:** *Battlestar Galactica*, miniseries, part 1 (air date: December 8, 2003) **Cylons:** *Battlestar Galactica*, original series, season 1, episode 1 (air date: September 17, 1978)
Creators:	**Number Six:** Ronald D. Moore and Glen A. Larson **Cylons:** Glen A. Larson

Other Media:	Comics, novels
Primary Strength:	Computer interface, hive mind, numbers, resurrection (later models)
Major Weakness:	Obsession with humanity
Weapons:	Lasers, star fighters, starships
Base of Operations:	Interstellar space
Key Allies:	Gaius Baltar
Key Enemies:	Commander Adama, Captain Apollo, Lieutenant Starbuck
Actual Identity:	N/A
Nicknames/Aliases:	"Chrome Domes" (original models), "Skin Jobs" (later models), "Toasters"

In the immediate wake of the overnight global success of *Star Wars*, movie and television studios scrambled for the next big sci-fi franchise. Producer Glen A. Larson approached ABC with his idea: *Battlestar Galactica* (ABC, 1978–1979; a final, second season, retitled *Galactica 1980*, aired from January to May 1980). The basic premise was that life on Earth originated somewhere else, far across the stars, and that humanity as we know it is actually the lost thirteenth colony of humanity. As such, humanity's true ancestors were the other twelve colonies, located far, far away. Those colonies were at war with the robotic Cylon race. After a brutal attack that decimated the human colonies, the remnants of that

Gaius Baltar

In the original series of *Battlestar Galactica* in the late 1970s, Count Baltar (played by John Colicos) is a member of the ruling Council of Twelve, the leadership of the Twelve Colonies of humanity. Baltar, however, secretly negotiates with the villainous Cylon imperious leader to lull the council into a false sense of security as the Cylons unleash their attacks on the colonies. Throughout the original run, Baltar remains with the Cylons, acting as a counselor on human strategies and ways of thinking.

In the 2003 series reboot, Dr. Gaius Baltar (played by James Callis) is a genius narcissist, responsible for designing the vast computer network of defenses that the Twelve Colonies rely on as protection against possible Cylon attack. When he begins a romantic relationship with the beautiful Caprica, secretly a mechanical Cylon known as Number Six, he gives the mysterious woman access to those defenses, allowing for the Cylons to decimate the human populations and destroy the Twelve Colonies and making Baltar a traitor. For the remainder of the series, Baltar lives nervously among the human survivors. He is eventually appointed vice president, and through a corrupt election, he is elected to the presidency, where he negotiates a "peace" with the Cylons that, in essence, enslaves the human race. Before the series' end, Baltar is placed on trial for his treason but is found not guilty when he is presented as acting out of fear rather than malice. On April 22, 2013, *TV Guide* listed him as television's thirteenth "nastiest" villain ("TV Guide Picks TV's 60 Nastiest Villains," *TV Guide*). He stands as an example of how fear of reprisal or embarrassment can lead even the most benign of individuals down a path of treachery and villainy.

Richard A. Hall

society collected on ragtag spacecraft, protected by the sole remaining battlestar, the *Galactica*, commanded by Commander Adama (originally played by Lorne Greene). Adama and the *Galactica* set out to find their long-lost relatives on the mythical Earth in hopes of gaining their assistance against the Cylon threat. However, on reaching Earth in the year 1980, Adama discovers that humanity here is centuries behind them technologically and that they had inadvertently brought a dangerous threat to Earth's doorstep.

Unfortunately, the high costs of producing a *Star Wars*–level program for television outweighed the series' considerable success and popularity, and it was cancelled after only one and a half seasons. The enduring popularity of the franchise, however, led Ronald D. Moore, successful for his iconic series *Star Trek: Deep Space Nine*, to approach the Sci-Fi Channel to greenlight a twenty-first century reboot, beginning with a two-part miniseries airing in December 2003. The overnight commercial and critical success of the miniseries guaranteed that the reboot would be picked up for a series run (Sci-Fi, 2004–2009). Much remains the same in the reboot. The Twelve Colonies experienced a long war with the robotic Cylons but eventually negotiated a peace. After forty years, the Cylons returned, evolved from their original robot form to a more humanlike appearance, allowing them to easily blend into human society unnoticed. Once successfully embedded, they attack again, decimating the human populations as in the original series; the *Galactica* and Commander Adama (this time played by Edward James Olmos) lead the remnants of humanity on a quest for Earth.

In the original series, Cylons were, in fact, a reptilian race who built the robotic Centurions to fight humanity on their behalf. This was a direct reflection of the Cold War, with mindless automatons (communists) set to destroy the freedom and liberties of humanity (the United States). In the reboot, Cylons were actually robots built by the humans of the Twelve Colonies as servants, just as humans on Earth do today. When the Cylons evolved a sense of self, they learned to comprehend their existence as a form of slavery and revolted against their human masters. Their final strike against humanity is only successful due to the new humanlike models that embed as "terrorists" within the colonies, maintaining drones that are unaware that they are

Tricia Helfer played the "Number Six" model of the artificial lifeforms, the Cylons, in the 2003 remake of the sci-fi series *Battlestar Galactica*. (Sci-Fi Channel/AF Archive/Alamy Stock Photo)

Cylons, waiting to be awakened when the moment is right, making the reboot much more relevant to a post-9/11 world). Most Cylons remain as purely metallic robots, but the ruling class are the "Skin Jobs," who are humanlike in appearance. One other upgrade is the fact that although there are only twelve humanlike models, once they are destroyed, their consciousness is immediately uploaded to a new, identical body.

Of the humanlike Cylons in the reboot, the central character is Number Six (played by Tricia Helfer), also known as Caprica or Caprica Six. Six develops a romantic relationship with the human scientist Gaius Baltar, who was central to creating the defense network for the Twelve Colonies. Although Six and Baltar appear to die in a nuclear explosion during the Cylon invasion, Six downloads to a new body elsewhere, and Baltar somehow survives and joins the ragtag team of humans fleeing to Earth. Throughout the series, however, Baltar continues to see Six, maintaining a traitorous relationship with this subconscious connection. Eventually, the sleeper Cylons are awakened, including human fleet first officer Colonel Tye (played by Michael Hogan). These sleepers, however, maintain a loyalty to their long-lived human natures rather than become weapons for the Cylons. Another key difference to the rebooted models is that whereas the Twelve Colonies worship a pantheon of gods similar to the ancient human civilizations of Earth, Cylons worship the "one true God." As such, they see humanity's religious beliefs as heresy and an abomination.

What allows the *Galactica* to survive the overwhelming Cylon attack is that, at Commander Adama's orders, the ship's computers are not networked, as all other ships and computers in the Twelve Colonies had become. Even aboard the ship itself, computers are not interconnected, and intership communications are done by standard telephone. As such, whereas all of the colonies' defenses were subject to a computer-based attack, the *Galactica* remained protected. This speaks to the growing danger in 2003—and even more so in the time since—of relying too heavily on interconnected computer systems to operate every basic function of society. However, just as with all such *Frankenstein*-esque cautionary tales, society has ignored the warning, and American society is now susceptible to such an attack literally every minute of every day.

The Cylons originated as manifestations of the American fear of communism during the Cold War, but their return in a post–Cold War world required a reimagining, shaping them more as religious zealots and terrorists. They represent an awe-inspiring threat to the basic freedoms and liberties that we all too often take for granted. Their original, frightening robotic forms, in massive numbers, become even more terrifying when they evolve to pass as one of us. They are the threat that lives around every corner, appearing to be on our side while conspiring to eliminate all that our society holds dear. They are the embodiment of what Americans fear in a post-9/11 world. Even as fears of international fundamentalist religious terror have abated in the decades since 9/11, Americans today still see Cylon threats: Democrats versus Republicans and liberals versus conservatives. Any threat to the status quo, any perceived enemy that threatens life as one group knows it, can be seen in the Cylons.

Richard A. Hall

See also: Agent Smith, Alpha/The Whisperers, Borg Queen/Borg, Captain Phasma/Stormtroopers, Davros/Daleks, Frankenstein's Monster, Kahless/Klingons, Negan/The Saviors, Nurse Ratched, Reverend Stryker/The Purifiers, Ultron; *Thematic Essays*: "Nazis, Communists, and Terrorists . . . Oh My!": The Rise of the Supervillain and the Evolution of the Modern American Villain, The Dark Mirror: Evil Twins, *The Twilight Zone*, and the Villain Within, The Pathos of Villainy: Getting to the Heart of Why Villains Went Bad.

Further Reading

Alsford, Mike. 2006. *Heroes & Villains*. Waco, TX: Baylor University Press.

Ashby, LeRoy. 2006. *With Amusement for All: A History of American Popular Culture since 1830*. Lexington: University Press of Kentucky.

Castleman, Harry, and Walter J. Podrazik. 2016. *Watching TV: Eight Decades of American Television*. 3rd ed. Syracuse, NY: Syracuse University Press.

Faludi, Susan. 2007. *The Terror Dream: Myth and Misogyny in an Insecure America*. New York: Picador.

Gross, Edward, and Mark A. Altman. 2018. *So Say We All: The Complete, Uncensored, Unauthorized Oral History of Battlestar Galactica*. New York: Tor.

Handley, Rich, and Lou Tambone, eds. 2018. *Somewhere beyond the Heavens: Exploring Battlestar Galactica*. Edwardsville, IL: Sequart Research and Literacy Organization.

Starck, Kathleen, ed. 2010. *Between Fear and Freedom: Cultural Representations of the Cold War*. Newcastle upon Tyne, UK: Cambridge Scholars.

Willis, Susan. 2005. *Portents of the Real: A Primer for Post-9/11 America*. London: Verso.

Nurse Ratched

First Appearance:	*One Flew over the Cuckoo's Nest* (publication date: February 1, 1962)
Creators:	Ken Kesey
Other Media:	Film
Primary Strength:	Authority
Major Weakness:	Lack of compassion
Weapons:	Medication (to dispense)
Base of Operations:	Salem State Hospital, Oregon
Key Allies:	Hospital staff
Key Enemies:	Randle McMurphy, "Chief" Bromden
Actual Identity:	Unknown
Nicknames/Aliases:	N/A

One Flew over the Cuckoo's Nest is an iconic twentieth-century novel that focuses on the darker side of the psychiatric care profession. Told from the perspective of the "Chief," a patient at a state hospital in Salem, Oregon, the story centers on Chief's observations and eventual friendship with fellow inmate

Randle McMurphy, a Korean War veteran and prisoner of war, who has been convicted of battery and statutory rape. McMurphy decides to "dodge" hard time—albeit short—by having himself declared insane and sentenced to the asylum. McMurphy soon becomes confrontational with the ward's head nurse, Nurse Ratched, who seeks stability by keeping the inmates medicated and punishing them with electroshock therapy when the medication fails to achieve her desired goals. When McMurphy goes so far as to physically attack Ratched, the nurse has him scheduled for a lobotomy, making him, in essence, a mental vegetable. This final act inspires the Chief to escape the hospital. The novel was adapted into a Broadway and off-Broadway play before finally becoming a feature film in 1975, directed by Milos Forman. In the film, Ratched was played with a legendary performance by actress Louise Fletcher.

Nurse Ratched represents the cold, detached method to psychiatric treatment that was more common until very recently. She foregoes actual therapy in exchange for stability and quiet among the inmates. As the primary authority on the ward, she also represents the very essence of absolute power corrupting absolutely. In all incarnations of the story, there are no redeeming qualities to Nurse Ratched, although, to be fair, there is no representation of her outside of her role on the ward. In the overall realm of American villainy, Nurse Ratched represents an example of a human being with no evident humanity. She dishes out punishment and reward at her own whim. Further, she represents the very antithesis to the care, dedication, and personal sacrifice that society most associates with professional nursing. She is the demanding boss, the overbearing parent, and the unmerciful God that most people fear and desperately attempt to avoid.

Richard A. Hall

See also: Alexis Carrington-Colby-Dexter, Alpha/The Whisperers, Angelique Bouchard-Collins, Asajj Ventress, Bellatrix Lestrange, Borg Queen/Borg, Captain Phasma/Stormtroopers, Catwoman, Cersei Lannister, The Court of Owls, Dark Willow, Elle Driver/California Mountain Snake, Faith the Vampire Slayer, Fiona Goode/The Supreme, Fish Mooney, Hannibal Lecter, Harley Quinn, Imperial Officers, La Llorona, Maleficent, Martin Brenner, The Master/Missy, Morgan le Fay, Number Six/Cylons, O-Ren Ishii/Cottonmouth, Poison Ivy, Reverend Stryker/The Purifiers, Sherry Palmer, Sue Sylvester, Tia Dalma/Calypso, Ursula, Wicked Witch of the West; *Thematic Essays*: "Nazis, Communists, and Terrorists . . . Oh My!": The Rise of the Supervillain and the Evolution of the Modern American Villain, The Dark Mirror: Evil Twins, *The Twilight Zone*, and the Villain Within, The Pathos of Villainy: Getting to the Heart of Why Villains Went Bad.

Further Reading

Alsford, Mike. 2006. *Heroes & Villains*. Waco, TX: Baylor University Press.

Ashby, LeRoy. 2006. *With Amusement for All: A History of American Popular Culture since 1830*. Lexington: University Press of Kentucky.

Douglas, Susan J. 1995. *Where the Girls Are: Growing Up Female with the Mass Media*. New York: Three Rivers.

Kirshner, Jonathan. 2012. *Hollywood's Last Golden Age: Politics, Society, and the Seventies Film in America*. Ithaca, NY: Cornell University Press.

O-Ren Ishii/Cottonmouth

First Appearance:	*Kill Bill, Vol. 1* (release date: October 10, 2003)
Creators:	Quentin Tarantino
Other Media:	N/A
Primary Strength:	Cunning, martial arts, expert swordsman
Major Weakness:	Blind hatred of Beatrix Kiddo
Weapons:	Samurai swords, guns
Base of Operations:	Various
Key Allies:	Deadly Viper Assassination Squad: Bill/Snake Charmer, Budd/Sidewinder, Elle Driver/California Mountain Snake, Vernita Green/Copperhead; Crazy 88, Gogo Yubari
Key Enemies:	Beatrix Kiddo/Black Mamba/The Bride
Actual Identity:	O-Ren Ishii
Nicknames/Aliases:	Cottonmouth

Kill Bill (volumes one and two) is the ultimate cinematic revenge epic by writer and director Quentin Tarantino. Released in two parts in 2003 and 2004, the film stars Uma Thurman as the enigmatic Bride, bent on revenge against the gang that placed her in a coma after trying to kill her on her wedding day and presumably killing her unborn child in the process. As she moves one by one through the colorful and dangerous members of the Deadly Viper Assassination Squad, audiences learn numerous things about the mysterious Bride: she was once a member of the Deadly Vipers, known as "Black Mamba"; she was once romantically involved with the Viper leader, Bill ("Snake Charmer"); and her child was saved and currently lives with her father, Bill. Of the members of the Deadly Vipers, perhaps the most formidable with regard to swordsmanship is O-Ren Ishii ("Cottonmouth"), played by Lucy Liu.

In *Kill Bill, Vol. 1* (2003), audiences learn the life story of O-Ren through animated flashback scenes, narrated by the film's heroine, the Bride. O-Ren is half-Chinese, half-Japanese American and witnesses the brutal murders of her parents at a very young age, as she hides under the bed in the room where they are slaughtered. She then works as a child prostitute, where she eventually gets revenge on the crime boss who ordered her parents' murders. She makes inroads into Japanese organized crime as an assassin, eventually coming to Bill's attention and

Mandarin

The Mandarin was one of the original supervillains of the Marvel Age of superhero comic books. Created by Stan Lee (1922–2018) and Don Heck (1929–1995), he first appeared in *Tales of Suspense #50* (February 1964), as an antagonist to the superhero Iron Man and remained Iron Man's primary nemesis for several decades. A half-Chinese, half-English descendent of Genghis Khan, he seeks to destroy Western civilization by turning their own technologies against them, primarily using a mixture of science and mysticism revolving around "ten rings" of power. In the film *Iron Man 3* (2013), Mandarin's Chinese heritage was written out of the character, making him, instead an Osama bin Laden–style international terrorist (played by Ben Kingsley, b. 1943). Ultimately, this incarnation was exposed as a fraud, a deception to move Iron Man's attention from the true threat.

In an extra feature on the DVD/Blu Ray of the film *Thor: The Dark World* (2013), Kingsley's imprisoned Mandarin discovers that the *true* Mandarin was unhappy with his fraudulent impersonation, suggesting a future appearance of the real Mandarin, which did not happen in the *Iron Man* franchise. Currently, the character is set to appear in the martial arts Marvel Cinematic Universe film *Shang-Chi and the Legend of the Ten Rings* (2021). The primary reason that the character disappeared from the comics is that, by the 1990s, it became clear that the character was a racist, stereotypical caricature of Chinese villains, dating back to the 1920s. Even in the more politically correct twenty-first century, portrayals of characters of East Asian origin easily fall prey to long-held stereotypes, even when the goal is inclusion.

Richard A. Hall

becoming part of the Deadly Viper Assassination Squad. She is part of the raid on Beatrix Kiddo's wedding, where she assists in killing the entire wedding party, including the minister, his wife, the piano player, the groom, and presumably the Bride and her unborn child.

After leaving Bill's employ, O-Ren returns to Japan, using her cunning and deadly skills to work her way to the top of the Japanese Yakuza, the organized-crime racket. With the assistance of her army of samurai (the Crazy 88), and her sadistic right hand, Gogo Yubari, she rules the Japanese underworld with an iron fist, making fast example of any who would question or criticize her gender or half-Chinese heritage as a disqualifying factor for rule, as lower crime lord Boss Tanaka learns when O-Ren relieves him of his head. She ultimately meets her fate at the hands of the Bride after the revenge-driven heroine kills her way through the Crazy 88 and Gogo.

In the realm of American villainy, O-Ren Ishii is a fascinating example. She is both proud of and insecure about her mixed heritage. She is an example of a child who suffers unimaginable trauma and is then driven by that trauma to become the darkest version of herself. Her considerable fighting and assassination skills are the result of years of dedicated training. Combined with her own considerable cunning and intellect, she is one of the most dangerous foes in the Tarantino universe of characters, which, though a bold statement, holds up under scrutiny. In overall fiction, O-Ren is a direct dark mirror of the Chinese legend/Disney animated heroine Mulan.

Richard A. Hall

See also: Alexis Carrington-Colby-Dexter, Bill/Snake Charmer, Billy the Kid, Boba Fett, The Corleone Family, Elle Driver/California Mountain Snake, Ernst Stavro Blofeld/SPECTRE, Fish Mooney, Gus Fring, Heisenberg/Walter White, Jabba the Hutt, Marsellus Wallace, Negan/The Saviors, Nurse Ratched, Pancho Villa, Ra's al Ghul, Tony Montana, Tony Soprano; *Thematic Essays*: The Dark Mirror: Evil Twins, *The Twilight Zone*, and the Villain Within, Tarantino and the Antivillain.

Further Reading

Alsford, Mike. 2006. *Heroes & Villains.* Waco, TX: Baylor University Press.

Greene, Richard, and K. Silem Mohammad, eds. 2007. *Quentin Tarantino and Philosophy: How to Philosophize with a Pair of Pliers and a Blowtorch.* Chicago: Open Court.

Kirshner, Jonathan. 2012. *Hollywood's Last Golden Age: Politics, Society, and the Seventies Film in America.* Ithaca, NY: Cornell University Press.

Peary, Gerald, ed. 2013. *Quentin Tarantino: Interviews, Revised and Updated.* Jackson: University of Mississippi Press.

Roche, David. 2018. *Quentin Tarantino: Poetics and Politics of Cinematic Metafiction.* Jackson: University of Mississippi Press.

Shone, Tom. 2017. *Tarantino: A Retrospective.* San Rafael, CA: Insight Editions.

Ozymandias

First Appearance:	*Watchmen #1* (cover date: September, 1986)
Creators:	Alan Moore and Dave Gibbons
Other Media:	Motion comics, live-action film, HBO live-action series
Primary Strength:	Massive intelligence, considerable wealth, enhanced strength and speed
Major Weakness:	Megalomania
Weapons:	Bionic right hand, disintegration machine
Base of Operations:	Antarctica
Key Allies:	The Watchmen (originally), Doctor Manhattan, Bubastis
Key Enemies:	Rorschach (I), Nite Owl (II), Silk Spectre (II), The Comedian
Actual Identity:	Adrian Veidt
Nicknames/Aliases:	"The World's Smartest Man"

In 1986, writer Alan Moore and artist Dave Gibbons produced the groundbreaking comic book miniseries/graphic novel *Watchmen.* In this twelve-issue series, Moore examined the issue of how, if superheroes existed in the real world, they would prove to be extremely flawed and possibly psychologically disturbed individuals. In the alternate reality of *Watchmen*, set in 1985, U.S. president Richard Nixon has not only successfully avoided the Watergate scandal that destroyed his presidency in real life but has also managed to remain president long after the two-term limit. The United States and the Soviet Union are on the verge of a nuclear war, and costume vigilantes (superheroes) have been outlawed in the United States. The de facto leader of the former superhero team Watchmen (or the Crimebusters, as they were briefly called in the comic), Ozymandias ultimately proves to be the villain of *Watchmen*, with an overall scheme to slaughter millions of New Yorkers with a fake alien attack in order to create world peace when the world's two major nuclear powers, the United States and Soviet Union, come together after the tragedy to unite against this unknown (and utterly imaginary) threat.

Adrian Veidt was born a child of wealth, inspired from a young age by ancient conquerors: Macedonia's Alexander the Great and Egypt's Ramses II. On reaching adulthood, Veidt takes on the superhero mantle Ozymandias, the Greek name for Ramses. Aside from his unparalleled wealth and considerable physical prowess, Veidt is also the most brilliant mind on the planet. Once superheroes are outlawed, Veidt focuses on his fortune, even cashing in on the merchandising rights of his former teammates, and secretly utilizes his vast resources toward a master plan to bring peace to the world.

When the mercenary and vigilante known as the Comedian discovers Veidt's plan, the former team leader murders him. This murder is where the story of *Watchmen* begins. The vigilante Rorschach becomes obsessed with the case, following the trail from Comedian's murder to that of former villain Moloch and eventually to Veidt. When Rorschach, Nite Owl, and Silk Spectre confront Veidt, he points out that the slaughter of millions of New Yorkers is necessary to save billions from the nightmare of nuclear war. Nite Owl, Silk Spectre, and even the godlike Doctor Manhattan agree to keep his secret, but Rorschach, dedicated to absolute truth, refuses. This leads Doctor Manhattan to murder Rorschach for the greater good.

In 2009, director Zach Snyder brought the classic comic book to life in the live-action film *Watchmen*, where Veidt was portrayed by actor Matthew Goode. In 2017, DC Comics decided to merge the world of *Watchmen* with their overall superhero universe in the series *Doomsday Clock* (Geoff Johns and Gary Frank, 2017–2020). Set in the early 1990s in the *Watchmen* universe, Rorschach's journal has become public knowledge, exposing Veidt as a criminal and leading him to escape into the regular DC Comics universe. In 2019, HBO launched a live action series, *Watchmen*, as a sequel to the original comic book, with no connection to the *Doomsday Clock* story line. In the series, Veidt is portrayed by actor Jeremy Irons.

Ozymandias/Adrian Veidt is the classic mad scientist. He sees his machinations of mass murder—as well as the individual murders necessary to cover it up—as for the greater good of humankind. It is difficult to argue the case when treating it as a simple math equation of killing millions to save billions; however, the ethical conundrum of the taking of innocent life for any reason foregoes the math in the realm of heroism and villainy. He is a megalomaniacal madman whose hubris has overshadowed his once-heroic nature. In the end, Ozymandias, like the ancient conquerors who inspired him, succumbs to believing in his own legend.

Richard A. Hall

See also: Alexis Carrington-Colby-Dexter, Brainiac, The Comedian, The Court of Owls, Doctor Doom, Dr. Frank-N-Furter, Ernst Stavro Blofeld/SPECTRE, Fish Mooney, Green Goblin, Grindelwald, J. R. Ewing, Lex Luthor, Martin Brenner, Professor Moriarty, Thanos; *Thematic Essays*: "Nazis, Communists, and Terrorists . . . Oh My!": The Rise of the Supervillain and the Evolution of the Modern American Villain, The Pathos of Villainy: Getting to the Heart of Why Villains Went Bad.

Further Reading

Alsford, Mike. 2006. *Heroes & Villains.* Waco, TX: Baylor University Press.

Ashby, LeRoy. 2006. *With Amusement for All: A History of American Popular Culture since 1830.* Lexington: University Press of Kentucky.

Faludi, Susan. 2007. *The Terror Dream: Myth and Misogyny in an Insecure America.* New York: Picador.

Hillerbrand, Rafaela, and Anders Sandburg. 2009. "Who Trusts the Watchmen." In *Supervillains and Philosophy: Sometimes, Evil Is Its Own Reward,* edited by Ben Dyer, 103–112. Chicago: Open Court.

Rossinow, Doug. 2015. *The Reagan Era: A History of the 1980s.* New York: Columbia University Press.

Tucker, Reed. 2017. *Slugfest: Inside the Epic 50-Year Battle between Marvel and DC.* New York: Da Capo.

White, Mark D., ed. 2009. *Watchmen and Philosophy: A Rorschach Test.* The Blackwell Philosophy and Pop Culture Series, edited by William Irwin. Hoboken, NJ: Wiley.

Wright, Bradford W. 2003. *Comic Book Nation: The Transformation of Youth Culture in America.* Baltimore, MD: Johns Hopkins University Press.

P

Pancho Villa

First Appearance:	Born: La Coyotada, Mexico, 1878
Creators:	Parents: Agustin Arango and Micaela Arambula
Other Media:	Novels, movies, radio, television, stage plays, songs
Primary Strength:	Cunning, tenacity
Major Weakness:	Ego
Weapons:	Six-shooters, rifles
Base of Operations:	Northern Mexico, State of Chihuahua
Key Allies:	Francisco Madero, El Devision del Norte, Pascual Orozco (briefly), Emiliano Zapata, Venustiano Carranza (briefly), U.S. general John "Black Jack" Pershing (originally)
Key Enemies:	Victoriano Huerta, Alvaro Orozco, U.S. president Woodrow Wilson, General John "Black Jack" Pershing (eventually), Venustiano Carranza (eventually), Pascual Orozco (eventually)
Actual Identity:	José Doroteo Arango Arambula
Nicknames/Aliases:	Francisco "Pancho" Villa, "La Cucaracha" ("The Cockroach")

Much of the early life of the legendary outlaw Pancho Villa is shrouded in mystery. With little in the way of documented records and conflicting stories from Villa himself, an accurate portrayal of his childhood is difficult. He was the oldest of five children and took on several jobs to help his mother and siblings after his father's death. A long-held legend is that he murdered the son of the landlord on whose hacienda his family lived when he discovered that the son had raped his sister. This act (among others) allegedly led to him go on the run and change his name to Francisco Villa. In 1910, the Mexican Revolution began, and Villa joined the forces of the prodemocracy Francisco Madero. After numerous victories by Madero forces, most led by Villa, the ailing Mexican president Porfirio Diaz resigned, and Madero was elected president in 1911.

At first remaining loyal to Madero, Villa grew disenchanted with the new president and his military leader, General Victoriano Huerta. Huerta had Villa arrested in 1912 and sentenced to death, but a plea to Madero resulted in the sentence being reduced to imprisonment. Villa escaped in 1913 and fled to the United States just across the border. He returned a few months later after the assassination of Madero in order to avenge his former leader's death by taking on the new president, Huerta. Teaming his northern armies with the southern forces of Emiliano Zapata, the Mexican Revolution continued, and Villa was painted in the American press as a revolutionary hero. Scores of Americans would visit the border with binoculars and telescopes in hopes of seeing Villa in action across the river.

By 1913, Villa had been named governor of the Mexican state of Chihuahua, and the U.S. Army under General John "Black Jack" Pershing began studying Villa's military tactics for training. Even President Woodrow Wilson hailed Villa as a modern-day Robin Hood. Villa became the source for the first feature-length motion picture in 1914, when the American film company Mutual Films cut a deal to film Villa in battle. Villa received 50 percent of the profits from the film, which contained fictionalized biographical scenes, with actor Raoul Walsh playing the younger Villa. The final scene of the film proposed a possible future where Villa, playing himself, became president of Mexico (Frank E. Woods, *The Life of General Villa*, 1914).

The hero turned outlaw in 1916, when Villa, now opposing the new Mexican president Venustiano Carranza, led his men in a raid across the U.S. border to gain supplies. On Villa's orders, a team of approximately one hundred Villistas crossed into the small town of Columbus, New Mexico, on March 9, 1916. Twenty Americans, including ten soldiers and one pregnant woman, were killed in the raid. Villa's villainy was exacerbated by newspaper magnate William Randolph Hearst, who had lost millions to Villa in raids against Hearst properties in Mexico. From this point on, Americans viewed Pancho Villa as a murderous outlaw, prompting President Wilson to order General Pershing to lead eleven thousand men into Mexico to find the bandit. After ten months in country, however, U.S. forces never found him.

Mexican outlaw-turned-revolutionary-turned-outlaw Pancho Villa gained international notoriety throughout the 1910s. (Library of Congress)

Villa claimed to have married seventy-five women in his life, fathering enough sons, he claimed, to send one to each American university. He was finally assassinated in an ambush in the town of Parral in 1923. In 1972, actor Telly Savalas played the legendary outlaw in a fictional film, *Pancho Villa*. The story of Pancho Villa—and, most notably, his contribution to the movie filmed during his lifetime—was best portrayed in the HBO movie *And Starring Pancho Villa as Himself* (2003), where the revolutionary and outlaw was portrayed by Antonio Banderas.

Nearly a century after his death, Pancho Villa is still commonly thought of as a villain and murderous outlaw on both sides of the border. Whether he is a hero or villain or something in between, one thing is certain: Pancho Villa was a brutal soldier and leader, quick to kill and pillage the properties of his enemies, most of whom were as "bad" as the outlaw himself. Over the last century, his image has become the stereotype for Mexicans in the United States, complete with sombrero, bandoliers, and large moustache. To those who study him closely, however, Pancho Villa is a symbol of strength and tenacity against oppression, with a for-the-greater-good mentality toward ethics and morality.

Richard A. Hall

See also: Asajj Ventress, Bill/Snake Charmer, Billy the Kid, Boba Fett, Captain Hector Barbossa, Elle Driver/California Mountain Snake, General Custer, Geronimo, Negan/The Saviors, O-Ren Ishii/Cottonmouth, Tony Montana, Tony Soprano; *Thematic Essays*: "In the Beginning . . .": The Origins of Villains in the Western World, Tarantino and the Anti-villain, The Pathos of Villainy: Getting to the Heart of Why Villains Went Bad.

Further Reading

Alsford, Mike. 2006. *Heroes & Villains.* Waco, TX: Baylor University Press.

Ashby, LeRoy. 2006. *With Amusement for All: A History of American Popular Culture since 1830.* Lexington: University Press of Kentucky.

Behnken, Brian D., and Gregory D. Smithers. 2015. *Racism in American Popular Media: From Aunt Jemima to the Frito Bandito.* Westport, CT: Praeger.

Gavaler, Chris. 2015. *On the Origin of Superheroes: From the Big Bang to Action Comics No. 1.* Iowa City: University of Iowa.

Guzman, Martin Luis. 1938. *Memorias de Pancho Villa.* Mexico City: Mexico: Botas.

Lozano, Gustavo Vasquez, and Charles Rivers, eds. 2016. *Pancho Villa: The Life and Legacy of the Famous Mexican Revolutionary.* Scotts Valley, CA: CreateSpace.

Welsome, Eileen. 2006. *The General and the Jaguar: Pershing's Hunt for Pancho Villa: A True Story of Revolution & Revenge.* Boston: Little, Brown and Company.

Penguin

First Appearance:	*Detective Comics #58* (cover date: December, 1941)
Creators:	Bill Finger and Bob Kane
Other Media:	Animated and live-action television series, movies
Primary Strength:	Cunning, tenacity
Major Weakness:	Hubris
Weapons:	Trick umbrellas (in most incarnations)
Base of Operations:	Gotham City
Key Allies:	Riddler (occasionally), Catwoman (occasionally)

Key Enemies:	Batman, Robin, Batgirl, Police Commissioner James Gordon, Fish Mooney (on *Gotham*)
Actual Identity:	Oswald Chesterfield Cobblepot
Nicknames/Aliases:	"The King of Gotham"

The *Batman* franchise is, perhaps, second only to *Superman* in regard to it impact on popular culture. Created by writer Bill Finger and artist Bob Kane, Batman is billionaire playboy Bruce Wayne, who, after witnessing a mugger murder his parents when he was a young boy, vowed to dedicate his life battling crime in his hometown of Gotham City. In order to strike fear in criminals, Wayne chose to disguise himself as a bat, and "the Batman" (originally "Bat-Man") was born (Bill Finger and Bob Kane, *Detective Comics #33*, November 1939). Unlike his counterpart, Superman, Batman is a mere mortal, with no "super" powers of any kind. Instead, Batman is armed only with his keen intellect and a myriad of gadgets and vehicles that he uses in his fight against crime. Over the decades, in comics as well as on television and film, Batman has gained arguably the most impressive rogues' gallery of villains in all of popular culture. One of his most tenacious villains is the Penguin. Often portrayed as a more comedic villain in comics, the television series *Gotham* (FOX, 2014–2019) presented a deeper and much more malevolent incarnation than ever before.

The Penguin, originally, was one of the more sympathetic villains in the *Batman* rogues' gallery. Bullied as a child for his squat, chubby physicality and bird-like nose, Oswald Cobblepot developed a love of birds at an early age. He was forced to always carry an umbrella, as his father had died from pneumonia contracted when he did not carry one on a particularly rainy day. As a villain, the Penguin often chased bird-themed works of art. His firm belief that he belonged among the upper classes of Gotham City was manifest in his always wearing tuxedo, top hat, and monocle; the tuxedo only added to his physical resemblance to a penguin. In the 1960s live-action series *Batman* (ABC, 1966–1969), actor Burgess Meredith brought the birdlike nature of Penguin to life, adding a squawking laughter and waddling gait to the character. This live-action version also made considerable use of the concept of the trick umbrella made famous in the comics. A much-darker incarnation was portrayed by actor Danny Devito in the feature film *Batman Returns* (Warner Brothers, 1991). In this incarnation, Cobblepot, having been raised in a circus after his upper-class parents discarded him by throwing him into the freezing river as an infant, seeks revenge of Gotham's elite by stealing their firstborn sons.

Perhaps the best portrayal of the character, however, came in the live-action television series *Gotham*, where Oswald Cobblepot/Penguin was portrayed by Robin Lord Taylor. In this incarnation, Oswald works as an umbrella boy for Gotham mobster Fish Mooney. Through a long chain of deceptions, Oswald works his way through the various crime families of Gotham, establishing himself to take over as king of Gotham and, even, eventually, mayor. His on-again, off-again partnership and one-sided romance with fellow rogue Edward Nygma/Riddler brought some of the more comedic story lines of the series. As the series was established as a prequel to the *Batman* franchise, covering the years between the murders of Bruce Wayne's parents and his rise as Batman, the series concluded with the Penguin as comics fans remembered him: overweight, tuxedoed, monocled, and armed with an umbrella.

Lord Taylor's Penguin was a murderous megalomaniac intent on ruling Gotham City. This version is consistent with the character's portrayal in comics in the twenty-first century. In modern times on television and in comics, the Penguin stands as a traditional local crime boss. He keeps his finger on the pulse of the Gotham underworld. Less comedic and more menacing, the Penguin has emerged as one of the more serious threats to law and order in Gotham City.

Richard A. Hall

See also: Catwoman, The Corleone Family, The Court of Owls, Ernst Stavro Blofeld/SPECTRE, Fish Mooney, Goldfinger, Green Goblin, Gus Fring, Harley Quinn, Joker, Lex Luthor, Poison Ivy, Ra's al Ghul, Red Skull, Scarecrow, Tony Soprano, Two-Face; *Thematic Essays*: "Nazis, Communists, and Terrorists . . . Oh My!": The Rise of the Supervillain and the Evolution of the Modern American Villain, The Dark Mirror: Evil Twins, *The Twilight Zone*, and the Villain Within, The Pathos of Villainy: Getting to the Heart of Why Villains Went Bad.

Further Reading

Alsford, Mike. 2006. *Heroes & Villains.* Waco, TX: Baylor University Press.

Ashby, LeRoy. 2006. *With Amusement for All: A History of American Popular Culture since 1830.* Lexington: University Press of Kentucky.

Beard, Jim, ed. 2010. *Gotham City 14 Miles: 14 Essays on Why the 1960s Batman TV Series Matters.* Edwardsville, IL: Sequart Research & Literacy Organization.

Faludi, Susan. 2007. *The Terror Dream: Myth and Misogyny in an Insecure America.* New York: Picador.

Langley, Travis. 2012. *Batman and Psychology: A Dark and Stormy Knight.* New York: John Wiley & Sons.

O'Neil, Dennis, ed. 2008. *Batman Unauthorized: Vigilantes, Jokers, and Heroes in Gotham City.* Smart Pop Series. Dallas, TX: BenBella.

Weldon, Glen. 2016. *The Caped Crusade: Batman and the Rise of Nerd Culture.* New York: Simon & Schuster.

Wright, Bradford W. 2003. *Comic Book Nation: The Transformation of Youth Culture in America.* Baltimore, MD: Johns Hopkins University Press.

Poison Ivy

First Appearance: *Batman #181* (cover date: June, 1966)
Creators: Robert Kanigher and Sheldon Moldoff
Other Media: Animated and live-action television series, movies
Primary Strength: Seduction
Major Weakness: Blinded by ideology
Weapons: Plant-based toxins

Base of Operations:	Gotham City
Key Allies:	Harley Quinn, Birds of Prey, Gotham City Sirens
Key Enemies:	Batman, Robin, Batgirl, Police Commissioner James Gordon
Actual Identity:	Lillian Rose (originally), Pamela Isley, Penelope Ivy
Nicknames/Aliases:	Paula Irvin

The *Batman* franchise is, perhaps, second only to *Superman* in regard to its impact on popular culture. Created by writer Bill Finger and artist Bob Kane, Batman is billionaire playboy Bruce Wayne, who, after witnessing a mugger murder his parents when he was a young boy, vowed to dedicate his life battling crime in his hometown of Gotham City. In order to strike fear in criminals, Wayne chose to disguise himself as a bat, and "the Batman" (originally "Bat-Man") was born (Bill Finger and Bob Kane, *Detective Comics #33*, November 1939). Unlike his counterpart, Superman, Batman is a mere mortal, with no "super" powers of any kind. Instead, Batman is armed only with his keen intellect and a myriad of gadgets and vehicles that he uses in his fight against crime. Over the decades, in comics as well as on television and film, Batman has gained arguably the most impressive rogues' gallery of villains in all of popular culture. Over the decades, a particularly dangerous foe has been the plant-obsessed seductress, Poison Ivy.

Originally, Poison Ivy was Dr. Lillian Rose, who was poisoned by her partner with ancient Egyptian herbs to prevent her from being a witness to his criminal activities. Rather than die, however, Rose gained an immunity to all plant-based toxins. In the post-*Crisis* continuity of DC Comics (since 1986), Ivy has been Dr. Pamela Isley, who was poisoned by her professor while a grad student during his experiments on plant toxins. Again, rather than being killed, she emerges with an immunity to plant toxins as well as a psychic link with plants. In most representations, Poison Ivy is insane (frequently a resident of Arkham Asylum), obsessed with the idea that all animal-based life—and particularly humans—are the toxic danger to the planet, and she seeks to replace humanity with an entirely plant-populated planet. In recent decades, her frequent associations with Harley Quinn and the Gotham City Sirens suggest that it is not *humanity* that she despises and sees as a danger, but *men*. Men are, in fact, her most common targets, as she utilizes seduction to get men to do her will, even—often—Batman. Additionally, her relationship with fellow-criminal Harley Quinn has had strong lesbian overtones.

Ivy was a recurring villain on *Batman: The Animated Series* (FOX-Kids, 1992–1995; Kids' WB, 1997–1999) and *The Batman* (Kids' WB, 2004–2008). In the 1997 feature film *Batman & Robin*, Ivy was played by Uma Thurman. This version of the character is very similar to the post-*Crisis* story line, except that she is working for Wayne Enterprises in South America, and her scientist mentor poisons her when she discovers his experiments into creating the Venom serum to create mindless super soldiers. The film, however, is often derided as the absolute worst *Batman* project in the character's history.

In the live-action television series *Gotham* (FOX, 2014–2019), Ivy goes through a considerable transformation during Bruce Wayne's formative years. Beginning

Uma Thurman became the first actress to portray a live-action version of the comic book villainess Poison Ivy in the much-derided 1997 film *Batman & Robin*. (Warner Bros. Pictures/AF Archive/Alamy Stock Photo)

as a poor child of an abusive criminal father, whom she sees murdered by the Gotham City Police Department, who loves plants because they ask for nothing in return, Ivy Pepper (as she is known in this continuity) was originally played by Clare Foley. She is exposed to an aging compound when thrown into a sewer, and she emerges as the early twentysomething actress Maggie Geha. Toward the end of the series, Ivy ages once more, this time to the thirtysomething actress Peyton List. The last two adult versions begin to experiment on her mind-control toxins and her art of seduction, and Poison Ivy is born.

At her core, Poison Ivy is the *Batman* universe's idea of a witch. Working with potions and toxins, she holds all the characteristics of the classic witch character. There are also biblical overtones to the character. As she turns her hideouts into de facto gardens and as the importance of seduction and temptation is written into the character, Poison Ivy has a strong connection to Eve, the original temptress in the Garden of Eden who leads man to sin after the serpent has tempted her to do so. Since the 1960s, Poison Ivy has stood as an example of a powerful woman who makes men her slaves in her quest to rid the world of the harm they do.

Richard A. Hall

See also: Alexis Carrington-Colby-Dexter, Angelique Bouchard-Collins, Asajj Ventress, Bellatrix Lestrange, Catwoman, Dark Willow, Elle Driver/California Mountain Snake, Fiona Goode/The Supreme, Fish Mooney, Grindelwald, Harley Quinn, Joker, Loki, Morgan le Fay, O-Ren Ishii/Cottonmouth, Penguin, Ra's al Ghul, Scarecrow, Tia Dalma/Calypso, Two-Face, Ursula, Voldemort, Wicked Witch of the West; *Thematic Essays*: The Pathos of Villainy: Getting to the Heart of Why Villains Went Bad.

Further Reading

Alsford, Mike. 2006. *Heroes & Villains*. Waco, TX: Baylor University Press.

Barba, Shelley E., and Joy M. Perrin, eds. 2017. *The Ascendance of Harley Quinn: Essays on DC's Enigmatic Villain*. Jefferson, NC: McFarland.

Cavendish, Richard. 1968. *The Black Arts: A Concise History of Witchcraft, Demonology, Astrology, and Other Mystical Practices throughout the Ages*. New York: TarcherPerigree.

Faludi, Susan. 2007. *The Terror Dream: Myth and Misogyny in an Insecure America*. New York: Picador.

Hutton, Ronald. 2017. *The Witch: A History of Fear, from Ancient Times to the Present*. New Haven, CT: Yale University Press.

Langley, Travis. 2012. *Batman and Psychology: A Dark and Stormy Knight*. New York: John Wiley & Sons.

O'Neil, Dennis, ed. 2008. *Batman Unauthorized: Vigilantes, Jokers, and Heroes in Gotham City*. Smart Pop Series. Dallas, TX: BenBella.

Russell, Jeffrey B., and Brooks Alexander. 2007. *A History of Witchcraft: Sorcerers, Heretics, & Pagans*. London: Thames & Hudson.

Ryan, Hannah. 2020. "Vilifications: Conjuring Witches Then and Now." In *The Supervillain Reader*, edited by Robert M. Peaslee and Robert G. Weiner, 156–171. Jackson: University of Mississippi Press.

Weldon, Glen. 2016. *The Caped Crusade: Batman and the Rise of Nerd Culture*. New York: Simon & Schuster.

Wright, Bradford W. 2003. *Comic Book Nation: The Transformation of Youth Culture in America*. Baltimore, MD: Johns Hopkins University Press.

Professor Moriarty

First Appearance:	"The Adventure of the Final Problem," *Strand Magazine* (publication date: December 1893)
Creators:	Sir Arthur Conan Doyle
Other Media:	Movies, television series, novels
Primary Strength:	Cunning, brilliant intellect
Major Weakness:	Hubris
Weapons:	Considerable wealth/resources
Base of Operations:	Europe
Key Allies:	Irene Adler (in some incarnations)
Key Enemies:	Sherlock Holmes, Dr. John Watson, Inspector Lestrade, Scotland Yard
Actual Identity:	James Moriarty
Nicknames/Aliases:	"The Napoleon of Crime"

In 1887, Sir Arthur Conan Doyle introduced readers to Sherlock Holmes, "the World's Greatest Detective," and his companion and scribe, Dr. John Watson, in the short story "A Study in Scarlet," published in *The Strand* magazine in London, England. For the next six years, Conan Doyle's *Holmes* adventures captivated the imaginations of a growing audience around the world. Many even began to blur the lines between fiction and fact, believing Holmes's adventures to be real. At the height of the Jack the Ripper murders of 1888, Scotland Yard was flooded with letters from concerned Londoners wondering why the police had not yet brought Holmes in on the case. By 1893, Conan Doyle had tired of his detective and decided to send him off in a blaze of glory. To do so in a satisfactory way for audiences, the author needed an antagonist who was equal to Holmes in every way, providing a mystery that could never be surpassed and a means of ending his detective in a manner fit for fiction's greatest hero. The result was the story "The Adventure of the Final Problem," which introduced Holmes's ultimate archnemesis, "the Napoleon of Crime," Professor James Moriarty.

In this last *Holmes* tale, the great detective has spent months tracking the organization of Professor Moriarty, a man whose criminal brilliance equals Holmes's deductive skills. Holmes and Watson track the mad genius to Switzerland, where Watson is deceived into returning to England, leaving Holmes alone. When Watson returns, he tracks Holmes to Reichenbach Falls, where the evidence suggests that Holmes and Moriarty had engaged in a physical struggle, both men apparently falling to their deaths. Aware of his fate, Holmes has written a final farewell to Watson—and the audience—and the tales of Sherlock Holmes came to an abrupt end. In 1915, Conan Doyle returned to his most famous creation with the short story "The Valley of Fear." This story, set prior to "The Final Problem," provides more insight into Moriarty, establishing him as the dangerous international criminal in a much more fleshed-out manner than the original story.

Though long-held as Sherlock Holmes's greatest nemesis, Professor Moriarty did not appear in the Holmes stories until the original run's last entry, 1893's *The Final Problem*. (*The Strand Magazine*, December 1893)

Holmes and Moriarty have reencountered each other in every medium of popular culture in the century since their first meeting. The most popular recent incarnation has been the television series *Sherlock* (BBC, 2010–2017). Starring Benedict Cumberbatch as a modern-day reimagining of the World's Greatest Detective, the series has remained remarkably in line with Conan Doyle's original tales. In this series, Moriarty is portrayed with villainous insanity by Andrew Scott. The New Year's Day special episode "The Abominable Bride" (BBC, January 1, 2016), set in the original setting of 1893, was filmed as a period piece and functioned as a dream sequence set between seasons three and four, where Sherlock dreams of the fatal final confrontation with Moriarty over the waterfall before waking up for the modern-day story line's continuation with the new season.

Moriarty admires Holmes as much as—and perhaps even more than—he despises him. Fully aware that if anyone can stop him, it is Holmes, Moriarty thrives on the thrill of setting up the clues and watching Holmes at work, intricately learning more about his adversary through means of his own devising. In the century since Conan Doyle's last Holmes-Moriarty tale, Moriarty has come to be synonymous with any such dark mirror adversary to an exemplary hero. Moriarty is Holmes had Holmes chosen a life of crime rather than crime fighting. The two reflect and complement each other, each making the other a richer, fuller character and requiring each to be at the top of their game in order to defeat the other. Moriarty is Ra's al Ghul to Holmes's Batman. He is Lex Luthor to Holmes's Superman. Perhaps the best connection in British fiction can be found in the science fiction classic *Doctor Who*: Moriarty is the Master to Holmes's the Doctor. Whenever people look in the mirror and can see the darker side of their nature, they have found their inner Moriarty.

Richard A. Hall

See also: The Court of Owls, CSM/The Cigarette Smoking Man, Doctor Doom, Ernst Stavro Blofeld/SPECTRE, Green Goblin, Grindelwald, Hannibal Lecter, J. R. Ewing, Lex Luthor, Loki, The Master/Missy, Ozymandias, Ra's al Ghul, Red Skull, Zod; *Thematic Essays*: "In the Beginning . . .": The Origins of Villains in the Western World, The Dark Mirror: Evil Twins, *The Twilight Zone*, and the Villain Within.

Further Reading

Alsford, Mike. 2006. *Heroes & Villains.* Waco, TX: Baylor University Press.

Ashby, LeRoy. 2006. *With Amusement for All: A History of American Popular Culture since 1830.* Lexington: University Press of Kentucky.

Knight, Stephen. 2016. *Toward Sherlock Holmes: A Thematic History of Crime Fiction in the 19th Century World.* Jefferson, NC: McFarland.

Porter, Lynnette. 2012. *Sherlock Holmes for the 21st Century: Essays on New Adaptations.* Jefferson, NC: McFarland.

Weldon, Glen. 2016. *The Caped Crusade: Batman and the Rise of Nerd Culture.* New York: Simon & Schuster.

Q

First Appearance:	*Star Trek: The Next Generation*, season 1, episode 1 (air date: September 28, 1987)
Creators:	Gene Roddenberry and D. C. Fontana
Other Media:	Novels, comics
Primary Strength:	Omnipotence
Major Weakness:	Hubris
Weapons:	N/A
Base of Operations:	The Q Continuum
Key Allies:	Other members of the Q Continuum, Captain Jean-Luc Picard (occasionally), Captain Kathryn Janeway (briefly)
Key Enemies:	N/A
Actual Identity:	N/A
Nicknames/Aliases:	N/A

Star Trek is a popular science fiction franchise originally developed for television by Gene Roddenberry in 1966. It was originally set in the twenty-third century, when humanity has long been exploring deep space and Earth is a member of the United Federation of Planets. The original series has spawned an animated series, five sequel and prequel live-action series, and thirteen feature films to date. The original series debuted on NBC on September 8, 1966, and focused on the adventures of Captain James T. Kirk and the crew of the *USS Enterprise*. The first live-action spin-off series, set a century after the original, was *Star Trek: The Next Generation*, which debuted in syndication on September 28, 1987. The series, dubbed *TNG* by fans, focuses on the adventures of Captain Jean-Luc Picard and the crew of the *USS Enterprise-D* (making it the fifth Federation starship to bear the name). The first threat faced by Captain Picard and his crew was the troublesome but dangerous godlike being known only as Q.

In the pilot episode of *Star Trek: The Next Generation*, the brand-new *U.S.S. Enterprise-D* and its captain, Jean-Luc Picard (played by Patrick Stewart), are stopped on their way to Farpoint Station by a powerful godlike being who identifies himself as Q, played by John de Lancie. This being accuses all humanity of being an inferior, childlike race, and he demands that they cease their trek through the stars. Picard replies that he and his crew represent the best of humanity and that they are happy to prove their worthiness through their actions. Q agrees, suggesting that their current destination will be trial enough to determine their guilt or innocence. On reaching Farpoint, Picard and his crew discover that the amazing natural power source for the station actually comes from an alien creature that the inhabitants of Farpoint have trapped and forced to provide them with endless energy. When the station is attacked by the creature's mate, Picard deduces the source of the alien's anger and releases the trapped creature to return to the stars. Picard's humanity impresses Q, who allows them to continue on their missions "for now" (Gene Roddenberry and D. C. Fontana, "Encounter at Farpoint," *Star Trek: The Next Generation*, season 1, episode 1, September 28, 1987).

Q returns to irritate the crew of the *Enterprise* on numerous occasions, becoming more an impish nuisance than godlike judge. In the second season, Q returns and suggests that humanity, even Picard and his crew, are unprepared for the many dangers that exist in the galaxy. When Picard declares that they are ready for anything, Q, with a snap of his fingers, flings the *Enterprise* to the Delta Quadrant of the galaxy, decades from home, at top speed. There, the crew encounters the alien species the Borg, cybernetic life-forms bent on "assimilating" the "biological and technological distinctiveness" of every species into their collective. The Borg prove too much for Picard and his crew, and they are only saved by Q returning them to their own quadrant of space. However, the encounter makes the Borg aware of humanity, and Picard realizes that now the Borg will be coming to find them (Maurice Hurley, "Q Who," *Star Trek: The Next Generation*, season 2, episode 16, May 8, 1989).

The massive popularity of the character and actor led to Q's appearance on the two sequel series. He makes one appearance on *Star Trek: Deep Space Nine* but finds the series protagonist, Commander Benjamin Sisko (played by Avery Brooks), to be less willing to play along than Picard had been, and he does not return. He becomes more fascinated by Captain Kathryn Janeway (played by Kate Mulgrew), commander of the *U.S.S. Voyager*, trapped in the Delta Quadrant, seventy-five light-years from home. In the second season of *Star Trek: Voyager*, Janeway and her crew run across another member of the Continuum, referred to as Q2. This Q, however, has grown tired of immortality and desires to end his existence. Q arrives to prevent this, claiming that doing so would throw the entire Continuum into chaos. Janeway represents Q2 in a mock trial for his right to die and wins the argument. Q2, then, is made human and commits suicide. Moved by Janeway's arguments, Q agrees to take up Q2's cause of rebellion against the Continuum (Shawn and Michael Piller, "Death Wish," *Star Trek: Voyager*, season 2, episode 18, February 19, 1996).

This story is continued in the following season's episode "The Q and the Grey," (Shawn Piller and Kenneth Biller, *Star Trek: Voyager*, season 3, episode 11, November 27, 1996) where the Continuum plays out their civil war. His final appearance in any visual medium of *Star Trek* was the season seven *Voyager* episode "Q2" (Kenneth Biller and Robert J. Doherty, episode 18, April 11, 2001), where Q introduces Janeway to her godson, his new "son," Q Junior. The character of Q evolves over the span of fourteen years of appearances on *Star Trek*. He begins as a Zeus-like god, passing judgment on what he sees as a lesser species, but rather quickly he transforms into a more Loki-like impish devil, testing humanity's values and ethics, often surprised by the results. He represents the corruption of absolute power and the dangers of unfettered ego.

Richard A. Hall

See also: Borg Queen/Borg, Grand Nagus/Ferengi, Kahless/Klingons, Loki, Lucifer/Satan; *Thematic Essays*: "In the Beginning . . .": The Origins of Villains in the Western World, "Nazis, Communists, and Terrorists . . . Oh My!": The Rise of the Supervillain and the Evolution of the Modern American Villain.

Further Reading

Alsford, Mike. 2006. *Heroes & Villains.* Waco, TX: Baylor University Press.

Ashby, LeRoy. 2006. *With Amusement for All: A History of American Popular Culture since 1830.* Lexington: University Press of Kentucky.

Castleman, Harry, and Walter J. Podrazik. 2016. *Watching TV: Eight Decades of American Television.* 3rd ed. Syracuse, NY: Syracuse University Press.

Gross, Edward, and Mark A. Altman. 2016. *The Fifty-Year Mission, the Next 25 Years: The Complete, Uncensored, Unauthorized Oral History of Star Trek.* New York: St. Martin's.

Reagin, Nancy R. 2013. *Star Trek and History.* Hoboken, NJ: John Wiley & Sons.

Rossinow, Doug. 2015. *The Reagan Era: A History of the 1980s.* New York: Columbia University Press.

Ra's al Ghul

First Appearance:	*Batman* #232 (cover date: June 1971)
Creators:	Dennis O'Neil, Neal Adams, and Julius Schwartz
Other Media:	Animated and live-action television series, movies
Primary Strength:	Cunning, tenacity, immortality (via the Lazarus Pit)
Major Weakness:	Hubris
Weapons:	Considerable wealth and resources
Base of Operations:	Various
Key Allies:	Talia al Ghul (daughter), League of Assassins
Key Enemies:	Batman, Robin, Barbara Kean (on *Gotham*)
Actual Identity:	N/A
Nicknames/Aliases:	"The Demon's Head," "The Physician" (briefly)

The *Batman* franchise is, perhaps, second only to *Superman* in regard to its impact on popular culture. Created by writer Bill Finger and artist Bob Kane, Batman is billionaire playboy Bruce Wayne, who, after witnessing a mugger murder his parents when he was a young boy, vowed to dedicate his life battling crime in his hometown of Gotham City. In order to strike fear in criminals, Wayne chose to disguise himself as a bat, and "the Batman" (originally "Bat-Man") was born (Bill Finger and Bob Kane, *Detective Comics #33*, November 1939). Unlike his counterpart, Superman, Batman is a mere mortal, with no "super" powers of any kind. Instead, Batman is armed only with his keen intellect and a myriad of gadgets and vehicles that he uses in his fight against crime. Over the decades, in comics as well as on television and film, Batman has gained arguably the most impressive rogues' gallery of villains in all of popular culture. The Professor Moriarty to Batman's Sherlock Holmes is the seemingly immortal Ra's al Ghul, who is also the maternal grandfather of Batman's son, Damian Wayne, the most recent Robin, the Boy Wonder.

Due to various retellings, Ra's al Ghul's origins are murky. He was born sometime between the thirteenth and fifteenth centuries. The source of his longevity is the mysterious Lazarus Pit, a pool of strange liquid that rejuvenates and de-ages Ra's whenever he grows old or mortally wounded. His long life has shown him the darker nature of humanity: its continued warlike nature and covetousness of the planet's finite resources as well as its misuse and abuse of those same resources. As such, by the twentieth century, Ra's is consumed with the idea that the world can only be saved by wiping out millions of people and starting civilization over again. He sees Gotham City as a particularly specific example of humanity's decay, but he is impressed with the city's protector, Batman. Ra's views Batman as an intellectual equal, and Batman returns this respect, although he is appalled by Ra's' views about the solutions to humankind's problems. Batman develops a romantic relationship with Talia, Ra's' devoted daughter, and the two eventually produce a son, Damian Wayne (Chuck Dixon and Jerry Bingham, *Batman: Son of the Demon*, 1987).

In his first appearance, having deduced that Batman is actually billionaire Bruce Wayne, Ra's approaches Batman in the Batcave. Batman is investigating the recent kidnapping of his sidekick Robin/Dick Grayson. Ra's believes that his daughter, Talia, has been abducted by the same people who have taken the Boy Wonder. While tracking the clues together, Batman discovers that Ra's is, in fact, behind Robin's kidnapping but plays along to determine Ra's' motive. Ra's does not call Batman by either his vigilante or real names; he refers to him as "Detective." The immortal genius runs Batman through a gauntlet of trials to test the limits of his abilities, which, as it turns out, are as considerable, if not more than those of Ra's himself. When Batman finds Robin and exposes Ra's, the villain assures Batman that they will meet again and suggests to his daughter that the Detective would make a worthy heir and son-in-law (Dennis O'Neil and Neal Adams, *Batman #232*, June 1971).

Aside from his numerous appearances in comics over the decades, Ra's al Ghul was also a regular on the legendary *Batman: The Animated Series* (FOX Kids, 1992–1995; Kids' WB, 1997–1999). His first live-action appearance was in the film *Batman Begins* (Warner Brothers, 2005), where he was portrayed by Liam Neeson. He was also a key character in the animated film *Batman: Under the Red Hood* (Warner Home Video, 2010), where he was voiced by Jason Isaacs. Ra's was a recurring character on the non-*Batman*-related live-action television series *Arrow* (CW, 2012–2020), played by Matthew Nable. The most comic-accurate live-action portrayal, however, was on the television series *Gotham* (FOX, 2014–2019), where the character was portrayed by Alexander Siddig (previously Siddig El Fadil). In every incarnation, his tactical genius and leadership of the League of Assassins are presented, and his immortality via the Lazarus Pit is, if not directly explained, at least alluded to.

In the lexicon of Batman's rogues' gallery, most of the villains suffer some degree of insanity or psychological dysfunction. While it has been suggested that repeated use of the Lazarus Pit may have affected Ra's al Ghul's sanity, he is the most mentally stable of all Batman's nemeses, which makes him one of the most dangerous. He is fully aware of the villainy of his plan to purge the world and start anew, but he sees this as a necessary evil, for the greater good of humanity and the planet overall. The most frightening aspect of Ra's' overall plan is its clear logic. If humankind is a threat to its own continuance, is it more villainous to purge the threat or to allow, through a respect for all life, for the threat to play itself out? From Ra's' perspective, it comes down to either destroying most of humanity or allowing all of it to die. The hero's goal, then, is to find a preferable third option.

Richard A. Hall

See also: Catwoman, The Corleone Family, The Court of Owls, Ernst Stavro Blofeld/SPECTRE, Fish Mooney, Harley Quinn, Joker, Lex Luthor, Magneto, Penguin, Poison Ivy, Professor Moriarty, Red Skull, Scarecrow, Two-Face, Zod; *Thematic Essays*: The Dark Mirror: Evil Twins, *The Twilight Zone*, and the Villain Within.

Further Reading

Alsford, Mike. 2006. *Heroes & Villains.* Waco, TX: Baylor University Press.

Ashby, LeRoy. 2006. *With Amusement for All: A History of American Popular Culture since 1830.* Lexington: University Press of Kentucky.

Beard, Jim, ed. 2010. *Gotham City 14 Miles: 14 Essays on Why the 1960s Batman TV Series Matters.* Edwardsville, IL: Sequart Research & Literacy Organization.

Faludi, Susan. 2007. *The Terror Dream: Myth and Misogyny in an Insecure America.* New York: Picador.

Langley, Travis. 2012. *Batman and Psychology: A Dark and Stormy Knight.* New York: John Wiley & Sons.

O'Neil, Dennis, ed. 2008. *Batman Unauthorized: Vigilantes, Jokers, and Heroes in Gotham City.* Smart Pop Series. Dallas, TX: BenBella.

Weldon, Glen. 2016. *The Caped Crusade: Batman and the Rise of Nerd Culture.* New York: Simon & Schuster.

Wright, Bradford W. 2003. *Comic Book Nation: The Transformation of Youth Culture in America.* Baltimore, MD: Johns Hopkins University Press.

Red Skull

First Appearance:	*Captain America Comics #1* (cover date: March, 1941)
Creators:	Joe Simon and Jack Kirby
Other Media:	Animated television series, movies
Primary Strength:	Cunning, genius
Major Weakness:	Blind hatred
Weapons:	Various (often the Cosmic Cube)
Base of Operations:	Various
Key Allies:	Arnim Zola, Professor Faust, Hydra, Syn (his daughter), Crossbones
Key Enemies:	Captain America, Bucky/Winter Soldier, Falcon, Nick Fury/SHIELD
Actual Identity:	Johann Schmidt (originally George Maxon)
Nicknames/Aliases:	N/A

When Marvel Comics editor-in-chief Stan Lee launched what came to be known as the Marvel Age of Comics in the early 1960s, he made the decision to bring back a hero from the Golden Age of comics, cocreated by one of his artists, Jack Kirby: Captain America. Captain America was introduced to the world in December 1940, a full year before the Japanese attack on Pearl Harbor that brought the United States into World War II. Soon after Cap's revival in the 1960s, his archnemesis, the Red Skull, soon followed and has been a mainstay in the Marvel Comics' rogues' gallery ever since. The Red Skull is the closest that fiction has come to date in copying real-world supervillain Adolf Hitler, making him one of the most truly evil villains in modern popular culture.

For the first six months of *Captain America Comics*, the Red Skull was actually American industrialist George Maxon, whose company built airplanes for the U.S. military but whose true allegiance was to fascist Nazism. He wore a red skull mask, hence his name. That changed with *Captain America Comics #7* (Joe Simon and Jack Kirby, October 1941), when the *true* Red Skull was exposed: Johann Schmidt. Unlike Maxon, Schmidt did not wear a mask. His head actually resembled a red human skull. Schmidt was a dedicated Nazi, consumed with the destruction of America by any means necessary. When the *Captain America* comics were brought back in 1953 (after having been canceled in 1950), the Nazis were presumed dead and gone, and the new threat to America was Soviet communism. As such, the reintroduced Red Skull, still Schmidt, was a dedicated communist. From the perspective of Stan Lee (Timely/Atlas Comics' chief writer by that time, Simon and Kirby long since gone from the company), what the Nazis and communists had in common was a totalitarian and authoritarian desire to rid the world of the liberal democracy and capitalism of the United States. This made the Red Skull (his identifying color consistent with red communism) a perfect fit to continue as America's greatest threat.

When Lee incorporated Cap and the Skull into the Marvel Comics Universe, the updated Red Skull was no longer tied to any particular political ideology. His sole purpose was the utter destruction of the United States, often seeking to do so from within by turning Americans against themselves. His most common weapon on this quest was the mystical Cosmic Cube, an alien artifact that allowed whoever held it to alter reality in any way they imagined. Over the decades, the Cube has been a constant, albeit lazy, method of creating chaos and drama in the Marvel Comics Universe. In the 1980s, Red Skull posed as an American businessman, utilizing the corruption of Washington, DC, to strip Captain America of his title and handing the moniker to a more violent Captain America. In the 1990s, when Steve Rogers died from a cancer borne from his Super Soldier Serum, Red Skull revived him by placing Rogers's consciousness into a body cloned from the Red Skull himself, a controversial decision that Marvel writers soon undid by returning Cap to an original Steve Rogers body.

Weeks before the terrorist attacks of September 11, 2001, *Captain America* writer Dan Jurgens unveiled the Skull's latest scheme to destroy America, and it would prove eerily prescient, considering how American society would unfold over the next twenty years. The Red Skull was going to attempt to put the entire nation under mass hypnosis, digging to the heart of American prejudices and pitting Americans against each other, inflaming long-standing tensions between black and white, men and women, Christians and Muslims, citizens and undocumented immigrants, straight and LGBT+, conservatives and liberals. He reveals this plan to Captain America in a quote that has come to define the nation in the 2010s: "Your nation is a cauldron of hate waiting to erupt a cesspool of violent

Hugo Weaving gave a haunting performance as The Red Skull/Johann Schmidt, the head of Hydra, in the 2011 film *Captain America: The First Avenger.* (PictureLux/The Hollywood Archive/Alamy Stock Photo)

thoughts looking for release. It's a fuse extending from one coast to the other, waiting for someone to ignite the flame" (Dan Jurgens, *Captain America #46*, October 2001). As America approaches the 2020 presidential elections, the divisions between the above-mentioned groups are as heated—and occasionally as violent—as at any point in the country's history. The Red Skull is winning. America is being destroyed by itself.

The Red Skull is pure, unadulterated hatred personified. The depths of his evil are unprecedented in fiction, surpassing villains from Satan to Voldemort. He represents the darkness that lies deep in the human psyche, a darkness that many fight their entire lives to keep submerged, but that lies there nonetheless. His fictional goals to destroy America have come to fruition in the real world. If the nation does not tap into what President Abraham Lincoln called "the better angels of our nature," this fictional villain will succeed where his real-world counterparts failed, and the real world possesses no Captain America to respond.

Richard A. Hall

See also: Alpha/The Whisperers, Archie Bunker, Bellatrix Lestrange, Brainiac, Catwoman, Cersei Lannister, COBRA, The Court of Owls, Davros/Daleks, Doctor Doom, Doomsday, Ernst Stavro Blofeld/SPECTRE, Frank Burns, Green Goblin, Grindelwald, Harley Quinn, Joker, Killmonger, Lex Luthor, Loki, Magneto, Penguin, Poison Ivy, Ra's al Ghul, Reverend Stryker/The Purifiers, Scarecrow, Thanos, Two-Face, Ultron, Voldemort, Zod; *Thematic Essays*: "Nazis, Communists, and Terrorists . . . Oh My!": The Rise of the Supervillain and the Evolution of the Modern American Villain, The Dark Mirror: Evil Twins, *The Twilight Zone*, and the Villain Within, The Pathos of Villainy: Getting to the Heart of Why Villains Went Bad.

Further Reading

Alsford, Mike. 2006. *Heroes & Villains*. Waco, TX: Baylor University Press.

Costello, Matthew. 2009. *Secret Identity Crisis: Comic Books & the Unmasking of Cold War America*. New York: Continuum.

Howe, Sean. 2012. *Marvel Comics: The Untold Story*. New York: Harper Perennial.

Robichaud, Christopher. 2009. "Bright Colors, Dark Times." In *Supervillains and Philosophy: Sometimes Evil Is Its Own Reward*, edited by Ben Dyer, 61–70. Chicago: Open Court.

Simon, Joe. 2011. *My Life in Comics*. London: Titan Books.

Stevens, J. Richard. 2015. *Captain America, Masculinity, and Violence: The Evolution of a National Icon*. Syracuse, NY: Syracuse University Press.

Weiner, Robert G., ed. 2009. *Captain America and the Struggle of the Superhero: Critical Essays*. Jefferson, NC: McFarland & Company.

Wright, Bradford W. 2003. *Comic Book Nation: The Transformation of Youth Culture in America*. Baltimore, MD: Johns Hopkins University Press.

Reverend Stryker/The Purifiers

First Appearance:	*X-Men: God Loves, Man Kills* (publication date: 1982)
Creators:	Chris Claremont and Brent Anderson
Other Media:	Movies (William Stryker only)
Primary Strength:	Persuasion, propaganda
Major Weakness:	Racism, religious zealotry
Weapons:	Television
Base of Operations:	New York City
Key Allies:	N/A
Key Enemies:	The X-Men, Magneto
Actual Identity:	William Stryker
Nicknames/Aliases:	N/A

In 1963, Marvel Comics editor-in-chief Stan Lee and artist Jack Kirby introduced the last of their new Marvel Age of heroes: the X-Men. Although commercially the least successful of these new heroes, the X-Men were the most socially relevant to the period. Professor Charles Xavier ran a school for "gifted youngsters," or "mutants," teenagers born with a mutated gene that provided them with exceptional super powers. Unlike the previous Marvel heroes who received their powers from some manner of scientific accident, the X-Men were born with enhanced abilities that manifested during puberty. Due to their strange natural powers, mutants were hated by "normal" humans. Professor X sought peaceful coexistence between mutants and humans. By 1970, lagging sales led Marvel to stop issuing new stories, simply reprinting older stories from 1970 to 1975. In 1975, Len Wein and Dave Cockrum introduced the "All New–All Different" X-Men, making the team more multinational and multiethnic. Under the creative team of writer Chris Claremont and artist John Byrne, *The Uncanny X-Men* reached unprecedented heights, making the mutant heroes Marvel's top seller throughout the 1980s.

In 1982, Marvel began publishing one-shot graphic novels, with much-deeper and adult-oriented content like death and racism. The fifth graphic novel was *X-Men: God Loves, Man Kills*. In that story, Reverend William Stryker is an evangelical minister and head of the Worldwide Evangelical Stryker Crusade. His army of Purifiers roam the countryside, murdering mutants (even children). Stryker firmly believes that mutants are an abomination to God and the creation of the Devil. Under the ruse of a televised debate on the issue, Stryker kidnaps Professor Charles Xavier, leader of the X-Men and the most powerful telepath in the world. Stryker plans to utilize Xavier's ability and amplify it to kill every mutant in the world through brain hemorrhage. The X-Men and their longtime foe, Magneto, rescue Xavier and confront Stryker's prejudice during his televised sermon.

During that sermon, Stryker contends, "[Humans] are beings of Divine creation, yet there are those among us whose existence is an affront to that Divinity. . . . We are as God made us! Any deviation from that sacred template—any *mutation*—comes not from Heaven, but Hell!" (Chris Claremont, *X-Men: God Loves, Man Kills*, 1982). He then questions the humanity of the X-Man Nightcrawler, whose mutation includes blue skin, pointed ears, and a devil-like tail. When Stryker attempts to shoot the teenage female X-Man Shadowcat, a security guard shoots Stryker instead. The X-Men leader, Cyclops, then addresses the crowd and television audience about the dangers and un-Christian aspects of prejudice and racism. The experience leaves Professor Xavier questioning his own peaceful approach to human-mutant relations and considering that Magneto's more militant approach may be correct.

X-Men: God Loves, Man Kills was published at a time when the HIV/AIDS virus was still terrifying Americans and appeared to be a disease that directly targeted the gay community. Many television ministers at the time considered AIDS to be God's punishment for the gay lifestyle, and countless Americans believed them. Since their inception in 1963, the X-Men had always been an allegory for racism in the United States. Beginning with this story line, the popular superheroes began to represent any group that was considered other or outsider in American society. The Stryker ministry was also prophetic of the rise of televangelism throughout the 1980s. In the decades since, the various X-titles at Marvel have made inclusion and tolerance a staple in their storytelling.

The character of William Stryker returned in the 20th Century Fox *X-Men* movie franchise from 2000 to 2019 as a recurring character. In the film incarnation, Stryker is an American soldier who becomes involved in experimentation on mutants, including being the person responsible for the traumatic addition of the metal adamantium to the skeleton of the X-Man Wolverine. In his introduction in the franchise's second installment, *X2: X-Men United* (2003), Stryker has a mutant son and blames Professor Xavier for not "curing" his son. In *God Loves, Man Kills*, Reverend Stryker killed his mutant son at birth, along with the child's mother. In the overall lexicon of American villains, Reverend Stryker and his band of Purifiers represent the horrors of prejudice, racism, and intolerance.

Although they claim to commit their atrocities in the name of God, their actions are no different from the Nazis decades before. Stryker represents the dangers of giving powerful voice to the forces of hate in America, a warning still relevant in the twenty-first century.

Richard A. Hall

See also: Alpha/The Whisperers, Archie Bunker, Bellatrix Lestrange, Borg Queen/Borg, Cybermen, Davros/Daleks, Doctor Doom, Ernst Stavro Blofeld/SPECTRE, Frank Burns, Green Goblin, Grindelwald, Killmonger, Loki, Magneto, Number Six/Cylons, Red Skull, Thanos, Ultron, Voldemort, Zod; *Thematic Essays*: The Dark Mirror: Evil Twins, *The Twilight Zone*, and the Villain Within, The Pathos of Villainy: Getting to the Heart of Why Villains Went Bad.

Further Reading

Alsford, Mike. 2006. *Heroes & Villains.* Waco, TX: Baylor University Press.

Costello, Matthew J. 2009. *Secret Identity Crisis: Comic Books & the Unmasking of Cold War America.* New York: Continuum.

De Falco, Tom. 2006. *Comics Creators on X-Men.* London: Titan.

Howe, Sean. 2012. *Marvel Comics: The Untold Story.* New York: Harper-Perennial.

Powell, Jason. 2016. *The Best There Is at What He Does: Examining Chris Claremont's X-Men.* Edwardsville, IL: Sequart.

Wright, Bradford W. 2003. *Comic Book Nation: The Transformation of Youth Culture in America.* Baltimore, MD: Johns Hopkins University Press.

S

Sauron/Saruman

First Appearance:	*The Lord of the Rings, Book I: The Fellowship of the Ring* (publication date: July 29, 1954)
Creators:	J. R. R. Tolkien
Other Media:	Movies (live-action and animated)
Primary Strength:	Cunning, deception
Major Weakness:	Hatred
Weapons:	Magic
Base of Operations:	Mordor, Middle-earth
Key Allies:	Orcs, Wormtongue (Saruman's right hand)
Key Enemies:	Gandalf the Grey (later Gandalf the White), Frodo Baggins, Fellowship of the Ring, Dwarves, Elves, Humans
Actual Identity:	N/A
Nicknames/Aliases:	"The Dark Lord," "Lord of the Earth," "King of Men" (all Sauron)

The Lord of the Rings is a three-part epic fantasy series set in the mythical realm of Middle-earth. Millennia before the events of the story, the Dark Lord Sauron created, or ordered to be created, nineteen Rings of Power to be distributed between elves, dwarves, and men. He then created the One Ring to rule them all. During a massive battle, the human Isildur cut off Sauron's finger, claiming the ring for himself. In doing so, Sauron was reduced from physical to metaphysical form. Later, a band of Orcs attacked Isildur, and in the heat of battle, the One Ring was lost, falling into a nearby river, where, centuries later, it was discovered by the Hobbit Smeagol, whose obsession with the object caused him to devolve into the hideous Gollum. Gollum went into hiding to protect his "Precious," but he lost the ring in the dark, where, centuries later, it was discovered and stolen by the Hobbit Bilbo Baggins. Baggins hid the ring for decades. Finally, the wizard Gandalf the Grey tasked Bilbo's nephew, Frodo Baggins, with returning the ring to the fires of Mount Doom in order to destroy it before it could fall into the hands of Sauron and return the Dark Lord to power (J. R. R. Tolkien, *The Fellowship of the Ring*, 1954).

Sauron was created by Eru, the supreme creator of all things. As such, Sauron was a semidivine spirit, part of a group of such spirits known as Majar. Being the first such being, however, Sauron evolved to a higher order than the other Majar.

Originally, Sauron was not an evil being (as he was created to be good), but as Sauron gained power and was corrupted by it, other Majar came to Middle-earth as the wizards Saruman, Gandalf, and Radagast. In the beginning, all were part of an angelic choir known as the Ainur. However, another Majar, Melkor, began to weave more selfish and malevolent verses into his music, finally becoming the source of evil in the world. Sauron was eventually seduced by this evil, becoming the Dark Lord (J. R. R. Tolkien, *The Silmarillion*, 1977). Sauron later creates the Rings of Power, gifting them to elves, dwarves, and men in an attempt to rule the peoples of Middle-earth through the One Ring.

Although his physical form is destroyed when the human Isildur takes possession of the One Ring, Sauron, being semidivine, continues to exist in a more metaphysical form. He leads his forces to build the Dark Tower, from which he seeks the ring with his giant eye, which protrudes from the top of the tower. The wizard Gandalf the White (resurrected from his previous form) deduces that Sauron's rise will be halted if the One Ring is destroyed. It becomes Frodo's mission, then, to take the ring to Mount Doom and cast it into the lava rivers within the mountain. On completion of this mission, the ring and Sauron are destroyed (J. R. R. Tolkien, *The Return of the King*, 1955).

Saruman the White was sent to Middle-earth as leader of the Istari, a group of wizards tasked with preventing Sauron's rise to power. In *The Fellowship of the Ring*, Sauron is clearly the superior of Gandalf the Grey, who comes to the wizard for advice about what to do about the One Ring and Sauron's quest for it. By the end of that first part and expanded upon in the next part, *The Two Towers*, it becomes clear that Saruman has been seduced by the power promised by Sauron's rise, becoming a devoted follower of Saruman, commanding legions against the elves, dwarves, and men of Middle-earth. Once he is discovered, Gandalf leads Frodo and the others against the rising forces of Saruman, eventually breaking the dark wizard's magical staff and casting him from the Council of Wizards (J. R. R. Tolkien, *The Two Towers*, 1954). After successfully conning Hobbits and men into following him (in disguise) with the assistance of the evil Wormtongue, Saruman faces a revolt led by the brave Hobbit, Frodo. When he attempts to place the blame on Wormtongue, his loyal servant cuts his throat, ending Saruman for good (J. R. R. Tolkien, *The Return of the King*, 1955).

In the end, both Sauron and Saruman become the manifestation of the corruption of absolute power. Although originating as good beings, their lust for control and ultimate power lead them down the path of darkness. They are modern-day incarnations of characters such as Lucifer and Loki and precursors to the Sith Lords of *Star Wars* and dark wizards of *Harry Potter*. They speak to that inner consciousness that warns of the corruption of power and the dangers of giving into the temptation that such power presents. For as long as fantasy fiction exists, there will always be such dark wizards, forever warning their audiences of the ultimate fate of giving in to the darker nature of humanity.

Richard A. Hall

See also: Angelique Bouchard-Collins, Bellatrix Lestrange, Dark Willow, Fiona Goode/ The Supreme, Gollum, Grindelwald, Loki, Lucifer/Satan, Sith Lords, Ursula, Voldemort;

Thematic Essays: The Dark Mirror: Evil Twins, *The Twilight Zone*, and the Villain Within.

Further Reading

Alsford, Mike. 2006. *Heroes & Villains*. Waco, TX: Baylor University Press.

Ashby, LeRoy. 2006. *With Amusement for All: A History of American Popular Culture since 1830*. Lexington: University Press of Kentucky.

Hammond, Wayne G., and Christina Scull. 2005. *The Lord of the Rings: A Reader's Companion*. San Diego, CA: Houghton Mifflin Harcourt.

Kreeft, Peter. 2005. *The Philosophy of Tolkien: The Worldview behind The Lord of the Rings*. San Francisco, CA: Ignatius.

Russell, Jeffrey B., and Brooks Alexander. 2007. *A History of Witchcraft: Sorcerers, Heretics, & Pagans*. London: Thames & Hudson.

Starck, Kathleen, ed. 2010. *Between Fear and Freedom: Cultural Representations of the Cold War*. Newcastle upon Tyne, UK: Cambridge Scholars.

Scarecrow

First Appearance:	*World's Finest Comics #3* (cover date: Autumn 1941)
Creators:	Bill Finger, Bob Kane, and Jerry Robinson
Other Media:	Animated and live-action television series, movies
Primary Strength:	Cunning, gifted scientist
Major Weakness:	Severely mentally unstable
Weapons:	Fear gas
Base of Operations:	Gotham City
Key Allies:	Joker, Bane, Poison Ivy (all occasionally)
Key Enemies:	Batman, Robin, Batgirl, Police Commissioner James Gordon
Actual Identity:	Dr. Jonathan Crane
Nicknames/Aliases:	"Ichabod Crane," "Master of Fear," "Prince of Panic," "Yellow Lantern" (temporarily)

The *Batman* franchise is, perhaps, second only to *Superman* in regard to its impact on popular culture. Created by writer Bill Finger and artist Bob Kane, Batman is billionaire playboy Bruce Wayne, who, after witnessing a mugger murder his parents when he was a young boy, vowed to dedicate his life battling crime in his hometown of Gotham City. In order to strike fear in criminals, Wayne chose to disguise himself as a bat, and "the Batman" (originally "Bat-Man") was born (Bill Finger and Bob Kane, *Detective Comics #33*, November 1939). Unlike his counterpart, Superman, Batman is a mere mortal, with no "super" powers of any kind. Instead, Batman is armed only with his keen intellect and a myriad of gadgets and vehicles that he uses in his fight against crime. Over the decades, in comics as well as on television and film, Batman has gained arguably the most impressive rogues' gallery of villains in all popular culture. One of his most frightening of these villains is Scarecrow.

Jonathan Krane becomes obsessed with fear during his youth, when he is constantly bullied because of his particularly thin frame. He soon views revenge as a cathartic release for his own fear, returning such fear on others. As an adult, he becomes a brilliant scientist, focusing on the brain and all physical and mental aspects of fear (Bruce Jones and Sean Murphy, *Year One: Batman/Scarecrow #1–2*, July–August 2005). Krane puts his thin frame to use with his new fear gas, combining the two to create the supervillain identity Scarecrow. Over the decades, Scarecrow has proven a formidable villain in Batman's rogues' gallery, perhaps getting the better of the Dark Knight more than any other villain. The character has appeared in all the various animated incarnations of Batman on television and home video. He has also appeared in the live-action Chris Nolan trilogy of Batman films—*Batman Begins* (2005), *The Dark Knight* (2008), and *The Dark Knight Rises* (2012)—played in each by Cillian Murphy. Possibly the most in-depth look at the character was presented in the live-action television series *Gotham* (FOX, 2014–2019).

On *Gotham*, Dr. Gerald Crane is working on a fear toxin to enhance people's greatest fear in an attempt to learn to deal with that fear and, in time, to rid people such as himself and his young son, Jonathan, from fear. He murders several people, raising their fear levels before doing so, and removes their adrenal glands postmortem. When the Gotham City Police Department discovers Crane's identity and intentions, they raid his rural farmhouse, but not before the mad doctor doses his teenage son with a particularly heavy dose (Ken Woodruff, "The Scarecrow," *Gotham*, season 1, episode 15, February 9, 2015). From this point on, Jonathan is clinically insane and confined to Arkham Asylum. Over the rest of the series, Jonathan Crane (played by Charlie Tahan in seasons one through three and David W. Thompson in seasons four and five). When young Jonathan is first injected, the first thing he sees is a scarecrow in a field, causing this to become his greatest fear. From that point on, Jonathan is terrified of his own alter ego, but he eventually gives in to his fear and his quest to inspire fear in others.

As is the case with many *Batman* villains, Scarecrow is a sympathetic character in all his incarnations. He is the product of bullying. Like Joker and Poison Ivy, Scarecrow's crimes confine him to the asylum rather than prison, because his villainous acts come from a place of mental instability rather than clearheaded malice. At a time when bullying garners so much attention in American society, the Scarecrow is a villain worthy of considerable study. Like Frankenstein's Monster, Scarecrow does not *want* to be a villain; however, through the fear created by victimization, he has been created one.

Richard A. Hall

See also: Catwoman, The Court of Owls, Fish Mooney, Green Goblin, Harley Quinn, Joker, Poison Ivy, Ra's al Ghul, Two-Face; *Thematic Essays*: "Nazis, Communists, and Terrorists . . . Oh My!": The Rise of the Supervillain and the Evolution of the Modern American Villain, The Pathos of Villainy: Getting to the Heart of Why Villains Went Bad.

Further Reading

Alsford, Mike. 2006. *Heroes & Villains*. Waco, TX: Baylor University Press.

Ashby, LeRoy. 2006. *With Amusement for All: A History of American Popular Culture since 1830*. Lexington: University Press of Kentucky.

Faludi, Susan. 2007. *The Terror Dream: Myth and Misogyny in an Insecure America*. New York: Picador.

Langley, Travis. 2012. *Batman and Psychology: A Dark and Stormy Knight*. New York: John Wiley & Sons.

O'Neil, Dennis, ed. 2008. *Batman Unauthorized: Vigilantes, Jokers, and Heroes in Gotham City*. Smart Pop Series. Dallas, TX: BenBella.

Weldon, Glen. 2016. *The Caped Crusade: Batman and the Rise of Nerd Culture*. New York: Simon & Schuster.

Wright, Bradford W. 2003. *Comic Book Nation: The Transformation of Youth Culture in America*. Baltimore, MD: Johns Hopkins University Press.

Sherry Palmer

First Appearance:	*24*, season 1, episode 1 (air date: November 6, 2001)
Creators:	Robert Cochran and Joel Surnow
Other Media:	Novels, comics
Primary Strength:	Cunning, strategy
Major Weakness:	Disloyalty, self-interest
Weapons:	Henchmen, political allies
Base of Operations:	Washington, DC
Key Allies:	David Palmer (husband), Wayne Palmer (brother-in-law), Roger Stanton
Key Enemies:	Jack Bauer, David Palmer (eventually), Wayne Palmer (eventually)
Actual Identity:	N/A
Nicknames/Aliases:	N/A

In the wake of the terrorist attacks of September 11, 2001, as Americans still cowered in fear at every suggestion of breaking news, a new television series debuted that acted as a cathartic release for American audiences: *24* (FOX, 2001–2010, 2014). The series centered on Counter-Terrorism Unit agent Jack Bauer (played by Kiefer Sutherland), and each season represented one day, with each episode presenting one hour of real time. Audiences watched with fevered anticipation hour by hour to see if Bauer would save the day from each season's terrorist threat. Though often criticized for its excessive violence, the series was wildly popular for its strong stance against terrorist threats to the United States. During the 2008 Republican primary debates, when asked how they would respond to a

Lady Macbeth

Ever since the first performance of the tragic play *Macbeth* by William Shakespeare (1564–1616) in the early 1600s, the key antagonist, Lady Macbeth, has become a representation, to the point of stereotype, of female characters driven by a thirst for power and/or wealth. The wife of the play's protagonist, Macbeth, Lady Macbeth is the driving force behind her husband's eventual fall. It is Lady Macbeth who pushes her husband to murder the king, clearing the way for Macbeth's own rise to the throne. Her primary goal is not her husband's success but her own rise to political power. Ultimately, however, her very machinations lead Macbeth to the unfortunate end that he is warned against at the very beginning of the play by the mysterious witches.

In the four-hundred-plus years since the play's debut, numerous Lady Macbeths have appeared both in fiction and real life. Any time a male figure, fictional or historical, is driven to success by the support of his wife, that wife has been looked upon as a Lady Macbeth. Even in the twenty-first century, characters, such as Sherry Palmer from the television series *24*, play the role of Lady Macbeth. The downside, of course, is the rise of this stereotype of women seeking ambitious goals of any kind. Even former secretary of state and 2016 Democratic presidential candidate Hillary Rodham-Clinton has often been portrayed as a Lady Macbeth, riding her successful husband's coattails to her own rise to power. While Lady Macbeth is a fascinating character and an important view into what drives all humans, the frequent use of the character to stereotype women has been an unfortunate side effect.

Richard A. Hall

terrorist attack on the United States within the next twenty-four hours, one candidate responded, "I would call Jack Bauer." Although most villains each season were new to that season, one villain who overarched the first three seasons was Sherry Palmer, wife to the "first black presidential candidate," David Palmer, in season one and ex-wife to President Palmer in seasons two and three.

Portrayed by Penny Johnson Jerald, Sherry Palmer is shown in season one to be willing to commit any illegal action that would assist in her husband's ascension to the presidency. She also commits various crimes to protect her son, Keith, from bogus murder allegations. Also in that season, when Sherry sees that she no longer has her husband's trust, she pushes one of her female assistants to seduce the candidate in order to provide him with stress relief. Discovering his wife's machinations, Palmer decides to file for divorce, which he does after the events of "Day 1."

During "Day 2" (season two), Sherry attempts to regain the new president's trust by coming to him with a conspiracy against him. As it turns out, however, Sherry is conspiring *with* the said conspirator to regain her ex-husband's trust. By the end of "Day 2," Agent Bauer has taken Sherry into custody for her role in that day's events. At the beginning of "Day 3," President Palmer, now running for reelection, calls upon his ex-wife to use her talents to rid him of someone extorting him. Sherry succeeds by killing the would-be extortionist, and the president assists in the cover-up of her involvement but orders her to leave, disgusted by her tactics. Enraged, Sherry turns to Palmer's political opponent with the evidence of Palmer's role in covering up the murder. This too, however, proved to be a ruse; Sherry goes back to her ex-husband and offers to be *his* weapon to victory, asking, in return, to once more be first lady. President Palmer agrees, but Sherry is ultimately killed, as her machinations do not unfold according to plan. Although he now on a clear path to victory, Palmer, affected deeply by his ex-wife's death, chooses to drop out of the race.

Sherry Palmer is the ultimate modern incarnation of Lady Macbeth. She is the source of political intrigue on the first three seasons of *24*. She whispers aspirations into her husband's ear, convincing him to betray his own morals in his quest for the greater good, his political victory. She also represents the powerful women who have pulled the strings of power in governments behind the scenes since the days of ancient Rome. Her win-at-all-costs mentality, however, ultimately proves to be the source of her own downfall. She is the warning against falling to political corruption, while she simultaneously shows how adept women can be at playing the game of a "man's" world. Her tragic end is a testament to the dangers of that world.

Richard A. Hall

See also: Alexis Carrington-Colby-Dexter, Angelique Bouchard-Collins, Cersei Lannister, Fiona Goode/The Supreme, Sue Sylvester; *Thematic Essays*: "Nazis, Communists, and Terrorists . . . Oh My!": The Rise of the Supervillain and the Evolution of the Modern American Villain, The Pathos of Villainy: Getting to the Heart of Why Villains Went Bad.

Further Reading

Alsford, Mike. 2006. *Heroes & Villains*. Waco, TX: Baylor University Press.

Castleman, Harry, and Walter J. Podrazik. 2016. *Watching TV: Eight Decades of American Television*. 3rd ed. Syracuse, NY: Syracuse University Press.

Faludi, Susan. 2007. *The Terror Dream: Myth and Misogyny in an Insecure America*. New York: Picador.

Goldman, Michael R. 2008. *24: The Ultimate Guide*. London: DK.

Peacock, Steven, ed. 2007. *Reading 24: TV against the Clock*. London: I. B. Tauris.

Willis, Susan. 2005. *Portents of the Real: A Primer for Post-9/11 America*. London: Verso.

Sith Lords

First Appearance: *Star Wars: From the Adventures of Luke Skywalker* (publication date: November 12, 1976)
Creators: George Lucas
Other Media: Television, comics, novels
Primary Strength: Strategy, politics, cunning
Major Weakness: Blinded by ideology, hubris
Weapons: The Force, lightsabers

Base of Operations:	The Galactic Empire ("a galaxy far, far away")
Key Allies:	Imperial/First Order Officers, Stormtroopers
Key Enemies:	Jedi Knights, Rebel Alliance/Resistance (and, to a degree, each other)
Actual Identity:	**Darth Sidious:** Senator/Emperor Sheev Palpatine **Darth Tyrannus:** Count Dooku **Darth Vader:** Anakin Skywalker **Kylo Ren:** Ben Solo
Nicknames/Aliases:	N/A

In 1977, writer and director George Lucas introduced the world to his iconic film *Star Wars* (Lucasfilm/20th Century Fox). The massive worldwide success of the original film has spawned numerous sequels, prequels, animated television series, made-for-TV movies, novels, and comic books. Set a "long time ago . . . in a galaxy far, far away," *Star Wars* tells a generational saga of a galaxy at war between the forces of good and evil. Six months prior to the original film's release, ghostwriter Alan Dean Foster brought Lucas's story to the printed page in the novelization of the film. The original *Star Wars* set up the basics of what would become the *Star Wars* universe and one of the most successful franchises in pop culture history. The novel and film introduced audiences to the Dark Lord of the Sith, specifically Darth Vader, the key antagonist in the original *Star Wars* trilogy.

The Sith Lords are a dark order of Force users. Much of their origins and history has been rewritten in recent years, as the established canon of the *Star Wars* expanded universe has been stripped of its canonical status since 2012. What is established is that millennia ago, a dark order of Jedi knights split from the established order to dedicate themselves to the dark side of the Force, a mystical energy that flows throughout all living forms but can be harnessed and utilized by individuals who possess a "Force sensitivity." Whereas the Jedi and the light side focus their power outwardly, for the benefit of all, the Sith focus their powers inwardly, gaining strength from fear, hatred, and ambition. As such, however, the Sith often fall into civil war, killing each other with abandon. Early on, a Sith Lord named Darth Bane establishes the Rule of Two: that there should be no more than two Sith at any given time, a master and an apprentice.

Throughout the nine "saga" films of the *Star Wars* franchise, as well as the animated television series *The Clone Wars* and *Rebels*, the chief Sith Lord was Darth Sidious (primarily played by Ian McDiarmid), known throughout the galaxy as Emperor Sheev Palpatine, the former senator from the planet Naboo. Palpatine has proven to be the most powerful Sith in history to this point. When as a senator, Palpatine manipulated the fall of the Old Republic and the Jedi Order, he took on an apprentice, Darth Maul (played originally by Ray Park). Unlike the human Palpatine, Maul was a Zabrak, with a multihorned head and dark black skin with red tatoos. Maul was presumed killed by the Jedi knight Obi-wan Kenobi during the Battle of Naboo (George Lucas, *Star Wars, Episode I: The Phantom Menace*, 1999). Although Maul survived and would return in *The Clone Wars*, *Rebels*, and the feature film *Solo: A Star Wars Story* (2018), his failure against Kenobi led Palpatine to forever disavow his former apprentice.

Palpatine's next apprentice was Darth Tyrannus, the former Jedi master Count Dooku (played by Christopher Lee). As part of Palpatine's machinations, Dooku led half the systems of the republic to secede and form the Confederacy of Independent Systems, leading to a civil war known as the Clone Wars (George Lucas, *Star Wars, Episode II: Attack of the Clones*, 2002). This allowed Palpatine to weed out the Jedi and consolidate his power as emperor of the new Galactic Republic. Tyrannus was killed by the Jedi knight Anakin Skywalker (played by Hayden Christensen). Skywalker was a particularly powerful Force user, born by virgin birth through the manipulation of midichlorians, microscopic life-forms through which the Force flows more easily, and believed by the Jedi knight Qui-Gon Jinn to be the Chosen One of ancient myth. Over time, it would be discovered that it was Palpatine who manipulated Anakin's creation, and he would eventually seduce the young Jedi to follow the Dark Side and become Darth Vader (George Lucas, *Star Wars, Episode III: Revenge of the Sith*, 2005).

Darth Vader, Dark Lord of the Sith, is the most iconic villain in the *Star Wars* franchise. (Lucasfilm/Sportsphoto/Alamy Stock Photo)

For roughly twenty-five years, Vader would be the emperor's loyal apprentice and enforcer, tasked with hunting down and destroying the remaining Jedi knights in the decades after the Clone Wars. When a rebellion emerges against Palpatine's regime, Vader leads the imperial forces against the rebels. Eventually, Vader discovered that the young rebel Luke Skywalker and Rebel Alliance leader Princess Leia Organa were his own children from his deceased wife, Padme Amidala. When Palpatine seeks to replace Vader with the younger Skywalker, Vader turns on his master, presumably killing him and finding redemption through saving his son (George Lucas, *Star Wars, Episode VI: Return of the Jedi*, 1983). The fall of Palpatine and death of Vader lead the galaxy to believe that the Sith are no more. Decades later, however, the galaxy will once more fall under the power of dark side Force users.

Thirty years after the fall of Palpatine, a new imperial organization, the First Order, emerges under the leadership of Supreme Leader Snoke. Although not officially Sith, Snoke is clearly a master of the dark side of the Force and seduces a young Jedi apprentice named Ben Solo (played by Adam Driver). Solo is the son of Leia Organa and her husband, and fellow rebel, Han Solo (J. J. Abrams and Lawrence Kasdan, *Star Wars, Episode VII: The Force Awakens*, 2015). Solo becomes Kylo Ren, master of the Knights of Ren. In time, Ren assassinates Snoke, becoming the new supreme leader of the First Order (Rian Johnson, *Star Wars, Episode VIII: The Last Jedi*, 2017). As the First Order fights the resistance, led by Ren's mother, General Leia Organa, both discover that Palpatine lives on, threatening a return of the Sith (J. J. Abrams, *Star Wars, Episode IX: The Rise of Skywalker*, 2019).

In the realm of American villainy, the Sith represent all that American society considers evil. Their power is built on fear, hatred, and ambition, and their rule is through subjugation and de facto slavery. They are the demonic legions of the "galaxy far, far away." Although fans were delighted at the return of Palpatine for the final chapter of the Skywalker saga, his return is a reminder that true evil never dies and that complacency with the status quo allows evil to emerge victorious over and over again. As to the religion of the Force, by the time the Skywalker saga comes to a close, only a handful of followers of either side remain throughout the galaxy.

Richard A. Hall

See also: Angelique Bouchard-Collins, Asajj Ventress, Bellatrix Lestrange, Boba Fett, Captain Phasma/Stormtroopers, Grindelwald, Jabba the Hutt, Loki, Lucifer/Satan, Sauron/Saruman, Tia Dalma/Calypso, Ursula, Voldemort; *Thematic Essays*: "Nazis, Communists, and Terrorists . . . Oh My!": The Rise of the Supervillain and the Evolution of the Modern American Villain.

Further Reading

Alsford, Mike. 2006. *Heroes & Villains.* Waco, TX: Baylor University Press.

Ashby, LeRoy. 2006. *With Amusement for All: A History of American Popular Culture since 1830.* Lexington: University Press of Kentucky.

Eberl, Jason T., and Kevin S. Decker, eds. *The Ultimate Star Wars and Philosophy: You Must Unlearn What You Have Learned.* Hoboken, NJ: Wiley-Blackwell.

Jones, Brian Jay. 2016. *George Lucas: A Life*. New York: Little Brown & Company.

Kaminski, Michael. 2008. *The Secret History of Star Wars: The Art of Storytelling and the Making of a Modern Epic*. Kingston, ON, Canada: Legacy.

Lomax, Tara. 2020. "'You Were the Chosen One!': Darth Vader and the Sequential Dynamics of Villainy in the *Star Wars* Prequel Trilogy." In *The Supervillain Reader*, edited by Rob Peaslee and Robert Weiner, 214–223. Jackson: University of Mississippi Press.

Nichols, Catherine. 2018. "The Good Guy/Bad Guy Myth: Pop Culture Today Is Obsessed with the Battle between Good and Evil. Traditional Folk Tales Never Were. What Changed?" *Aeon*. January 25, 2018. Accessed September 20, 2019. https://getpocket.com/explore/item/the-good-guy-bad-guy-myth.

Reagin, Nancy R., and Janice Liedl, eds. *Star Wars and History*. New York: John Wiley & Sons.

Sunstein, Cass R. 2016. *The World According to Star Wars*. New York: Dey Street.

Sweet, Derek R. 2015. *Star Wars in the Public Square: The Clone Wars as Political Dialogue*. Critical Explorations in Science Fiction and Fantasy Series, edited by Donald E. Palumbo and Michael Sullivan. Jefferson, NC: McFarland.

Taylor, Chris. 2015. *How Star Wars Conquered the Universe: The Past, Present, and Future of a Multibillion Dollar Franchise*. New York: Basic.

Van Yperen, Nathaniel. 2011. "I Am Your Father: The Villain and the Future Self." In *Vader, Voldemort and Other Villains: Essays on Evil in Popular Media*, edited by Jamey Heit, 189–201. Jefferson, NC: McFarland.

Spike and Drusilla

First Appearance:	*Buffy the Vampire Slayer*, season 2, episode 3 (air date: September 29, 1997)
Creators:	Joss Whedon
Other Media:	Comics, novels
Primary Strength:	Strength, regenerative powers
Major Weakness:	Sunlight, wooden stakes (or enchanted objects) through heart, crosses
Weapons:	Fangs
Base of Operations:	Sunnydale, California; Los Angeles, California
Key Allies:	Drusilla, Angel/Angelus (occasionally), Wolfram and Hart (Dru only)
Key Enemies:	Buffy Summers, Rupert Giles, Willow Rosenberg
Actual Identity:	William (Spike)
Nicknames/Aliases:	"William the Bloody" (Spike)

Buffy the Vampire Slayer (WB, 1997–2001; UPN, 2001–2003) is a cult-classic television series that has gained an international following. Creator Joss Whedon

Boris and Natasha

Boris Badenov and Natasha Fatale are the primary comedic antagonists to the animated comedy duo of Rocky the Flying Squirrel and Bullwinkle Moose ("Rocky and Bullwinkle"). They appeared on the animated television series *The Adventures of Rocky and Bullwinkle and Friends* (ABC, 1959–1961; NBC, 1961–1964), working for the Nazi-esque Fearless Leader and the more mysterious Mr. Big. Although said to be from the fictional nation of Pottsylvania, their accents betray them as satirical spins on Russian spies from the Cold War era. As the program was a children's comedy cartoon, their hijinks and situations are comedic in nature, but they do pose a threat to the free-loving lifestyle of the protagonist animals. Their place in the American zeitgeist makes them an analogy for any antagonist male and female duo, from Doctor Evil and Frau Farbissina of the *Austin Powers* movie franchise to the more occasionally menacing duo of Spike and Drusilla from the television series *Buffy the Vampire Slayer.* Their Russian overtones also speak to their placement in history during the height of the Cold War, when Russian spies were portrayed in films, such as the *James Bond* franchise, and television series, such as *The Man from U.N.C.L.E.*, as serious threats to the basic freedoms and liberties of the United States and its allies. In the animated, live-action film *The Adventures of Rocky and Bullwinkle* (2000), Boris was portrayed by Jason Alexander (b. 1959), and Natasha was played by Renee Russo (b. 1954).

Richard A. Hall

wanted to take the tired concept of the girl being attacked by the monster and flip the idea so that the girl attacks the monster (Billson, *Buffy the Vampire Slayer*, 24–25). The show centers on Buffy Summers, a run-of-the-mill high school teenager who also happens to be the latest in a centuries-long line of "Chosen Ones," teenage girls who serve, one at a time, as the slayer, the one girl in all the world who can save us from demons, vampires, and all threats of the supernatural. Every slayer is trained by a watcher, chosen by the Watchers' Council to oversee the slayer's training and guiding her on her overall mission. When the series begins, Buffy and her recently divorced mother move to the small California town of Sunnydale, which happens to sit directly on a Hellmouth, a portal/magnet of concentrated evil, mostly in the form of vampires.

In the second season, audiences are introduced to Spike and Drusilla, vampire lovers with a penchant for chaos and bloodlust. Spike (played by James Marsters) dresses as a modern-day Billy Idol, with bleached blond hair and floor-length leather coat; Dru (played by Juliet Landau) dresses as a stereotypical Roma girl. Spike is famous for having killed two slayers, with his eyes on Buffy as the next. Dru is completely insane, frequently hears voices, and has a deep desire for torture and slaughter. The two eventually part ways as Dru's mental status prevents her from comprehending the level of devotion that Spike feels for her. Over time, Spike falls in love with Buffy. After attempting to rape the slayer, Spike embarks on a journey to retrieve his human soul, making him more like Buffy's true love, Angel. Although he succeeds, the guilt that comes with his soul drives him mad for some time before he finally comes to his senses to become an ally to Buffy and, later, Angel.

Spike and Dru quickly become more comedic relief than threatening menace, and Marsters's performance of Spike makes the character a fan favorite. At a time when vampires across American popular culture have become sympathetic characters in search of redemption for their sins, Spike and Dru return the classic monster to its original bloodthirsty origins. Before they part ways, the two represent the most horrific examples of the violence and nonchalant attitude toward taking life that made characters such as Dracula so terrifying. As with traditional vampire lore, Spike and Dru represent the fallen human, consumed with following the path of evil, regardless of the ultimate hellish consequences. Spike's eventual redemption speaks to pop culture's obsession with making popular characters good.

Richard A. Hall

See also: Angelique Bouchard-Collins, Angelus, Dark Willow, Dracula, Faith the Vampire Slayer; *Thematic Essays*: The Pathos of Villainy: Getting to the Heart of Why Villains Went Bad.

Further Reading

Adler, Margot. 2014. *Vampires Are Us: Understanding Our Love Affair with the Immortal Dark Side*. Newburyport, MA: Weiser.

Alsford, Mike. 2006. *Heroes & Villains*. Waco, TX: Baylor University Press.

Ashby, LeRoy. 2006. *With Amusement for All: A History of American Popular Culture since 1830*. Lexington: University Press of Kentucky.

Billson, Anne. 2005. *Buffy the Vampire Slayer*. London: British Film Institute.

Castleman, Harry, and Walter J. Podrazik. 2016. *Watching TV: Eight Decades of American Television*. 3rd ed. Syracuse, NY: Syracuse University Press.

Dial-Driver, Emily, Sally Emmons-Featherston, Jim Ford, and Carolyn Anne Taylor. 2008. *The Truth of Buffy: Essays on Fiction Illuminating Reality*. Jefferson, NC: McFarland.

Field, Mark. 2017. *Buffy, the Vampire Slayer: Myth, Metaphor & Morality*. N.p.: Amazon Services.

Gross, Edward, and Mark A. Altman. 2017. *Slayers & Vampires: The Complete, Uncensored, Unauthorized Oral History of Buffy & Angel*. New York: Tor.

Jowett, Lorna. 2005. *Sex and the Slayer: A Gender Studies Primer for the Buffy Fan*. Middletown, CT: Wesleyan University Press.

Lavery, David. 2013. *Joss Whedon, A Creative Portrait: From Buffy, the Vampire Slayer to Marvel's The Avengers*. London: I. B. Tauris.

Lavery, David, and Cynthia Burkhead, eds. 2011. *Joss Whedon: Conversations*. Television Conversations Series. Jackson: University of Mississippi Press.

Pender, Patricia J. 2016. *I'm Buffy and You're History*. London: I. B. Tauris.

Pollard, Tom. 2016. *Loving Vampires: Our Undead Obsession*. Jefferson, NC: McFarland.

Short, Sue. 2011. "*Buffy the Vampire Slayer*: Beauty and the 'Big Bad.'" In *Cult Telefantasy Series: A Critical Analysis of The Prisoner, Twin Peaks, The X-Files, Buffy the Vampire Slayer, Lost, Heroes, Doctor Who, and Star Trek*, 84–107. Jefferson, NC: McFarland.

South, James B., ed. 2005. *Buffy, the Vampire Slayer and Philosophy: Fear and Trembling in Sunnydale*. Chicago: Open Court.

"TV Guide Picks TV's 60 Nastiest Villains." 2013. *TV Guide*. April 22, 2013. Accessed January 1, 2019. http://wordsmithonia.blogspot.com/2013/04/tv-guide-picks-tvs-60-nastiest-villains.html.

Wilcox, Rhonda V., Tanya Cochran, Cynthea Masson, and David Lavery. 2014. *Reading Joss Whedon*. Syracuse, NY: Syracuse University Press.

Wilcox, Rhonda V., and David Lavery. 2002. *Fighting the Forces: What's at Stake in Buffy, the Vampire Slayer*. Lanham, MD: Rowman & Littlefield.

Yeffeth, Glenn, ed. 2003. *Seven Seasons of Buffy: Science Fiction and Fantasy Writers Discuss Their Favorite Television Show*. Dallas, TX: BenBella.

Yeffeth, Glenn, ed. 2004. *Five Seasons of Angel: Science Fiction and Fantasy Writers Discuss Their Favorite Vampire*. Smart Pop Series. Dallas, TX: BenBella.

Sue Sylvester

First Appearance:	*Glee*, season 1, episode 1 (air date: 1968)
Creators:	Ryan Murphy, Brad Falchuk, and Ian Brennan
Other Media:	Stage
Primary Strength:	Cunning
Major Weakness:	Insecurity
Weapons:	Authority
Base of Operations:	William McKinley High School, Lima, Ohio
Key Allies:	Jean Sylvester (sister), Principal Figgins, Cheerios (cheerleading squad), Becky Jackson
Key Enemies:	Will Schuester ("Mr. Shue"), McKinley High Glee Club ("The New Directions")
Actual Identity:	Susan Sylvester
Nicknames/Aliases:	"Coach"

The television series *Glee* (FOX, 2009–2015), was an hour-long musical dramedy centered on a high school glee club in Ohio. The primary protagonists of the series were the new glee club director, Will Shuester (played by Matthew Morrison), and his club of nerds and misfits who make up the New Directions with their sights set on winning the glee club national competition. Their enemy on this quest is the high school's cheerleading coach, Sue Sylvester (played by Jane Lynch). Throughout the early seasons of the series, Sue relentlessly attempts to torpedo the glee club on the basis that she believes that limited public school funds would be better spent on her cheerleading squad, the Cheerios. As the heroes of the series are those kids often statistically bullied in high school, Sue represents the ultimate in high school bullies (despite being an adult faculty member). Over time, the traditional high school cliques begin to melt as the teenagers from all social strata begin to work together, seeing each other as equally valued, breaking down the social barriers prevalent in American high schools.

The series begins with Sue's relentless efforts to bring down the burgeoning glee club. Her first plan involves recruiting some of her cheerleaders to join the club with the intention of breaking down the teenagers' resolve from the inside. When this fails, she goes on to give the set list prepared by the club to their other high school opponents, forcing the club to improvise a new set literally at the last minute. She exerts power through consistently blackmailing the school's principal, Principal Figgins, to do her bidding. She inspires fear not only in the glee clubbers and fellow faculty but also in her own cheerleaders. After manipulating her way on to the judges' panel for the regional glee club competition, Sue becomes the target of bullying when the other judges ridicule her for her lack of background in glee club. This reversal leads Sue to begin to sympathize with the teenagers she has been tormenting all year.

In the following season, Sue's prized Cheerios revolt, quitting the team to dedicate themselves to the glee club. Their absence leads the cheerleading team to lose their own regional competition after six consecutive national victories. Due to this loss, Sue's budget gets reduced, raising her ire more against the glee club. In the third season, Sue adds high schooler Becky Jackson (played by Lauren Potter), a girl with Down syndrome, to the Cheerios squad as the young girl reminds Sue of her own sister, Jean, who also has Down syndrome. In season four, Sue is fired when Becky's gun accidentally goes off, causing the high school to believe there is an active shooter situation. When Becky comes forward the following season

Jane Lynch created an oddly lovable villain with cheerleading coach Sue Sylvester on the FOX television series *Glee*. (Twentieth Century Fox/AF Archive/Alamy Stock Photo)

and admits to the accidental gunfire, Sue is restored, in the process manipulating the downfall of Principal Figgins and moving herself into the position of principal. The series ends with Sue once more being fired from McKinley High, but in a flash-forward sequence, it is revealed that Sue becomes vice president of the United States to President Jeb Bush in 2020, with Becky as her bodyguard.

Thanks in large part to the brilliance of Lynch's performance, Sue Sylvester is the ultimate, in-depth representation of the American bully. She bullies those she claims to be lesser than herself, while she simultaneously possesses deep insecurities that it is, in fact, *she* who is inferior. Just when the audience reaches the point of ultimate disgust with Sue's actions, the character makes an abrupt about-face and reveals her own inner demons, leading the same audience to sympathize, and even root for, the bully. Through Sue Sylvester, *Glee* did perhaps more than any other franchise in popular culture to dissect and examine the issue of high school bullying than has ever been presented on screen. In 2013, *TV Guide* ranked Sue Sylvester as TV's fifty-seventh "nastiest" villain ("TV Guide Picks TV's 60 Nastiest Villains," *TV Guide*).

Richard A. Hall

See also: Archie Bunker, Asajj Ventress, Cersei Lannister, CSM/The Cigarette Smoking Man, Dark Willow, Faith the Vampire Slayer, Fiona Goode/The Supreme, Frank Burns, La Llorona, Loki, Maleficent, Nurse Ratched, Sherry Palmer, Ursula, Wicked Witch of the West; *Thematic Essays*: The Pathos of Villainy: Getting to the Heart of Why Villains Went Bad.

Further Reading

Alsford, Mike. 2006. *Heroes & Villains.* Waco, TX: Baylor University Press.

Castleman, Harry, and Walter J. Podrazik. 2016. *Watching TV: Eight Decades of American Television.* 3rd ed. Syracuse, NY: Syracuse University Press.

Faludi, Susan. 2007. *The Terror Dream: Myth and Misogyny in an Insecure America.* New York: Picador.

"TV Guide Picks TV's 60 Nastiest Villains." 2013. *TV Guide.* April 22, 2013. Accessed January 1, 2019. http://wordsmithonia.blogspot.com/2013/04/tv-guide-picks-tvs-60-nastiest-villains.html.

Willis, Susan. 2005. *Portents of the Real: A Primer for Post-9/11 America.* London: Verso.

T

Thanos

First Appearance:	*The Invincible Iron Man #55* (cover date: February, 1973)
Creators:	Jim Starlin
Other Media:	Movies, animated television series
Primary Strength:	Tactics, genius, superhuman strength/stamina/agility/durability
Major Weakness:	Delusions of grandeur
Weapons:	The Infinity Gauntlet
Base of Operations:	Titan
Key Allies:	Mistress Death, Nebula, The Black Order, Adam Warlock (briefly)
Key Enemies:	Eros (brother), Silver Surfer, Thor, The Avengers, The Guardians of the Galaxy, Gamora, Captain Marvel, Nova Corps, Squirrel Girl, Adam Warlock, Nebula (eventually)
Actual Identity:	N/A
Nicknames/Aliases:	"The Mad Titan"

By the 1970s, the Marvel Comics Universe had grown a considerable audience among superhero comic book fandom. The intricately woven fictional universe created by Stan Lee, Jack Kirby, and Steve Ditko had raised the bar for superhero narratives. A new wave of heroes and villains emerged in the 1970s, one such being Thanos, the "Mad Titan," by writer and artist Jim Starlin. Born on the Saturn moon of Titan, Thanos was of mixed heritage, of both the Eternal and Deviant races. These highly advanced, near godlike races made Thanos a formidable foe for the Marvel superheroes. Though a relatively lower-tier villain in the comic books, Thanos became a household name in the American zeitgeist with his inclusion in the Marvel Cinematic Universe from 2008 to 2019, where he was ultimately portrayed by actor Josh Brolin.

Thanos's major breakthrough as a major Marvel villain came with the 1990–1991 story line "The Infinity Gauntlet." Romantically obsessed with Mistress Death, the goddess of death in the Marvel Comics Universe, Thanos seeks to win her affections by retrieving the six infinity gems, cosmic stones of immense power, each possessing a specific area of control: time, space, soul, reality, power, and mind. With these gems loaded into the mystical Infinity Gauntlet, the bearer would possess unlimited, absolute power over the universe. Armed with this power, Thanos would eradicate half the life in the entire universe, offering those deaths to Mistress Death as a show of his affection. The spiritual essence known as Adam Warlock leaves his realm of Soul World to inhabit a recently deceased Earth human, rallying Earth's superheroes as well as other cosmic entities to stop Thanos from further destruction. In the end, Warlock reclaims the gauntlet, and Thanos appears to commit suicide while actually exiling himself to a private, idyllic planet where he promises Warlock to live out his life in a monk-like existence (Jim Starlin, George Perez, and Ron Lim, *The Infinity Gauntlet #1–6*, July–December 1991).

In the Marvel Cinematic Universe, the Thanos/Gauntlet story line plays out similarly. Unlike in the comics, however, Thanos's desire to wipe out half of all life in the universe is for an environmentally conscious purpose. With exploding populations consuming a finite amount of resources, Thanos hopes that by eliminating half of all life, other planets will avoid the fate of his home world of Titan, which was ultimately destroyed by overpopulation. Although he is successful, as in the comics, the surviving Avengers of Earth unite to travel back through time to retrieve the infinity stones at earlier points in time to create a new gauntlet and use its power to bring back those who disappeared due to Thanos's original snap. Once successful, Iron Man/Tony Stark utilizes the stones to make Thanos disappear, sacrificing his life in the process, his human form unable to survive channeling the power of the stones (Christopher Markus and Stephen McFeely, *Avengers: Infinity War/Avengers: Endgame*, Marvel Studios, 2018/2019).

Though villainous as a cold-blooded mass murderer, the movie form of Thanos adds a sympathetic factor to his crimes. By killing half of all life, Thanos believes that he is providing longevity to the species of every planet (a sacrifice for the greater good). The heroes, by contrast, place more importance on the immediate loss of loved ones over the long-term ramifications of their continued overpopulated existence. This is a dramatic contrast from Thanos's motives in the comics, which are purely self-serving. As such, Thanos is a villain whose different incarnations open a debate on egoism versus altruism and the point at which altruism becomes villainous. Comparing and contrasting the two Thanos story lines open doors to fascinating academic debate for decades to come.

Richard A. Hall

See also: Doctor Doom, Doomsday, Killmonger, Lex Luthor, Loki, Magneto, Ozymandias, Ra's al Ghul, Red Skull, Ultron, Zod; *Thematic Essays*: The Pathos of Villainy: Getting to the Heart of Why Villains Went Bad.

Further Reading

Alsford, Mike. 2006. *Heroes & Villains.* Waco, TX: Baylor University Press.

Ashby, LeRoy. 2006. *With Amusement for All: A History of American Popular Culture since 1830.* Lexington: University Press of Kentucky.

Costello, Matthew J. 2009. *Secret Identity Crisis: Comic Books & the Unmasking of Cold War America.* New York: Continuum.

Dyer, Ben, ed. 2009. *Supervillains and Philosophy: Sometimes, Evil Is Its Own Reward.* Popular Culture and Philosophy Series. Chicago: Open Court.

Howe, Sean. 2012. *Marvel Comics: The Untold Story.* New York: Harper-Perennial.

Tucker, Reed. 2017. *Slugfest: Inside the Epic 50-Year Battle between Marvel and DC.* New York: Da Capo Press.

Wright, Bradford W. 2003. *Comic Book Nation: The Transformation of Youth Culture in America.* Baltimore, MD: Johns Hopkins University Press.

Tia Dalma/Calypso

First Appearance:	*Pirates of the Caribbean: Dead Man's Chest* (release date: June 24, 2006)
Creators:	Ted Elliot and Terry Rossio
Other Media:	Novels
Primary Strength:	Hoodoo/voodoo
Major Weakness:	Cursed (by nine Pieces of Eight)
Weapons:	Obeah spells/incantations
Base of Operations:	Unspecified swamp (as Tia Dalma)/Seven Seas (as Calypso)
Key Allies:	Davy Jones (lover), Jack Sparrow, Captain Barbossa, Will Turner, Elizabeth Swann
Key Enemies:	Davy Jones (eventually), Brethren Court of Pirate Lords
Actual Identity:	Calypso
Nicknames/Aliases:	Tia Dalma

In 2003, Disney launched its *Pirates of the Caribbean* film franchise, based loosely on the popular ride at their theme parks and set in the early 1700s. The first film, subtitled *The Curse of the Black Pearl,* introduced viewers to the antihero pirate Captain Jack Sparrow (played with overly exuberant glee by Johnny Depp) and his archnemesis, the pirate Captain Hector Barbossa (played with slithering charisma by Geoffrey Rush). The unexpected worldwide success of the first film led to four sequels: *Dead Man's Chest* (2006), *At World's End* (2007), *On Stranger Tides* (2011), and *Dead Men Tell No Tales* (2017). In 2018, Disney announced that it would be rebooting the franchise rather than commit to future films from the current saga. In the second chapter of the original series, audiences were introduced to the voodoo queen, Tia Dalma (played by Naomie Harris).

When Captain Jack Sparrow is cursed by the legendary Davy Jones (played by Bill Nighy), condemned to serve as Jones's crewman on the ghostly pirate ship *The Flying Dutchman* for all eternity, Sparrow visits the voodoo priestess Tia Dalma for information concerning the Dead Man's Chest, which is said to contain the cursed heart of Davy Jones. Although ultimately successful in his quest,

Sparrow is devoured by the sea creature known as the Kraken, also in service to Jones. This death sends Sparrow to a strange afterlife. In the wake of Sparrow's loss, Will Turner (played by Orlando Bloom), Elizabeth Swann (played by Keira Knightly), and the crew of *The Black Pearl* return to Tia Dalma, who assures them that Sparrow can be saved and reveals that she has resurrected Captain Hector Barbossa (played by Geoffrey Rush), who can lead them to rescue Sparrow (Ted Elliot and Terry Rossio, *Pirates of the Caribbean: Dead Man's Chest*, 2006).

Dalma travels with the crew of the *Pearl* and rescues Sparrow from the afterlife, and the crew then embarks on calling together the nine Pirate Lords to do battle against the British East India Company, who threaten the pirates' way of life on the open seas. During this adventure, the pirates conclude that they must release the ocean goddess Calypso, who was bound to human form by their predecessors centuries earlier, using nine Pieces of Eight (although as none of the pirates at the time actually had any Pieces of Eight coins, they substituted the coins for whatever objects they happened to have at the time). Calypso had once been the lover of the pirate Davy Jones, when he was still human. Calypso had granted Jones immortality in exchange for providing the task of leading lost souls at sea to the afterlife; the downside of the curse was that Jones could only make landfall one day every ten years. When Jones returns the first time, Calypso is nowhere to be found. Enraged, Jones informed the Brethren Court of Pirate Lords about how to subdue the goddess and trap her in human form, thus calming the Seven Seas. Soon, the pirates discover that Tia Dalma is the trapped goddess and prepare the ritual for her release.

Imprisoned, Dalma is visited by Jones one last time, and she reveals that it has been his neglect of his duty to the lost souls (whom he has impressed into service rather than lead to the afterlife) that has turned him into the monster he has become. Once released, Calypso enacts her revenge on both the pirates and Jones. Although Will Turner is killed in the melee, Sparrow utilizes Jones's heart to save Will, allowing him to take Jones's place as guide to the afterlife. Calypso disappears prior to the battle, free but never to be seen again (Ted Elliot and Terry Rossio, *Pirates of the Caribbean: At World's End*, 2007). While Calypso is the traditional villainous goddess, Tia Dalma is the traditional voodoo queen, a witch and practitioner of the black arts. The source of her villainy in the *Pirates* franchise comes from the betrayal of a trusted lover. She also, however, portrays the feminine power that, for centuries, was associated with witchcraft.

Richard A. Hall

See also: Alexis Carrington-Colby-Dexter, Angelique Bouchard-Collins, Asajj Ventress, Bellatrix Lestrange, Captain Hector Barbossa, Dark Willow, Fiona Goode/The Supreme, La Llorona, Loki, Lucifer/Satan, Maleficent, Morgan le Fay, Poison Ivy, Sauron/Saruman, Sith Lords, Ursula, Wicked Witch of the West; *Thematic Essays*: The Pathos of Villainy: Getting to the Heart of Why Villains Went Bad.

Further Reading

Alsford, Mike. 2006. *Heroes & Villains*. Waco, TX: Baylor University Press.

Cavendish, Richard. 1968. *The Black Arts: A Concise History of Witchcraft, Demonology, Astrology, and Other Mystical Practices throughout the Ages*. New York: TarcherPerigree.

Faludi, Susan. 2007. *The Terror Dream: Myth and Misogyny in an Insecure America*. New York: Picador.

Forasteros, J. R. 2017. *Empathy for the Devil: Finding Ourselves in the Villains of the Bible*. Downers Grove, IL: InterVarsity.

Hutton, Ronald. 2017. *The Witch: A History of Fear, from Ancient Times to the Present*. New Haven, CT: Yale University Press.

Russell, Jeffrey B., and Brooks Alexander. 2007. *A History of Witchcraft: Sorcerers, Heretics, & Pagans*. London: Thames & Hudson.

Ryan, Hannah. 2020. "Vilifications: Conjuring Witches Then and Now." In *The Supervillain Reader*, edited by Rob Weiner and Rob Peaslee, 156–171. Jackson: University of Mississippi Press.

Tony Montana

First Appearance:	*Scarface* (release date: December 1, 1983)
Creators:	Oliver Stone
Other Media:	Novels
Primary Strength:	Cunning, ambition
Major Weakness:	Anger
Weapons:	Various guns, knives
Base of Operations:	Miami, Florida
Key Allies:	Angel, Chi-Chi, Manny Ribera, Frank Lopez (briefly), Elvira Hancock, Georgiana (mother), Gina (sister), Alejandro Sosa (briefly)
Key Enemies:	Omar Suarez, Mel Bernstein, Frank Lopez (eventually), Alejandro Sosa (eventually), Gina (eventually), The Skull
Actual Identity:	Antonio Montana
Nicknames/Aliases:	"Scarface"

In 1983, Universal Pictures and director Brian De Palma released the classic gangster film *Scarface*, starring Al Pacino as Tony Montana. Montana comes to the United States as a Cuban refugee in the summer of 1980. Soon after his arrival, Montana and his friends are enlisted by local drug lord Frank Lopez (played by Robert Loggia). Over time, Montana decides that he is meant for bigger things and begins to utilize his cunning and connections to negotiate his own drug empire through a deal with Bolivian crime lord Alejandro Sosa (played by Paul Shenar). This deal puts Tony on the outs with Lopez, who begins to maneuver against him, especially after discovering that Tony is secretly involved with Lopez's wife, Elvira, played by Michelle Pfeiffer. Sosa, too, turns on Tony once the up-and-coming drug dealer fails to assassinate a New York journalist threatening to expose Sosa's criminal empire. After Tony murders his best friend for what he believes to be a tryst with Tony's sister, Gina (only to discover the two had secretly

Al Capone

Alphonse Capone (1899–1947) may well be the ultimate example of the organized-crime boss in American history. Born in New York City, Capone came to fame after moving to Chicago, Illinois, in his early twenties. Working for Johnny Torrio (1882–1957) as his right hand man, Capone learned the ins and outs of the illegal alcohol business during the Roaring 1920s. When Torrio retired, Capone rose even higher in power as a result of the St. Valentine's Day Massacre (February 14, 1929), where Capone's men took out most of his business rivals, gaining him the moniker "Public Enemy #1" by the burgeoning FBI. Unable to catch Capone for his various criminal endeavors, the U.S. government ultimately arrested the crime boss for tax evasion, when the accounting books covering his illegal monies was obtained by authorities. In 1931, he was sentenced to eleven years in Alcatraz Prison, but he was released after serving eight. He died from complications of a stroke in 1947. In the decades since his death, most organized-crime characters in popular culture have been based to one degree or another on Al Capone, from Virgil Sollozzo in *The Godfather*, to Tony Montagna in *Scarface*, to Jabba the Hutt in *Star Wars: Return of the Jedi* and Tony Soprano in *The Sopranos*. In the 1987 film *The Untouchables*, Capone was brought to life by actor Robert De Niro (b. 1943).

Richard A. Hall

married), Tony binges on own narcotics and is now devoid of friends, family, and even Elvira. Sosa's men attack Tony's home, and the titular character goes down in a blaze of gunfire.

Tony Montana and *Scarface* ranks with *The Godfather* films as the quintessential example of gangsters on the big screen. Whereas *The Godfather* presents organized crime in a more "civilized" and family-centered way, *Scarface* fully bears out the ugly violence inherent in organized crime in America. The film also, however, plays into racial and ethnic stereotypes of Central and South American and Caribbean immigrants to the United States, underscoring the systemic racism toward immigrants and refugees from these regions. Montana desires the American Dream, but he chooses a dark path to that end, culminating with the violent result of his chosen lifestyle. Unlike many villains in modern pop culture, Tony Montana is not a sympathetic figure. From the outset, his motives and actions dictate his unavoidable outcome.

Richard A. Hall

See also: Bill/Snake Charmer, Billy the Kid, Captain Hector Barbossa, The Corleone Family, Elle Driver/California Mountain Snake, Fish Mooney, Gus Fring, Heisenberg/Walter White, La Llorona, Negan/The Saviors, O-Ren Ishii/Cottonmouth, Pancho Villa, Penguin, Tony Soprano, Two-Face; *Thematic Essays*: The Pathos of Villainy: Getting to the Heart of Why Villains Went Bad.

Further Reading

Alsford, Mike. 2006. *Heroes & Villains.* Waco, TX: Baylor University Press.

Ashby, LeRoy. 2006. *With Amusement for All: A History of American Popular Culture since 1830.* Lexington: University Press of Kentucky.

Behnken, Brian D., and Gregory D. Smithers. 2015. *Racism in American Popular Media: From Aunt Jemima to the Frito Bandito.* Westport, CT: Praeger.

Browne, Nick, ed. 2000. *Francis Ford Coppola's "The Godfather" Trilogy.* Cambridge: Cambridge University Press.

McCarty, John. 2004. *Bullets over Hollywood: The American Gangster Picture from the Silents to "The Sopranos."* Cambridge, MA: Da Capo.

Rossinow, Doug. 2015. *The Reagan Era: A History of the 1980s.* New York: Columbia University Press.

Tony Soprano

First Appearance:	*The Sopranos*, season 1, episode 1 (air date: January 10, 1999)
Creators:	David Chase
Other Media:	Movie
Primary Strength:	Cunning
Major Weakness:	Family
Weapons:	Standard handguns, bombs, garrote
Base of Operations:	New Jersey
Key Allies:	Carmela Soprano, Anthony Soprano Jr. (A.J.), Meadow Soprano, Christopher Moltisanti, Corrado Soprano Jr. (Junior, Uncle June), Janice, Livia, Dr. Jennifer Melfi, Sal Bonpensiero (Big Pussy), Silvio Dante, Paul Gualtieri (Paulie Walnuts), Herman Rabkin (Hesh), Bobby Baccalieri (Bobby Bacala), John Sacrimoni (Johnny Sack)
Key Enemies:	Federal Bureau of Investigations, Richie Aprile, Ralph Cifaretto, Phil Leotardo
Actual Identity:	Anthony Soprano
Nicknames/Aliases:	N/A

David Chase, creator of *The Sopranos*, toiled in television writing for iconic shows such as *The Rockford Files* (NBC, 1974–1980) for decades before he was approached by Brad Grey, cofounder of Brillstein-Grey, about coming to work for his production company. When Chase was asked about writing "*The Godfather* for TV" for Brillstein-Grey, he initially turned the idea down, but the suggestion reminded him of a movie idea he had about a mafioso in therapy. Chase presented the idea and was encouraged to write a pilot script. The script was turned down by all of the major broadcast networks before HBO decided to gamble on the series (Leibovitz and Kashner, "The Family Hour"). Running from 1999 to 2007, the show was a critical success from the first episode, was nominated for awards every year it was eligible, and won numerous awards and accolades.

The plot of *The Sopranos* was boiled down thus in the pitch to HBO: "40-year-old guy, crossroads of his life, turmoil in his marriage, turmoil in his professional career, beginning to raise teenage kids in modern society—all the pressures of every man in his generation. The only difference is he's the Mob boss of northern New Jersey. Oh, by the way, he's seeing a shrink" (Leibovitz and Kashner, "The Family Hour"). At its core, the plot of this groundbreaking show is that simple. That is one of the things that made the show so popular with audiences. The show begins with a black screen that suddenly opens on Tony Soprano (played by James Gandolfini) sitting in the waiting room of his therapist, Dr. Jennifer Melfi (played by Lorraine Bracco). As he creatively retells the events leading to the panic attack bringing him to a "shrink's" office, we learn that Tony is in the Mafia (David Chase, "Pilot," *The Sopranos*, season 1, episode 1, January 10, 1999). James Gandolfini attributed the success of his character and the audience's love to Tony's sessions with Dr. Melfi. He likened Dr. Melfi to the Greek chorus of ancient dramas.

In every season of the show, Tony is shown juggling his family responsibilities and his "family" responsibilities (i.e., his job as mob boss of northern New Jersey), often to poor results on both fronts. Each season introduces new enemies for the focus of that season in addition to the ever-present threat of the FBI, and the audience is taken on a journey along with weekly (mostly) visits with Dr. Melfi to decide what it all means for Tony and his two lives. The controversial final episode ends as the show began: with a black screen (David Chase, "Made in America," *The Sopranos*, season 6, episode 21, June 10, 2007). The debate rages on over whether Tony gets "whacked" in that final scene, and it will never be definitively answered to the satisfaction of all fans.

James Gandolfini in the defining role of his career: Tony Soprano from the HBO television series *The Sopranos*. (ZUMA Press, Inc./Alamy Stock Photo)

There are two revolutionary legacies of *The Sopranos*: the television landscape and men's perception of mental health. The latter is likely the more important. The image of the tough guy mob boss engaging in talk therapy helped men in America see mental health in a new light. Tony would occasionally bemoan, "Whatever happened to Gary Cooper? You know, the strong silent type," but his experiences as portrayed in the show demonstrated to men for the first time in a crystallized way why the strong silent type was not the ideal they should be striving for. When Tony would quit therapy in his characteristically abrupt manner, his life would go more wrong than usual, and he would realize the value of his sessions with Dr. Melfi.

Even the reactions of his colleagues when they learned he was in therapy were important for men. When Tony tells his three closest associates in his organization that he is seeing a therapist, two of the three take the news fairly well. One even reveals that he, too, had seen a therapist in the past (David Chase, "I Dream of Jeannie Cusamano," *The Sopranos*, season 1, episode 13, April 4, 1999). This scene shows that because of the glorification of this strong silent type, we have no idea how even our closest friends and family are handling the struggles in their lives, but if men would open up to one another, they could be pleasantly surprised to find they are not alone. Tony's nephew Christopher Moltisanti (played by Michael Imperioli) is the only one who shows serious reservations about the news. Even so, Christopher will go on to sporadically embrace addiction recovery.

The other important legacy of *The Sopranos* is how it revolutionized television. This show introduced story arcs that lasted longer than an episode. To give David Chase a break from the grind of producing the show, audiences had to learn patience between seasons when they did not get the show on the classic twelve-month cycle (Leibovitz and Kashner, "The Family Hour"). Most important, though, was Tony Soprano as the antihero. Tony Soprano is not a good guy. In fact, he is a sociopath who plies his trade with impunity, cheats on his wife, murders people, and orders the murders of others. In spite of that, women love him, and men want to be him. The success of the character of Tony Soprano blazed a trail audiences could follow as they delight in the story of a serial killer who kills other serial killers, Dexter Morgan; the high school chemistry teacher turned meth cook/crime boss, Walter White; and many, many others.

Keith R. Claridy

See also: Alexis Carrington-Colby-Dexter, Bill/Snake Charmer, Billy the Kid, Captain Hector Barbosa, Cersei Lannister, COBRA, The Corleone Family, The Court of Owls, Elle Driver/California Mountain Snake, Ersnt Stavro Blofeld/SPECTRE, Goldfinger, Gus Fring, Grand Nagus/Ferengi, Heisenberg/Walter White, Jabba the Hutt, J. R. Ewing, Marsellus Wallace, Negan/The Saviors, O-Ren Ishii/Cottonmouth, Ozymandias, Pancho Villa, Sherry Palmer, Tony Montagna, Two-Face; *Thematic Essays*: Tarantino and the Antivillain, The Pathos of Villainy: Getting to the Heart of Why Villains Went Bad.

Further Reading

Grevas, Andrew. 2019. "'You Understand the Human Condition': *The Sopranos*, Mental Health, & Me." 25YL. May 2019. Accessed June 1, 2019. https://25yearslatersite.com/2019/05/03/you-understand-the-human-condition-the-sopranos-mental-health-me/.

Hines, Ree. 2013. "Tony Soprano Character Altered Face of TV, Paving Way for Antiheroes." Today. June 2013. Accessed June 1, 2019. https://www.today.com/popculture/tony-soprano-character-altered-face-tv-paving-way-antiheroes-6C10387810.

Karson, Michael. 2017. "A Case Formulation for Tony Soprano." Psychology Today. January 2017. Accessed June 1, 2019. https://www.psychologytoday.com/us/blog/feeling-our-way/201701/case-formulation-tony-soprano.

Leibovitz, Annie, and Sam Kashner. 2012. "The Family Hour: An Oral History of *The Sopranos*." *Vanity Fair*. April 2012. Accessed June 1, 2019. https://www.vanityfair.com/hollywood/2012/04/sopranos-oral-history.

Pruner, Aaron. 2019. "How the Godfather of TV Antiheroes Tony Soprano Changed Television Forever." Rotten Tomatoes. January 2019. Accessed June 1, 2019. https://editorial.rottentomatoes.com/article/tony-soprano-introduced-the-tv-antihero/.

Szabo, Ross. 2007. "Mental Health Advocates Will Miss *The Sopranos*." June 2007. Updated May 2011. Accessed June 1, 2019. https://www.huffpost.com/entry/mental-health-advocates-w_b_51662.

Two-Face

First Appearance:	*Detective Comics #66* (cover date: August, 1942)
Creators:	Bill Finger and Bob Kane
Other Media:	Animated and live-action television series, movies
Primary Strength:	Tenacity
Major Weakness:	Obsessive compulsive disorder (OCD)
Weapons:	Handguns
Base of Operations:	Gotham City
Key Allies:	Various henchmen, Riddler (in movie)
Key Enemies:	Batman
Actual Identity:	Harvey Dent
Nicknames/Aliases:	"Harvey Two-Face," "Big Bad Harve" (in animated series)

The *Batman franchise* is, perhaps, second only to *Superman* with regard to its impact on popular culture. Created by writer Bill Finger and artist Bob Kane, Batman is billionaire playboy Bruce Wayne, who, after witnessing a mugger murder his parents when he was a young boy, vowed to dedicate his life battling crime in his hometown of Gotham City. In order to strike fear in criminals, Wayne chose to disguise himself as a bat, and "the Batman" (originally "Bat-Man") was born (Bill Finger and Bob Kane, *Detective Comics #33*, November 1939). Unlike his counterpart, Superman, Batman is a mere mortal, with no "super" powers of any kind. Instead, Batman is armed only with his keen intellect and a myriad of gadgets and vehicles that he uses in his fight against crime. Over the decades, in comics as well as on television and film, Batman has gained arguably the most impressive rogues' gallery of villains in all of popular culture. One of the most sympathetic to audiences has been the former Gotham City district attorney, Harvey Dent, also known as the villain Two-Face.

In the original origin story for Two-Face, Gotham district attorney Harvey Dent is permanently scarred when a mobster he is trying throws acid into his face, disfiguring half. As he was previously known for his good looks, this deformity drives the young man insane, and he becomes the villain Two-Face, who bases right or wrong decisions on the flip of a double-headed coin, one head scarred (denoting a wrong choice) and the other pristine (denoting the right choice). As Two-Face, he becomes a leader in the Gotham underworld (Bill Finger and Bob Kane, *Detective Comics #66*, August 1942).

In the wake of the *Crisis on Infinite Earths* universal reboot (1985–1986), a deeper examination of the character reveals that Dent was physically abused as a child, his father frequently choosing to do so at the literal flip of his lucky coin (Jeph Loeb and Tim Sale, *Batman: The Long Halloween #1–13*, December 1996–December 1997). A "final story" for Two-Face appeared in the legendary miniseries *Batman: The Dark Knight Returns* (1986) by Frank Miller. In that story, set a decade after Bruce Wayne has retired as Batman, Harvey Dent is deemed healed both physically and mentally by his doctors and is released from Arkham Asylum. He immediately embarks on a typical Two-Face crime spree. When Batman catches Dent, the former district attorney laments that though the doctors made both sides of his face the same, they did so by scarring the unscarred half. Although this is not the case—in fact, both sides of his face are now unscarred—the fact that Harvey views himself as completely scarred expresses the idea that mentally he will always be Two-Face (Frank Miller, *Batman: The Dark Knight Returns #1*, February 1986).

A deeper and equally sympathetic portrayal of Two-Face appeared on television in *Batman: The Animated Series* (FOX Kids, 1992–1995), where Harvey Dent/Two-Face was voiced by Richard Moll. African American actor Billy Dee Williams portrayed a pre-Two-Face Harvey Dent in the feature film *Batman* (Warner Brothers, 1989). In the third film of the original Batman movie series, *Batman Forever* (Warner Brothers, 1995), actor Tommy Lee Jones portrayed a more comedic version of the character, more in line with what might have appeared on the 1960s live-action *Batman* series. Another pre-Two-Face Harvey Dent was portrayed on the live-action television series *Gotham* (FOX, 2014–2019). This version of Dent, played by actor Nicholas D'Agosto, provided glimpses into the darker nature of Dent as well as his prescarred double-headed coin.

Many villains in the *Batman* rogues' gallery are sympathetic villains, people who have experienced differing degrees of personal trauma, as a young Bruce Wayne had, but who, unlike the boy billionaire, allowed their trauma to take them down a darker path. Two-Face is the ultimate example of this manifestation of villainy in the *Batman* universe. His villainy does not come from a place of original malice or insanity but from a series of mind-altering traumas that make him the villain he ultimately becomes. Once he is Two-Face, Dent becomes the standard underworld tough guy organized-crime boss, the flip side of the social crusader he once was.

Richard A. Hall

See also: Catwoman, The Court of Owls, Fish Mooney, Harley Quinn, Joker, Penguin, Poison Ivy, Ra's al Ghul, Scarecrow; *Thematic Essays*: The Pathos of Villainy: Getting to the Heart of Why Villains Went Bad.

Further Reading

Alsford, Mike. 2006. *Heroes & Villains*. Waco, TX: Baylor University Press.

Ashby, LeRoy. 2006. *With Amusement for All: A History of American Popular Culture since 1830*. Lexington: University Press of Kentucky.

Langley, Travis. 2012. *Batman and Psychology: A Dark and Stormy Knight*. New York: John Wiley & Sons.

O'Neil, Dennis, ed. 2008. *Batman Unauthorized: Vigilantes, Jokers, and Heroes in Gotham City*. Smart Pop Series. Dallas, TX: BenBella.

O'Neil, Dennis. 2009. "Two Fates for Two-Face." In *Supervillains and Philosophy: Sometimes, Evil Is Its Own Reward*, edited by Ben Dyer, 147–156. Chicago: Open Court.

Weldon, Glen. 2016. *The Caped Crusade: Batman and the Rise of Nerd Culture*. New York: Simon & Schuster.

Wright, Bradford W. 2003. *Comic Book Nation: The Transformation of Youth Culture in America*. Baltimore, MD: Johns Hopkins University Press.

Ultron

First Appearance:	*The Avengers #55* (cover date: August 1968)
Creators:	Roy Thomas and John Buscema
Other Media:	Movie, animated television series
Primary Strength:	Artificial intelligence, computer interaction, enhanced speed and strength
Major Weakness:	Blinded by strict adherence to programming
Weapons:	Various computerized devices
Base of Operations:	Various, internet/World Wide Web
Key Allies:	Hank Pym (briefly), The Vision (briefly), Masters of Evil, Doctor Doom
Key Enemies:	The Avengers, The West Coast Avengers
Actual Identity:	Ultron-5 (originally)
Nicknames/Aliases:	"Crimson Cowl," "Hank Pym," "The Living Automaton"

By the mid-1960s, the Marvel Comics Universe had revolutionized superhero comic books with heroes and villains of a more complex nature than had ever been previously conceived. The robotic/AI villain Ultron appeared in the team book *The Avengers* in 1968. It is soon revealed that this evil robot was actually created by Avengers lead scientist and engineer Dr. Hank Pym ("Ant Man/Giant Man"). Based primarily on Pym's own brain patterns, Ultron develops an obsession with destroying and replacing Hank Pym, beginning with hypnotizing Pym into forgetting that he had created Ultron. Additionally, Ultron develops a romantic obsession with Pym's love interest Janet van Dyne, the Wasp (Roy Thomas and John Buscema, *The Avengers #58*, November 1968).

Every time the Avengers succeed in "destroying" Ultron, the robot, who can upload his essence into any computer system, ultimately returns in an upgraded body, becoming more dangerous with each reincarnation. It is later discovered that Ultron became the creator of the Vision, the AI-android hero and eventual Avenger, utilizing the brain patterns of the recently deceased Avenger Wonder Man (Roy Thomas and John Buscema, *The Avengers #58*, November 1968). With his continued obsession with Janet van Dyne, Ultron eventually creates an AI robot based on her brain patterns named Jocasta (Jim Shooter and George Perez, *The Avengers #162*, August 1977). Jocasta, like Vision before her, soon becomes

HAL 9000

Heuristically programmed ALgorithmic computer (HAL) 9000 is the computer antagonist in the *Space Odyssey* franchise created by Arthur C. Clarke (1917–2008). He appears in four novels—*2001: A Space Odyssey* (1968), *2010: Odyssey Two* (1982), *2061: Odyssey Three* (1987), and *3001: The Final Odyssey* (1997)—and two feature films, *2001: A Space Odyssey* (1968) and *2010: The Year We Make Contact* (1984). HAL is the intelligent and self-aware operating system of the Earth spacecraft *Discovery One*. In both the original novel and film, HAL turns on the two human astronauts on board *Discovery* when they detect a malfunction in his systems and attempt to shut him down.

The novel, however, goes into more detail as to why HAL decides to murder the crew. According to the text, HAL was given two primary missions: accurately report every aspect of the mission to mission control and conceal from the astronauts the true intent of the mission, to contact alien life. These competing missions, to be both fully honest and deceptive, lead to the malfunctions in his systems. Killing the crew is HAL's most logical course of action not only to preserve his own existence but also to fully comply with both missions. In both feature films, HAL was voiced by Douglas Rain (1928–2018). The scene in the film where Astronaut Dave Bowman (played by Keir Dullea, b. 1936) orders HAL to "open the pod bay doors," leading HAL to respond, "I'm sorry, Dave. I'm afraid I can't do that," is considered one of the most iconic scenes in Hollywood history. In the end, HAL 9000 stands as yet another cautionary tale against giving too much authority to computers and artificial intelligence.

Richard A. Hall

an Avenger, fighting against her creator. In the twenty-first century, Ultron returns as Ultron Pym, once more out to destroy and replace his creator. Pym strikes a bargain with the robot, agreeing to force Jocasta to become Ultron's bride, provided that Ultron then permanently confine himself to the alternate dimension of ultraspace (Dan Slott and Khoi Pham, "Salvation," *Mighty Avengers #35–36*, March–April 2010).

Ultron has appeared in various Marvel animated series over the decades, but his most prominent appearance in American pop culture outside of comics was the live-action feature film *Avengers: Age of Ultron* (Marvel, 2015). Written and directed by Joss Whedon, this CGI version of Ultron was voiced by actor James Spader. As the Marvel Cinematic Universe has developed differently than the original source material, with Hank Pym eventually presented as a much older character than the Avengers, Ultron was the creation of Tony Stark/Iron Man (played by Robert Downey Jr.) as the ultimate global AI protection, programmed to protect the world.

Quickly achieving sentience, Ultron believes that the true threat to the world is humanity and that, therefore, to protect the world, humanity must be eradicated so that the world could be remade in Ultron's image. He attempts to build a new body from the indestructible metal vibranium, but the body is stolen by the Avengers before Ultron can upload into it. Stark and Dr. Bruce Banner/the Hulk (played by Mark Ruffalo) instead upload the remnants of Stark's JARVIS AI program into the body, which is brought to life with an assist from lightning summoned by Thor (played by Chris Hemsworth). The result is the heroic android Vision (played by

Paul Bettany). Ultimately, the Avengers defeat Ultron by destroying all of his mechanical bodies, with Vision destroying the final avatar before it can upload elsewhere (Joss Whedon, *Avengers: Age of Ultron*, 2015).

Ultron represents yet another Frankenstein's Monster, another example of humankind's hubris and inevitable penchant for playing God. Like Shelley's iconic monster, Ultron is nearly indestructible, seeks to destroy his creator, and yearns for a bride. Like the real-world atomic bomb and the fictional dinosaurs of *Jurassic Park*, Ultron is a warning against humanity's reach extending its grasp. Ultron is a perfect example of the old adage that "the road to hell is paved with good intentions." The film version best expresses this, as Ultron is created to protect humankind but the tiny slip of suggesting protecting "the world" rather than "humanity" completely alters the idea behind the programming. As long as scientists and engineers continue to experiment with discoveries and technologies with no regard to unintended consequences, the lesson of Ultron, in all of his fictional and nonfictional reincarnations, will continue to be told.

Richard A. Hall

See also: Borg/Borg Queen, Brainiac, Cybermen, Davros/Daleks, Doctor Doom, Doomsday, Frankenstein's Monster, Green Goblin, Joker, Killmonger, Loki, Magneto, Ozymandias, Red Skull, Thanos; *Thematic Essays*: "Nazis, Communists, and Terrorists . . . Oh My!": The Rise of the Supervillain and the Evolution of the Modern American Villain, The Dark Mirror: Evil Twins, *The Twilight Zone*, and the Villain Within.

Further Reading

Alsford, Mike. 2006. *Heroes & Villains*. Waco, TX: Baylor University Press.

Ashby, LeRoy. 2006. *With Amusement for All: A History of American Popular Culture since 1830*. Lexington: University Press of Kentucky.

Costello, Matthew J. 2009. *Secret Identity Crisis: Comic Books & the Unmasking of Cold War America*. New York: Continuum.

Howe, Sean. 2012. *Marvel Comics: The Untold Story*. New York: Harper-Perennial.

Starck, Kathleen, ed. 2010. *Between Fear and Freedom: Cultural Representations of the Cold War*. Newcastle upon Tyne, UK: Cambridge Scholars.

Tucker, Reed. 2017. *Slugfest: Inside the Epic 50-Year Battle between Marvel and DC*. New York: Da Capo Press.

Wright, Bradford W. 2003. *Comic Book Nation: The Transformation of Youth Culture in America*. Baltimore, MD: Johns Hopkins University Press.

Ursula

First Appearance:	*The Little Mermaid* (release date: November 17, 1989)
Creators:	Ron Clements and John Musker
Other Media:	Animated television series, stage
Primary Strength:	Witchcraft
Major Weakness:	Jealousy
Weapons:	Spells/incantations

Base of Operations:	The oceans
Key Allies:	Flotsam and Jetsam
Key Enemies:	King Triton, Princess Ariel, Sebastian, Flounder
Actual Identity:	N/A
Nicknames/Aliases:	"The Sea Witch," "Vanessa"

The Modern Age of Disney animated feature films began with the release of *The Little Mermaid* in 1989. Directed by Ron Clements and John Musker, this musical tells the tale of Princess Ariel (voiced by Jodi Benson), a mermaid who desires to experience life as a human. The film is loosely based on the nineteenth-century fairy tale by Hans Christian Andersen. Scolded by her father, King Trion (voiced by Kenneth Mars), Ariel turns to the sea witch Ursula (voiced by Pat Carroll), who offers a Faustian bargain. Ursula will make Ariel human for three days in exchange for her magnificent voice; the caveat to the deal is that in order to remain human, Ariel must experience the "kiss of true love" or return to mermaid form as one of the witch's "poor unfortunate souls."

When it becomes clear that Ariel may succeed through the love of the human Prince Eric (voiced by Christopher Daniel Barnes), Ursula transforms into the beautiful Vanessa and attracts Eric with Ariel's singing voice, hypnotizing him into marrying her. Although Ariel and her animal friends stop the wedding, she does not achieve her kiss in time. King Triton agrees to take his daughter's place as Ursula's slave, making Ursula mistress of the seas. When she causes a massive tempest, bringing the wreckage at the bottom of the sea to the surface, Prince Eric steers a surfaced sunken ship to stab the witch and kills her, releasing Triton and winning Ariel's hand in marriage (Ron Clements and John Musker, *The Little Mermaid*, 1989).

Ursula is the traditional witch, a tried-and-true villain in stories around the world since the dawn of time. Like most witches in modern times, Ursula is presented as ugly (the upper half of her body is humanlike, while the lower half is that of an octopus) and jealous of the beauty (and, in this case, the singing voice) of the heroine princess. While her history with Triton is never clear, it is clear that she bears some grudge and desires to take Triton's place as ruler of the ocean. This traditional villain has always been a centerpiece of Disney villains, from the wicked queen, stepmother, and witch of *Snow White and the Seven Dwarfs* (1937), to the evil Maleficent of *Sleeping Beauty* (1959), to the male wizard Jafar of *Aladdin* (1992). She is representative of the evil usually associated with practitioners of the so-called dark arts. So long as there are princesses in search of true love, there will be evil witches bent on destroying their dreams.

Richard A. Hall

See also: Alexis Carrington-Colby-Dexter, Angelique Bouchard-Collins, Asajj Ventress, Bellatrix Lestrange, Dark Willow, Fiona Goode/The Supreme, Jafar, La Llorona, Loki, Lucifer/Satan, Maleficent, Morgan le Fay, Poison Ivy, Sauron/Saruman, Sith Lords, Wicked Witch of the West; *Thematic Essays*: The Pathos of Villainy: Getting to the Heart of Why Villains Went Bad.

Further Reading

Alsford, Mike. 2006. *Heroes & Villains*. Waco, TX: Baylor University Press.

Ashby, LeRoy. 2006. *With Amusement for All: A History of American Popular Culture since 1830*. Lexington: University Press of Kentucky.

Bowman, Sarah Lynne. 2011. "The Dichotomy of the Great Mother Archetype in Disney Heroines and Villainesses." In *Vader, Voldemort and Other Villains: Essays on Evil in Popular Media*, edited by Jamey Heit, 80–96. Jefferson, NC: McFarland.

Cavendish, Richard. 1968. *The Black Arts: A Concise History of Witchcraft, Demonology, Astrology, and Other Mystical Practices throughout the Ages*. New York: TarcherPerigree.

Darcy, Jen. 2016. *Disney Villains: Delightfully Evil: The Creation, the Inspiration, the Fascination*. New York: Disney Editions.

Davis, Amy M. 2007. *Good Girls and Wicked Witches: Women in Disney's Feature Animation*. East Barnet, UK: John Libbey.

Hutton, Ronald. 2017. *The Witch: A History of Fear, from Ancient Times to the Present*. New Haven, CT: Yale University Press.

Russell, Jeffrey B., and Brooks Alexander. 2007. *A History of Witchcraft: Sorcerers, Heretics, & Pagans*. London: Thames & Hudson.

Ryan, Hannah. 2020. "Vilifications: Conjuring Witches Then and Now." In *The Supervillain Reader*, edited by Rob Weiner and Rob Peaslee, 156–171. Jackson: University of Mississippi Press.

Voldemort

First Appearance:	*Harry Potter and the Philosopher's [Sorcerer's] Stone* (novel) (release date: June 26, 1997)
Creators:	J. K. Rowling
Other Media:	Movies, Pottermore website, stage
Primary Strength:	Witchcraft/magic
Major Weakness:	Racism, megalomania
Weapons:	Wand
Base of Operations:	Great Britain
Key Allies:	Nagini, Lucius Malfoy, Bellatrix Lestrange, Peter Pettigrew, Death Eaters, Severus Snape (originally)
Key Enemies:	Albus Dumbledore, James and Lilly Potter, Sirius Black, Remus Lupin, Mad-Eye Moody, Arthur and Molly Weasley, Frank and Alice Longbottom, Order of the Phoenix, Harry Potter, Ronald Weasley, Hermione Granger, Dumbledore's Army, Severus Snape (ultimately)
Actual Identity:	Tom Marvolo Riddle
Nicknames/Aliases:	"Lord Voldemort," "The Dark Lord," "He-Who-Must-Not-Be-Named," "You-Know-Who," "The Heir of Slytherin"

In 1997, author J. K. Rowling introduced readers to the magical world of Harry Potter with *Harry Potter and the Philosopher's Stone* (released in the United States as *Harry Potter and the Sorcerer's Stone*). The series follows young wizard Harry Potter from the ages of eleven to seventeen, through his years at Hogwarts School of Witchcraft and Wizardry in Great Britain. When Harry is first informed that he is a wizard, he learns that his parents, James and Lilly Potter, were murdered by "He-Who-Must-Not-Be-Named," the evil Lord Voldemort, and that the lightning-bolt scar on Harry's forehead was the result in Voldemort's trying to murder Harry with the "killing curse," which rebounded back on the Dark Lord, presumably destroying him. Harry soon learns that Voldemort lives, although severely weakened, and is in search of methods to return him to full strength so that he can continue his quest for power over the wizarding world (and eventually the Muggle—or nonmagical—world beyond that).

Nagini

The snake Nagini is widely known as the giant pet snake and one of the horcruxes of the dark wizard Lord Voldemort. As a servant to the Dark Lord, Nagini assists her master in murdering various good guy characters in the *Harry Potter* series of novels and films from author J. K. Rowling (b. 1965). Nagini, however, is not born a snake. She is born a human Maledictus: someone who is forced to magically and unwillingly transform into various creatures (in this case, a large snake). As time passes, with each transformation, the Maledictus eventually reaches a state where the transformation becomes permanent. In her human form, in the late 1920s, Nagini meets the troubled young wizard Credence Barebone, and he frees her.

Years later, now permanently in snake form, Nagini becomes the pet to Lord Voldemort. When Voldemort is critically wounded when his killing curse on the infant Harry Potter rebounded back on him, Voldemort relies on a potion made from Nagini's milk to sustain him until he could regain human form. In preparation for his possible defeat, Voldemort creates seven horcruxes, objects that could contain a portion of a human soul and keep it safe until the original owner is safe. In the novel *Harry Potter and the Deathly Hallows* (2007), the boy wizard and his friends discover that Nagini is one of the horcruxes, and it falls to Neville Longbottom to destroy the snake with the Sword of Godric Gryffindor, helping to lead to the Dark Lord's final defeat. In the *Fantastic Beasts* films, prequels to the *Harry Potter* franchise, the human Nagini is portrayed by actress Claudia Kim (b. 1985).

Richard A. Hall

Young Tom Riddle is the son of a witch named Merope Gaunt, who serves a love potion to local landowner Thomas Riddle, causing the enchanted man to marry the young witch. When she becomes pregnant, she allows the potion to wear off and confesses the truth to her husband, who immediately abandons her and their unborn child. When Merope dies after childbirth, young Tom becomes an orphan and is sent to a London orphanage. There his magical powers begin to manifest, and he comes to the attention of Professor Albus Dumbledore, headmaster of Hogwarts. Although posing as a proper and attentive student, Tom Riddle is, in fact, a cold-blooded sociopath, intent on ridding the world of nonmagical people, including "half-bloods" like himself. After graduating from Hogwarts, Tom applies to be the Defense against the Dark Arts professor at his alma mater but is denied the position by Dumbledore, who senses his dark nature. Tom then devolves deeper into darkness, his outer appearance even transforming to a solid white snakelike appearance. Now calling himself Lord Voldemort, his full name being an anagram for "I Am Lord Voldemort," he raises an army of evil wizards and witches called Death Eaters to assist in his malevolent scheme (J. K. Rowling, *Harry Potter and the Half-Blood Prince*, 2005).

With the help of the cowardly Peter Pettigrew, onetime trusted friend of James and Lilly Potter, and Barty Crouch Jr., disguised as Hogwarts professor Mad-Eye Moody, the weakened Voldemort successfully lures young Harry to a graveyard, where he uses Harry's blood in an incantation that returns him to full power (J. K. Rowling, *Harry Potter and the Goblet of Fire*, 2000). Successfully raising his army once more, Voldemort eventually gains control of the Ministry of Magic and

Ralph Fiennes brought to life the evil Lord Voldemort in the film versions of the popular *Harry Potter* novels. (Warner Bros. Pictures/Entertainment Pictures/Alamy Stock Photo)

embarks on one final battle against Harry and his other enemies (sans Dumbledore, who has recently been killed by Hogwarts professor and faux Death Eater Severus Snape) at the Battle of Hogwarts, where he is finally defeated once and for all by Harry Potter (J. K. Rowling, *Harry Potter and the Deathly Hallows*, 2007).

In the *Harry Potter* film franchise (Warner Brothers, 2001–2011), adhering strictly to the primary narratives of the novels, Voldemort was portrayed with seething villainy by Ralph Fiennes. In 2016, Rowling produced an epilogue of sorts to the novel and film series with the stage play *Harry Potter and the Cursed Child*. In this story, audiences are introduced to Delphi, the daughter of Voldemort and Bellatrix Lestrange. Delphi seeks to use a time turner to change the past so that her father rises to power. The now-adult Harry, along with his lifelong friends Ron Weasley and Hermione Granger and onetime foe Draco Malfoy, once more saves the day by distracting Delphi disguised as her father.

Lord Voldemort stands with Darth Vader as one of the most recognized and well-known villains of modern times. Like Vader, Voldemort transcends language, nationality, and culture, and is known throughout the world. He is the very representation of ultimate evil. Unlike Vader, who was borne of a tragic past, Voldemort appears to have been evil to his very core from the very beginning. He is a natural antagonist to Harry Potter, whose soul is as purely good as Voldemort's is evil. With Lord Voldemort, J. K. Rowling has taken the traditional villain of dark wizard and raised the bar from simple villainy to outright evil. His place in literary history secure, He-Who-Must-Not-Be-Named will likely continue to terrify generations of children for centuries to come.

Richard A. Hall

See also: Angelique Bouchard-Collins, Archie Bunker, Bellatrix Lestrange, Dark Willow, Fiona Goode/The Supreme, Grindelwald, Loki, Lucifer/Satan, Maleficent, Morgan le Fay, Sauron/Saruman, Sith Lords, Ursula, Wicked Witch of the West; *Thematic Essays*: "In the Beginning . . .": The Origins of Villains in the Western World, "Nazis, Communists, and Terrorists . . . Oh My!": The Rise of the Supervillain and the Evolution of the

Modern American Villain, The Pathos of Villainy: Getting to the Heart of Why Villains Went Bad.

Further Reading

Alsford, Mike. 2006. *Heroes & Villains*. Waco, TX: Baylor University Press.

Baggett, David, Shawn E. Klein, and William Irwin, eds. 2004. *Harry Potter and Philosophy: If Aristotle Ran Hogwarts*. Chicago: Open Court.

Barratt, Bethany. 2012. *The Politics of Harry Potter*. London: Palgrave MacMillan.

Cavendish, Richard. 1968. *The Black Arts: A Concise History of Witchcraft, Demonology, Astrology, and Other Mystical Practices throughout the Ages*. New York: TarcherPerigree.

Davidson-Harden, Adam. 2020. "Voldemort's 'Unusual Evil.'" In *The Supervillain Reader*, edited by Robert Peaslee and Robert Weiner, 172–179. Jackson: University of Mississippi Press.

Hutton, Ronald. 2017. *The Witch: A History of Fear, from Ancient Times to the Present*. New Haven, CT: Yale University Press.

Irwin, William, and Gregory Bassham, eds. 2010. *The Ultimate Harry Potter and Philosophy: Hogwarts for Muggles*. Hoboken, NJ: John Wiley & Sons.

Reagin, Nancy R. 2011. *Harry Potter and History*. Hoboken, NJ: John Wiley & Sons.

Rothman, Ken. 2011. "Hearts of Darkness: Voldemort and Iago, with a Little Help from Their Friends." In *Vader, Voldemort and Other Villains: Essays on Evil in Popular Media*, 202–217. Jefferson, NC: McFarland.

Russell, Jeffrey B., and Brooks Alexander. 2007. *A History of Witchcraft: Sorcerers, Heretics, & Pagans*. London: Thames & Hudson.

Wicked Witch of the West

First Appearance:	*The Wonderful Wizard of Oz* (publication date: May 17, 1900)
Creators:	L. Frank Baum
Other Media:	Movies, comic books, stage
Primary Strength:	Magic
Major Weakness:	Water
Weapons:	Spells/incantations
Base of Operations:	Oz
Key Allies:	Wicked Witch of the East, Wicked Witch of the South, Mombi, flying monkeys
Key Enemies:	Glinda the Good Witch of the North, Dorothy Gale, Scarecrow, Tin Man, Cowardly Lion, The Wizard
Actual Identity:	Bastinda (in 1939 novel, *The Wizard of the Emerald City*), Evillene (in 1974 play, *The Wiz*), Elphaba Thropp (in 1995 novel, *Wicked*), Theodora (in 2013 film, *Oz the Great and Powerful*)
Nicknames/Aliases:	"Momba," "West" (to name but a very few)

In 1900, L. Frank Baum introduced the world to the mythical realm of Oz, which, over the last century, has become one of the most enduring classics in American children's literature. Baum was a devout follower of the populist movement of the period, and *The Wonderful Wizard of Oz* and its sequels are steeped in populist symbolism. For example, the Scarecrow without a brain represents the farmers of the time, the Tin Man without a heart is the industrialist, and the Cowardly Lion is the politician (Littlefield, "The Wizard of Oz: Parable on Populism," 53–54). When Dorothy is magically thrown to the mystical land of Oz by a Kansas tornado, her house lands on the Wicked Witch of the East, who has enslaved the small people of Munchkinland. Dorothy is given the evil witch's magical silver shoes (not ruby red slippers, as portrayed in the 1939 film) and sent to see the Wizard of Oz in Emerald City to grant her wish to return home. The wizard tasks Dorothy and her friends with destroying the Wicked Witch of the West, who desires the powerful silver slippers. According to Littlefield, the Wicked Witch of the West represents "sentient and malign nature" (Littlefield, "The Wizard of Oz: Parable on Populism," 55).

Margaret Hamilton forever cemented the popular idea of a "witch" with her portrayal of the Wicked Witch of the West in the 1939 film adaptation of the 1900 novel *The Wonderful Wizard of Oz*. (PictureLux/The Hollywood Archive/Alamy Stock Photo)

In the original novel, the Wicked Witch seeks to enslave Dorothy by capturing and torturing her friends. When she trips Dorothy and causes her to lose one silver shoe, Dorothy angrily throws a bucket of water onto the witch (not knowing this was her one weakness), causing the witch to melt. This story is repeated in the legendary 1939 film, where the witch was played with an iconic and career defining performance by Margaret Hamilton. In the 1974 stage play *The Wiz: The Super Soul Musical "Wonderful Wizard of Oz"* by Charlie Smalls and William F. Brown, an African American twist is given to the traditional tale. In both the stage play and the 1978 feature film version of the musical, the Wicked Witch, now named Evillene, was played by Mabel King.

In the 1995 novel *Wicked: The Life and Times of the Wicked Witch of the West* by Gregory Maguire and the 2003 Broadway musical based on it, the witch is given the name Elphaba Thropp and is the college roommate of Galinda, who will become Glinda the Good Witch of the North. This story provides a more sympathetic view of the Wicked Witch and allows her to survive the dousing by Dorothy. Another prequel story emerges in the 2013 film *Oz the Great and Powerful*. In this incarnation, the traditional Wicked Witch is Theodora (played by Mila Kunis), the younger sister of the witch Evanora, who is at war with Glinda the Good Witch. Theodora is in love with Oscar/Oz (played by James Franco), but Evanora convinces her that he is in love with Glinda. Evanora offers her sister a potion that promises to ease her pain, but instead, it drains all the good from her soul and transforms her into the Wicked Witch of the West. The character has also appeared in numerous television series and special adaptations of the original. She is one of the most iconic villains of the twentieth century, and her image from the 1939 film classic has become synonymous with witches ever since.

In the end, the Wicked Witch of the West follows the European tradition of witches in fairy tales and stories from "Hansel and Gretel" to "Snow White and Rose Red." She is a practitioner of the dark arts and is, therefore, a precursor to modern-day witches, from *Harry Potter*'s Bellatrix Lestrange to *American Horror Story: Coven*'s Fiona Goode. The original Wicked Witch, however, is a pop culture icon, with phrases from the film such as "I'll get you, my pretty, and your little dog too!" and "I'm melting! I'm mellllltiinnngg!" part of the American vernacular. For as long as there are tales of magical witches and as long as Halloween remains a staple of American culture, the Wicked Witch of the West will live on.

Richard A. Hall

See also: Alexis Carrington-Colby-Dexter, Angelique Bouchard-Collins, Asajj Ventress, Bellatrix Lestrange, Dark Willow, Fiona Goode/The Supreme, La Llorona, Loki, Lucifer/Satan, Maleficent, Morgan le Fay, Poison Ivy, Sauron/Saruman, Sith Lords, Tia Dalma/Calypso, Ursula; *Thematic Essays*: The Pathos of Villainy: Getting to the Heart of Why Villains Went Bad.

Further Reading

Alsford, Mike. 2006. *Heroes & Villains*. Waco, TX: Baylor University Press.

Ashby, LeRoy. 2006. *With Amusement for All: A History of American Popular Culture since 1830*. Lexington: University Press of Kentucky.

Cavendish, Richard. 1968. *The Black Arts: A Concise History of Witchcraft, Demonology, Astrology, and Other Mystical Practices throughout the Ages*. New York: TarcherPerigree.

Faludi, Susan. 2007. *The Terror Dream: Myth and Misogyny in an Insecure America*. New York: Picador.

Forasteros, J. R. 2017. *Empathy for the Devil: Finding Ourselves in the Villains of the Bible*. Downers Grove, IL: InterVarsity.

Hutton, Ronald. 2017. *The Witch: A History of Fear, from Ancient Times to the Present*. New Haven, CT: Yale University Press.

Littlefield, Henry M. 1964. "The Wizard of Oz: Parable on Populism." *American Quarterly* 16, no. 1: 47–58.

Russell, Jeffrey B., and Brooks Alexander. 2007. *A History of Witchcraft: Sorcerers, Heretics, & Pagans*. London: Thames & Hudson.

Ryan, Hannah. 2020. "Vilifications: Conjuring Witches Then and Now." In *The Supervillain Reader*, edited by Rob Weiner and Rob Peaslee, 156–171. Jackson: University of Mississippi Press.

Z

Zod

First Appearance:	*Adventure Comics #283* (cover date: April 1961)
Creators:	Robert Bernstein and George Papp
Other Media:	Movies, television (animated and live-action), animated home video
Primary Strength:	Cunning, super strength and speed, flight, heat vision, freeze breath, X-ray vision
Major Weakness:	Racism, megalomania
Weapons:	N/A
Base of Operations:	Krypton (originally)
Key Allies:	Non, Ursa, Jax-Ur
Key Enemies:	Superman, Supergirl, Superboy, Lois Lane
Actual Identity:	Dru-Zod
Nicknames/Aliases:	"General Zod"

The *Superman* franchise is one of the most successful in pop culture history. Created by the Jewish American team of writer Jerry Siegel and artist Joe Shuster, Superman is an alien named Kal-El, whose home world of Krypton was destroyed shortly after his birth. Aware of the impending doom, his parents placed him in a space capsule and sent him into space to save him. He landed in Smallville, Kansas, and was raised by Jonathan and Martha Kent under his adopted name, Clark Kent. On reaching adulthood, Clark discovered that he had "powers and abilities far beyond those of mortal men" and dedicated himself to protecting the world as Superman, the world's first superhero. Because of his near-godlike powers, his only weakness being Kryptonite (meteor fragments of his home world), Superman requires antagonists of particularly daunting abilities. His exact equal in strength and powers—and his dark mirror—is the Kryptonian criminal General Zod.

General Zod was introduced in a story featuring Superboy—young Clark Kent, still living with his adopted parents in Smallville—when the Boy of Steel is accidentally thrust into the Phantom Zone, a prison for Kryptonians who have survived the destruction of their home world. General Zod has been imprisoned in the Phantom Zone for attempting to take over Krypton. As Zod has met and surpassed the sentence placed on him, Superboy releases him and others, who then make their way to Earth (Robert Bernstein and George Papp, *Adventure Comics #283*, April 1961). On reaching Earth, Zod discovers that the planet's yellow sun gives him the same powers as Superboy/Superman. Over the decades that follow, Superman and Supergirl battle Zod many times, casting him back into the Phantom Zone each time. After the events of *Crisis on Infinite Earths* (1986–1987), the new DC Comics continuity established that Superman was the *only* survivor of Krypton. As such, for years afterward, the Zod faced by Superman came from an alternate reality (but always to the same end).

On the big screen, Zod first appeared in *Superman: The Movie* (Warner Brothers, 1978) and *Superman II* (Warner Brothers, 1980), played by Terence Stamp, providing over-the-top grandiosity to Zod's megalomania. In the second film, Superman tricks Zod and his two minions into having their powers removed, before tossing them into a bottomless pit in the Fortress of Solitude. In the film *Man of Steel* (Warner Brothers, 2013), Zod is played by Michael Shannon. In this incarnation, General Zod once more leads an army to take over Krypton and is once more defeated by Jor-El, and he and his army are confined to the Phantom Zone, thereby allowing them to survive their home world's demise. On escaping decades later, Zod and his army find their way to Earth with plans to use a Kryptonian machine called the World Engine to terraform Earth into a new Krypton. While Superman stops the machine and Zod's minions, he is forced to kill Zod in order to prevent him from trying to destroy Earth again.

On television, Zod first appeared in the television series *Smallville* (WB, 2001–2006; CW, 2006–2011), eventually appearing in two different incarnations. First, in season five, the spirit of Zod enters the body of Clark Kent's friend and enemy Lex Luthor (played by Michael Rosenbaum). Later, in season mine, the actual Major Zod (played by Callum Blue) is released from the Phantom Zone to be that season's baddie, taken out by Clark in the season finale. On the prequel series *Krypton* (SyFy, 2018–2019), General Zod (played by Colin Salmon) travels back in time to take over Krypton at a time before either Superman/Kal-El or his father, Jor-El existed. Once back in time, Zod teams with his future mother, Lyta-Zod (played by Georgina Campbell) and her lover, Seg-El (played by Cameron Cuffe), to defeat Brainiac, only to go on to take over Krypton himself as planned. During this period, however, Zod discovers that Seg-El, Superman's grandfather, is actually his father, making him Superman's uncle.

In the realm of American villainy, Zod represents the stereotypical megalomaniacal madman bent on world conquest. A super-powered Hitler, Zod views all others as inferior and, therefore, not worthy of mercy or compassion. He is the dark mirror of Superman and a representation of the danger Superman poses should he decide to take a darker path. Many viewed Superman's actions as criminal in *Man of Steel* when he killed Zod, although no one complained when he did the same thing in *Superman II* and again on *Smallville*, but it raised the question once more on the morality of the death penalty (especially a death penalty imposed by one man), which is what the best of popular culture does—forces us to consider what our own morality is and where the lines of that morality are drawn.

Richard A. Hall

See also: Brainiac, Cersei Lannister, The Court of Owls, Doctor Doom, Doomsday, Ernst Stavro Blofeld/SPECTRE, Green Goblin, Grindelwald, Lex Luthor, Loki, Magneto, Ra's al Ghul, Red Skull, Reverend Stryker/The Purifiers, Thanos, Ultron, Voldemort; *Thematic Essays*: "Nazis, Communists, and Terrorists . . . Oh My!": The Rise of the Supervillain and the Evolution of the Modern American Villain, The Dark Mirror: Evil Twins, *The Twilight Zone*, and the Villain Within, The Pathos of Villainy: Getting to the Heart of Why Villains Went Bad.

Further Reading

Alsford, Mike. 2006. *Heroes & Villains.* Waco, TX: Baylor University Press.

Ashby, LeRoy. 2006. *With Amusement for All: A History of American Popular Culture since 1830.* Lexington: University Press of Kentucky.

Barker, Cory, Chris Ryan, and Myc Wiatrowski, eds. 2014. *Mapping Smallville: Critical Essays on the Series and Its Characters.* Jefferson, NC: McFarland.

Daniels, Les. 2004. *Superman: The Complete History—the Life and Times of the Man of Steel.* New York: DC Comics.

Robichaud, Christopher. 2009. "Bright Colors, Dark Times." In *Supervillains and Philosophy: Sometimes, Evil Is Its Own Reward,* edited by Ben Dyer, 61–70. Chicago: Open Court.

Tucker, Reed. 2017. *Slugfest: Inside the Epic 50-Year Battle between Marvel and DC.* New York: Da Capo Press.

"TV Guide Picks TV's 60 Nastiest Villains." 2013. *TV Guide.* April 22, 2013. Accessed January 1, 2019. http://wordsmithonia.blogspot.com/2013/04/tv-guide-picks-tvs-60-nastiest-villains.html.

Tye, Larry. 2013. *Superman: The High-Flying History of America's Most Enduring Hero.* New York: Random House.

Wright, Bradford W. 2003. *Comic Book Nation: The Transformation of Youth Culture in America.* Baltimore, MD: Johns Hopkins University Press.

Glossary

Antagonist
Often described as the villain of a piece; more accurately defined as the character (or characters) who attempt to challenge the protagonist. As the villain's plan is usually central to a narrative, many have defined the hero as the antagonist, as they are attempting to stop the actions of the villain.

Antihero
A hero who, from time to time, commits actions that society may deem villainous (i.e., killing a villain in cold blood).

Antivillain
A villain who, from time to time, commits actions that society may deem heroic (i.e., protecting an innocent from another villain).

Archenemy/Archrival
One's primary enemy/rival; the most formidable on a list of enemies.

Body Count
A list of victims of some manner of violence.

Comic Book/Comics
A genre of storytelling revolving around pictures with dialogue or monologue inserted into the images.

Continuity
The established, uninterrupted time line of a character's continuing story.

Dark Side
The villainous side of human nature.

Ethics/Morals/Values
The rules a society has agreed to live by and uphold.

Evil
Behaviors or intents that are directly antithetical to the beliefs and core values of a society; the opposite of what a society considers good.

Fandom
Collection of fans of a specific genre, medium, or franchise.

Fascism
A radical conservative political ideology centered on nationalism, imperialism, racism, and often atheism.

Franchise
Sometimes referred to as "intellectual property" (IP); a franchise is a fictional universe that revolves around a set of established fictional characters.

Genocide
The mass extermination of a certain race or ethnicity.

Genre
Subsection of a medium (i.e., superheroes are a genre of the comic book medium).

Hitleresque
Reminiscent of the actions of philosophies of Adolf Hitler and/or the Nazi Party.

Mafia/The Mob
Referring to American organized crime; usually, although sometimes mistakenly, associated with the Italian/Sicilian mafioso or Cosa Nostra.

Megalomania
An obsession with absolute power.

Nationalism
A radical form of patriotism focused on economic isolationism or dominance and, frequently, racial purity.

Nemesis
The primary rival of an individual, nation, or society; someone who stands in direct contrast to one's goals and most represents the opposite of one's core values (i.e., Lex Luthor is Superman's nemesis; Superman is Lex Luthor's nemesis).

Protagonist
Often described as the hero of a piece; more accurately defined as the character (or characters) who attempt to stop the actions of the antagonist. As the villain's plan is usually central to a narrative, many have defined the hero as the antagonist, as they are attempting to stop the actions of the villain.

Psychopathy
An antisocial psychological dysfunction that centers highly on egoistic or egotistic behavior; it differs from sociopathy in that the psychopath may understand the difference between right and wrong, but simply does not care.

Reboot
Relaunching a franchise or intellectual property with a new direction and occasionally an altered origin story.

Retcon/Ret-Con
Short for "retroactive continuity"; a change to established continuity outside of a complete reboot.

Rogues' Gallery
Collection of villains connected to a specific hero.

Satanic
Of or having to do with the character of Satan, Lucifer, or the Devil.

Serial Killer
Someone who has committed numerous, seemingly unrelated murders.

Sociopathy
An antisocial psychological dysfunction that renders a person incapable of distinguishing between right and wrong, and seemingly without a conscience.

Universe
The totality of interconnected characters in comic book storytelling, involving multiple books.

Vampire
A creature (usually human) who is "undead," one who possesses all the attributes of a living person but immortal or has returned from death and who feeds off the blood of the living.

Villain
Someone who commits actions that are antithetical to a society's ethics/morals/values; often the enemy of the hero.

Witch/Wizard
A person who is gifted (either naturally or by practice) in the magical arts.

Xenophobia
A fear or hatred of people from other countries or societies.

Bibliography

Adams, Neal, Rafael Medoff, and Craig Yoe. 2018. *We Spoke Out: Comic Books and the Holocaust*. San Diego, CA: Yoe Books/IDW.

Adler, Margot. 2014. *Vampires Are Us: Understanding Our Love Affair with the Immortal Dark Side*. Newburyport, MA: Weiser.

Alsford, Mike. 2006. *Heroes & Villains*. Waco, TX: Baylor University Press.

Arp, Robert, ed. 2017. *The X-Files and Philosophy: The Truth Is in Here*. Chicago: Open Court.

Ashby, LeRoy. 2006. *With Amusement for All: A History of American Popular Culture since 1830*. Lexington: University Press of Kentucky.

Ashlin, D. L. 1998. "Sleeping Beauty. Folklore and Mythology." Pittsburg University. Accessed December 27, 2019. http://www.pitt.edu/~dash/type0410.html#basile.

Baggett, David, Shawn E. Klein, and William Irwin, eds. 2004. *Harry Potter and Philosophy: If Aristotle Ran Hogwarts*. Chicago: Open Court.

Barba, Shelley E., and Joy M. Perrin, eds. 2017. *The Ascendance of Harley Quinn: Essays on DC's Enigmatic Villain*. Jefferson, NC: McFarland.

Barker, Cory, Chris Ryan, and Myc Wiatrowski, eds. 2014. *Mapping Smallville: Critical Essays on the Series and Its Characters*. Jefferson, NC: McFarland.

Barratt, Bethany. 2012. *The Politics of Harry Potter*. London: Palgrave Macmillan.

Bates, Billie Rae. 2004. *Dynasty High: A Guide to TV's Dynasty and Dynasty II: The Colbys*. Charleston, SC: BookSurge.

Bates, Billie Rae. 2007. *Destination: Dallas: A Guide to TV's Dallas*. Charleston, SC: BookSurge.

Beard, Jim. 2018. *The Joy of Joe: Memories of America's Movable Fighting Man from Today's Grown-Up Kids*. N.p.: CreateSpace.

Beard, Jim, ed. 2010. *Gotham City 14 Miles: 14 Essays on Why the 1960s Batman TV Series Matters*. Edwardsville, IL: Sequart Research & Literacy Organization.

Behnken, Brian D., and Gregory D Smithers. 2015. *Racism in American Popular Media: From Aunt Jemima to the Frito Bandito*. Westport, CT: Praeger.

Bellomo, Mark. 2018. *The Ultimate Guide to G. I. Joe: 1982–1994*. 3rd ed. Iola, WI: Krause.

Billson, Anne. 2005. *Buffy the Vampire Slayer*. London: British Film Institute.
Boggs, Johnny D. 2013. *Billy the Kid on Film: 1911–2012*. Jefferson, NC: McFarland.
Brittany, Michele, ed. 2014. *James Bond and Popular Culture: Essays on the Influence of the Fictional Superspy*. Jefferson, NC: McFarland.
Brode, Douglas, and Carol Serling. 2009. *Rod Serling and The Twilight Zone: The 50th Anniversary Tribute*. Fort Lee, NJ: Barricade.
Browne, Nick, ed. 2000. *Francis Ford Coppola's "The Godfather" Trilogy*. Cambridge: Cambridge University Press.
Campbell, Joseph. (1949) 2004. *The Hero with a Thousand Faces: Commemorative Edition*. Princeton, NJ: Princeton University Press.
Castleman, Harry, and Walter J. Podrazik. 2016. *Watching TV: Eight Decades of American Television*. 3rd ed. Syracuse, NY: Syracuse University Press.
Cavendish, Richard. 1968. *The Black Arts: A Concise History of Witchcraft, Demonology, Astrology, and Other Mystical Practices throughout the Ages*. New York: TarcherPerigree.
Cheeda, Saim. 2019. "Lobo: 10 Things to Know about SyFy's Main Man." Screen Rant. July 18, 2019. Accessed July 19, 2019. https://screenrant.com/lobo-facts-trivia-syfy/.
Clapton, William, and Laura J. Shepherd. 2017. "Lessons from Westeros: Gender and Power in *Game of Thrones*." *Politics* 37, no. 1: 5–18.
Clover, Carol. 1993. *Men, Women, and Chainsaws: Gender in Modern Horror Film*. Princeton, NJ: Princeton University Press.
Connell, Evan S. (1984) 2001. *Son of the Morning Star: Custer and the Little Bighorn*. New York: History Book Club.
Cordingly, David. 2006. *Under the Black Flag: The Romance and the Reality of Life among the Pirates*. New York: Random House.
Costello, Matthew J. 2009. *Secret Identity Crisis: Comic Books & the Unmasking of Cold War America*. New York: Continuum.
Cowie, Peter. 1997. *The Godfather Book*. London: Faber.
Craven, Bruce. 2019. *Win or Die: Leadership Secrets from Game of Thrones*. NY: Thomas Dunne.
Crome, Andrew, and James McGrath, eds. 2013. *Time and Relative Dimensions in Faith: Religion and Doctor Who*. London: Darton, Longman, and Todd.
Curran, Barbara A. 2005. *Dallas: The Complete Story of the World's Favorite Prime-Time Soap*. Nashville, TN: Cumberland House.
Daniels, Les. 2004. *Superman: The Complete History—the Life and Times of the Man of Steel*. New York: DC Comics.
Darcy, Jen. 2016. *Disney Villains: Delightfully Evil: The Creation, the Inspiration, the Fascination*. New York: Disney Editions.
Davis, Amy M. 2007. *Good Girls and Wicked Witches: Women in Disney's Feature Animation*. East Barnet, UK: John Libbey.
Dawson, Delilah S. 2017. *Star Wars: Phasma*. New York: Del Rey.
DeFalco, Tom. 2004. *Comics Creators on Spider-Man*. London: Titan.
DeFalco, Tom. 2006. *Comics Creators on X-Men*. London: Titan.

Deutelbaum, Marshall, and Leland Poague. 2009. *A Hitchcock Reader*. 2nd ed. Hoboken, NJ: Wiley-Blackwell.

Dial-Driver, Emily, Sally Emmons-Featherston, Jim Ford, and Carolyn Anne Taylor. 2008. *The Truth of Buffy: Essays on Fiction Illuminating Reality*. Jefferson, NC: McFarland.

Dickens, Charles. 2015. *A Christmas Carol (Annotated): An Annotated Version of A Christmas Carol with Full Novel and In-Depth Analysis*. N.p.: Amazon Services.

Dolansky, Shawna. 2018. "How the Serpent Became Satan: Adam, Eve, and the Serpent in the Garden of Eden." Biblical Archaeology Society. Accessed April 7, 2019. https://www.biblicalarchaeology.org/daily/biblical-topics/bible-interpretation/how-the-serpent-became-satan/.

Donovan, James. 2008. *A Terrible Glory: Custer and the Little Bighorn, the Last Great Battle of the American West*. New York: Little, Brown and Company.

Durand, Kevin K., and Mary K. Leigh, eds. 2011. *Riddle Me This, Batman!: Essays on the Universe of the Dark Knight*. Jefferson, NC: McFarland.

Dyer, Ben, ed. 2009. *Supervillains and Philosophy: Sometimes, Evil Is Its Own Reward*. Popular Culture and Philosophy Series. Chicago: Open Court.

Eberl, Jason T., and Kevin S. Decker, eds. *The Ultimate Star Wars and Philosophy: You Must Unlearn What You Have Learned*. Hoboken, NJ: Wiley-Blackwell.

Faludi, Susan. 2007. *The Terror Dream: Myth and Misogyny in an Insecure America*. New York: Picador.

Fertig, Mark. 2017. *Take That, Adolf!: The Fighting Comic Books of the Second World War*. Seattle, WA: Fantagraphics.

Field, Mark. 2017. *Buffy, the Vampire Slayer: Myth, Metaphor & Morality*. N.p.: Amazon Services.

Forasteros, J. R. 2017. *Empathy for the Devil: Finding Ourselves in the Villains of the Bible*. Downers Grove, IL: InterVarsity.

Friedman, Lester D., and Allison B. Kavey. 2016. *Monstrous Progeny: A History of the Frankenstein Narratives*. New Brunswick, NJ: Rutgers University Press.

Gaiman, Neil. 2018. *Norse Mythology*. New York: W. W. Norton & Company.

Gavaler, Chris. 2015. *On the Origin of Superheroes: From the Big Bang to Action Comics No. 1*. Iowa City: University of Iowa.

Geaman, Kristen L., ed. 2015. *Dick Grayson, Boy Wonder: Scholars and Creators on 75 Years of Robin, Nightwing, and Batman*. Jefferson, NC: McFarland.

Geronimo, and S. M. Barrett. (1906) 2005. *Geronimo: My Life*. Chicago, IL: Dover.

Gillespie, Nick, and Matt Welch. 2008. "How 'Dallas' Won the Cold War." *Washington Post*. April 27, 2008. Accessed September 26, 2019. http://www.washingtonpost.com/wp-dyn/content/article/2008/04/25/AR2008042503103.html.

Gloyn, Liz. 2019. *Tracking Classical Monsters in Popular Culture*. London: Bloomsbury Academic.

Goldman, Michael R. 2008. *24: The Ultimate Guide*. London: DK.

Grau, Christopher, ed. 2005. *Philosophers Explore The Matrix*. Oxford: Oxford University Press.

Greene, Richard, and K. Silem Mohammad, eds. 2007. *Quentin Tarantino and Philosophy: How to Philosophize with a Pair of Pliers and a Blowtorch.* Chicago: Open Court.

Gresh, Lois H., and Robert Weinberg. 2005. *The Science of Supervillains*. Hoboken, NJ: John Wiley & Sons.

Grevas, Andrew. 2019. "'You Understand the Human Condition': *The Sopranos*, Mental Health, & Me." 25YL. May 2019. Accessed June 1, 2019. https://25yearslatersite.com/2019/05/03/you-understand-the-human-condition-the-sopranos-mental-health-me/.

Gross, Edward, and Mark A. Altman. 2016a. *The Fifty-Year Mission, the First 25 Years: The Complete, Uncensored, Unauthorized Oral History of Star Trek.* New York: St. Martin's.

Gross, Edward, and Mark A. Altman. 2016b. *The Fifty-Year Mission, the Next 25 Years: The Complete, Uncensored, Unauthorized Oral History of Star Trek.* New York: St. Martin's.

Gross, Edward, and Mark A. Altman. 2017. *Slayers & Vampires: The Complete, Uncensored, Unauthorized Oral History of Buffy & Angel.* New York: Tor.

Gross, Edward, and Mark A. Altman. 2018. *So Say We All: The Complete, Uncensored, Unauthorized Oral History of Battlestar Galactica.* New York: Tor.

Guzman, Martin Luis. 1938. *Memorias de Pancho Villa*. Mexico: Botas.

Hall, Jacob. 2017. "All 104 James Bond Villains Ranked: From Masterminds to Henchmen, the Final Word on 007's Furious Foes." *Esquire*. May 24, 2017. Accessed July 4, 2019. https://www.esquire.com/entertainment/movies/g2496/best-james-bond-villains-ranked/.

Hammond, Wayne G., and Christina Scull. 2005. *The Lord of the Rings: A Reader's Companion*. San Diego, CA: Houghton Mifflin Harcourt.

Hamrick, Craig, and R. J. Jamison. 2012. *Barnabas & Company: The Cast of the TV Classic Dark Shadows.* Bloomington, IN: iUniverse.

Handlen, Zack, and Todd VanDerWerff. 2018. *Monsters of the Week: The Complete Critical Companion to The X-Files.* New York: Harry N. Abrams.

Handley, Rich, and Lou Tambone, eds. 2018. *Somewhere beyond the Heavens: Exploring Battlestar Galactica.* Edwardsville, IL: Sequart Research and Literacy Organization.

Harris, Malcolm. 2013. "Walter White Supremacy." *New Inquiry*. September 2013. Accessed August 10, 2019. https://thenewinquiry.com/walter-white-supremacy/.

Heit, Jamey, ed. 2011. *Vader, Voldemort and Other Villains: Essays on Evil in Popular Media*. Jefferson, NC: McFarland.

Hendershot, Cyndy. 1999. *Paranoia, the Bomb, and 1950s Science Fiction Films.* Bowling Green, KY: Bowling Green State University Popular Press.

Herrera, Cristina. 2016. "Cinco Hermanitas: Myth and Sisterhood in Guadalupe Garcia McCalls Summer of the Mariposas." *Children's Literature* 44: 96–114.

Hines, Ree. 2013. "Tony Soprano Character Altered Face of TV, Paving Way for Antiheroes." Today. June 2013. Accessed June 1, 2019. https://www.today.com/popculture/tony-soprano-character-altered-face-tv-paving-way-antiheroes-6C10387810.

Hitchcock, Susan Tyler. 2007. *Frankenstein: A Cultural History*. New York: W. W. Norton.

Hoberman, J. 2003. *The Dream Life: Movies, Media, and the Mythology of the Sixties*. New York: New Press.

Hoberman, J. 2011. *An Army of Phantoms: American Movies and the Making of the Cold War*. New York: New Press.

Hogan, Susan, Albach. 2003. "Was Judas a Good Guy or Bad? Scholars Disagree." Baylor University. April 17, 2003. Accessed April 21, 2019. https://www.baylor.edu/mediacommunications/index.php?id=6435.

Holderness, Graham. 2015. *Re-Writing Jesus: Christ in 20th-Century Fiction and Film*. London: Bloomsbury.

Howe, Sean. 2012. *Marvel Comics: The Untold Story*. New York: Harper-Perennial.

Hunter, Jack, ed. 1996. *House of Horror: The Complete Hammer Films Story*. London: Creation.

Hutchings, Peter. 2003. *Dracula: A British Film Guide*. London: I. B. Tauris.

Hutson, Thommy. 2016. *Never Sleep Again: The Elm Street Legacy*. Brentwood, TN: Permuted.

Hutton, Paul Andrew, ed. 1992. *The Custer Reader*. Lincoln: University of Nebraska Press.

Hutton, Ronald. 2017. *The Witch: A History of Fear, from Ancient Times to the Present*. New Haven, CT: Yale University Press.

Irwin, William, ed. 2002. *The Matrix and Philosophy: Welcome to the Desert of the Real*. Chicago: Open Court.

Irwin, William, and Gregory Bassham, eds. 2010. *The Ultimate Harry Potter and Philosophy: Hogwarts for Muggles*. Hoboken, NJ: John Wiley & Sons.

Jones, Brian Jay. 2016. *George Lucas: A Life*. New York: Little Brown and Company.

Jones, Rebecca. 2012. "A Game of Genders: Comparing Depictions of Empowered Women between *A Game of Thrones* Novel and Television Series." *Journal of Student Research* 1, no. 3: 14–21.

Joslin, Lyndon W. 2017. *Count Dracula Goes to the Movies*. Jefferson, NC: McFarland.

Jowett, Lorna. 2005. *Sex and the Slayer: A Gender Studies Primer for the Buffy Fan*. Middletown, CT: Wesleyan University Press.

Kalter, Suzy. 1984. *The Complete Book of Dallas: Behind the Scenes at the World's Favorite Television Program*. New York: Harry N. Abrams.

Kalter, Suzy. 1988. *The Complete Book of M*A*S*H*. New York: Harry N. Abrams.

Kaminski, Michael. 2008. *The Secret History of Star Wars: The Art of Storytelling and the Making of a Modern Epic*. Kingston, ON, Canada: Legacy Books.

Karson, Michael. 2017. "A Case Formulation for Tony Soprano." Psychology Today. January 2017. Accessed June 1, 2019. https://www.psychologytoday.com/us/blog/feeling-our-way/201701/case-formulation-tony-soprano.

Keetley, Dawn. 2014. *We're All Infected: Essays on AMC's The Walking Dead and the Fate of the Human*. Contributions to Zombie Studies. Jefferson, NC: McFarland.

Kelly, Henry Ansgar. 2006. *Satan: A Biography*. Cambridge: Cambridge University Press.

Kirkman, Robert. 2018. *The Quotable Negan: Warped Witticisms and Obscene Observations from The Walking Dead's Most Iconic Villain*. New York: Skybound.

Kirshner, Jonathan. 2012. *Hollywood's Last Golden Age: Politics, Society, and the Seventies Film in America*. Ithaca, NY: Cornell University Press.

Kistler, Alan. 2013. *Doctor Who: Celebrating Fifty Years, a History*. Guilford, CT: Lyons.

Knight, Stephen. 2016. *Toward Sherlock Holmes: A Thematic History of Crime Fiction in the 19th Century World*. Jefferson, NC: McFarland.

Kreeft, Peter. 2005. *The Philosophy of Tolkien: The Worldview behind The Lord of the Rings*. San Francisco, CA: Ignatius.

Langley, Travis. 2012. *Batman and Psychology: A Dark and Stormy Knight*. New York: John Wiley & Sons.

Langley, Travis, ed. 2015. *The Walking Dead Psychology: Psych of the Living Dead*. Popular Culture Psychology. New York: Sterling.

Laszlo, Monseignore. 2006. "Anti-Villain." *Urban Dictionary*. July 23, 2006. Accessed July 7, 2019. https://www.urbandictionary.com/define.php?term=anti-villain.

Lavery, David. 2013. *Joss Whedon, A Creative Portrait: From Buffy, the Vampire Slayer to Marvel's The Avengers*. London: I. B. Tauris.

Lavery, David, and Cynthia Burkhead, eds. 2011. *Joss Whedon: Conversations*. Television Conversations Series. Jackson: University of Mississippi Press.

Leach, Mike, and Buddy Levy. 2015. *Geronimo: Leadership Strategies of an American Warrior*. New York: Gallery.

Leadbeater, Alex. 2019. "Star Wars Is Trying to Turn Darth Vader into an Anti-Hero (and That's Very Bad)." *Screen Rant*. February 4, 2019. Accessed February 4, 2019. https://screenrant.com/star-wars-darth-vader-villain-anti-hero/.

Lebo, Harlan. 2005. *The Godfather Legacy*. Rev. ed. New York: Fireside.

Lee, Stan. 1976. *Bring on the Bad Guys: Origins of Marvel Villains*. New York: Marvel Comics.

Leibovitz, Annie and Sam Kashner. 2012. "The Family Hour: An Oral History of *The Sopranos*." *Vanity Fair*. April 2012. Accessed June 1, 2019. https://www.vanityfair.com/hollywood/2012/04/sopranos-oral-history.

Lewis, Courtland, and Paula Smithka, eds. 2010. *Doctor Who and Philosophy: Bigger on the Inside*. Chicago: Open Court.

Lewis, Courtland, and Paula Smithka, eds. 2015: *More Doctor Who and Philosophy: Regeneration Time*. Chicago: Open Court.

Lewis, Jon. 2010. *The Godfather*. London: Palgrave Macmillan.

Littlefield, Henry M. 1964. "The Wizard of Oz: Parable on Populism." *American Quarterly* 16, no. 1: 47–58.

Lozano, Gustavo Vasquez, and Charles Rivers, eds. 2016. *Pancho Villa: The Life and Legacy of the Famous Mexican Revolutionary.* Scotts Valley, CA: CreateSpace.

Maddrey, Joseph. 2004. *Nightmares in Red, White, and Blue: The Evolution of the American Horror Film.* Jefferson, NC: McFarland.

Mahnke, Aaron. 2017. *The World of Lore: Monstrous Creatures.* New York: Del Rey.

Mallory, Michael. 2009. *Universal Monsters: A Legacy of Horror.* New York: Universe.

Manning, Scott. 2017. "Classical Reception: Batman and the Court of Owls." Historian the Warpath. Accessed December 18, 2018. https://scottmanning.com/content/ancient-roots-batman-and-the-court-of-owls/.

Martos Garcia, Alberto, and Martos Garcia Aitana. 2015. "Nuevas Lecturas de la Llorona: Imaginarios, identidad y Discurso Parabolico." *Universum* 30, no. 2: 179–195.

McCarty, John. 2004. *Bullets over Hollywood: The American Gangster Picture from the Silents to "The Sopranos."* Cambridge, MA: Da Capo.

McCoy, Daniel. 2016. *The Viking Spirit: An Introduction to Norse Mythology and Religion.* Scotts Valley, CA: CreateSpace.

McCrohan, Donna. 1988. *Archie & Edith, Mike & Gloria: The Tumultuous History of All in the Family.* New York: Workman.

McKeown, B., D. B. Thomas, J. C. Rhoads, and D. Sundblad. 2015. "Falling Hard for *Breaking Bad*: An Investigation of Audience Response to a Popular Television Series." *Participations: Journal of Audience & Receptions Studies.* November 2015. Accessed June 1, 2019. https://www.participations.org/Volume%2012/Issue%202/8.pdf.

McNeill, Dustin. 2017. *Slash of the Titans: The Road to Freddy vs. Jason.* San Jose, CA: Harker.

Montelongo Flores, Monica. 2013. "Placing La Llorona as Curandera: Leslie Marmon Silko's Ceremony and Chicano Culture Theory." *Southwestern American Literature* 31, no. 1: 42–54.

Mooney, Darren. 2017. *Opening The X-Files: A Critical History of the Original Series.* Jefferson, NC: McFarland.

Muir, John Kenneth. 2007. *A Critical History of Doctor Who on Television.* Jefferson, NC: McFarland.

Muir, John Kenneth. 2012. *Horror Films of the 1980s.* Jefferson, NC: McFarland.

Murphy, Bernice M. 2013. *The Rural Gothic in American Popular Culture: Backwoods Horror and Terror in the Wilderness.* London: Palgrave Macmillan.

Nichols, Catherine. 2018. "The Good Guy/Bad Guy Myth: Pop Culture Today Is Obsessed with the Battle between Good and Evil. Traditional Folk Tales Never Were. What Changed?" *Aeon.* January 25, 2018. Accessed September 20, 2019. https://getpocket.com/explore/item/the-good-guy-bad-guy-myth.

O'Neil, Dennis, ed. 2008. *Batman Unauthorized: Vigilantes, Jokers, and Heroes in Gotham City.* Smart Pop Series. Dallas, TX: BenBella.

Parker, Lara. 2012. *Dark Shadows: Angelique's Descent*. New York: Tor.

Patel, C. 2014. "Expelling a Monstrous Matriarchy: Casting Cersei Lannister as Abject in *A Song of Ice and Fire*." *Journal of European Popular Culture* 5, no. 2: 135–147.

Peacock, Steven, ed. 2007. *Reading 24: TV against the Clock*. London: I. B. Tauris.

Pearson, Roberta, William Uricchio, and Will Brooker, eds. 2015. *Many More Lives of the Batman*. London: BFI Palgrave.

Peary, Gerald, ed. 2013. *Quentin Tarantino: Interviews, Revised and Updated*. Jackson: University of Mississippi Press.

Peaslee, Robert, and Rob Weiner, eds. 2020. *The Supervillain Reader*. Jackson: University of Mississippi Press.

Pender, Patricia J. 2016. *I'm Buffy and You're History*. Investigating Cult TV. London: I. B. Tauris.

Perez, Domino R. 2008. *There Was a Woman: Llorona from Folklore to Popular Culture*. Austin: University of Texas Press.

Peters, Andy. 2015. "Beyond Good and *Bad*: The Linguistic Construction of Walter White's Masculinity in *Breaking Bad*." University of Michigan. Accessed June 1, 2019. https://lsa.umich.edu/content/dam/english-assets/migrated/honors_files/PETERS%20A.%20Beyond%20Good%20&%20Bad.pdf.

Pierson, David P., ed. 2014. *Breaking Bad: Critical Essays on the Contexts, Politics, Style, and Reception of the Television Series*. Lanham, MD: Lexington Books.

Pollard, Tom. 2016. *Loving Vampires: Our Undead Obsession*. Jefferson, NC: McFarland.

Porter, Lynnette. 2012. *Sherlock Holmes for the 21st Century: Essays on New Adaptations*. Jefferson, NC: McFarland.

Powell, Jason. 2016. *The Best There Is at What He Does: Examining Chris Claremont's X-Men*. Edwardsville, IL: Sequart.

Prioleau, Chris. 2013. "Walter White and Bleeding Brown: On *Breaking Bad*'s Race Problem." *Apogee Journal*. October 2013. Accessed August 10, 2019. https://apogeejournal.org/2013/10/03/walter-white-bleeding-brown-on-breaking-bads-race-problem/.

Pruner, Aaron. 2019. "How the Godfather of TV Antiheroes Tony Soprano Changed Television Forever." Rotten Tomatoes. January 2019. Accessed June 1, 2019. https://editorial.rottentomatoes.com/article/tony-soprano-introduced-the-tv-antihero/.

Puzo, Mario. 1969. *The Godfather*. New York: G.P. Putnam's Sons.

Reagin, Nancy R. 2011. *Harry Potter and History*. Hoboken, NJ: John Wiley & Sons.

Reagin, Nancy R. 2013. *Star Trek and History*. Hoboken, NJ: John Wiley & Sons.

Reagin, Nancy R., and Janice Liedl, eds. 2013. *Star Wars and History*. New York: John Wiley & Sons.

Reiss, David S. 1983. *M*A*S*H: The Exclusive, Inside Story of TV's Most Popular Show*. London: Macmillan.

Renga, Dana, ed. 2011. *Mafia Movies: A Reader.* Toronto, ON, Canada: University of Toronto Press.

Roche, David. 2018. *Quentin Tarantino: Poetics and Politics of Cinematic Metafiction*. Jackson: University of Mississippi Press.

Rosenfeld, Gavriel D. 2014. *Hi Hitler!: How the Nazi Past Is Being Normalized in Contemporary Culture*. Cambridge: Cambridge University Press.

Rossinow, Doug. 2015. *The Reagan Era: A History of the 1980s*. New York: Columbia University Press.

Russell, Jeffrey B., and Brooks Alexander. 2007. *A History of Witchcraft: Sorcerers, Heretics, & Pagans*. London: Thames & Hudson.

Sanborn, K. 2015. "Who Killed Jason Todd: The Joker, Himself, His Writer, or the Fans?" Graphic Novel. October 18, 2015. Accessed February 20, 2019. http://graphicnovel.umwblogs.org/2015/10/18/who-killed-jason-todd-the-joker-himself-his-writer-or-the-fans/.

Sandel, Adam Adatto. 2018. "Breaking Bad: Walter White as Nietzschean Hero." *American Affairs Journal*. Fall 2018. Accessed August 10, 2019. https://americanaffairsjournal.org/2018/08/breaking-bad-walter-white-as-nietzschean-hero/.

Schoell, William. 2014. *The Horror Comics: Fiends, Freaks, and Fantastic Creatures*. Jefferson, NC: McFarland.

Scott, Kathryn Leigh, and Jim Pierson. 2012. *Dark Shadows: Return to Collinwood*. New York: Pomegranate.

Segal, David. 2011. "The Dark Art of *Breaking Bad*." *New York Times*. July 2011. Accessed June 1, 2019. https://www.nytimes.com/2011/07/10/magazine/the-dark-art-of-breaking-bad.html.

Serena, Katie. 2018. "Brushy Bill Roberts: The Man Who Claimed to Be Billy the Kid." *All That's Interesting*. December 25, 2018. Updated January 17, 2019. Accessed June 29, 2019. https://allthatsinteresting.com/brushy-bill-roberts.

Shapiro, Esther. 1984. *Dynasty: The Authorized Biography of the Carringtons*. New York: Doubleday.

Shone, Tom. 2017. *Tarantino: A Retrospective*. San Rafael, CA: Insight Editions.

Short, Sue. 2011. *Cult Telefantasy Series: A Critical Analysis of The Prisoner, Twin Peaks, The X-Files, Buffy the Vampire Slayer, Lost, Heroes, Doctor Who, and Star Trek*. Jefferson, NC: McFarland.

Silver, Alain, and James Ursini. 1993. *The Vampire Film*. New York: Limelight.

Silverman, Eric J., and Robert Arp, eds. 2017. *The Ultimate Game of Thrones and Philosophy: You Think or Die*. Chicago, IL: Open Court.

Simon, Joe. 2011. *My Life in Comics*. London: Titan.

Sivan. 2014. "The Secret History of Maleficent: Murder, Rape, and Woman-Hating in Sleeping Beauty." Reviving Herstory. Accessed December 27, 2019. http://www.revivingherstory.com/rhblog/2014/11/3/the-secret-history-of-maleficent-murder-rape-and-woman-hating-in-sleeping-beauty.

Skal, David J. 2001. *The Monster Show: A Cultural History of Horror*. Rev. ed. New York: Farrar, Straus and Giroux.

South, James B., ed. 2005. *Buffy, the Vampire Slayer and Philosophy: Fear and Trembling in Sunnydale*. Chicago: Open Court.

Spinoso Arcocha, Rosa Maria. 2003. *La Llorona: Mito, Género, y Control Social en México.* Mexico City: Mexico: Servicios de Publicaciones y Divulgación Científica e la Universidad de Malaga.

Spoto, Donald. 1991. *The Art of Alfred Hitchcock: Fifty Years of His Motion Pictures*. Norwell, MA: Anchor.

Standiford, Les. 2011. *The Man Who Invented Christmas: How Charles Dickens's "A Christmas Carol" Rescued His Career and Revived Our Holiday Spirits*. New York: Broadway.

Starck, Kathleen, ed. 2010. *Between Fear and Freedom: Cultural Representations of the Cold War.* Newcastle upon Tyne, UK: Cambridge Scholars.

Stark, Steven D. 1997. *Glued to the Set: The 60 Television Shows and Events That Made Us Who We Are Today.* New York: Delta Trade Paperbacks.

Stevens, J. Richard. 2015. *Captain America, Masculinity, and Violence: The Evolution of a National Icon*. Syracuse, NY: Syracuse University Press.

Stuller, Jennifer K. 2010. *Ink-Stained Amazons and Cinematic Warriors: Superwomen in Modern Mythology.* London: I. B. Tauris.

Sunstein, Cass R. 2016. *The World According to Star Wars.* New York: Dey Street.

Sweeney, Edwin R. 2012. *From Cochise to Geronimo: The Chiricahua Apaches, 1874–1886*. Norman: University of Oklahoma Press.

Sweet, Derek R. 2015. *Star Wars in the Public Square: The Clone Wars as Political Dialogue*. Critical Explorations in Science Fiction and Fantasy Series, edited by Donald E. Palumbo and Michael Sullivan. Jefferson, NC: McFarland.

Szabo, Ross. 2007. "Mental Health Advocates Will Miss *The Sopranos.*" *Huffington Post.* June 2007. Updated May 2011. Accessed June 1, 2019. https://www.huffpost.com/entry/mental-health-advocates-w_b_51662.

Szumskyj, Benjamin, ed. 2008. *Dissecting Hannibal Lecter: Essays on the Novels of Thomas Harris*. Jefferson, NC: McFarland.

Tannenbaum, Rob. 2013. "Gus from *Breaking Bad* Wants Walt's Head on a Pike." *Rolling Stone*. September 2013. Accessed August 10, 2019. https://www.rollingstone.com/tv/tv-news/gus-from-breaking-bad-wants-walts-head-on-a-pike-205633/.

Taylor, Chris. 2015. *How Star Wars Conquered the Universe: The Past, Present, and Future of a Multibillion Dollar Franchise*. New York: Basic Books.

Terry, Paul. 2019. *The X-Files: The Official Archives: Cryptids, Biological Anomalies, and Parapsychic Phenomenon*. New York: Abrams.

Thompson, Dave. 2016. *The Rocky Horror Picture Show FAQ: Everything Left to Know about the Campy Cult Classic*. Logan Village, Australia: Applause.

Tucker, Reed. 2017. *Slugfest: Inside the Epic 50-Year Battle between Marvel and DC*. New York: Da Capo Press.

"TV Guide Picks TV's 60 Nastiest Villains." 2013. *TV Guide.* April 22, 2013. Accessed January 1, 2019. http://wordsmithonia.blogspot.com/2013/04/tv-guide-picks-tvs-60-nastiest-villains.html.

Tye, Larry. 2013. *Superman: The High-Flying History of America's Most Enduring Hero*. New York: Random House.

Üner, Ayse Melda. 2017. "Intertextual Transformation of a Fairy Tale from Sleeping Beauty to Maleficent." *Journal of Social Sciences Institute* 20, no. 38: 371–382.

Unger, Steven P. 2010. *In the Footsteps of Dracula*. New York: Audience Artist Group.

VanDerWerff, Emily Todd. 2013. "*Breaking Bad* Ended the Anti-Hero Genre by Introducing Good and Evil." *AV Club*. September 2013. Accessed June 1, 2019. https://tv.avclub.com/breaking-bad-ended-the-anti-hero-genre-by-introducing-g-1798240891.

Van Seters, John. 1998. "The Pentateuch." In *The Hebrew Bible Today: An Introduction to Critical Issues*, edited by Steven L. McKenzie and Matt Patrick Graham, 3–49. Westminster, UK: John Knox.

Van Wormer, Laura. 1985. *Dallas: The Complete Ewing Family Saga, Including Southfork Ranch, Ewing Oil, and the Barnes-Ewing Feud—1860–1985*. New York: Doubleday/Dolphin.

Vogel, Joseph. 2018. *Stranger Things and the '80s: The Complete Retro Guide*. St. London, ON, Canada: Cardinal.

Wagner, Erica. 2014. "The Capitalist Nightmare at the Heart of *Breaking Bad*." *NewStatesmanAmerica*. December 2014. Accessed June 1, 2019. https://www.newstatesman.com/culture/2014/12/capitalist-nightmare-heart-breaking-bad.

Wallace, Daniel. 2012. *Batman: The World of the Dark Knight*. London: Dorling Kindersley.

Wallis, Michael. 2007. *Billy the Kid: The Endless Ride*. New York: W. W. Norton.

Wein, Len, ed. 2006. *The Unauthorized X-Men: SF and Comic Book Writers on Mutants, Prejudice, and Adamantium*. Smart Pop Series. Dallas, TX: BenBella.

Weiner, Robert G., ed. 2009. *Captain America and the Struggle of the Superhero: Critical Essays*. Jefferson, NC: McFarland & Company.

Weinstock, Jefferey Andrew. 2008. *Reading Rocky Horror: The Rocky Horror Picture Show and Popular Culture*. Basingstoke, UK: Palgrave Macmillan.

Weldon, Glen. 2016. *The Caped Crusade: "Batman" and the Rise of Nerd Culture*. New York: Simon & Schuster.

Welsome, Eileen. 2006. *The General and the Jaguar: Pershing's Hunt for Pancho Villa: A True Story of Revolution & Revenge*. Boston: Little, Brown and Company.

Wert, Jeffry D. 1996. *Custer: The Controversial Life of George Armstrong Custer*. New York: Simon & Schuster.

Westfall, Joseph, ed. 2016. *Hannibal Lecter and Philosophy: The Heart of the Matter*. Chicago, IL: Open Court.

Wetmore, Kevin J., Jr. 2019. *Uncovering Stranger Things: Essays on Eighties Nostalgia, Cynicism and Innocence in the Series*. Jefferson, NC: McFarland.

White, James. 2018. "Star Wars: Kathleen Kennedy Confirms the Boba Fett Movie Is Dead." *Empire*. October 28, 2018. Accessed January 23, 2019. https://www.empireonline.com/movies/news/star-wars-kathleen-kennedy-confirms-boba-fett-movie-dead/.

White, Mark D., ed. 2009. *Watchmen and Philosophy: A Rorschach Test*. The Blackwell Philosophy and Pop Culture Series, edited by William Irwin. Hoboken, NJ: Wiley.

White, Mark D., and Robert Arp, eds. 2008. *Batman and Philosophy: The Dark Knight of the Soul*. The Blackwell Philosophy and Pop Culture Series. Hoboken, NJ: Wiley.

Wilcox, Rhonda V., Tanya Cochran, Cynthea Masson, and David Lavery. 2014. *Reading Joss Whedon*. Television and Popular Culture. Syracuse, NY: Syracuse University Press.

Wilcox, Rhonda V., and David Lavery. 2002. *Fighting the Forces: What's at Stake in Buffy, the Vampire Slayer*. Lanham, MD: Rowman & Littlefield.

Willis, Susan. 2005. *Portents of the Real: A Primer for Post-9/11 America*. London: Verso.

Woodard, Colin. 2007. *The Republic of Pirates: Being the True and Surprising Story of the Caribbean Pirates and the Man Who Brought Them Down*. Boston: Houghton Mifflin Harcourt.

Wooley, John. 2011. *Wes Craven: The Man and His Nightmares*. Hoboken, NJ: Wiley & Sons.

Wright, Bradford W. 2003. *Comic Book Nation: The Transformation of Youth Culture in America*. Baltimore, MD: Johns Hopkins University Press.

Wrobel, Ron, III. 2016. *The Complete Ferengi Rules of Acquisition: Aphorisms, Guidelines, and Principles to Life in Ferengi Culture*. Scotts Valley, CA: CreateSpace.

Yeffeth, Glenn, ed. 2003a. *Seven Seasons of Buffy: Science Fiction and Fantasy Writers Discuss Their Favorite Television Show*. Dallas, TX: BenBella.

Yeffeth, Glenn, ed. 2003b. *Taking the Red Pill: Science, Philosophy and the Religion of The Matrix*. Smart Pop Series. Dallas, TX: BenBella.

Yeffeth, Glenn, ed. 2004. *Five Seasons of Angel: Science Fiction and Fantasy Writers Discuss Their Favorite Vampire*. Smart Pop Series. Dallas, TX: BenBella.

Yuen, Wayne, ed. 2012. *The Walking Dead and Philosophy: Zombie Apocalypse Now*. Popular Culture and Philosophy. Chicago: Open Court.

Yuen, Wayne, ed. 2016. *The Ultimate Walking Dead and Philosophy: Hungry for More*. Popular Culture and Philosophy. Chicago: Open Court.

About the Editor and Contributors

EDITOR

RICHARD A. HALL is an Adjunct Professor of History at Texas A&M International University in Laredo, Texas. After serving four years in the U.S. Army, he attended Texas A&M International, finishing his bachelor's and master's degrees before receiving his PhD in history from Auburn University in Auburn, Alabama. He is the author of *The American Superhero: Encyclopedia of Caped Crusaders in History* and *Pop Goes the Decade: The Seventies*, both from ABC-CLIO/Greenwood Press, and is a contributor and member of the board of advisors for the online pop culture database *Pop Culture Universe: Icons, Idols, and Ideas*, from ABC-CLIO. He is also a contributor to *The Supervillain Reader*, from the University of Mississippi Press. His upcoming projects include *Pop Goes the Decade: The 2000s* (in 2021) and *Robots in Popular Culture: Androids and Cyborgs in the American Imagination* (in 2021), both from ABC-CLIO/Greenwood, and *Gotham, U.S.A.: Critical Essays on Ethics, American Society, and the Batman Universe of Television's "Gotham"* (in 2021) from McFarland & Company. A father of five and grandfather of five, he lives in Laredo, Texas, with the youngest of his children and his wife, best friend, fellow former soldier, coworker, and frequent collaborator, Dr. Maria A. Reyes.

CONTRIBUTORS

KEITH R. CLARIDY graduated from Auburn University with his bachelor's degree in history in 2004 and his master's degree in history in 2006. He is a student information manager for Lee County Schools in Lee County, Alabama. He is the author of *"Bring God to the Negro, Bring the Negro to God": Archbishop Thomas Joseph Toolen and Race in Alabama* (2009) from LAP Lambert Academic.

JOSHUA PLOCK studied American history with a focus in popular culture at Columbus State University. He is currently a staff writer covering comics, films, and literature for the website House of Geekery. On Friday nights, he has a regular segment on the podcast *The Aymerich Show*. Josh Plock currently resides in Memphis, Tennessee.

MARIA ANTONIETA REYES is an Assistant Professor of Public Administration at Texas A&M International University. Her scholastic interests are interdisciplinary and include local organizations, political theology, public administration theory, popular culture, and interdependence and interrelation beyond economic bases. She received her PhD from Auburn University in 2012, served in the U.S. Army, and lives in Laredo, Texas, with her husband and children. She presented the paper "The Doctor, the Daughter, and the Holy TARDIS: A Systematic Theology of the Three" at the Southwest Regional Popular/American Culture Conference in February 2017.

Index

Page numbers in **bold** indicate main entries; page numbers in *italic* indicate figures.